Asheville, North Carolina City Directory 1913

(Volume XII)

Ernest H. Miller

Alpha Editions

This edition published in 2020

ISBN : 9789354043031

Design and Setting By
Alpha Editions
www.alphaedis.com
email - alphaedis@gmail.com

As per information held with us this book is in Public Domain.
This book is a reproduction of an important historical work. Alpha Editions uses the best technology to reproduce historical work in the same manner it was first published to preserve its original nature. Any marks or number seen are left intentionally to preserve its true form.

Asheville, North Carolina
CITY DIRECTORY

Vol. XII.   **1913**   Vol. XII.

Including West Asheville, South Asheville, Biltmore, South Biltmore, Woolsey, Grace, Chunn's Cove, Bingham Heights, Richmond Hill, Kenilworth, Vernon Hill, Etc.

Contains a General Business and Street Directory of Asheville and much useful information classified as Miscellaneous.

Piedmont Directory Company
INCORPORATED

Publishers

Home Office   ASHEVILLE, N. C.

Member Association of American Directory Publishers

See General Index, Page 9

Price, ... $6.00

ISSUED ANNUALLY, November 1st

THE PIEDMONT SERIES

66 AMER. NAT'L BANK BLDG.   ASHEVILLE, N. C.

Name, Contents, General Arrangement, and Classifications of each Department Copyright Sept., 1912 by PIEDMONT DIRECTORY CO., [INC.] All rights reserved.

Compiled by ERNEST H. MILLER

Hackney & Moale Co.   Printers, Asheville, N. C.

Wachovia Bank & Trust Co.

Home Office:
WINSTON-SALEM, N. C.

Asheville, North
Carolina Office

Capital and Surplus, $1,650,000.00

| Banking Department | Saving Department |
| Trust Department | Insurance Department |

4% Interest Paid in Savings Dept., Compounded Quarterly

4% PAID ON TIME CERTIFICATES

T. S. MORRISON, Chairman & Vice-Pres.
W. B. WILLIAMSON, Cashier   S. M. HANES, Asst Cashier
P. R. ALLEN, Mgr. Insurance Dept.

P. R. MOALE   J. MOORE CHILES

Moale & Chiles

PHONE 661   Real Estate Brokers   **PHONE 661**

Fire Insurance

27 Patton Ave., 2nd fl.   ASHEVILLE, N. C.

City and Suburban improved property, timber, mineral and farm lands; also several fine country estates for sale.
HOUSES FOR RENT—Modern houses, furnished, $40 to $100 per month; unfurnished, $15 to $100 per month
BUSINESS OPPORTUNITIES—Parties desiring to engage in business or establish factories in Western North Carolina should write us. We can secure local co-operation and capital for deserving enterprises. Loans negotiated.
GENERAL AGENTS U. S. FIDELITY & GUARANTY CO.

When writing advertisers mention the directory

GENERAL INDEX

Abbreviations 65	Hotels 415-416
Advertisers' Special Directory....2-24	Judiciary 511
Alphabetical List of Names....65-393	Military 518
Banks .... 397 and 513	Miscellaneous Directory 509-520
Board of Trade 514	Objects of Directory Publishers
Boarding Houses 398-399	Assn 496
Building & Loan Associations..... 400	Organizations 514
Business Directory 395-438	Police Department 509-510
Cemeteries .... 401 and 514	Post Office 512-513
Christian Associations 514	Preface 13
Churches 514-515	Private Schools and Colleges..... 517
City Government 509	Public Schools 517
Clergymen 402-403	Rural Routes and Carriers 513
Clubs 403-404	Schools and Colleges 433
County Government 510	Secret Societies 518-520
Courts 511	State Government 511
Educational 516-517	Street Directory 439-495
Fire Alarm Boxes 510	Suburbs 497-508
Fire Department 510	Title Page 5
Fraternal Organizations 518	United States Court and Officers..512
General Directory 65-393	United States Government 512
Hospitals, Homes and Charities..517	

Asheville Dray, Fuel & Construction Co.

Moving Furniture a Specialty

COAL

Wood and Kindling Stone and Sand

HEAVY HAULING OF ALL KINDS

WE FURNISH BUILDING STONE

6 1-2 S. MAIN   Phone 223

INDEX TO ADVERTISERS

Albemarle Park Co............page 17
Alexander Louis I
　　card at name and at optometrists
Allanstand Cottage Industries
　　card at name
Allen Industrial Home and Asheville Academy ....page 23
American National Bank
　　front cover and page 12
Amiss J Taylor...............page 20
Arbogast Motor Co
　　left side lines and Fly A
Asheville Academy...........page 23
Asheville Business College
　　card at name
Asheville Cleaning and Pressing
　　Club ....left bottom lines
Asheville Coal Co......right top lines
Asheville Dray, Fuel & Construction Co...left top lines and page 9
Asheville Dry Cleaning Co
　　left bottom lines
Asheville Electrical Co...left side lines
Asheville Paint & Glass Co back cover
Asheville Power & Light Co
　　right side lines

Asheville Sign Co........card at name
Asheville Steam Laundry
　　right top small side lines
Asheville Supply & Foundry Co
　　card at Founders in Bus Directory
Asheville & East Tenn R R Co
　　front cover and left top lines
Baird-Wilford Realty Co......page 24
Barbee S A..............back cover
Battery Park Bank (The)
　　front cover and left bottom lines
Belmont ....page 20
Belvedere (The)..............page 18
Blue Ridge B & L Assn..back Fly A
Bowles R L...................page 5
Bradford J M................page 24
Brown-Carter Realty Co
　　left small bottom side lines
Brown Chas L...............page 24
Brown H A & Co
　　left small bottom side lines
Brown's Undertaking Parlor
　　right top small side lines
Cansler P U Mrs..............page 20
Carolina Coal & Ice Co..right top lines

Index to Advertisers Con'td

Carolina Machinery Co
    right bottom lines
Carter Joe................opp biz dept
Central Bank & Trust Co
    marginal line front cover
Chapel Cottages...............page 20
Cherokee Inn..................page 19
Citizens Bank................front cover
Club Cafe & Candy Kitchen
    left top lines
College Street Dye Works
    opp biz dept
Crisp N L............card at Grocers
Day Mary Frances Miss.......page 12
Elton (The)...................page 16
Emanuel School of Shorthand
    card at name
English Lumber Co...right top lines
Enterprise Machine Co
    bottom line back cover and page 14
Faulkner Bennie P Mrs opp biz dept
Finkelstein H L
    top marginal line back cover
Galer E E............left bottom lines
Goodlake A M.........card at name
Gruner Sanitarium (The)
    cards at Sanitariums and Baths
Guffey Jno A........card at Dry Goods
Hackney & Moale Co..insert at name
Hall S D small right bottom side lines
Harville Belle Mrs.............page 24
Haskell H S...................page 12
Highland Hotel................page 18
Hill's Market
    bottom marginal line front cover
Honess Chas H
    small bottom right side lines
Hotel Oxford......right bottom lines
Hughes Transfer & Livery Co, right
    side lines and card at Transfer Cos
Hyams M.....................back cover
Imperial Mutual Life and Health
    Ins Co.............right side lines
Jackson B J small lower left side lines
Jackson Daisy M..opp business dept
Johnson T P & Co
    upper right small side lines
Jones W M......................page 3
Kübler & Whitehead...right bot lines
Knickerbocker (The).........page 15
Life Insurance Co of Va.left top lines
Loftain C S Mrs................page 5
Louisiana (The)...............page 18
Love F P & Son ½ page opp biz dept
Lyon J M & Co..insert opp bus dept
McPherson J C......left bottom lines

Magnolia Cottage..............page 15
Manor (The)...................page 17
Meriwether Hospital............page 6
Messler F M..................back cover
Mildred E Sherwood Home..page 4
Miller C H Dr
    right bot small side lines and pg 21
Moale & Chiles
    right bottom lines and page 8
Montagne Mnfg Co
    right top lines and bet pages 188-189
Moore E J K Miss card at Art Goods
Moore Plumbing Co
    lower left small side lines
Mountain City Laundry, outside
    marginal lines front and back cover
Nevercel F J..........back Fly A
Normal & Collegiate Institute
    inside back cover and opp
North State Fitting School...page 12
Piedmont Directory Co........insert
Piedmont Electric Co...left side lines
Reliable Cleaning & Pressing Club
    insert at name
Rockett O N..................page 22
St Genevieve College
    insert at name (2 sides)
Sanitary Home Laundry
    right top and bottom lines
Sartor J R...........see opp Bus dept
Sherwood Mildred E Home...page 4
Southern Coal Co, tab insert at name
Star Market
    top marginal line front cover
Stevens Saml M.........card at name
Swannanoa-Berkeley Hotel
    backbone and page 16
Swannanoa Laundry
    marginal line back cover
Tillman Jas A........right top lines
Trakas N S & Co...............page 5
Trexler D...small left top side lines
Viniarski B A.................page 22
Wachovia Bank & Trust Co Ins
    Dept (P R Allen)....card at names
Wachovia Bank & Trust Co
    stencils and page 8
Western Carolina Realty Co
    right top small side lines
Whiteside E W..........page insert
Whitmore Sanitarium..........page 11
Williams-Brownell Planing Mill Co
    left top lines and right top lines
Wilson E F...................page 24
Woodward & Son
    right top lines and bet pages 188-189

Mr. Merchant: Do you know that about the only Establishment that makes money without Advertising its business is the Mint?

Whitmore Sanitarium

For the Treatment of

Paralysis, Rheumatism, Gout, Kidney, Liver and Stomach troubles, Bronchitis, Asthma, Hay Fever, Neuralgia, Neuritis, Neurasthenia, Insomnia, Melancholia, and Special Diseases of Men and Women.

Lovely Park, Tennis, Croquet, etc., Non-Uric-Acid-Diet, Curative Gymnastics, Rest Cure, Effort Cure, Naturopathy, Hydro-therapy, Psychotherapy, Chiropractic, Massage, Electricity in various forms, Vapor, Shower, Sitz and Electric-Light Baths.

Take Patton Avenue Car.

408 Haywood St.   Asheville, N. C.
Phone 1020

Haskell's Pepsi-Cola Co.

Manufacturers and Wholesale Shippers of
"CASCADE" Brand of

Ginger Ale Soda
and Mineral Waters in SIPHONS

Factory 217 Haywood St.   Phone 170   Asheville, N. C.

North State Fitting School

J. M. ROBERTS, A. M., PRINCIPAL

A SELECT SCHOOL FOR BOYS   EXPERIENCED TEACHERS
BOARDING AND DAY PUPILS   INDIVIDUAL ATTENTION

Thorough Work and Manly Conduct Insisted Upon
Beautiful and Healthful Location at 157 Church Street

Asheville, N. C.   Phone 1374

MISS M. FANNIE DAY
TEACHER OF
Piano, Pipe Organ, Theory, Harmony

Finished course at Oberlin Conservatory of Music. Number of years experience as teacher. Address **NORTH STATE FITTING SCHOOL, 157 Church Street.**
Phone 1374

The American National Bank
OF ASHEVILLE

UNITED STATES DEPOSITARY
CAPITAL $300,000

OFFICERS:

L. L. JENKINS, Pres., C. J. HARRIS, V-Pres., HENRY REDWOOD, V Pres., J. G. MERRIMON, V Pres., ARTHUR E. RANKIN, Asst. Cashier, R. E. CURRENCE, Asst. Cashier.

We solicit the accounts of banks, corporations, merchants and individuals strictly upon our merits as an Institution where patrons are assured every courtesy consistent with sound banking and where their business will receive prompt and careful attention.

PRO BONO PVBLICO

PREFACE

In submitting Volume XII of the Asheville City Directory, it is gratifying to note the progress that is being made in industries and growth of population.

A great factor in the upbuilding of any city is its civic pride; the fact that your citizens stand as a unit on everything that affects the prosperity of your city is worthy of commendation.

The City Directory is one of the foremost enterprises of any city; it is generally referred to by the press of the whole country as a semi-public institution of great value.

The Directory is more than a mere list of names of residents, giving their various occupations and addresses; it is an infallible guide to your city, for your people and for the stranger within your gates. It not only deals with your people, but with your government, your institutions and various other organizations. It is a recognized standard work of reference and becomes the most reliable history of your city and its citizens. As there is no other publication in the world which gives the information as contained in the City Directory, there is probably no other publication in which all the people are so vitally interested.

To gather the data and compile a volume of this character is no easy task. It requires much time, a well defined system, the patience of Job and incurs no little expense. Few people have any idea of the work it means and the tenacity it takes to publish a reliable directory.

In preparing this book the publishers have spared neither time nor expense, and if errors occur or a single name is omitted which should appear in the work, it is generally the fault of the public and not of the publisher, as every house is visited and it is not the publisher's or canvasser's fault if some one fails to give all the information or gives it incorrectly. The intentions of the reliable publisher are always for improvement, and you can always count on getting as accurate a directory as circumstances will permit.

The estimate of the population of a city is a matter necessarily enjoined upon the directory publisher; such estimates, however, are not merely theoretical, but based on facts, sustained by the contents of the publication.

This volume contains 13,450 names of individuals; using the conservative multiple 2½ times, to represent the names of married women and children not counted, indicates a population of

(This does not mean simply population inside the city limits, but takes into consideration all suburbs included in the Directory.)

In concluding, we desire to thank our patrons for their support and to extend our thanks to the public in general for the courteous way in which nearly every one supplied our canvassers with the desired data. We shall continue this publication from time to time to meet the demand.
Yours truly,
PIEDMONT DIRECTORY CO., ERNEST H. MILLER, Pres.

PRO BONO PVBLICO

Enterprise Machine Co.

67-69-71 MAIN STREET

FIREPROOF GARAGE

Electric, Steam and Gasoline Automobiles

Automobile Accessories of All Kinds

Storage Battery Charging System

══Specialists in══

Designing and construction of scientific instruments and mechanical models.

Dealers in Metal Working Machinery

THE KNICKERBOCKER

77 College Street, on Charlotte Street Car Line

All Modern Improvements. Steam Heat, Etc. Rates on Application

Phone 153   M. H. HARRIS

Special Department of Select Hotels and Boarding Houses

INDEX

PAGE	PAGE
Belvedere (The).........18	Knickerbocker (The) see above
Bonniview (The)........20	
Cansler P U Mrs.........20	Louisiana Cottage see below
Chapel Cottages 20	
Cherokee Inn 19	Manor (The) 17
Elton (The) 16	Swannanoa-Berkeley
Highland Hotel 18	Hotel 16
Hotel Oxford......bot lines	

Magnolia Cottage
[TAKE CHARLOTTE STREET CAR]

PRIVATE BOARD

First Class Rooms   ::   Excellent Table   ::   Rates Reasonable

MRS. K. L. DuREN, Proprietress

Phone 1828   72 College St., ASHEVILLE, N. C.

When writing advertisers mention the directory.

SWANNANOA-BERKELEY
Asheville, N. C.

The most modern and up-to-date Family and Commercial Hotel in the city.
Strictly American Plan

COLONIAL entrance, tiled office, lobby, writing and lounging room, hot and cold running water or private bath in every room. Local and long distance telephones. Large convention and dancing hall. Ideal for conventions. Electric cars from depot and all sections. Electric elevator. Central location, one block from public square.

RATES—$2.50 to $4 a Day

Frank Loughran, Owner-Proprietor

An Ideal Place to Stop

Choice Rooms
Best Table
Beautiful Lawn
PHONE 958
Rates Reasonable

The Elton
45 N. Spruce Street
Asheville, N. C.

The Manor
An Exclusive Inn

Albemarle Park
Asheville, N. C.

¶ Situated on Charlotte Street near Golf Links; Private Club House within the Park :: ::

¶ Numerous Attractive Cottages for Family Parties :: ::

¶ Accommodations and Table are of the Best

Albemarle Park Company

"BELVEDERE"
Formerly RAVENSCROFT

Nicely Furnished
Steam Heat
Reasonable Rates
Modern Conveniences
Large Airy Rooms
Everything First Class
No Consumptives

Mrs. Nellie W. Hyman

95 Church St., Asheville, N.C.
Phone 468

HIGHLAND HOTEL
(RAILROAD HEADQUARTERS)
MRS. EMMA ELSE, Propr.

Rates: $1.50 per day   Weekly $6.00

Catering to Transient and Commercial Trade

Electric Lights   ::   Baths, Etc., Etc.

368 Depot Street   ::   Phone 1097

THE LOUISIANA
PRIVATE BOARD

MRS. D. O. RAY, Propr.

51 College St., ASHEVILLE, N. C.

First Class Table
Large Airy Rooms
Hot and Cold Water
Rates on Application
Special Rates to Families
No Sick People Taken   Phone 1777

CHEROKEE INN

Oak, Corner Woodfin

Asheville, N. C.

The nearest and most desirable Family Hotel in Asheville, its commanding location, beautiful grounds, and extensive verandas make it very popular as a tourist resort.

Moderate Rates

Phone 395   D. W. Misenheimer, Proprietor

When writing advertisers mention the directory.

SPECIAL ADVERTISERS' DIRECTORY

CHAPEL COTTAGES

41 Victoria Road :: Phone 55

Convalescent Invalids
in Separate Cottage

Miss E. E. Moore ∴ Asheville, N. C.

MRS. P. U. CANSLER

Select Boarding

Modern Coveniences   Rates Reasonable
76 College Street :: Phone 816

BONNIVIEW

PARTIES desirous of superior Board and Accomodations in a refined and exclusive household in the most attractive and convenient section of Asheville, at reasonable rates, will find such advantages at Bonniview, where the views are unsurpassed and only cultivated guests are accepted. Rooms are large and well furnished, and the table exceptionally fine.

No Tuberculosis

Mrs. J. Taylor Amiss

Phone 1553   128 Haywood

BELMONT

57 Spruce Street :: Asheville, N. C.

FOR NERVOUS AND STOMACH DISEASES AND CONVALESCENTS :: :: :: ::

No Tuberculous or Communicable Case Accepted

BERTRAND HOUSER, M. D., B. S.
— Manager —
Phone 840

When writing advertisers mention the directory.

Chas. L. Brown
GENERAL BLACKSMITHING

Wagons Built to Order, Wagon and Carriage Woodworking, Scientific Horse Shoeing, Planing and Ripsawing, Rubber Tireing, Axe Grinding Headquarters for Automobile Springs, we put New Spokes and Rims in all makes of Auto Wheels.

21-27 North Lexington Ave. :: Phone 681

DR. C. H. MILLER

Graduate American College of Mechano-Therapy

HOURS BY ENGAGEMENT

14 N. Spruce St. Asheville, N. C.

PHONE 979

HEALTH IS COMBUSTION

My business is aiding nature to dispose of this unwelcome abnormality. I accomplish this by means of a physiological, scientific system of manual manipulation of the structure which, by accelerating the circulation, increases combustion and so facilitates the natural elimination of a diseased condition. In short, I make it possible for the body to purify itself by improving the circulation. This is the object and certain result of Mechano Therapy.

I do not disparage the noble art of the physician and surgeon, and if your sickness is not amenable to Mechano Therapy, I shall tell you so frankly.

J. M. BRADFORD
Carriage, Automobile and Coach Painting of Every Description
Work of Superior Quality

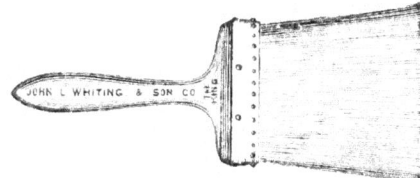

I use Valentine's Varnishes

25-27 N. Lexington Avenue

Phone - 681

When writing advertisers mention the directory

Champion Shoe Repair Shop

Your Old Shoes Made Like New Ones

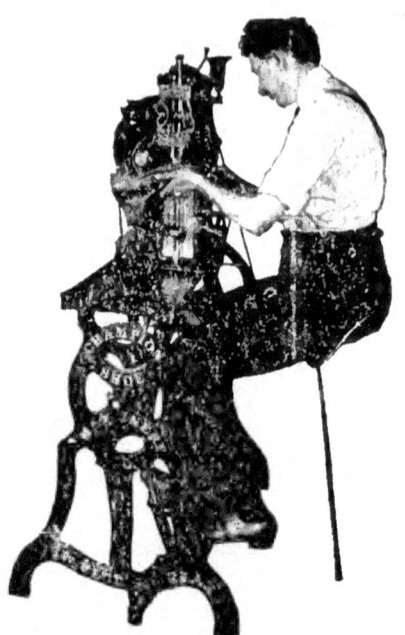

Men's Shoes half-soled, sewed, and heels straightened . . . 90c

Ladies' Shoes half-soled, sewed . . . 50c

30 W. College St.

O. N. ROCKETT

Watchmaker and Jeweler

All Work Guaranteed  29 North Main Street

Watch Cleaning	50c	Watch Glasses fitted	15c
Main Spring	50c	Hands, each	5c
Hair Spring, fitted and regulated	75c	Gold Rings Soldered	15c
Roller Jewel	50c	Gold Spectacles Soldered	15c
Balance Jewel	50c	Eight Day Clocks Cleaned	50c
Balance Staffs fitted	75c	Thirty-Six Hour Clocks Cleaned	25c

☞ Prompt attention given to Jewelry Repairing of every description. Stone Setting, Mounting, etc., etc.

When writing advertisers mention the directory.

ESTABLISHED 1887

Asheville Academy and Allen Industrial Home For Colored Girls

Under the auspices of the Woman's Home Missionary Society of the Methodist Episcopal Church.

Spacious Buildings with modern equipment. All grades from primary through normal.

Music, Domestic Science, Dress-Making and plain Sewing.

Home care for the girls. Fine climate. Rates resonable.

MISS ALSIE B. DOLE, Superintendent

241 College Street ·:· ·:· Asheville, N. C.

When writing advertisers mention the directory.

MRS. BELLE HARVILLE
FASHIONABLE DRESSMAKER

172 Haywood St. -:- Telephone 1496

E. F. WILSON

Successor to C. C. BROWN

Livery and Sale Stable

Fine Saddle Horses a Specialty

53 S. Main St.   Telephone 709

CHAS. W. BAIRD   I. B. WILFORD

Baird-Wilford Co.

ROOM: 206 OATES BUILDING

Real Estate, Investments

Fire Insurance, Brokerage

Talk With Us Today -:- We Can Interest You

Office Phone 938 -:- -:- Residence Phone 1308

THE ASHEVILLE, N. C.
City and Suburban Directory

Including Asheville, South Asheville, West Asheville,
Biltmore, South Biltmore, Kenilworth,
Woolsey and Grace.

Vol. XII.   **1913**   Vol. XII.

THE PIEDMONT SERIES

ABBREVIATIONS USED IN THIS WORK.

adv—advertisement.	cor—corner.	mkr—maker.	rms—rooms.
Add—Addition	cot byr—cotton buyer.	mkt—market.	R R—Railroad.
agt—agent.	ct—court.	mldr—moulder.	Ry—railway.
al—alley.	ctr—cutter.	mlnr—milliner.	s—south.
appr—apprentice.	dep—deputy.	mnfg—manufacturing.	sec—secretary.
assn—association.	dept—department.	manfr—manufacturer.	servt—servant
asst—assistant.	dlr—dealer.	mngr—manager.	ship—shipping.
atty—attorney.	e—east.	msgr—messenger.	slsmn—salesman.
av—avenue.	emp—employment.	mstr—master.	smstrs—seamstress.
bartndr—bartender	electrn—electrician.	n—north.	Sou—Southern.
bds—boards.	engnr—engineer.	nr—near.	solr—solicitor.
bkkpr—bookkeeper.	ext—extension.	off—office.	sp—space.
Bldg—building.	flgmn—flagman	opp—opposite.	spl—special.
bldr—builder.	flr—floor.	opr—operator.	sq—square.
blksmith—blacksmith.	frt—freight.	paperhngr—paperhanger	stengr—stenographer.
brkmn—brakeman.	ftr—fitter.	passgr—passenger.	supt—superintendent.
cabtmkr—cabinetmaker.	gen'l—general.	photog—photographer.	tchr—teacher.
carp—carpenter.	h—house.	pl—place.	tel opr—telegraph operator.
chf—chief.	int rev—internal revenue.	plstr—plasterer.	trav—traveling.
clk—clerk.		plmbr—plumber.	treas—treasurer.
co—county.	ins—insurance.	P O—post office.	uphr—upholsterer.
collr—collector.	inspr—inspector.	pres—president.	v-pres—vice-president.
comr—commissioner.	la—lane.	prin—principal.	w—west.
com mer—commission merchant.	lab—laborer.	propr—proprietor.	whol—wholesale.
	laund—laundry.	(r)—rear.	wid—widow.
condr—conductor.	lyr—layer.	R M S—railroad mail service.	wkr—worker.
confr—confectioner.	mchst—machinist.		wks—works.
contr—contractor.	mdse—merchandise.	rd—road.	

☞ The classification by business will be found after the alphabetical arrangement of names. For full indices to the contents of the work, see index. Names marked * are those of colored persons except where a * is used to denote a certain occupation or special business heading.

ASHEVILLE [1913] DIRECTORY   65

A

Abbey Willis P (Lila R), clk Ry M S, h 44 Clayton
*Abbott Jas (Annie), candy mkr, h 47 Hazzard
*Abbott Lewis (Minnie), lab, h 166 Beaumont
*Abbott Maggie, cook, h 86 Curve
Abbott Thos J (Daisy), trav slsmn, h 20 Jefferson Drive
*Abernathy Caroline, dom, h 94 Southside av
Abernathy Chas (Martha), electrn, h Biltmore Park
Abernathy Freda Miss, maid 296 Montford av
*Abernathy Julius C (Janie B), sexton All Souls Church, h 27 Clemmons

WORDS OF WISDOM

Do not advertise and stop,
But advertise and stay,
For those who saw your ad last year,
Will look for it to-day.

CAROLINA MACHINERY CO.
—US when you want machine work of any kind . . .

Founders Machinists and Jobbers of Mill Supplies
When in the market for heavy castings such as columns or building plates get our prices. **Phone 590**

The Life Insurance Co. of Virginia
ORGANIZED 1871   RICHMOND, VA.

ISSUES ALL THE MOST APPROVED FORMS OF LIFE INSURANCE CONTRACTS from $500.00 to $25,000.00, with premiums payable quarterly, semi-annually and annually

J. V. Moon, Superintendent, Rooms 3-4-5 Maxwelton Bldg., Asheville, N. C.

D. TREXLER TIN SHOP

All Kinds of Roofing, Gutter and Conductor Work.

Phone 862

159 South Main St.

DR. C. H. MILLER

MECHANO-THERAPIST

14 N. Spruce St.
Phone 979
ASHEVILLE, N. C.

Hours by engagement

Drugless Healing of Disease

Abernathy Robt S (Amelia), flgmn Sou Ry, h 104 Bartlett
*Abernathy Sarah, dom, h 2 Catholic av
Abrahams Annie C Miss, student, h 187 Montford av
Abrahams Annie K Mrs, wid Dr Wm T, h 187 Montford av
Abrahams Clyde A Lieut, U S A Commandant Bingham School, rms same
Academy School (City), s Main extd
Acee Jno M (Ethel T), claim agt Sou Ry, h 20 Baird
*Adair Siss, laund, h 78 Pine
Adair & Baker (E M Adair, C P Baker), proprs Dew Drop Candy Parlor, 32 Patton av
Adams Anthony (Hattie A), h nr Hazel Mill rd, W Ashev
Adams Eugene T, engnr Sou Ry, h 115 Bartlett
Adams Georgia Miss, nurse 36 Haywood, h same
Adams Hamilton J, mchst, h 80 Josephine
*Adams Hennie, dom, h 159 College
ADAMS JNO S (Merrimon, Adams & Adams), h Bingham Heights
ADAMS JUNIUS G (Helen B) (Merrimon, Adams & Adams) and police justice, h 17 Cullowhee
Adams Lillian A Miss, h 3 Angle, Biltmore
*Adams Lucy, dom 62 Orange
Adams Olando E (Racie D), condr Sou Ry, h 21 Jefferson Drive
Adams Walter S, mining, h 3 Angle, Biltmore
Adams Wm M (Katherine), real estate, h 80 Josephine
*Addington Jas A W (Maggie), waiter, h 16 Weaver
Adelaide Building, Offices, 33-35 Haywood
Adickes Emily B Mrs, "Westdale" Vernon Hill
Adickes Henning F (Emily B), ins, h "Westdale" Vernon Hill
Adickes Henning F Jr, atty, h "Westdale" Vernon Hill
Adickes Sarah S Miss, h "Westdale" Vernon Hill
Adickes Wm Clawson, h "Westdale" Vernon Hill
Aetna Insurance Co, 5-6 Paragon Bldg, Geo E Lee agt
Aiken Arabel Miss, rms Hotel Paxton
Aiken Chas F (Bertha E), slsmn Rogers Grocery Co, h 369 Southside av
Aiken J Patrick (Nora), laundryman, h 65 Starnes av
*Aiken Janie, laund, h (r) 41 Pine
Aiken Marguerite Miss, nurse Aiken Cottage, rms same
*Aikens Frank (Stella), janitor, h 167 Hill
AKERS ARTHUR K (Watt), mngr Postal Tel-Cable Co, h 30 College Park
Akers Clara Mrs, tchr High Schl, h 30 College Park

....Asheville Cleaning and Pressing Club....
Tailoring That Satisfies and Prices That Please
Steam and French Dry Cleaning of all delicate and fine wearing apparel for ladies and gentlemen. MESSENGER SERVICE IN THE CITY.

J. C. WILBAR, Prop.   4. N. Pack Square   PHONE 389

Akers Mary Mrs, tchr, h 30 College Park
Alabama (The), boarding, 127 Haywood, Mrs Carrie B Campbell propr
Albea Geo L, clk Langren Hotel
Albemarle Club, Albemarle Park, T D Raoul pres, A H Malone sec
Albemarle Park, Charlotte nr City Limits
ALBEMARLE PARK CO, builders and renters, Albemarle Park and proprs The Manor, Charlotte nr City Limits—phone 513, Thos W Raoul pres, Wm G Raoul treas, A H Malone sec (see p 17)
Alberts Jos, bkkpr Field's, rms 28 Technical Bldg
Albright Frank J (Catherine A), trav slsmn, h 60 Cumberland av
Albright Ruth E Miss, h 60 Cumberland av
Albright Susan Miss, asst in music Normal & Collegiate Inst
Aldrich Lester P (Nora), engnr Sou Ry, h 95 Ora
*Alexander Adolphus, driver E C Jarrett, h 19 Catholic av
Alexander Alice M Miss, tchr, h 147 Ashland av
*Alexander Amos (Bettie), driver E C Jarrett, h 19 Catholic av
Alexander Beatrice Miss, clk G Alexander, h 218 Patton av
Alexander B V, clk A C Jackson, bds Hazel Mill rd
Alexander Celeste J Mrs, h 159 Hillside
*Alexander Chas (Kate), cook, h 16 Latta
Alexander Edith Miss, asst prin Grace School, bds Billows Rest
Alexander Edith Mrs, mlnr H B Hood, h 68 Church
Alexander Edith A Miss, h 33 Orange
Alexander Edith I Miss, h 255 s Main
*Alexander Emma, h 23 Catholic av
*Alexander Frank (Kate), fruits 12 Eagle, h 12 Baxter al
*Alexander Geo (Laura), eating house 17 Eagle, h 16 same
Alexander Gustave (Minnie), jeweler 33 Patton av, h 218 same
Alexander Hester V Miss, h 33 Orange
Alexander J Mason, student, h 124 Montford av
Alexander J Thos (Addie), emp Burton & Holt, h 275 College
*Alexander Jas A (Belle), fireman, h 40 Catawba
ALEXANDER JAS L (Florence M), propr Battery Park Hotel, h 124 Montford av
Alexander Jas M (Edith), agt Imp Mut L & H Ins Co, bds 68 Church

Asheville Dray, Fuel & Construction Co. — **COAL** — Wood and Kindling, Stone and Sand
6 1-2 South Main   PHONE - 223

68 ASHEVILLE [1913] DIRECTORY

Alexander Jas R (Eva C), cotton planter, h 60 Montford av
Alexander Julia Miss, h 218 Patton av
Alexander Lewis E (Celia), foreman, h Broadway av, W Ashev
ALEXANDER LOUIS I (Gertrude), optometrist and optician, 78 Patton av—phone 92, h 136 w Chestnut—phone 1705

See Us For The Best of Everything **OPTICAL**

We Grind Our Own Lenses

ALEXANDER
Optometrist and Optician

78 PATTON AVENUE
Next to Palace Theatre

Alexander Mark, carp, bds 16 s Spruce
*Alexander Mattie, dom, h 10 Greer's Row
Alexander May Miss, tchr Asheland av Schl, h 255 s Main
Alexander Nannie J Miss, h Haywood rd, W Ashev
*Alexander O G (Mary), lab, h 19 (1) Mountain
Alexander Paul E, sec-treas Asheville Concrete Pipe & Block Co, h 255 s Main
*Alexander Pearl, laund, h 37 Catholic av
*Alexander Peter (Clarissa), meat ctr, h 17 Catholic av
Alexander Rebecca D, wid J M, h 255 s Main
Alexander Robt L (Sallie E), carp, h Brevard rd, W Ashev

When Writing to Advertisers Please Mention the City Directory

*Alexander Rufus B (Julia), barber P A Goins, h 69 Seney
Alexander Ruth Miss, h 159 Hillside
Alexander Serena D Miss, h 159 Hillside
*Alexander Sherman E (Hester), eating hse, 103 Pine, h 115 n Main
Alexander Wm J, h 40 Flint
*Alexander Wm M (Etta), gro Max cor Haid, h 23 Catholic
Alger Bertram H, clk H T Rogers, h 34 Asheland av
Alger Thos, clk, bds 34 Asheland av
All Souls Protestant Episcopal Church, Angle cor Swan, Biltmore, Rev R R Swope rector

---

EVER READY FLASHLIGHTS
Piedmont Electric Company
ASHEVILLE, N. C.
64 PATTON AVENUE

J. C. McPHERSON
SLATE AND TIN ROOFING
Galvanized Iron Work   Hot Air Furnaces
35-37 EAST COLLEGE STREET

PLUMBING STEAM AND HOT WATER **HEATING**
PHONE 133

Yellow Pine / White Pine / Hardwoods
See bet. pgs. 188-189

LUMBER
SASH, BLINDS, DOORS

WOODWARD & SON
Ninth and Arch Streets
RICHMOND - VIRGINIA

ASHEVILLE [1913] DIRECTORY 69

ALLANSTAND COTTAGE INDUSTRIES, art crafts, 33 Haywood; Miss F L Goodrich pres, Miss H C Wilkie mngr

ALLANSTAND COTTAGE INDUSTRIES
Handwoven Rugs, Portieres, Coverlets, Baskets

MISS FRANCES L. GOODRICH, - - President
MISS HARRIET C. WILKIE, - - - Manager

SALESROOM:
THE ADELAIDE
33 Haywood Street -:- ASHEVILLE, N. C.

*Allen Albert, chauffeur, "Klondyke," Montford av
Allen Chas J Genl (Elizabeth W), Genl U S A, h Victoria rd
Allen Clara G Miss, propr The Pines, h 112 Pearson Drive
Allen Ella C Miss, mngr Hotel Paxton, rms same
Allen Grace Miss, h Victoria rd
Allen H Edwin, student, h 237 Montford av
Allen Harry L, bds 112 Pearson Drive
Allen Herbert C (Alice G), mngr Ashev Transfer & Storage Co, h 237 Montford av
*ALLEN INDUSTRIAL HOME and Asheville Academy under auspices Woman's Home Missionary Society M E Church, 241 College, Miss Alsie B Dole supt (see page 23)
Allen Jas (Sarah C), boarding 51 Penland, h same
Allen Jno A, painter, h 135 n Main
Allen M Althea Mrs, boarding 135 n Main, h same
*Allen Mary, laundress, h 17 Wallach
Allen P A, clk, rms 11 Maxwelton Bldg
ALLEN P R, mngr insurance dept Wachovia Bank & Trust Co—phone 166, rms 11 Flint

Representing All Lines of Insurance

FIRE	LIFE	LIABILITY
HEALTH	ACCIDENT	BONDING

*Allen Walter A (Emma), cook, h 45 Mountain
*Allan Wesley (Ella), lab, h (r) 330 w Haywood

What Have You in Real Estate that You Don't Want?

What do You Want in Real Estate that You Haven't?

WESTERN CAROLINA REALTY CO.
J. W. Wolfe, Sec. & Treas.
On the Square
PHONE 974
10 N. PACK Sq.

H. A. BROWN & Co.
General Contractors
23 Temple Court Bldg.
Phone 341

—DEALERS IN—

Rough Building
and
all Kinds of
Crushed Stone

—OUR SPECIALTIES—

STONE
FOUNDATIONS
CONCRETE WORK
and
EXCAVATING

Moale & Chiles Real Estate and Insurance
27 Patton Ave., [2d fl] Phone 661
City and Suburban Property FARMS and TIMBER LANDS

Club Cafe and Candy Kitchen
"A GOOD PLACE FOR REFRESHMENT"

The standards we work to in our Restaurant Department are: Cooking, perfect; Service, prompt and cheerful; Prices, moderate; Menu, everything in season. Parties and Banquets, Teas and Dinners. 19 and 21 Haywood St. Phones 110 and 111.

Brown's Undertaking Parlors

S. H. BROWN

50 Patton Avenue
ASHEVILLE, N. C.

Lady Assistant When Desired

Phone 193-2 Rings

THE MOORE Plumbing Company

16 N. Pack Square

PHONE 1025

Sanitary Plumbing, General Tin and Metal Work, Hot Air Furnaces

---

70 ASHEVILLE [1913] DIRECTORY

Alley Chas S (Sarah C), chauffeur, h 20 n French Broad av
Alley Sarah C Mrs, propr The Richelieu, h 20 n French Broad av
Allison Alma Miss, rms 210 College
Allison Andrew B, trav slsmn Harris-Barnett Dry Goods Co, res Webster N C
Allison Argus (Florence), pressman The Inland Press, h 376 w Haywood
*Allison Belle, cook, h 48 McDowell
Allison Coleman N (Bessie), supt Balfour Quarry Co, h 605 Montford av
ALLISON'S DRUG STORE (T B Allison), 43 Patton av opp Church st—phone 556
Allison Ernest B (Kate), foreman, h 240 Southside av
Allison Erwin (May B), clk C A Walker, h 150 Asheland av
Allison Florence E Mrs, clk Bon Marche, h 376 w Haywood
Allison G D (S Edna), gro 225 Merrimon av, h same
*Allison Hattie, cook, h 48 McDowell
Allison Irvin (Callie), engnr Sou Ry, h 59 Bartlett
Allison L Canie (Celia), painter Excel P & P Hse, h 332 n Main
Allison Louise Mrs, rms 35 Turner
Allison Maggie Miss, h 99 Jefferson Drive
*Allison Nancy, laund, h 7 Greer's Row
Allison Oliver T, lab, h Lester rd, W Ashev
Allison Saml, student, h 59 Bartlett
Allison T Birch (Rosalie), (Allison's Drug Store), h 104 s French Broad
Allison Thos C, lab, h Lester rd, W Ashev
*Allison Wm, driver, h 72 Market
Allman Harriet Miss, h Woolsey (R F D 1)
Allman Jas T (May), driver, h Woolsey (R F D 1)
Allman Zoe Miss, h 169 Patton av
Allman Willie K Miss, h Woolsey (R F D 1)
Allport Frances D Mrs, furn rms 18 Oak, h same
Allport J Hobart (Frances D), mngr, h 18 Oak
Allport Myrtle C, wid Andrew, h 18 Oak
Allport Susanna N Miss, h 18 Oak
Ambler Building, 72 n Main
AMBLER CHASE P (Harriet B), physician, office 72 n Main—Tel 306, h 412 Merrimon av—Tel 241
American Dairy Lunch Restaurant, 1½ s w Pack Sq, Chakales & Pilalas proprs
American Furniture Buyers Assn, 37-38-39 Amer Natl Bank Bldg, F S Kennett mngr

---

The Battery Park Bank

Capital - - $100,000.00
Surplus and Profits, $110,000.00

ASHEVILLE, N. C. City, County and State Depositary

J. A. TILLMAN — Jeweler — 17 N. Main St.
I carry a nice line of Watches, Clocks and Jewelry, and make a specialty of repair work. Satisfaction guaranteed

American Furniture Manufacturing Co, 37-38-39 Amer Natl Bank Bldg; H Miller pres, J C Pritchard v-pres, F S Kennett sec-treas
American Furniture Mnfg Co, plant Riverside Drive
AMERICAN NATIONAL BANK (The), 44 Patton av s e cor Church; L L Jenkins pres, C J Harris v-pres, Henry Redwood v-pres, J G Merrimon v-pres, A E Rankin asst cashr, R E Currance asst cashr (see front cover)
AMERICAN NATIONAL BANK BUILDING, offices, 44 Patton av
American Tailors (Inc), 25 Patton av, F Y McConnell mngr
AMERICAN WAGON CO (J C Wallace, J H Weaver), builders of American Dump and Asheville Farm Wagons, repairing and horseshoeing, 65-67 s Main—phone 262
AMISS J TAYLOR MRS, propr The Bonniview, h 128 Haywood—phone 1553 (see p 20)
Anandale Purity Dairy, W Asheville
Anders Alfred B (Alice), carp, h nr Smith's Bridge, W Ashev
Anders Benj F (Loretta), carp, h 15 Seney
Anders Henry, emp city, h 242 n Main
Anders J Burgin (McLean & Anders), h 242 n Main
Anders Jas J (Irene), motorman, bds 39 Clingman av
Anders Jettie M Miss, inspr, h nr Smith's Bridge, W Ashev
Anders Jno H, carp, h 242 n Main
Anders Jno H (Eliza), tanner, h Haywood rd, W Ashev
Anders Lewis (Nancy), lab, h 79 Hall
Anders Martha Miss, h 242 n Main
Anders Martha, wid Jno, h Haywood rd, W Ashev
Anders Philip (Julia), h Haywood rd, W Ashev
Anders Teddy C (Lillian), mtrmn St Ry, h 71 Conestee
Anders Verda Miss, h Haywood rd, W Ashev
☞Anders see also Andrews
*Anderson Andrew (Catherine), janitor Maxwelton Bldg, h 69 Mountain
Anderson Arthur C (Emma B), yd condr Sou Ry, h 655 Oakland av
Anderson Augusta Miss, prin Grace School, bds Billows Rest
Anderson Chas G (Fannie), farmer, h Asheville av, W Ashev
Anderson Clara Belle Miss, tchr Normal & Collegiate Inst, rms same
*Anderson David (Adeline), lab, h 115 Wallach

INSURANCE
INSURE YOUR SALARY WITH US
NEVER CARRY YOUR OWN RISK
SAFETY IS THE BEST POLICY
UNLESS YOU ARE A CAPITALIST
REST EASY IF YOU HAVE
AN ACCIDENT WE WILL
NOT KEEP YOU WAITING TO
COLLECT YOUR CLAIM
EVERY CLAIM PROMPTLY PAID

Imperial Mutual Life & Health Insurance Co.

Home Office: ASHEVILLE, N. C.
Phone 495

HOTEL OXFORD — Asheville, N. C.
Redecorated and Refitted throughout. Recently enlarged to 60 rooms. Centrally located. Depot cars stop at entrance. Long distance telephone office upstairs. American and European plan. Rates 50c, 75c and $1 per day; special rates by week or month. C. H. Branson & Sons, Proprietors. Phone 1887. 50-54 South Main St.

Anderson Edith Miss, tchr Asheland av School
*Anderson Ella E, tchr Mountain St Schl, h 27 Furman av
Anderson Geo E, driver Sou Exp Co, h W Asheville
Anderson Gudder, driver, h Grace
*Anderson Hattie, dom, h 12 Cumberland av
*Anderson Henry, lab, h 38 Wallach
*Anderson Henry (Minnie), lab, h Biltmore rd, S Biltmore
*Anderson Hettie, laund, h 12 Cumberland av
*Anderson Isabella, dom, h 53 Church
*Anderson Jas (Amanda), lab, h 127 Clingman av
ANDERSON JAS G (Lottie L), physician 14-15 Morsell Bldg, office hours 10 to 12 and 3 to 5—phone 568, h W Asheville—phone 568
Anderson Jno, clk Sou Ry, h Main st, W Ashev
*Anderson Jno (Rosa), lab, h 12 Blanton
Anderson Jno B (Sarah E), (Stevens & Anderson), h 332 Montford av
*Anderson Jos (Cora), lab, h 19 s Grove
*Anderson Lewis (Malinda), h Chunns Cove
Anderson Margaret, wid E Ross, h 38 Atkinson
Anderson N M (Asheville School), h Haywood rd (5 m w)
*Anderson Rose, cook Mrs E H Radeker, rms same
Anderson Rufus L (Rosa), blksmith A B Bishop, h Haywood rd, W Ashev
Anderson Sallie J, wid Locke M, boarding 655 Oakland av, h same
*Anderson Sandy (Jennie), lab, h 26 Bay
Anderson Vinnie Miss, mlnr Sproat's, h 268 Chestnut
*Anderson Walter (Henrietta), lab, h 127 Clingman av
*Anderson Wm M Rev (Ella), presiding elder A M E Zion Church, h 27 Furman av
*Anderson Zan, lab, h 81 Roberts
Andrews Geo W (Olive), carp, h 82 Hall
Andrews Lockie, h 76 Blanton
Andrews Margaret F, wid D B, h 62 Josephine
Andrews Terrell M (Cora J), carp, h Brevard rd, W Ashev
Andrews Warren J, clk Nichols Shoe Co, Inc, bds 128 s Main
   Andrews see also Anders
*Angel Georgia, laundress, h 46 Smith
*Angel Jno (Hattie), lab, h 46 Smith
Angel Melvin Y (Frances), police, h Valley cor Eagle
Anglin Zebulon B, trav slsmn, rms 3 Barnard Bldg
*Anthony Dianah M, dom, h 31 Max
*Anthony Jos (Lizzie), gro 23 Hazzard, h same

Maple Flooring and Poplar Siding

English Lumber Co.
PHONE . . 321

ASHEVILLE [1913] DIRECTORY

Antiseptic Barber Shop (R C Parkins, C M Williams), 1 Patton av
Apostolic Holiness Church, Buxton nr Park av
Apperson Helen Miss, tchr, bds Cherokee Inn
Arany Chas, jeweler C E Hednerson, h 173 s Main
Arbogast Clifford, student, h 108 Montford av
Arfbogast Eula M Miss, h 108 Montford av
Arbogast Jno C (Ida M), mngr Champion Lbr Co, h 108 Montford av
ARBOGAST MOTOR CO (Ralph B Arbogast), automobiles and supplies, 52-60 n Main—phones 1728 and 303 (see left side lines)
ARBOGAST RALPH B (Arbogast Motor Co), h 108 Montford av
Archer Chas (Dora), carp, h 100 Avery
*Archer Lindsey (Lizzie), porter, h 42 Ridge
Arcouet Leah H Miss, h 85 St Dunstan's rd
Arcouet Mary E, wid Casimir, h 85 St Dunstan's rd
"Ardmion," residence of O C Hamilton, Carroll av
Argintarter Benny (Argintarter Bros), h 70 College
Argintarter Bros (Sanders and Benny), ladies' suits, 43 College
Argintarter Sanders (Argintarter Bros), h 18 Central av
Argoe Robt T (Winnie L), h 97 Broad
Armory Hall, Penland nr Walnut
Armour & Co, provisions, 375 Depot, Eugene Carland mngr
Armstrong — Mrs, rms 31 Grove
*Armstrong Annie, laund, h 19 Bay
*Armstrong Ethel, maid, h 19 Bay
Armstrong Flora, wid Eugene, h Chunns Cove
*Armstrong Jesse C (Eula), lab, h 19 Bay
Armstrong Kathleen M Miss, cashr M V Moore & Co, h 31 Grove
Armstrong Wilbur W, h Chunns Cove
Arnett Eugene, bds 153 n Main
Arney Chas, watchmkr, bds 173 s Main
*Arnold Alice, laund, h 35 Ocala
*Arnold Jas (Iona), porter Ashev Gro Co, h 14 Magnolia av
*Arnold Jno, presser Eagle Street Pressing Club, h 17 Atkin
*Arnold Lula, dom, h 35 Ocala
*Arnold Oscar (Sadie), waiter, h 166 Hill
*Arnold Robt L (Margaret), waiter, h 35 Ocala
*Arnold Stella, dom, h 123 Valley
Arrowood Columbus C (Mary), mtrmn St Ry, h 15 Seney
Arthur Cecil C, emp Sou Ry, h 105 Asheland av

BIGGEST BUSIEST BEST
Asheville Steam Laundry

Phones:
1936 and 1937

43 to 47
W. College Street

CHARLES H. HONESS
OPTOMETRIST
AND
OPTICIAN

Exclusive maker of
ATLAS SHUR-ON
EYE GLASSES

THE
Home of Ce-Rite
Toric Lenses

We make a specialty of correcting optical defects with properly fitted glasses.

54 Patton Avenue
Opposite Postoffice

IF in the market for a Gas Engine let us make you prices.
its heavy castings, such as columns or building plates, see us.
its a skilled mechanic for boiler work, see us.
you want machine work of any kind phone 590.

CAROLINA MACHINERY CO.

FOUNDERS
MACHINISTS and
Jobbers of Mill
Supplies

Life Insurance Company of Virginia
ORGANIZED 1871
Home Office - Richmond, Va.

Has won the hearty approval and active support of the people by its promptness and fair dealing during the **FORTY-TWO YEARS** of its operation

J. V. Moon, Superintendent, Rooms 3-4-5 Maxwelton Bldg., Asheville, N. C.

T. P. JOHNSON & CO.

SHEET METAL WORKERS

All Kinds of Roofing Guttering and Conductor Work Metal Ceilings, Skylights and Galvanized Iron Cornices

OFFICE and SHOP: 69-71 S. MAIN

Phone 325

DR. C. H. MILLER

Mechano-Therapist

14 N. Spruce Street
ASHEVILLE, N. C.

PHONE 979

Hours by Engagement

DRUGLESS HEALING OF DISEASE

Arthur Fannie V Miss, h 324 College
Arthur Geo S, mngr Biltmore Vegetable Garden, h Biltmore Estate
Arthur J Waller (Ellie G), condr St Ry, h 56 Gaston
Arthur Jas N, emp Sou Ry, h 105 Asheland av
Arthur Jno P, atty at law, 29 Morsell Bldg, h 324 College
Arthur Jno W L (Sophie B), lumber dlr, h 105 Asheland av
Arthur Wm, opr Postal Tel-Cable Co, h 105 Asheland av
Arthur Wm H (Minnie M), tinner A L McLean & Co, h 158 Blanton
Artus Endora (Julia), gardener, rms Zealandia
*Asbury Sidney A (Anna), propr Y M I Pressing Club, h 74 Market
Ashe Chas B, cutter, h 72 Ralph
*Ashe Hugh L Rev (Nannie), dist supt Western Dist M E Church, h 20 Hildebrand
Ashe Ida M Miss, h 99 Jefferson Drive
Ashe May L Miss, picker, h 72 Ralph

```
Correct Advertising
    Brings results all ways and always;
    and your City Directory is at your
    instant command for correctness.
```

Asheland Avenue Graded School, 186-216 Asheland av, A H King prin
Asheville Abbatoir, W Asheville
ASHEVILLE ACADEMY AND ALLEN INDUSTRIAL HOME, under auspices Woman's Home Missionary Society M E Church, 241 College, Miss Alsie B Dole supt (see p 23)
Asheville Auditorium, Haywood at junction of Flint, G W Bailey mngr
Asheville Auto Co, 15-17 s Lexington av, E C Sawyer propr
Asheville Barber Shop, 14 Patton av, T Perry Young propr
ASHEVILLE BARBERS' SUPPLY CO (Inc), a full line barbers' supplies, 23 n Main—phone 432; B T Tiller pres, J T Tiller sec
ASHEVILLE BASE BALL CLUB (Inc), 201-202 Legal Bldg; Fergus Stikeleather pres, V L Wells v-pres, T M Duckett sec-treas
ASHEVILLE BOARD OF TRADE, 6-7-8 Temple Ct Neptune Buckner sec

---

ASHEVILLE CLEANING and PRESSING CLUB

TAILORING THAT SATISFIES and PRICES THAT PLEASE

Hats cleaned, banded and bound. Silk hats ironed. Buttons made to order in all sizes. Plain or with rims. **PHONE 389**

DYEING IN ALL SHADES Cleaned. Messenger Service.

Kid Gloves, Slippers and Plumes. Fancy Jabots and Ties, French Dry Cleaned. Ladies' and Gentlemen's suits Steam Cleaned.

J. C. Wilbar, Prop. 4 NORTH PACK SQ.

ASHEVILLE COAL CO.
6 North Pack Sq. Phone 40

M. & W. COAL

Gas Ranges — **Asheville Power and Light Co.** PHONE 69

ASHEVILLE BUSINESS COLLEGE, 8 n Pack Sq (3d fl), H S Shockley prin

Asheville Business COLLEGE Oldest in the State

Third Floor, Revell-Wagner Building
N. PACK SQUARE

Full Business, Shorthand and Typewriting courses. Also courses in Salesmanship and Postal Examinations. Two Thousand Graduates holding responsible positions in Ten States. This is not a cheap College, offering partial courses only. For full information, call on or address the principal,

HENRY S. SHOCKLEY, Asheville, N. C.

Asheville Cabinet Co (D C Collins, T G Williams), furn repairers, 17½ Church
Asheville Candy Kitchen, 13 s Main, Geo Gianakos propr
Asheville Carpet House, 18-20 Church, O M Coston propr
Asheville Cavalry Governor's Guards, Paragon Bldg, R R Reynolds capt
Asheville Cemetery, Cemetery Drive, W S Cornell supt
Asheville Cemetery Co, s Pack Sq cor Main; J P Sawyer pres, Haywood Parker sec-treas
Asheville Children's Home, Woolsey
ASHEVILLE CITIZEN (The), (Daily, Sunday and Weekly), 8 Battery Park pl, The Citizen Co proprs; Robt S Jones bus mngr, Jas H Caine mng editor
ASHEVILLE CITY DIRECTORY (Piedmont Directory Co), 66 and L Amer Natl Bank Bldg, Ernest H Miller genl mngr
ASHEVILLE CITY OFFICIALS (see City Officials)
ASHEVILLE CLEANING & PRESSING CLUB, 4 n Pack Sq—phone 389, J C Wilbar propr (see bottom lines)
Asheville Club, Haywood cor Battery Park pl; Jos W Sluder pres, J Gibbon Merrimon v-pres, Jno S Adams sec-treas
Asheville Club Building, 24 Battery Park pl
ASHEVILLE COAL CO, dealers, 6 n Pack Sq—phone 40, F M Weaver mngr (see top lines)

Meats **Kiibler & Whitehead**
CITY MARKET   PHONES, 195 and 694

Asheville Concrete Pipe & Block Co, 6½ s Main; R M Ramsey pres, P E Alexander sec-treas

Asheville Cotton Mills (Inc), w Haywood and Sou Ry; F W Cone pres, J E Harden v-pres, M D Long sec-treas

Asheville Country Club, Golf Links, Charlotte extd

ASHEVILLE DRAY, FUEL & CONSTRUCTION CO (Inc), 6½ s Main—phone 223, yards Depot and Roberts; R M Ramsey pres, W H Bird v-pres, J F Keith sec-treas (see top lines and p 9)

Asheville Dray, Fuel & Construction Co, yds, Roberts nr Clingman av

ASHEVILLE DRY CLEANING CO, n e cor n Main & College sts—phones 835 and 836, E S Paine propr (see bottom lines)

Asheville Dry Goods Co, 10-12 Patton av

ASHEVILLE ELECTRICAL CO, 74 Central av, W Mansfield Booze mngr (see side lines)

Asheville F P Gas Machine Co (Louis Fragge and Nicholas Blau), dlrs, 62 s Main

ASHEVILLE FIRE DEPARTMENT, City Hall—phone 1000

Asheville Fish Co, City Market, C E Sorrels propr

ASHEVILLE FURNITURE CO, 29 s Main, C M Cohen, propr

ASHEVILLE GAZETTE-NEWS (The), (daily except Sunday), 4 n Pack Sq, The Evening News Publishing Co publishers; W A Hildebrand editor, J R Law sec-treas

ASHEVILLE GRAIN & HAY CO, wholesale feed dealers, Depot cor Roberts—phone 197, Earle & Nelson proprs

ASHEVILLE GROCERY CO, wholesale 385 Depot, H C Johnson propr—phones 881 and 886

Asheville Harness Co (Inc), mnfrs, 33 s Main; J P Coston pres, Chas Glass v-pres, C N Webster sec-treas

Asheville High School, Oak n e cor College, R V Kennedy prin

Asheville Hook and Ladder No 1, City Hall

Asheville Hose Co No 1, City Hall

Asheville Hose Co No 2, City Hall

ASHEVILLE ICE CO (J A Nichols, A W Faulkner), 8 Market—phone 72

ASHEVILLE LIBRARY, 4 s Park Sq, Miss Grace McH Jones, librarian

Asheville Light Infantry, Armory

Asheville Lodge K of P, Paragon Bldg (3d fl)

MAPLE FLOORING
HARDWOOD LUMBER OF ALL KINDS

WOODWARD & SON
9th and Arch Sts., Richmond, Va.
See Adv. Opposite Page 188

Asheville Lumber Co, 14 Temple ct; W N Cooper pres, T J Cooper v-pres, J E Dickerson sec-treas
Asheville Marble Works, 170 Patton av, H D Gentry propr
ASHEVILLE MERCANTILE AGENCY, 27 Amer Nat'l Bank Bldg; W McDowell sec-treas, G T Hawes mngr
ASHEVILLE MERCHANTS ASSN, 6-8 Temple Ct, J E Rector sec
Asheville Mica Co (W Vance and S H Brown), 26-28 Market
Asheville Mica Co, warehouse, Lyman cor Avery, Wade Morgan supt
Asheville Milling Co, 530 w Haywood, W E Collins mngr
Asheville Mission Hospital, 5 Charlotte, Mrs Martha Carvin supt
Asheville Mission Hospital, Nurses Home, 17 Charlotte
Asheville Packing Co (S Sternberg, G Lichtenfels, F Zimmerman), meat packers and mnfrs, fertilizers, office 353 Depot, plant W Asheville
Asheville Printing & Engraving Co, 15 Church; Dr S Westray Battle pres-genl mngr, O H Page v-pres, L M Bourne sec, M V Moore treas

---

When writing to advertisers please mention the City Directory

---

ASHEVILLE PAINT & GLASS CO, 4-6 n Main—phone 292; S O Bradley pres-treas, B C Carpenter v-pres, O R S Pool sec (see back cover)
Asheville Piano Co, 118 Patton av, J W Davis propr
ASHEVILLE POLICE COURT, City Hall, J G Adams, justice
ASHEVILLE POWER & LIGHT CO, Patton av s e cor Asheland av; C E Johnson pres, H W Plummer v-pres and genl mngr—phone 69 (see side lines)
ASHEVILLE POWER & LIGHT CO, gas plant 140 Avery, Jno D Caldwell supt
ASHEVILLE POWER & LIGHT CO, power plant 131-151 Avery, M P Lawrence chf engnr
Asheville School (The), Haywood rd, 5 miles w of city, N M Anderson and C A Mitchell prins
Asheville School for Girls, 2 Woodfin, Miss E K Ford prin
Asheville School of Musical Art, Auditorium Bldg, F F Harker director
Asheville Shoe Shine Parlor, 4 Patton av, Chakales & Pilalas proprs

---

What Have You in Real Estate that You Don't Want?

What do You Want in Real Estate that You Haven't?

WESTERN CAROLINA REALTY CO.
J. W. Wolfe, Sec. & Treas.

On the Square
PHONE 974
10 N. PACK SQ.

Brown-Carter Realty Co.
REAL ESTATE
23 TEMPLE COURT
PHONE 341
ASHEVILLE   N. C.

FLORIDA SPECIALTIES
Grazing, Timbered, Farm Lands, Orange Groves, Turpentine Locations and Phosphate Lands.

NORTH CAROLINA SPECIALTIES
Orchard, Farm and Timbered Lands, City Property, Rent Collections.

Moale & Chiles Real Estate and Insurance
27 Patton Ave., (2d fl)   Phone 661
General Agents United States Fidelity & Guaranty Co.

Club Cafe and Candy Kitchen
"A GOOD PLACE FOR REFRESHMENT"

Our Ice Cream manufacturing plant is absolutely clean and sanitary.
Prompt family delivery. Phones 110 and 111.
Catering for large parties and receptions. Special Creams.

Brown's Undertaking Parlors S. H. BROWN Lady Assistant When Desired Phone 193-2 Rings 50 Patton Avenue Asheville, N. C. --- Established 1894 **B. J. JACKSON** Carefully Selected Fruits and Vegetables Stall No. 11, City Market BUSINESS PHONES: 86 and 101 RESIDENCE PHONE 1596	ASHEVILLE SIGN CO, 25-27 n Lexington av—phone 681, G E Mitchell pres & genl mngr, W G Jenkins sec-treas # Asheville Sign Company ## SIGNS ### "OF THE TIMES" 25-27 N. Lexington Ave. -:- Asheville, N. C. Asheville Steam Bakery, 110-112 Patton av, A A Buehrer mngr ASHEVILLE STEAM LAUNDRY, 43 w College—phones 1936 & 1937, J A Nichols mngr (see side lines) Asheville Steam Vulcanizing Co (W E Kennerly), 7 College ASHEVILLE SUPPLY & FOUNDRY CO (Inc), machinists 18-22 Market—phone 155; D S Hildebrand pres, W C Britt sec-treas, G W Donnan mngr (see index for adv) ASHEVILLE TELEPHONE & TELEGRAPH CO (Inc), 32 Walnut, M A Erskine dist coml mngr Asheville Tobacco Co, 35 w Walnut, W W Barnard propr Asheville Transfer & Storage Co, 60 Patton av, H C Allen mngr Asheville Transfer Moving & Storage Co, whol, Main cor Atkin ASHEVILLE & EAST TENNESSEE RAILROAD CO, 7 n Main—phone 715; J S Coleman pres, Stanley Howland v-pres-genl mngr, Reginald Howland treas, G W Epps sec (see front cover and top lines) Ashton Agnes, wid Jas, h 91 Seney Ashton Chas B (Mary R), drug clk, h 99 Merrimon av Ashton J F Lang, student, h 99 Merrimon av Ashton Jas (Kelley), driver, h 91 Seney Ashton Lena, wid Webster, h 35 Southside av Ashton Saml, driver, h 91 Seney Ashton Sarah E Miss, h 99 Merrimon av ☞ Ashton see also Aston Ashworth Ralph P, clk E S Galyean, rms Y M C A

Furniture and China Carefully Prepared for Shipment

Mahogany Furniture Hand Made & Carefully Reproduced | **E. E. GALER** 114 PATTON AVE. | Upholstering and Refinishing PHONE - 1674

Askew Ira (Eulalia), yd supt Natl Casket Co, h 251 Flint
Askew Jno Mc C (Sadie), train dispr Sou Ry, h 79 Cumberland av
Askew Wm A (Nancy), h 444 Depot
Aspery Jos (Julia), iron wkr, h 195 Patton av
Ast Chas, wkr Ashe Mica Co, h 72 Relph
Ast May Miss, wks Ashev Mica Co, h 72 Ralph
Aston Cordelia, wid E J, h 45 Church
Aston Park (City), s French Broad av opp Philip
ASTON, RAWLS & CO (C T Rawls, Fergus Stikeleather), genl ins, real estate, 22-23 Amer Natl Bank Bldg—phone 387
Atkin Susan G, wid Thos W, dress mkr, h 34 Monroe pl
Atkins Augusta Mrs, phone opr Battery Park Hotel, rms same
Atkins Bertha L Miss, h 174 s Main
Atkins Carrie Miss, h 108 Avery
Atkins Dock (Ethel), painter R E Bowles, h 36 s Spruce
Atkins Edwd, painter Excelsior P & P House, h Woodfin st
Atkins Elsie F Miss, music tchr 136½ s Main, h same
Atkins Emma Miss, h 108 Avery
Atkins Jno (Laura), h 34 Highland
Atkins Laura, wid Thos, h 108 Avery
Atkins Margaret I Miss, dom, h 34 McDowell
Atkins Margaret M Miss, china decorator and superv drawing city schls, 136½ s Main, rms same
Atkins Sarah, wid Wm M, h 34 McDowell
Atkins Thos (Josephine), painter R E Bowles, h 174 s Main
Atkins Thos N, painter, h 34 McDowell
Atkinson Edwd B (Annie J) (Natt Atkinson Sons' Co), h Haywood rd, W Asheville
Atkinson Edwd N, h Haywood rd, W Asheville
Atkinson Harriett N, wid Natt, h Haywood rd, W Asheville
Atkinson Jack, h Haywood rd, W Asheville
Atkinson Julia E Miss, h Haywood rd, W Asheville
Atkinson Mary R Miss, h Haywood rd, W Asheville
Atkinson Philip G, h Haywood rd, W Asheville
Atkinson Natt Sons' Co (Edwd B Atkinson), real estate, 5 w Pack Sq
Atwell Wm, electrn, bds Shanks' Hotel
AUDITORIUM (The), Haywood Junction of Flint
*Austell Lawrence (Dora), bellman, rms 86 Eagle
*Austin ——, waiter The Winyah, h 166 Church
*Austin Della, cook, h 180 Hill
*Austin Ella, laund, h 58 Ralph

Mrs. Wilder's SANITARY HOME LAUNDRY turns out first class work in Laundering and Dry Cleaning. No. 7 Montford Ave., Phone 1354

Austin Elsie Miss, wks Ashev Mica Co, h 13 Buttrick
Austin Emma B Miss, h 102 s Main
Austin Emma J, wid O O, h 102 s Main
Austin Frank J (Alice), clk Ashev P & G Co, h 60 Conestee
Austin Grover L, switchman, bds Highland Hotel
Austin Harriet A, wid G P, h 26 Buttrick
*Austin Henry (May), tchr, h 231 Flint
Austin J Frank (Alice), clk, bds 60 Conestee
*Austin Louvinia, h 109 Beaumont
Austin Lyman T, carp, h 27 Atkinson
Austin Mittie C Mrs, clk Peerless Dept Store, h 100 s Main
Avanmore (The), boarding, 107 Haywood, Mrs Josephine Baker propr
*Avery Amanda, cook, h 64 Hill
*Avery Anna, cook, h 64 Hill
*Avery Anna, laund, h 26 Pearson Drive
*Avery Caroline, laund, h 126 Eagle
*Avery Edwd (Harley), driver, h 62 Mountain
*Avery Harper (Handsome), driver, h 93½ n Lexington av
*Avery Jennie, h 27 Curve
*Avery Jno, driver, 435 Pearson Drive
*Avery Malinda, waitress, h 36 Ocala
Avery Mary Mrs, h Lester rd, W Asheville
*Avery Rosa, cook, h Bingham Heights
Avery Street M E Church, 85 Avery, Rev Jno Carver pastor
*Avery Tempie, h 26 Pearson Drive
*Avery Wm (Addie), lab, h s Asheville
Azalea Woodworking Co, planing mill Azalea N C, W O Riddick mngr

B

*Babb Arglee, h 19 Maiden la
*Babb Jno (Texie), driver Ashev Gro Co, h 19 Maiden la
Baber Willie, student, bds 255 s Main
Bachelder Edna Miss, student, h 137 Woodfin
Bachelder Syvil Miss, student, h 137 Woodfin
*Bacon Jas (Viney), porter, h (r) 45 n French Broad av
BACTERIO-THERAPEUTIC LABORATORY, Winyah Sanatorium, Dr Karl Von Ruck director
Bagur Peter E (Diana), h 17 Clyde
Bagwell Clarence L, clk G D Allison, h 98 Cherry
Bagwell Ella G, wid W L, h 98 Cherry
Bagwell Irvin G (Julia D), dist dept, h 76 Cherry

BUICK MAXWELL'S OLDSMOBILE DETROIT ELECTRIC
ARBOGAST MOTOR COMPANY
ACCESSORIES AND SUPPLIES
52-60 N. Main   Phones 302 and 1728

Asheville Dry Cleaning Co.
Telephones 835-836, All Dep't
MAIN, N. E. COR. COLLEGE

THE CLEANERS
Our Department for Oriental Rugs and Carpet Cleaning is prepared to serve you in all its branches.
E. S. Paine   O. E. Hansen

For Kindling "What am Kindling" Call
ENGLISH LUMBER COMPANY   Phone 321

Bagwell Wilton H, mchst, h 98 Cherry
*Bailey C B, genl agt Royal Fraternal Assn, res Charlotte N C
*Bailey Caroline, h W Asheville (R F D3)
Bailey Cordie M Miss, h 331 Southside av
Bailey Doylas, lab, bds Riverside Drive nr n Main
*Bailey Edwd, porter baggage Sou Ry
*Bailey Edwd (Anna), lab, h 13 Wallach
*Bailey Frank (Maggie), lab, h 45 Velvet
*Bailey Geo (Nancy), pedler, h 58½ Mountain
Bailey Geo W (Isabele), mngr Ashev Auditorium, bds 107 Haywood
Bailey Gersh T (Belle M), rustic mkr, h W Asheville
Bailey Jas, lab, bds Riverside Drive nr n Main
*Bailey Jas (Ella), huckster, h 47 Fredrick
*Bailey Jas D (Christine), lab, h 73 Ridge
*Bailey Joel (Daisy), lab, h 28 Sassafras
*Bailey Julia, cook, h 60 Valley
*Bailey Lillie, dom, h 52 Mountain
*Bailey Nancy, dom, h 52 Mountain
Bailey Saml S (Annie M), mchst Western Carolina Auto Co, h W Asheville
*Bailey Thos (Beatrice), lab 50 Reed
Bailey Thurman, lineman, bds 56 Penland
Bailey Vennia Mrs, h Swannanoa av, W Asheville
Baird Annie Laurie Miss, h 54 Central av
*Baird Calvin (Matilda), lab, h 44 McDowell
BAIRD CHAS W (Nancy) (Baird-Wilford Realty Co), h 73 Cumberland av—phone 1308
*Baird David (Leila), presser, h 130 Lexington
Baird David E, clk, h 54 Central av
*Baird Gay M (Lelia), pressing 51 East, h 57 Fulton
*Baird Hannah, h 44 McDowell
Baird Harriet L, wid Elisha, h 54 Central av
Baird Jas R (Epsie), clk Rogers Gro Co, h Beaver Dam (R F D 1)
*Baird Jno (Lottie), janitor, h 48 Curve
*Baird Jno B (Annie), horseshoer, h 21 Bay
Baird Jno T (Sallie), broker, 2 Morsell Bldg, h 80 Cumberland av
*Baird Mary, laund, h 110 Eagle
Baird Mary E Miss, student, h 54 Central av
Baird Sallie L, wid J R, h 135 Asheland av
BAIRD THURMAN G (Alice F), groceries and provisions 152 Montford av—phone 224, h 140 same

BIGGEST **B**USIEST **B**EST

Phones 1936 and 1937
ASHEVILLE STEAM LAUNDRY
43 to 47 W. COLLEGE

S. D. HALL REAL ESTATE AGENT

Money Loaned

Notary Public

32 PATTON AVENUE

Phone 91

Founders, Machinists and Jobbers of Mill Supplies
PHONE 590 — When in the market for pipe and fittings, let us make you Prices.
Carolina Machinery Co.
PHONE 590 — If it's a Gas Engine let us figure with you, also on other kinds of machinery

LIFE INSURANCE COMPANY OF VA. OLDEST, LARGEST STRONGEST Southern Life Insurance Co.

ORGANIZED 1871
RICHMOND, VIRGINIA

Issues Industrial Policies from $8.00 to $900.00, with Premiums Payable WEEKLY on persons from two to seventy years of age

J. V. Moon, Superintendent, Rooms 3-4-5 Maxwelton Bldg., Asheville, N. C.

D. TREXLER TIN SHOP

All Kinds of Roofing, Gutter and Conductor Work.

Phone 862

159 South Main St.

DR. C. H. MILLER

MECHANO-THERAPIST

14 N. Spruce St.
Phone 979
ASHEVILLE, N. C.

Hours by engagement

Drugless Healing of Disease

Baird Wilburn A, foreman W H Westall & Co, h 135 Asheland av
BAIRD-WILFORD REALTY CO (Chas W Baird, Isaac B Wilford), real estate, insurance, loans and investments, 206 Oates Bldg (see p 24)
Baity Ada Miss, clk Palais Royal, h W Asheville
Baity Jas W (Georgia A), carp, h Pennsylvania av, W Asheville
Baity M Ada Miss, clk, h Pennsylvania av, W Asheville
Baker Addie Mrs, furn rooms 71 Woodfin, h same
*Baker Alfred (Fannie), lab, h 31 Cole
*Baker B, driver E C Jarrett
*Baker Beulah, h 70 Hill
*Baker Callie, dom, 1 Catholic av
Baker Chas P (Adeline), Dew Drop Candy Parlor, h 71 Woodfin
Baker F Ruggles, cashr Prudential Ins Co of Amer, rms 18 Vance
Baker Hamilton D (Louisiana A), h 330 w Haywood
*Baker Henry, lab, h 29 Cole
Baker Jno A, h 328 w Haywood
Baker Josephine Mrs,, propr The Avonmore, h 107 Haywood
Baker M Brownson (Etta), farmer, h Haywood rd, W Ashe
*Baker Melinda, laund, h (r) 114 Poplar
Baldwin C Lee (Beulah), condr St Ry, h 375 s Main
Baldwin David P (Mamie), condr St Ry, h 30 Philip
BALDWIN PENROSE L (Annie N), mngr Grant's Pharmacy, h 21 s Ann
Baldwin Pressley (Alice), driver, h (r) 20 Ralph
Baldwin Sarah, wid Pinkney, h Lester rd, W Asheville
Balfour Quarry Co (Inc), 7-8 Electrical Bldg, G R Collin pres, W B Valentine sec-treas
Ball Carrie Miss, bkkpr Dunhams Music House, h 118 Cherry
Ball D Edwd (Annie), painter, h Haywood rd, W Asheville
Ball Eleanor Miss, stengr, bds 58 East
Ball Enoch G (A Irene), barber 8 Roberts, h 23 Factory Hill
Ball H C (Mattie), lab, h 475 w Haywood
Ball Jno (Flora), lab, bds 16 s Spruce
Ball Jno E (Beethelda), barber Wm W Young, h W Asheville
Ball Julia Miss, h W Asheville (R F D 3)
Ball Lena Miss, stengr Ashev Barber Supply Co, h 58 East

....**Asheville Cleaning and Pressing Club**....
Tailoring That Satisfies and Prices That Please
Steam and French Dry Cleaning of all delicate and fine wearing apparel for ladies and gentlemen. MESSENGER SERVICE IN THE CITY.

J. C. WILBAR, Prop.   4. N. Pack Square   PHONE 389

CAROLINA "M & W" INDIAN Prompt Delivery  **COAL** **& ICE CO.** PHONE 130 50 PATTON AVE. WEIGHTS ACCURATE

ASHEVILLE POWER AND LIGHT COMPANY — St. Rw'y — Electric Light and Power — PHONE 69 — Gas

Ball Leroy R (Alice), plmbr, h Josephine cor Cornelia
Ball Louise M Miss, stengr, h 40 East
Ball Sebron J (Ida M), flgmn Sou Ry, h Arlington st, W Asheville
Ball Victoria J, wid Thos, boarding 10½ Pack Sq, h same
Ball Wm A, cashr Slayden Fakes & Co Inc, rms 17 Medical Bldg
Balllrd Albert M, phys, 208 Haywood, h same
Ballard Claud C (Ellen), gardner, h W Asheville
Ballard Cora, wid Rome, h (r) Maiden la
Ballard Emmett, clk Crystal Cafeterian, rms 29 Flint
Ballard Eugene R (Mary), tmstr, h Haywood rd, W Ashev
Ballard Geo (Mary), h 32 Turner
Ballard Hilliard D (Flora), engnr Sou Ry, h 337 s French Broad av
Ballard Howard A (Dalton), engnr Power Plant Ashev P & L Co, h 165 Grove
Ballard Jno A (Bertha), clk, h 60 Conestee
Ballard Lucas, clk Crystal Cafeterian, rms 29 Flint
Ballard Lucius, carp, bds 34½ n Main
Ballard Mary Miss, h 32 Turner
Ballard Norman, clk Crystal Dairy Lunch, h 16 Flint
Ballard Paul, driver, h (r) 40 Maiden la
Ballard Rachel C, wid Wm, h 88 s French Broad av
Ballard Robt (Dovie), driver, h 100 Biltmore rd
Ballard Robt (Emma), lab, h 15 Factory Hill
Ballard Robt B, emp Water Dept, h 32 Turner
Ballard Solomon C (F Eliza), farmer, h Hazel Mill rd, W Ashev
Ballew Dess S, carp, h Main st, W Ashev
Ballew Francis R, fnhr, h Main st, W Ashev
Ballew Jas M (Mary), lab, h Main st, W Ashev
Ballew Wm W, wood carver, h Main st, W Ashev
Ballinger Carrie M Miss, smstrs, h Haywood rd, W Ashev
Ballinger Jas J (Miriam), gardener, h Haywood rd, W Ashev
Ballinger Jno S, miller, h Haywood rd, W Ashev
Ballinger Wm I, miller, h Haywood rd, W Ashev
Balm Grove M E Church, Haywood rd, W Asheville, Rev Zeb E Barnhardt pastor
Baltimore Cafe, 412 Depot, A J Kantsios mngr
Baltimore Installment House, 244 Patton av, Abram Bane propr
Bame J M, engnr Balfour Quarry Co, Inc, h Richmond Hill
Bame L Jackson (Annie), engnr, h Richmond Hill

Poultry Kiibler & Whitehead CITY MARKET PHONES, 195 and 694

Asheville Dray, Fuel and Construction Co.

Heavy Hauling of all kinds — 61-2 South Main — WE FURNISH BUILDING STONE — Moving Furniture a Specialty — PHONE - 223

DYNAMOS & MOTORS

Piedmont Electric Co.

64 Patton Av.
ASHEVILLE, N.C.

Bame Thos A (Lula), h Richmond Hill
Bamford Carl, doorkpr Princess Theatre
Bane Abram, propr Baltimore Installment House, rms 242 Patton av
Banfield Iona Miss, clk R E Mumpower, h 58 Haywood
Bankhardt Maude Miss, h 403 Merrimon av
Banks Alfreda Miss, bds 107 Haywood
*Banks Alice, dom, h 113 Black
Banks Annette, wid Rev Henry H, h 35 Charlotte
Banks Catherine E, wid Fred'k E, clk Peerless Dept Store, h 107 Haywood
Banks Chas (Martha), clk, h 424 n Main
Banks Estella Miss, h Swannanoa av, W Ashev
Banks Etta Miss, bds 56 Penland
Banks G Bryce (Harriett), lab, h 454 Pearson Drive
Banks Gaither, lab, h 454 Pearson Drive
Banks Gay V (Lillie C), lab Water Dept, h 130 Poplar
*Banks Geo (Lizzie), porter Dr P H Ringer, h 62 w Chestnut
Banks J Oscar (Tessie), weaver, h 3 Factory Hill
Banks Jas A (Loretta), plstr, h 3d av, W Ashev
Banks Jno G (T Elizabeth), lab, h Swannanoa av, W Ashev
Banks Jos W (Lucy), lab, h Swannanoa av, W Ashev
Banks Minnie Miss, h 437 n Main
Banks N Osborne (Lula), carp, h 242 Patton av
Banks Ragan D (Mary), lab, h 437 n Main
Banks Victor S (Maggie), carp, h 23 North
Banks Walter, lab, h 437 n Main
*Banks Wiley H (Bessie), lab, h 120 Roberts
Banks Woodfin, lab, h 454 Pearson Drive
Banning Jas (Julia A), carp, h Brevard rd, W Ashev
Banning Jessie Miss, clk Morris Levitt, h W Asheville
Banning M Josephine Miss, clk, h Brevard rd, W Ashev
Banning R Pearl Miss, clk, h Brevard rd, W Ashev
Baptist Mission Sunday School, French Broad cor Bartlett, J L Sams supt
BARBEE SEATON A, cigars, tobacco, newspapers and periodicals, 14 Patton av (see back cover)
Barber B Geo (Stella), (The Inland Press), h 156 Hillside
Barber Frank A (The Inland Press), h St Petersburg Fla
Barber Jas M (Mae A), electrn, bds Cherokee Inn
*Barber Jane, dom, h 3 Greer's Row
Barber Lawrence, student, h 17 Cullowee
Barber Warren (Patsy), emp Tannery, h 219 Asheland av
Barclay F Walker (Dora), farmer, h 5 Factory Hill

J. C. McPHERSON
SLATE AND TIN ROOFING
Galvanized Iron Work   Hot Air Furnaces
35-37 EAST COLLEGE STREET

PLUMBING STEAM AND HOT WATER HEATING
PHONE 133

Bard Chas I (Elsie M), sign painter, 23 Arlington, h same
Barger Taylor, h 41 Bearden av
Barker Ellen M Miss, tchr, h 47 Starnes av
Barker Estelle Miss, student, h 64 Summit, S Biltmore
Barker Jno J (Bettie), pastor S Biltmore Methodist Church, h 64 Summit, S Biltmore
Barker Jno J Jr, collr Burton & Holt, h 64 Summit, S Biltmore
Barker Mary Miss, student, h 64 Summit, S Biltmore
Barker Mary C, wid Thos M, h 47 Starnes av
Barker Thos, solr, h 47 Starnes av
Barkley Sarah D, wid R A, stewardess Sou Ry Dining Room, rms Florence Hotel
BARNARD ALFRED S (Jessie M), (Merrick & Barnard), h 37 Watauga
Barnard Building, offices, 1 Patton av
Barnard Florence Miss, h 167 Chestnut
Barnard Jas A, student, h 167 Chestnut
*Barnard Jas W, h 92 Pine
*Barnard Sallie, cook, h 92 Pine
Barnard Susie Miss, h 167 Chestnut
Barnard W Oscar, clk Biltmore Estate Genl Office, h Merrimon av
Barnard Wm W (Cornelia), propr Ashev Tobacco Co, h 167 Chestnut
☞Barnard see also Bernard
Barnes Ada E Miss, h 20 Clyde
Barnes Frank, tanner, h 59½ Avery
Barnes McKinley, mill opr, h 59½ Avery
*Barnes Mamie, cook, Merrimon av cor Hillside
Barnes Reed (Lillie), mill opr, h 59½ Avery
Barnes W E & Co (W E Barnes, C S Lowe), produce, 34 n Lexington av
Barnes Wm E (Dora), (W E Barnes & Co), h 20 Central av
Barnes Wm M Rev, h 23 Central av
Barnett Asbury G (Eva), v-pres Harris-Barnett Dry Goods Co (Inc), h 179 Charlotte
Barnett Emma K Miss, violinist, h 23 Highland
Barnett Jones (Katie M), trav slsmn, h 23 Highland
Barnett Wm E (Carrie A), foreman, h 346½ Bartlett
Barnett Wm L (Lula), gro 37 n Main, h 10½ n Pack Sq
Barnhardt Zeb E Rev (Kate), pastor Balm Grove M E Ch, h Jarrett av, W Ashev (R F D 3)
*Barnum Jno R Rev (Eva A), pastor St James A M E Ch, h 42 Hildebrand

Candy Kitchen and Club Cafe
"A GOOD PLACE FOR REFRESHMENT"

Hot drinks on cold days. Cold drinks on hot days. The best drinks every day. Pure fruits and syrups blended "just right," served daintily. Our Ice Cream and Soda Water Department, Restaurant and Candy Departments are always kept up to the standard of nearest perfection. Phones 110 and 111. 19 and 21 Haywood St.

Brown's Undertaking Parlors

S. H. BROWN

50 Patton Avenue
ASHEVILLE, N. C.

Lady Assistant When Desired

Phone 193-2 Rings

THE MOORE Plumbing Company

16 N. Pack Square

PHONE 1025

Sanitary Plumbing, General Tin and Metal Work, Hot Air Furnaces

---

Baron A Zeta, wid Henry, h Kenilworth Park
*Barr Nellie, h 128 Pearson Drive
*Barr Tillie, dress mkr, h 128 Pearson Drive
Barrett Jas F (Lula), lino opr Ashev Gazette-News, h 16 Seney
Barrett Jerome J (Nora), lather, h 441 w Haywood
Barrett Jos, bag mstr Sou Ry, bds 186 Asheland av
Barrett Loren F, chauffeur, h Brevard rd, W Ashev
Barrett Wm G, h Arlington st, W Asheville
Barrus J Alex, rms Y M C A
BARTLETT C HENRY (Essie R), city tax collr, office City Hall, h 21 Starnes av
Bartlett Clara C Mrs, wid Wm C, h 123 Chestnut
Bartlett Jno W, painter R E Bowles, h 272 Southside av
Bartlett Mary Mrs, h 16 Marjorie
Bartlett Mary L, wid Wm, h 272 Southside av
Bartlett Wm, painter T J Perkinson
Bartlett Woodfin, emp J M Westall & Co, h Reems Creek
*Barton Geo H (Harriet), lab, h nr Hazel Mill rd, W Ashev
Barton Jennie Mrs, dressmkr 167 Patton av, h same
*Barton Lee (Minnie), cook, h 45 Short
*Barton Mack H (Minnie), cook, h 166 Hill
*Barton Major H (Florence), lab, h nr Hazel Mill rd, W Ashev
*Bason Henry, lab, h 52 Short
Baskerville Geo S (Fannie), clk G F Stradley, h W Ashev
Bass Frank (Lillie), laundryman, h 4 Hunt Hill
Bass Hardy, lab, h (r) 326 s Main
Bass J Gordon, cashr Natl Biscuit Co, h 32 College Park pl
Bass Jno (Clara), lab, h (r) 326 s Main
*Bass Laura, laund, h (r) 78 Pine
Bass Wm, lab Ashev Grain & Hay Co
Bassett Henry G (Bertha), collr J R Davis, h Grace
Bassett Jas M (Louise), farmer, h 304 Riverside Drive
Bassett Minnie Miss, mill wkr, h 304 Riverside Drive
Bassett Roberta Miss, mill wkr, h 304 Riverside Drive
Bassett Wm, driver, h 304 Riverside Drive
Bateman Walter C (Lottie), pharmacist Carmichael's Pharmacy, h 208 Montford av
Bates Andrew (Hester), helper Water Dept, h 119 Poplar
Bates David (Susie), lab, h 49 North
*Bates Edgar (Maggie), waiter, h 35 Ridge
Bates L C, bkkpr, rms 331 Southside av
Batson Alice, wid Jas S, h 29½ s Main
Batterham E Rose Miss, tchr High Schl, h 82 Church

The Battery Park Bank   Capital - - $100,000.00
                               Surplus and Profits, $110,000.00
ASHEVILLE, N. C.   City, County and State Depositary

J. A. TILLMAN — I carry a nice line of Watches, Clocks and Jewelry, and make a specialty of repair work. Satisfaction guaranteed. **Jeweler — 17 N. Main St.**

Batterham Harry (Eleanor A), real estate Library Bldg (basement), h 82 Church
Batterham Lily Mary Miss, tchr High Schl, h 82 Church
Batterham Susan R, wid Wm, h 74 Hillside
Batterham W Forster, student, h 82 Church
Battery Park (private), Haywood cor Patton av
BATTERY PARK BANK (The), 15 Patton av; T C Coxe pres, E C Sluder v-pres, J E Rankin cashr, C Rankin asst cashr (see front cover and bottom lines)
Battery Park Cottage, res Mrs Josephine Millard, Haywood cor Battery Park pl
BATTERY PARK HOTEL, Patton av and Haywood, J L Alexander propr
Battery Park Hotel, sample room, 93 Patton av
Battery Park Hotel Barber Shop, Battery Park Hotel, Jas A Williamson propr
Battery Park Hotel Billiard & Pool Room, Battery Park
Battery Park Hotel News & Cigar Stand, Battery Park Hotel, Jas V Sevier Jr propr
"Battle Bungalow," Beaumont Ridge
Battle S Westray Dr (Battle & Clemenger), and pres-genl mngr Ashev Ptg & Engrav Co, bds Battery Park Hotel
*Battle Sarah, h 18 Cumberland av
Battle & Clemenger (Drs S W Battle, F J Clemenger), phys Halthenon Bldg
*Baugh C A, tchr Southside Schl
Baughn Chas R (Ida), clk Bon Marche, h 5 Brook, Biltmore
Baughnight Wm, ins, bds 94 Cherry
Baumberger Elsie Miss, h 102 Ralph
Baumberger Jno E, fireman, h 102 Ralph
Baumberger Kitty V Miss, h 102 Ralph
Baumberger Lina E Miss, h 102 Ralph
Baumberger Margaret, wid Julius, boarding 102 Ralph, h same
Baumgardner Chas B (Sallie), clk Sou Ry, h 8 Biltmore rd, S Biltmore
Baumgardner Fay Miss, student, h 80 Central av
Baumgardner Harry L, student, h 80 Central av
Baumgardner Hattie L, wid L M, h 80 Central av
*Baxter Carrie, h 194 s Main
*Baxter Clinton, lab, h (r) 118 Church
Baxter Della Miss, h 92 Jefferson Drive
Baxter Jos M, foreman St Dept, h 1 Aston Park
*Baxter Worthy, laund, h (r) 123 Mountain
Bayless Rebecca Miss, stengr, 301 Legal Bldg, bds Chestnut

INSURANCE
Insure your salary with us
Never carry your own risk
Safety is the best policy
Unless you are a capitalist
Rest easy if you have
An accident we will
Not keep you waiting to
Collect your claim
Every claim promptly paid

Imperial Mutual Life & Health Insurance Co.
Home Office: ASHEVILLE, N. C.
Phone 495

HOTEL OXFORD — Redecorated and Refitted throughout. Recently enlarged to 60 rooms. Centrally located. Depot cars stop at entrance. Long distance telephone office upstairs. American and European plan. Rates 50c, 75c and $1 per day; special rates by week or month. C. H. Branson & Sons, Proprietors. Phone 1887. 50-54 South Main St. **Asheville, N. C.**

Williams-Brownell Planing Mill Company — **Hardwoods**

Lumber---Rough and Dressed — Flooring a Specialty — Moulding, Interior Finish, Etc.
Office, Plant and Yards on Southern Railway, Near Biltmore Station
WHITE PINE — Phone 729 — YELLOW PINE

Asheville Electrical Company
W. Mansfield Booze, Manager
74 CENTRAL AVE.
HEADQUARTERS
Phone 377

88 ASHEVILLE [1913] DIRECTORY

*Bayson Wm (Cecelia), porter, h 12 Ridge
Beacham Edwd M (Bessie M), condr, h Asheville av, W Ashev
Beacham Thos C (Abbie), propr Maple Leaf Dairy, h Main st, W Ashev
Beacham Thos L (Sarah E), carp, h nr Smiths Bridge, W Ashev
Beacham Wm B (Mollie), condr, h 75 Tiernan
Beachboard Arthur, tinner A L McLean, h 333 w Haywood
Beachboard Callie Miss, laund, h 333 w Haywood
Beachboard Calvin G, emp Green Bros, h 333 w Haywood
Beachboard Geo, lab, h 38 William
Beachboard Jno A (Martha), lab, h 38 William
Beachboard W Martin (Alice), carp, h 333 w Haywood
BEADLE CHAUNCEY D (Margaretta), supt Biltmore Estate Genl Office, h Biltmore Estate
Beadles Catherine E Miss, h 146 Charlotte
Beadles Nicholas N, sec-treas Coca-Cola Bottling Co of Ashev, h 146 Charlotte
Beadles Robt M (Addie), trav slsmn, h 146 Charlotte
Beal Chas D (Lucy M), cabtmkr W M Jones, h 374 w Haywood
Beal Lemuel (Ellen), carp, h 374 w Haywood
Beal Nannie Mrs, h 391 w Haywood
Bean Allen J (Susan), engine inspr Sou Ry, h 58 Blanton
Bean Candas L, wid Jno R, h 10 Silver
Bean Carl N, appr S I Bean & Co, h 23 Seney
Bean Ervin R, stone ctr S I Bean & Co, h 23 Seney
Bean Hugh J (Clara J), mchst, h 27 Green
Bean Jno C (Scottie), mngr Murphy Div Sou Exp Co, h 165 Blanton
BEAN S I & CO (S I Bean, C S Gudger), marble and granite works, monuments and cut stone—phone 1102, 94 Patton av
BEAN SAM'L I (May C), (S I Bean & Co), h 23 Seney
Bean Saml T, printer, Whiteside Ptg Co, rms 27 Maxwelton Bldg
*Beard Amanda, dom, h Grace
*Beard Ernest (Hattie), lab, h 121 Wallach
*Beard Julia, dom, h Grace
Beard Pearle Miss, h 36 Vivian
Beard Richd, clk S D Pelham, h 346½ Depot
Beard Wm, flgmn Sou Ry, bds 346½ Depot
Beard see also Baird
Bearden Amelia R, wid Marcus J, h 124 Flint

Asheville Dry Cleaning Co.
Telephones 835-836, All Dep't
MAIN, N. E. COR. COLLEGE

THE CLEANERS
Our Department for Oriental Rugs and Carpet Cleaning is prepared to serve you in all its branches.
E. S. Paine — O. E. Hansen

FOR BOX SHOOKS — Call English Lumber Co. PHONE 321

Bearden Eugene M (Mary), trav slsmn, rms 35 Church
Bearden Wm R (Madeline), mdse broker, h 124 Flint
*Bearman Missouri, cook, h 17 Mountain
*Beasley Wister (Hattie), porter, h Scott nr Hibernia
*Beatty Jno W Rev (Harriet), h 21 Black
*Beatty Monroe (Nellie), care taker "Witchwood," h same
Beaumont Furniture Co, 27 s Main; W C Hawk pres, Frank Loughran v-pres, W B Taylor sec-treas-mngr
*Beaumont Hotel, 77 Mountain, R P Jones propr
Beaumont Lodge, Beaucatcher Mountain
Beaver Chas E (Lydia), fireman, h 446 Depot
*Beazley Amy, h 12 McDowell
Beck Anna M Miss, tchr, h 14 Blake
Beck Geo W (Mattie), pattern mkr, h 63 Blanton
Beck H Ada Miss, student, h 63 Blanton
Beck Jacob F (Jennie), carp, h 66 Pine Grove av
Beck W Burgin, clk, h 63 Blanton
Beck Walter S (Margaret), carp, h 78 Atkinson
BEERS CHAS DR, solr Western Carolina Realty Co, h 52 Merrimon av
Beerworth Jesse A (Mabel A), motorman, h 91 Starnes av
Bell Chas C (Edith), inspr, h Woolsey (R F D 1)
*Bell Chas W (Susie), baker, h 20 Oakdale av
Bell Clarence C (Gertrude), condr, h 300 Southside av
Bell Edwd (Malinda A), carp, h W Ashev (R F D 3)
Bell Eliza Miss, clk Bon Marche, rms The Henrietta
Bell Jas H (Mollie), condr St Ry, h 160 Grove
Bell Jno A, motorman, h 153 Blanton
Bell Jno B (Estella), carp, h Haywood rd, W Ashev
Bell Jno K (Neita), clk frt office Sou Ry, h 28 Oak
Bell Landon C, atty at law 308-309 Oates Bldg rms Y M C A
Bell Laura A Mrs, rms 90 Starnes av
Bell Mack C (Julia), h 3 Cameron
Bell Martha A, wid Jno, h W Ashev (R F D 3)
Bell May Miss, clk Peerless Dept Store, bds 20 Adams
Bell O B (Agnes), condr St Ry, h 69½ Blanton
Bell Octavia, wid Jno M, h Main st, W Ashev
Bell Thos (Anna), clk, h Biltmore Park
Bell Thos, driver Brown's Creamery, bds 16 Orchard
Bell Wm, engnr, bds 308 Depot
Bellew Paul, fireman, bds 346½ Depot
Bellew W Pitt (Sallie), engnr, bds 96 Bartlett
BELMONT, 57-65 n Spruce, for nervous and stomach diseases and convalescents — phone 840, Bertrand Houser M D B S mngr see p 20)

Biggest Busiest Best Asheville Steam Laundry
Phones: 1936 and 1937
43 to 47 W. College Street

CHARLES H. HONESS OPTOMETRIST AND OPTICIAN
Exclusive maker of ATLAS SHUR-ON EYE GLASSES
THE Home of Ce-Rite Toric Lenses
We make a specialty of correcting optical defects with properly fitted glasses.
54 Patton Avenue
Opposite Postoffice

Carolina Machinery Co. Founders, Machinists and Jobbers of Mill Supplies. We make all kinds of Castings in Iron, Brass or Aluminum.
WE ALSO FURNISH SKILLED MECHANICS FOR BOILER REPAIRS — PHONE 590

LIFE INSURANCE COMPANY OF VA.
ORGANIZED 187
Richmond -:- Virginia
J. V MOON, Superintendent
Rooms 3-4-5- Maxwelton Bldg., Asheville, N. C.

All claims paid IMMEDIATELY upon receipt of satisfactory proofs of Death. Total payment to policyholders since organization, over $12,000,000.00. Is paying its Policyholders over $1,000,000.00 annually.

T. P. JOHNSON & CO.

SHEET METAL WORKERS

All Kinds of Roofing Guttering and Conductor Work Metal Ceilings, Skylights and Galvanized Iron Cornices

OFFICE and SHOP:
69-71 S. MAIN
Phone 325

DR. C. H. MILLER

Mechano-Therapist

14 N. Spruce Street
ASHEVILLE, N. C.

PHONE 979

Hours by Engagement

DRUGLESS HEALING OF DISEASE

---

90 ASHEVILLE [1913] DIRECTORY

Belote Edwd T (Mary E), contr 188 Flint, h same
*Below Kate, laund, h 90 Hazzard
*Belt Maria, cook, h 7 Hiawassee
*Belt M, carpet clnr, bds 48 McDowell
BELVEDERE (formerly Ravenscroft), (Mrs Nellie W Hyman), 95 Church—phone 468 (see page 18)
Bender Fred (Minnie), rms 106 Asheland av
Benedict Evangeline G Mrs, tchr Peace Memorial House
*Benjamin Joanna, laund, h (r) 330 w Haywood
Benjamin Marvin, fireman, bds 418 Southside av
*Benjamin Postell, lab, h (r) 328 w Haywood
Bennett Benj F (Elsie), lab, h 289 Charlotte
Bennett Frank V, lab, h 14 Roberts
*Bennett Geo Rev (Maude), h 81 Ridge
Bennett Oscar K, atty at law 10½ n Pack Sq, bds 9 Louie
Bennett Poston R Dr (Jeanette C), h 1 Panola
Bennett Penelope, wid Jos, h 165 Hillside
Benson Annie P Miss, h 69 Victoria av
*Benson Effie, dom, h 63 Valley
Benson Matthew M (Annie M), lumberman, h 69 Victoria av
Benson Sallie Miss, house kpr, h Haywood rd, W Asheville
Bentley Lucretia M, wid Wm W, h nr Smiths Bridge, W Asheville
*Benton Anna, laund, h 121 Black
*Berger Frank, lab, h Cherry st
Berkeley Pool Room, 17 n Lexington av, Wm H Zurburg mngr
Bernard Lizzie Miss, tchr Orange St School, h Hollywood pl
BERNARD SILAS G, atty at law 201-202 Legal Bldg—phone 1160 and sec Blue Ridge Develop Co, h 56 Hollywood—phone 1654
Bernecker Amelia Miss, bkkpr The Cash Grocery, h 60 n Spruce
Bernecker Annie Miss, h 60 n Spruce
Bernecker Bertha Miss, h 60 n Spruce
Bernecker Clara Miss, h 60 n Spruce
BERNECKER FRIEDA MISS, modiste 60 n Spruce, h same
Bernecker Julius, cabt mkr W M Jones, h 60 n Spruce
Bernhard Carl H Rev (Helen), pastor Emanuel Evangelical Lutheran Church, h 44 Philip
*Bernhardt Creola, cook, h 154 Hill
Berry Alice Miss, dom, 36 Starnes av

ASHEVILLE CLEANING and PRESSING CLUB

TAILORING THAT SATISFIES and PRICES THAT PLEASE

Hats cleaned, banded and bound. Silk hats ironed. Buttons made to order in all sizes. Plain or with rims. PHONE 389

DYEING IN ALL SHADES Cleaned. Messenger Service.

Kid Gloves, Slippers and Plumes. Fancy Jabots and Ties, French Dry Cleaned. Ladies' and Gentlemen's suits Steam Cleaned.

J. C. Wilbar, Prop. 4 NORTH PACK SQ.

*Berry Alonzo, waiter, rms 74 Eagle
Berry B Maud Miss, stengr Martin, Rollins & Wright, h 102 Haywood
*Berry Carrie, laundress, h 56 Wallach
*Berry Darkey, lab, h 21 Oliver
*Berry Edwd (Elizabeth), lab, h 81 Roberts
*Berry F Alex, lab, h 23 Ingle
*Berry Hester, cook, h 56 Wallach
*Berry J Alex Rev (Mollie), pastor Providence Baptist Church, h 23 Ingle
*Berry Jas, lab, h 97 Market
Berry Pinckney W (Goldie), h 485 n Main
*Berry Temple M E Church, 246 College, Rev J P Morris pastor
Berry Walter L (Etta), engnr, h 18 Clingman av
Bertolett Mamie T Mrs, propr Montford Cottage, h 103 Montford av
Beth Ha Teplulla Synagogue, Spruce nr Woodfin
Bethel M E Church (South), Blanton cor Phifer, Rev H H Robbins pastor
*Bethel Rebecca, cook, h s Asheville
Betts Fannie W Mrs, h 143 Pearson Drive
Betts Rich'd W (Nora), bkkpr Ashev Coal Co, h 15 Jefferson Drive
*Bias Ada, dom, h 19 Wallach
*Bias Ida, dom, 12 Aston pl
Bickercholem Synagogue, s Liberty nr Woodfin, Ellis Fox Rabbi
Bickerstaff Ella A Miss, tchr Normal Schl, h Livingston nr Oliver
*Big Four Pressing Club (The), Oates Bldg (basement), R P Jones propr
BIGGS ANDREW C DR (Ambra W), propr Biggs Sanitorium 104 Woodfin, h same—phone 179
Biggs Bertha Miss, mill wkr, h 28 Logan
Biggs Sallie S, wid Jas, h 28 Logan
BIGGS SANITARIUM, 104 Woodfin—phone 179, Dr A C Biggs propr
"Billows Rest," boarding, Grace, Mrs Elsie Culvern propr
Biltmore Baptist Church, S Biltmore
Biltmore Box Factory, mnfrs packing boxes Sou Ry nr Biltmore Sta, R P Foster propr
Biltmore Dairy, Biltmore Estate, Dr A S Wheeler mngr
Biltmore Drug Store, 10 Plaza Biltmore, Dr T C Smith propr

WEAVERVILLE LINE NINE MILES BY TROLLEY FROM PACK SQUARE TO WEAVERVILLE

ASHEVILLE AND EAST TENNESSEE RAILROAD CO.

7 NORTH MAIN STREET — ASHEVILLE N. C.

Electrical Supplies — PIEDMONT ELECTRIC COMPANY — 64 PATTON AVE. — ASHEVILLE, N. C.

BILTMORE ESTATE, General Office, Plaza cor Lodge, Biltmore—phone 68, C D Beadle supt
Biltmore Estate Industries, 8-9 Plaza—phone 1026, Biltmore, Misses E P Vance and C L Yale mngrs
Biltmore Farms (Including Dairy and Stock Farms), Dr A S Wheeler supt
Biltmore Fire Department, Biltmore
Biltmore Graded School, Biltmore rd (S B)
Biltmore Hospital, Village la, Miss M H Trist supt
Biltmore Hospital, Nurse Home, 3 Plaza, Biltmore
Biltmore House, Biltmore Estate—phone 545, res of Geo W Vanderbuilt
Biltmore Nursery, Biltmore Estate
Biltmore Parish House, Angle nr Swan, Biltmore
Biltmore Post Office, 1 Brook, Biltmore, B J Luther postmstr
Biltmore Roller Mills, flour, Hickory Nut Gap rd, C S Reed propr
Biltmore Shops, blksmiths, Biltmore rd, D B Lipe propr
Biltmore Station (Sou Ry), Brook nr Plaza, G A Digges agt
Biltmore Supply Co, genl mdse, Biltmore rd cor Lula, W H Maney mngr
Biltmore Vegetable Garden, Biltmore Estate, G S Arthur mngr
BINGHAM ROBT COL (Violet), supt Bingham School, h Bingham Heights—phone 264
BINGHAM SCHOOL (The) (military), Bingham Heights—phone 264, Col Robt Bingham supt, Maj R T Grinnan v-supt (see inside front cover)
*Birchett Jno F (Carrie L), waiter, h 32 Catholic av
Bird G Bonham, purchasing agt Ashev P & L Co, h Biltmore
Bird Harriet Miss, h 60 Central av
Bird Lillian S Miss, h 277 s Main
Bird Louisa A, wid Chas, boarding 60 Central av, h same
BIRD WM H (Hattie), v-pres Asheville Dray, Fuel & Construction Co and chf inspr City Sanitary Dept, h 277 s Main
☞ Bird see also Byrd
"Birdwood Cottage," Sunset Drive
Birkemyer Catherine Miss, h 25 Spears av
Birmingham Ervin B (Stella), switchman, bds 480 Depot
Birmingham Realty Co, 27 Patton av, J M Stoner pres, P R Moale v-pres, J M Chiles sec-treas

CONTRACTOR and BUILDER
STEEL RANGES — **J. C. McPHERSON** — 35-37 E COLLEGE ST. PHONE 133
PLUMBING STEAM AND HOT WATER HEATING

MAPLE FLOORING
HARDWOOD LUMBER OF ALL KINDS

WOODWARD & SON
9th and Arch Sts., Richmond, Va.
See Adv. Opposite Page 188

Birmingham Realty Co, 27 Patton av
Bishop Amalie Miss, h Woolsey
Bishop Andrew B (Sallie), meat mkt and blksmith Haywood rd, W Asheville, h W Asheville
Bishop C Ralph, painter, h Arlington st, W Asheville
Bishop David M (Dora), paper hngr T J Perkinson, h 36 s Spruce
Bishop Eliza Mrs, quilter, h 13 Brick
Bishop Elmer, repr F J Nevercel, h Woolsey
Bishop Ernest H, driver, h Arlington st, W Ashev
Bishop Grace A, wid Geo W, boarding 348½ Depot, h same
Bishop Jas B (Bessie B), painter T J Perkinson, h 358 s Main
Bishop Jas P (Mary A), carp, h Arlington st, W Ashev
Bishop Jno L (Carrie L), engnr Sou Ry, h 169 Bartlett
Bishop Larkin (Mary), h W Asheville
Bishop Ralph, painter R E Bowles, h W Asheville
Bishop Richard (Pearle), painter, h 180 s Main
Bishop Tennie Miss, h Woolsey
Bishop Thos H (Mattie), slsmn Haskell's Pepsi-Cola Bot Wks, h Woolsey
Bishop Thos P, painter R L Fitzpatrick & Son, h 180 s Main
Bishop Thos T (Josephine J), city fumigator, h Riverside Drive nr William
Bishop Wm B (Minnie), flgmn Sou Ry, h 169 Asheland av
Bishop Wm H (May), painter, h 425 s Main
*Bivins Henry, lab, h 15 Turner
Bivings Minnie A, wid S J, h 191 Chestnut
Bivings Pauline E Miss, student, h 191 Chestnut
Bizzell A Donan (Effie G), farmer, h Hazel Mill rd, W Ashev
Bizzell Adrain H, farmer, h Hazel Mill rd, W Ashev
Bizzell Robt M (Edith B), foreman, h Hazel Mill rd, W Ashev
*Black Anderson Rev (Ellen), lab, h 107 Clingman av
Black Bertha Miss, rms 8 College Park
*Black Della, dom, h S Asheville
Black Elsie J, wid Jas A, h 25 Rector
Black Essie Miss, h 339 w Haywood
Black Fredk R, bricklyr, h 10 s Spruce
Black H B, barber 418 Depot, bds Windsor Hotel
Black Hiram, mngr Windsor Cafe, h Weaverville N C
Black Horace C (Lizzie), driver Zindel's Model Bakery, h W Asheville (R F D 3)
Black Jas M (Sarah), gro 337 w Haywood, h 339 same

What Have You in Real Estate that You Don't Want?

What do You Want in Real Estate that You Haven't?

WESTERN CAROLINA REALTY CO.
J. W. Wolfe, Sec. & Treas.

On the Square
PHONE 974
10 N. PACK SQ.

Brown-Carter Realty Co.
REAL ESTATE
23 TEMPLE COURT
PHONE 341
ASHEVILLE   N. C.

FLORIDA SPECIALTIES
Grazing, Timbered, Farm Lands, Orange Groves, Turpentine Locations and Phosphate Lands.

NORTH CAROLINA SPECIALTIES
Orchard, Farm and Timbered Lands, City Property, Rent Collections.

Moale & Chiles Real Estate and Insurance
27 Patton Ave., (2d fl)   Phone 661
General Agents United States Fidelity & Guaranty Co.

Candy Kitchen and Club Cafe
"A GOOD PLACE FOR REFRESHMENT"

The very best ingredients with sanitary conditions in our Candy Manufacturing Department make possible the dainty, crisp confections sold here.

Bon Bons and Chocolates made every day, put up in neat, attractive boxes. Phones 110 and 111. 19 and 21 Haywood St.

Brown's Undertaking Parlors

S. H. BROWN

Lady Assistant When Desired

Phone 193-2 Rings

50 Patton Avenue
Asheville, N. C.

Established 1894

B. J. JACKSON

Carefully Selected Fruits and Vegetables

Stall No. 11, City Market

BUSINESS PHONES:
86 and 101

RESIDENCE PHONE
1596

ASHEVILLE [1913] DIRECTORY

Black Jos (Mary J), lab, h 23 Buxton
Black Jos N (Janie E), meat ctr, h 351 w Haywood
Black Pitt, car inspr, bds 26 Spring
Black Thos P (Mattie), bricklyr, h 10 s Spruce
Black Tracy E, switchman, h 23 Buxton
Black Wiley P (Saphronia), propr Windsor Hotel, h Weaverville N C
Black Wm A (Agnes M), engnr Sou Ry, h 227 s French Broad av
*Blackburn Jno, firemn, h 18 Ralph
Blackburn Mattie C Mrs, h 46 Panola
Blackburn Nellie Miss, h 46 Panola
Blackburn Rankin, mchst, h 46 Panola
Blackford Wm C, painter R E Bowles, h Gaston st
Blackstock Thos E (Nancy W), (Greenwood & Blackstock) ,h 22 Courtland av
Blackwelder Jas M (Lois), carp, h 91 Broad
*Blackwell Alex (Y M I Drug Store Co), h 98 Pine
Blackwell Benj F (Fynette), janitor City Hall, h 3 s Spruce
Blackwell Della Miss, maid 287 Pearson Drive
Blackwell Donnie Miss, matron Police Dept, h 3 s Spruce
Blackwell Dorcas D, wid J D, h 71 Madison av
Blackwell Elmer (Margaret), lab, h 421 n Main
Blackwell Francis (Vestie), lab, h Haywood rd, W Ashev
*Blackwell Frank, lab, h 98 Pine
*Blackwell Henry (Neta), lab, h (r) 512 s French Broad av
Blackwell Julia Miss, h 71 Madison av
Blackwell Margaret Miss, h 3 s Spruce
Blackwell Pollie Miss, h 71 Madison av
*Blackwell Virgie, dom, h 98 Pine
Blackwell W Scott (Cornelia), lab, h 421 n Main
Blackwell Zachariah A, mtrmn St Ry, rms 32 n Ann
Blackwood Jas C (Alice), mchst, h 26 Ora
Blackwood Martha, wid Jno T, h 56 Asheland av
Blackwood Wm C (Laura K), painter, h 69 Gaston
*Blaine Frazier A (Mattie), waiter The Gladstone, h 45 Mountain
Blair Alex B (Mollie E), engnr Sou Ry, h 418 Southside av
Blair Clarence (Elvira), painter, h 38 McDowell
Blair Estelle V Miss, h 418 Southside av
Blair Eva Miss, laund, h 38 McDowell
Blair Fannie, wid Jno, laund, h 38 McDowell
*Blair Frank (Annie M), lab, h 82 Pine
Blair Hilliard H, painter, rms 11½ n Main
Blair Jno O (Jennie), clk Ashev Dry Gds Co, bds Woolsey

Yᵉ OLD BOOK SHOP
114 Patton Ave.   Phone 1674
BOOKS BOUGHT, SOLD OR EXCHANGED

Blair Mollie E Mrs, boarding 418 Southside av, h same
Blair Sophie C Miss, h 418 Southside av
Blake Blanche Miss, h 127 Chestnut
*Blake Chas, butler, 255 Haywood
Blake Frank A (Virginia A), mngr Gladstone Hotel Cafe, h 409 Depot
Blake J Heath, drug clk Allison's Drug Store, h 66 Asheland
*Blake Mary, cook, h 101 n Lexington av
Blake Virginia A Mrs, propr Gladstone Hotel, h same
*Blakely Heywood (Roxey), lab, h 97 n Main
Blalock Alice E Miss, clk Peerless Dept Store, h 189 Asheland av
Blalock Lester L, pressman, h 189 Asheland av
Blalock Wm C (Carrie), stone mason, h 189 Asheland av
Blanchard Artie X, mngr Crystal Cafeterian, rms 36 Oak
Blanchard Jas, waiter, h 83 Hall
Blanchard Lula, wid Jas, h 83 Hall
Blanchard M, lab, h 83 Hall
Blanchard Ruth E Miss, musician, h 38 Spears av
*Bland Mabel, tchr Catholic Hill School
Blankenship ——, h 37 Orange
Blankenship Chas G (Helen), tel opr W U T Co, Battery Park Hotel, h Beaver Dam
Blankenship Jas M (Effie), fireman, h 394½ Southside
Blankenship Lorenzo M, watchman Ashev P & L Co, h Grace
Blankenship Maria Miss, wks Ashev Mica Co, h 32 Carter
Blau Nicholas (Ashev F P Gas Mch Co), h 55 Starnes av
Blauvelt Wm H (Bessie L), drug clk C A Raysor, h 44 Hiawassee
Bledsoe Jas T (Maude T), (Donnahoe & Bledsoe), h 179 Merrimon av
Blodgett Dorothy Miss, tchr High School
Blomberg Aaron (Sara), propr The Racket Store h 30 Charlotte
Blomberg Freda Miss, h 31 Woodfin
Blomberg Helen G Miss, clk The Racket Store, h 30 Charlotte
Blomberg Jacob L, clk The Racket Store, h 30 Charlotte
Blomberg Louis, cigars and sporting goods and propr Phoenix Hotel, 15 Patton av, h 31 Woodfin
Blomberg Saml I (Hannah G), dry goods 13 n w Pack Sq, h 54 Charlotte
Blomberg Sigmund, clk, h 31 Woodfin
*Blow Wm C (Venia), porter A M Field Co, h 74 Circle

Mrs. Wilder's SANITARY HOME LAUNDRY turns out first class work in Laundering and Dry Cleaning. No. 7 Montford Ave., Phone 1354

Blue Mary Mrs, h W Asheville
Blue Saml H, lab, h nr Smith's Bridge, W Ashev
BLUE RIDGE BUILDING & LOAN ASSN, 1 Haywood; J H Rankin pres, H T Rogers v-pres, E L Ray sec-treas A H Cobb acct (see back fly A),
Blue Ridge Development Co, 201-202 Legal Bldg; Jno S Taylor pres, N W Ulmer v-pres, S G Bernard sec, G A Petteway treas
*Blueford Fred (Emma), waiter, h 128 Livingston
*Blueford Mary, laund, h 128 Livingston
☞ **Bluford see also Buford**
Board of County Commissioners, Court House
BOARD OF TRADE, 6-7-8 Temple Court, N Buckner sec
Boardman Cornelia A Miss, h 40 Arlington
Boardman Hattie E Miss, h 40 Arlington
*Bobo Floyd, lab, h 25 Lyman
Bocook F H, photog, h 64 McDowell
Bogart Walter E, bds 326 s Main
*Boger Martin (Minnie), barber, h 21 Weaver
*Bogle Arthur (Maria), porter Green Bros, h 34 Ridge
*Bogle Marshall B (Sarah), porter Green Bros, h 13 Dundee
*Bohannon Jas (Samantha), emp hotel, h 187 s Beaumont
*Bolden Andrew (Jane), barber W T Conley, h 12 Short
*Bolden Jos (Minnie), lab, h 152 Hill
*Bolden Wallace (Margaret), tmstr, h 12 Short McDowell
*Bolden Walter (Kate), emp Sou Ry, h 12 Short McDowell
Boling Elsie Miss, stengr, h 33 Asheland av
Boling Elura J, wid Jno W, h 33 Asheland av
Boling Roy F, ticket counter Ashev P & L Co, h 33 Asheland av
Bollinger Ethel C Miss, student, h 8 Grady
Bollinger Mary E, wid Robt C, h 8 Grady
Bollinger Rhetta B Miss, clk Mrs M C Denoon, h 8 Grady
Bolton Lizzie, wid Geo, h 173 Chestnut
Boman C E Mrs, matron Childrens Home, h Grace
"Bon Air" (The), boarding 66 Asheland av, Mrs S T Willie propr
BON MARCHE, department store, 19-23 Patton av—phone 338, S Lipinsky propr
Bonafield Ruby C Miss, stengr Prudential Ins Co of America, bds The Henrietta
Boney Jane, wid David, h 289 College
Bonham Catherine Y, wid Jas, h 146 Bartlett
Bonham R Carl (Grace), agt Ashev Transfer & Storage Co, bds 56 Oak

OLDSMOBILE DETROIT ELECTRIC
ARBOGAST MOTOR COMPANY
ACCESSORIES AND SUPPLIES
Phones 302 and 1728
52-60 N. Main
BUICK MAXWELLS

Asheville Dry Cleaning Co.
Telephones 835-836, All Dep't
MAIN, N. E. COR. COLLEGE

THE CLEANERS
Our Department for Oriental Rugs and Carpet Cleaning is prepared to serve you in all its branches.
E. S. Paine   O. E. Hansen

Bonney Eli W (Eula), serg U S Army Recruiting Station, bds 91 Woodfin
BONNIVIEW (THE), boarding, 128 Haywood—phone 1553, Mrs J Taylor Amiss propr (see p 20)
Book Chas (Gussie), clk H Seigle, h 68 s Liberty
*Booker Fred, lab, h 108 Eagle
*Booker Wm, lab, h 108 Eagle
Boone A Mrs, h 306 Chestnut
Boone Adolphus (Janie), painter, h 35 East
Boone Cyrus A (Elizabeth), engnr, h 193 s French B Broad
Boone Herbert, painter T J Perkinson, h 26 Jefferson Drive
Boone Lillian Miss, cook, h 15 Jefferson Drive
Boone Martha L, wid Geo, h 12 Seney
Boone Mary Miss, linen rm kpr Battery Park Hotel, rms same
Boone W Herbert (Hattie), painter, h 26 Jefferson Drive
Boothe Nannie, wid Geo, housekpr 129 Broad
*Boozer Jas (Fannie), gro Biltmore rd, S Biltmore, h same
*Boozer Myrtle, dom, h 36 Hill
BOOZE W MANSFIELD (Minnie), mngr Asheville Electrical Co, h 74 Central av (see side lines)
*Borden Mary, laund, h 23 McDowell
Boring Amna Miss, clk Ashev Dry Gds Co, bds The Henrietta
BORNE WILLIS G, cartoonist The Ashev Citizen, rms 21 Technical Bldg
Bosse Jno H, h 27 Blake
Bosse Lena C Miss, h 27 Blake
Bosse Rose K Miss, h 27 Blake
Bostic Jos T (Attie), supt of streets 100 City Hall, h 71 Central av
Bostic Lalia E Miss, tchr, h 71 Central av
Bostic Nettie M, wid Plato B, h 49 s French Broad av
Bostick Elizabeth, wid B R, h 11 All Souls Crescent, Biltmore
BOSTICK V BUREN, mngr Estate of Frank Coxe, rms 20-21 Medical Bldg—phone 163
Bostick Wilbur A (Crusia), (B J Luther & Co), h 1 Church, S Biltmore
*Bost Martin L (Mary), grdnr, h 63 Curve
Boston Shoe Store (The), 30 Patton av; J R Clements pres, W M Lambright treas, H S Chambers sec
Boswell Thos S, supt Murphy Div Sou Ry, old yd office Sou Ry, rms 195 s French Broad av
Botts Anna N Mrs, h Marigold Cottage, Albemarle Park

The Life Insurance Co. of Virginia
ORGANIZED 1871 RICHMOND, VA.

ISSUES ALL THE MOST APPROVED FORMS OF LIFE INSURANCE CONTRACTS from $500.00 to $25,000.00, with premiums payable quarterly, semi-annually and annually

J. V. Moon, Superintendent, Rooms 3-4-5 Maxwelton Bldg., Asheville, N. C.

D. TREXLER TIN SHOP

All Kinds of Roofing, Gutter and Conductor Work.

Phone 862

159 South Main St.

DR. C. H. MILLER

MECHANO-THERAPIST

14 N. Spruce St.
Phone 979
ASHEVILLE, N. C.

Hours by engagement

Drugless Healing of Disease

Bouknight Frank N, agt Life Ins Co of Va, h 94 Cherry
Bourne Frances C, student, h 16 Bearden av
Bourne Fred T, lab, h 460 s Main
Bourne Henry Mc, student, h 16 Bearden av
Bourne Jas D (Sallie), carp, h 460 s Main
Bourne Jas D Jr, trav slsmn The Piedmont Elec Co, h 460 s Main
BOURNE LOUIS M (Emily C), (Bourne, Parker & Morrison), and sec Ashev Ptg & Engrav Co, h 16 Bearden
Bourne Louis M Jr, U S N, h 16 Bearden av
BOURNE, PARKER & MORRISON (L M Bourne, Haywood Parker, A T Morrison), attys at law, s Pack Sq cor Main—phone 514
Bouters Jno (Katherine), adjutant Salvation Army, h 3 Aston Park
Bouters Wesley, clk, h 3 Aston Park
Bowden T Gilmer (Louise B), shoemkr 26 e College, h 51 Atkins
Bowen Louanna Miss, h 39 Clingman av
Bowles Carrie L Miss, h 190 Woodfin
Bowles Edwin, painter R E Bowles, h 190 Woodfin
BOWLES ROBT E (Marie L), paints, oils, colors, varnishes, stains, brushes, etc, 1 e Pack Sq—phone 407, h 190 Woodfin (see p 5)
Bowles Robt E Jr, painter R E Bowles, h 190 Woodfin
Bowles Wm R, painter, h 190 Woodfin
*Bowman Bessie, cook, 296 Montford av
Bowman Ira (Cora), collr L O Golightly, h Grace
*Bowman Jno W, barber 5 n w Pack Sq, h 76 Chunn
Bowman Mary E Miss (Bowman & Wright), h 21-25 Reed Bldg
*Bowman Nora, cook, 182 Cumberland av
*Bowman Robt (Emma), cook, h 67 Gudger
*Bowman Wm J (Willie), barber, h 76 Chunn
Bowman & Wright (Miss M E Bowman, Mrs Sarah Wright), dressmkrs 21-25 Reed Bldg
*Boyce Henry, lab, h 27 Scott
Boyce Sallie R, wid Wm A, h 187 Haywood
*Boyd Benj (Carrie), lab, h nr Hazel Mill rd, W Ashev
Boyd Camey C, lab, 34 Spring
Boyd Carl M, clk W H Wyatt, h 508 w Haywood
Boyd Coatsworth P (Martha), mill wkr, h 25 Roberts
Boyd Edwd D, condr, bds 376 Southside av
Boyd Elizabeth A, wid Saml M, h Arlington st, W Ashev
Boyd Erwin A (Florence), painter, h (r) 5 Aston Park

....Asheville Cleaning and Pressing Club....
Tailoring That Satisfies and Prices That Please

Steam and French Dry Cleaning of all delicate and fine wearing apparel for ladies and gentlemen. MESSENGER SERVICE IN THE CITY.

J. C. WILBAR, Prop. 4. N. Pack Square **PHONE 389**

Boyd Hardy W (Mary), fruits, h 508 w Haywood
Boyd Ivan (Leona), peddler, h 47 Spring
Boyd Jno R (Julia), carp, h 111 Seney
Boyd Marinda Miss, laund, h 47 Spring
BOYD ROBT LEE (Ida M), pres-treas Swannanoa Drug Co, h 55 Pearson Drive—phone 1944
Boyd Rosa Miss, stengr U S Furn Mnfg Co, h S Biltmore
Boyd Stella Miss, h 47 Spring
*Boyd Wm, lab, h nr Hazel Mill rd, W Ashev
Boyd Wm H (Mary), eating hse 515 w Haywood, h 508 same
Boyd Wm M (Louise), carp, h Haywood rd, W Ashev
Boyd Wm W, clk Sou Exp Co, bds 34 Spring
*Boyden Jno, helper Hollar Motor Co, h 17 McDowell
Boyles Bessie Mrs, clk Morris Levitt, h Woolsey
Boyles Edwd J (Kate H), foreman W M Jones, h Jarrett av, W Ashev
Boyles Hallie Miss, bds The Henrietta
Boyles Lallie M Miss, stengr, h Jarrett av, W Ashev
Boynton A Gray (Dorothy), civil engnr Biltmore Estate, h 7 Brook, Biltmore
Boynton Frank (Mary), mngr, h Biltmore Park
*Bozeman Fred, lab, h 10 Hibernia
*Bozeman Jas, waiter, h 10 Hibernia
*Bozeman Otis, waiter, h 10 Hibernia
Brackett Gaither (Mary), mill wkr, h 25 Logan
Brackett Hardy (Alice), lab, h 128 Poplar
*Brackett Lou, lab, h S Asheville
*Brackett Raymond (Anna), driver, h S Asheville
Brackett Robt B (Rosa), driver, h 55 Clingman av
Brackett Thos (Eliza), lab city, h 120 Poplar
Bradburn Jos H (Mary), gro Haywood rd, W Ashev h same
Bradfield Annie Miss, asst supt Ashev Mission Hospital, h 5 Charlotte
Bradford Howell W, plstr, h 31 Reed, S Biltmore
Bradford Jas B (Annie L), clk P O, h 84 Penland
BRADFORD JOS C (Annie M), asst U S Pastmaster, h 38 Hiawassee
BRADFORD JOSEPH M (Mamie), automobile, carriage and wagon painter 25-27 n Lexington av—phone 681, h 356 n Main (see p 21)
Bradford Mary S Miss, h 38 Hiawassee
Bradford Mary S, wid Chas, h 36 Hiawassee
Bradford Wiley (Cora), painter J M Bradford, bds 356 n Main

Bradford Wm C, plstr, h 31 Reed, S Biltmore
*Bradley Baylis (Anna), lab, h 12 Blanton
Bradley Bessie Miss, h 65 Charlotte
*Bradley Bessie, dom, h W Ashev
Bradley Callie, wid Fate, h Haywood rd, W Ashev
Bradley Clyde B, clk frt office Sou Ry, h W Asheville
Bradley F Ellis (Margaret), lab, h 34 View
*Bradley Geo, lab, h 47 Black
Bradley Geo D (Emeline T), farmer, h nr Hazel Mill rd, W Ashev
BRADLEY GORDON B, treas Dixie Mutual Life Ins Co, bds 65 Charlotte
Bradley Grace Miss, h 65 Charlotte
Bradley Hiram, meat ctr Marlow Bros, h 304 College
Bradley J Milton, lab, h Riverside Drive nr William
*Bradley Jas (Alice), gardener, h Herren av, W Ashev
Bradley Jeannette G Mrs, tchr West Ashev Schl, h W Asheville
Bradley Jeter C, clk, bds 50 Asheland av
*Bradley Jno (Rosa), lab, h 190 Scott
*Bradley Jno (Rachel), gardener, h nr Hazel Mill rd, W Ashev
Bradley Jno N (Lula), gro 527 w Haywood and police, h 26 Logan
Bradley Jno W (Jeanette), prin West Ashev School, h Hill st, W Ashev
Bradley Jos (Gertrude), lab, h 11 Spring
BRADLEY JOSEPH S (Dora), pres Dixie Mutual Life Ins Co, h 65 Charlotte
Bradley L Elizabeth Mrs, h W Asheville (R F D3)
Bradley Leona Miss, h nr Hazel Mill rd, W Asheville
Bradley Lonnie C (Bertha), clk Sou Exp Co, h 25 Phifer
*Bradley Louise, h Haywood rd, W Asheville
Bradley Martha J, wid Jno, h 52 Woodfin
Bradley Mollie Miss, h nr Hazel Mill rd, W Asheville
*Bradley Mollie, laund, h 47 Black
Bradley Napoleon B, eating hse 523 w Haywod, h W Asheville
Bradley Parley P (Harriet), driver J M Westall, h Woolsey
Bradley Rebecca Mrs, h nr Hazel Mill rd, W Asheville
*Bradley Robt (Georgia), bottler Pepsi-Cola Botg Wks, h 36 Gudger
BRADLEY SAM'L O (Crimora), pres-treas Ashev Paint & Glass Co and sec Swannanoa Drug Co, h 1 Summit cor Hillside

Bradley Squire W (Nancy), h 27 Atkinson
Bradley Virgil B (Ada), painter, h nr Haywood rd, W Asheville
Bradley Wm, tmstr, h 304 College
*Bradshaw Green (Matilda), lab, h 180 Beaumont
BRADSHAW HARRY R (Daisy E) (Brown-Northup & Co), h 99 East
Bragaw Winifred A, wid Richard, h 39 Washington rd
Bragg Wm M (Nancy), route agt Sou Expr Co, h 15 Baird
Braman Herbert O (Alice), driver Swannanoa Laundry, h 41 Atkin
Braman Herbert O Jr (Florida), emp Champion Fibre Co, h 131 Blanton
Bramlett Marcus M, farmer, h Haywood rd, W Asheville
Bramlett Philip H (Nancy A), h Haywood rd, W Asheville
Bramlett Wm R (Glenn), farmer, h Haywood rd, W Ashev
Branagan Jno J (Florence), tailor, h 374 s Main
Branch Louise L Miss, clk P O, h Margo Terrace
BRANCH PATRICK H (Grace), propr Margo Terrace, h same
Branch Thos W, clk Margo Terrace, h same
BRANDLE ANDREW C (Mae) (Theobold & Brandle), h 48 Cherry
Brandl Jos A, city milk inspr, h 48 Cherry
Brandl Katherine C Miss, propr The Tallulah, h 48 Cherry
Brandt Jos B, discount clk Amer Natl Bank, bds The Knickerbocker
Brank Albert V (Virgil), carp, h 23 Eloise
Brank Bascombe, clk, h 23 Eloise
Brank Carl B (Minnie,) driver, h 16 View
Branks E Curtis (Jennie), driver Caro Coal & Ice Co, h 103 Clingman av
Branks J Bastian, driver Sou Dray, h Hall st
Branks Martin, driver Mustin-Robertson Co Inc, h 103 Depot
Brannogan Jno J, tailor Whitlock Clo Co, h 374 s Main
Brannon Chas R (Allen B), trav slsmn, h 38 Carter
*Brannon Dorcas, h 15 Short
BRANSON C H & SONS (Chas H and F Edwd Branson), proprs Hotel Oxford (see side lines)
BRANSON CHAS H (Alice P) (C H Branson & Sons), h Hotel Oxford
Branson Chas H Jr, student, h Hotel Oxford
BRANSON F EDWD (C H Branson & Sons) and mngr Hotel Oxford Cafe, h Hotel Oxford

Club Cafe and Candy Kitchen "A GOOD PLACE FOR REFRESHMENT" — The standards we work to in our Restaurant Department are: Cooking, perfect; Service, prompt and cheerful; Prices, moderate; Menu, everything in season. Parties and Banquets, Teas and Dinners. 19 and 21 Haywood St. Phones 110 and 111.

Brown's Undertaking Parlors
S. H. BROWN
50 Patton Avenue
ASHEVILLE, N. C.
Lady Assistant When Desired
Phone 193-2 Rings

THE MOORE Plumbing Company
16 N. Pack Square
PHONE 1025
Sanitary Plumbing, General Tin and Metal Work, Hot Air Furnaces

---

Branton Edith Miss, h W Asheville
Branton Ella Miss, h W Asheville
Braswell Alonzo F (Paradine), lumber, h 120 Broad
Braswell Estelle Miss, h 120 Broad
Braswell Forest (Madonna), photog, h 120 Broad
Bratman Max (Regina), tailor S T Logan, h 33 Orchard
Bratman Regena Mrs, h 33 Orchard
Braun Adam (Amanda A), h 36 Carter
Braun H Ernest (Ellis), slsmn, h 25 Bearden av
Braun Milton L, clk, h 36 Carter
Braun Raymond A, clk G F Stradley, h 36 Carter
*Brazil Sarah, cook, h 53 Gudger
Breazeal Katherine M Mrs, h 211 Patton av
BREESE W E JR, pres Greater Western N C Assn, h Brevard N C
Bregstein Ralph, clk H L Finkelstein, rms Phoenix Hotel
Brendle David B (Rosa), engnr Sou Ry, h 391 s French Broad av
Brevard S Merta Miss, dress mkr Mrs H B Freezor, h Biltmore
Brewer A Jack, collr, h 59 Charlotte
Brewer Alex H, farmer, bds R P Potts, W Asheville
Brewer Ida Miss, h 15 Green
Brewer Sadie W, wid A J, h 59 Charlotte
Brewer Sarah Mrs, h Herren av, W Asheville
*Brewton Jno (Gertrude), lab, h 303 Ashland av
Bridges G Carson, brkmn, bds 430 Depot
*Bridges Carson (Mary), hackman 104 Choctaw, h same
Bridges Genevieve, clk Bon Marche, h 182 Flint
Bridges Jno M (Genevieve), clk C Sawyer, h 182 Flint
Bridges Roy, brkmn, bds 430 Depot
Bridgett Luther, switchman, bds 30 Jefferson Drive
Briggs Chas (Phoebe), real est, h 2 Hunt Hill
Briggs Chas C (Mattie), clk frt office Sou Ry, h W Asheville
Briggs Chas W, driver Coca-Cola Bot Co, h 17 Merrimon
Briggs Clarence O (Myrtle C), undtkr, h 16 s Ann
Briggs Dillard W (Lillie), mtrmn St Ry, h Vivian extd
Briggs Ellis, lab, h 475 w Haywood
Briggs F Bertha Miss, student, h Haywood rd, W Asheville
Briggs Gordon, hostler S D Robinson, bds 62 Pender
Briggs Harriet Miss, dress mkr 17 Merrimon av, h same
BRIGGS HENRY H (Attie), physician 73 Haywood—phone 608; office hours 9 a m to 1 p m, h Swannanoa Drive

---

The Battery Park Bank
ASHEVILLE, N. C.   City, County and State Depositary
Capital - - $100,000.00
Surplus and Profits, $110,000.00

J. A. TILLMAN I carry a nice line of Watches, Clocks and Jewelry, and make a specialty of repair work. Satisfaction guaranteed **Jeweler** **17 N. Main St.**

ASHEVILLE [1913] DIRECTORY

Briggs J Frank, lab, h Haywood rd, W Asheville
Briggs Jas, lab, h 475 w Haywood
Briggs Jno (Vici), lab, h 35 Catawba
Briggs Jos W (Mary), driver Swannanoa Ldy, h 81 East
Briggs Laura L Miss, h 17 Merrimon av
Briggs M Luther (Delia), driver, h 475 w Haywood
Briggs Milton (Jennie), carp, h 17 Merrimon av
Briggs Nellie Miss, h 17 Merrimon av
Briggs Pierre (Huldah), boarding 146 s French Broad av, h same
Briggs Richard, clk Yates & McQuire
Briggs Ross, lab, h 475 w Haywood
Briggs Theresa Miss, student, h 146 s French Broad av
Briggs Thos, mtrmn St Ry, h 17 Merrimon
Bright Alfred L (Mary M), genl mdse Haywood rd, W Asheville, h Brevard rd
Bright Sarah H, wid Isaiah, h 176 Woodfin
Brigman Garry, emp Langren Pool Rom
*Brigman Jas C (Cora L), butler, h 72 Ridge
Brigmon Caroline C, wid D I, h 172 Haywood
Brigmon Etta B, wid Jas, boarding 16 Hilliard la, h same
Brigmon Fred'k, driver, h 16 Hilliard la
Brigmon Guy, lumber inspr, h 16 Hilliard la
Brigmon Jodie Mrs, emp Ashev Mica Co, h 9 Reed Bldg
Brigmon Wilburn, clk, h 16 Hilliard la
*Brinder Elvira, h 94 Grove
Brinkley Alonzo, driver Owenby & Son, h Bingham Hghts
Brister Saml L (Daisy), phys, h 147 Charlotte
*Bristol Jas L (Jane), lab, h 92 Curve
Brith J Henderson (Nora), lab, h 12 View
British Woolen Mills, tailors, 28 s Main, T W Charles mngr
Britt Carmen Miss, h 48 Woodfin
Britt Cline, press feeder Ashev Ptg & Engrav Co, h 29 Silver
Britt Geo E (Nancy), farmer, h Hazel Mill rd, W Asheville
Britt Geo W, student, h 48 Woodfin
Britt Mary Miss, cook O N Rockett, h 55½ n Main
Britt Mary L, wid Geo, h 60 Blanton
Britt Horace C (Mamie), driver N C Oil Co, h 60 Blanton
Britt W E & Co (W E Britt, Gay Green), livery, 32 w College
BRITT WALTER C (Shirley), sec-treas Ashev Supply & Fdy Co, h 31 Josephine
Britt Wm W (Luna), police, h 48 Woodfin
Britt Worley E (Mary I) (W E Britt & Co), h Haywood rd, W Asheville

INSURANCE

INSURE YOUR SALARY WITH US
NEVER CARRY YOUR OWN RISK
SAFETY IS THE BEST POLICY
UNLESS YOU ARE A CAPITALIST
REST EASY IF YOU HAVE
AN ACCIDENT WE WILL
NOT KEEP YOU WAITING TO
COLLECT YOUR CLAIM
EVERY CLAIM PROMPTLY PAID

Imperial Mutual Life & Health Insurance Co.

Home Office:
ASHEVILLE, N. C.

Phone 495

HOTEL OXFORD Redecorated and Refitted throughout. Recently enlarged to 60 rooms. Centrally located. Depot cars stop at entrance. Long distance telephone office upstairs. American and European plan. Rates 50c. 75c and $1 per day; special rates by week or month. C. H. Branson & Sons, Proprietors. Phone 1887. 50-54 South Main St. **Asheville, N. C.**

Williams-Brownell Planing Mill Company — *Hardwoods*

Lumber---Rough and Dressed Flooring a Specialty Moulding, Interior Finish, Etc.

Office, Plant and Yards on Southern Railway, Near Biltmore Station

WHITE PINE   **Phone 729**   YELLOW PINE

Brittain Martha A, wid F Barto, h 30 Blake
Brittner Jno J, pressman The Inland Press, h 293 Asheland av
Brittner Richard V (Maggie), shoe repr T L Hyndman, h 293 Ashland av
Britton Frank, condr Sou Ry, bds 308 Depot
Broadwight Florence Miss, governess "Klondyke" Montford av
Brock Ignatius W (Ora) (N Brock), h Woolsey (R F D1)
Brock N (Ignatius Brock), photogrs Mosell Bldg (3d fl)
Brohun Carrie B, wid Robt, h 55 Victoria av
Brohun Florida B Miss, h 55 Victoria av
Brohun Jno P, h 55 Victoria av
Brohun Matthew S, student, h 55 Victoria av
Brohun Thos D, civ engnr, h 55 Victoria av
Brohun Wm Leroy, trav slsmn, h 55 Victoria av
Brooks Alfred (Mira A), dentist, h 42 Atkinson
*Brooks Annie, dom, h 47 Brick
*Brooks Butler (Lucinda), driver Carolina C & I Co, h 177 Clingman av
Brooks Geo (Ordie), driver, h 90 Avery
*Brooks Henry (Alice), lab, h 125 Roberts
Brooks Ida Miss, h Lester rd, W Ashev
*Brooks Jno, lab, h 46 Pine
Brooks Julia Miss, h Lester rd, W Ashev
*Brooks L (Emma), bellman, h 177 Clingman av
*Brooks Lillie, dom, h 27 Jordan
Brooks Luther (Carrie), lab, h 7 Velvet
Brooks Malissa Miss, laund, h 28 Ralph
Brooks Mary B Miss, stengr J S Styles, h W Asheville
Brooks Minnie Miss, laund, h 28 Ralph
*Brooks Tena, cook, h 148 Hill
*Brooks Vernon (Ida), lab, h 177 Clingman av
Brooks Virginia Miss, h nr Main st, W Ashev
*BROOKS W P MRS, mngr Eagle Street Pressing Club, h 242 s Beaumont
*Brooks Wm (Annie), lab, h 20 Short McDowell
*Brooks Wm P (Wilhelmina E), barber 8 Eagle, h 242 Beaumont
Brookshire Chas W (Maggie), engnr Power Plant Ashev P & L Co, h 137 Grove
Brookshire Frank, h Bingham Hghts
Brookshire Fredk, helper, h 18 Asheland av
Brookshire Geo, driver Ashev Ice Co, h Avery st
Brookshire Horace L (Mattie), lab, h 560 s Main

Asheville Electrical Company
W. Mansfield Booze, Manager
74 CENTRAL AVE.
HEADQUARTERS
Phone 377

Asheville Dry Cleaning Co.
Telephones 835-836, All Dep't
MAIN, N. E. COR. COLLEGE

THE CLEANERS
Our Department for Oriental Rugs and Carpet Cleaning is prepared to serve you in all its branches.   :-:   :-:   :-:

E. S. Paine   O. E. Hansen

Maple Flooring and Poplar Siding

English Lumber Co.
PHONE . . 321

Brookshire Jas M (Etta), h "Overbrook," Summit st, S Biltmore
Brookshire Jno V, student, h "Overbrook," Summit st, S Biltmore
Brookshire Julia Miss, student, h "Overbrook," Summit st, S Biltmore
Brookshire Laura Mrs, housekpr Winsor Hotel, rms same
Brookshire Julia A, wid Jno A, rooming hse, 39 s French Broad av, h same
Brookshire Lonnie L (Tennie V), collr J L Smathers & Sons, h 130 s French Broad av
Brookshire Thos J (Emma), tmstr Ashev P & L Co, h 18 Asheland av
"Brookwood Bungalow," res Mrs N M Watson, "Edgemont"
Brown Ada T Mrs, rms Adelaide Bldg
Brown Albert E Rev (Lamanda), supt Mountain School Dept Home Mission Board So Baptist Convention, h W Asheville (R F D 3)
Brown Alberta Miss, student, h Haywood rd, W Ashev
Brown Alex, sign painter, 32 McDowell, h same
*Brown Anna, laund, h 384 College
*Brown Augustus (Lizzie), lab, h 29 Sorrell
Brown B Gene Miss, h 31 s French Broad av
Brown Barbara C Miss, stengr Murray Lbr Co, bds 57 Cherry
*Brown Belton (Susie), waiter, h 24 Short McDowell
Brown Bessie E Miss, h 293 s Main
*Brown Bettie, cook, h 74 Circle
Brown Book Co (Inc), 66 Patton av; E L Brown Jr pres-mngr, T J Harkins v-pres, Owen Gudger sec, J G Stikeleather treas
Brown Building, offices, 10½ n Pack Sq
Brown C E Graham (Myrtle), bkkpr Battery Park Bank, h Sand Hill rd, W Ashev
Brown Canie B (Emma), hackman, 293 s Main, h same
BROWN CANIE N (Allie B), propr Swannanoa Laundry, h 135 Haywood—phone 146
Brown Carl B, student, h Emma N C
BROWN-CARTER REALTY CO (H A Brown, G D Carter and T W Smith), real estate and collections, 23 Temple ct—phone 341 (see side lines)
*Brown Chas, agt, h 67 Hill
*Brown Chas (Florence), lab, h 125 Roberts
Brown Chas B, hackman, h 293 s Main

ASHEVILLE [1913] DIRECTORY 105

BIGGEST
BUSIEST
BEST

Asheville Steam Laundry

Phones:
1936 and 1937

43 to 47
W. College Street

CHARLES H. HONESS
OPTOMETRIST
AND
OPTICIAN

Exclusive maker of
ATLAS SHUR-ON
EYE GLASSES

THE
Home of Ce-Rite
Toric Lenses

We make a specialty of correcting optical defects with properly fitted glasses.

54 Patton Avenue
Opposite Postoffice

IF in the market for a Gas Engine let us make you prices.
its heavy castings, such as columns or building plates, see us.
its a skilled mechanic for boiler work, see us.
you want machine work of any kind phone 590.

CAROLINA MACHINERY CO.

FOUNDERS
MACHINISTS and
Jobbers of Mill
Supplies

Life Insurance Company of Virginia
ORGANIZED 1871
Home Office - Richmond, Va.

Has won the hearty approval and active support of the people by its promptness and fair dealing during the **FORTY-TWO YEARS** of its operation

J. V. Moon, Superintendent, Rooms 3-4-5 Maxwelton Bldg., Asheville, N. C.

T. P. JOHNSON & CO. SHEET METAL WORKERS All Kinds of Roofing Guttering and Conductor Work Metal Ceilings, Skylights and Galvanized Iron Cornices OFFICE and SHOP: 69-71 S. MAIN Phone 325 **DR. C. H. MILLER** Mechano-Therapist 14 N. Spruce Street ASHEVILLE, N. C. PHONE 979 Hours by Engagement DRUGLESS HEALING OF DISEASE	BROWN CHAS L (Maggie M), general blacksmith and horseshoeing, 25-27 n Lexington av—phone 681, h 26 Chestnut (see p 21) BROWN CHAS W (Josephine R), pres Central Bank & Trust Co, Brown-Miller Shoe Co and v-pres Noland, Brown & Co, h Grove Park Brown Clara, wid Geo W, matron Whitmore Sanitarium, rms same Brown Clara D Miss, clk Dr W L Dunn, h Brevard rd, W Ashev *Brown Clarence, lab, h 38 Wallach *Brown Clarence, propr Railroad Men's Pressing Club Brown Claude V (Nannie L), clk P O, h W Asheville (R F D 3) BROWN'S CREAMERY (see Carolina Creamery) *Brown David, lab, porter Bon Marche, h 27 Hazzard Brown David C (Bonnie), painter, h 324 Pearson Drive Brown Donna M Miss, emp Dr T C Smith, h 44 Clingman Brown Dovie Miss, stengr Ashev Citizen, h 42 Starnes av BROWN EDWD B (Bessie F), genl sec Y M C A, h 178 Haywood BROWN EDWARD E (Mittie), propr Brownhurst Greenhouses and florist, Murdock av opp Grove Park—phone 497, h 34 Oak Brown Edwin L (Eva F), mnfrs agt, h 204 Woodfin Brown Edwin L Jr (Jane S), pres-mngr Brown Book Co, and v-pres Brown Hdw Co, h 144 Chestnut *Brown Eliza, cook, h 60 Eagle Brown Elmo L, student, h 34 Oak Brown Elsie M Miss, h 293 s Main *Brown Emanuel (Daisy), lab, h 23 Green's Row *Brown Ernest (Annie), barber J A Wilson, h 73 Eagle *Brown Essie, laund, h 13 Lincoln av *Brown Estella, cook, h 40 Maiden la Brown Eva F Miss, stengr, h 204 Woodfin Brown Frances E, wid Dr T E W, h 231 Haywood *Brown Frank B (Violet), barber C T Howell, h 60 Eagle Brown Frank F (Lena), trav slsmn, h 139 Haywood Brown Garrett W, appr Union Plumbing Co, h 13 Seney Brown Genevieve R Miss, h 34 Oak BROWN GEO E (Leona), with Brown-Miller Shoe Co, h 170 w Chestnut Brown Geo H (Ellen), painter, h 7 Park pl Brown Gertrude S, wid Jas J, h 218 Cumberland av Brown Grace L Miss, soloist, h Emma N C

ASHEVILLE CLEANING and PRESSING CLUB

TAILORING THAT SATISFIES and PRICES THAT PLEASE. Hats cleaned, banded and bound. Silk hats ironed. Buttons made to order in all sizes. Plain or with rims. PHONE 389

DYEING IN ALL SHADES Cleaned. Messenger Service. Kid Gloves, Slippers and Plumes. Fancy Jabots and Ties. French Dry Cleaned. Ladies' and Gentlemen's suits Steam

J. C. Wilbar, Prop. 4 NORTH PACK SQ.

Brown Gustavus (Lizzie), emp City Stable, h 29 Sorrell
BROWN H A & CO (H A Brown, T W Smith), genl contrs 23 Temple ct—phone 341 (see side lines)
BROWN HARDWARE CO (Inc), wholesale and retail 25 n Main; F M Weaver pres, E L Brown Jr v-pres, J H Cathey sec, H C Brown treas-genl mngr
*Brown Henry (Della), lab, h (r) 78 Pine
Brown Hester E Mrs, nurse Main st, W Ashev, h same
BROWN HORACE A (Jennie G), (Brown-Carter Realty Co), and (H A Brown & Co), h Haywood rd, W Asheville—phone 1721
BROWN HUGH C, treas and genl mngr Brown Hdw Co, h 204 Woodfin
Brown Ira D, foreman, h Haywood rd, W Ashev
Brown Isham B (Jane), lab, h 41 Catawba
Brown J Floyd (Lenora), horse trader, h Haywood rd, W Ashev
BROWN J LATT, mngr, h Emma N C
Brown Jas H (Nancy M), liveryman, h W Asheville
Brown Jas M (Laura), mchst, h 44 Clingman av
Brown Jas M (Rebecca), motorman, bds 585 Montford av
BROWN JAS V (Susie H), (Brown Undertaking Co), h 115 Haywood
Brown Jane, wid Jas, h 356 w Haywood
Brown Jennie L Miss, rms Adelaide Bldg
Brown Jessie P Miss, student, h 13 Seney
Brown Jno, lab, h 49 Spring
Brown Jno H (Lucy E), laundryman, h 116 Clingman av
Brown Josephine G Miss, h 13 Seney
Brown Jos A (Sophia), h 200 Montford av
*Brown Judge B, shoemkr 60 Sycamore, h 40 Tuskee
*Brown Julia, waitress, h S Asheville
BROWN JULIAN T, with Carolina Creamery, rms 271 Haywood
BROWN L V (Amanda H), (Brown-Northup & Co), h 231 Haywood
Brown Laura H Miss, h 204 Woodfin
*Brown Lelia, h 47 Velvet
Brown Lila M Miss, student, h 26 Chestnut
Brown Lillie O Miss, h Sand Hill rd, W Ashev
*Brown Lizzie, h 43 Velvet
*Brown Lula, cook 44 Watauga
Brown M Alice Miss, h 218 Cumberland av
Brown Maggie Mrs, h 32 McDowell
*Brown Malinda, laund, h 384 College

*Brown Mamie, cook, h 24 Gibbons
Brown Margaret Miss, h 60 Montford av
Brown Margaret Miss, h W Asheville (R F D 3)
Brown Maria T Miss, h 182 Cumberland av
Brown Marion, lab, bds 119 Park av
Brown Mark W (L Eugenia), atty at law, 4-5 Temple Court h 38 n Spruce
Brown Mary J, wid Milton M, h Sand Hill rd, W Ashev
Brown Matthew, driver, h 13 Seney
*Brown Mattie, cook, h 224 Flint
Brown May Miss, clk Jno A Guffey, h Harmony N C
*Brown Milan A (Nancy), lab, h 41 Tuskee
BROWN-MILLER SHOE CO, shoes for the whole family, 47 Patton av—phone 710; C W Brown pres, U S Miller v-pres, H B Voorhies sec
*Brown Naomi, laund, h 74 Circle
BROWN-NORTHUP & CO (W B and H K Northup, H R Bradshaw, R M Miller, W H and L V Brown), hardware, 33 Patton av—phone 142
Brown Oscar D, mngr E F Wilson, h 58-60 s Main
Brown Paul P, bkkpr Amer Natl Bank, h Chunns Cove
Brown Pender B (Daisy), firemn Sou Ry, h 149 Bartlett
*Brown Pinckney B (Edna), cook, h 37 Hill
Brown Port V, trav inspr Natl Cash Register Co, rms 3 Aston Place
Brown Rachel, wid Jno, h 317 n Main
*Brown Ralph (Evelyn), lab, h 109 Mountain
BROWN REX U (Jessie M), propr Carolina Creamery, h 159 Woodfin
Brown Robt S, mngr Pack Sq Book Co, h 204 Woodfin
Brown Roy P (Myrtle), clk P O, h 152 Flint
Brown S Herbert (Ashev Mica Co), h 182 Cumberland av
*Brown Sallie, dom, h 40 Maiden la
Brown Saml (Minnie), h Richmond Hill
Brown Sandiford W, student, h Emma N C
BROWN SUSAN H MRS, propr Brown's Undertaking Parlors, h 116 Haywood
Brown T Caney, h 89 Montford av
Brown Theo H, sec-treas Hose Co No 1 A F D, rms A F D
BROWN'S UNDERTAKING PARLORS, 50 Patton av, Mrs Susan H Brown propr (see right side lines)
*Brown W Alex (Lelah), caretaker Edgewood Park h same
Brown W Vance (Daphne), (Asheville Mica Co), h 177 Cumberland av
*Brown Walter, cook, h 238 Asheland av

Brown Walter M (Essie G), foreman Swannanoa Ldy, h 178 w Chestnut
BROWN WILEY B (Laura J), live stock, 11 Lexington av —phone 104, h Emma N C (R F D 3)
*Brown Wm (Maggie), cook Langren Hotel, h 238 Asheland av
*Brown Wm Jr, h 238 Asheland av
Brown Wm A (Elizabeth), mtrmn St Ry, h 13 Seney
Brown Wm C (Alice), slsmn, h 31 s French Broad av
Brown Wm C Jr, clk, h 31 s French Broad av
BROWN WM H (Clara), (Brown-Northup & Co), h W Asheville
*Brown Wm M, porter, Drs Purefoy & Powell
Brown Wm P (Alice), atty at law, 208 Oates Bldg, h 104 Central av
Brown Z Yates, msgr Murphy Div Sou Exp Co, bds 23 n Ann
*Brown Zelmer (Minnie), brkmn, h 127 Roberts
Brown & Smith, stone quarry Lester rd, W Ashev
BROWNELL ELNATHAN P JR (Lillian M), sec-treas Noland, Brown & Co and pres Williams-Brownell Planing Mill Co, h 19 Grove—phone 1216
BROWNHURST GREENHOUSES, Murdock av opp Grove Park—phone 497, E E Brown propr
Brownsberger Ethel Miss, dom, 49 Zillicoa
Brownson Allen R, student, h Haywood rd, W Ashev
Brownson Victor C, student, h Haywood rd, W Ashev
BROWNSON WM C (Elizabeth H), physician, rms 1-2 Medical Bldg—phone 1177, office hours 10 a m to 12, 4 to 5 p m, h W Asheville (R F D 3)
Brownson Wm C Jr, student, h W Asheville (R F D 3)
Broxton Wm M (Pearl), trav slsmn, h 105 College
Broyles Delphia Miss, laundress, Chunn's Cove
Broyles Earnie E (Bessie), clk The Racket Store, h Chunns Cove
Bruce Arthur W, farmer, h W Asheville (R F D 3)
Bruce E O, farmer, h W Ashev (R F D 3)
*Bruce Lacy, porter, h 16 Dundee
Bruce Maude, mad, h 18 Eagle Terrace
Bruce Mitchell A (Lillie B), farmer, h W Ashev (R F D 3)
Bruce Walter M, farmer, h W Ashev (R F D 3)
Brunner Edwd H (Cora I), propr Champion Shoe Hospital, h 126 Cherry
Brunner Fred L (May), shoemkr Champion Shoe Hospital, h 125 Cherry

Club Cafe and Candy Kitchen
"A GOOD PLACE FOR REFRESHMENT"

Our Ice Cream manufacturing plant is absolutely clean and sanitary.
Prompt family delivery. Phones 110 and 111.
Catering for large parties and receptions. Special Creams.

Brown's Undertaking Parlors

S. H. BROWN

Lady Assistant When Desired

Phone 193-2 Rings

50 Patton Avenue
Asheville, N. C.

Established 1894

B. J. JACKSON

Carefully Selected Fruits and Vegetables

Stall No. 11, City Market

BUSINESS PHONES:
86 and 101

RESIDENCE PHONE
1596

Bruns H Ernest (Ellis), clk H Redwood & Co, h 25 Bearden
Bruton D Ella Miss, h 65 Park av
Bruton Daniel W (Rachel E), real est, h 65 Park av
*Bruton Florence, laund, h 61 Lincoln av
*Bruton Lillie, laund, h 61 Lincoln av
*Bruton Maggie, h 61 Lincoln av
*Bruton Minnie, dom, h 61 Lincoln av
*Bruton Ora, cook, h 20 Smith
*Bruton Rena, laund, h 488 s French Broad av
*Bruton Theodosia, cook, h 132 Hill
Brux Cecil, clk H B Brux, bds 101 Victoria rd
Brux Gussie E Miss, h 101 Victoria rd
Brux Harry D, clk H B Brux, bds 101 Victoria rd
Brux Henry B (Helena), paper dlr, 57 s Main, h 101 Victoria rd
Brux Willa W Miss, stengr H B Brux, bds 101 Victoria rd
Bryan Frank A (Anna), trav slsmn, h 172 Asheland av
*Bryan Julius (Mattie I), janitor, h 71 Hill
*Bryan Mattie I, dressmkr 71 Hill, h same
Bryant Chas S (Edith M), sec-treas Champion Fibre Co, h 35 Cullowhee
Bryant Edwd, mchnst, bds 39 Clingman av
Bryant Francis, driver J F Sims, h 20 Jefferson Drive
Bryant Geo H (Sallie), electrn, h 20 Jefferson Drive
Bryant Jacob K, lab, h 36 s Spruce
Bryant M L Mrs, tchr Montford av Schl
Bryant Marie C, wid B Allen, stengr, h 69 Flint
Bryant Martin L Rev (Elizabeth), h 201 Merrimon av
Bryant Olive Miss, clk, bds 76 Starnes av
*Bryant Reuben H (Fannie E), phys 18 Eagle, h 195 s Main
*Bryant Robt W (Annie), (Bryant & Clarke), h 235 Flint
Bryant Sallie, wid Barnet, h 36 s Spruce
*Bryant & Clarke (R W Bryant, S S Clarke), cleaning and pressing, 94 Haywood
Bryce Mallissa A, wid M H, h 33 Buxton
Bryce Saml P (May), gro 34 Roberts, h 33 Buxton
*Bryson Bessie, h 46 Curve
Bryson Clarence C (Sadie), flagman, h 18 Buncombe
Bryson Cora Mrs, boarding 34½ n Main, h same
*Bryson Ernest, presser J C Wilbar, h 60 Eagle
Bryson Fannie Miss, picker Ashev Mica Co, h W Asheville
Bryson Glenn Miss, student, h 102 Blanton
Bryson Harry, lab, bds Hotel Warren
Bryson Hattie M Miss, clk, h 102 Blanton
Bryson Julius A (Jane), horse dlr, h Haywood rd, W Ashev

Furniture and China Carefully Prepared for Shipment

Mahogany Furniture Hand Made & Carefully Reproduced

E. E. GALER
114 PATTON AVE.

Upholstering and Refinishing
PHONE - 1674

*Bryson Kate, dom, h S Asheville
*Bryson Mamie, dom, h 152 Church
Bryson S Avery, horse dlr, h Haywood rd, W Ashev
Bryson Ulysses S (Cora), hackman 34½ n Main, h same
Bryson W Atley (Jessie), slsmn McConnell Bros, h 284 College
Bryson Wilbur V, student, h 102 Blanton
Bryson Wm C (Loduskie), condr Sou Ry, h 102 Blanton
Buchanan Bessie Mrs, boarding 34 Asheland av, h same
Buchanan I Bayley (Leona), plmbr J R Rich Co, h 59 Asheland av
Buchanan J Frank (Bessie), bricklyr, h 34 Asheland av
Buchanan Jas, h 262 s Main
Buchanan Julius (Callie), h 34 Asheland av
Buchanan Sarah E, wid Wm A, h 262 s Main
Buchanan W T, driver J E Johnson, h Grace
Buchanan Wm A, h 262 s Main
Buck Clara E, wid S C, h Woolsey (R F D 1)
Buck Ione W Miss, stengr, bds 111 Montford av
*Buckeye Sanitary Shaving Parlor, 11½ s Main, Frazier & Martin proprs
Buckeye Water Co, Haywood rd (R F D 3), W Ashev; R P Hayes pres, Mrs L P Hayes sec
Buckner Albert S (Dora A), clk frt office Sou Ry h W Asheville nr Smith's bridge
Buckner Alfred L (Easter), lab, h 353 Hillside
Buckner Annie Miss, bds A B Anders, W Ashev
Buckner C Baxter (Ida), mchst, h 14 Roberts
Buckner Clementine Miss, stengr Board of Health, h 11 Soco
Buckner Cletus D (Minnie), mill wkr, h 12 Factory Hill
Buckner Eleanor Miss, phone opr, bds 60 Conestee
Buckner Eliza, wid M A, h Woolsey (R F D 1)
Buckner Ella I Mrs, boarding 41 Oak, h same
Buckner Fannie Miss, cook, 48 Starnes av
Buckner Geo, mchst, h Brevard rd, W Ashev
Buckner H Jefferson (Mira), carp, h Brevard rd, W Ashev
BUCKNER HORACE C (Ella), head pressman Hackney & Moale Co, h 41 Oak
Buckner Horace G (Annie), fireman, h 22 Nelson av
Buckner Jacob, carp, bds 34½ n Main
Buckner Jacob G (Susan), carp, h 79 Washington rd
Buckner Jacob H (Anna), foreman, h Haywood rd, W Ashev
Buckner Jas R (Miley), lab, h 20 Fagg

Mrs. Wilder's **SANITARY HOME LAUNDRY** turns out first class work in Laundering and Dry Cleaning. **No. 7 Montford Ave., Phone 1354**

ASHEVILLE [1913] DIRECTORY

Buckner Jane, wid Mitchell, h 12 Roberts
Buckner L Monroe, wid Wm, h 511 n Main
Buckner Marguerite C Mrs, h 35 Clingman av
BUCKNER NEPTUNE (Lena), sec Board of Trade, h 7 Aston pl
Buckner Nimrod, h 11 Soco
Buckner Robt B (Sarah), carp, h 28 Ralph
Buckner Robt W (Florence), carp, h 585 Montford av
BUCKNER RUFUS G, physician (eye, ear, nose, and throat), 7-8 Medical Bldg, h 11 Soco
Buckner Sallie Miss, h Brevard rd, W Ashev
Buckner Starling (Caroline), carp, h 6 Factory Hill
Buckner Thula J Miss, h 511 n Main
Buckner Veach, driver, bds 511 n Main
Buckner W W (Emma), mtrmn, h 242 n Main
Buckner Wilburn G (Lena), baker, h 33 Central av
Buckner Wm N (Hester), mchst, h 327 Hillside
Buehrer Albert A, mngr Ashev Steam Bakery, 110-112 Patton av, h 160 Flint
Bugg David (Zora), mill wkr, h 8 Factory Hill
Bull Henry K (Marguerite), h Victoria rd
☞Bumgardner see Baumgardner
BUNCOMBE COUNTY OFFICIALS (see County Officials)
BUNDY JOSEPHINE MISS, associate prin Home Indus Schl, rms same
"Bungalow" (The), Summit cor Hillside, res Dr W L Dunn
Bunn Adrian, plmbr, h Woolsey (R F D 1)
Bunn Albert (Katharine), brick mnfr, h 15 Clayton
Bunn Albert Jr, U S N, h 15 Clayton
Bunn Jno G, clk Ashev P & G Co, h 15 Clayton
Bunn Roland (Annie), bricklyr, h Woolsey (R F D 1)
Burbage Jno H (Florrie L), h 19 e Spears av
Burbank Emma W, wid P M, h 202 Charlotte
Burbank Helen Miss, h 202 Charlotte
Burbank Malcolm W, student, h 202 Charlotte
Burbank Marcia B Miss, h 202 Charlotte
Burchell Jno B, meat ctr Hill's Market, h 26 Oak
Burchfield Clemson L, condr, bds 308 Depot
Burdick Julia W, wid Harry L, h 216 Pearson Drive
*Burgess Geo, lab, bds 488 s French Broad av
*Burgess Jennie L, nurse 13 Ridge, h same
Burgess Jno, emp Sou Ry, h Haywood rd, W Ashev
*Burgin Agnes, cook, h 27 Jordan
Burgin Allie P (Nannie L), condr Sou Ry, h 34 John

OLDSMOBILE — **DETROIT ELECTRIC**
ARBOGAST MOTOR COMPANY
ACCESSORIES AND SUPPLIES
Phones 302 and 1728
52-60 N. Main
BUICK — **MAXWELLS**

Asheville Dry Cleaning Co.
Telephones 835-836, All Dep't
MAIN, N. E. COR. COLLEGE

THE CLEANERS
Our Department for Oriental Rugs and Carpet Cleaning is prepared to serve you in all its branches.
E. S. Paine   O. E. Hansen

Burgin Beulah Miss, ticket seller Princess Theatre
*Burgin Carrie, dom, h 11 Wallach
*Burgin Champ (Ethel), lab, h 69 Chunn
*Burgin Claude, cook, h 27 Jordan
*Burgin Delia, dom, h S Asheville
*Burgin Edwd, lab, h S Asheville
*Burgin Jackson (Lizzie), lab, h 73 Chunn
*Burgin Julia, h S Asheville
*Burgin Luther (Mamie), driver, h 7 Atkin
*Burgin Mary, laund, h 27 Jordan
*Burgin Nora, laund, h 514 s French Broad av
*Burgin Ollie, laund, h (r) 140 Pine
*Burgin Wm (Margaret), lab, h S Asheville
Burgin Wm B (Jessie), condr Sou Ry, h 44 John
*Burk Lillian, dom, h Woolsey (R F D 1)
Burk Nelson, tinner, h Woolsey (R F D 1)
Burke Helen L, wid W W, h 155 Charlotte
*Burnett Chas (Lizzie), lab, h 7 Hiawassee
Burnett Donna Miss, dom, 22 Broad
*Burnett Jackson (Ella), waiter, h 370 Magnolia av
Burnett Luther (Mary), inspr, h Haywood rd, W Ashev
Burnett Roscoe, driver W B Nixon, h 289 Charlotte
Burnett Thos R (Lalla L), engnr Sou Ry, h 51 Bartlett
Burnett Wm, chauffeur O K Auto Supply & Transit Co, bds 16 Hilliard la
Burnette C Belle Miss, boarding 157 Patton av, h same
Burnette Lou J, wid Z Taylor, h 157 Patton av
*Burnham Floyd (Susan), lab, h 19 Oliver
*Burnon Wm (Ella), fireman, h 5 Hibernia
Burns Dana B (Clara D), civ engnr 321 Legal Bldg, h 132 s Main
Burns Millinery Store, 10 Church
Burns Nora, wid J M, h 47 Orange
Burns Wilson, lab, h 41 Velvet
Burrell Balfour, cabt mkr E E Galer, h Pearson Drive
Burrell D Andrew (Lula), lab, h 68 Hall
Burrell Edwd E (Stella), fireman Sou Ry, rms 57 Cherry
Burrell Edgar C (Bessie), uphr E E Galer, h 250 Pearson Drive
Burrell Ettie Miss, mica assorter, h 68 Hall
Burrell Jas, mill opr, h 46 Avery
Burrell Jas (Maggie), mason, h Grace
Burrell Jane Miss, emp Ashev Mica Co, h 176 s Main
Burrell Jerome (Emma), weaver, h 54 Avery
Burrell Lena Miss, emp Ashev Mica Co, h 176 s Main

LIFE INSURANCE COMPANY OF VA. OLDEST, LARGEST STRONGEST Southern Life Insurance Co.

ORGANIZED 1871
RICHMOND, VIRGINIA

Issues Industrial Policies from $8.00 to $900.00, with Premiums Payable WEEKLY on persons from two to seventy years of age

J. V. Moon, Superintendent, Rooms 3-4-5 Maxwelton Bldg., Asheville, N. C.

D. TREXLER TIN SHOP

All Kinds of Roofing, Gutter and Conductor Work.

Phone 862

159 South Main St.

DR. C. H. MILLER

MECHANO-THERAPIST

14 N. Spruce St.
Phone 979
ASHEVILLE, N. C.

Hours by engagement

Drugless Healing of Disease

Burrell Milford, mill opr, h 46 Avery
Burrell Minnie, wid Calvin, h 324 Pearson Drive
Burrell Perry D (Mollie), mill opr, h 54 Avery
Burriss Wm, mldr, bds W P Ford, W Asheville
Burroughs Jas A Miss, h Edgemont
Burroughs Rich'd A, bkkpr T J Perkinson, h 36 Clingman
Burrows Florence Mrs, cashr Carmichael's Pharmacy, h 72 s Liberty
Burrows Harry S (Florence), tailors 1-2 Paragon Bldg, h 72 s Liberty
Burt Aden (Celestia), millwright, h 114 Charlotte
BURT C H, asst sec Y M C A, rms same
Burt Clinton S (Nettie), engnr Sou Ry, h 222 s French Broad av
Burt Fern Miss, milliner Paris Millinery Shop, h 114 Charlotte
*Burton Emma H, h 160 Hill
*Burton Geo Washington (Mary), driver C Sawyer, h 160 Hill
*Burton Harriet, laund, h 11 Clemmons
Burton Jno A, drayman, h 29 Rector
*Burton Jos, driver Ashe Ice Co, h 28 Sassafras
*Burton Lelia, cook, h Haywood rd, W Ashev
*Burton Lucinda, laund, h 167 Hill
*Burton Saml (Carrie), driver Ashe Ice Co, h 28 Sassafras
BURTON SAM'L P (Ella C), (Burton & Holt), h 291 Haywood
Burton Saml S (Marguerite C), drayman, h 29 Rector
BURTON & HOLT (S P Burton, S D Holt), furniture, 2 s Main cor Pack Sq—phone 980
Butler Dock (Jane), lab, h Biltmore rd, S Biltmore
Butler Jas F (Jennie), waiter, h 43 Clemmons
Butler Jas H (Mary), shoemkr Nichols Shoe Co, h 24 Nelson av
*Butler Maggie, dom, h 78 Phifer
Butler Nellie M Miss, bds 28 Clingman av
Butler Wm, furn mkr, bds 502 Depot
*Butler Wm (Odessa), lab, h 78 Phifer
Butler Wm S (Alice E), condr Sou Ry, h 51 Ora
Buttrick Eula F Miss, tchr Park av Schl, h Emma N C
Buttrick Martha A, wid Jas, h Emma N C
Buttrick Mary E Miss, tchr, h Emma N C
Buttrick Nena A Miss, tchr, h Emma N C
Buttrick W Turner (Bertha), asst sec Va-Carolina Coal Co, h 24 Vance

---

....Asheville Cleaning and Pressing Club....
Tailoring That Satisfies and Prices That Please
Steam and French Dry Cleaning of all delicate and fine wearing apparel for ladies and gentlemen. MESSENGER SERVICE IN THE CITY.

J. C. WILBAR, Prop. 4. N. Pack Square **PHONE 389**

Buxton Mary R Miss, propr "Buxton Place," h 157 Church
"Buxton Place," 157 Church, Miss Mary R Buxton propr
Byas Ida Miss, h 44 Clyde
Byas Wm M, carp, h 44 Clyde
Byerly C C, wid Clarence, h 357 n Main
Byerly Chas W, mchst, h 91 Clingman av
Byerly Ephraim (Ella M), carp, h 91 Clingman av
Byerly Herman B, lab, h 91 Clingman av
Byerly Roy P, clk, h 91 Clingman av
*Byers Chas, cook, h 29 Gray
Byers Harriett Miss, sec-treas Faith Cottage Rescue Home, h same
*Byers Jno, cook, h 249 Beaumont
Byers Katherine S Mrs, tchr Peace Memo House, rms same
Bynum Annie E, wid J T, h 64 Orchard
*Bynum Jas, driver Carolina Coal & Ice Co
*Bynum Jos B (Myra), driver Ashev Ice Co, h 29 Oakdale
Bynum W Emmett, clk W U Tel Co, h 64 Orchard
Byrd Chas W Rev (Hattie), pastor Central M E Church (South), h 35 Church
Byrd Oscar (Georgia), overseer, h 26 Jefferson Drive
*Byrd Sallie, h 41 Velvet
☞ Byrd see also Bird
Byrne Mary W, wid Dr Jno, h Milfoil Cottage, Albemarle Park
Byrne Rosa M Miss, h Milfoil Cottage, Albemarle Park

C

Cabe Margaret C Mrs, furn rms, 72 Ralph, h same
Cabe Thos J (Margaret C), blksmith Amer Wagon Co, h 72 Ralph
Caddy Jno G (Cora L), contr, h 296 College
Cafeterian (The), n Pack Sq, M M Sullivan propr
Cain Alex (Annie), tinner, h 60 Madison av
Cain J Berkeley (Edith), dep clk Superior Court, h Haywood rd, W Ashev
Cain Jno A (Annie), tinner, h 60 Madison av
Cain Walter S Rev (Elizabeth L), rector Grace Memorial Episcopal Church, h 36 Watauga
CAINE JAS H (Nona), v-pres The Citizen Co and mng editor The Ashev Citizen, h 87 Elizabeth—phone 401
*Caldwell Alonzo (Bessie), porter, h 112 Pine
*Caldwell Augusta, clk, h 22 Latta
*Caldwell Augustus, lab, h Lincoln av cor Latta

Asheville Dray, Fuel and Construction Co.

Heavy Hauling of all kinds
61-2 South Main

WE FURNISH
BUILDING STONE

Moving Furniture a Specialty
PHONE - 223

DYNAMOS & MOTORS

Piedmont Electric Co.

64 Patton Av.
ASHEVILLE, N.C.

Caldwell Catherine S, wid Wm K, h 157 Park av
Caldwell Edwd S, pres Carolina Abstract & Title Co
*Caldwell Ella, nurse, h 224 Flint
*Caldwell G Haven Rev, pastor West Asheville M E Ch, h Hazel Mill rd, W Ashev
*Caldwell Geo (Pearle), lab, h 112 Pine
*Caldwell Geo W, mngr Greenlee & Loder, h 18 Eagle
Caldwell J Albert, condr Sou Ry, bds 96 Bartlett
*Caldwell Jas (Minnie), waiter Sou Ry Dining Room, h 179 Livingston
*Caldwell Jeremiah, agt N C Mutual & Prov Assn, h 15 Hildebrand
*Caldwell Jno, driver, h 31 Haid
Caldwell Jno D (Marion M), supt Gas Plant Ashev P & L Co, h 128 Flint
*Caldwell Louise, dom, h 310 Asheland av
*Caldwell Louise, maid, 36 n French Broad av
*Caldwell Minnie, cook, h Lincoln av cor Latta
*Caldwell Paul, cook, h 15 Hildebrand
Califf Louis, barber Wm W Young, h Asheland av
Call D Herman (Eliabeth), fireman Sou Ry, h 331 Southside
Call Jno E (Dora T), trav slsmn, h 175 Cumberland av
☞ **Call see also McCall**
Callahan Addie R (Naomi), barber C U Monday, h 59 Park Sq
Callahan C Vernon (Mollie), h 483 w Haywood
Callan Alice Mrs, hair dresser, bds 49 Clayton
CALLOWAY ARTHUR W (Charlotte L), physician 16 Medical Bldg—phone 352, office hours 10:30 a m to 1 p m and 4 to 5 p m, Sunday by appointment, h 274 Merrimon av (White Oak)—phone 716
Calloway Gus, linotype opr Hackney & Moale Co, rms Fire Dept
Calloway Henry (Cecelia), lab, h Riverside Drive
Calloway Jas M (Mary), pedler, h 33 Roberts
Calloway Jno (Cynthia), driver, h Haywood rd, W Ashev
*Calloway Shade (Lona), lab, h 56 Mountain
Calloway Smithia Miss, machine hd Sou Mica Co, h W Asheville
Calloway Wm (Maude), mill opr, h 40 Avery
Calloway Wm E (Lula), blksmith Riverside Drive nr Quarry, h 33 Roberts
Calvary Baptist Church, W Asheville
*Calvary Presbyterian Church, Eagle cor Velvet, Rev C B Dusenbury pastor

---

J. C. McPHERSON
SLATE AND TIN ROOFING
Galvanized Iron Work   Hot Air Furnaces
35-37 EAST COLLEGE STREET

PLUMBING
STEAM AND HOT WATER
HEATING
PHONE 133

Cameron Mary Miss, nurse Mildred E Sherwood Home, rms same
Camp Elizabeth P Miss, h 403 Merrimon av
Camp Jos B (Olive), driver, h 12 View
Campbell Alonzo C, h 32 Panola
Campbell Belle Miss, nurse 63 Clayton, h same
Campbell Carrie B Mrs, tchr Ashev Bus College, h 127 Haywood
Campbell Colin (Ella E), stone mason, h 169 Park av
Campbell Emilie Miss, h 101 s Main
Campbell Emma B Miss, bds 403 Pearson Drive
*Campbell Essie, h 104 Grove
*Campbell Francis S, gro Eagle cor Valley, h 87 Eagle
Campbell Frank M (Florence), plmber, h 25 Victoria rd
Campbell Grace E Miss, student, h 127 Haywood
Campbell J F Mrs, tchr Ashev Business College, h 127 Haywood
Campbell J Milton (Carrie B), trav slsmn, h 127 Haywood
Campbell Jas A, student, h 146 Victoria rd
Campbell Jas A (Bessie), engnr, h Asheville av, W Ashev
Campbell Jas N (Mary), carp, h 146 Victoria rd
CAMPBELL JNO A (Mary R), cashr Citizens Bank, h 255 Cumberland av
Campbell Jno M (Margaret J), real estate 212-214 Legal Bldg, h 105 s Main
Campbell M Burroughs, student, h 127 Haywood
Campbell Mary E, wid Wm, dressmkr 114 Poplar, h same
Campbell Nora P Miss, dressmkr 153 s Main, h same
Campbell Richmond W (Marguerite), engnr, h 169 Park av
*Campbell Robt (Evelyn), plstr, h 60 n Lexington av
Campbell Robt F Rev (Sallie M), pastor First Presby Ch, h 6 Pearson Drive
Campbell W A Ruffner, h 6 Pearson Drive
Campbell Wm, press feeder Ashev Ptg & Engrav Co, h 114 Popular
Campbell Wm A (E Grace), plmber, h Livingston nr Oliver
Campbell Wm R (Forbes & Campbell), bds The Manor
Canada Herman C (Minnie L), warehouseman Mustin-Robertson Co, h W Asheville (R F D 3)
Canady Wm M (Jeanette), h 201 Merrimon av
Candler Jas H, carp, h 144 Park av
*Candler Jno G (Mamie), lab, h 150 Hill
Candler Lloyd (Nannie), lab, h Lester rd, W Asheville
*Candler Odessa, cook, h 154 Hill
*Candler Richard (Annie), lab, h 12 Sorrell

Candy Kitchen and Club Cafe
"A GOOD PLACE FOR REFRESHMENT"

Hot drinks on cold days. Cold drinks on hot days. The best drinks every day. Pure fruits and syrups blended "just right," served daintily. Our Ice Cream and Soda Water Department, Restaurant and Candy Departments are always kept up to the standard of nearest perfection. Phones 110 and 111. 19 and 21 Haywood St.

Brown's Undertaking Parlors

S. H. BROWN

50 Patton Avenue
ASHEVILLE, N. C.

Lady Assistant When Desired

Phone 193-2 Rings

THE MOORE Plumbing Company

16 N. Pack Square

PHONE 1025

Sanitary Plumbing, General Tin and Metal Work, Hot Air Furnaces

---

118 ASHEVILLE [1913] DIRECTORY

Candler Robbie Mae Miss, laund, h 144 Park av
Candler Saml (Belle M), lab, h Arlington st, W Ashev
Candler Tennie, wid Geo W, h 144 Park av
*Candler Wallace, fireman, h 154 Hill
*Candy Isaac (Sallie), lab, h 326 Asheland av
CANDY KITCHEN (see Theobold & Brandl)
☞Cane see Cain and Caine
*Cannon Alice, cook, h 124 Church
Cannon Chas (Ellen), lab, h 493 w Haywood
Cannon Chas W (Ruth), (Cannon & Haynes), h 560 n Main
Cannon Claude, mill wkr, h 8 Logan
Cannon Dollie M Miss, h 560 n Main
Cannon Effie M Miss, h 560 n Main
Cannon Katie Miss, clk, h 560 n Main
*Cannon Robt B (Daisy E), (Cannon & Oglesby), h 18 Sassafras
Cannon Thos (Ida), helper, h 45 East
Cannon & Haynes (C W Cannon, M E Haynes), gros, 467 n Main
*Cannon & Oglesby (R B Cannon, Thos Oglesby), real estate, 44 Market
Cansler Genoese A Miss, h 76 e College
CANSLER P U MRS, boarding, 76 e College—phone 816, h same (see p 20)
Cansler Peter U (Vincent L), h 76 e College
Canter Annie Miss, dom, h 19 Zillicoa
Capehart Emma Miss, waitress, h 242 Patton av
Capehart Ivy (Cornelia), clk, h 23 Central av
Capehart Joanna A Miss, emp Asheville Mica Co, h 336 n Main
Capehart Louis (Rhoda), carp, h 434 n Main
Capehart Margaret D, wid Francis M, h 336 n Main
Capell Carlton W (Eva J), pressman, h 80 Flint
Capell Eva J Miss, clk M V Moore & Co, h 80 Flint
Capps Della Miss, h 22 Jefferson Drive
Capps Edgar H, lab, h Edgemont
Capps Jas (Besse), shoemkr Boston Shoe Store, h 91 Wallach
Capps Jas E, student, h Edgemont
Capps Jno A (Daisy), lab, h Edgemont
Capps Meariett C Jr, clk C Sawyer, h 162 s Main
Capps Meariett R (Nancy), farmer, h 162 s Main
Capps Pearle Miss, h Edgemont
Capps Wakefield (Callie), helper, h 396 Southside av
Capps Wm C (Elizabeth), mchst, h 22 Jefferson Drive

The Battery Park Bank

Capital - - $100,000.00
Surplus and Profits, $110,000.00

ASHEVILLE, N. C.   City, County and State Depositary

J. A. TILLMAN — **Jeweler** — **17 N. Main St.**
I carry a nice line of Watches, Clocks and Jewelry, and make a specialty of repair work. Satisfaction guaranteed

Capps Wm R (Carrie R), carp, h W Ashev (R F D 3)
Carey Andrew J, printer Ashev Ptg & Engrav Co, bds 107 Haywood
Carland Carrie Miss, wkr Ashev Mica Co, h W Asheville
Carland Carrie C Miss, h Hazel Mill rd, W Ashev
Carland Eugene (Lucy), mngr Armour & Co, h 56 Chestnut
Carland Harley (Mary), mchst O K Auto Supply & Transit Co, h 173 s Main
Carland Jas T (Sarah A), carp, h Hazel Mill rd, W Ashev
Carland Jno, wood, h 93 Wallach
Carland Jno D (Nora), carp, h Hazel Mill rd, W Ashev
Carland Robt R, lab, h Hazel Mill rd, W Ashev
Carland Wm A (Estella), carp, h Hazel Mill rd, W Ashev
*Carlos Washington, butler A F Rees, Kenilworth
Carlton Lottie B, wid Guy, h 134 Hillside
Carmichael Anna F Miss, tchr Orange Schl, h 129 s Main
Carmichael Eleanor Miss, h 129 s Main
Carmichael R Edgar (Minnie), trav slsmn, h 114 s French Broad av
CARMICHAEL WHITFIELD C (Carmichael's Pharmacy), h 129 s Main—phone 305
Carmichael Whitfield C Jr, student, h 129 s Main
CARMICHAEL'S PHARMACY (W C Carmichael), 1 n w Pack Sq—phone 19
Caroleen (The), boarding, 94 e College, Miss Lena Mendel
CAROLINA ABSTRACT & TITLE CO (Inc), 312 Legal Bldg; Edwd S Caldwell pres, F T Meriwether Jr v-pres, Geo H Wright sec-treas
Carolina Amusement & Investment Co, 11 n w Pack Sq (2d fl), S A Lynch pres and genl mngr
CAROLINA COAL & ICE CO (Inc), office 50 Patton av—phone 130, yards Roberts at junction Depot—phone 144; F M Weaver pres, Harmon A Miller treas and genl mngr (see top lines)
Carolina Commercial School, office 301 Legal Bldg, Miss Pearl L Holman prin
Carolina Coupler Co, s Pack Sq cor Main
CAROLINA CREAMERY, ice and dairy products, 252-258 Patton av—phone 296
Carolina Dairy Farm, Weaverville rd nr new bridge, Rex U Brown propr
Carolina Electric Vehicle Co, 2 Electrical Bldg, G S Powell pres-mngr
Carolina Hardwood Lumber Co, 12 Temple Court, N J Warner Sou mngr

INSURANCE
INSURE YOUR SALARY WITH US
NEVER CARRY YOUR OWN RISK
SAFETY IS THE BEST POLICY
UNLESS YOU ARE A CAPITALIST
REST EASY IF YOU HAVE
AN ACCIDENT WE WILL
NOT KEEP YOU WAITING TO
COLLECT YOUR CLAIM
EVERY CLAIM PROMPTLY PAID

Imperial Mutual Life & Health Insurance Co.
Home Office: ASHEVILLE, N. C.
Phone 495

HOTEL OXFORD — **Asheville, N. C.**
Redecorated and Refitted throughout. Recently enlarged to 60 rooms. Centrally located. Depot cars stop at entrance. Long distance telephone office upstairs. American and European plan. Rates 50c, 75c and $1 per day; special rates by week or month. C. H. Branson & Sons, Proprietors. Phone 1887. 50-54 South Main St.

Williams-Brownell Planing Mill Company — *Hardwoods*

Lumber---Rough and Dressed Flooring a Specialty Moulding, Interior Finish, Etc.
Office, Plant and Yards on Southern Railway, Near Biltmore Station
WHITE PINE Phone 729 YELLOW PINE

Asheville Electrical Company
W. Mansfield Booze, Manager
74 CENTRAL AVE.
HEADQUARTERS
Phone 377

Carolina Industry Co, Temple Ct, J E Rector, counsel
CAROLINA MACHINERY CO (Inc), Avery and Sou Ry; W F Decker pres, S Sternberg v-pres, F A Lindsey sec-treas—phone 590 (see bottom lines)
Carolina Supply Co, jobbers 200-202 Oates Bldg, J C Arbogast mngr
CARPENTER BARTO C (Carrie), v-pres Ashev Paint & Glass Co
CARPENTER JAS E (Mabel E), jeweler and watchmkr 8 n Pack Sq, h 4 Carroll av
Carpenter Jas L (Carrie), h 10 Chunn
CARPENTER W B, rec teller Battery Park Bank
Carr Caroline E Miss, student, h 15 Furman av
Carr Claudius T (Annie R), prin Montford av Schl, h 143 Montford av
Carr Janie V Miss, stengr J M English & Co, h 135 Furman av
Carr Jonas J (Viola), h 15 Furman av
Carr Mary D Miss, stengr Ashev Mica Co, h 15 Furman av
Carr Omar (Blanche K), chemist, h 14 Watauga
*Carr see also Kerr
CARRIER A HEATH (Sarah), (Smith & Carrier Co), h 25 Broad
Carrier Building, College n e cor Market
Carriker Susanna Miss, nurse Highland Hosp, h same
*Carrington Fannie, laund, h Haywood rd, W Ashev
Carroll Heloise Miss, student, h 75 Zillicoa
Carroll Jno B, clk, h 243 Chestnut
Carroll Jno L (Ora), phys 11 Church, h 243 Chestnut
CARROLL ROBERT S DR (Lydia), medical director Highland Hospital and physician—phone 421, h 75 Zillicoa—phone 1036
Carscaddon O Clyde, pressman, h 64 Woodfin
Carson Adolphus, laund, h 16 Starnes pl
*Carson Alfred (Amanda), gas mkr, h 71 Black
Carson Chas G (Mary L), emp W M Jones, h Brevard rd, W Ashev
*Carson David (Henrietta D), lab, h 9 (175) Velvet
*Carson Davis (Mattie), lab, h 24 Gibbons
*Carson Fannie, cook, h 52 Clemmons
Carson Henry B, msngr rms 36½ s Main
Carson Jos W, clk, J H Jenkins, h 211 Merrimon av
*Carson Louisa cook, h 20 McDowell
*Carson Mary, laund, h 115 Poplar
Carson Queen M Miss, prin Park av Schl, h 182 Haywood
*Carson Robt C (Annie), vet surg, h 240 Flint

Asheville Dry Cleaning Co.
Telephones 835-836, All Dep't
MAIN, N. E. COR. COLLEGE

THE CLEANERS
Our Department for Oriental Rugs and Carpet Cleaning is prepared to serve you in all its branches.
E. S. Paine   O. E. Hansen

FOR BOX SHOOKS | **Call English Lumber Co. PHONE 321**

*Carson Rufus, trucker, h 20 McDowell
Carter Amy L Miss, h W Asheville
Carter Bruce, clk Carmichael's Pharmacy, h S Biltmore
Carter Caleb, h 32 n French Broad av
Carter Carrie Miss, h 257 Montford av
*Carter Clyde, lab, h 26 Pearson Drive
*Carter Dillard, lab, h 16 Lincoln av
*Carter Elizabeth, h 36 Maiden la
*Carter Ella, dom, h 26 Pearson Drive
*Carter Emma, laundress, h 304 Asheland av
*Carter Eva, dom, h 26 Pearson Drive
Carter Fannie, wid Bruce, clk Bon Marche, h Biltmore Park
Carter Frank (Florence M), judge Superior Court of N C, h 440 Montford av
Carter Florence H Miss, h 32 n French Broad av
CARTER GARRETT D (Sallie L), (Brown-Carter Realty Co), h W Asheville—phone 635
Carter Garrett N (Flata), lumber, h Woolsey (R F D 1)
Carter Guy R, clk W R Carter, h 24 Seney
Carter H Bascom (Laura), atty at law 10½ n Pack Sq, h 31 Clayton
Carter H Bascom Jr, student, h 31 Clayton
*Carter Henry (Maggie), lab, h (r) 255 s Main
Carter J Emery (Addie), farmer, h Haywood rd, W Ashev
Carter J Robt (Manda), carp, h 65 Penland
Carter Jno H (Roberta M), h 288 Montford av
***CARTER JOE** (Jennie), horseshoeing, 4 Penland, h 175 s Beaumont (see opp bus dept)
Carter Kate, dom, h Edgemont
Carter Louella Miss, dom, h 225 Merrimon av
Carter Louise Miss, h 31 Clayton
Carter Marie Miss, waitress, Cherokee Inn, rms same
Carter Mary Miss, h 31 Clayton
*Carter Mary, dom, h 26 Pearson Drive
*Carter Mary, dom, 224 Chestnut
Carter Mary R Miss, h 32 n French Broad av
Carter Melvin E, rodman, h 32 n French Broad av
Carter Mildred Miss, h 32 n French Broad av
Carter Nancy B Miss, tchr Asheland av Schl, h 31 Clayton
*Carter Preston (Jane), lab, h 68 Gudger
Carter Susie E Miss, h 32 n French Broad av
Carter Susie R, wid M E, h 32 n French Broad av
Carter Wiley R (Sallie A), gro Haywood rd, W Ashev, h 24 Seney
Carter Wm H, h Grace

Biggest Busiest Best Asheville Steam Laundry

Phones: 1936 and 1937

43 to 47 W. College Street

CHARLES H. HONESS OPTOMETRIST AND OPTICIAN

Exclusive maker of ATLAS SHUR-ON EYE GLASSES

THE Home of Ce-Rite Toric Lenses

We make a specialty of correcting optical defects with properly fitted glasses.

54 Patton Avenue
Opposite Postoffice

Carolina Machinery Co. Founders, Machinists and Jobbers of Mill Supplies. We make all kinds of Castings in Iron, Brass or Aluminum.

WE ALSO FURNISH SKILLED MECHANICS FOR BOILER REPAIRS —— **PHONE 590**

LIFE INSURANCE COMPANY OF VA.
ORGANIZED 187
Richmond -:- Virginia
J. V. MOON, Superintendent
Rooms 3-4-5- Maxwelton Bldg., Asheville, N. C.

All claims paid IMMEDIATELY upon receipt of satisfactory proofs of Death. Total payment to policyholders since organization, over $12,000,000.00. Is paying its Policyholders over $1,000,000.00 annually.

T. P. JOHNSON & CO.

SHEET METAL WORKERS

All Kinds of Roofing Guttering and Conductor Work Metal Ceilings, Skylights and Galvanized Iron Cornices

OFFICE and SHOP:
69-71 S. MAIN
Phone 325

DR. C. H. MILLER

Mechano-Therapist

14 N. Spruce Street
ASHEVILLE, N. C.

PHONE 979

Hours by Engagement

DRUGLESS HEALING OF DISEASE

ASHEVILLE [1913] DIRECTORY

Cartmell Katharine Miss, h 71½ Magnolia av
Cartwright Herbert (Emma S), clothing, h 74 Courtland av
Cartzendafner Edmond C, bds 51 n Main
Carver Baxter J (Nina), mill wkr, h 3 Factory Hill
Carver Geo W (Mary), coach clnr, h nr Haywood rd, W Ashev
Carver Jno Rev, pastor Avery Street M E Church, h 38 Turner
Carver Jno M, h 308 Southside av
Carver Jno W (Louise), tanner, h 54 Buxton
Carver Mallie H (Ellen), mill wkr, h 7 Factory Hill
Carver Nancy S Mrs, h 283 College
Carver Walter C, mill wkr, h 54 Buxton
Carver Wiley F, tanner, h 54 Buxton
Carvin Martha Mrs, supt Mission Hospital, h same
☞Carwell see Caldwell
Cascaddan Clyde, pressman Ashev Gazette-News, h 64 Woodfin
Case A Roy, trav slsmn, h 49 Clayton
Case Adelaide J Miss, h 5 Edgehill av
Case Arthur (Margaret), h (r) 40 Maiden la
Case Arthur H, bkkpr, h 5 Edgehill av
Case Benj H, mining and civil engnr, h 5 Edgehill av
Case Clyde E, plmbr S M Stevens, h 95 Cumberland av
Case Ella A Miss, nurse, 6 Battery Park pl, h same
Case Evelyn D Miss, h 5 Edgehill av
Case Gertrude, wid J Howard, h 118 Woodfin
Case Harriet D, wid Wm H, h 5 Edgehill av
Case Jas H (Katharine), trav slsmn, h 49 Clayton
Case Jno (Sarah), driver, h Haywood rd, W Ashev
Case Kathleen L Miss, h 111 Broad
Case Mildred E Miss, h 111 Broad
Case Roscoe C, painter, h 111 Broad
Case W Benj (Zennie), lineman, h Haywood rd, W Ashev
*Cash Alice, dom, h 12½ Aston pl
Cash Grocery (The), 1 s w Pack Sq, Pat'k McIntyre propr
*Cash Isabella, laundress, h 12½ Aston pl
Cash Sherman, clk, h 147 Grove
Cashatt Wm H (Alice B), engnr, h 57 John
Caslar Sol, cider and vinegar, Sycamore cor Market, rms 10 Technical Bldg
Cassada Maggie Mrs, boarding 14 s Spruce, h same
Cassada Robt E (Maggie), carrier P O, h 14 s Spruce
*Cassell Wm M (Alpha), lab, h 61 Madison av
*Castion Eugene, gro 67 Hill, h same

ASHEVILLE CLEANING and PRESSING CLUB

TAILORING THAT SATISFIES and PRICES THAT PLEASE
Hats cleaned, banded and bound. Silk hats ironed. Buttons made to order in all sizes. Plain or with rims. PHONE 389

DYEING IN ALL SHADES Cleaned. Messenger Service.

Kid Gloves, Slippers and Plumes, Fancy Jabots and Ties, French Dry Cleaned. Ladies' and Gentlemen's suits Steam

J. C. Wilbar, Prop. 4 NORTH PACK SQ.

Cathey Barton S, h 289 College
Cathey Geo, h 23 Pearson Drive
*Cathey Jno (Sarah), cabt mkr, h 29 Gibbons
CATHEY JNO H (Ida), sec Brown Hdw Co (Inc), h 16 Blair
*Catholic Hill School, 11 Catholic av cor Valley, W S Lee prin
Cauble Albert E, bds 101 Haywood
Cauble Daniel W (Susan H), blksmith 425 n Main, h 436 same
Cauble Daniel W Jr, plmbr, h 436 n Main
CAUBLE J CLAUDE (Edna), (Union Plumbing Co), h 124 Charlotte
Cauble J Edwd, asst ticket agt Sou Ry, h 436 n Main
Cauble Julia M Miss, clk Palais Royal, h 436 n Main
Cauble Mary A Miss, clk, h Hickory Nut Gap rd
Cauble Ora Mrs, propr The Ninety Nine, h 101 Haywood
Cauble P Archie (Ora), condr The Pullman Co, h 101 Haywood
Cauble Pinckney L (Hattie), mngr Biltmore Roller Mills, h Hickory Nut Gap rd
Cauble Wm T (Stella), switchman, bds 655 Oakland av
Causey Eva V Miss, stengr Williams, Brownell Planing Mill Co, bds The Henrietta
Cawley C W Prof, tchr The Asheville School, rms same
Cedar Hill Baptist Church, W Asheville, Rev Thos M Cole pastor
Cefalu Helen Miss, h 49 Broad
Cefalu Jno B (M Blanche), h 49 Broad
Centerfit Wm H (Alice K), police, h 264 Haywood
CENTRAL BANK & TRUST CO, Legal Bldg, s Pack Sq; C W Brown pres, W B McEwen v-pres, Wallace B Davis cashr (see marginal line front cover)
Central Cafe (The), 5 s w Pack Sq, Peroulas Bros proprs
Central Labor Union Hall, 39 Patton av (3d fl)
Central M E Church (South), Church nr Patton av, Rev Chas W Byrd pastor
Chaffee Roland F (Mabel), supt Amer Furn Mnfg Co, h Riverside Drive
Chakales Peter (Sarah), (Chakales & Pilalas), h 156 n Main
Chakales & Pilalas (Peter Chakales, Geo Pilalas), proprs Ashev Shoe Shine Parlor and pool, 4 and 56½ Patton av and proprs Amer Dairy Lunch, 1½ w Pack Sq
Chalens F N, propr Public Service & Motor Co
*Chambers Allie T, h 190 Livingston

WEAVERVILLE LINE NINE MILES BY TROLLEY FROM PACK SQUARE TO WEAVERVILLE

ASHEVILLE AND EAST TENNESSEE RAILROAD CO.

7 NORTH MAIN STREET   ASHEVILLE N. C.

Chambers Bathilda, wid R W, h Woolsey (R F D 1)
*Chambers Cam, helper, h 23 McDowell
Chambers Canie J (Minor), collr Beaumont Furn Co, h 13 Atkinson
Chambers Chas E (Susan), mill hd, h 126 Short Roberts
Chambers Corrie Miss, h 32 Vance
Chambers E Ogburn, dentist 4-6 Harkins Bldg, h Woolsey (R F D 1)
CHAMBERS ELBERT C (Clara A), (Chambers & Weaver), h 123 Asheland av—phone 98
Chambers Florence Miss, h Woolsey (R F D 1)
*Chambers Geo (Mattie), lab, h 190 Livingston
Chambers Hardy S, sec Boston Shoe Co, h 32 Vance
*Chambers Hester, cook 29 Jefferson Drive
*Chambers J F, agt N C Mutual & Prov Assn, h Elk Park
Chambers Jno K (Eva), livery 39-41 n Lexington av, h 32 Vance
*Chambers Jno W (Ella), barber, h 33 Circle
Chambers Jos M (Margaret), lab 13 Reed Bldg
Chambers Mamie Miss, h 32 Vance
Chambers Robt W, student, h Woolsey (R F D 1)
Chambers S Gregg (Amanda), h 70 Conestee
CHAMBERS & WEAVER (E C Chambers and Dick Weaver), livery, feed and sale stables, Aston (Willow) s e cor Lexington av—phone 18
Champion Fibre Co (The), mnfrs of wood pulp, Canton N C, R B Robertson mngr
Champion Harriett A Miss, h 4 Maple
Champion Lumber Co, 200-202 Oates Bldg, J C Arbogast mngr
Champion Shoe Hospital (E H Brunner), 42 s Main
CHAMPION SHOE REPAIR SHOP, 30 w College, B A Viniarski propr (see index for adv)
Chance Eva L Mrs, boarding 68 Church, h same
Chance Isaac C (Eva L), collr Marsteller & Co, h 68 Church
Chance Robt L, slsmn Bon Marche, h 68 Church
Chance Wm, lab, bds 434 Depot
Chandel Lloyd, engnr, bds 102 Ralph
Chandler Lilburn, clk C A Walker, h 346 w Haywood
Chandler T Catherine, wid Isaac, boarding 346 w Haywood, h same
Chandler Theo, emp Ashev Citizen, h 346 w Haywood
Chandley Everett O (Pearle), clk frt office Sou Ry, h 207 s French Broad av
*Chaney Ida, h 55 Bay

CONTRACTOR and BUILDER
STEEL RANGES   **J. C. McPHERSON**   35-37 E COLLEGE ST. PHONE 133
PLUMBING STEAM AND HOT WATER **HEATING**

Electrical Supplies — **PIEDMONT ELECTRIC COMPANY**, ASHEVILLE, N. C., 64 PATTON AVE.

MAPLE FLOORING

HARDWOOD LUMBER OF ALL KINDS

WOODWARD & SON

9th and Arch Sts., Richmond, Va.

See Adv. Opposite Page 188

ASHEVILLE [1913] DIRECTORY

CHAPEL COTTAGES, boarding, 41 Victoria rd—phone 55, Miss A E Moore propr (see p 20)
Chapman C Brewster, v-pres, rms Asheville Club
Chapman Chas (Berdie), emp Tannery, h W Ashev (Biltmore R F D 3)
Chapman Helen Miss, h 392 Charlotte
Chapman Leicester, student, h 392 Charlotte
Chapman Millard (Effie), emp Tannery, h W Asheville
CHAPMAN S FRANK (Minnie), lumber and timber lands 3-5 Technical Bldg—phone 1693, h 392 Charlotte—phone 1350
Chappell Clarence J, student, h 147 Grove
Chappell Daisy M, student, h 147 Grove
Chappell Floyd E, harness mkr Ashev Harness Co, h 147 s Grove
Chappell Viola, wid J W, h 147 Grove
Charles Eugene E, student, h 206 e Chestnut
Charles Jas A, draymn, h 15 Centre
Charles Jessie M Mrs, h W Asheville (R F D 3)
Charles Louisa C Miss, h 15 Centre
Charles Mattie E Miss, h 15 Centre
Charles Robt H, h 15 Centre
Charles T Wray, mngr British Woolen Mills, bds 16 Hilliard la
Chase Elizabeth H, wid Wm, h 166 e Chestnut
Chatham (The), boarding 55 College, Mrs Lucy E Meadows propr
*Chatman Edwd, porter, h 70 Ridge
*Chavis Emma E, tchr, h 16 Davidson
*Chavis Jno C (Mary), janitor Medical Bldg, h 40 Brick
*Cheatham Gaston, waiter, h 23 Aston pl
*Cheatham Nora, laundress, h 23 Aston pl
Chedester Hugh C, atty at law 412-415 Legal Bldg, rms 21 Meriwether Bldg
Chedester M H, student, h 51 s French Broad av
Chedester Saml H (Annie), h 51 s French Broad av
Cheek Amanda E Mrs, boarding 87 Ora, h same
Cheek Jno H (Amanda E), weigh mstr, h 87 Ora
Cheek Laura W, wid Dr B A, h 327 Southside av
Cheek Wm B, h 327 Southside av
Cheesborough Elizabeth P Miss, h 60 Baird
Cheesborough Thos P (Alice C), phys 107-108 Citizen Bldg, h Victoria rd
Cheetham Mary L, wid Fredk C, h 403 Merrimon av
Cheever Frank A, bds 54 Oak

What Have You in Real Estate that You Don't Want?

What do You Want in Real Estate that You Haven't?

WESTERN CAROLINA REALTY CO.

J. W. Wolfe, Sec. & Treas.

On the Square

PHONE 974

10 N. PACK SQ.

Brown-Carter Realty Co.

REAL ESTATE
23 TEMPLE COURT
PHONE 341
ASHEVILLE   N. C.

FLORIDA SPECIALTIES

Grazing, Timbered, Farm Lands, Orange Groves, Turpentine Locations and Phosphate Lands.

NORTH CAROLINA SPECIALTIES

Orchard, Farm and Timbered Lands, City Property, Rent Collections.

Moale & Chiles Real Estate and Insurance
27 Patton Ave. (2d fl)   Phone 561
General Agents United States Fidelity & Guaranty Co.

Candy Kitchen and Club Cafe
"A GOOD PLACE FOR REFRESHMENT"

The very best ingredients with sanitary conditions in our Candy Manufacturing Department make possible the dainty, crisp confections sold here. Bon Bons and Chocolates made every day, put up in neat, attractive boxes. Phones 110 and 111. 19 and 21 Haywood St.

Brown's Undertaking Parlors

S. H. BROWN

Lady Assistant When Desired

Phone 193-2 Rings

50 Patton Avenue
Asheville, N. C.

Established 1894

B. J. JACKSON

Carefully Selected Fruits and Vegetables

Stall No. 11, City Market

BUSINESS PHONES:
86 and 101

RESIDENCE PHONE
1596

"Cherokee Cottage," Albemarle Park
CHEROKEE INN, Oak n e cor Woodfin, D W Misenheimer propr (see p 19)
Cherry Claude M, bkkpr, R E Bowles, h 19 Technical Bldg
Cherry Lossie S Miss, h 136 Asheland av
Cherry Pattie B, wid A B, h 136 Asheland av
Cherry Virginia Mrs, clk Palais Royal, h 136 Asheland av
*Chesser Maggie, dom, h Grace
Child Herbert D (T S Morrison & Co), bds Forest Hill
Child Mary E, wid Wm S, h 265 Pearson Drive
CHILDS EDWARD P PROF (Sada H), pres Normal & Collegiate Institute, h 86 Victoria rd—phone 864
Childs Edwd P Jr, student, h 86 Victoria rd
Childs Wm F (Laura), coachman H K Bull, h same
CHILES J MOORE (Jane), (Moale & Chiles), and sec-treas Birmingham Realty Co, h "Sunup," Forest Hill—phone 611
Chiles Jake M, v-pres-treas Kenilworth Development Co, office 61 Amer Natl Bank Bldg, h 3 Grove Park
Chilton Jos, trav slsmn, rms 16-22 Technical Bldg
Chipley Dudley (Louise), civ engnr 78 Patton av, bds Montford av
Chisolm Anna M Mrs, h 53 Orange
*Chisolm Chas, porter, h 165 College
*Chisolm Thos (Bettie), waiter, h 40 Tuskee
☞Chockley see Shockley
Christian Church of Asheville, Haywood opp Flint, Rev P H Mears pastor
Christian Science Reading Room, 68 Patton av
Christopher Altha E Miss, emp Ashev Mica Co, h Haywood rd, W Ashev
Christopher C Knox (Hattie), chauffeur, h 296 Southside av
Christopher Calvin F (Louise J), inventor, h 226 Asheland
Christopher Minnie O Miss, wks Ashev Mica Co h W Asheville
Christopher Robt E, fireman Sou Ry, h 226 Asheland av
Christopher Sallie L, wid Wm H, h Haywood rd, W Ashev
Chunn Bessie L Miss, student, h Haywood rd, W Ashev
Chunn Chas H (Nannie), architect 32 Patton av, h Haywood rd, W Ashev
Chunn Clorinda D, wid Cicero, h 386 s French Broad av
Chunn's Cove Baptist Church, Chunns Cove
Chunn's Cove Episcopal Church, Chunns Cove
Chunn's Cove School, Chunn's Cove
Chunn J Leslie, h 161 Haywood

Yᵉ OLD BOOK SHOP
114 Patton Ave.   Phone 1674
BOOKS BOUGHT, SOLD OR EXCHANGED

Chunn Jos S (Sarah), contr, h 161 Haywood
Chunn M Locke (Lillian), flgmn Sou Ry, h 386 s French Broad av
Church Garfield A (Ida), huckster, h 481 n Main
Church Jas L (Maggie), lab, h 108 Centre
Church Pearl Miss, h 108 Centre
Church Wm F (Leona), lab, h 108 Centre
CITIZEN'S BANK, 55 Patton av cor Haywood; E L Ray pres, G A Murray v-pres, Jno A Campbell cashr (see front cover)
CITIZEN'S BANK BUILDING (see Paragon Bldg)
CITIZEN BUILDING (offices), 8-14 Battery Park pl
CITIZEN CO (The), publishers The Asheville Citizen, 8 Battery Park pl—phones bus office 80, editorial 207; Robt S Jones pres-treas, J H Caine v-pres, W A Kindel sec
CITIZEN'S LUMBER CO, lumber and builders' supplies, 20-24 e College—phone 60; J M English pres, C H Hobbs v-pres, Walter P Taylor sec-treas
Citizens Transfer Co, 48 Patton av, stables 35 and 42 s Lexington av, J A Woodcock propr
CITY DIRECTORY OF ASHEVILLE N C, office 66 and L Amer Natl Bank Bldg, Ernest H Miller mngr
CITY FIRE DEPARTMENT, City Hall, e Pack Sq, J H Wood chf
City Fish Market (H G McKenzie), City Market
CITY GOVERNMENT (City Hall)
    Attorney—J F Glenn
    Auditor—J M Clark
    Bacteriologist—L M McCormick
    Building Inspector— C B Leonard
    Chief of Police—D K Lyerly
    Chief of Fire Dept—J H Wood
    City Clerk—Laurence W Young
    City Engineer—B M Lee
    City Laboratory—204 City Hall
    Council Chambers—203 City Hall
    Electrician—R B Hampton
    Fire Department—J H Wood chf
    Health Officer—Dr L B McBrayer
    High School—Oak cor College, R V Kenney prin
    Hospital (for contagious diseases)—Riverside Drive
    Mayor's Office—J E Rankin mayor
    Meat and Milk Inspector—L M McCormick
    Park—Flint cor Magnolia

Mrs. Wilder's **SANITARY HOME LAUNDRY** turns out first class work in Laundering and Dry Cleaning. **No. 7 Montford Ave., Phone 1354**

128 ASHEVILLE [1913] DIRECTORY

Plumbing Inspector—E M Israel
Police Court—Junius G Adams justice
Reservoir—College nr Poplar
Sanitary Inspector—W H Bird
School Committee—office 61 City Hall
Stables—Valley cor Beaumont, J C Swink foreman
Superintendent of Schools—Prof R J Tighe
Superintendent of Streets—J T Bostic
City Tax Collector—C H Bartlett
Tool House—Eagle cor Velvet
Treasurer—J Bulow Erwin
Water Department—Wm Francis Supt

CITY HALL, e Pack Sq
City Market, e Pack Sq, T J Mitchell supt
Claiborne Robt R, fireman, bds 29 Jefferson Drive
Clampet Benj J (Julia), shoemkr, h 10 Philip
Clampet Josephine, wid J C, h 286 Southside av
Clancy Margaret Miss, bds 107 Haywood
Clapp Edgar B Rev, h 11 Reed, S Biltmore
Clapp Edith B Miss, student, h 11 Reed, S Biltmore
Clapp Frank F, h 170 w Chestnut
Clapp Lena M Miss, dressmkr, h 11 Reed, S Biltmore
Clapp Pearl L Miss, clk H Redwood & Co, h 11 Reed, S Biltmore
Clapp Wm R (Annie), clk, h 11 Reed, S Biltmore
Clarence Barker, Memorial Hospital, Biltmore
*Clarey Sumter, cook, h 20 Ralph
*Clark Andrew (Lula), lab, h S Asheville
Clark Bessie A Miss, h 19 Roberts
Clark Dock C (Tennie), carp, h 167 Asheland av
*Clark Douglas (Mary E), hatter J C Wilbar, h 79 Clemmont
Clark Duncan, musician Princess Theatre
Clark Earl R, electrn, h 51 Starnes av
*Clark Eliza, laund, h 56 Short
*Clark Ella, dom, h 64 Ralph
Clark Ellis G (Lula), hostler Sou Ry, h Haywood rd, W Ashev
Clark Harley (Maude), hostler Sou Ry, h Haywood rd, W Ashev
Clark Herman C (Blanche S), clk C Sawyer, h 283 s Main
Clark Jas, lab, h W Asheville
*Clark Jas (Ella), driver, h 156 Church
Clark Jas C B (Grace L), lab, h Hazel Mill rd, W Ashev
Clark Jane Miss, stengr Margo Terrace, rms same

BUICK — **OLDSMOBILE**
ARBOGAST MOTOR COMPANY
ACCESSORIES AND SUPPLIES
52-60 N. Main Phones 302 and 1728
MAXWELLS — DETROIT ELECTRIC

Asheville Dry Cleaning Co.
Telephones 835-836, All Dep't
MAIN, N. E. COR. COLLEGE

THE CLEANERS
Our Department for Oriental Rugs and Carpet Cleaning is prepared to serve you in all its branches.
E. S. Paine   O. E. Hansen

Clark Jesse L, h 144 n Main
CLARK JESSE M (May H), city auditor, office 202, h Brevard rd, W Ashev
Clark Jno N (Eliza), bicycle repr J M Hearn & Co, h 15 Clingman av
Clark Jos W (Dovie), foreman, h 19 Roberts
Clark Lloyd, lab, h 19 Roberts
Clark May Miss, mica picker, bds 485 w Haywood
Clark Mitchell (Lina), driver, h 23 Clingman
*Clark Otis (Bessie), lab, h 99 Roberts
Clark Thos A, lab, h 19 Roberts
Clark Thos G (Edna F), bkkpr G L Guischard, h 99 Starnes
CLARK THOS S (Fannie), with S A Barbee, h 144 n Main
Clark Wm (Cinda), h Richmond Hill
Clark Wm C (Amanda), stone mason, h 98 Flint
Clark Wm H (Minnie A), clk, h 51 Starnes av
Clark Winifred D Mrs, h 135 Charlotte
Clarke Albert B, clk frt office Sou Ry, h 252 s French Broad
Clarke Chas D (Agnes), station mstr Sou Ry, h 98 Asheland
Clarke Chas D Jr, clk W U Tel Co, h 98 Asheland av
Clarke D Viola, wid R S, h 229 Asheland av
Clarke Dutch Miss, h 98 Asheland av
Clarke Eugene, weaver, h 493 w Haywood
Clarke Harris H (Elizabeth), painter, rms 37 Chestnut
Clarke Henry, student, bds 25 Asheland av
*Clarke Ida, h 49 West
Clarke Jno J (Edith), engnr Sou Ry, h 131 Asheland av
Clarke Louise Miss, h 252 s French Broad av
*Clarke Mary J, h 49 West
Clarke Michael F, h Carroll av
*Clarke Nellie, cook, h 48 Hill
Clarke Rose Miss, h 98 Asheland av
Clarke Rose A Miss, h Carroll av
Clarke Sarah E, wid Robt, h 1 Biltmore rd, Biltmore
*Clarke Sherman S (Maria), (Bryant & Clarke), h 93 Hazzard
Clarke Wm E, chf clk to supt Sou Ry, h 252 s French Broad
Clarke Wm M (Marie), timekpr Sou Ry, h 252 s French Broad av
Claudius Henry F (Adelaide), archt, h 40 Dortch av
Claudwoody Franklin C (Jettie), driver, h Hazel Mill rd, W Ashev
Claverie Jos S (Marthe), drug clk Grant's Pharmacy, h 38 Arlington
*Clayborne Hardwell (Bevel), waiter, h 77 Eagle

The Life Insurance Co. of Virginia
ORGANIZED 1871   RICHMOND, VA.

ISSUES ALL THE MOST APPROVED FORMS OF LIFE INSURANCE CONTRACTS from $500.00 to $25,000.00, with premiums payable quarterly, semi-annually and annually

J. V. Moon, Superintendent, Rooms 3-4-5 Maxwelton Bldg., Asheville, N. C.

D. TREXLER TIN SHOP

All Kinds of Roofing, Gutter and Conductor Work.

Phone 862

159 South Main St.

DR. C. H. MILLER

MECHANO-THERAPIST

14 N. Spruce St.
Phone 979
ASHEVILLE, N. C.

Hours by engagement

Drugless Healing of Disease

ASHEVILLE [1913] DIRECTORY

*Clayborne Isabelle, cook, h (r) 27 Buttrick
*Clayborne Odessa, cook, h (r) 27 Buttrick
Clayton Edna E Miss, student, h 50 Highland
CLAYTON EPHRAIM S (Bethel J), supt Williams, Brownell Planing Mill Co, h 53 w Walnut
Clayton Geo H (Laura D), lineman, h 161½ s Main
Clayton Howard P, carp, bds 12 Hilliard la
Clayton Jesse (Angeline), lab, h S Asheville
Clayton Jno (Laura), lab, h 15 Haid
Clayton Thad E (Louise), slsmn T S Morrison & Co, h 43 Arlington
Clayton Wm B (Ellen), carp, h 50 Highland
*Claytor Annie, dom, h 90 Southside av
Clee Frank W (Katie A), barber Antiseptic Barber Shop, h 95 Starnes av
Clegg Emma Miss, rms 74 Haywood
Cleland J Agnes Miss, milliner, h 126 Seney
Cleland Mary, wid Edwd, h 126 Seney
"Clematis Cottage," Albemarle Park
Clemenger Francis J (Daisy S), (Drs Battle & Clemenger), bds Battery Park Cottage
Clement Bertha C Miss, nurse 16 s French Broad av, h same
Clement Elizabeth Miss, student, h 16 s French Broad av
Clement Geo W (Elizabeth), contr, h 16 s French Broad av
*Clement Janie, laund, h 124 Church
Clement L Exum, bkkpr, h 16 s French Broad av
Clement Nancy R Miss, wood carver, h 16 s French Broad
Clement Ray (May), engnr, h 131 Park av
Clement Thos D (Adele), ins, rms 36 Philip
*Clements Frank, lab, h 19 Short Valley
Clements Jesse R (Irlene), pres The Boston Shoe Store, h 76 s Liberty
Clemmons Eugene T, engnr Hominy Sta, Ashev Power & Light Co
*Clemmons Otis (Maude), massage 18 Hilliard la, h same
*Clemons Sarah, laundress, h 12½ Aston pl
Cleveland Elizabeth J, wid J S, h 12 Village la, Biltmore
Clevenger Erastus H, lineman W U Tel Co, h Charlotte cor Clayton
Clevenger Jas F (Lyda E), farmer, h 23 Arlington, W Ashev
Clevenger Matilda, wid Allen, h 62 Charlotte
Cleverston Jno, mason, bds 49 n Main
Click Amelia, wid J N, h 480 Depot
Click Sidney M (Nonnie), h 480 Depot

....Asheville Cleaning and Pressing Club....
Tailoring That Satisfies and Prices That Please
Steam and French Dry Cleaning of all delicate and fine wearing apparel for ladies and gentlemen. MESSENGER SERVICE IN THE CITY.
J. C. WILBAR, Prop.   4. N. Pack Square   PHONE 389

Cliff Horace G (Julia), clk Ry M S, h 113 Asheland av
*Clifton Dora, cook, h 101 Market
Cline David W (Annie), watchman, h 32 Reed
*Cline Francis E, clk F S Campbell, h 388 College
Cline Jno W (Emma), engnr Sou Ry, h 208 s French Broad
*Cline Oma, h 388 College
Cline Robt F (Ella S), engnr, h 11 Flint
Cline Thos L (Hattie E), mngr Swannanoa-Berkeley Barber Shop, h 54 Vance
*Cline Walter (Annie), cook, h 388 College
*Cline Wm, lab, h 388 College
☞ Cline see also Kline
*Clinton Daisy, laund, h 48 Ralph
"Clio Cottage," Albemarle Park
Clodfelter Jas F (Beulah), car inspr, bds Dr J G Anderson, W Ashev
Clontz Brown, lab, h 44 View
Clontz Elizabeth Miss, h 44 View
Clouse Jas H (Annie), motorman, h 32 n Ann
"Clover Cottage," Albemarle Park
*Clowney Lewis (Lillie), waiter, h 15 Knob
CLUB CAFE & CANDY KITCHEN, 19-21 Haywood—phones 110-111, Theobold & Brandl proprs (see top lines)
Clyde Earl Mrs, mlnr Sproat's, bds Grey Gables
*Coachman Chas (Bettie), butler "Ardmion," h 264 s Beaumont
Coachman Eula H Miss, h Victoria rd
Coachman Jno W (Eula H), h Victoria rd
Coachman Kendrick P, student, h Victoria rd
COBB ALPHONSO H (Margaret), auditor Blue Ridge B & L Assn, h 133 Montford av
COBB J MONROE, supt Dixie Mutual Life Ins Co, bds 16 n Spruce
Cobb Jos F (Hanie E), lab, h 269 s Main
Cobb Perry D (Nell), h 3 Summit
Coca-Cola Bottling Co of Ashev, 90-92 s Main; R L Ellis pres, N N Beadles sec-treas
Coche Alonzo, painter R E Bowles, h 85 Hall
Coche E Zebulon (Bonnie), drayman, h 43 Hall
Coche Jos J (Rosa), painter R L Fitzpatrick & Son, h 85 Hall
Cochran Paul (Bonnie), painter, h 105 Biltmore rd, S Biltmore
Cochrane Annie L Miss, stengr, h 8 Biltmore rd, S Biltmore

Asheville Dray, Fuel & Construction Co.
6 1-2 South Main

COAL

Wood and Kindling
Stone and Sand
PHONE - 223

EVER READY FLASHLIGHTS
Piedmont Electric Company
ASHEVILLE, N. C.
64 PATTON AVENUE

Cochrane Carl V, clk, h 8 Biltmore rd, S Biltmore
Cochrane G Hal (Addie), asst supt Asheville Cemetery, h 107 Church
Cochrane Girdwood (Minnie), trav solr, h 16 Buncombe
Cochrane Hannah J, wid Jas, h 8 Biltmore rd, S Biltmore
Cochrane Jas G (Jessie), slsmn Harris-Barnett Dry Goods Co, h 106 Biltmore rd, S Biltmore
Cochrane Jessie Mrs, clk Peerless Dept Store, h Biltmore
Cochrane Mack D (Ernestine), barber, h 8 Biltmore rd, S Biltmore
Cochrane Virgil Miss, h Merrimon av extd (R D 1)
Cocke Ada G Mrs, h 15 Soco
Cocke Chas H, phys, h 216 Pearson Drive
Cocke Eugene, student, h 149 s French Broad av
Cocke Jere E (Freda), (Reynolds & Cocke), h 218 Cumberland av
Cocke Philip C, atty at law, 212 Legal Bldg, rms Asheville Club
Cocke Rowena L Miss, h 216 Pearson Drive
Cocke Rowena L, wid Chas H, h 216 Pearson Drive
Cocke Timothy D, h 15 Soco
Cocke Wm J (Nola D), atty at law 212-214 Legal Bldg, h 149 s French Broad av
Coday Chas, clk, h 98 Flint
Coday P Henry (Parthenia), h 98 Flint
Cody Mark, painter Excelsior P & P House
Coffey Ivey R (Zora), livery and blksmith 28-30 e College, h 11½ n Main
Coffey Zora Mrs, furn rooms 11½ n Main, h same
Cogburn Mack, chauffeur, bds 16 Hilliard la
Cogdill Fate, lab, bds 49 n Main
Cogwell Frank V (Frances), waiter, h 38 Pine
COHEN SANDFORD H, mngr Greater Western N C Assn bds Margo Terrace
Cohn Chas M (Tilly), propr Ashev Furn Co, h 39 s Liberty
Cohn Rosa B Miss, student, h 39 s Liberty
Colboch Wm, lab, bds 511 w Haywood
COLBY C D W, physician with Dr Wm L Dunn, 18 Battery Park pl, rms 12-13 Medical Bldg
Cole Daisy R Mrs, h 84 Clingman av
Cole Edom C (Della), farmer, h Asheville av, W Ashev
Cole Fulton, music tchr 51 n Main, h same
Cole Jno D (Laura), condr, h 11 Madison av
Cole Maggie D, wid Oscar, h 278 College
Cole Margaret, wid Richard, h 11 Soco

J. C. McPHERSON
SLATE AND TIN ROOFING
Galvanized Iron Work   Hot Air Furnaces
35-37 EAST COLLEGE STREET

PLUMBING
STEAM AND HOT WATER
HEATING
PHONE 133

*Cole Richard (Pearle), lab, h 45 Short
Cole Thos M Rev (Annie), pastor Cedar Hill Baptist Ch, h Main st, W Ashev
Cole W E Rex (Kate F), clk A M Field Co, h W Asheville
Coleman Annie K Miss, h 36 Montford av
Coleman Chas, weaver, h 2 Factory Hill
*Coleman Chas (Sereptha), driver Patton & Stikeleather, h 59 Hazzard
Coleman Frank, weaver, h 2 Factory Hill
Coleman Fred, car clnr, h 2 Factory Hill
Coleman Jas M, student, h 36 Montford av
COLEMAN JAS S (Gladys C), (Coleman, Robinson & Co), and pres Ashev & E Tenn R R Co, h "Willanow"
Coleman Margaret W Miss, h 36 Montford av
Coleman Mary Miss, h 36 Montford av
Coleman Mary J, wid Jno K, h 36 Montford av
Coleman, Robinson & Co (J S Coleman and C K Robinson), lumber, 4 Morsell Bldg
Coleman Saml, helper, h 2 Factory Hill
*Coleman Thos (Louisa), lab, h 33 Black
Coleman Wm, bkkpr Ashev Transfer Co, h 36 Montford av
Coley Bert L (Corye B), fireman, h 115 Park av
*Coley Martha, dom, h Grace
*Collanter Peter (Lizzie), foreman, h S Asheville
College Street Bakery, 37 e College, A G Fuller propr
***COLLEGE STREET DYE WORKS AND MERCHANT TAILORS**, 35½ College, Forney & Jones proprs—phone 981 (see opp bus dept)
*Collett Thos (Kate), waiter, h 49 Pine
*Colley Henry (Sallie), gro 1 Mountain, h same
*Colley Lizzie, h 20 Weaver
Colley Wm W, painter, h 20 Weaver
Collins Agnes R Miss, h W Asheville
Collins Annie H Miss, h 42 Chunn
Collins Benj M (Sallie), police, h 80 West
*Collins Chas (Mary), cook, h 132 Hill
Collins Clarence, emp J M Westall & Co, h Hall st
Collins David C (Maggie M), (Ashev Cabinet Co), h W Asheville
*Collins Dora, dom, h 19 w Chestnut
*Collins Ernest (Mattie), porter, h 19 w Chestnut
Collins Euphie Miss, student, h 89 Grove
Collins Geo R, pres Balfour Quarry Co, h Salisbury, N C
Collins Henry T (Harriet R), (Ashev Milling Co), h 295 s French Broad av

Club Cafe and Candy Kitchen
"A GOOD PLACE FOR REFRESHMENT"

The standards we work to in our Restaurant Department are: Cooking, perfect; Service, prompt and cheerful; Prices, moderate; Menu, everything in season. Parties and Banquets, Teas and Dinners. 19 and 21 Haywood St. Phones 110 and 111.

Brown's Undertaking Parlors

S. H. BROWN

50 Patton Avenue
ASHEVILLE, N. C.

Lady Assistant When Desired

Phone 193-2 Rings

THE MOORE Plumbing Company

16 N. Pack Square

PHONE 1025

Sanitary Plumbing, General Tin and Metal Work, Hot Air Furnaces

---

Collins Henry T Jr, student, h 170 Cumberland av
*Collins June (Martha), h Haywood rd, W Ashev
Collins Lewis Rev (Elizabeth P), h 42 Chunn
Collins Lourey Miss, h 303 s Main
*Collins Nellie, laund, h 19 w Chestnut
Collins Richard, lab, h 140 Hall
*Collins Russell, porter B J Jackson, h Livingston st
*Collins Selina, cook, h 19 w Chestnut
*Collins Theodore, barber, h 19 w Chestnut
Collins Willis E (Louise), (Ashev Milling Co), h 170 Cumberland av
Collister Andrew J, clk Windsor Hotel
Collister Eugene E (Lula H), propr The Roselawn, h 52 Merrimon av
Colonial (The), boarding 70 n Main, Mrs Olive J Neville propr
*Colter Geo W (Susan), lab, h 47 Catholic av
"Columbus Cottage" Albemarle Park
Colvin Annie M Miss, h 95 Woodfin
Colvin Jas G (Janet) (Colvin & Davidson), h 95 Woodfin
Colvin Jas G Jr, student, h 95 Woodfin
Colvin Jno K, civ engnr, Colvin & Davidson, h 95 Woodfin
Colvin & Davidson (Jas G Colvin, Geo H Davidson), contrs 95 Woodfin
Colwell Algernon E (Mary), h 232 Haywood
Colyer Amy Miss, h Sunset Drive
Colyer Chas T (Mary E), landscape gardener, h Sunset Drive
Colyer Julia B Miss, h Sunset Drive
Coman Laura A, wid Jas R, h Haywood rd, W Asheville
Comber Wm Geo (Belle), engnr, rms Harkins Bldg
*Compton Jas L (Onnie), plmbr, h 139 Clingman av
COMPTON LUCIUS B REV (Etta), evangelist and supt Faith Cottage Rescue Home, h 53 Atkinson
Conder Frank L (Maude), segt police, h 165½ s Main
Cone F W, pres Asheville Cotton Mills, h Balto Md
Confederate Hall, Court House, Col Jas M Ray custodian
*Conley Alex (Mary), lab, h 22 Davidson
*Conley Douglas (Alice), lab, h 249 Asheland av
*Conley Geo, brick lyr, h Herren av, W Asheville
*Conley Hannah, h 12 Cumberland av
*Conley Laura, cook, h 12 Cumberland av
*Conley Lee, barber 13 n Main, h 22 Eagle
Conley Montiville S (Lethia), farmer, h Broadway av, W Asheville

---

The Battery Park Bank

Capital - - $100,000.00
Surplus and Profits, $110,000.00

ASHEVILLE, N. C. City, County and State Depositary

J. A. TILLMAN I carry a nice line of Watches, Clocks and Jewelry, and make a specialty of repair work. Satisfaction guaranteed **Jeweler** **17 N. Main St.**

*Conley Patsy, laund, h 30 Maiden la
*Conley Wm, porter Bon Marche
*Conley Wm T (Eliza), barber 8 w College, h 100 Grove
Connally Alice T, wid Jno K, h "Fernihurst" Victoria rd
Connally-Cox Mary Mrs, h "Fernihurst" Victoria rd
Connally Tench F, student, h "Fernihurst" Victoria rd
*Connelly Dempsey, driver, h 302 Asheland av
*Conner David W (Mary), farmer, h 21 Ridge
Conner Robt H (Lydia), driver McConnell Bros, h 352 w Haywoood
Constantine Harry B (Blanche H), h 146 Hillside
CONTINENTAL CASUALTY CO of Chicago Ill, 3 Harkins Bldg, S A Scott dist mngr
CONTINENTAL CASUALTY OF CHICAGO ILL (Com'l Dept), 1 Harkins Bldg, Thos W Osteen agt
Conway Violette D Mrs, manicure Langren Barber Shop, h 49 Walnut
Cook Annie Miss, picker Ashev Mica Co, h 40 Roberts
Cook Barbara, wid Marvel, h 40 Roberts
Cook Daniel, shoe mkr J H Tilson, h 151 Grove
*Cook Della, cook, h 3 Clemmons
Cook Eli (Annie), mica mnfr, h 40 Roberts
*Cook Ernestine, laund, h 21 Catholic av
Cook Etta Miss, h 27 Courtland av
Cook Geo (Cora), clk L O Maxwell, h W Asheville
Cook Julia N, wid Henry, h Haywood rd, W Asheville
Cook Luvenia Miss, emp Ashev Mica Co, h 258 College
*Cook Mary, laund, h S Asheville
Cook Mary Miss, student, h 4 Clayton
Cook Nina Miss, mica picker, h Haywood rd, W Asheville
*Cook Olin, h S Asheville
Cook Robt L (Laura), foreman, h 40 Roberts
Cook Roxie, mad, h 24 Eagle Terrace
Cook Thos L, emp Tannery, h 151 Grove
Cook Vena Miss, wks Ashev Mica Co, h 258 College
Cook Wade R, wood wkr, h Haywood rd, W Asheville
Cook Wm M (Nannie), h 27 Courtland av
Cooke Daisie V Miss, h 27 Chunn
Cooke Geo (Cora B), shoe mkr, h nr Arlington st, W Ashev
Cooke Geo (Isabella), lumber, h 27 Chunn
Cooke Horace E (Texie), condr, h 241 s Main
Cooley Olive Miss, Manicurist Ashev Barber Shop, h Livingston nr Oliver
*Coon Augustus (Susan), lab Sou Coal Co, h (r) 330 w Haywood

INSURANCE

INSURE YOUR SALARY WITH US
NEVER CARRY YOUR OWN RISK
SAFETY IS THE BEST POLICY
UNLESS YOU ARE A CAPITALIST
REST EASY IF YOU HAVE
A**N** ACCIDENT WE WILL
NOT KEEP YOU WAITING TO
COLLECT YOUR CLAIM
EVERY CLAIM PROMPTLY PAID

Imperial Mutual Life & Health Insurance Co.

Home Office:
ASHEVILLE, N. C.
Phone 495

HOTEL OXFORD Redecorated and Refitted throughout. Recently enlarged to 60 rooms. Centrally located Depot cars stop at entrance. Long distance telephone office upstairs. American and European plan. Rates 50c, 75c and $1 per day; special rates by week or month. C. H. Branson & Sons, Proprietors. Phone 1887. 50-54 South Main St. **Asheville, N. C.**

Williams-Brownell Planing Mill Company   *Hardwoods*

Lumber---Rough and Dressed   Flooring a Specialty   Moulding, Interior Finish, Etc.
Office, Plant and Yards on Southern Railway, Near Biltmore Station
WHITE PINE   Phone 729   YELLOW PINE

*Coon Robt, lab, h 6 Cole
Cooper Albin N, clk M V Moore & Co, bds 50 Walnut
COOPER C DURAND, mngr Arbogast Motor Co, bds 50 Walnut
Cooper C Seldon (Fannie), h 33 Hiawassee
Cooper Claud D, electn Dreamland Theatre, rms 40 Hiawassee
Cooper Dr, rms 1 Reed, S Biltmore
Cooper Emma, mad, h 22 Eagle Terrace
Cooper Geo W (Estelle), lino mchst Ashev Citizen h 44 Oak
Cooper Hannah G, wid A D, h 50 Walnut
Cooper Jno M, student, h 50 Walnut
Cooper Mabel Miss, student, h 50 Walnut
Cooper McKee, h 50 Walnut
Cooper Otho W (Alice), track supt Ashe P & L Co, h 165 Asheland av
Cooper Thos J, v-pres Ashe Lbr Co, Temple Ct
Cooper Waverly P, lab, h 25 Rector
Cooper Wm M, bkkpr, h 50 w Walnut
Cooper Wm N, pres Ashe Lbr Co, rms 36 Temple Ct
*Copeland Della, laundress, h 17½ Wallach
*Copeland Thos, lab, h 19 Wallach
*Copening Geo, chauffer, h 36 Sassafras
*Copening Harvey (Mary), driver, h 36 Sassafras
*Copening Mamie, h 38 Cumberland av
*Copening Mattie, cook, h (r) 6 Depot
COPSES ERNEST G, mngr N S Trakas & Co, h 31 s Main
Corbett Chas F (Stella), switchman, bds 480 Depot
Corbin Jno T (Allie), stone ctr, h 38 Clingman av
Corsoran Annie M Miss, h 68 Haywood
Corcoran Mary J Mrs, propr The Rock Ledge, h 68 Haywood
Corcoran Patrick J (Mary J), granite ctr, h 68 Haywood
Cordell Claudia Miss, dom 35 s French Broad av
Cordell Jno, driver Hughes Transfer & Livery Co, rms 401 Southside av
Corland Beulah Miss, nurse Biltmore Hosp, rms same
Corn Claude H, clk J C Wilbar, h 77 East
Corn Claude H, pressing, 77 East
Corn Geo W (Anna L), carp, h nr Murphy Junction, W Asheville
Corn Jas (Fannie E), fireman Sou Ry, h 12 Green
Corn Noah P (Lillie), carp, h 77 East
Corn Rosa M Miss, maid, h Haywood rd, W Asheville
Corn Vera E Miss, phone opr Batery Park Hotel, h 77 East

Asheville Electrical Company
W. Mansfield Booze, Manager
74 CENTRAL AVE.
HEADQUARTERS
Phone 377

Asheville Dry Cleaning Co.
Telephones 835-836, All Dep't
MAIN, N. E. COR. COLLEGE

THE CLEANERS
Our Department for Oriental Rugs and Carpet Cleaning is prepared to serve you in all its branches. :-: :-: :-:
E. S. Paine   O. E. Hansen

Cornell Erner V Miss, h Haywood rd, W Ashev
Cornell Harriet A, wid Harrison T, gro Haywood rd, W Ashev, h same
Cornell Wm S (Mary), supt Asheville Cemetery, h Woolsey (R F D 1)
Corner Pool Room (The), Patton av cor Pack Sq, B A Woodfin mngr
Cornwell Fred'k R (May), atty, h Daffodil Cottage, Albemarle Park
*Cornwell Lula, maid, 112 Pearson Drive
Corpening Clifford C, clk Battery Park Hotel, rms same
Corpening Florence Miss, mngr, h Florence Hotel
*Corpening Harrison (Dora), lab, h Dewey nr Jordan
Corpening Wm G, propr Hotel Florence 436 Depot, h same
*Correll Susan, h (r) 29 Clingman av
Cortino Theresa Miss, clk Bon Marche, h 46 Haywood
*Cory Lula, laund, h 63 Max
Cory Wm O Maj, retired maj U S A, h 19 Zillicoa
Cosby Benj H (Maude), jeweler 70 Patton av, h 54 Clingman av
Cosby Helen E Miss, h 54 Clingman av
Cosby Jno C, designer, h 54 Clingman av
Cosgrove Thos A Rev (Mary), pastor Oakland Heights Presby Church, h 515 Biltmore rd
Costello Michael J Dr (Nora), h 74 e College
*Coston Bertha, dom, h Edgemont
*Coston Columbus, porter MacKay's Pharmacy
Coston Jas A, slsmn Asheville Auto Co, rms 20 Church
Coston Jesse P (Constance E), pres Ashev Harness Co, h 90 Church
Coston Oscar M (Susan M), propr Ashev Carpet House, h 365 Merrimon av
Councell Margaret D, wid R H T, h 401 s Main
Councill Cora Mrs, housekpr, Margo Terrace, rms same
*Counts Thos (Mary), waiter Sou Ry Dining Room, h 12 Ralph
County Court House, 57-67 College
COUNTY GOVERNMENT—offices Court House
    Attorney—J E Swain
    Auditor—E M Lyda
    Board of Commissioners—E W Patton chmn
    Board of Education—W H Hipps supt
    Coroner—Dr E R Morris
    Home of the Aged and Infirm—7 miles from City on Leicester rd, B F Merrell keeper

Life Insurance Company of Virginia
ORGANIZED 1871
Home Office - Richmond, Va.

Has won the hearty approval and active support of the people by its promptness and fair dealing during the FORTY-TWO YEARS of its operation

J. V. Moon, Superintendent, Rooms 3-4-5 Maxwelton Bldg., Asheville, N. C.

T. P. JOHNSON & CO.

SHEET METAL WORKERS

All Kinds of Roofing Guttering and Conductor Work Metal Ceilings, Skylights and Galvanized Iron Cornices

OFFICE and SHOP: 69-71 S. MAIN

Phone 325

DR. C. H. MILLER

Mechano-Therapist

14 N. Spruce Street
ASHEVILLE, N. C.

PHONE 979

Hours by Engagement

DRUGLESS HEALING OF DISEASE

---

138 ASHEVILLE [1913] DIRECTORY

　Register of Deeds—J J Mackey
　Road Engineer—J C M Valentine
　Sheriff—Chas F Williams
　Solicitor (15th Jud Dist)—R R Reynolds
　Superior Court—Marcus Erwin clk
　Superior Court Judge—Hon Frank Carter
　Superior Court Stenographer—A E Eve
　Supt of Health—6½ s Main, Dr D E Sevier
　Tax Collector—B A Patton
　Treasurer—T M Duckett
County Jail, Marjorie nr Spruce, J B Jordan jailor
Court House (County), 57-71 College
Courtney Harry S (Marche), trav slsmn, bds 111 Montford
Courtney Michael P (Sarah A), farmer, h Brevard rd, W Ashev
Courtney Pink, furn mkr, bds 502 Depot
Cowan Aleene Miss, smstrs, h Haywood rd, W Ashev
*Cowan Ernest O Rev, pastor Varick Chapel (A M E Zion) h 9 Maiden la
Cowan Eugene, driver McConnell Bros, h W Asheville
Cowan Ida Miss, smstrs, h Haywood rd, W Ashev
Cowan Jas G, h 258 Haywood
Cowan Jas K (Florence D), R R contr, h 258 Haywood
Cowan Jas W (Josephine), contr, h Haywood rd, W Ashev
Cowan Jno C, pres Farmer's Union, h W Asheville (R F D 3)
Cowan Lucy E Miss, stengr Dr G D Gardner, h Haywood rd, W Ashev
Cowan Margaret Miss, h 258 Haywood
Cowan Robt (Sophia R), carp, h nr Hazel Mill rd, W Ashev
Cowan Thos H (Grace), ship clk McConnell Bros, h W Asheville
*Cowan Wm, fireman, h 219 s Main
Coward Geo, bds 434 Depot
Cowdery Catherine V Miss, student, h 15 All Souls Crescent, Biltmore
Cowdery Lewis W (Florence V), h 15 All Souls Crescent, Biltmore
Cowgill Anna, wid Jno H, propr Western Hotel, h 11½ s w Pack Sq
Cowley Alexander Mrs, h 249 Cumberland av
Cox Fountin M (Margaret), piano tuner, h 481 w Haywood
Cox Frank, fireman, bds 308 Depot
Cox Leona Miss, h 194 Charlotte
Cox Lila Mrs, h Broadway av, W Ashev

ASHEVILLE CLEANING and PRESSING CLUB

TAILORING THAT SATISFIES and PRICES THAT PLEASE

Hats cleaned, banded and bound. Silk hats ironed. Buttons made to order in all sizes. Plain or with rims. PHONE 389

DYEING IN ALL SHADES

Kid Gloves, Slippers and Plumes. Fancy Jabots and Ties, French Dry Cleaned. Ladies' and Gentlemen's suits Steam Cleaned. Messenger Service. **J. C. Wilbar, Prop.**

4 NORTH PACK SQ.

Cox Norma Miss, h 194 Charlotte
Coxe Building (office), 4-6 Battery Park pl
COXE FRANK (Estate of), offices 10 Battery Park pl—phone 163, V B Bostick mngr
COXE TENCH C (Sara), pres Battery Park Bank and trustee The Estate of Frank Coxe, h "Klondyke," Montford av
Cozad Marcus E (Margaret S), timber, bds 23 Woodfin
Craddock Jos E (Margaret), lumber, h 450 Montford av
Craddock Thos E Dr (Viola), h 80 Arlington
Craig Arthur B, student, h 169 Montford av
Craig Cappitolia Miss, stengr Rogers Grocery Co, bds Y W C A
Craig Carlyle, student, h 169 Montford av
*Craig Caroline, laund, h 12 w Woodfin
Craig Geo W, student, h 169 Montford av
Craig Locke Hon (Annie B), (Craig, Martin & Thomason), h 169 Montford av
Craig, Martin & Thomason (Locke Craig, J H Martin, G A Thomason), attys at law, 403-405 Oates Bldg
Crank Jno C (Ellen), grader, h 443 n Main
*Crawford C Jefferson (Daisy), waiter, h Valley nr College
Crawford Edwd, condr, bds 17 Ora
Crawford Guy, train dispr, bds Glen Rock Hotel
*Crawford Jno (Elvria), gardener, h 34 Maiden la
*Crawford Lillian, laund, h 133 Roberts
*Crawford Maria, dom, h 41 Catholic av
*Crawford Wm L (Mary), waiter, h 117 Cherry
Crawley Lola B, wid Jas, h 7½ s Main
Creasman Bertha A, wid W B, h 76 Flint
Creasman Edwd T (Ella), engnr Hominy Sta Ashev P & L Co, h W Asheville
Creasman Elistus C (Lura), driver, h Haywood rd W Ashev
Creasman Eliza, wid Lorenzo A, h Biltmore rd, S Biltmore
*Creasman Emily, h 60 n Lexington av
Creasman Fred O (Mary), driver, h Van st, W Ashev
Creasman Geo W (Bessie), plmbr, h 285½ College
*Creasman Hannah, maid, h 60 n Lexington av
Creasman Henry (Ethel), mchst Asheville Auto Co, h 6 Victoria av
Creasman Hattie, wid Robt, weaver, h Lester rd, W Asheville
Creasman Jas H (Maude), stables 9 Walnut, h 53½ n Main
Creasman Jeannette Miss, h Biltmore rd, S Biltmore
Creasman Jos, helper Dr P V Orr, h W Asheville

WEAVERVILLE LINE NINE MILES BY TROLLEY FROM PACK SQUARE TO WEAVERVILLE

ASHEVILLE AND EAST TENNESSEE RAILROAD CO.

7 NORTH MAIN STREET   ASHEVILLE N. C.

ELECTRIC FIXTURES

Piedmont Electric Co.

64 PATTON AVE.
ASHEVILLE, N.C.

*Creasman Kate, nurse 60 n Lexington av, h same
Creasman Kate B Miss, h Asheville av, W Ashev
Creasman Lawrence N (Gladys), mchst Western Carolina Auto Co, h 97 Josephine
Creasman Lewis W (Eliza), barber, h Haywood rd, W Ashev
Creasman Listus (Laura), clk J L Welch & Co, h W Ashev
Creasman Mayme C Miss, h 76 Flint
Creasman Manley A (M Lou), justice of peace and notary Oates Bldg (basement), h 76 Flint
Creasman Oscar F (Effie), cabt mkr, h 32 Summit, S Biltmore
Creasman Owen (Mary), driver J B Ingle, h W Asheville
Creasman Robt A (Lillian E), sawyer, h nr Hazel Mill rd, W Ashev
Creasman Sue Miss, h Biltmore rd, S Biltmore
Creasman Thos F (Amanda), care taker Golf Links, h Asheville av, W Ashev
Creasman Zebulon V (Mollie), contr, h Biltmore rd, S Bilt
*Credle Green (Rosa), bellmn, h 70 Circle, Battery Park
Creech R S, collr J M Hearn & Co, bds Chestnut st
Creek Emma Miss, h 40 Josephine
Creek Martha, wid M C, h 40 Josephine
Creek Mattie Miss, h 40 Josephine
Crenshaw Jas W (Elizabeth), h Chunns Cove
Crescent Jewelry Co, 16 Patton av, H L Finkelstein propr
*Crescent Lunch Room, 16 Eagle, Geo Alexander propr
*Crews Robt, driver Asheville Dry Cleaning Co, h W Ashev
CRISP N L (Myrtle), groceries 305 w Haywood, h 23 Depot (see card in classified)
Crompton Arthur, driver Felmet Bros, h 16 Jefferson Drive
Crompton Betty, wid Francis M, dressmkr, h 16 Jefferson Drive
Crompton Chas E (May), driver Felmet Bros, h 16 Jefferson Drive
Crompton Lloyd, driver Felmet Bros, h 16 Jefferson Drive
Crompton Mayme Miss, h 16 Jefferson Drive
Crompton Wm P (Della), trouble man Sou Bell Tel & Tel Co, h 15 Green
☞ Crompton see also Compton
Crook Edwd, h Chunn's Cove
Crook Harriet Miss, laund, h nr Smith's Bridge, W Ashev
Crook Henry T (Bertha), mchst, h 94 Jefferson Drive
Crook Jas R (Julia A), h Allen st, W Ashev
Crook Jesse, h Chunn's Cove

CONTRACTOR and BUILDER

STEEL RANGES   **J. C. McPHERSON**   35-37 E COLLEGE ST. PHONE 133

PLUMBING STEAM AND HOT WATER HEATING

Crook Jno E (Dovie), barber 513 w Haywood, h W Asheville
Crook Lillian J Miss, clk, h 15 Rector
Crook Lyda (Lola E), switchman, h Main st, W Ashev
Crook Ober Miss, bkkpr Brown Book Co, h W Asheville
Crook Opall Miss, h Allen st, W Ashev
Crook Rebecca E, wid Jasper A, h nr Smiths Bridge, W Ashev
Crook Richard L (Roberts & Crook), and barber 342 w Haywood, h W Asheville
Crook Robt L, driver Sou Exp Co, bds 102 Patton av
Crook Thos (Mollie), lab, h Lester rd, W Asheville
Crook Vinie Miss, clk College Street Bakery, rms 20 Marjorie
Crook Wm J (Matilda J), driver, h 15 Rector
*Crosby Ira T (Rosa), lab, h 48 Gudger
*Crosby Isaac, wood dlr 99 Market, h same
Crosby Lois Miss, h Edgemont
*Cross Lizzie, laund, h 11 Haid
Cross Robah D Rev (Virginia), h Haywood rd, W Ashev
*Crow Clarence, lab, h 17 Oakdale av
Crowder Mollie Miss, h 60 Starnes av
Crowell Alma Miss, waitress, h 30 Short Roberts
Crowell Jos A (Sallie), bricklyr, h 40 Seney
Crowell Paul B (Birdie), pressman Ashev Ptg & Engrav Co h 22 Vivian av
CROWELL RUSSELL CHURCHILL (Lottie), ex-county tax collector, office Court House, h Acton N C
Crowell Ruth E Miss, clk, h 40 Seney
*Crowle Walter, waiter, h 23 Aston pl
"Crows Nest Cottage," Albemarle Park
Cruise Johnnie B Miss, hair goods 25 Haywood, bds 107 same
*Crump Archie, butler 312 Montford av
*Crump Benj (Charity), driver, h 62 Mountain
*Crump Lizzie, cook, h 112 Church
*Crump Richard (Annie), lab, h 63 Eagle
Crystal Cafeterian, 8 n Pack Sq, M M Sullivan propr
Crystal Dairy Lunch, 56 Patton av, Frank Pons mngr
Cudahy Packing Co, whol prov 351 Depot, Eli Mustin agt
Culvern Frank M, student, h "Billows Rest," Grace
Culvern Geo W (Elsie), propr "Billows Rest," h Grace
Culvern Lula B Miss, h "Billows Rest," Grace
*Cummings Lucy, cook, h 89 Circle
Cunningham Chas E, h 6 Battery Park pl

Club Cafe and Candy Kitchen
"A GOOD PLACE FOR REFRESHMENT"

Our Ice Cream manufacturing plant is absolutely clean and sanitary.
Prompt family delivery. Phones 110 and 111.
Catering for large parties and receptions. Special Creams.

Brown's Undertaking Parlors

S. H. BROWN

Lady Assistant When Desired

Phone 193-2 Rings

50 Patton Avenue
Asheville, N. C.

Established 1894

B. J. JACKSON

Carefully Selected Fruits and Vegetables

Stall No. 11, City Market

BUSINESS PHONES: 86 and 101

RESIDENCE PHONE 1596

Cunningham Emma Miss, h 6 Battery Park pl
Cunningham Hester O. wid S E, h 6 Battery Park pl
Cunningham Jason F (Kittie C), carrier P O, h 21 Louisa
Cunningham Kate Miss, h 6 Battery Park pl
Cuthbert Margaret Miss, cashr H Redwood & Co, h 10 Locust
*Cuthbertson Baxter (Irene), lab, h Grace
*Cuthbertson Ira, h Grace
Cuthbertson T Walter (Essie), brkmn Sou Ry, h 342 s French Broad av
*Cureton Jas (Lula), lab, h 89 Black
CURRENCE ROBT E (Cliffie S), asst cashr Amer Natl Bank, h 82½ Cumberland av
*Currents Leroy (Eunice), cook, h 26 Gibbons
Currier Hazel M Miss, h 218 e Chestnut
Currier Wm M (Hattie), lumberman, h 218 Chestnut
Curry Elizabeth Miss, clk, h 43 Chestnut
Curry Giles S, emp Ashev Citizen, h 139 Grove
Curry Grace Miss, h 41 Victoria rd
Curry Saml J (Mary), h 43 Chestnut
Curtis Julia Miss, h Victoria rd
Curtis Lottie Miss, h 291 Merrimon av
Curtis M Gertrude Miss, stengr, h 69 Flint
CURTIS T EUGENE (Mayme), pres J R Rich Co (Inc), h 69 Flint
CURTIS ZEB F (Kathryn S), atty at law and notary 3-4 Library Bldg, h 212 Chestnut

D

"Daffodil Cottage," Albemarle Park
"Dahlia Cottage," Albemarle Park
*Dailey Mary, h 48 Madison
Dale H T, fireman, bds 430 Depot
*Dale Jones F (Willie), fireman, h 17 Oakdale av
Dale Lee (Elizabeth L), asst Drs Sinclair, h 42 Starnes av
Dallas Rhea F Miss, tchr, h Sand Hill rd, W Ashev
*Dalrymple Larkin (Eulah), painter (r) 14 n Spruce
Dalton General R (Cora), loom fixer, h Swannanoa av, W Ashev
Dalton Geo L (Mary R), carp, h 387 Cumberland av
Dalton Grace D Miss, h 329 s Main
Dalton Howard B, lab, h 387 Cumberland av
Dalton J Baxter, painter, h 329 s Main
Dalton Jas T (Delia A), steward, h 329 s Main

Furniture and China Carefully Prepared for Shipment

Mahogany Furniture Hand Made & Carefully Reproduced | **E. E. GALER** 114 PATTON AVE. | Upholstering and Refinishing PHONE - 1674

Dalton Jno (Olive), h Bingham Hghts
Dalton Rebecca, wid Patrick; h Haywood rd, W Ashev
Dalton Sarah Mrs, wkr Ashev Mica Co, h 488 w Haywood
Dalton Thos S (Sarah), bldg contr 167 s Main, h same
*Dalton Wm (Lucy), lab, h S Asheville
Dalton Wm A, agt, h 329 s Main
Dalton Worth, h 167 s Main
Daniel Danl C, stengr, bds 24 n Spruce
Daniel Robt C, private sec Hon J C Pritchard, bds The Belvedere
Daniel Sophronia, wid Jas, h 197½ Asheland av
Daniel Wm H, court reporter and atty at law 3 Temple Ct, rms Y M C A
Daoulas Geo, mngr New York Fruit Stand, 404 Depot
Darby Jas (Fannie E), clk The Cash Grocery, h 34 Carter
Darby Jas A (Fannie), clk, h 34 Carter
DARDEN ALLEN W (Reliable Cleaning & Pressing Club), h 55 College
*Darden Jacob B (Nettie), cook, h 48 Short
*Darden Texas, cook, h 1 Hazzard
Dark Saml H, barber Langren Barber Shop, h 15 Spruce
*Davenport Allie, cook, rms 86 Eagle
Davenport Doris Miss, h 31 Panola
*Davenport Minnie, cook, 39 Border
Davenport Otis M (Zoe), police, h 349 Hillside
Daves Alfred D (Minnie), clk H J Olive, h W Ashev
Daves Clara L Miss, h Haywood rd, W Ashev
Daves Eugene E, slsmn H J Olive, h W Asheville
Davidson Elizabeth A, wid Allen T, h 265 Pearson Drive
Davidson Geo H (Elizabeth), (Colvin & Davidson), h 147 Woodfin
*Davidson Geo H (Ada), hostler, h 223 s Main
Davidson Jno (Mathilda), emp The Tannery, h 22 s French Broad av
*Davidson Lawrence, h Chunn's Cove
*Davidson Robt, driver L A Murphy
Davidson Robt (Agnes), carp, h "Zealandia Cottage"
Davidson S Kate Miss, stengr Wells & Swain, h 135 Asheland
DAVIDSON THEO F (Sarah L C), atty, h 61 n Liberty
Davies Henry D (Helen B), h 20 Clayton
Davies Ida E Miss (Kenilworth Hall), h s Main extd
Davies Wm M, atty at law, 17 Library Bldg, h same
Davis Aaron P (Nancy L), farmer, h nr Smiths Bridge, W Ashev

Mrs. Wilder's SANITARY HOME LAUNDRY turns out first class work in Laundering and Dry Cleaning. No. 7 Montford Ave., Phone 1354

*Davis Ada, cook, 21 s Ann
*Davis Agnes, student, h 74 Eagle
Davis Alice M, wid Benj K, h 83 w Chestnut
Davis Anna Miss, clk Palais Royal, h 12 Hilliard la
Davis Anna E Miss, spooler, h nr Smith's Bridge, W Ashev
Davis Annie E Miss, h 58 Cherry
Davis Arah W Miss, clk, h 302 s French Broad av
Davis Ardie Miss, stengr Ashev Mercantile Agcy, h 59 Blanton
Davis Armand, clk H Redwood & Co, h 83 w Chestnut
Davis B Cleo Miss, clk Bon Marche, h 64 n French Broad av
Davis Benj, lab, h Grace
*Davis Benj (Mamie), barber, h 63 Max
Davis Benj R (Sallie), blksmith C L Brown 25 n Lexington av
Davis Bessie Miss, stengr, bds 6 Phifer
Davis Blanche M Miss, h 80 Penland
Davis Bonnie Miss, stengr, bds 226 Asheland av
Davis Carrie V Miss, h 58 Cherry
Davis Chas, musician The Dreamland, h 58 Cherry
Davis Chas S (Minnie), sec Slayden, Fakes & Co, Inc, h 58 Cherry
Davis Clarence B, clk Ashev Grain & Hay Co, h 83 w Chestnut
Davis Claude (Elizabeth), lab, h 22 Atkinson
Davis Claude L (Maud), lab, h 42 Jefferson Drive
Davis D Frank (Nancy L), lab, h nr Smith's Bridge, W Ashev
Davis Drayton, stengr J L Smithers & Sons, h 80 Penland
Davis Edwd M, clk R S Finley, bds Florence Hotel
Davis Ella Mrs, clk Peerless Dept Store, h 302 s French Broad av
*Davis Ellen, tchr, h 74 Eagle
*Davis Emma, dressmkr 29 Hillside, h same
Davis Ernest W (Myrtle), ship clk Slayden, Fakes & Co, Inc, h 51 Hiawassee
Davis Estus S, student, h 64 n French Broad av
Davis Eva K Mrs, wid Walter, h 128 Cumberland av
Davis Everett C, mch opr A L McLean & Co, h 459 n Main
Davis Ezekiel, lab Woolsey Greenhouses, h Woolsey (R F D 1)
Davis Faye Miss, h 449 n Main
Davis Florida Miss, emp Poole Bros, h 57 Church
Davis Furman G, bookbndr Hackney & Moale, h Woolsey
Davis Geo, foreman, h 64 n French Broad av

BUICK — ARBOGAST MOTOR COMPANY — MAXWELLS
OLDSMOBILE — ACCESSORIES AND SUPPLIES — DETROIT ELECTRIC
52-60 N. Main   Phones 302 and 1728

Asheville Dry Cleaning Co.
Telephones 835-836, All Dep't
MAIN, N. E. COR. COLLEGE

THE CLEANERS
Our Department for Oriental Rugs and Carpet Cleaning is prepared to serve you in all its branches.
E. S. Paine   O. E. Hansen

For Kindling "What am Kindling" Call
ENGLISH LUMBER COMPANY   Phone 321

ASHEVILLE [1913] DIRECTORY

Davis Geo W (Ella P), notions 426 Depot, h 302 s French Broad av
Davis Geo W (Julia), foreman, h 96½ Haywood
Davis H Elizabeth, wid L Dowd, h 42 Jefferson Drive
Davis Hall (Mary), emp Amer Wagon Co, h E Biltmore
Davis Harriet E, wid Lorenzo D, h 376 w Haywood
Davis Harriet H Mrs, phys, h 135 Charlotte
Davis Harry M, stage mngr Palace Theatre, h 175 Grove
*Davis Herman, porter B J Jackson, h Hibernia st
Davis Herman B, student, h Woolsey (R F D 1)
Davis Hugh, lab, h Woolsey (R F D 1)
Davis Ilean Miss, stengr T E Davis, h 34 Hillside
Davis Ivory Miss, h 22 Atkinson
Davis J Arthur (Sallie), lab, h 42 Jefferson Drive
*Davis J Calvin, meat ctr The Star Market, h 30 Hill
Davis Jas A (Addie), lab, h 158 Park av
Davis Jas P (Mary), lab, h 176 Grove
Davis Jno (Clara), carp, h 464 s Main
Davis Jno H (Jane), carp, h 449 n Main
Davis Jno P (Alice), mill wkr, h 11 Factory Hill
DAVIS JNO R (Maude H), furniture 37 s Main—phone 1707, h 174 Charlotte—phone 1615
Davis Jno W, collr Montague Loan Co, rms 12 n Pack Sq
Davis Jno W (Carrie), propr Ashev Piano Co, h 173 Asheland av
*Davis Jos (Caroline), butcher, h 30 Hill
Davis Jos S, bkkpr Battery Park Bank
Davis Latimer (Hattie), lab, h 1 New
Davis Lee E (Jennie E), dentist, h Brevard rd, W Ashev
*Davis Lettie, laund, h S Asheville
Davis Lillian M Miss, clk H Redwood & Co, h 83 w Chestnut
Davis Linnie Ward, wid Albert C, h 121 Flint
Davis Louisa, wid Jno, h 99 Jefferson Drive
Davis Lucy E Miss, tchr, h 58 Park av
Davis M Drayton, stengr, h 80 Penland
Davis Mamie Miss, spinner, h nr Smith's Bridge, W Ashev
Davis Manie, lab, h nr Smith's Bridge, W Ashev
Davis Mattie Miss, tchr Park av Schl, h 58 Park av
*Davis Mattie, h 9 (175) Velvet
Davis Merritt (Nannie), mill wkr, h 10 Factory Hill
*Davis Moses, porter, h 20 Hill
Davis Myrtle M Miss, h Woolsey
*Davis Nathaniel C (Lizzie), farmer, h Haywood rd, W Ashev

BIGGEST **B**USIEST **B**EST

Phones 1936 and 1937
ASHEVILLE STEAM LAUNDRY
43 to 47 W. COLLEGE

S. D. HALL
REAL ESTATE AGENT
—
Money Loaned
—
Notary Public
—
32 PATTON AVENUE
—
Phone 91

Founders, Machinists and Jobbers of Mill Supplies
PHONE 590 When in the market for pipe and fittings, let us make you Prices.
Carolina Machinery Co.
PHONE 590 If it's a Gas Engine let us figure with you, also on other kinds of machinery

LIFE INSURANCE COMPANY OF VA. OLDEST, LARGEST STRONGEST Southern Life Insurance Co.

ORGANIZED 1871
RICHMOND, VIRGINIA

Issues Industrial Policies from $8.00 to $900.00, with Premiums Payable WEEKLY on persons from two to seventy years of age

J. V. Moon, Superintendent, Rooms 3-4-5 Maxwelton Bldg., Asheville, N. C.

D. TREXLER TIN SHOP

All Kinds of Roofing, Gutter and Conductor Work.

Phone 862

159 South Main St.

DR. C. H. MILLER

MECHANO-THERAPIST

14 N. Spruce St.
Phone 979
ASHEVILLE, N. C.

Hours by engagement

Drugless Healing of Disease

---

146   ASHEVILLE [1913] DIRECTORY

Davis Osborne (Minnie), lab, h 2 New
Davis Perch Mrs, bds 88 Penland
*Davis Randolph, coachman, Merrimon av cor Hillside
*Davis Reuben (Ida), lab, h 229 Southside av
Davis Russell C, clk Battery Park Bank, h 121 Flint
Davis Sallie R, wid J E, boarding 80 Penland, h same
Davis Saml F (Minnie), lab, h 81 Seney
Davis Saml N (Mabel F), slsmn Slayden, Fakes & Co, Inc, h 29 Livingston
Davis Simon P (Minnie), slsmn Slayden, Fakes & Co, Inc, h 58 Park av
*Davis Sisley, boarding, 74 Eagle, h same
Davis Sylla Miss, clk H Redwood & Co, h 176 Park av
Davis Thos, lab, bds 52 Woodfin
Davis Thos, driver J E Johnson, h Grace
*Davis Thos (Emma), lab, h 3 Hibernia
Davis Thos E (Sarah E), archt 20½ s Spruce, h 34 Hillside
Davis Truxton, student, h 302 s French Broad av
DAVIS WALLACE B (Kate L), cashr Central Bank & Trust Co, h 155 Hillside
Davis Whit, lab Woolsey Greenhouse, h Charlotte extd
Davis Whitney E, mchst, h 58 Park av
Davis Wm (Nellie), lab, h Woolsey (R F D 1)
*Davis Wm (Annie), lab, h 21 Oliver
*Davis Wm (Mary), lab, h Chunn's Cove
Davis Wm A, gro 41 s Main, h Woolsey (R F D 1)
Davis Wm J, plmbr, h 64 s French Broad av
Davis Wm M (Elizabeth), dryman, h 175 Grove
Davis Wm V, lumberman, bds 80 Penland
*Dawkins Ruth, presser J R Sartor, h 22 McDowell
*Dawkins Saml (Belle), waiter, h 100 Hazzard
Dawl Claude A, photog, h 18 Central av
Dawl Daniel D (Emma), artist, h 18 Central av
Dawson Nellie Miss, h 556 n Main
Dawson Rufus (Emma), mngr, h 556 n Main
Day Charlotte B, wid A H S, h 32 Philip
*Day Jno (Callie), cabt mkr Ashev Cabinet Co, h 16 Sorrell
DAY MARY FRANCES MISS, tchr piano, pipeorgan theory and Harmony, 157 Church—phone 1374, h same (see p 12)
Dayton Jno H (Fannie), lab, h 485 w Haywood
Dayton Thos J (Neta), barber C U Monday, h 8 View
Dayton Thos L (Elizabeth), mill wkr, h 85 Atkinson
Dayton Walter W (Hattie L), mchst, h Arlington st, W Ashev

....Asheville Cleaning and Pressing Club....
Tailoring That Satisfies and Prices That Please

Steam and French Dry Cleaning of all delicate and fine wearing apparel for ladies and gentlemen. MESSENGER SERVICE IN THE CITY.

J. C. WILBAR, Prop.   4. N. Pack Square   PHONE 389

Deal Everett, emp Hughes Transfer & Livery Co, rms 401 Southside av
Deal Jno (Lottie), lab, h Grace
Deal Obe H (Minnie E), compositor Ashev Gazette-News, and musician, h 42 Cumberland av
Deal Oscar, clk, h Grace
Deal Ralph, lab, h Grace
Dean Chas H (Tembte), h 79 Central av
Dean Mary S Miss, h 79 Central av
Deaver Burgin, emp Sou Ry, bds 51 Penland
Deaver Ethel E Miss, h 23 Woodfin
DeBrew Henrietta Mrs, laund, h 13 Gray
DeBrew Jno (Eskew L), tanner, h nr Smith's Bridge, W Ashev
DeBruhl Geo W (Hattie), condr St Ry, h 181½ Asheland
DECKER WM F, pres Carolina Machinery Co, rms Asheville Club
Del Rosa Farm, Grace, Mrs M J Way propr
*Dellinger Chas, lab, h 63 Eagle
Dellinger Chas W, jeweler J E Carpenter, rms Y M C A
*DeLoach Moses (Mary L), janitor Trinity Episcopal Ch, h 118 Church
*DeLoach Wm, porter Jno A Guffey, h 118 Church
Dennis Geo C, h Woolsey
Dennis Lee E Miss, tchr Orange St Schl, h Woolsey
Dennison Jack, rms Y M C A
Denoon Mabel C Mrs, art goods 17 Haywood, h 8 Grady
Denton Jas F (Mollie), landscape gardener, h 5 Biltmore rd, S Biltmore
Denton Jas F Jr, painter, h 5 Biltmore rd, S Biltmore
Denton McKibben K (Minnie), ins, h 144 East
DEPLANCK MOTHER, in charge St Genevieve College, Victoria rd
Depot Drug Co (The), 400 Depot; Dr G D Gardner pres, Dr J G Anderson v-pres, S D Pelham sec-mngr
*Depot Pressing Club, 424 Depot, I W Kerns propr
Dermid Junius W (Coila R), condr, h 28 n Ann
Dermid S Eliza, wid M P, h 15 Clayton
*Derumpley Larkin (Eula), painter, h 28 Lincoln av
*Derumpley Lizzie, dom, h 33 Mountain
*Derumpley Prelow (Cora), lab, h 27 Hildebrand
*Deruncle Cora, cook Western Hotel, h 27 Hildebrand
De Vault Benj (Mattie), solr, h 14 Sassafras
De Vault Chas W (Laura), mnfr flavoring extracts 70 Patton av, h Chunn's Cove

Asheville Dray, Fuel and Construction Co.

Heavy Hauling of all kinds — WE FURNISH BUILDING STONE — Moving Furniture a Specialty

61-2 South Main PHONE - 223

DYNAMOS & MOTORS

Piedmont Electric Co.

64 Patton Av.
ASHEVILLE, N.C.

De Vault E Ray, clk Felmet Bros, h 361 w Haywood
De Vault Katherine M Miss, h 361 w Haywood
De Vault W Bertsie, chf call boy Sou Ry, h 361 w Haywood
De Vault Wm W (Kate), engnr Sou Ry, h 361 w Haywood
Devenish Alice G Miss, public stengr 8 Paragon Bldg, h 148 Charlotte
Devenish David G (Elizabeth), bkkpr, h 148 Charlotte
Devenish Mona Miss, bkkpr A M Field Co, h 148 Charlotte
Devenish Nora A Miss, h 148 Charlotte
Devine H P Furniture Co (H P Devine and C H Thompson), 315 w Haywood
Devine Hugh P (Mattie A), (H P Devine Furn Co), h 90 Jefferson Drive
De Vine Wm (Hattie), canvasser, h 26 Spring
*Devinie Robt (Laura), lab, h 118 Valley
Dew Drop Candy Parlor, 32 Patton av, Adair & Baker propr
Deweese Elizabeth, wid Wesley, h 557 n Main
Deweese Elizabeth, wid Humphrey M, h 46 Clyde
Deweese R Lee, clk msgr Sou Exp Co, bds 9 Louie
Dewey Chas, plmbr, h 18 Buncombe
Dewey Edwd C (Sarah), clk, h 18 Buncombe
Dewey Edwd C Jr, h 18 Buncombe
De Young Jno T (Fannie), slsmn Haskell's Pepsi-Cola Bot Wks, h 27 Crescent
Dial Ada, wid J H, h 334½ w Haywood
Dial J Ira, clk Dew Drop Candy Parlor, h 334½ w Haywood
Dial Robt, cashr Bon Marche
Diamond Annie Miss, clk Ashev Dry Gds Co, h 40 Merrimon av
Diamond Jennie, wid Simon, h 40 Merrimon av
Diamond Morris (Dora), clothing 14 Eagle, h 33 s Liberty
Diamond Rose Miss, clk Bon Marche, h 160 s Main
Diamond Sadie Miss, clk Bon Marche, h 160 s Main
*Dickerson Amos, lab, h 58 Poplar
Dickerson Arizona Miss, h 341 Hillside
Dickerson Geo W (Annie), driver Burton & Holt, h Woolsey
Dickerson Jas N, driver, h 341 Hillside
Dickerson Jos E (Frances B), sec-treas Asheville Lbr Co, h 81 Charlotte
*Dickerson Louetta, laund, h 58 Poplar
Dickerson Martha J, wid G W, h 341 Hillside
Dickerson Myrtle Miss, clk Peerless Dept Store, h 341 Hillside
Dickerson Stokley J, lab, h 341 Hillside

J. C. McPHERSON
SLATE AND TIN ROOFING
Galvanized Iron Work   Hot Air Furnaces
35-37 EAST COLLEGE STREET

PLUMBING STEAM AND HOT WATER HEATING
PHONE 133

Dickinson Clarence D (Ella), ship clk Armour & Co, h 245 s Grove
Dickinson Edgar C (Willie), propr Woolsey Greenhouse, h 16 Josephine
Dickinson Minnie Mrs, h Highland Hotel
*Dickson David, porter, h 133 Valley
*Dickson Hattie, h 47 Velvet
*Dickson Henry, porter, h 133 Valley
*Dickson Isaac (Delia), janitor Battery Park Bank, h 133 Valley
*Dickson Jas Bryant, porter, h 133 Valley
*Dickson Letitia, dom, h 121 Wallach
Dickson Matilda Mrs, h 45 Roberts
*Dickson Silas (Leo), porter, h 12 Dundee
DICKSON W SAML, asst city editor Ashev Gazette News, h Haywood nr Flint
☞ Dickson see also Dixon
Diggs Alex P, student, h 644 s Main
Digges Atwood, clk, h Biltmore Rd
Diggs Daniel C, student, h 644 s Main
Digges Geo A (Annie), agt Sou Ry Biltmore Station, h 644 s Main
Digges Geo A Jr, clk Sou Ry Biltmore Sta, h 644 s Main
Digges M Estelle Miss, student, h 644 s Main
Diggs A Leigh, stengr Temple Ct, rms Y M C A
DILL HARRY M (Catherine), physical director Y M C A, bds 94 College
Dill Jno A (Eliza), driver, h (r) 269 s Main
Dill Jno E, collr Jno C Moore, h 269 s Main
Dillard J P, emp U S Furn Factory, h 6 Brook, Biltmore
*Dillard Matilda, laund, h 43 Circle
Dillingham D C, clk Langren Hotel Grill Room, rms 55 Penland
*Dillingham Della, dom, bds 433 Depot
Dillingham E Carl (Jessie), mngr Union Dairy Lunch, h 18 Fulton
Dillingham Grace E Mrs, boarding 55 Penland, h same
Dillingham H G, clk Langren Hotel
Dillingham H Tildon (Grace), overseer, h 55 Penland
Dillingham Lizzie Miss, 156 Hillside
Dillon Albert S, driver, h Woolsey
Dillon Carmi F (Fannie), driver, h Woolsey
Dillon Cora Miss, h 165½ s Main
Dillon Jeremiah, printer The Gazette, h 165½ s Main
Dillon Jno W (Mollie), carp, h 165½ s Main

Candy Kitchen and Club Cafe
"A GOOD PLACE FOR REFRESHMENT"

Hot drinks on cold days. Cold drinks on hot days. The best drinks every day. Pure fruits and syrups blended "just right," served daintily. Our Ice Cream and Soda Water Department, Restaurant and Candy Departments are always kept up to the standard of nearest perfection. Phones 110 and 111. 19 and 21 Haywood St.

Brown's Undertaking Parlors

S. H. BROWN

50 Patton Avenue
ASHEVILLE, N. C.

Lady Assistant When Desired

Phone 193-2 Rings

THE MOORE Plumbing Company

16 N. Pack Square

PHONE 1025

Sanitary Plumbing, General Tin and Metal Work, Hot Air Furnaces

---

150   ASHEVILLE [1913] DIRECTORY

Dillon Mae Miss, h Woolsey
Dills Claude M (Dovie C), trav slsmn, h 47 Panola
Dilworth Sarah J, wid Jas C, h 149 s French Broad av
*Dinkins Belle, cook Crescent Lunch Room, h 147 Valley
Dinkins Lucille, h 69 Bartlett
DIRECTORY LIBRARY (directories of over 100 cities for free use of all directory patrons), 66 Amer Natl Bank Bldg
DIRECTORY OF ASHEVILLE, office 66 & L Amer Natl Bank Bldg, E H Miller mngr
Divelbiss Jos E (May), engnr Sou Ry, h 97 Blanton
Dixie (The), boarding, 15 n Spruce, Mrs Bessie Hatchell propr
DIXIE MUTUAL LIFE INSURANCE CO, of Asheville N C, 408-414 Legal Bldg; J S Bradley pres, Chas H E Moran v-pres-genl mngr, F M Vaughan sec, G B Bradley treas
*Dixon Jno, clk Shade's Pharmacy, h Poplar st
Dixon Luke, trav solr Ashev Gazette-News, h Charlotte extd
Dixon Norman A (Vallie), ship clk Dr T C Smith, h 40 Woodfin
Dixon R E Prof, tchr The Asheville Schl, rms same
☞Dixon see also Dickson
*Dizer Geo (Lula), butler, h 47 Circle
*DOBBINS JAMES (Stella), hackman 56-64 Valley, h same
*Dobbins Jno (Maggie), lab, h 117 Black
*Dobbins Jos F, porter, rms 22 Eagle
*Dobbins Rachel, laund, h 117 Black
Dobson Lula R Miss, nurse 84 s French Broad av, rms same
Dockery Cyrus, student, h Grace
Dockery Elbert J (Maggie), lab, h Grace
Dockery J Edwd (Mary), dairyman Brown's Creamery, h Grace
Dockery Pearl Miss, h Grace
Dockery Thos L (Julia), plstr, h 312 n Main
DODD ERNEST W (Mary C), optometrist C H Honess, h 5 Angle, Biltmore
*Dodd Jos P (Gena), driver, h 48 Ridge
Dodd Thos L (Mary A), meat and vegetables, 4 Plaza, Biltmore, h 5 Angle, same
*Dodson Earl J, barber W T Conley, h 167 e College
Dodson Kriemhild Miss, tchr North State Fitting School, h 157 Church

---

The Battery Park Bank

Capital - - $100,000.00
Surplus and Profits, $110,000.00

ASHEVILLE, N. C.   **City, County and State Depositary**

J. A. TILLMAN — Jeweler — 17 N. Main St. I carry a nice line of Watches, Clocks and Jewelry, and make a specialty of repair work. Satisfaction guaranteed

"Dogwood Cottage," Albemarle Park
DOLE ALSIE B MISS, supt Allen Industrial Home and Asheville Academy, h 241 College (see p 23)
Donald J Clinton, genl supt Ashev P & L Co, rms 16 Medical Bldg
Donald J McDowell (Leila), (Donald & Donald), h 202 s French Broad av
Donald Sidney G (Donald & Donald), h 202 s French Broad
Donald & Donald (J M and S G), furniture, 14 s Main
Donaver Wm, bricklyr, bds 98 Patton av
Donnan Frank W (Mary O), mchst, h 6 Battery Park pl
DONNAN GEO W (Mary), mngr Ashev Supply & Fdy Co, h 157 Asheland av
Donnan Georgia M Miss, student, h 157 Asheland av
Donnan Mary O Mrs, dressmkr, 6 Battery Park pl, h same
Donnahoe Claude E, soda clk C A Raysor, h 206 Merrimon
DONNAHOE OLLIE N (Reliable Cleaning & Pressing Club), h 206 Merrimon av
Donnahoe Prince A (Kate), (Donnahoe & Bledsoe), h 206 Merrimon av
Donnahoe Roy B, student, h 206 Merrimon av
Donnahoe & Bledsoe), real est, s Pack Sq cor Main
Donnell Wm H, genl sales mngr Wm S Whiting, h 170 Montford av
Dorland Harry P (Nettie), helper, h Haywood rd, W Ashev
Dorn Ellen Miss, housekpr Battery Park Hotel, rms same
*Doster Henry (Mary A), gro 104 Pine, h same
Dougherty Gordon W (Ruby D), money clk Sou Exp Co, h W Asheville
Dougherty Jos M (Annie), engnr Sou Ry, h 163 Park av
Dougherty Katharine E Miss, propr Hillside, Edgewood and Ville Roye Cottages, h Sunset Drive
Douglas Cicero, fireman, bds 444 Depot
Douglas Geo J (Adelaide), solr F M Messler, h 79½ Washington rd
*Douglas Jno, lab, bds 39 Pearl
*Douglas Jno, lab, h (r) 39 Clingman av
*Dover Rebecca, laund, h 62 Ralph
*Dowden Bettie, dom, h 147 Southside av
Dowell Ernest G, plmbr, h 77 Victoria av
*Downes Rachel, dom, h 34 Magnolia av
Downing Melvin (Ara E), clk H T Rogers, h 83 Elizabeth
*Downs Jno W (Susie), gardener, h 35 Curve
Dowtin Robt G (Agnes), gro, h 8 Summit, S Biltmore
Doyle Anna B Mrs, h Sunnybank, Oakland av nr Victoria rd

INSURANCE
Insure your salary with us
Never carry your own risk
Safety is the best policy
Unless you are a capitalist
Rest easy if you have
An accident we will
Not keep you waiting to
Collect your claim
Every claim promptly paid

Imperial Mutual Life & Health Insurance Co.

Home Office:
ASHEVILLE, N. C.
Phone 495

HOTEL OXFORD — Asheville, N. C. Redecorated and Refitted throughout. Recently enlarged to 60 rooms. Centrally located. Depot cars stop at entrance. Long distance telephone office upstairs. American and European plan. Rates 50c, 75c and $1 per day; special rates by week or month. C. H. Branson & Sons, Proprietors. Phone 1887. 50-54 South Main St.

Williams-Brownell Planing Mill Company — *Hardwoods*
Lumber---Rough and Dressed   Flooring a Specialty   Moulding, Interior Finish, Etc.
Office, Plant and Yards on Southern Railway, Near Biltmore Station
WHITE PINE   Phone 729   YELLOW PINE

Dozier Ruth Miss, clk Langren Hotel
Drake Arlena T Mrs, h W Asheville (R F D 3)
Drake Jack F, mngr meter dept Ashev Power & Light Co, h W Asheville
Drake Jno R (Hannah), condr St Ry, h 319 n Main
Drake Wm H (Mildred), carp, h 30 Philip
Dreamland (The), moving pictures, 81 Patton av, Adolf Kohn mngr
Drennan Fay Miss, stengr, bds 127 Haywood
Drhumor Building (offices), 48-50 Patton av
Driver Harry L (Pauline C), h 93 Starnes av
Drummond Cameron Miss, h 71 Magnolia av
Drummond Cora L Miss, h 71 Magnolia av
Drummond Grover C (Willie), fireman Sou Ry, h 118 s French Broad av
DRY CLEANING CO, THE ASHEVILLE, n e cor Main & College sts—phones 835 and 836, E S Paine propr (see bottom lines)
Duck Danl J (Ida), fruit shipper, h 65 Penland
Ducker Jeanette Miss, cook, h Haywood rd, W Ashev
Ducker Zack T, gro and restaur 16-18 w College, h Biltmore
Duckett Alonzo L (Gertrude), foreman linemen Ashev P & L Co, h 163 Patton av
Duckett Audry M Miss, h Hazel Mill rd, W Ashev
Duckett Bertha Miss, h Hazel Mill rd, W Ashev
*Duckett Collier, lab, h 39 Max
Duckett Cora L Miss, h Haywood rd, W Ashev
Duckett Emma A, wid H B, h 303 s Main
Duckett Ernest, delivery clk, The Cash Grocery, h W Asheville
Duckett Furman F (Florence), plstr, h Allen st, W Ashev
Duckett H Walter (Mary), police, h Haywood rd, W Ashev
Duckett Herbert (Johnnie), miller, bds 173 s Main
Duckett Jno W (Maggie), contr Hazel Mill rd, W Ashev, h same
Duckett Martha E, wid Thos, h 88 s French Broad av
Duckett R F, clk W U Tel Co, h W Asheville
Duckett Rex B, student, h 303 s Main
Duckett Robt L (M Elizabeth), carp, h Allen st, W Ashev
Duckett T C, rms 29 Meriwether Bldg
DUCKETT THOS M, county treas, office Court House and sec-treas Ashev Baseball Club, h 88 s French Broad av
Duckett Walter H, watchman Riverside Park Ashev P & L Co, h W Asheville
*Duffy Walter (Mollie), lab, h Beaumont nr College

Asheville Electrical Co. Electrical Contractors
HEADQUARTERS 74 CENTRAL AVENUE
W. Mansfield Booze, Manager
PHONE 377

Asheville Dry Cleaning Co.
Telephones 835-836, All Dep't
MAIN, N. E. COR. COLLEGE

THE CLEANERS
Our Department for Oriental Rugs and Carpet Cleaning is prepared to serve you in all its branches.
E. S. Paine   O. E. Hansen

Dufour Elise R, wid A J, h 120 Charlotte
Dufour Rhett R, timekpr Sou Ry, h 120 Charlotte
Dugan Jno S (Ida), boarding 434 Depot, h same
Dukes A F, printer H T Rogers, bds 102 Patton av
Dukes Elizabeth J, wid Charlton, h 14 Pearson Drive
Dukes Mary L Miss, h 14 Pearson Drive
Dukes Susan C Miss, tchr Montford av Schl, h 14 Pearson Drive
*Dukes Warren (Sallie), lab, h 64 Ralph
*Dunbar Saml, janitor Legal Bldg, h 6 Sassafras
Duncan Anderson F (Jennie), steam ftr Rhinehardt Bros, h Woolsey
Duncan Beccalie Miss, h 67 Josephine
Duncan Cora L Miss, cashr The Racket Store, h 392 n Main
Duncan Dora Miss, h Morsell Bldg
Duncan Elizabeth Mrs, laund, h 5 Madison
*Duncan Fred (Martha), janitor, h 10 Aston pl
Duncan Jos, h Woolsey (R F D 1)
Duncan Lettie Miss, h 15 William
Duncan Nathaniel, h 15 William
Duncan Vera Miss, h Woolsey (R F D 1)
Duncan Waitie Miss, clk Ashev Dry Gds Co, bds 67 Josephine
Duncan —— Mrs, h Morsell Bldg
DUNCAN WM F (Josephine), teller Citizens Bank, h 246 Montford av
DUNHAM HARRY A (Ella H), propr Dunham's Music House, h 224 Patton av
Dunham Maude O Miss, clk Dunham's Music House, h 224 Patton av
DUNHAM'S MUSIC HOUSE, musical mdse, 14 n Pack Sq H A Dunham propr
*Dunlap Jno, brkmn, h 64 Ralph
Dunn ——, h 57 Summit, S Biltmore
Dunn Albert C, bkkpr Mt City Ldy, h 37 Arlington
Dunn Chas W (Josephine), trav slsmn, h 37 Arlington
Dunn Edwd E (Elizabeth G), embalmer Red Cross Undertaking Co, h 37 Arlington
Dunn Eliza C Mrs, h 84 Penland
Dunn Elsie C, wid Alfred (The London Shop), Legal Bldg
Dunn J C, supt Ashev Elec Co, power plant
Dunn Jno W (Elizabeth), broker, rms 75 Church
Dunn Lee, bds 26 Logan
Dunn Louella F Miss, stengr, h 84 Penland
Dunn May E Miss, bkkpr, h 37 Arlington

LIFE INSURANCE COMPANY OF VA.
ORGANIZED 187
Richmond -:- Virginia
J. V MOON, Superintendent
Rooms 3-4-5- Maxwelton Bldg., Asheville, N. C.

All claims paid IMMEDIATELY upon receipt of satisfactory proofs of Death. Total payment to policyholders since organization, over $12,000,000.00. Is paying its Policyholders over $1,000,000.00 annually.

T. P. JOHNSON & CO.

SHEET METAL WORKERS

All Kinds of Roofing Guttering and Conductor Work Metal Ceilings, Skylights and Galvanized Iron Cornices

OFFICE and SHOP:
69-71 S. MAIN

Phone 325

DR. C. H. MILLER

Mechano-Therapist

14 N. Spruce Street
ASHEVILLE, N. C.

PHONE 979

Hours by Engagement

DRUGLESS HEALING OF DISEASE

---

154 ASHEVILLE [1913] DIRECTORY

Dunn Thos A (Aldeba), h "Bungalow," Hillside cor Summit
DUNN WM L (Myrtle), physician Medical Bldg, Battery Park pl—phone 818, office hours 11 a m to 12:30 p m and 3 to 4 p m, h "Bungalow," Hillside cor Summit—phone 773
DU REN KATE L, wid J W, propr Magnolia Cottage, 72 e College, h same
Durham Benj J (Fannie), dentist 10-11 Medical Bldg, h Woolsey (R F D 1)
Durham Beulah T Miss, artist H W Pelton, bds 100 Asheland av
*Durham Elmer (Nora), porter, h 24 Curve
*Durham Jane, h 119 Valley
Durow Estella Mrs, clk Peerless Dept Store, h 27 Highland
Durow Wm E (Estella), h 27 Highland
*Dusenbury Chas B Rev (Lula B), pastor Calvary Presbyterian Church, h 71 Eagle
*Dusenbury Chas Jr, h 71 Eagle
*Dusenbury Viola, h 71 Eagle
Dustin Mary Miss, h 162 w Chestnut
DUVALL C LE ROY (Helen), adv mngr The Ashev Citien, h 54 Highland
Dwelle Edwd C (Fay Ross), h 230 Montford av
Dye Dollie Mrs, h 7½ s Main

E

Eagan Jno S, foreman Ashev Citizen, bds 42 Walnut
*Eagle Street Pressing Club, 28 Eagle, Mrs W P Brooks mngr
Eagles' Hall, 33½ s Main
Eames Anna L Miss, bds 68 e College
Earle Addie C Miss, bkkpr Ashev Grain & Hay Co, h 139 Montford av
Earle J Daniel (Bessie J), (Asheville Grain & Hay Co), h W Asheville (R F D 3)
*Earle Jos (Mollie), lab, h 52 Max
*Earle Martha, laund, h 41 Catholic av
*Earle Nancy, dom, h 139 Poplar
*Earle Zillie, laundress, h 83 Valley
EARLE & NELSON (J D Earle, J D Nelson), proprs Asheville Grain & Hay Co, Roberts cor Depot
Early Dora D, wid Wm, h 7½ s Main

ASHEVILLE CLEANING and PRESSING CLUB

TAILORING THAT SATISFIES and PRICES THAT PLEASE

Hats cleaned, banded and bound. Silk hats ironed. Buttons made to order in all sizes. Plain or with rims. PHONE 389

DYEING IN ALL SHADES Cleaned. Messenger Service.

Kid Gloves, Slippers and Plumes, Fancy Jabots and Ties, French Dry Cleaned. Ladies' and Gentlemen's suits Steam

J. C. Wilbar, Prop. 4 NORTH PACK SQ.

Early Sion T (Hattie L), pres Southside Furniture Co, h 11 John
Earwood Chester, painter Excelsior P & P House, h Woolsey
Earwood W Riley (Susan), farmer, h nr Haywood rd, W Ashev
Easley Jno H (Hattie), pipe ftr, h 283 College
*East Mamie, laund, h 121 Black
EASTMEAD GEO E, asst sec-treas Hans Rees Sons (Inc)
Eaton Cecil L, student, h 80 Ora
Eaton Geo E, engnr, h 26 Pearl
*Eaton Jas (Fannie), lab, h 326 Asheland av
Eaton Jno H (Elizabeth), plstr, h 26 Pearl
Eaton Maude Miss, h 26 Pearl
Eaton Ronald G, bkkpr, h 80 Ora
Eaton Saml C (Julia), lumber inspr, h 80 Ora
Eaton Troy, laundryman, h 26 Pearl
Eaves Paul, trav slsmn, rms 25 Technical Bldg
Ebbs Jno A (Emma), car inspr, h Allen st, W Ashev
Eberman Edwin (Annie), mngr Citizens Lumber Co, h Woolsey
Echerd E Ralph, clk, h 43 s French Broad av
Echols Paul C, switchman, bds 655 Oakland av
Eckel Oscar F, phys 17 Church, rms 23 McAfee Bldg
*Eddings C Arthur (Emma), lab, h nr Hazel Mill rd, W Ashev
*Edgerton Bessie, cook, h 24 Ralph
*Edgerton Fannie, h 20 Cumberland av
*Edgerton Julia, laund, h 13 Haid
*Edgerton Mack, bellmn, h 21 Haid
"Edgewood Cottage," Sunset Drive, Miss K E Doughty, propr
Edmonds Deliah, wid Andrew, h 431 w Haywood
Edney Georgie A Miss, housekpr A C Mc Bee, W Ashev
Edson J W Mrs, clk M V Moore & Co, h 371 w Haywood
Edwards Bowley, carp, rms 1 Barnard Bldg
Edwards Chas, lab, h 557 n Main
*Edwards Eliza, h 27 Scott
Edwards Eugene (Pearl), carp, h 247 s Grove
Edwards Eva L, wid Jas N, h Hazel Mill rd, W Ashev
Edwards Frank O (Bessie), clk Felmet Bros, h 44 Magnolia
Edwards Gwynn (Annie M), real estate 11 Temple Ct, h Jarrett av, W Ashev
Edwards J Flavius (Lelia), driver, h Haywood rd, W Ashev
Edwards J Horace (Gertrude), driver, h Main st, W Ashev

Edwards Jno A (Carrie), mchst, h 327 Southside av
Edwards Laura, wid L G, h 557 n Main
Edwards Lillie Miss, h 361 n Main
Edwards Lucius E (Janie), slsmn H Redwood & Co, h 361 n Main
Edwards Luther D, trav slsmn Ashev Gro Co, h Mars Hill
Edwards Mallie Miss, h 557 n Main
Edwards Olive Miss, dom, h 557 n Main
Edwards Oscar, barber, h 19 Buxton
Edwards Robt B (Rosa), tchr West Ashev School, h W Ashev (R F D 3)
Edwards Susan Miss, h 19 Buxton
Edwards T Vernon, barber R L Crook, h 19 Buxton
Edwards Wm, driver, h Hazel Mill rd, W Ashev
Edwards Wm S (Dora A), trav slsmn, h 385 w Haywood
Efird Wm A (Jennie), train mstr Sou Ry, h 163 Blanton
Egerton Jas A (Annie), bkkpr Slayden, Fakes & Co, Inc, h 108 Central av
☛Egerton see also Edgerton
Egerton Laura F Miss, student, h 108 Central av
*Eidson Douglas (Mary), watchman, h 118 Livingston
Eidson J Wm (Helen), dep tax collr, rms 371 w Haywood
EK AUGUSTUS W, sec Imperial L & H Ins Co (Inc), res Wilmington N C
*Elbert Elvira, dom, h 12 Aston pl
Eldridge Emery, h 327 Montford av
Electrical Building, offices 64 Patton av
ELIAS BERNARD (Elias & Hopson) rms 18 Medical Bldg
Elias Donald S, treas Virginia-Carolina Coal Co and Fork Ridge Coal Co, rms 18 Medical Bldg
ELIAS LEWIS W (Frances), physician 19-20 Morsell Bldg office hours 12 a m to 1:30 p m and by appointment—phone 985, h 5 All Souls Crescent, Biltmore—phone 1327
ELIAS & HOPSON (Bernard Elias, J S Hopson), merchant tailoring and custom shirts, 68 Patton av—phone 393
Elkins Chas Y Jr, lab, h Hazel Mill rd, W Ashev
Elkins Fannie B Mrs, h Hazel Mill rd, W Ashev
Elkins Harrison J (Burgin), lab, h Hazel Mill rd, W Ashev
Elkins Harvey, lab Woolsey Greenhouse, h Grace
Elkins Herbert E, mch opr Princess Theatre, h nr Murphy Jct, W Asheville
Elkins Jno (Augusta), lab, h nr Hazel Mill rd, W Ashev
Elkins L D Mrs, asst matron Childrens Home, h Grace

Elkins Mark C (Mollie), clk H J Olive, h 441 w Haywood
Elkins Robt N (M Elizabeth), carp, h Hazel Mill rd, W Ashev
Elkins Susanna, wid Chas Y, h Hazel Mill rd, W Ashev
Elkins U Eugene (Stella), coach clnr, h Haywood rd, W Ashev
Elkins Wm C (Finettie), blksmith, h nr Murphy Junct, W Ashev
ELKS CLUB, 53 Haywood, W Marsteller exalted ruler
ELKS HOME CO; F R Hewitt pres, F W Thomas sec, office of sec 33 Amer Natl Bank Bldg
Ellege Andrew J (Cordie), emp Tannery, h Broadway av, W Ashev
Ellege Garfield C (Carrie), emp Tannery, h Haywood rd
Ellege Jno W (Lillie), loom fxr, h 61 Park Sq
Ellege Nellie, wid J W, h 16 Green
Ellenburg Henry (Lillie), lab, h Lester rd, W Ashev
Ellenburg Jerome T (Maggie), emp W M Jones, h Lester rd, W Ashev
Eller Benj L (Katharine), mail contr P O, h 181 Asheland
Eller Eugene E (May), carp, h 67 Josephine
Eller J Frank, driver B L Eller, h 181 Asheland av
Eller Jos P, driver B L Eller, h 181 Asheland av
Eller M Pearl Miss, h 181 Asheland av
Eller Nannie, wid Jno C, h Asheville av, W Asheville
Eller Thos N (Florence), mchst, h 362 w Haywood
Eller Y Delcie, wid J A, h 87 Broad
Ellington Augusta Mrs, h 17 Coleman
ELLIOTT CHAS J (Lillian), mngr Underwood Typewriter Co, h 288 Charlotte
Elliott Matilda D, wid J W, h 44 Atkin
Elliott W Avery (Addie), trav slsmn, h 31 Pearl
Ellis Robt L (Nancy), pres Coca-Cola Bottling Co, rms 111 s Main
Ellis Thos Mrs, bds 327 Montford av
Ellison J E, helper Ashe Supply & Fdy Co
Elm (The), boarding, 42 Walnut, Mrs P J Johnson propr
Elmore Ada G Miss, clk Ashev Steam Bakery, h 1 Buxton
Elmore Ernest (Kate), driver, h Haywood rd, W Asheville
Elmore Geo E (Fannie B), driver, h Haywood rd, W Ashe
Elmore Jno M (Louisa), clk Burton & Holt, h 1 Buxton
*Elrod Thos M (Mattie L), prin West Ashe Schl, h 85 Circle
Else Clarence, clk Highland Hotel, rms same
ELSE EMMA, wid Henry, propr Highland Hotel, h 368 Depot

Candy Kitchen and Club Cafe
"A GOOD PLACE FOR REFRESHMENT"

The very best ingredients with sanitary conditions in our Candy Manufacturing Department make possible the dainty, crisp confections sold here.

Bon Bons and Chocolates made every day, put up in neat, attractive boxes. Phones 110 and 111. 19 and 21 Haywood St.

---

158 ASHEVILLE [1913] DIRECTORY

Brown's Undertaking Parlors	
S. H. BROWN	
Lady Assistant When Desired	
Phone 193-2 Rings	
50 Patton Avenue Asheville, N. C.	

Else Frankie Miss, h Highland Hotel
ELTON (THE) BOARDING, 45 n Spruce—phone 958, Mrs S N Watkins propr (see p 16)
Elwell Selia M Mrs, mlnr H B Hood, h Woolsey
Elwood (The), boarding, 119 Haywood, Mrs Mary Morrison propr
Ely Marion E Miss, h 146 Hillside
Emanuel Evangelical Lutheran Church, French Broad cor Philip, Rev C H Bernhard pastor
EMANUEL SADIE MISS (Emanuel School of Short Hand) and public stenographer 16 Drhumor Bldg, h 132 w Chestnut
EMANUEL SCHOOL OF STENOGRAPHY AND TYPEWRITING, 16 Drhumor Bldg, Miss Sadie Emanuel prin

---

Stenography   Typewriting

Emanuel School of Shorthand

OFFICE: No. 16 Drhumor Building

Phone 1100   48-50 Patton Ave.

Embler Connie, driver McConnell Bros, h 352 w Haywood
Embler Henry C, clk W A Davis, h Woolsey
Embler Jos M (Harriet), lineman Ashe P & L Co, h 356 w Haywood
Embler T Grover, lineman Ashe P & L Co, h 356 w Haywood
☞Embler see also Ambler
Emery Noah, lab, h W Asheville
Emery Thos (Annie), lab, h Haywood rd, W Asheville
Emler Pearn J, lineman Ashe P & L Co, rms 18 Asheland av
Emmons Lewis, jeweler A M Field Co, h Western Hotel
Emmons Loren E, rms 12 Technical Bldg
Enderlaine Alfonso, boiler mkr, bds 102 Ralph
*England Edwd (Lizzie), lab, h 9 Mountain
☞Engle see Ingle
English Alma Miss, h "Reedcrest", Biltmore
English Edwin B, h "Reedcrest", Biltmore

Established 1894

B. J. JACKSON

Carefully Selected Fruits and Vegetables

Stall No. 11, City Market

BUSINESS PHONES: 86 and 101

RESIDENCE PHONE 1596

Yᵉ OLD BOOK SHOP

114 Patton Ave.   Phone 1674

BOOKS BOUGHT, SOLD OR EXCHANGED

English Effie Mrs, h Haywood rd, W Asheville
*English Horace, lab, rms Louie nr Depot
ENGLISH ISAAC McCALL (Annie M), v-pres and sec English Lbr Co, h 37 Orchard
English J M & Co (J M English), lumber 16-17 Temple Ct
ENGLISH JAS M (Blanche B) (J M English Lbr Co), and pres Citizens Lumber Co, h 206 Chestnut
ENGLISH JNO LUCIUS (Cora), pres and genl mngr English Lbr Co, h "Reedcrest", Biltmore—phone 528
English Laurie Miss, h "Reedcrest", Biltmore
ENGLISH LUMBER CO (Inc), wholesale dealers and mnfrs of lumber, Avery and Sou Ry—phone 321, J L English pres and genl mngr, J Mc English v-pres and sec (see top lines)
English Roy R, h "Reedcrest", Biltmore
Enloe Andrew C (Frances), engnr Sou Ry, h 244 s French Broad av
Enloe Arthur L, engnr, bds 29 Jefferson Drive
Enloe Benj F, fireman, bds 29 Jefferson Drive
Ennes Gertrude A Miss, tchr High School, h 5 Flint
Ennes Howard W, student, h 5 Flint
Ennes U Retta R, wid I R, propr The Uleeta, h 5 Flint
Enoch Jas L (Jennie), plmbr, h 56 Josephine
Ensley Edwd E (Fannie), clk, bds 87 Ora
ENTERPRISE MACHINE CO (J E and J B Rumbough), automobiles, metal working and electrical power machinery and scientific instruments a specialty, 67-69-71 n Main (see line back cover and p 14)
Ensley R Arthur (Lillie), lab, h 24 Nelson av
Enthoffer Edwd J (Edith), h 50 Vance
Enthoffer Elizabeth Miss, h 50 Vance
Epley Jno N (Daisy L), fireman, h 17 John
Epley Mary M, wid Chas R, h Arlington st, W Asheville
Epps Annette L Miss, h 102 n Holland
*Epps G W, elev opr The Langren, h 194 s Main
EPPS GILBERT W, sec Ashe & East Tenn R R Co and sec Weaverville Elec Co, office 7 n Main, h 102 n Holland
EQUITABLE LIFE INSURANCE CO OF N Y, 26 Amer Natl Bank Bldg, F M Messler agt
*Erby Amos, tanner, h 150 Livingston
Ericsson Eric (Christine), supt U S Furn Co, h 1 All Souls Crescent, Biltmore
Ericsson Ione E Miss, student, h 1 All Souls Crescent, Biltmore

Mrs. Wilder's SANITARY HOME LAUNDRY turns out first class work in Laundering and Dry Cleaning. No. 7 Montford Ave., Phone 1354

ERSKINE MICHAEL A (Irene), dist coml mngr Ashev Tel & Tel Co, h 62 Courtland av
*Erwin Addie, laund, h 84 Black
*Erwin Leila, clk S W Walker, h 33 Mountain
*Erwin Addie, cook, h 76 Gudger
ERWIN ANN T MISS, asst librarian Pack Memorial Library, h 174 w Chestnut
Erwin Ella, wid J B, h 174 w Chestnut
Erwin Jno A, flgmn, bds 87 Ora
ERWIN J BUELOW, city treas, office 100 City Hall, h 174 w Chestnut
*Erwin Maggie, dom, h 15 Hildebrand
Erwin Marcus (Susie H), clk Superior Court, office Court House, h 101 Furman av
Erwin Mollie Miss, h 174 w Chestnut
Erwin Nannie Miss, h 174 w Chestnut
*Erwin Robt, lab, h 15 Hildebrand
Erwin Robt C (Paralee), condr Sou Ry, h 41 Montford av
*Erwin Virgil (Rachel), lab, h 15 Hildebrand
Erwood Alice Mrs, h 38 East
Eshbaugh Newton T, mchst O K Auto Supply & Transit Co, bds Marquette Hotel
Esley Jno, lab, city water dept
Esmery Marie Mrs, tchr, bds 29 Cumberland
Essig Norman (Mercy), dentist, h 21 n Liberty
Estes Ollie N A, wid Jno L J, h Haywood rd, W Asheville
Estes P Richard (Margaret), condr Sou Ry, h 17 Ora
Estes Poindexter D, pool 316½ Depot, h 17 Orr
Eubanks Susan, wid Jas M, h Leicester rd, W Ashev
Eureka (The), boarding 153 n Main, Miss Sarah L Shoup propr
European Hotel, 118½ Depot, J A White propr
*Evans Arthur B (Masaline), porter Ashev Club, h 20 Hill
Evans Chas A (L Jane), lab, h 38 Spring
Evans Dorcas, wid Chas A, h Jarrett av, W Ashev
*Evans Edwd (Amanda), driver, h 226 Beaumont
EVANS EDWD J (Kate), dentist 3 s w Pack Sq, h 126 Broad
Evans Eva Mrs, bkkpr Yates & McGuire, h Woolsey
Evans Geo (Georgiana), mtrmn, h 26 Morgan av
Evans Geo E, ship clk The Piedmont Electric Co, h Woolsey
*Evans Hannabel, cook N Murrough, h 45 Pine
Evans Henry H (Mary), condr Pigeon Ry, rms 31 Grove
Evans Hester Miss, nurse 21 Jefferson Drive, h same

BUICK MAXWELLS OLDSMOBILE DETROIT ELECTRIC
ARBOGAST MOTOR COMPANY
ACCESSORIES AND SUPPLIES
52-60 N. Main
Phones 302 and 1728

Asheville Dry Cleaning Co.
Telephones 835-836, All Dep't
MAIN, N. E. COR. COLLEGE

THE CLEANERS
Our Department for Oriental Rugs and Carpet Cleaning is prepared to serve you in all its branches.
E. S. Paine   O. E. Hansen

Evans J Pinckney (Lubergia), driver, h 8 North
Evans Jas (Callie), bricklyr, h 415 w Haywood
Evans Jno(plstr, h 449 n Main
Evans L Miss, h 105 College
Evans Lonnie E (Sidney), driver, h 146 Hall
Evans P P (Ella), agt Met Life Ins Co, h 406 Montford av
Evans Saml, appr G L Guischard, h 415 w Haywood
Evans Solomon, supt Standard Oil Co, rms 19 Medical Bldg
*Evans Solomon G (Ella), driver, h 45 Pine
Eve A Emerson, stengr Superior Court, h Bingham rd
Eve Bessie Miss, h Bingham rd
Eve Chas W (Kate E), h Bingham Hghts
Eve Paul R, asst mngr Mustin-Robertson Co, Inc, h Bingham Heights
EVENING NEWS PUBLISHING CO, publrs Asheville Gazette News, 4 n Pack Sq; W A Hildebrand pres, J R Law sec-treas
Everett Jas (Myrtle), lab, h 100 Cherry
Everhart Nelson (Alice), bkkpr Burton & Holt, h Chunn's Cove
*Eves Carrie, cook, h 48 Pine
*Eves Chas, emp Greenlee & Loder, h 139 Wallach
Evers Mattie Miss, nurse Winyah Sanatorium, rms same
Ewell Jno L, h 22 Orange
Excelsior Paint & Paper House (The), 34 n Main; F M Johnson propr, Chas M Johnson mngr

F

Fagan Max (Rebecca), gro 36 Mountain, h 474 s French Broad av
*Faggart Mary, laundress, h 78 Wallach
Fain Nathaniel W (Myra), carrier P O, h 73 Montford av
Fair Anna Mae Miss, h 23 Catawba
*Fair Cora L, laund, h 32 Grail
Fair Jas R (Kate), stone mason, h 23 Catawba
*Fair Jessie, dom, h 32 Grail
Fair Jos O (Mattie), painter, h 35 Catawba
*Fair Josephine, laund, h 32 Grail
Fairchild Geo W (Eunice), gro Haywood rd, W Ashev, h Van st, W Ashev
Fairchild Robt, lab, bds 135 n Main
Fairchild Roy D, mchst, h Van st, W Ashev
Fairchild Ruth Miss, h Van st, W Ashev
Fairfield Rose Miss, tchr, bds 346½ Depot

The Life Insurance Co. of Virginia
ORGANIZED 1871   RICHMOND, VA.

ISSUES ALL THE MOST APPROVED FORMS OF LIFE INSURANCE CONTRACTS from $500.00 to $25,000.00, with premiums payable quarterly, semi-annually and annually

J. V. Moon, Superintendent, Rooms 3-4-5 Maxwelton Bldg., Asheville, N. C.

D. TREXLER TIN SHOP

All Kinds of Roofing, Gutter and Conductor Work.

Phone 862

159 South Main St.

DR. C. H. MILLER

MECHANO-THERAPIST

14 N. Spruce St.
Phone 979
ASHEVILLE, N. C.

Hours by engagement

Drugless Healing of Disease

FAITH COTTAGE RESCUE HOME, 53 Atkinson; Rev L B Compton supt, Miss Janet MacGregor matron
"Fairview Cottage," Sunset Drive, Miss K E Doughty propr
Fakes Betheaniel R (Martha A), v-pres-treas Slayden, Fakes & Co, Inc, h 174 Montford av
FALK CASIMER PROF, propr Falk's Music House, h 45 Blanton
Falk Louisa Miss, h 45 Blanton
FALK'S MUSIC HOUSE, pianos and organs, 21 s Main—phone 206, Prof Casimer Falk propr
*Falls Lulu, laund, h 52 Short
Fanning E Homer (Ina F), clk Ry M S, h 43 s French Broad av
Fanning Francis J, civ engnr, 106 Citizens Bldg
Fanning Frank A (Harriet S), trav slsmn, rms Adelaide Bldg
Fanning Grace W Miss, 1st v-pres M Webb Co, Ashev Club Bldg
Fanning Leslie (Katherine), contr, h 32 Panola
Farlow Flora Miss, h 484 w Haywood
Farlow Harley (Ennice), helper, h 488 w Haywood
Farlow Lathan A (Pattie), mill wkr, h 484 w Haywood
Farlow Oscar W, driver Ashev Ice Co, h 484 w Haywood
Farm School (for boys), Swannanoa N C
Farman Ida Miss, h 140 Merrimon av
Farmer Elsie L Mrs, dressmkr 10 s Main, h same
Farmer Jos, helper, h 7½ s Main
Farmer Josephine E, wid W A, h 7½ s Main
Farmer M Elizabeth, wid Wesley, h 212 s French Broad av
Farmer Mamie Miss, h 10 s Main
Farmer's Union, genl mdse 55 n Main; J C Cowan pres, E P Stradley sec-treas
Farmer Virginia Miss, h 283 College
Farmer Walter, h 7½ s Main
*Farnsworth Rosa, cook, 311 Montford av
Farnsworth Wm, driver Yates & McGuire
Farow Addie Miss, h 7½ s Main
*Farr Josephine, eating house 86 Pine, h same
Farr Susan, wid M F, h Merrimon av, Woolsey
FARR WM (Eva), pres-mngr The Piedmont Electric Co, h Merrimon av, Woolsey (R F D 1)
Farris Moses Frank (Bessie), gro 250 Patton av, h 18 Clingman av
Fater David H (Bessie G), propr Sunny Smoke Shop, h 18 Blake

....Asheville Cleaning and Pressing Club....
Tailoring That Satisfies and Prices That Please
Steam and French Dry Cleaning of all delicate and fine wearing apparel for ladies and gentlemen. MESSENGER SERVICE IN THE CITY.
J. C. WILBAR, Prop.   4. N. Pack Square   PHONE 389

*Faucett Giles, h 79 Ridge
Faucette Jno W (Ethel T), dentist 16-17 Electrical Bldg, h h 112 College
Faulkner Abner W (Sarah), (Ashev Ice Co), h 187 Pearson Drive
FAULKNER BENNIE P MRS, Massuese and hair goods 39½ s ain—phone 1883, h same (see opp bus dept)
FAULKNER ABNER W (Sarah H), mngr Ashev Ice Co, h 183 Pearson Drive
Faulkner Bros, meats, city market, V F Hawkins mngr
Faulkner Jas H (Mamie), clk The Cash Grocery, h 49 Walnut
Featherston Ambrose A (Clara M), gro 19 n Main, h 23 Woodfin
Featherston Cameron, evangelist, h 174½ s Main
Featheston Clara M Mrs, boarding 23 Woodfin, h same
Featherston E Cameron, clk P O, h 26 Blake
Featherston Horace, clk, h 174½ s Main
Featherston S Merrimon (Mary), clk A A Featherston, h 174½ s Main
Featherstone Emma Miss, h 180 Charlotte
*Featherstone Kate, h 144 Pearson Drive
Featherstone Mamie E Miss, h 180 Charlotte
FEDERAL BUILDING, Patton av cor Haywood
Feezor Hepsie B Mrs, dressmkr 18 s Main, h Biltmore N C
*Feimster Clarence (Elnora), lab, h 78 Wallach
*Feimster Robt (Rebecca), farmer, h W Asheville
Felmet Andrew H (Ellen L), dep city tax collr, h 391 w Haywood
Felmet Bros (Claude L, Wm V, Fred M), gros 349 w Haywood
Felmet Carl H (Iva), clk Bon Marche, h 391 w Haywood
Felmet Claude L (Estelle), (Felmet Bros), h Grace (R D 1)
Felmet Fred M (Fannie F), (Felmet Bros), h 379 w Haywood
Felmet Wm V (Alice), (Felmet Bros), h Penna av, W Asheville
Felthaus Annie K Miss, student, h 36 Clayton
Felthaus Anton (Lillie), plmbr, 36 Clayton, h same
Felthaus Genevieve Miss, cashr C Sawyer, h 36 Clayton
Fender J David (Zella), mtrmn St Ry, rms 17-18 Harkins Bldg
*Fenderson Emma H, prin Mountain Street Schl, h 123 Poplar
*Fenderson Wm B, porter, h 123 Poplar

*Ferguson Callie, dom, h 56 Ridge
*Ferguson Florence, h (r) 35 Clingman av
*Ferguson Henry (Ida), lab, h 26 Smith
Ferguson Kenneth G (Olga), condr, h 21 Bearden av
Ferguson S A Miss, clk Bon Marche
"Fernihurst," res Mrs A T Connally, Victoria rd
*Few Thos (Kate), lab, h 11 Maiden la
Field A M Co, jewelers Patton av cor Church; A M Field pres, David Gudger sec-treas
Fields Andrew J (Roxie), blksmith C L Brown, h 50 Madison av
Field Arthur M (Isabella), pres A M Field Co, h 58 Grove
Field Isabella Mrs, sec Pack Memorial Library Assn, h 58 Grove
*Fields Arthur, oiler, bds 88 Eagle
Fields Ella Mrs, dom, 134 Flint
☞ Fifer see Phifer
*Figgins Wm (Harriet), fireman, h 177 Black
Fincher Albers J, trav slsmn Harris-Barnett Dry Goods Co (Inc), h Canton N C
Finestein Saml, clothing 12 n Main, h 41 s Liberty
Finger E J, clk The Racket Store, h 92 e Church
*Finger Luther, chauffeur Mrs A T Connally
Fink H Leon, stengr Sou Exp Co, bds 102 Patton av
FINKELSTEIN HARRY L (Fannie), (Crescent Jewelry Co), and propr Finkelstein's Pawn Shop and dealer in watches, bags, suit cases, etc, 23-25 s Main—phone 887, h 167 n Main—phone 419 (see back cover)
Finkelstein Jesse (Bessie), clk, rms 125 Cherry
Finley Gray B, mngr West End Drug Store, h 270 Patton av
*Finley Josephine, laund, h 444 Greens Row
Finley Robt S (Willie), druggist 408 Depot, h Florence Hotel
*Finney Ada, cook 14 Watauga
FIRE DEPARTMENT, City Hall—phone 1000
First Baptist Church, College cor Spruce, Rev Calvin B Waller pastor
*First Baptist Church, Pine cor Hazzard, Rev J F Hughes pastor
First Church Christ Scientist, 66 n French Broad av
First Presbyterian Church, Church nr Patton, Rev R F Campbell pastor
Fish Helen D Miss, tchr Home Industrial Schl, rms same
Fisher Anna Miss, nurse 287 Chestnut, h same
Fisher Chas C (Elizabeth), bag mstr, h 112 Clingman av

Fisher Florence E Miss, stengr, h 287 Chestnut
Fisher Harry L (Laura E), confr 9 s Main, h 29 Vance
Fisher Jas E (Maggie M), blksmith D H Webb, h 25 Atkinson
Fisher Janet L Miss, nurse 287 Chestnut, h same
Fisher Luther, bkkpr Felmet Bros, h 40 Buxton
Fisher R Z, rms 22 Meriwether Bldg
Fisher Saml J (Mary), h 287 Chestnut
Fisher Saml J Jr, storekpr Ashev P & L Co, h 287 Chestnut
*Fisher Tina, laundress, h 302 Asheland av
Fisher Wm C, h 287 Chestnut
*Fisher Wm M (Lula), porter A M Field Co, h 85 Circle
Fitcher Robt R (Mamie), bkkpr and cashr Ashev Ptg & Engrav Co, h 126 Woodfin
Fite Geo, carp, bds 173 s Main
Fitzgerald Alice C Mrs, h Maxwell nr Main
Fitzgerald Martha Miss, h 75 Park av
Fitzgerald Mary Mrs, h 75 Park av
Fitzgerald May Miss, h 75 Park av
Fitzgerald Olive L Jr (Maude), clk P O, h 39 Charlotte
Fitzgerald Wm J, h 397 Montford av
Fitzgerald Wm E (Laura), carrier R F D 1, h 91 Woodfin
Fitzpatrick Lola R Miss, student, h 28 Orange
Fitzpatrick Mittie L Miss, nurse, 28 Orange, h same
Fitzpatrick Ossie H (R L Fitzpatrick & Son), res Everett, Washington
Fitzpatrick R L & Son (Robt L and Ossie H), paints, oils, etc, 53 n Main
Fitzpatrick Robt L (Elizabeth), (R L Fitzpatrick & Son), h 28 Orange
FITZPATRICK RUFO M (Cornelia), div supt Mutual Life Ins Co of N Y, h 87 St Dunstan's rd
*Flack Alex (Eliza), lab, h 29 Hildebrand
*Flack Anna J, boarding, 16 Davidson, h same
*Flack J Edwin, barber W P Brooks, h 242 Beaumont
*Flack Thos (Maude), h 151 Short Pine
*Flack Wm M, h 16 Davidson
*Flax Ida, h 47 Velvet
*Flax Pearl (Anna), mngr Greenlee & Loder, h (r) 33 Clingman av
*Fleming Jane, laundress, h 19 Wallach
*Fleming Jos, lab The Moore Plumbing Co, h 19 Wallach
*Fleming Lee Anna, laund, h 45 Lincoln av
*Fleming Loula, cook 43 Chunn
*Fleming Wm, porter Boston Shoe Store, h Chunn's Cove

lub Cafe and Candy Kitchen
"A GOOD PLACE FOR REFRESHMENT"

The standards we work to in our Restaurant Department are: Cooking, perfect; Service, prompt and cheerful; Prices, moderate; Menu, everything in season. Parties and Banquets, Teas and Dinners. 19 and 21 Haywood St. Phones 110 and 111.

Brown's Undertaking Parlors

. H. BROWN

0 Patton Avenue
SHEVILLE, N. C.

Lady Assistant When Desired

hone 193-2 Rings

THE MOORE Plumbing Company

6 N. Pack Square

PHONE 1025

Sanitary Plumbing, General Tin and Metal Work, Hot Air Furnaces

166 ASHEVILLE [1913] DIRECTORY

Flenniken J McCoy (Josie), with A T & T Co, h 108 Biltmore rd, S Biltmore
Fletcher Anna, wid Jeremiah, h 303 s Main
*Fletcher David F (Ella), lab, h S Asheville
*Fletcher Edwd, lab, h 35 w Chestnut
FLETCHER FRANCIS O'C (Lucy G), bkkpr The Piedmont Electric Co, h 91 Elizabeth
*Fletcher Henrietta, laund, h 21 Hildebrand
Fletcher Lillian E Miss, h 199 Haywood
Fletcher Mamie Miss, h 124 Broad
Fletcher Marshall H (Jessie W), phys 17 Church, h 199 Haywood
*Fletcher Pearl, laund, h (r) 11 Depot
*Flint Frank (Etta), lab, h 54 Wallach
Florence Hotel, 436 Depot, W G Corpening propr
Florida House (The), furn rooms 41½ s Main, Mrs H B Hudson propr
Florio Caryl, musician, 37 Patton av (3d fl)
Flower Mission and Associated Charities and Free Medical Dispensary, 20 s Pack Sq, Mrs F P Wild genl sec
*Floyd Albert (Hester), butler, h 102 s Main
Floyd Andrew J (Juno), barber Antiseptic Barber Shop, h 47 Central av
*Floyd Annie R, clk Dr R H Bryant, h 9 Blanton
Floyd Jno W (Annie M), painter, h 2d av, W Ashev
Floyd M Josephine, wid J, h 55 Bartlett
Floyd Richard C (Josephine), flgmn Sou Ry, h 55 Bartlett
*Floyd Theresa, eating house, 88 Eagle, h 22 (92) Gibbons
Flynn Edwin J, agt Life Ins Co of Va, h 51 College
Fogleman Wm D Rev (Elizabeth), pastor Methodist Protestant Church, h 176 Flint
Fogus Clinton R (Gresham & Fogus), rms Florence Hotel
Foister Adelaide M Miss, stengr, h 23 Park av
Foister C Frank (Elizabeth), engnr Ice Factory, h 23 Park
Foister Ellen K Miss, h 23 Park av
Foister Mabel Miss, nurse Biltmore Hosp, h 23 Park av
Foller Jno J, tailor 32 Patton av, rms Franklin Hotel
*Folse Thos, butler, 382 Montford av
Folsom Chas, civil engnr, h 14 Clayton
Folsom Chas, lab, bds 348½ Depot
Folsom Eleanor E, wid Harris H, h 14 Clayton
Forbes Clifford, Envoy Salvation Army, h 38½ s Main
Forbes Gordon, student, h Edgemont
Forbes Saml L (Ada R), (Forbes & Campbell), and sec-treas Home B & L Assn, h "Edgemont"

The Battery Park Bank Capital - $100,000.00
Surplus and Profits, $110,000.00
ASHEVILLE, N. C.   City, County and State Depositary

J. A. TILLMAN — **Jeweler** — **17 N. Main St.**
I carry a nice line of Watches, Clocks and Jewelry, and make a specialty of repair work. Satisfaction guaranteed

Forbes & Campbell (S L Forbes, W R Campbell), real estate, 2 Dhrumor Bldg
Ford Albert L (Ethel), mldr, h Arlington st, W Ashev
Ford Bessie A Miss, bkkpr T H Lawing, h Hazel Mill rd, W Ashev
Ford Elizabeth Mrs, smstrs, h 28 Short Roberts
Ford Elizabeth K Miss, prin Ashev Schl for Girls, h 137 Woodfin
*Ford Eugene (Sadie), driver, h 12 Catholic av
Ford Floyd, clk W P Ford & Son, h nr Smith's Bridge, W Asheville
Ford Jno, engnr, bds 308 Depot
Ford Jno T (May E), (W P Ford & Son), h W Asheville
Ford Jos F (Mattie), (Lee & Ford), h 46 Arlington
Ford Laura Miss, nurse 84 s French Broad av, rms same
*Ford Leo (Rosa), waiter, h 71 Ridge
Ford Logan B (Nola), barber, h 179 n Main
Ford Lora Miss, h nr Smith's Bridge, W Ashev
Ford Mary A Miss, tchr, h 137 Woodfin
Ford Rebecca L, wid Frank, h 137 Woodfin
*Ford Rosa, cook, h 79 Ridge
Ford W P & Son (Wm P and Jno T Ford), gros 348 Depot
Ford Wm G (Ida), peddler, h Hazel Mill rd, W Ashev
Ford Wm P (Sarah J), (W P Ford & Son), h W Asheville
Fordham Montgomery G (Irene), mason, h Swannanoa av, W Ashev
Fore A Robt (Susan A), h Biltmore
Fore Ernest G, lab, h Haywood rd, W Ashev
Fore Wiley, lab, bds J A Kuykendall, W Ashev
Fore Wm J (Mary), lab, h Haywood rd, W Ashev
*Foreman Charlotte, h Herren av, W Ashev
*Foreman Maggie, cook, h 52 Davidson
*Foreman Edna, laund, h 18 Frederick
Foreman J W Dr (Edith S), dentist 17½ Church, h 27 Soco
Forest Hill, boarding s Main extd, Mrs W Talbot Penniman
Forestburg Mathias (Nettie), (D S Watson & Co), h 49 Madison av
Forester Jno H (Martha), trav slsmn, h 106 Broad
Fork Ridge Coal Co (Inc), 24 Amer Natl Bank Bldg; W J Sproles pres, F C Todd sec, D S Elias treas
*Forney Bessie, cook, h 4 Hibernia
*Forney Eloise, cook, h 31 Haid
*Forney Henrietta, laund, h 16 Short
*Forney Jas (Emma), lab, h 135 Poplar
*Forney Julia, laund, h 52 Clemmons

INSURANCE
Insure your salary with us
Never carry your own risk
Safety is the best policy
Unless you are a capitalist
Rest easy if you have
An accident we will
Not keep you waiting to
Collect your claim
Every claim promptly paid

Imperial Mutual Life & Health Insurance Co.
Home Office: ASHEVILLE, N. C.
Phone 495

HOTEL OXFORD — **Asheville, N. C.**
Redecorated and Refitted throughout. Recently enlarged to 60 rooms. Centrally located. Depot cars stop at entrance. Long distance telephone office upstairs. American and European plan. Rates 50c, 75c and $1 per day; special rates by week or month. C. H. Branson & Sons, Proprietors. Phone 1887. 50-54 South Main St.

Williams-Brownell Planing Mill Company — *Hardwoods*

Lumber---Rough and Dressed   Flooring a Specialty   Moulding, Interior Finish, Etc.
Office, Plant and Yards on Southern Railway, Near Biltmore Station
WHITE PINE   Phone 729   YELLOW PINE

168 ASHEVILLE [1913] DIRECTORY

*Forney Luther (Louisa), cook, h 32 Catholic av
*Forney Maria, dom, h 31 Haid
*Forney Pearson, driver, h 214 Beaumont
*Forney Pearson, driver, h 214 Beaumont
*Forney Stanley (Willie), messgr U S Court, h 15 Blanton
*Forney Thos (Annie), plstr, h 214 Beaumont
*Forney Wm (Cora), lab, h 37 Sycamore
*FORNEY WM C (Forney & Jones), h 52 Clemmons
*FORNEY & JONES (W C Forney, J E Jones), proprs College Street Dye Works and Merchant Tailors, 35½ e College (see index for adv)
Forster Jno P (Sarah E), bkpr M H Kelly, h 194 College
Forster Jno S (Adella), gro 162 Southside av, h 264 Depot
☞ Forster see also Foster
Fort Phoebe Mrs, h 3 s Spruce
Fort W Henry (Myra L), mchst Asheville Auto Co, h Arlington st, W Ashev
Fortner Mary Mrs, asst matron Pease Memorial House, rms same
Fortner Mary Mrs, asst matron Pease Memorial House, rms same
Fortune Burgin, foreman Grove Park Inn
*Fortune Callie, cook, 182 Montford av
*Fortune Estelle, cook, rms 88 Eagle
Fortune Gary R, clk Ashev P & G Co, h 45 Bartlett
*Fortune Giles Rev (Regina), h 9 Choctaw
Fortune Mary J, wid A B, h 178 Haywood
*Fortune Regina, tchr Southside Schl, h 9 Choctaw
Fortune Robt G (Nellie), mngr Palais Royal, h 23 n Spruce
Fortune Wm G (Marie), (Fortune & Roberts), h 45 Bartlett
Fortune & Roberts (W G Fortune and E Gallatin Roberts), attys at law, 11-12 Library Bldg
*Foster Amy, maid Battery Park Cottage, rms same
*Foster Arthur (Jessie), waiter, h 143 Livingston
Foster Benj J, slsmn Mrs Lynch & Son, h 55 Woodfin
Foster Bertha L Miss, clk J S Foster, h 262 Depot
*Foster Betsy, cook, h 22 Ralph
*Foster Chas, lab, h 25 Short Valley
*Foster Chas (Annie), lab, h 103 Choctaw
*Foster Elva, cook, h 103 Choctaw
*Foster Essie, cook, h 64 Hill
*Foster Ethel, hairdresser 272 Asheland av
*Foster Evelyn, h Edgemont
Foster Florence A Miss, physical director Y W C A, h 78 s Main

Asheville Electrical Company
W. Mansfield Booze, Manager
74 CENTRAL AVE.
HEADQUARTERS
Phone 377

Asheville Dry Cleaning Co.
Telephones 835-836, All Dep't
MAIN, N. E. COR. COLLEGE

THE CLEANERS
Our Department for Oriental Rugs and Carpet Cleaning is prepared to serve you in all its branches.

E. S. Paine   O. E. Hansen

Maple Flooring and Poplar Siding **English Lumber Co.** PHONE . . 321

*Foster Frank, lab, h 90 Mountain
Foster Frank S (Annie), gro 356 Depot, h 205 Bartlett
Foster Geo M (Clara), clk P O, h Hillside cor Washington rd
Foster Harley (Susan), condr, h 18 Ora
*Foster Henry C (Nannie), bricklyr, h 272 Asheland av
*Foster Isaac, lab, rms 91 Black
*Foster Jas, driver Dr T C Smith, rms 184 Chestnut
*Foster Jeannette, cook 398 Montford av
Foster Jerome (Claudis), clk, h 55 Woodnfi
Foster Jno S (Della E), gro 262 Depot, h same
*Foster Jos, lab, h 12 Lincoln av
*Foster Julia, h 26 Pearson Drive
*Foster Lena, laund, h 90 Mountain
*Foster Lucinda, h 7 Knob
Foster M Florence Miss, h 71 Woodfin
Foster Mary A Mrs, nurse 29 Clingman av, h same
*Foster Nancy, maid, h 103 Choctaw
*Foster Napoleon, lab, h 9 Short Valley
*Foster Narcissa, h 4 Sorrell
Foster Omega H, supt Biltmore Box Factory, h 53 Walnut
*Foster Oliver (Annie), lab, h 207 Southside av
*Foster Paul, bellman, h 143 Livingston
*Foster Polnef (Pearl), baker Zindel's Model Bakery, h 25 Aston la
Foster Robt P (Love), propr Biltmore Box Factory, h 111 s Main
Foster Robt P Jr, student, h 111 s Main
Foster Rosella Miss, opr, h 29 Clingman av
*Foster Sallie, laund, h Valley nr College
Foster Wade, lab, h (r) 180 s Main
Foster Wm, del clk The Reliable Cleaning & Pressing Co, h Depot st
Foster Zebulon (Nancy), lab, h (r) 180 s Main
Foster Zebulon, clk, bds 25 Asheland av
☞ Foster see also Foister and Forster
Fountain Building, offices 16½ n Pack Sq
*Fowler Chas F (Johanna), lab, h 98 Pine
*Fowler Eliza J, laund, h 98 Pine
Fowler Emma Miss, dom 180 Charlotte
Fowler Fred B (Eleanor), painter, h 14 Roberts
*Fowler Fred F, porter, h 98 Pine
Fowler J B Morris (Druscilla M), ydman Citizens Lbr Co, h Penna av, W Ashev
*Fowler Jno S (Ida), barber W P Brooks, h 48 Poplar

BIGGEST **B**USIEST **B**EST

Asheville Steam Laundry

Phones:
1936 and 1937

43 to 47
W. College Street

CHARLES H. HONESS
OPTOMETRIST AND OPTICIAN

Exclusive maker of
ATLAS SHUR-ON EYE GLASSES

THE
Home of Ce-Rite Toric Lenses

We make a specialty of correcting optical defects with properly fitted glasses.

54 Patton Avenue
Opposite Postoffice

IF in the market for a Gas Engine let us make you prices.
its heavy castings, such as columns or building plates, see us.
its a skilled mechanic for boiler work, see us.
you want machine work of any kind phone 590.

CAROLINA MACHINERY CO.

FOUNDERS
MACHINISTS and
Jobbers of Mil
Supplies

Life Insurance Company of Virginia
ORGANIZED 1871
Home Office - Richmond, Va.

Has won the hearty approval and active support of the people by its promptness and fair dealing during the FORTY-TWO YEARS of its operation

I. V. Moon, Superintendent, Rooms 3-4-5 Maxwelton Bldg., Asheville, N. C.

T. P. JOHNSON & CO.

SHEET METAL WORKERS

All Kinds of Roofing Guttering and Conductor Work Metal Ceilings, Skylights and Galvanized Iron Cornices

OFFICE and SHOP:
69-71 S. MAIN

Phone 325

DR. C. H. MILLER

Mechano-Therapist

14 N. Spruce Street
ASHEVILLE, N. C.

PHONE 979

Hours by Engagement

DRUGLESS HEALING OF DISEASE

Fowler Thos M, clk Gladstone Hotel, h 346½ Depot
Fowlkes Ruby Miss, h 23 Highland
Fox Clayton, h 35 Catawba
Fox Ellis Rabbi, Bickercholim Synagogue, h Central av nr Woodfin
Fox Hammoleketh J, wid Robt F, h 21 Rector
Fox Herschel A, solr Ashev Citizen, h 21 Rector
Fox Hubert H, tinner, h 21 Rector
Fox Jesse A (Nannie J), tmstr, h Haywood rd, W Asheville
Fox Jno H (Manda), farmer, h W Asheville
Fox Jno M (Lula), blksmith D W Cauble, h 35 Catawba
Fox Jos C (Elizabeth), stone mason, h 18 Factory Hill
Fox Landon N (Arrie), farmer, h W Asheville
Fox Lessie M Miss, h Haywood rd, W Asheville
Fox Marian H Miss, clk H Redwood & Co, h 21 Rector
Fox Norman McC, chf clk div frt agt Sou Ry, bds——
Fox Wm M (Lucinda), plmbr G L Guischard
Frady Edgar R (Leona), h 18 Olive
Frady G Frank (Hannah), clk Singer Sewing Mch Co, h 47 Seney
Frady Garrett B, deliveryman, h 315 s Main
Frady Grace M Miss, bkkpr T P Johnson, h 59 Woodfin
Frady Hall F (Rosa), condr St Ry, h 60 Phifer
Frady Henry M (Susan), mtrmn St Ry, h 10 Buttrick
Frady J Benj (Creola), foreman St Dept, h 315 s Main
Frady Lawrence M, clk Michalove, h 1 Reservior
Frady Robt E (Ethel), lineman Ashev P & L Co, h 58 Summit, S Biltmore
Frady Wm B (Dora), driver A F D, h 1 Reservior
Fragge Louis (Veronica) (Ashev F P Gas Mch Co), h 415 Merrimon av
*Francis Ella, laund, h 24 Ralph
*Francis Jas (Hattie), lab, h 16 Ralph
Francis Robt L (Marguerite F), engnr, h 130 Park av
FRANCIS WM (Nellie F), supt water dept, office 103 City Hall, h 111 College
Frank Ralph R, clk frt office Sou Ry, h 23 Phifer
Franklin Emma Mrs, smstrs Whitlock Clo Co, h 17 Merrimon av
Franklin Hotel, s Pack Sq cor Main, F V Roberts propr
Franklin Jas C, clk Ashev Gro Co, h 12 Village la, Biltmore
*Franklin Jno (Rebbeca), eating hse 227 Clingman av, h 123½ same
Franklin Lucian, clk Ashev Gro Co, h 12 Village la, Biltmore

ASHEVILLE CLEANING and PRESSING CLUB

TAILORING THAT SATISFIES and PRICES THAT PLEASE

Hats cleaned, banded and bound. Silk hats ironed. Buttons made to order in all sizes. Plain or with rims. PHONE 389

DYEING IN ALL SHADES Cleaned. Messenger Service.

Kid Gloves, Slippers and Plumes. Fancy Jabots and Ties. French Dry Cleaned. Ladies' and Gentlemen's suits Steam

J. C. Wilbar, Prop. 4 NORTH PACK SQ.

Franklin Mary, wid Wm, h 390 Southside av
Franklin Melvin W (Addie), car repr, h 125 Bartlett
Franklin Oscar G (Effie), painter, h W Asheville (R F D 3)
Franklin Percy E, student, h 12 Village la, Biltmore
Franklin Sidney, painter R L Fitzpatrick & Son
Franks F H, tchr High School
Frasier D Henry (Ellen), weaver, h 8 Factory Hill
Frasier Jas H, mill wkr, h 8 Factory Hill
Fratenal Order of Eagles, Aerie No 1377, 33½ s Main
Frazer Thompson (Julia), phys 6-7 Citizen Bldg, h Charlotte extd
*Frazier Sandy D (Rosa) (Frazier & Martin), h 34 Hill
*Frazier & Martin (S D Frazier, K R Martin), proprs Buckeye Sanitary Shaving Parlor, 11½ s Main
Freck Carrie, wid Adolph, furn rooms, 153 s Main, h same
Freck Chas B (Emma), plmbr, h (r) 153 s Main
Freck Dollie, wid Chas, h 155½ s Main
*Fredwell Houston B (Mary), cook, h 73 Eagle
*Fredwell Mary, dress mkr, 73 Eagle, h same
*Free Will Baptist Church, 149 Livingston, Rev Lee Harshaw pastor
Freedlander Florence Miss, h 104 n Liberty
Freedlander S A (Jennie), optician, h 104 n Liberty
Freedlander Saml A, student, h 104 n Liberty
Freeman Adolphus E (Mary E), gardener, h (r) 330 w Haywood
Freeman Alex L (Ella), foreman, h Arlington St, W Asheville
Freeman Anna Miss, weaver, h Arlington St, W Asheville
Freeman Annie L Miss, stengr, h 16 Grove
Freeman Aurora B, dep colr int revenue, h 66 Asheland av
Freeman Estes G, stengr, h 51 Orchard
Freeman Eva Miss, weaver, h Arlington St, W Asheville
Freeman F May Miss, h Hazel Mill rd, W Asheville
Freeman Gertrude Miss, clk Amer Natl Bank
Freeman Jessie L Miss, mica picker, h Hazel Mill rd, W Asheville
*Freeman Jno (Leola), lab, h 101 Roberts
Freeman Jno C, lab, h 51 Orchard
*Freeman Jos, porter Dr T C Smith, h 89 Poplar
*Freeman Julia, waitress Crescent Lunch Room, rms 32 Davidson
Freeman Julia E, wid Bruce, h 16 Grove
Freeman Laura A, wid P Marion, h Hazel Mill rd, W Ashev
Freeman May Miss, mica picker, h W Asheville

WEAVERVILLE LINE NINE MILES BY TROLLEY FROM PACK SQUARE TO WEAVERVILLE

ASHEVILLE AND EAST TENNESSEE RAILROAD CO.

7 NORTH MAIN STREET   ASHEVILLE N. C.

ELECTRIC FIXTURES

Piedmont Electric Co.

64 PATTON AVE.
ASHEVILLE, N.C.

Freeman Ray C (Clara E), bkkpr, h 51 Orchard
Freeman Robt E L (Marguerite A), clk West End Grocery, h 340 Haywood
Freeman Wm I Rev, evanglist, h (r) 330 w Haywood
Freeny Henry B (Grace E), (no address)
French Broad Quarry Building Material Co, Riverside Drive W Frank Rogers mngr
*Friday Jno (Worthy), hostler, h 52 Catholic av
*Friday Minnie L, dom, h 92 Eagle
Friend J W, bds 173 s Main
Fritchey Emil (Julia), plmbr, h Woolsey
Frost Herbert M, jeweler 15 Church, h 14½ Church
Frost Theo V (Amy), painter, h 40 Cherry
Fry H Allen (Alice), painter, h 298 n Main
Fry H Love, clk P W Lowe & Son, bds 98 Patton av
Fruchey Fred'k J (Anna), h 2 Carroll av
Fulbrecht Zora S Miss, h 216 College
Fulbright Artie B, wid T Oscar, h 22 Grady
Fulbright Columbus, lab Highland Hotel, bds same
Fulbright F W Mrs, clk Bon Marche
Fulgham Jos E, sec-asst mngr The Murray Lbr Co, bds 50 Chunn
Fullam Beatrice L Miss, student, h Asheville av, W Ashe
Fullam Clarence (Eva), painter, h 140 Park av
Fullam Jno S (Dora J), condr, h Asheville av, W Asheville
*Fullenwider Alice, cook, h 30 Davidson
Fuller Aldridge G, propr College Street Bakery, rms 20 Marjorie
Fuller Claud (Corinne), trav slsmn, h 59 Penland
Fuller Jeanie S Miss, sec to prin Home Industrial Schl, rms same
*Fuller Jeffrey E (Mattie), barber, h 23 Short
*Fuller Jno H (Minnie), janitor, h (r) 4 Sorrell
*Fuller Wm (Theresa), lab, h 26 Gaither
Fulton Rosa W, wid Saml, h 44 Atkin
*Fulton Willie L, tchr Catholic Hill Schl, h Eagle st
*Funches Georgianna, laund, h 13 Haid
Furey Smith J, mchst Ashe Supply & Fdy Co
Fussell Herman, clk Pack Sq Book Co Inc, bds Hiawassee

G

Gaddy Georgia Miss, clk Morris Levitt, h Woolsey
Gaddy Jas, driver, h W Asheville
Gage E Regina, h 26 Oakdale av

CONTRACTOR and BUILDER

STEEL RANGES | **J. C. McPHERSON** | 35-37 E COLLEGE ST. PHONE 133

PLUMBING STEAM AND HOT WATER HEATING

Yellow Pine		WOODWARD & SON
White Pine	**LUMBER**	Ninth and Arch Streets
Hardwoods	SASH, BLINDS, DOORS	RICHMOND - VIRGINIA
See bet. pgs. 188-189		

Gaines Edmund T, asst mngr Singer Sewing Mch Co, h Weaverville
Gaines Emma Miss, nurse Highland Hosp, rms same
*Gaines Lillie, cook, h 49 Sycamore
*Gaines Thaddeus (Mattie), shoe shiner, h 70 Ridge
*Gaines Ulysses H, waiter, h 82 Pine
*Gaither Adeline, laund, h 36 Maiden la
*Gaither Alfred (Allie), waiter, h 18 Gaither
*Gaither Geo, lab, h 36 Maiden la
*Gaither Jas (Rosa), lab, h (r) 60 Clingman av
*Gaither Jennie, h 7 Sorrell
*Gaither Jessie, cook, h 47 Short
*Gaither Lucy, cook, h 105 Roberts
"Galax Cottage", Albemarle Park
*Galbraith Sallie, dom, h 128 Southside av
Galbraith Seaborne J (Bessie), clk, h 84 Bartlett
Galer Cora A Miss, h 49 w Chestnut
Galer Edwd J, student, h 49 w Chestnut
GALER EMMETT E (Anna G), cabt mkr, upholstr and furn repr, furniture crated for shipment, 114 Patton av, h 49 w Chestnut (see bottom lines)
Gales Priscilla, wid T L, supt Sanitary Home Ldy, h 18½ Cherry
Gallamore Jennie Miss, h 282 Cumberland av
Galloway Arthur M (Doska), car inspr Sou Ry, h 31 Gaston
Galloway Lyda E Miss, nurse 31 Gaston, h same
Galloway Mayes W (Vaughtie), driver Donald & Donald, h W Asheville
Galloway Susan K, wid J M, h 31 Gaston
Galloway Zelma Miss, house kpr, h Haywood rd, W Ashe
Galvin Jno H (Dorcas I), mchst, h 34 Ora
Galyean Ernest S (Sallie), confr 405 Depot, h 61 Phifer
*Gammon Jas, lab, bds (r) 328 w Haywood
Gant Butler, emp Brown & Smith, h nr Leicester rd, W Asheville
Gardner Frank K (Myra B), optician 43 s Main, h 8 Aston pl
GARDNER GARRETT D (Frances L), 266½ Patton av—phone 139, office hours 11 a m to 1 p m, 4 to 6 p m, h W Asheville
*Gardner Grace, dom, h 180 Valley
*Gardner Lillie, laund, h 180 Eagle
*Gardner Quess (Georgiana), lab, h 33 Weaver
*Gardner Taylor (Susan), lab, h 5 Short Pine
Garland Andrew, student, h Grace

What Have You in Real Estate that You Don't Want?

What do You Want in Real Estate that You Haven't?

WESTERN CAROLINA REALTY CO.

J. W. Wolfe Sec. & Treas.

On the Square
PHONE 974
10 N. PACK SQ.

Brown-Carter Realty Co.
REAL ESTATE
23 TEMPLE COURT
PHONE 341
ASHEVILLE   N. C.

FLORIDA SPECIALTIES
Grazing, Timbered, Farm Lands, Orange Groves, Turpentine Locations and Phosphate Lands.

NORTH CAROLINA SPECIALTIES
Orchard, Farm and Timbered Lands, City Property, Rent Collections.

Moale & Chiles Real Estate and Insurance
27 Patton Ave., (2d fl)   Phone 661
General Agents United States Fidelity & Guaranty Co.

Club Cafe and Candy Kitchen
"A GOOD PLACE FOR REFRESHMENT"

Our Ice Cream manufacturing plant is absolutely clean and sanitary.
Prompt family delivery. Phones 110 and 111.
Catering for large parties and receptions. Special Creams.

---

174 ASHEVILLE [1913] DIRECTORY

Brown's Undertaking Parlors
S. H. BROWN

Lady Assistant When Desired

Phone 193-2 Rings

50 Patton Avenue
Asheville, N. C.

Established 1894

B. J. JACKSON

Carefully Selected Fruits and Vegetables

Stall No. 11, City Market

BUSINESS PHONES:
86 and 101

RESIDENCE PHONE
1596

Garland Elbert F (Mary), lab, h Grace
Garland G Ervin (Wrenn & Garland), h Grace
Garland Jas (Mattie), clk, h Grace
Garland Jno N (Sarah), carp, h Grace
Garland Julia Miss, h Grace
Garland Lillian Miss, h Grace
Garland Willie Miss, h Grace
Garman Wm H (Coressa), trav slsmn, rms 90 Church
Garren Augustus G (Lucinda), carp, h 52 Centre
Garren Edwd (Bessie), driver, h 435 s Main
Garren Geo, tinner, h 52 Centre
Garren Jno H (Martha), plmbr J R Rich Co, h 87 East
Garren May Miss, bds 443 s Main
Garren Saml M (Annie), R F D Carrier, h Biltmore rd, S Biltmore
Garren Virginia Mrs, h 425 s Main
Garren Wm H, tinner, h 87 East
*Garrett Anna, maid, rms 115 n Main
*Garrett Archie, waiter, h 55 Max
*Garrett Ethel, laundress, h 215 s Main
*Garrett Josie, cook, rms 115 n Main
*Garrett Mollie, laundress, h 215 s Main
Garrett Robt U (Adeline), real estate and loans 9 Electrical Bldg, h 2 Oakland rd, Victoria
*Garrett Vina, h 55 Max
Garrett Wm E (Willie), propr Patton Hotel, h 20 Patton av
Garrison Annie Miss, dom, h Woolsey (R F D 1)
Garrison Carl, lab, h 78 Avery
Garrison Chas E, engnr French Broad Quarry, bds 31 Spring
Garrison Henry H (Kate), plumber, h 78 Avery
Garrison Olive Miss, maid 240 Pearson Drive
Garrisson Jacob, car repr, h 119 Park av
Garvin Fletcher B (Ollie), tel opr, h Main st, W Asheville
Garvin Margaret M, wid M M, h 82 Woodfin
*Gash Doctor (Dora), lab, h 33 Catholic av
Gash Flora M Miss, h 50 Orange
Gash Fred, mchst Asheville Auto Co, rms 17 s Lexington av
*Gash Jas (Amanda), driver The Star Market, h 24 Miller
Gasperson Chas (May), lab, h Swannanoa av, W Asheville
Gasperson Geo B (Clara), drayman, h 472 s French Broad
Gasperson Wm O (Martha B), farmer, h W Asheville
*Gaston Alex H (Fredericka), armature winder Ashev P & L Co, h 24 Richard
GASTON EDWIN L (Daisy H), sec-treas Williams-Brownell Planing Mill Co, h 162 Cumberland av

---

Furniture and China Carefully Prepared for Shipment

Mahogany Furniture Hand Made & Carefully Reproduced | **E. E. GALER** 114 PATTON AVE. | Upholstering and Refinishing PHONE - 1674

*Gaston Wm (Ella), lab, h 92 Eagle
Gates Mary C, wid Jas W, h 114 Poplar
Gates Thos L (Margaret A), carp, h 94 Livingston
*Gather Chas, lab, h 3 Greer's Row
☞Gather see also Gaither
*Gatlin Jas, lab, h 29 Black
Gatlin Jno P, lab, h 45 Summit, S Biltmore
Gatiln Jos S, emp Planing Mill, h 45 Summit, S Biltmore
Gatlin Mattie l, wid J W, h 45 Summit, S Biltmore
*Gay Frank (Mattie), brakeman, h 56 Wallach
*Gay Frank (Mattie), lab, h 29 Black
*Gay Lewis, waiter, h 27 Max
Gearhart Paul H, surveyor, rms 33 McAfee Bldg
Gee Harry M (Katherine), lumber, h 52 Arlington
Gee Harry M Jr, h 52 Arlington
Gee Nellie R Miss, h 52 Arlington
Geiger Elizabeth E, wid David W, boarding 18 College pl
Gelula Max (Rose), h 83 Centre av
Gem Clothing Store (The), 6 Patton av, Ike Swartzberg propr
Gem Lunch Room, 388 Depot, T J Harrison propr
*General Emma, dom 129 s Main
General Supply Co, mnfrs agts, 51 Asheland av, C P Southerland mngr
Gentile Paul F (Beatrice), tailor S T Logan, bds 28 s Ann
Gentry Claude S (Dixie), clk S Finestein, h 62 Hall
Gentry Everett R, clk J C Gentry, h 40 Cumberland av
Gentry Georgia Miss, h 244 s French Broad av
Gentry H Claude (Viola), lab, h 142 Hall
Gentry Hazel Miss, h 140 Hall
Gentry Houston D (Emma), propr Asheville Marble Works h 169 Charlotte
Gentry J Cornelius (Mary V), dry goods 22 s Main, h 40 Cumberland av
Gentry J Wiley (Ethel), clk Asheville Fish Co, h 306 n Main
Gentry Joanna, wid Chas A, h 8 View
Gentry Jno W (N Malissia), lab, h nr Smith Bridge, W Asheville
Gentry Jones, lab, bds 49 n Main
Gentry Lillie Miss, h 140 Hall
Gentry Millard, marker Ashe Stm Ldyq, bds 18 Factory Hill
Gentry Sarah E Miss, sinner, h nr Smith Bridge, W Ashe
Gentry Wm M (Mary), blksmith, h 10 Spring
Gentry Wyatt T (Clarissa), emp French Broad Quarry, h 140 Hall

Mrs. Wilder's SANITARY HOME LAUNDRY turns out first class work in Laundering and Dry Cleaning. No. 7 Montford Ave., Phone 1354

176 ASHEVILLE [1913] DIRECTORY

George Earl O (Helen), sales agt Natl Cash Register Co, h 150 Cumberland av
George Marguerite Miss, h "Knowllacre" Victoria rd
George Wm C, pottery, h "Knowllacre" Victoria rd
George Wm S (Annie), pottery, h "Knowllacre" Victoria rd
GEORGIA TALC CO (Inc), 215 Legal Bldg, E B Glenn pres, C F Glenn v-pres, J F Glenn sec-treas—phone 117
Gerst Max, tailor S T Logan, h 40 Merrimon av
Gheen Stella, wid Wm E, h W Asheville
Gianakos Geo, propr Ashev Candy Kitchen, h Henderson N C
Gianakos Pete, mngr Ashe Candy Kitchen, rms 13 s Main
Gibbon Corinna M, wid Dr Robt, h 193 Montford av
*Gibbs A Lee (Julia), lab, h 15 Margaret
Gibbs Corrie E Mrs, sec Womans Exchange, h 3 Aston pl
Gibbs Chas B (Anna), carp, h 16 Hillside
Gibbs Mary D Miss, stengr Battery Park Bank, h 176 Merrimon av
Gibbs Minnie Miss, nurse 71 Central av, rms same
Gibbs Saml H (Sarah D), ins, h 176 Merrimon av
Gibbs W Augustus (Zora), mtrmn, h 56 East
*Gibbs W May, dress mkr, h 21 Bay
*Gibbs Wm (Mary), lab, h 21 Bay
Gibson Eliza, wid Richmond, h 110 Seney
*Gibson Eva, laund, h 100 n Lexington av
Gibson Geo, optician, bds 51 College
*Gibson Hardy, stone mason, h 70 Curve
*Gibson Henrietta, laund, h 214 Beaumont
Gibson Jos A (Sallie E), gro nr Smith's Bridge, W Ashe, h Haywood rd, W Asheville
Gibson Nada Miss, cashr Bon Marche, h 110 Seney
*Gibson Wm (Mary), h 227 Southside av
*Gibson Wm M (Mary), lab, h 40 Curve
Gideon Nannie J, wid Ollie, dress mkr 57 East, h same
Gilbert Mary Mrs, h "Edwin Place" Grove Park
Gilden Chas N (Mattie), engnr P & L Co, h W Asheville
Giles Nora Miss, bds 216 Haywood
*Giles Thos, porter Antiseptic Barber Shop, h 57 Short
Gilkey Edwd P, mngr C A Raysor, rms Harkins Bldg
Gillespie Edgar J, agt Imp Mut L & H Ins Co, h 23 Asheland av
Gillespie Fred E (Julia), driver, h 393 Merrimon av
Gillespie G Reagan (N Elizabeth), mill wkr, h 54 Buxton
Gillespie Homer G, clk Glen Rock Hotel, bds same
Gillespie J Marvin, chauffeur, h 29 Jefferson Drive

BUICK — ARBOGAST MOTOR COMPANY — MAXWELLS
ACCESSORIES AND SUPPLIES
52-60 N. Main Phones 302 and 1728
DETROIT ELECTRIC

Asheville Dry Cleaning Co.
Telephones 835-836, All Dep't
MAIN, N. E. COR. COLLEGE

THE CLEANERS
Our Department for Oriental Rugs and Carpet Cleaning is prepared to serve you in all its branches.
E. S. Paine   O. E. Hansen

For Kindling "What am Kindling" Ca
ENGLISH LUMBER COMPANY   Phone 32

ASHEVILLE [1913] DIRECTORY 177

Gillespie Roy F, tanner, h 54 Buxton
*Gillespie Seay, porter Swannonoa-Berkeley Hotel Pool Room, bds Davidson st
Gilliam Ada, wid P T, h Grove Park
Gilliam Andrew J, carp, h 34 Asheland av
*Gilliam Emanuel (Amanda), lab, h 27 Short
*Gilliam Giles (Elizabeth), lab, h 27 Short
*Gilliam Jno (Mattie), driver J L Smathers & Sons, h 116 Livingston
Gilliam Louella Miss, h Grove Park
Gilliam Mary C Miss, h 34 Asheland av
*Gilliam Richard (Sarah), lab, h 41 Ocola
Gilliland Latta, slsmn, bds 92 Church
GILLIS DONALD (Woodcock & Gillis) and atty at law pres Pack Memorial Library Assn, h 134 Montford av
Gillis Eliza W, wid Calvin, h 134 Montford av
Gillis Robt (Minnie), foreman, h 41 Spring
Gillis Waddell Miss, h 134 Montford av
Gilreath Cleveland H (Martha C), h 68 Clingman av
*Gist Jno (Viola), helper, h 179 Livingston
Gladstone Hotel, 409 Depot, Mrs Virginia A Blake propr
Gladstone Hotel Cafe, 409 Depot, Frank A Blake mngr
*Glascow Mary, boarding 194 s Main, h same
Glaser I W (Rebecca), clothing 18 Patton av, h 578 Montford av
Glass Chas (Amanda), v-pres Ashe Harness Co Inc, h 37 Hiawassee
Glass Chas Jr, clk, h 37 Hiawassee
Glass Edwd L (Sophronia), saddler Ashe Harness Co, h 56 Josephine
Glass Fred'k J (Jessie), condr The Pullman Co, h 128 w Chestnut
Glass Fred S (Jessie), condr Sou Ry, h 130 w Chestnut
Glass Helen A Miss, h 128 w Chestnut
Glass Helen A Miss, h 130 w Chestnut
Glazner Ada Miss, bkkpr, bds 23 Asheland av
Glen Rock Barber Shop, 402 Depot, J W Jacoke propr
GLEN ROCK HOTEL, 400 Depot opp Sou Depot—phone 76, J H Lange propr
GLEN ROCK STATION of POST OFFICE, 372 Depot, J C Melton clk in charge
Glenn Blanche A Mrs, h 264 Patton av
GLENN CASSIUS F DR (Maggie), v-pres Georgia Talc Co and dentist, 9-10-11 New Sondley Bldg, office hours 9 to 1 and 2 to 5—phone 90, h 45 Panola pl—phone 1708

BIGGEST BUSIEST BEST

Phones 1936 and 1937
ASHEVILLE STEAM LAUNDRY
43 to 47 W. COLLEGE

S. D. HALL
REAL ESTATE AGENT
—
Money Loaned
—
Notary Public
—
32 PATTON AVENUE
—
Phone 9

Founders, Machinists and Jobbers of Mill Supplies
PHONE 590
When in the market for pipe and fittings, let us make you Prices.
Carolina Machinery Co.
PHONE 590
If it's a Gas Engine let figure with you, also other kinds of machiner

[LIFE] INSURANCE COMPANY OF VA. OLDEST, LARGEST STRONGEST Southern Life Insurance Co.

ORGANIZED 1871
RICHMOND, VIRGINIA

Issues Industrial Policies from $8.00 to $900.00, with Premiums Payable WEEKLY on persons from two to seventy years of age

[.] V. Moon, Superintendent, Rooms 3-4-5 Maxwelton Bldg., Asheville, N. C.

[.] TREXLER

TIN SHOP

All Kinds of Roofing, Gutter and Conductor Work.

Phone 862

59 South Main St.

DR. C. H. MILLER

MECHANO-THERAPIST

14 N. Spruce St.
Phone 979
ASHEVILLE, N. C.

Hours by engagement

Drugless Healing of Disease

GLENN EUGENE B (Elizabeth E Lumpkin), physician, 1-2-3 New Sondley Bldg, office hours 12 to 1 p m and 4 to 5 p m—phone 54, and pres Georgia Talc Co, h 41 Starnes av—phone 701
Glenn Fes C, plmbr, h Woolsey (R F D 1)
Glenn Frank (Lucy), fireman, bds 102 Ralph
GLENN J FRAZIER (Eunice F), atty at law 215 Legal Bldg—phone 117, corporation counsel and sec-treas Georgia Talc Co, h 51 Montford av
Glenn Jno T, fireman, h 376 Southside av
Glenn M Fillmore (Jennie), h 376 Southside av
Glenn Marshall R Dr (Georgia), h Woolsey (R F D 1)
Glenn Orr T, contr, h Woolsey (R F D 1)
Glenn Robt B (Joannah), mdse, h Woolsey (R F D 1)
Glenn Wm C (Dora), elctrn, bds 14 s Spruce
Glenn Wm E Dr (Minnie L), h 36 Starnes av
Globe Furniture Co, 52 s Main, J W Ramsey mngr
Globe Market, meats, City Market, J A Penland propr
Globe Sample Co, shoes, 32 s Main, L H Pollock propr
*Glover Chas, lab, h 33 Wallach
*Glover David (Mabel), fireman, h 188 Livingston
Glover Jefferson, painter R E Bowles, h Flat Rock N C
*Glover Mary, laund, h 133 Roberts
Glover Murray (Mollie E), tmstr, bds C E Lawing, W Asheville
Glover Murry (Mollie), driver, h 18 Factory Hill
*Glymp Wm (Annie), lab, h (r) 123½ Clingman av
GODBEY EARL, mng editor Ashev Gazette-News, h 162 Charlotte
Godfrey Jno (Vinie), foreman, h 33 Louie
Goff Chas Mc D, planer, h 6 Connolly's Ridge
Goff Hattie M Miss, h 6 Connolly's Ridge
Goff Jno, lab, h 6 Connolly's Ridge
Goff Mary Miss, h 6 Connolly's Ridge
Goff Waits A, vegetables City Market, h 12 n Spruce
Goforth Jas A (Elizabeth S), mchst, h 63 Ora
*Goins Marshal, lab, h 16 Hazzard
*Goins Prince A (Lucy), barber 11 Eagle, h 241 s Beaumont
Golay Margaret M, wid Julius, h 167½ s Main
Solay Martha P Miss, clk J H Law, h 167½ s Main
Goldberg Max (Enna), trav slsmn, h 9 Central av
Goldberg Rebecca Miss, cashr Bon Marche, h 9 Central av
Goldsmith Carlos M (W W Goldsmith & Son), h 129 Broad
Goldsmith Edwd L (Fannie), mngr Langren Hotel Cigar Stand, h 38 Oak

---

...Asheville Cleaning and Pressing Club....
Tailoring That Satisfies and Prices That Please
[S]team and French Dry Cleaning of all delicate and fine wearing apparel for ladies and gentlemen. MESSENGER SERVICE IN THE CITY.
[.] C. WILBAR, Prop.   4. N. Pack Square   PHONE 389

CAROLINA "M & W" **INDIAN** Prompt Delivery **COAL** & ICE CO. PHONE 130 50 PATTON AVE. WEIGHTS ACCURATE

Goldsmith Franklin P, lab, h Hazel Mill rd, W Asheville
Goldsmith Lela Miss, h 37½ s Main
Goldsmith Maggie Mrs, collr Jno C Moore, h 37½ s Main
Goldsmith Robt F (Mattie A), lab, h 43 Rector
Goldsmith W W & Son (W W and Carlos M), jewelers 10 n Pack Sq
Goldsmith Wade, clk frt office Sou Ry
Goldsmith Wm, h 43 Rector
Goldsmith Wm W (W W Goldsmith & Son), h 129 Broad
Goldsmith Wm W Jr (Maggie), watchmkr 37 s Main, h 37½ s Main
Goldsmith Zebulon V (Sallie), police, h 29 Silver
Goldstein Robt C, tchr, atty at law Temple Ct, bds Cherokee Inn
Golightly Lewis O (Mamie), furn 16 n Pack Sq, h 2 Charlotte
Gooch Floyd, engnr, h 38 Jefferson Drive
Gooch Thos J (Etta), mngr, h 38 Jefferson Drive
Good Benj F (Clara V), carrier P O, h 90 Cherry
Goode Alma M Miss, h Edgemont
Goode Alson J (Ida), contr, h Edgemont
Goode Alson L, student, h Edgemont
Goode E C, student, h Edgemont
Goode Frances S Miss, public stengr 35 Amer Nat'l Bank Bldg, h 61 Vance
Goode J Lon, trav slsmn, h 61 Vance
Goode Jno C (Agnes), real est, h 61 Vance
*Goode Jno W (Cornelia), presser British Woolen Mills, h 138 Choctaw
Goode Mary, wid Wm C, smstrs, h 42 Jefferson Drive
Goodis Nathan (Clara), gro 80 Poplar, h same
GOODLAKE AUGUSTUS M (Olivia), contr and builder 22 s Pack Sq—phone 976, h 50 Clingman av

A. M. GOODLAKE
CONTRACTOR AND BUILDER
REINFORCED : CONCRETE : A : SPECIALTY

Office and Repair Shop:

22 SOUTH PACK SQUARE

Phone No. 976

Poultry **Kiibler & Whitehead**
CITY MARKET   PHONES, 195 and 694

ASHEVILLE POWER AND LIGHT COMPANY
St. Rw'y — Electric Light and Power — Gas
PHONE 69

Asheville Dray, Fuel and Construction Co.

Heavy Hauling of all kinds — WE FURNISH BUILDING STONE — Moving Furniture a Specialty
61-2 South Main — PHONE - 223

DYNAMOS & MOTORS

Piedmont Electric Co.

64 Patton Av.
ASHEVILLE, N.C.

Goodlake Burt E, plmbr, h 82 Livingston
Goodlake Carrol, stengr, rms 242 Patton av
Goodlake Claude A, auto repr Hollar Motor Co, bds 242 Patton av
Goodlake Edwd E, carp A M Goodlake, h 50 Clingman av
Goodlake Ella, wid Jno, h 82 Livingston
Goodlake J C, clk Ashe Tel & Tel Co, h 50 Clingman av
GOODMAN ALFRED C (Greene & Goodman), rms Y M C A
*Goodman E Zion, supt N C Mutual & Prov Assn, h 264 s Beaumont
Goodman Ida R Miss, stengr Merrick & Barnard, h 118 Woodfin
Goodman L Victor (Beulah), condr Sou Ry, h 153 Blanton
*Goodman Sallie, h 80 Baird
GOODRICH FRANCES L MISS, pres Allanstand Cottage Industries, h 89 Victoria rd
Goodrich Jos V (Katherine R), with Beaumont Furn Co, h 184 Woodfin
Goodrich Julia W Miss, h 89 Victoria rd
*Goodrum Columbus, cook, h 166 Church
*Goodrum Henry (Margaret), lab, h 144 Pearson Drive
*Goodrum Mary, laund, h 114 Mountain
*Goodrum Sandy (Julia), lab, h 41 Pine
*Goodrum Sophia, h 82 Mountain
Goodwill Bradley C (Abbie), h Edgemont
Goodwin Addie A Miss, stengr, h 14 Grove
Goodwin Jas W (Mary), printer, h 14 Grove
Goodwin Mamie Miss, clk, h 14 Grove
Goodwin Mattie T Miss, h 14 Grove
*Goodwin Thos, waiter, rms 50 McDowell
Goodwin Troy, driver, bds 94 Cherry
*Gordon Drucilla, dom, h 291 Merrimon av
Gordon J Edgar (Mahala), clk Carmichael's Pharmacy, h 38 Clingman av
GORDON JOS H, sec S & W H Northup Lbr Co (Inc), res Richmond Va
Gordon Jos W (Laura), h W Asheville
*Gore Victor (Hester), driver, h 67 Gudger
Gorham Gray, reporter Ashev Gazette-News, h 102 Cumberland av
Gorham J W Mrs, h 102 Cumberland av
Gorham Robt S, student, h 102 Cumberland av
Gorrell Jeanette B Miss, h 55 College
Gorrell Jeanette, wid Logan W, bds 55 College

J. C. McPHERSON
SLATE AND TIN ROOFING
Galvanized Iron Work — Hot Air Furnaces
35-37 EAST COLLEGE STREET

PLUMBING STEAM AND HOT WATER HEATING
PHONE 133

Gosnell Dora Miss, h 24 Cherry
Gosnold Wm E, engnr, bds 346 w Haywood
Gossett Carl T (Beatrice), fireman, h Asheville av, W Ashev
Gossett Ida C, wid Robt A, h Asheville av, W Asheville
Gossett Jno O, painter R L Fitzpatrick & Son, bds 51 n Main
Gossett Pearl E Miss, asst Dr E R Russell, h Asheville av, W Asheville
Gould Edith Miss, h 327 Montford av
Gould Edwd, h 327 Montford av
GOVERNMENT BUILDING, Patton av n w cor Haywood
Grace Julia T Miss, h 22 Broad
Grace Julia T, wid T E, h 22 Broad
Grace Memorial Episcopal Church, Merrimon av end of car line, Rev W S Cain rector
Grace Methodist Episcopal Church, Grace
Grace Public School, Grace, Miss Augusta Anderson prin
Gragg Finley E (Agnes), fireman, h Grace
Gragg Lillian Miss, h Grace
Gragg Robt L, student, h Grace
Gragg Viola Miss, h Grace
Graham Bessie Miss, h 5 Biltmore rd, S Biltmore
Graham Chas (Cora), driver, h 317 n Main
*Graham Daniel J (Nellie), fireman, h 73 Clingman av
Graham Geo W (Nettie B), foreman The Piedmont Electric Co, h W Asheville
Graham J Baxter (Mary J), tmstr, h (r) 269 s Main
Graham W Arthur (Katie), driver Swannanoa Ldy, h 26 Pearl
Grahl W Herbert (Julia), fireman, h Penna av, W Ashe
Grainger Ludie B Mrs, h 43 n Liberty
Grant Anna M, wid F Rogers, h 194 Montford av
*Grant Alex, driver Ashev Grocery Co
Grant Bessie W Miss, clk, h 69 Blanton
Grant Clara R Mrs, h 54 Madison
Grant David C, h 43 Arlington
Grant Florence V Miss, h 217 s Main
GRANT H F REALTY CO, 48 Patton av, W R McDermott v-pres, W A Rexford sec-treas
Grant J Thos (Sallie), lab, h Swannonoa av, W Asheville
Grant Jno H (Flonnie), clk, h 131 Blanton
Grant Katherine Miss, h 194 Montford av
Grant Leonard M, barber G W Johnson, h 25 Mountain
Grant Lewis F, agt Met Life Ins Co, h 69 Blanton

Candy Kitchen and Club Cafe
"A GOOD PLACE FOR REFRESHMENT"

Hot drinks on cold days. Cold drinks on hot days. The best drinks every day. Pure fruits and syrups blended "just right," served daintily. Our Ice Cream and Soda Water Department, Restaurant and Candy Departments are always kept up to the standard of nearest perfection. Phones 110 and 111. 19 and 21 Haywood St.

Brown's Undertaking Parlors

S. H. BROWN

50 Patton Avenue
ASHEVILLE, N. C.

Lady Assistant When Desired

Phone 193-2 Rings

THE MOORE Plumbing Company

16 N. Pack Square

PHONE 1025

Sanitary Plumbing, General Tin and Metal Work, Hot Air Furnaces

---

*Grant Mayme, h 37 Magnolia av
Grant Millard G, clk McPeeters & Mack, h 217 s Main
*Grant Nannie, cook, h 29 Poplar
GRANT'S PHARMACY, 10 s Main—phone 10, Penrose L Baldwin mngr
Grant Rose Miss, clk The London Shop, bds 5 Flint
Grant Rosa T, wid Murray, h 131 Asheland av
Grant Rufus M (Mary E), condr St Ry, h 217 s Main
Grant Saml J, tinner A L McLean & Co, h 217 s Main
Grant Wm B (Nora), contr, h 69 Blanton
Grant Wm T (Lura), jeweler, h W Asheville
Grarrettson Mary Miss, h Forest Hill
Grasty Robt M, tel opr, h nr Murphy Junction
Grasty Wiley, farmer, h nr Murphy Junction
*Graves Hattie, h Haywood rd, W Asheville
*Graves Jno (Pattie), lab, h Haywood rd, W Asheville
*Graves Mary, dom 435 Pearson Drive
*Graves Patti, cook, 435 Pearson Drive
*Gray Augustus (Sallie), lab, h 20 Blanton
Gray Florence Miss, milliner, h 58 Bartlett
"Gray Gables", boarding, 46-48 Walnut
*Gray Hattie, h S Asheville
*Gray Henry, furn repr 101 n Lexington av, h 25 Seney
*Gray Irene, laund, h 70 Ridge
*Gray Lucius, porter C T Howell, h Eagle st
*Gray Nellie, laund, h S Asheville
Gray Percy C (Belle), stage mngr The Dreamland, h 18 Central av
*Gray Porter, eating hse 40 Mountain, h same
*Gray Squire (Rachel), lab, h S Asheville
☞Gray see also Grey
Great Atlantic & Pacific Tea Co, 36 Oak, J S Handte mngr
GREATER WESTERN NORTH CAROLINA ASSN, 3-4 Electrical Bldg, W E Breese Jr pres, G S Powell treas, F W Miller sec, S H Cohen mngr
Greco Frank (Amelia), R R Contr 209 Oates Bldg, h 48 Philip
*Greecen Wm, lab, bds 488 s French Broad av
Green Archibald W (Ida), plmbr J R Rich Co, h 120 Clingman av
*Green Barney J, cook Harper Stiles, h 39 Black
Green Bettie, wid W H, h 36 w Haywood
GREEN BROS (Gay Green), furniture and house furnishings, 450 Patton av—phone 75
Green Carl, h Grace

The Battery Park Bank

Capital - - $100,000.00
Surplus and Profits, $110,000.00

ASHEVILLE, N. C.   City, County and State Depositary

J. A. TILLMAN   **Jeweler**   I carry a nice line of Watches, Clocks an Jewelry, and make a specialty of repa work. Satisfaction guaranteed   **17 N. Main St**

Green Doctor (Sophronia), crossing tender Sou Ry, h 495 Depot
*Green Dorcas, cook, h 12 Lincoln av
*Green Edith, matron Riverside Park Ashev P & L Co, h 2 Sorrell
GREEN GAY (Effie), (Green Bros), (W E Britt & Co), pres Imperial Mut L & H Ins Co, and Harris-Barnett Dry Goods Co, h 99 Asheland av—phone 916
Green Geo (Cora), carp, h (r) 269 s Main
Green Geo A (Annie), painter, h 113 Biltmore rd, S Biltmore
*Green Jas (Mary), cook, h 126 Pine
Green Jno F (Sue), fireman, h Grace
Green Kentucky, lab, h 495 Depot
Green Leta Miss, wks Ashev Mica Co, h 495 Depot
*Green Mary, dom, h 14 Aston pl
Green N Lois Miss, clk Peerless Dept Store, h 369 w Haywood
Green Ottis (Mary), propr Ottis Green Hdw Co, h 84 Church
Green Ottis Hardware Co, 11 s w Pack Sq, Ottis Green propr
Green P Jackson (Susan C), gro 246 Patton av, h 250 same
Green Paul, student, h Grace
Green Pearl Miss, h Grace
*Green Pleasant (Jennie), lab, h 141 Valley
Green Rose Miss, bkkpr Peerless Dept Store, h 369 w Haywood
*Green Theodore, gro 160 Beaumont, h 22 Hildebrand
Green W H, flgmn, bds 434 Depot
Green Walter, engnr Sou Ry, h 369 w Haywood
Green Wells H Jr (Pearle), clk Green Bros, h 59 Phifer
Green Willis W, bag clk Sou Ry, h 369 w Haywood
GREENE EDGAR C (Greene & Goodman), rms Y M C A
GREENE JOSEPH B (Sarah), physician (ear, nose and throat), 20 Battery Park pl—phone 1648, office hours, 10 a m to 1 p m, afternoon by appointment, h 40 Watauga—phone 1736
GREENE & GOODMAN (E C Greene, A C Goodman), real estate and insurance, 1½ s Main (2d fl)—phone 738
*Greenleaf Jas (Lola), lab Standard Oil Co, h 118 Hill
*Greenlee Geo L (Addie), (Greenlee & Loder), and (Wilson Undertaking Co), h (r) 177 Hill
*Greenlee Geo S (Sallie M), painter, h Haywood rd, W Ashev

INSURE YOUR SALARY WITH U
NEVER CARRY YOUR OWN RIS
SAFETY IS THE BEST POLIC
UNLESS YOU ARE A CAPITALIS
REST EASY IF YOU HAV
AN ACCIDENT WE WIL
NOT KEEP YOU WAITING T
COLLECT YOUR CLAI
EVERY CLAIM PROMPTLY PAI

Imperial Mu tual Life & Health Insurance Co

Home Office:
ASHEVILLE, N. C
Phone 49!

HOTEL OXFORD   **Asheville, N. C** Redecorated and Refitted throughout. R cently enlarged to 60 rooms. Centrally l cated Depot cars stop at entrance. Lor distance telephone office upstairs. American and European plan. Rates 50c, 75c and ! per day; special rates by week or month. C. H. Branson & Sons, Proprietors. Phone 1887. 50-54 South Main St.

*Greenlee Hattie, laund, h 54 Short
*Greenlee Hillman H, porter, h 8 Oakdale av
*Greenlee Jane, laund, h 514 s French Broad av
*Greenlee Letitia, h 21 Cumberland av
*Greenlee Madora, dom, h 8 Oakdale av
*Greenlee Matilda, laund, h 8 Oakdale av
*Greenlee S Woodfin (Essie), porter, h 8 Oakdale av
*Greenlee Wm, cook, h 8 Oakdale av
*Greenlee & Loder (G L Greenlee, R H Loder), pool 4 Eagle and 40 s Main
Greenwood Barbara L Miss, h 46 w Walnut
Greenwood E E Maj, tchr Bingham Schl, h Bingham Hghts
Greenwood Geo, lumberman, h Grace
Greenwood Jas G (Pearl), mchst, h Grace
Greenwood Jas H, propr Reed Farm Dairy, h w Chapel rd, Biltmore
Greenwood Ralph, student, h Grace
Greenwood Robt (Eliza) (Greenwood & Blackstock), h Grace
Greenwood Sallie, wid A B, h 10 s French Broad av
Greenwood & Blackstock (Robt Greenwood, T E Blackstock), hardwoods, 305 Oates Bldg
*Greer Allen (Minnie), driver C Sawyer, h 61 Hill
*Greer Barney, cook, h 37 Black
*Greer Henry (Clara), butler, h 34 Magnolia av
Greer L U, custodian Elks Home, h same
*Greer Louisa, maid, h 21 Maiden la
*Greer Otis, porter, h 21 Maiden la
Greer's Row, 81-93 n Lexington av
Gregg Pierce, student, h 312 Montford av
Gregory Andrew, lab, bds D F Hill, W Ashev
Gregory Carl, soda clk Allison's Drug Store, h 85 Penland
Gregory Ella, wid E J, h 85 Penland
Gregory Emma Miss, h 16 Cumberland av
Gregory Eugene, clk, h 22 Central av
Gregory Pearson, h 22 Central av
Gresham Clarence (Gresham & Fogus), h Mt Airy Ga
Gresham & Fogus (Clarence Gresham, C R Fogus), proprs Sou Ry Dining Room, Sou Ry Passngr Sta
*Grey Augustus (Sallie), lab, h 20 Blanton
*Grey Sallie, h 19 Cole
☞ Grey see also Gray
Grice Jno B (Nellie C), cotton weigher, h 66 Park Sq
*Griffin Annie, h 77 Eagle
Griffin Eliza C, wid Jno, h Brevard rd, W Ashev

FOR BOX SHOOKS | **Call English Lumber Co.** **PHONE 321**

Griffin Jno T (Evangeline), trav slsmn, h 10 All Souls Crescent, Biltmore
Griffin Jos F (Hester), lab, h 448 n Main
Griffin Jos, foreman St Dept, h n Main ext
*Griffin Pinckney (Beatrice), lab, bds 5 w Walnut
Griffin Rufus E, lab, h 448 n Main
*Griffin Saml, lab, h (r) 29 Clingman av
*Griffith Ellen, cook 578 Montford av
Griffith F Webb, phys, 20 Battery Park pl, rms 67 s French Broad av
Grimes Jas Walter (Mary), lime mnfr, h County
*Grimes Maria, laund, h 68 Mountain
Grimes Thos W, clk Ashev P & G Co, h 27 Spruce
Grimshawe Anna Miss, bkkpr Marsteller & Co h 211 Patton
Grimshawe Nellie Miss, h 211 Patton av
Grindstaff Claude, clk Carmichael's Pharmacy, bds 395 s French Broad av
Grindstaff E C, trav slsmn, rms 23 Technical Bldg
Grindstaff Lillie Mrs, wkr Ashev Mica Co, h 98 Patton av
Grindstaff Thos J (Mollie), driver, h Grace
GRINNAN R T MAJ (Sadie B), v-supt Bingham School, h Bingham Heights
GRISET ERNEST J (May), clk M Hyams, h 70 Charlotte
Griswold Florence Mrs, h 108 Montford av
*Groce Henry (Dora), cook, h 13 Miller
Groome Mary Miss, bds 41 Vance
Groome Russell L, bkkpr, bds 41 Vance
Groover Margaret Mrs, bds 327 Montford
Gross Albert, bkkpr, h 258 College
*Gross Alonzo, lab, h 55 Mountain
Gross David D (Minnie), mngr, h College Park
Gross Nola Mrs, boarding 51 n Main, h same
Gross Wiley W (Nola), h 51 n Main
Grove Automobile Co, office Grove Park
Grove Chas E (Maggie L), mngr Biltmore Drug Store, h 5 Reed, Biltmore
Grove Edwin W Dr (Gertrude), propr Grove Park, h 43 n Liberty
Grove Mary Miss, nurse Biltmore Hosp, rms same
Grove Park, end of Charlotte, W F Randolph supt
Grove Park Inn, ft of Sunset Mtn, Dr E W Grove pres, F L Seely mngr
Groves J A Grocery Co, 116 Patton av, J A Groves, propr
Groves Jno A (Retta), propr J A Groves Grocery Co, h 116 Patton av

Biggest Busiest Best Asheville Steam Laundry

Phones: 1936 and 1937

43 to 47 W. College Street

CHARLES H. HONESS OPTOMETRIST AND OPTICIAN

Exclusive maker of ATLAS SHUR-ON EYE GLASSES

THE Home of Ce-Rite Toric Lenses

We make a specialty of correcting optical defects with properly fitted glasses.

54 Patton Avenue
Opposite Postoffice

Carolina Machinery Co. Founders, Machinists and Jobbers of Mill Supplies. We make all kinds of Castings in Iron, Brass or Aluminum.

WE ALSO FURNISH SKILLED MECHANICS FOR BOILER REPAIRS —— **PHONE 590**

LIFE INSURANCE COMPANY OF VA.
ORGANIZED 187
Richmond -:- Virginia
J. V MOON, Superintendent
Rooms 3-4-5- Maxwelton Bldg., Asheville, N. C.

All claims paid IMMEDIATELY upon receipt of satisfactory proofs of Death. Total payment to policyholders since organization, over $12,000,000.00. Is paying its Policyholders over $1,000,000.00 annually.

T. P. JOHNSON & CO.

SHEET METAL WORKERS

All Kinds of Roofing Guttering and Conductor Work Metal Ceilings, Skylights and Galvanized Iron Cornices

OFFICE and SHOP:
69-71 S. MAIN

Phone 325

DR. C. H. MILLER

Mechano-Therapist

14 N. Spruce Street
ASHEVILLE, N. C.

PHONE 979

Hours by Engagement

DRUGLESS HEALING OF DISEASE

ASHEVILLE [1913] DIRECTORY

Groves P Raymond, printer The Inland Press, h 116 Patton
Grubb Edith Mrs, tailoress H P Petrie, h 480 Depot
Gruner B F Mrs, local mngr Spirella Corset Agency 21 s Main, h 45 Blanton
GRUNER EDWIN P DR, propr The Gruner Sanitarium (see classified Baths and Sanitariums)
GRUNER SANITARIUM (The), 29-31 Haywood, Dr Edwin P Gruner propr (see classified Baths and Sanitariums)
Gruver Mary Miss, stengr Guy Weaver, h 42 Walnut
Gryder Wm M (Martha), lab, h 27 Brick
Guarantee Shoe Store, 4 s Main, M L Roth mngr
*Guder Maria, cook 24 n Spruce
Gudger Alice L, wid H Lamar, h 89 Montford av
*Gudger Arnold, butler 210 Merrimon av
Gudger Bessie, wid Benj G, h 139 Montford av
GUDGER CASSIUS S (S I Bean & Co), rms Asheville Club
*Gudger Chas (Letha), driver, h 28 Smith
*Gudger Chas (Bertha), driver, h 137 Clingman av
Gudger Chas H (Olive E), driver, h 104 Bartlett
*Gudger Clarence, driver, h 200 Wallach
Gudger David S, sec-treas A M Field Co, h Asheville Club
*Gudger Eddie, cook, h 137 Southside av
Gudger Elsie F Miss, h 139 Montford av
Gudger Fannie G Miss, tchr, h 139 Montford av
Gudger Frank A (Ellen), clk A D Stoner, h Fairview rd
Gudger Henry C, student, h 139 Montford av
Gudger Herman A, atty at law 307 Oates Bldg, h 17 Soco
Gudger Hezekiah H Judge (Jennie), h 105 College
Gudger Horace M (Ella), clk A D Stoner, h Fairview rd
Gudger J Ernest, mica ctr Ashev Mica Co, h 26 Market
Gudger J Holland (Susan E), condr, h 30 Ora
*Gudger Jas (Julia), hostler, h 217 Clingman av
Gudger Jas M (Sarah), atty at law, 8 Short, h same
Gudger Jas M Jr (Kate M), congressman and atty at law, h 137 s French Broad av
*Gudger Jesse, lab, h 75 Wallach
Gudger Lillie M Mrs, dressmkr 145 s Main, h same
Gudger Maud Miss, h 89 Montford av
Gudger Myrtle Miss, h 89 Montford av
*Gudger Oscar, driver, h 200 Wallach
Gudger Owen (Haynes & Gudger), sec Brown Book Co, Inc, rms 35 Temple Ct
*Gudger Patton (Mary), driver, h 200 Wallach

ASHEVILLE CLEANING and PRESSING CLUB

TAILORING THAT SATISFIES and PRICES THAT PLEASE

Hats cleaned, banded and bound. Silk hats ironed. Buttons made to order in all sizes. Plain or with rims. PHONE 389

DYEING IN ALL SHADES Cleaned. Messenger Service.

Kid Gloves, Slippers and Plumes. Fancy Jabots and Ties, French Dry Cleaned. Ladies' and Gentlemen's suits Steam

J. C. Wilbar, Prop. 4 NORTH PACK SQ.

HACKNEY & MOALE CO.

E are the Printers and Binders of this Directory—We are prepared to print anything from a dodger to a daily paper—We use Linotypes in our composing room, which cast new type for each job—We have a full line of linen finish bond paper—envelopes to match; other papers we carry are Cranes, Old English, Deerfield Bond, H. & M. Bond and the best grades of ledger paper.

We operate in our press room two cylinders and five jobbers—Also a folder, stitcher and ruler—With such an equipment, backed by the very best and most experienced workmen, we feel confident that you will realize that you run no risk in placing orders with us.

We have, in connection with our printing office, a thoroughly equipped Bindery; we solicit orders for loose leaf ledgers, cash books, special ruling and all kinds of binding. We do as good work as you can get anywhere.

12 and 14 Lexington Ave.   Telephone 181

ASHEVILLE :: NORTH CAROLINA

HACKNEY & MOALE CO.

VERYTHING for the office—We are agents for Eaton, Crane & Pike's celebrated correspondence papers—We Carry all the new novels, and sell at 10 per cent less than publishers' prices—We sell and push the Waterman Ideal Fountain Pen, because we believe it to be the best on the market. We carry a full line of Rhododendron souvenirs, also novelties of every description; visitors will be especially interested in this department—We carry a greater variety of Souvenir Post Cards than all other dealers combined, having on hand from half a million to a million, at all times.

We sell new and re-built typewriters, all kinds of typewriter supplies, School Books and School Supplies; take orders for engraved and embossed stationery, wedding invitations, announcements, etc.

We are agents for the Yawman & Erbe Filing Cabinets, and all kinds of office furniture and devices.

We are agents for the celebrated Gunn and Macey Sectional Bookcases, which we consider the two best makes on the market.

3 West Pack Square   Telephone 242

ASHEVILLE :: NORTH CAROLINA

*Gudger Rachel, cook, h 40 Maiden la
Gudger S Lorena Miss, h 8 Short
*Gudger Susan, laundress, h 75 Wallach
*Gudger Thos (Francis), lab, h Valley nr College
Gudger Troy, driver G D Allison, h 94 Cherry
GUDGER VONNO L, atty at law 1-2-3 Brown-Gudger Bldg—phone 169, h 89 Montford av—phone 757
Gudger Walter R (Lillie M), justice of the peace and notary, 8 s Pack Sq (basement), h 145 s Main
*Gudger Wm (Zora), driver Carolina C & I Co, h 135 Clingman av
Guerard Albert S (Florence W), claim agt Sou Ry, h 79 Furman av
*Guess Henry, lab, h 20 Ralph
Guffey Adelaide (Baby), h 33 Aston
GUFFEY JOHN A (A Delilah), dry goods 9 s w Pack Sq—phone 471, h 33 Aston—phone 1376
Guffin Hallie I Miss, city missionary, h 19 Centre
Guffin Martha J, wid E M, h 19 Centre
Guffin Olive W Miss, stengr Board of Trade, h 19 Centre
Guffrey Frank (Lydia), lab, h 24 Ralph
Guischard Gustavus L (Laura O), plumber 22 s Pack Sq, h 187 Charlotte
Guischard Margaret R, wid Geo L, h 187 Charlotte
Guischard Marguerite L Miss, clk G L Guischard, h 187 Charlotte
Guthrie Donie Miss, rms 18 n Lexington av
Guthrie Ellen, wid Lewis, h 36 Bennett
Guthrie Hardy, h 36 Bennett
Guthrie Oscar M (Mamie), drayman, h 21 Atkinson
GUTHRIE RALPH N, solr Western Carolina Realty Co, h 64 n Spruce
Guthrie Robt W (Loretta), h Haywood rd, W Ashev
Guthrie T Kelley (Bertha), ship clk Mustin-Robertson Co Inc, h W Asheville
Guthrie W Arthur (Texie), driver Standard Oil Co, h W Asheville
Guy Jos L, whol produce and com mer, 32 n Lexington av, h 12 Blair
*Gwynn Harriett, laund, h 39 Magnolia av

H

Hackney Amy B Miss, h 22 Bearden av
Hackney F Minnie Miss, nurse, h 22 Bearden av

WEAVERVILLE LINE — NINE MILES BY TROLLEY FROM PACK SQUARE TO WEAVERVILLE

ASHEVILLE AND EAST TENNESSEE RAILROAD CO.
NORTH MAIN STREET — ASHEVILLE N. C.

Electrical Supplies — PIEDMONT ELECTRIC COMPANY, ASHEVILLE, N. C., 64 PATTON AVE.

ASHEVILLE [1913] DIRECTORY

HACKNEY GEO L, pres Knoxville Directory Co, res Lexington N C
Hackney Kate B Miss, tchr, h 22 Bearden av
Hackney Nell B Miss, nurse, h 22 Bearden av
Hackney Percy E, h Knoxville, Tenn
Hackney Wm N (Theresa), h 22 Bearden av
HACKNEY & MOALE CO (Inc), printers 10-12 s Lexington av, A E Swayne supt
Hackworth Frank, fireman, bds 348½ Depot
Haddon Fay Miss, clk Wm R Sluder, h 50 Highland
Haddon Henry B (Louisa), contr, h 50 Highland
*Haddon Thos G Rev (Ella), h 80 Valley
*Haden Rome (Amanda), lab, h 42 Black
Hagan Henry J, dental supplies 63 Amer Natl Bank Bldg, rms 36 n French Broad av
Hagenbach May Miss, superv of practice schl, Normal & Collegiate Institute, rms same
☞ **Hahn see Hawn and Hone**
Haines, Jones & Cadbury Co, plumbing supplies 1 Technical Bldg, Wm H Harrison Jr, local mngr
☞ **Haines see also Haynes**
*Hairston Robt P Rev (Mary), h 57 Short
*Hairston Vera, waitress, h 57 Short
☞ **Halcombe see Holcombe**
Hale Bonnie Miss, h Woolsey
Hale Carter R, bicycle repr J M Hearn & Co, h 84 Clingman
Haley Edwd L (Bonnie), pattern mkr, bds 172 Southside av
Hale Frank V, clk Sou Ry, h 65 Woodfin
Hale Jno H (Lenoir), lab, h Woolsey
Hale Lewis V, h Woolsey
Hale Pearl Miss, h Woolsey
Hale Sara H Miss, h 65 Woodfin
Hale Sara P, wid H Douglas, h 65 Woodfin
Hall Albert F (Bertha M), mngr Hardwood Lbr Co, h 249 Montford av
Hall Allie Miss, wks Ashev Mica Co, h 12 n Pack Sq
Hall Alvin A (Frances E), mngr Special Sales Co, h 132 w Chestnut
Hall Andrew J (Lillie), switchman, h Jarrett av, W Ashev
Hall Aven E, driver Brown's Creamery, h 7 Summit
Hall Farrell E, slsmn Boston Shoe Store, h 7 Summit
Hall Bascom, barber St Charles Barber Shop, h 107 Church
HALL BURWELL F, dentist 48-49 Amer Natl Bank Bldg—phone 803, rms 29 Technical Bldg
Hall C Edwd, trav slsmn, rms 41½ s Main

CONTRACTOR and BUILDER
J. C. McPHERSON
STEEL RANGES — 35-37 E COLLEGE ST. PHONE 133
PLUMBING STEAM AND HOT WATER HEATING

Hall Cebron E, carp A M Goodlake, h W Asheville
*Hall Chas (Hattie), driver, h Biltmore rd, S Biltmore
*Hall Cornelius, lab, h 7 Atkin
Hall Earle A, police, h 9 Summit
Hall Earle A (May), police, h 9 Summit
Hall Edwin S (Rosa L), mirrors resilvered 57 n Main, h 405 w Haywood
Hall Elijah H (Clara C), lumber, h 64 Bearden av
*Hall Ellen, laund, h 78 Mountain
Hall Geo L (O Jeanette), asst prin Carolina Coml Schl, h 88 Penland
Hall H Edwd, slsmn J M Westall & Co, h 7 Summit
Hall Howard (Elizabeth), lab, h Sunset Drive
*Hall Jas A (Eliza), carp, h 106 Livingston
Hall Julia Mrs, h 12 n Pack Sq (3d fl)
Hall Kate Miss, h 90 Church
Hall Lolan E, clk Brown-Miller Shoe Co, h 7 Summit
Hall M Irene Miss, h Brevard rd, W Ashev
Hall Maggie M Miss, h 405 w Haywood
*Hall Margaret, laundress, h 11 Wallach
Hall Martha Miss, h 22 Reed Bldg
Hall Marvin B (Cora), brakeman, h 24 Spring
Hall Mary Mrs, h Woolsey (R F D 1)
Hall Ohl J Mrs, propr The West Virginia, h 88 Penland
Hall Paralee, wid Mark, h 8 Redmon's al
Hall Philip B, bkkpr Amer Natl Bank
Hall Robt D (Kittie), janitor Court House, h 325 n Main
HALL SAM'L D (Lillie A), real estate and notary public, 32 Patton av (2d fl)—phone 91, h W Asheville (see side lines)
Hall Seabron C (Muncie), carp, h Van st, W Ashev
Hall Thaddeus (Gertrude), lab, h 71 Tiernan
Hall U Talmer, glazier J M Westall & Co, h 7 Summit
Hall Wm (Fannie), mchst, bds Hotel Florence
*Hall Wm (Estelle), lab, h 35 Buttrick
Hall Zilca B Miss, tchr Allen Industrial Home & Schl, h 241
Halpin Katherine Miss, maid, 103 Montford av
Halthenon Building, offices, 29-31 Haywood
Halyburton Alice Miss, tchr Orange St Schl, h Biltmore Estate
Halyburton Lillie, wid J A, h 4 Brook, Biltmore
Halyburton House, 430 Depot, J W Halyburton propr
Halyburton Jas W (Minnie), propr Halyburton House, h 430 Depot
Halyburton Nellie B, wid A G, h 80 Josephine

Candy Kitchen and Club Cafe
"A GOOD PLACE FOR REFRESHMENT"

The very best ingredients with sanitary conditions in our Candy Manufacturing Department make possible the dainty, crisp confections sold here. Bon Bons and Chocolates made every day, put up in neat, attractive boxes. Phones 10 and 111. 19 and 21 Haywood St.

Brown's Undertaking Parlors

S. H. BROWN

Lady Assistant When Desired

Phone 193-2 Rings

50 Patton Avenue
Asheville, N. C.

Established 1894

B. J. JACKSON

Carefully Selected Fruits and Vegetables

Stall No. 11, City Market

BUSINESS PHONES:
86 and 101

RESIDENCE PHONE
1596

---

190   ASHEVILLE [1913] DIRECTORY

Hames H Edwd (Eliza J), mchst Ashev Supply & Fdy Co, h W Asheville
*Hamilton Annie, waitress Wm Stinson, h 12 Ralph
Hamilton Earl P, emp Ashev Tel & Tel Co, rms 75 Church
Hamilton Ewart G (Emma), laundryman, h Woolsey
*Hamilton Geo F (Martha), waiter, h 45 Ridge
Hamilton Grace Miss, tchr Normal & Collegiate Inst
*Hamilton Henry (Clara), lab, h 22 Gaither
HAMILTON IDA MISS, society editor Ashev Citizen, h 18 Oak
Hamilton Ira, clk The Racket Store, bds 76 Starnes av
Hamilton Irene Miss, h 22 Summit, S Biltmore
*Hamilton Jack, porter, h (r) 129 s Main
*Hamilton Jas (Annie), porter, h 21 Sassafras
Hamilton Jas M (Rosamond), carp, h 22 Summit, S Biltmore
*Hamilton Jos, lab, h 15 Bay
*Hamilton Julia, dom, h 23 Gray
Hamilton Mary Miss, h "Ardmion," Carroll av
Hamilton O C (Katherine), h "Ardmion," Carroll av
*Hamilton Thos M, blksmith C L Brown, h 27 Aston pl
*Hamilton Walter (Beatrice), janitor, h Biltmore rd, S Biltmore
Hamilton Wm R B (Leah), contr, 31 Tiernan, h same
Hamiter Everett C, student, bds 50 Asheland av
Hamlet Avery A (Theodosia), surveyor, h 141 Flint
Hamlet H M, solr, rms Franklin Hotel
Hamlin Jacob (Elsie), leather, h Haywood rd, W Ashev
Hamlin Jas O (Nellie), h Haywood rd, W Ashev
HAMMERSLOUGH R W, asst sec Y M C A, h 55 w Chestnut
Hammett Augustus (Lula B), gro 502 w Haywood, h 36 Short Roberts
Hammett Harry, lab, h 36 Short Roberts
Hammett Jos T, fireman, bds 59 Ora
Hammett Spurgeon J, mngr P D Estes, h 59 Ora
Hammond Laura D, wid F C, propr The "Ozark," h 76 n Main
*Hammonds Wm H (Lois), waiter, h 19 Short
Hamner Clifton E, trav slsmn, h 194 Haywood
Hampton Annie Miss, bkkpr Asheville Dry Cleaning Co, rms 19 Harkins Bldg
Hampton Arthur B, mngr F B Hampton, h 46 Haywood
Hampton Bert A (Alice), condr Sou Ry, h 92 Jefferson Drive

Yᵉ OLD BOOK SHOP
114 Patton Ave.   Phone 1674
BOOKS BOUGHT, SOLD OR EXCHANGED

Hampton Chas G (Elizabeth), switchman, h 7 Connolly's Ridge
Hampton Chas M (Mary L), carp, h Asheville av, W Ashev
Hampton Delia Miss, h Woolsey (R F D 1)
Hampton E Rowley, ticket clk Sou Ry, h 257 s French Broad av
Hampton Eckles, usher The Dreamland, h 46 Haywood
Hampton Edna Miss, h 46 Haywood
Hampton Emmett, driver, bds 52 Woodfin
Hampton Fred B (Callie), bowling alley 12 w College, h 40 Haywood
*Hampton Geo (Laura), lab, h (r) 19 Mountain
Hampton Hattie Miss, h Woolsey (R F D 1)
Hampton Jno E (Julia), h 46 Haywood
Hampton Jno E Jr Dr (Emma), h 40 Haywood
Hampton Jno W (Annie), bkkpr Ideal Pressing Club, rms Harkins Bldg
*Hampton Laura, eating house 140 Valley, h 20 Mountain
Hampton Marcus F, h 151 Woodfin
Hampton Ralph B, city electrician, office 103 City Hall, h 46 Haywood
Hampton Saml A (Cordie), yd condr Sou Ry, h 60 Starnes
Hampton Wade, rms 34 Morsell Bldg
Hamrick Alex, helper J R Rich Co, h 55 Orchard
Hamrick Geo P (Carrie), gro 70 Charlotte, h 80 same
Hamrick Geo P Rev (Sallie L), pastor West End Baptist Church, h 51 Buxton
HAMRICK M WM (Mary), sec-treas J R Rich Co (Inc), h 55 Orchard
*Hamrick Pinkney (Ella), lab, h 164 Livingston
Handley Richard G (Annie), engnr, h 357 w Haywood
Handte Elta M Miss, h 36 Oak
Handte Jacob S (Fannie), mngr Great A & P Tea Co, h 36 Oak
HANES SULLIVAN M (Virginia), asst cashr Wachovia Bank & Trust Co, bds 94 College
☞Hanes see also Haines and Haynes
Haney ——, carp, bds 62 Penland
Haney Chas (Belle), lab, h 353 w Haywood
Haney Garfield W (Myrtle), lab, h 31 Buxton
Haney Jas E (Lena M), lab, h nr Murphy Junct
Haney Wm B (Jane), lab, h Lester rd, W Ashev
Hanley Margaret T Miss, bkkpr Ashev Mica Co, h 18 Oak
Hannah Wm W (Emma), yd mstr Sou Ry, h 370 w Haywood

Mrs. Wilder's SANITARY HOME LAUNDRY turns out first class work in Laundering and Dry Cleaning. No. 7 Montford Ave., Phone 1354

ARBOGAST MOTOR COMPANY
OLDSMOBILE — DETROIT ELECTRIC
BUICK — MAXWELLS
ACCESSORIES AND SUPPLIES
Phones 302 and 1728
52-60 N. Main

*Hannah Willie, h 35 Clemmons
Hanner Robt, lino opr Ashev Citizen, h 51 College
Hanner Robt, printer, rms 51 College
Hannon Jno T, mch opr Princess Theatre, h 6 Central av
Hannon Lou R, wid Chas, dressmkr, 6 Central av, h same
HANS REES SONS (Inc), tanners Sou Ry nr Passngr Sta (see Rees Hans Sons)
Hansen Jno (Chassie), lbr buyer, h Riverside Drive
HANSEN OLAF E, sec Asheville Dry Cleaning Co, bds 107 Haywood
*Happoldt Ivey, waitress, h 46 Short
*Harber Bessie, cook, h 22 Ralph
Harbin Jas (Delia), motorman, h 48 Buxton
Harbin Thos L, glazier W M Jones, h 14 Pearson Drive
Hardee Mattie, wid Chas J, h 44 Montford av
Hardee Montelas (Maude), fruit grower, bds 401 s Main
Harden Jno E, v-pres Ashev Cotton Mills, Inc, h Greensboro N C
Harden Robt W (Dorothy), carp, h 521 n Main
Hardin Monroe M (Mollie D), h Sand Hill rd, W Ashev
Hardin Sallie Miss, dressmkr W Asheville, h same
Harding Essie E Miss, student, h 80 Flint
Harding Geo W (Lettie), painter, h 26 Clyde
Harding M M, fireman W M Jones, h W Asheville
Harding Milton (Essie), contr, h 80 Flint
Harding Milton B, clk Dunham's Music House, h 80 Flint
Harding Sallie H Miss, h 17 Montford av
Harding Theodore C, brkmn Ga Central Ry, h 80 Flint
Hardwood Lumber Co, 31 Temple Ct; A F Hall mngr, F L McLean buyer
Hardwood Lumber Co, 31 Temple Ct, A F Hall mngr, F L McLean buyer
Hardegg Julius, watchmkr Victor Stern, bds 60 Spruce
*Hardy Jas (Minnie), butler, h 40 Tuskee
*Hardy Maggie, cook, h 488 Black
*Hardy Wm (Nannie), coachman, h 23 Short
Hare Chas F, mngr The Millard Livery Co, rms 33 n Main
Hare Patrick E (Lillian C) (Hare & Co), h 15 East
Hare Rich'd W (Kittie), wood wkr C L Brown, h Biltmore (R F D 2)
Hare & Co (P E Hare), undertakers, 21 s Main
*Hargrave Dock, cleaner and presser Y M I Pressing Club, h Y M I Bldg
*Hargrave Jonas (Annie), cleaner J C Wilbar, h 52 Hill
*Hargrace W I, presser J C Wilbar, h 33 Hill

Asheville Dry Cleaning Co.
Telephones 835-836, All Dep't
MAIN, N. E. COR. COLLEGE

THE CLEANERS
Our Department for Oriental Rugs and Carpet Cleaning is prepared to serve you in all its branches.
E. S. Paine   O. E. Hansen

ALL KINDS Hardwood Lumber — ENGLISH LUMBER CO. Phone 321

*Hargrave Malinda, laund, h (r) 26 Gudger
Harker Edith M Miss, voice tchr Ashe Schl of Musical Art, h Forest Hill
Harker F Flaxington (Edith M), director Ashe School of Musical Art, h Forest Hill
Harker Jno J, h "Oakwald" Forest Hill
Harkins Building, offices, 26-28 Patton av
Harkins Harry S, clk R W Harkins, h 324 Montford
Harkins Ralph W (Florence), gro 268 Patton av, h 390 w Haywood
Harkins Thos J (Margaret), h 121 Broad
HARKINS THOS J (Roxie), v-pres Brown Book Co and (Harkins & Van Winkle) and notary 9-11 Harkins Bldg—phone 1588, h 324 Montford av
Harkins Wm W (Jessie B), U S dep marshal, h Haywood rd, W Asheville
HARKINS & VAN WINKLE (T J Harkins, K Van Winkle), attys at law 9-10-11 Harkins Bldg—phone 1588
☞Harkins see also Hawkins
Harlan Julia C, wid Jno J, h 38 Oak
Harmon Annie Miss, cashr Bon Marche, h 98 Broad
Harmon Chas W (Lenora), contr, h 98 Broad
Harmon Herbert W, clk, h 10 Orchard
Harmon Robt T (Pauline), msgr Sou Exp Co, h 30 Bartlett
HARMON THOS J, asst supt Life Ins Co of Va, h 10 Orchard
Harp Edwd (Doris), painter R L Fitzpatrick & Son, h Sou Ry nr Biltmore
*Harper Albert, porter, rms 88 Eagle
*Harper Cordelia, laund, h 7 Atkin
Harper Emma Miss, emp Ashev Stm Ldy, bds 26 Buttrick
*Harper Henry, porter Y M C A, h 7 Atkin
*Harper Jos (Zora), lab, h 174 Livingston
Harper Robt, driver Sou Dray, h Spring st
Harper Wm (Mattie), driver, h Riverside Drive nr Bridge
*Harrell Lottie, dom, h 124 Church
Harren Edna Miss, clk, bds 34 Spring
Harrigan Mary Miss, smstrs Battery Park Hotel, h 111 College
*Harrington Estelle, tchr, h 240 Asheland av
*Harris Abbie, cook, h 158 Beaumont
Harris-Barnett Dry Goods Co (Inc), wholesale, 36 n Main, Gay Green pres, A G Barnett v-pres, Dell Harris sec-treas

BIGGEST **B**USIEST **B**EST

Phones 1936 and 1937

ASHEVILLE STEAM LAUNDRY

43 to 47 W. COLLEGE

S. D. HALL REAL ESTATE AGENT

Money Loaned

Notary Public

32 PATTON AVENUE

Phone 91

CAROLINA MACHINERY CO.
—US when you want machine work of any kind . . .

Founders Machinists and Jobbers of Mill Supplies
When in the market for heavy castings such as columns or building plates get our prices. **Phone 590**

The Life Insurance Co. of Virginia
ORGANIZED 1871   RICHMOND, VA.

ISSUES ALL THE MOST APPROVED FORMS OF LIFE INSURANCE CONTRACTS from $500.00 to $25,000.00, with premiums payable quarterly, semi-annually and annually

J. V. Moon, Superintendent, Rooms 3-4-5 Maxwelton Bldg., Asheville, N. C.

D. TREXLER TIN SHOP

All Kinds of Roofing, Gutter and Conductor Work.

Phone 862

159 South Main St.

DR. C. H. MILLER

MECHANO-THERAPIST

14 N. Spruce St.
Phone 979
ASHEVILLE, N. C.

Hours by engagement

Drugless Healing of Disease

Harris C F Mrs, h 9 Grady
*Harris Calvin (Esther), hostler, h 12 Haid
*Harris Carl (Mary), presser Asheville Dry Cleaning Co, h 7 Velvet
Harris Cecil R, student, h 54 Bartlett
HARRIS CHAS J, v-pres Amer Natl Bank, h Dillsboro N C
Harris Chester F Rev, asst pastor 1st Baptist Church, h 11 Grady
Harris Dell (Mary E), sec-treas Harris-Barnett Dry Goods Co, h 54 Bartlett
*Harris Edwd (Maggie), butler The Henrietta
*Harris Edwd (Bertha), porter, h 7 Lincoln av
*Harris Felix (Henrietta), janitor, h 223 Beaumont
*Harris Ina, laund, h 21 Haid
*Harris Irvin, lab, h 8 Bay
Harris Isabel G Miss, h 48 n French Broad av
Harris J Lee (Roberta), plstr, h 2 Victoria rd
Harris J Monroe, trav slsmn, h 92 Baird
Harris J Sidney, helper, h 21 Victoria rd
Harris Jno, lab, h 445 w Haywood
Harris Jno P (Mollie), switchman, h 13 Connolly's Ridge
*Harris Jos, lab, h 4 Greer's Row
*Harris Jos, (Marie), cook, h 152 Hill
Harris Louise Miss, h Jarrett av, W Asheville
*Harris Mabel, cook, h 48 Mountain
*Harris Maggie, dom The Henrietta
Harris Mary A, wid B F, h 135 Charlotte
Harris Mattie Miss, propr Mtn Meadows Inn, h same
*Harris Mattie, dom, h 40 Maiden la
HARRIS MINNIE H MRS, propr The Knickerbocker, h 77 College—phone 153 (see p 15)
Harris Pearl A (Myrtle), foreman, h 94 Clingman av
*Harris Robt, presser Depot Pressing Club, h 424 Depot
*Harris Saml (Amanda), butler, h 4 Brick
HARRIS THEO B, city reporter Ashev Citizen, h 48 n French Broad av
Harris W Randall (Laura B), trav slsmn, h 48 n French Broad av
*Harris Wm (Hattie), porter, h 23 Frederick
*Harris Wm H (Ella), plstr, h Herren av, W Ashev
Harrison Andrew A (Kate), jeweler, h Woolsey (R F D 1)
Harrison Bettie A, wid Jno W, h 151 Southside av
Harrison Caroline, wid Jesse, h Haywood rd, W Ashev
Harrison Eugenia Miss, tchr Montford av Schl, h 78 Starnes
Harrison Fannie W, wid Thos R, h 78 Starnes av

....Asheville Cleaning and Pressing Club....
Tailoring That Satisfies and Prices That Please

Steam and French Dry Cleaning of all delicate and fine wearing apparel for ladies and gentlemen. MESSENGER SERVICE IN THE CITY.

J. C. WILBAR, Prop.   4. N. Pack Square   **PHONE 389**

Harrison Henry B (Maggie), mtrmn, h 30 Philip
Harrison Jesse B, clk frt office Sou Ry, h 78 Starnes av
*Harrison Mamie, dom, h 74 Pine
*Harrison Moses (Matilda), driver Ashev Ice Co, h 74 Pine
Harrison Nathan A (Kittie), watchmkr H L Finkelstein, h Woolsey
*Harrison Peggie, laund, h 15 Max
Harrison Peter, clk Gem Lunch Room, h 492 Depot
Harrison Sallie K Miss, h 151 Southside av
*Harrison Sarah, cook, h 28 Campbell
*Harrison Thos, porter, h 22 Campbell
Harrison Thos J (Emma E), lab, h Haywood rd, W Ashev
Harrison Thos J (Mollie), propr Gem Lunch Room, h 492 Depot
*Harrison W Edgar (Henrietta), barber, h 44 Ridge
Harrison Wm H Jr (Mary J), local mngr Haines, Jones & Cadbury Co, h "Edgemont Park"
Harrison Wm V, mchst, bds 87 Ora
*Harroll Lottie, laundress J C Wilbar, h 134 Church
*Harshaw Lee Rev, pastor Free Will Baptist Church, h Black st
Hart Ellis P (Ellen), foreman Sou Ry, h 44 Seney
Hart Fred E, clk H Redwood & Co, h 44 Seney
Hart Geo G (Cordelia), lab, h 417 n Main
Hart J Luther, mtrmn, h 44 Seney
*Hart Minnie, dom, h 40 Wallach
Hart Wm S (Sallie), lab, h 22 Factory Hill
*Hartman Alice, dressmkr 78 Valley, h same
*Hartman Dennis, janitor, h 23 Mack
*Hartman Fannie, cook 15 Soco
*Hartman Thos (Alice), porter Dr T C Smith, h 78 Valley
Hartsell Frances Miss, h 96 Cumberland av
Hartsell Harry, ball player, h 96 Cumberland av
Hartsell Josephine M, wid Isaac A, h 96 Cumberland av
Hartsell Lula F Miss (Fredk K Rutledge & Co), h 96 Cumberland av
Hartshorn David O, h 167 Pearson Drive
Hartshorn Frank O, h 167 Pearson Drive
Hartshorn Frank O Jr, h 167 Pearson Drive
Hartwell Harry T (Anna), h Dahlia Cottage, Albemarle Park
Hartzog Hal L, student, h 41 Vance
Hartzog Percy G (Mamie V), trav slsmn, h 41 Vance
Harvey J F Mrs, state mngr Spirella Corset Agency, 21 s Main, h 45 Blanton

Asheville Dray, Fuel & Construction Co.
6 1-2 South Main

COAL

Wood and Kindling
Stone and Sand
PHONE - 223

EVER READY FLASHLIGHTS
Piedmont Electric Company
64 PATTON AVENUE **ASHEVILLE, N. C.**

HARVILLE C BELLE MRS, modiste 172 Haywood, h same—phone 1496 (see p 24)
Harville Lawrence, clk, bds 50 Asheland av
HASKELL HENRY S (Susan H), propr Haskell Pepsi-Cola Bottling Works, h 217 Haywood (see p 12)
Haskell M Elizabeth, wid Fredk H, tchr Park av Schl, h 217 Haywood
HASKELL'S PEPSI-COLA BOTTLING WORKS, 217 Haywood and 20 Gudger—phone 170, H S Haskell propr (see p 12)
HASKELL RAYMOND F, mngr Haskell's Pepsi-Cola Bottling Works, h 217 Haywood
Hatch Julia Miss, rms 15 Bearden av
Hatch Susan E Miss, h 30 Cumberland av
Hatch Walter N (Margaret), emp Amer Wagon Co, h 30 Cumberland av
Hatchell Bessie, wid O G, propr The Dixie, h same
Hatcher Alma Miss,———
Hatcher Kate S, wid W C, dressmkr,———
Hatcher Reginald W (Lucy W), h 30 Bearden av
*Hatchett Fred (Mary), lab, h 180 Green's Row
Hatler Homer (Mollie), lineman, bds 34 Asheland av
Hatley H C, lineman Postal Tel-Cable Co, h 34 Asheland av
*Hatten Geo A (Mary L), janitor High Schl, h 192 Beaumont
Havener Birtie L Miss, stengr, h 264 n Main
Havener Carl W, auto driver, h 44 Hillside
Havener Jno M (Elizabeth), contr, h 264 n Main
Havener Robt A (Pearl), furn repr 57 n Main, h 44 Hillside
Havener Walter R, clk Smith's Drug Store, h 44 Hillside
Haverson Janie Mrs, mngr Viavi Co, bds Langren Hotel
HAWES GEO T, mngr Ashev Mercantile Agency, h 23 Flint
Hawes Katherine R, wid E J, boarding 23 Flint, h same
Hawes Mary T Miss, h 23 Flint
HAWK WM C, pres Beaumont Furn Co, and asst mngr Swannanoa-Berkley Hotel, rms Swannanoa Hotel
Hawkins A Nelson (Altha), gro 326 s Main, h same
Hawkins Annie D, wid Patrick W, h 121 Bartlett
Hawkins Blanche Miss, opr, h 35 Clingman av
Hawkins Calvin (Margaret), clk, h 72 s Liberty
Hawkins Chas (Annice), clk Sou Ry, rms 371 w Haywood
Hawkins Clyde, plstr, h Haywood rd, W Ashev
Hawkins Dalthard H (Bertha), fireman, h Broadway av, W Ashev

J. C. McPHERSON
SLATE AND TIN ROOFING
Galvanized Iron Work   Hot Air Furnaces
35-37 EAST COLLEGE STREET

PLUMBING
STEAM AND HOT WATER
HEATING
PHONE 133

Hawkins J Frank, tin pressman A L McLean, h 35 Clingman av
Hawkins Jas L (Hester D), plstr, h Haywood rd, W Ashev
Hawkins Jno A, tinner The Moore Plumbing Co
*Hawkins Lawrence, waiter, rms 28 Davidson
*Hawkins Lucy, laund, h 77 Gudger
Hawkins Margaret Mrs, dep county register of deeds, h 72 s Liberty
Hawkins Martha L, wid Benj F, h 35 Clingman av
Hawkins Ralph C (Metta), slsmn Smathers Wholesale Produce, h W Asheville
Hawkins Robt C, clk Carmichael's Pharmacy, h 72 s Liberty
Hawkins Robt M (Salena), clk P O, h 19 Buttrick
Hawkins Vernon F (Hattie C), mngr Faulkner Bros, h 171 Haywood
Hawkins Wm A, plstr, h Haywood rd, W Ashev
Hawkins Wm F, clk Faulkner Bros, h 177 Woodfin
Hawkins Zebulon (Julia), lineman Ashev P & L Co, h W Asheville
☞Hawkins see also Harkins
Hawley Mary F Miss, h (r) 35 Charlotte
Hawley Oscar W, mngr Pack Square Bakery, rms Y M C A
Hawn Wesley H (Addie), carp, h 40 s Main
Haws Wm E (Edith), carp, h Biltmore rd, S Biltmore
Hawthorne Annie B Miss, h 208 Pearson Drive
Hawthorne Fannie V Miss, h 208 Pearson Drive
*Hawthorne Jas (Bettie), butler, h 6 Knob
Hawthorne Jas E (Elizabeth), dentist, h 170 Haywood
Hayes Annie Miss, clk Jno A Guffey, h Mars Hill
Hayes Burgin G (Launa), clk H J Olive, h 104 Asheland av
Hayes Carl S (Ella), gro 161 s Main, h 183 Ashland av
*Hayes Chas H (Annie), porter, h 48 Mountain
Hayes Chas L, meat ctr Kiibler & Whitehead, rms 2 Technical Bldg
Hayes Edgar (Sallie R), solr, h 98 Jefferson Drive
Hayes Ernest L (Elizabeth), carp Ashev P & L Co, h W Asheville
Hayes Julius F (Laura), propr North Asheville Grocery, h 277 n Main
Hayes Lucy P Mrs, sec Buckeye Water Co, h Haywood rd, W Ashev
Hayes Martha J, wid W J, h 284 College
Hayes Matthew M (Grave V), carrier P O, h 55 College
Hayes Rutherford P (Lucy P), sec Buckeye Water Co, h Haywood rd, W Ashev

Club Cafe and Candy Kitchen
"A GOOD PLACE FOR REFRESHMENT"

The standards we work to in our Restaurant Department are: Cooking, perfect; Service, prompt and cheerful; Prices, moderate; Menu, everything in season. Parties and Banquets, Teas and Dinners. 19 and 21 Haywood St. Phones 110 and 111.

Brown's Undertaking Parlors

S. H. BROWN

50 Patton Avenue
ASHEVILLE, N. C.

Lady Assistant When Desired

Phone 193-2 Rings

THE MOORE Plumbing Company

16 N. Pack Square

PHONE 1025

Sanitary Plumbing, General Tin and Metal Work, Hot Air Furnaces

---

198 ASHEVILLE [1913] DIRECTORY

Hayes Walter V (Susan E), chf clk Sou Ry frt depot, h 186 Asheland av
☞ Hayes see also Hays
*Haynes Alfonso, h 186 w Chestnut
Haynes Arthur L (Arizona), casket mkr, h 43 North
*Haynes Ester K, h 186 w Chestnut
*Haynes Geo, driver, h 10 Magnolia av
Haynes Ida Miss, h 61 Josephine
HAYNES J WALTER (Haynes & Gudger), rms 36 Temple Court
Haynes Jas (May), watchman, h 400 Pearson Drive
*Haynes Jonas S, pool, 10 Eagle, h 186 w Chestnut
*Haynes Lizzie, laund, h 89 Poplar
Haynes M Edwd (Hattie), (Cannon & Haynes), h 469 n Main
*Haynes Tolbert (Janie), lab, h 54 Black
Haynes Washington Rev, h Grace
Haynes Wm, bds 511 w Haywood
HAYNES & GUDGER (J W Haynes, Owen Gudger), attys at law, 18-19 Temple Court—phone 1678
Haynie Vasco V (Effie), gro and meat mkt, East cor Main, h 25 East
Hays Geo O (Ida), carp, rms 17 Montford av
Hays J M Capt, tchr Bingham Schl, rms same
Hays Lina E Mrs, dressmkr 102 Haywood, h same
☞ Hays see also Hayes
Haywood Street M E Church (South), w Haywood cor Patton av, Rev W A Newell pastor
Haywood Street Market, gros 336 w Haywood, P D Manley propr
Hazlewood Benj, barber Langren Barber Shop, h Candler Sta, N C
Hazzard Alice J Miss, h 11 Cullowhee
Hazzard Beaumont Miss, h 11 Cullowhee
Hazzard Elliott W, wid E W, h 11 Cullowhee
Hazzard Isabelle E Miss, h 11 Cullowhee
Head Chester G, driver I R Coffey, h 34½ n Main
Head Lula, wid Marion A, h 68 Poplar
Hearn J M & Co (James M Hearn), bicycles, 4 Battery Park pl
Hearn Jas M (Sue), (J M Hearn & Co), h 50 Montford av
*Heard Annie, h 306 Charlotte
*Heard Emma, hairdresser, h 130 Choctaw
*Heard Mattie, laund, h 11 Hiawassee
*Heard Nelson, emp E W Swepson, h 306 Charlotte

The Battery Park Bank
ASHEVILLE, N.C.

Capital - - $100,000.00
Surplus and Profits, $110,000.00

City, County and State Depositary

J. A. TILLMAN — **Jeweler** — **17 N. Main St.**

I carry a nice line of Watches, Clocks and Jewelry, and make a specialty of repair work. Satisfaction guaranteed

ASHEVILLE [1913] DIRECTORY

*Heath Edwd (Sarah), lab, h 205 Clingman av
*Heath Peter (Mayme), lab, h 81 Roberts
Hebard Ezra A (Charlotte A), h Broadway av, W Ashev
Hebrew Cemetery, end of Cemetery Drive
Heidtman Jno D (Eloise), trav slsmn, h 150 Chestnut
Heilig Jas H (Mattie), engnr Sou Ry, h 350 Southside av
*Helington Lucille, dom, h 38 Davidson
*Hellam Marjorie, cook, h 107 Roberts
*Hellams Mack C (Minnie), eating hse 5 w Walnut, h same
Hellas Harris, waiter U S Cafe, rms 11½ n Main
Helton Marion (Venie), tmstr, h 425 s Main
*Hemphill B Perry (Mary), h S Asheville
*Hemphill Carl, porter, h 6 Short McDowell
*Hemphill Cecelia, cook, h 63 Clemmons
*Hemphill Chas, porter St Charles Barber Shop, h 6 Short McDowell
*Hemphill Ella, laund, h 6 Short McDowell
*Hemphill Harrell, porter, h 6 Short McDowell
*Hemphill Jno, lab, h 118 Church
Hemphill Jno P (Eula), carp, h 458 Depot
Henderson Chas A (Margaret), lab, h 408 Pearson Drive
Henderson Chas E (Obie), jeweler 52 Patton av, h 50 Cumberland av
*Henderson Daisy, laund, h 92 Choctaw
Henderson Gale C, clk, h 32 s French Broad av
Henderson Geo (Orra M,) (McGuire & Co), h 48 Grove
Henderson Geo E (Henderson & Martin), h 304 College
Henderson Henry A (Texanna), carp, h 92 East
Henderson J Daniel (Jane), contr, h 304 College
Henderson Jas L (Addie), lab, h Lester rd, W Asheville
*Henderson Jas W Rev (Hattie R), pastor A M E Zion Church, h Haywood rd, W Ashev
Henderson Jno H (Bonnie), h (r) 21 Merrimon av
*Henderson Lafayette, lab, h 152 Church
Henderson M Carrie Miss, clk Ashev Dry Goods Co, h 32 s French Broad av
*Henderson Marilda, dom, h 16 Bay
*Henderson Mattie, laund, h 92 Choctaw
*Henderson May, laund, h (r) 38 Clingman av
Henderson May L Miss, bkkpr, h 32 s French Broad av
Henderson Orra M Miss, student, h 48 Grove
Henderson Ottis, h 408 Pearson Drive
Henderson Robt H (Lillian), carp 151 Woodfin, h same
Henderson Ryrd E Miss, h 48 Grove
Henderson Saml E (Ida P), ship clk, h 32 s French Broad

INSURANCE

INSURE YOUR SALARY WITH US
NEVER CARRY YOUR OWN RISK
SAFETY IS THE BEST POLICY
UNLESS YOU ARE A CAPITALIST
REST EASY IF YOU HAVE
AN ACCIDENT WE WILL
NOT KEEP YOU WAITING TO
COLLECT YOUR CLAIM
EVERY CLAIM PROMPTLY PAID

Imperial Mutual Life & Health Insurance Co.

Home Office: ASHEVILLE, N. C.

Phone 495

HOTEL OXFORD — Redecorated and Refitted throughout. Recently enlarged to 60 rooms. Centrally located. Depot cars stop at entrance. Long distance telephone office upstairs. American and European plan. Rates 50c, 75c and $1 per day; special rates by week or month. C. H. Branson & Sons, Proprietors. Phone 1887. 50-54 South Main St. **Asheville, N. C.**

Williams-Brownell Planing Mill Company — *Hardwoods*

Lumber---Rough and Dressed Flooring a Specialty Moulding, Interior Finish, Etc.
Office, Plant and Yards on Southern Railway, Near Biltmore Station
WHITE PINE Phone 729 YELLOW PINE

Henderson W Anson (Cordie), carp, h 5 Seney
Henderson W Burchard, sec to C D Beadle, supt Biltmore Estate, h Biltmore N C
Henderson W Porter, clk O Green Hdw Co, rms 33 Temple Court
Henderson Wm, lab, h Lester rd, W Asheville
Henderson Wm P (M Etta), agt Met Life Ins Co, h W Ashev
Henderson & Martin, automobiles 304 College
Hendley Jas B (Myrtle), fireman, h 82 Cumberland av
Hendley Mary J, wid Jas W, h 82 Cumberland av
Hendley Ray T (Sudie M), engnr, h Haywood rd, W Ashev
Hendrick J Frank (Mary C), h 234 Haywood
Hendricks Frank A (Carrie L), foreman Hackney & Moale Co
*Hendricks Jno (Frances), lab, h 24 Curve
*Hendricks P Fields, agt N C Mutual & Prov Assn, h Cullowhee st
*Hendricks Presley L (Laura), pres Piedmont Shoe Co, h 27 Eloise
Hendrix Jno W (Frankie), driver Stand Oil Co, h Hazel Mill rd, W Asheville
Hendrix Parley L (Kate), driver, h W Asheville
Hendrix Walter H (Cora), fireman, h W Asheville
Henninger Bessie Miss, clk Peoples Dept Store, h 20 Rector
Henninger Chas G (Ethel), clk, h 52 Hillside
Henninger Harry B, clk P O, h 20 Rector
Henninger Jos C (Laura), shoemkr 100 Patton av, h 20 Rector
HENRIETTA (The), (Y W C A), 78 s Main, Mrs M W Lance mngr
*Henry Adah, laund, h 3 Clemmons
Henry Arthur L (Mantie), carp, h W Asheville
*Henry Edwd, lab, h 42 Pine
Henry Edmund L (Mary), carrier P O, h 169½ Patton av
*Henry Eliza, h 12 Latta
*Henry Emanuel (Maggie), lab, h 42 Pine
*Henry Ethel, maid, h 42 Pine
*Henry Gaither, porter, h 133 Valley
*Henry Geo W (Addie), carp, h W Asheville
*Henry Lee (Cora), lab, h 42 Pine
*Henry Lewis, porter, h 42 Pine
Henry Lewis A (Mary), h 15 Madison av
Henry Lina M Mrs, h 96 e College
Henry M Athalia Miss, h 15 Madison av

Asheville Electrical Company
W. Mansfield Booze, Manager
74 CENTRAL AVE.
HEADQUARTERS
Phone 377

Asheville Dry Cleaning Co.
Telephones 835-836, All Dep't
MAIN, N. E. COR. COLLEGE

THE CLEANERS
Our Department for Oriental Rugs and Carpet Cleaning is prepared to serve you in all its branches.
E. S. Paine   O. E. Hansen

Henry Philip H (Annie), capitalist, h "Zealandia," Town Mountain
*Henry Robt, lab, h 42 Pine
Henry Thos N, clk P O, h 12 Pearl
Henry Violet R Miss, h "Zealandia," Town Mountain
Hensley Chas, emp Ashev Mica Co, bds 98 Patton av
Hensley Geo M (Mattie), carp, h W Asheville
Hensley Geo W (Rebecca), lab, h nr Smith's Bridge, W Ashev
Hensley Harrison, tanner, h 470 w Haywood
Hensley Isaac (Mollie), carp, h 16 Bennett
Hensley Jas H (Altha), driver, h 360 n Main
Hensley Mark E (Letha), carp, h 23 Central av
Hensley Oscar B, lab, h nr Smith's Bridge, W Ashev
Hensley S Monroe (Mayona), auto driver, h 320 n Main
Hensley T Milton, driver, h 9 Central av
Hensley W Berry (Callie), auto driver, h 360 n Main
Henson J Harrison, driver Ashe Ice Co, h 86 Avery
Henson Jos, driver, h 86 Avery
Henson Lillie Mrs, gro 86 Avery, h same
Henson Lizzie Miss, h 72 Avery
*Henton Saml, presser J C Wilbar, h 11 Bay
Herbert Wm P, phys, 16 Battery Park pl, bds The Manor
Hermann E A, flgmn, bds 430 Depot
Hermann Geo L (Ida Mae), linotype opr The Inland Press, h 36 Holland
Hermann Jno B, pool 9 s w Pack Sq (3d fl), h 149 s Main
Hermann Marie M Miss, h 149 s Main
Hern Nannie B Miss, nurse, 135 Asheland av, h same
Herndon Hannah M, wid E W, h 65 Woodfin
*Herrod Sarah E, h 42 Hildebrand
Herron Edwd (Lou), plmbr, h 51 Furman av
Herron Herbert M (Jane), condr St Ry, h 51 Furman av
Herron Jno R (Lizzie), clk, h Grace
Herron Kenneth H, student, h Grace
Herron Mary C, wid W J, rms 15 Woodfin
Herron Percy G (Lou), carp, h 78 Josephine
Herron Ruby V Miss, h Grace
Hess Erasmus A (Emma), yd mngr Carolina Coal & Ice Co, h 145 Flint
Hess Margaret, wid Chas, h 145 Flint
Hess Max, clk Crescent Jewelry Co, h 347 w Haywood
Hess Walter (Myrtle), emp Nursery, h Irwin cor Summit, S Biltmore
Hester Eugene G (Bessie), slsmn, h Edgemont

Life Insurance Company of Virginia
ORGANIZED 1871
Home Office - Richmond, Va.

Has won the hearty approval and active support of the people by its promptness and fair dealing during the FORTY-TWO YEARS of its operation

J. V. Moon, Superintendent, Rooms 3-4-5 Maxwelton Bldg., Asheville, N. C.

T. P. JOHNSON & CO.

SHEET METAL WORKERS

All Kinds of Roofing Guttering and Conductor Work Metal Ceilings, Skylights and Galvanized Iron Cornices

OFFICE and SHOP: 69-71 S. MAIN

Phone 325

DR. C. H. MILLER

Mechano-Therapist

14 N. Spruce Street
ASHEVILLE, N. C.

PHONE 979

Hours by Engagement

DRUGLESS HEALING OF DISEASE

---

202 ASHEVILLE [1913] DIRECTORY

Hester Frank, drug clk, bds Cherokee Inn
Hester Fred, slsmn C A Raysor, bds Cherokee Inn
Hester Mary C Miss, h Edgemont
Hester Wm R, student, h Edgemont
Hetchel Elizabeth, wid Fred F, h 30 Montford av
Hewitt Frank R (Frances M), pres Home B & L Assn, and Elks Home Co, h 311 Montford av
*Hewitt Willie, dom, h Woolsey
Heywood C K, lumberman, bds 186 Haywood
Hice C Columbus (Della L), h Hazel Mill rd, W Ashev
Hice Cora Miss, dom, h Woolsey (R F D 1)
HICKOK MARY MISS, prin Normal & Collegiate Institute, rms same
*Hicks Ada, laund, h 20 Green's Row
*Hicks Chas, lab, h 57 Black
*Hicks Jno (Katie), waiter, h 29 Gray
*Hicks Minnie, laund, h 57 Black
Hicks Riley, mch opr, bds 34½ n Main
*Hicks Wm (Beadie), boiler washer, h 138 Livingston
& Hicks see also Hix
Higgason Luther L (Fay), propr Higgason Studio, h 3 Carroll av
Higgason Studio, 18 n Pack Sq, L L Higgason propr
Higgins Carrie Miss, h 23 s Lexington av
*Higgins Richard H (Cynthia C), janitor, h 125 Clemmons
High School, Oak cor College, R V Kennedy prin
HIGHLAND HOSPITAL, Cumberland av and Zillicoa, Dr R S Carroll medical director
HIGHLAND HOTEL, 368-370 Depot—phone 1097, Mrs Emma Else propr (see p 18)
*Highs Rayford, lab, h 53 Gudger
Highsmith Zebulon F (Annie), optometrist, 9 Grady, h same
*Hightower Hattie, cook, h 78 Mountain
*Hightower Mary, laund, h 78 Mountain
Hildebrand Agnes E Miss, music tchr, h 5 Furman av
HILDEBRAND DAVID S (Oleatta), pres Ashev Supply & Fdy Co, h Chunn's Cove
Hildebrand Eleanor G Miss, tchr West Ashev Schl, h Chunn's Cove
Hildebrand Emma S, wid Arthur, h 5 Furman av
Hildebrand J Virgil, driver, bds 67 n Spruce
HILDEBRAND WALTER A (Helen), editor Ashev Gazette-News and pres Evening News Pub Co, h "Edgemont"

ASHEVILLE CLEANING and PRESSING CLUB

TAILORING THAT SATISFIES and PRICES THAT PLEASE

Hats cleaned, banded and bound. Silk hats ironed. Buttons made to order in all sizes. Plain or with rims. PHONE 389

DYEING IN ALL SHADES

Kid Gloves, Slippers and Plumes. Fancy Jabots and Ties. French Dry Cleaned. Ladies' and Gentlemen's suits Steam Cleaned. Messenger Service. **J. C. Wilbar, Prop.**

4 NORTH PACK SQ.

Hill Albert S, clk, h 361 s French Broad av
*Hill Alfred, lab, h 209 Clingman av
*Hill Annie M, laund, h 81 Eagle
*Hill Benj (Maude), driver, h 42 Brick
Hill Chas A, mchst, h 361 s French Broad av
Hill Chas O (Marie), clk Sou Ry, h 252 s French Broad av
*Hill Clarence D (Ella D), shoemkr 8 Eagle, h 24 Weaver
"Hill Cottage", boarding, 39 Clingman av, Mrs Theresa McCain propr
HILL DANIEL W, mngr Hill's Market, h 16 Vance
Hill Dock F (Ruth E), lab, h nr Haywood rd, W Asheville
HILL E D, mngr traffic dept Ashev Tel & Tel Co
HILL FRANK H, slsmn Hill's Market, rms A F D
*Hill Henry (Hattie), lab, h 45 Frederick
*Hill Hoke (Kate), lab C I & C Co, h 89 Choctaw
Hill J Francis (Mary E), gro 545 w Haywood, h W Ashe
*Hill Jas, porter Elks Club, h 81 Eagle
Hill Jas B (Delia), gro Haywood rd, W Asheville, h same
Hill Jno J, h 17 Coleman av
*Hill Julia, laund, h 11 Hiawassee
*Hill Logan (Emeline), lab, h S Asheville
Hill Margaret, wid Chas, h 361 s French Broad av
Hill Margaret A, wid Wm M, h 16 Vance
Hill Marie Mrs, clk Wachovia B & T Co, h 252 s French Broad av
HILL'S MARKET, meats, City Market—phones 4 and 359, D W Hill mngr (see bottom line front cover)
*Hill Martha, laund, h 37 Catholic av
Hill Mary Mrs, housekpr S S Bailey, h Haywood rd, W Asheville
Hill Minnie K Miss, h 351 w Haywood
HILL NELL S MISS, bkkpr Hill's Market, h 16 Vance
Hill R Finley, weaver, h Haywood rd, W Asheville
*Hill Saml (Annie), janitor, h 19 Tuskee
Hill Sophronia B Miss, h 16 Vance
*Hill Street School, 81 Hill, J H Michael prin
*Hill Street M E Church, 80 Hill
Hill Virgie S Miss, clk Bon Marche, h 17 Coleman
HILL W J, meat ctr Hill's Market, h 16 Vance
Hill Wm M (Lula), beamer, h Haywood rd, W Asheville
Hilliard Chas C, student, h 91 s Main
Hilliard Howard, clk Fred Hull, h 101 s Main
Hilliard Margaret E, wid Wm L, h 101 s Main
HILLSIDE CONVENT (St Genevieve College), Victoria rd, Sisters of Christian Education in charge

WEAVERVILLE LINE — NINE MILES BY TROLLEY FROM PACK SQUARE TO WEAVERVILLE

ASHEVILLE AND EAST TENNESSEE RAILROAD CO.

7 NORTH MAIN STREET — ASHEVILLE N. C.

ELECTRIC FIXTURES

Piedmont Electric Co.

64 PATTON AVE. ASHEVILLE, N.C.

"Hillside Cottage", 92 Baird
Hilton E Ruth Miss, h 30 Clayton
Hilton H Ward, tel opr, h 30 Clayton
Hilton Lee M (Ida), contr, h 30 Clayton
Hilton Murray D, student, h 30 Clayton
Hines Chas A (Grace), agt Life Ins Co of Va, h 235 Chestnut
*Hines Emerson (Della), lab, h 30 Oakdale av
Hines Herbert E (Cora), bag mstr, h 20 Adams
Hinkle Mamie L Mrs, h 18 s Main
☞ Hinson see Henson
Hinton D Saml, engnr Sou Ry, h 390 s French Broad av
Hinton Laura G Miss, student, h 390 s French Broad av
Hinton Maude Miss, h 390 s French Broad av
Hipp Eva L Mrs, dress mkr 64 Phifer, h same
Hipps Wm H, county supt of education, office Court Hse
Hirst Lillie Miss, nurse 109 Biltmore rd, S Biltmore, h same
Hiser Watsell, lab, bds 100 Avery
HITES C HARRY, city editor Ashev Citizen, bds 42 Walnut
Hobart Clarence Mrs, h Albemarle Park
HOBBS CHAS H, v-pres Citizens Lumber Co, office 24 e College, rms Y M C A
*Hobson Benj (Mary), porter Dunhams Music House, h 9 Miller
*Hobson Sarah, cook H K Bull, h same
Hodges Chas C (Fannie), supt Ashev Div Sou Ry, h 182 Montford av
Hodges Danl M (Clara P) (Hodges, Mitchell & Reynolds), h 168 Merrimon av
Hodges J Frank, msngr Sou Exp Co, bds 96 Bartlett
Hodges, Mitchell & Reynolds (D M Hodges, F E Mitchell, T P Reynolds), mngrs The Prudential Ins Co of America, 68 Patton av
Hodges Nena Miss, h 182 Montford av
HOFFMAN DAVID (Miriam), mngr The Star Market, h 41 Orchard
*Hoffman Henrietta, tchr Catholic Hill Schl
HOFFMAN M FRANK (Hoffman & Kent), rms Asheville Club
Hoffman Robt, bkkpr The Star Market, bds 68 Church
HOFFMAN & KENT (M Frank Hoffman, Fred Kent), proprs The Stare Market, City Market (see front cover)
Hoitt Chas A, sec-treas U S Furn Mnfg Co, h 5 Swan, Biltmore

CONTRACTOR and BUILDER

STEEL RANGES — **J. C. McPHERSON** — 35-37 E. COLLEGE ST. PHONE 133

PLUMBING STEAM AND HOT WATER HEATING

MAPLE FLOORING
HARDWOOD LUMBER OF ALL KINDS

WOODWARD & SON
9th and Arch Sts., Richmond, Va.
See Adv. Opposite Page 188

Holcombe Calvin L (Keturah T), carp, h W Asheville
Holcombe Carl C, painter R E Bowles, h W Asheville
Holcombe Chas A (Bonnie), condr St Ry, h 93 Grove
Holcombe Cleveland, lbr inspr, bds 16 Orchard
Holcombe Eugene, driver, bds Philip Anders
Holcombe Eugene S (Ethel E), condr Sou Ry, h 195 Bartlett
Holcombe Jno B (Faye), printer, h 182 w Chestnut
Holcombe Lee B, pressman The Inland Press, h W Ashe
Holcombe Mary J, wid Isaac, h 93 Grove
Holcombe Promethus, painter, h W Asheville
Holcombe Rosa, wid W H, h 386 n Main
Holcombe Thos B, condr, bds 32 n Ann
Holcombe Wm L (Beulah), printer, h W Asheville
*Holden Wade (Lula), h (r) 118 Church
Holder Claude B (Cora E), emblamer, h 17 Buncombe
Holiness Church, Buxton cor Park pl
*Holland Josephine, h Chunns Cove
Holland Walter (Silva), lab, h 93 Wallach
Hollar Bertha L Miss, cashr Hollar & Co, bds 418 Southside av
HOLLAR H RALPH (Hollar & Co), bds 418 Southside av
HOLLAR HENRY S (Carrie) (Hollar & Co) and mngr Hollar Motor Co, h 373 s French Broad av
HOLLAR MOTOR CO, 56 s Main, H S Hollar mngr
HOLLAR WALTER C (Hollar & Co), bds 196 Bartlett
HOLLAR & CO (H S, H R and W C Hollar), gro's 414 Southside av—phone 1017
*Holley Alex (Mayme), lab, h (r) 135 Clingman av
Hollifield Jefferson (Rena), driver, h Haywood rd, W Ashe
Hollingsworth Amelia Mrs, h nr Hazel Mill rd, W Asheville
Hollingsworth Chas, carp, h nr Hazel Mill rd, W Asheville
Hollingsworth Howell W (Laura), flgmn, h 4 Gaston
Hollingsworth Jno B, clk Ottis Green Hdw Co, h nr Hazel Mill rd, W Asheville
Hollingsworth Ralph S (Kate), driver, h nr Hazel Mill rd, W Asheville
Hollingsworth Saml O (Nettie), shoe mkr 303 s Main, h same
Hollins Chas, lab, bds Riverside Drive nr Caket Co
Hollins Mattie Miss, rms 90 Starnes av
Hollomon Janie, wid Robt B, h 157 Park av
*Holman Adam (Eliza), lab, h 55 Mountain
Holman Pearl L Miss, prin Carolina Coml Schl and stengr, h 8 College Park pl

What Have You in Real Estate that You Don't Want?

What do You Want in Real Estate that You Haven't?

WESTERN CAROLINA REALTY CO.
J. W. Wolfe Sec. & Treas.

On the Square
PHONE 974
10 N. PACK SQ.

Brown-Carter Realty Co.
REAL ESTATE
23 TEMPLE COURT
PHONE 341
ASHEVILLE   N. C.

FLORIDA SPECIALTIES
Grazing, Timbered, Farm Lands, Orange Groves, Turpentine Locations and Phosphate Lands.

NORTH CAROLINA SPECIALTIES
Orchard, Farm and Timbered Lands, City Property, Rent Collections.

Moale & Chiles Real Estate and Insurance
27 Patton Ave. (2d fl)   Phone 661
General Agents United States Fidelity & Guaranty Co.

Club Cafe and Candy Kitchen
"A GOOD PLACE FOR REFRESHMENT"

Our Ice Cream manufacturing plant is absolutely clean and sanitary.
Prompt family delivery. Phones 110 and 111.
Catering for large parties and receptions. Special Creams.

Brown's Undertaking Parlors

S. H. BROWN

Lady Assistant When Desired

Phone 193-2 Rings

50 Patton Avenue
Asheville, N. C.

Established 1894

B. J. JACKSON

Carefully Selected Fruits and Vegetables

Stall No. 11, City Market

BUSINESS PHONES: 86 and 101

RESIDENCE PHONE 1596

---

*Holmes Addie, laund, h 39 Frederick
*Holmes Carrie, laund, h 16 Sassafras
Holmes Clara L Miss, h 60 Baird
Holmes D O Mrs, h 155 Flint
Holmes David O, student, h 155 Flint
Holmes E I (Ann), trav slsmn, h 72 Baird
Holmes Edith C Miss, student, h 60 Baird
Holmes Janie C, wid E I, h 60 Baird
Holmes Maggie Miss, dom, h 385 Patton av
Holmes Wm C, student, h 60 Baird
Holt Ellerbe Miss, h 162 w Chestnut
HOLT SAML D (Catherine V) (Burton & Holt), h 162 w Chestnut
Holton Alfred E, U S dist atty P O Bldg, res Winston-Salem N C
Home Building & Loan Assn, 2 Drhumor Bldg, F R Hewitt pres, C W Brown v-pres, S L Forbes sec-treas
HOME INDUSTRIAL SCHOOL (Presbyterian School Campus), Biltmore rd, Victoria—phone 482, Miss Florence Stephenson prin
Honaker Henry C, lumber buyer, rms 54 Asheland av
HONESS CHAS H (Esther), optometrist 54 Patton av, h 40 Cumberland Circle (see side lines)
Honeycutt Joshua (Mary E), farmer, h W Asheville
Honeycutt Parlie L (Maggie), condr, h 195 Patton av
☛Honeycutt see also Hunnicutt
Hood Berdine, foundryman, bds 51 n Main
Hood Carl, mlnr H B Hood, h 50 Asheland av
Hood Ezekiel G (Mattie), h 39 Grove
Hood Henry B, millinery 5 Haywood, h 39 Grove
Hood Henry C, trimmer, bds 25 Asheland av
Hooker Harrison, lab, bds 79 Hall
*Hooper Avery (Carrie), driver, h 41 Magnolia av
Hoover V, stengr Green Bros, h 96 Bartlett
*Hopkins Chapel A M E Zion Church, 217 College, Rev J S Spurgeon pastor
Hopkins E B, clk Dr T C Smith, bds Patton Hotel
*Hopkins Isaac (Emma), lab, h 393 Asheland av
*Hopkins J W & Son (J W and J H), horse shoers, 7 Walnut
*Hopkins Jas W (Virginia), (J W Hopkins & Son), h 33 Buttrick
*Hopkins Jno H (J W Hopkins & Son), h 33 Buttrick
Hopson E Stanley, clk E C Jarrett, rms Harkins Bldg
HOPSON JOHN S (Elias & Hopson), h 115 Haywood

Furniture and China Carefully Prepared for Shipment

Mahogany Furniture Hand Made & Carefully Reproduced | **E. E. GALER** 114 PATTON AVE. | Upholstering and Refinishing PHONE - 1674

Hopson Sadie Miss, clk E C Jarrett, h 59 Josephine
☞Hopson see also Hobson
Horne Egbert P, emp Langren Hotel Grill Room, rms Y M C A
Horner Eva Miss, h "Schoenberger Hall," 135 Church
Horner Junius M Rev (Eva H), Bishop, h "Schoenberger Hall," 135 Church
Horner Susan C Miss, h 38 e Spears av
*Horshaw Arthur (Lizzie), packer, h 70 Circle
Horton Elizabeth A Miss, h 59 Vance
Horton Fredk L (Martha), tailor, h 59 Vance
Horton Wm J, clk Hotel Florence, h same
☞Hortsshorn see Hartshorn
*Hoskins Susie B, maid, h 101 n Lexington av
Hoskovitz Barnett H (Annie), shoemkr 2 Eagle and 418 Depot, h 347 w Haywood
Hoskovitz Harry, clk, h 347 w Haywood
Hoskovitz Max, clk, h 347 w Haywood
Hosrich Herman H (Christie), baker Ashev Stm Bakery, h 46 Madison av
Hotel Florence, 436 Depot, Wm G Corpening propr
HOTEL OXFORD CAFE, 50 s Main
HOTEL OXFORD, 50-54 s Main, European and American plan; C H Branson & Sons proprs—phone 1887 (see side lines)
Hotel Paxton, 26-28 s Main, J L Page propr
Hotel Warren, 39 n Main, B W Warren propr
Hough Alice B Miss, h 403 Pearson Drive
Hough Lydia, wid Geo, h 403 Pearson Drive
Hough Matilda, wid Wm R, h 359 w Haywood
House Margaret Miss, h Grace
HOUSER BETRAND A, M D, B S (Katherine), mngr Belmont, h 57 n Spruce—phone 840
Housman Ora G (Mamie), agt Sou Ry, h 47 Central av
Houston Kate G Miss, bds 55 College
*Houston Lee (Fannie), lab, h 23 Margaret
Houston Lida Miss, dressmkr, Mrs C B Harville, bds 68 Haywood
Houston Sophia A, wid Chas, bds 55 College
*Houston Wallace (Ella), lab, h 56 Max
Hovious Stonewall J (Ollie), ins agt, h 33 Victoria rd
*Howard Agnes, h 115 Beaumont
Howard Albert W, bds J R Teague, W Ashev
Howard H O, painter R E Bowles, bds 34 Asheland av
*Howard Herbert, hostler, h 99 Market

Mrs. Wilder's SANITARY HOME LAUNDRY turns out first class work in Laundering and Dry Cleaning. No. 7 Montford Ave., Phone 1354

---

*Howard Jesse (Stella), porter, h 22 Weaver
Howard Jessie E Miss, bds H A Wells, W Ashev
*Howard Sim (Sallie E), janitor Y M C A, h 263 College
Howard Thos, painter, bds 34 Asheland av
Howard Vernon B (Carrie), miller, h Haywood rd, W Ashev
Howard Wm A, h Haywood rd, W Ashev
Howard Wm E (Ella), trav slsmn, h Haywood rd, W Ashev
Howatt Jos P (Amelia), bkkpr, h 47 Vance
Howe Lealand Prof, pianist Princess Theatre, h 333 Merrimon av
Howell C B, slsmn Villa Heights Co, bds 107 Haywood
*Howell Chas T (Lottie C), barber 2 Eagle, h 74 Hill
Howell Chester R (Sara J), asst mngr Ashev Gro Co, h 28 Blake
Howell Frank F (Mary S), carp, h 33 Short
Howell Harriet Miss, h Woolsey
Howell Herbert S, opr W U Tel Co, h 33 Short
Howell Jas S, student, h 33 Short
*Howell Janie, cook, h 46 Pine
Howell Jos D, engnr, h 29 Jefferson Drive
Howell M Sadie Miss, h 33 Short
Howell Thaddeus N (Mabel), engnr Sou Ry, h 175 Bartlett
Howie Mamie G, wid T A, h 371 w Haywood
HOWLAND STANLEY, v-pres-genl mngr Ashev & E Tenn R R Co and pres Weaverville Elec Co, h "Dolobran," Sunset Drive
HOWLAND REGINALD, treas Ashev & E Tenn R R Co, and Weaverville Elec Co, h "Dolobran," Sunset Drive
Hoyer Susie G Miss, h 46 Soco
Hoyer Zoe M, wid Fred, h 46 Soco
Hoyle Chas R (Eva), carp, h 11 Pearl
Hoyle E Marvin Rev (Olive), h 58 Fulton
Hoyle Walter (Rita), carp, h 29 Clingman av
*Hubbard Mattie, laund, h 120 Pine
*Hubbard Zebulon D (Mammie), fireman, h 53 Hill
Hubert Carmella F Miss, bkkpr Singer Sewing Mch Co, h 25 Pearl
*Hudgens Meta, dom, 1 Summit
Hudgins Lee P (Ida), lab, h Riverside Drive nr Park
*Hudson Andrew (Lula), waiter, h 247 Flint
Hudson Florence Miss, dom, 45 Panola
Hudson Henry C, auto repr, h 41½ s Main
Hudson Hester B, wid Benj E, propr The Florida House, h 41½ s Main

---

OLDSMOBILE — DETROIT ELECTRIC
ARBOGAST MOTOR COMPANY
ACCESSORIES AND SUPPLIES
Phones 302 and 1728
52-60 N. Main
BUICK — MAXWELLS

Asheville Dry Cleaning Co.
Telephones 835-836, All Dep't
MAIN, N. E. COR. COLLEGE

THE CLEANERS
Our Department for Oriental Rugs and Carpet Cleaning is prepared to serve you in all its branches.
E. S. Paine   O. E. Hansen

For Kindling "What am Kindling" Call
ENGLISH LUMBER COMPANY   Phone 321

*Hudson Isaac G (Mamie), lab, h 321 Asheland av
Hudson Lawrence, helper Western Carolina Auto Co, h 41½ s Main
*Hudson Lee, lab, h 13 Short Valley
Hudson Wm C (Henrietta), dispr emp Sou Ry, h 244 e Chestnut
Hudson Wm D (Bertha), lab, h 80 Madison av
Huff Jesse W (Mary), (J H Huff & Son), h Chunn's Cove
Huff J H & Son (J H and J W), painters (r) 7 Aston
Huff Jno H (Ethel), (J H Huff & Son), h Chunn's Cove
Huff Paul J (Flora), condr, h 33 Louie
Huffaker Sallie P Mrs, h 23 Logan
Huffman Ara E (Bessie), tel opr, h 33 Highland
Huffman Beulah Miss, bds The Henrietta
☞ Huffman see also Hoffman
Huffsticker Jno J, waiter Windsor Cafe
*Huggins Walter (Laura), blksmith, h 30 Davidson
Hughes Anna J Miss, nurse, h Brevard rd, W Ashev
Hughes G Emmett (Love M), flgmn, h Pennsylvania av, W Ashev
Hughes Hannah M, wid Saml D, h Brevard rd, W Ashev
Hughes Jas R, lab, h Hazel Mill rd, W Ashev
*Hughes Jeremiah F Rev (Lillie), pastor First Baptist Ch. h 25 Ridge
Hughes Jno L, chf clk, rdmstr Sou Ry, h Florence Hotel
Hughes Mary M, wid C H, h 70 Madison av
Hughes Nancy, wid Robt Y, h Hazel Mill rd, W Ashev
Hughes Patrick H (Christina), h 111 College
HUGHES R PEARSON (Addie), (Hughes Transfer & Livery Co), h 401 Southside av—phone 1405
HUGHES TRANSFER & LIVERY CO (R P Hughes), autos for hire, trunks 25c to any part of the city, 401 Southside av—phone 1405 (see right side lines)
Hughes Wm H, gro Haywood rd, W Ashev, h same
Hughey Claude J, asst mngr, h 46 Walnut
Hughey Horace B (Beliva), meat ctr Globe Market, h 48 Walnut
Hughey Kelly M, asst stage mngr The Dreamland, bds 46 Walnut
Hughey Loretta Miss, dressmkr, 46 Walnut, h same
Hughey Ollie D Miss, h W Asheville
Hughey Robt W C (Dela), boarding 46 Walnut, h same
Hughey Wm C, h W Asheville
Hugill Frank B, electrn Piedmont Elec Co, h Brevard rd, W Ashev

Biggest Busiest Best

Phones 1936 and 1937

ASHEVILLE STEAM LAUNDRY

43 to 47 W. COLLEGE

S. D. HALL
REAL ESTATE AGENT

Money Loaned

Notary Public

32 PATTON AVENUE

Phone 91

Founders, Machinists and Jobbers of Mill Supplies

PHONE 590
When in the market for pipe and fittings, let us make you Prices.

Carolina Machinery Co.

PHONE 590
If it's a Gas Engine let us figure with you, also on other kinds of machinery

LIFE INSURANCE COMPANY OF VA. OLDEST, LARGEST STRONGEST Southern Life Insurance Co.
ORGANIZED 1871
RICHMOND, VIRGINIA
Issues Industrial Policies from $8.00 to $900.00, with Premiums Payable WEEKLY on persons from two to seventy years of age
J. V. Moon, Superintendent, Rooms 3-4-5 Maxwelton Bldg., Asheville, N. C.

D. TREXLER TIN SHOP

All Kinds of Roofing, Gutter and Conductor Work.

Phone 862
159 South Main St.

DR. C. H. MILLER
MECHANO-THERAPIST
14 N. Spruce St.
Phone 979
ASHEVILLE, N. C.
Hours by engagement
Drugless Healing of Disease

---

210 ASHEVILLE [1913] DIRECTORY

Hugill Henry C (Kate), carp, h Brevard rd, W Ashev
Hugill Homer, dynamo tndr, h Brevard rd, W Ashev
Hull's Flats, 80-82½ Cumberland av
Hull Fred A (Maria H), Natl Bank Examiner, 9 Medical Bldg, h 103 s Main
*Hull Garland (Della), cook, h (r) 18 Hilliard la
Hull Geo F, bridgemkr, h 122 Biltmore rd, S Biltmore
Hull Green D (Roxanna), bridgemkr, h 122 Biltmore rd, S Biltmore
Hull Louie W, emp Planing Mill, h 122 Biltmore rd, S Biltmore
Hulme Young M (Pearl S), h 20 Holland
Humble Edwd C (Nina), millwright, propr Birdwood Cottage, h Sunset Drive
Humphreville Ivy Miss, acct rdmstr Sou Ry, bds 83 Ralph
Hunnicutt Chester, lbr inspr, bds Riverside Drive nr Casket Co
Hunnicutt Jno W, driver, h 55 Ora
HUNNICUTT WM J (Johnnie E), physician, 19-20 Morsell Bldg, office hours, 11 a m to 1 p m and 4 p m to 5 p m—phone 985, h 55 Ora—phone 1444
☛Hunnicutt see also Honeycutt
*Hunt Annie, laund, h 108 Pine
*Hunt Butler (Love), farmer, h Herren av, W Ashev
*Hunt Clarence, emp Lutz Meat Co, h 374 Magnolia av
Hunt Flossie M Miss, h 302 s French Broad av
Hunt Fredk L (Janie), dentist 510 Legal Bldg, h 134 Hillside
*Hunt Hattie, dom, h 374 Magnolia av
Hunt Henry C, real est, h 162 s Main
Hunt Jno T (Sarah), gro 418 Depot, h 302 s French Broad
*Hunt Julia, h 63 Valley
Hunt Margaret Miss, mlnr, h 95 Church
Hunt Margaret Mrs, h 95 Church
Hunt Mary, wid Walter L, h 286 Depot
Hunt Mary E Miss, nurse, 36 College Park, h same
*Hunt Norman (Pearle), driver Patton & Stikeleather, h 108 Pine
*Hunt Perry (America), stone mason, h 125 Beaumont
*Hunt Sallie, laund, h 15 Short
*Hunt Sheridan S, lab, h Herren av, W Ashev
Hunt W Leroy, painter, h 286 Depot
Hunt W Lloyd (Laura G), real est, h 36 Grove
*Hunt Wooster (Belle), plstr, h 30 Miller
*Hunter Alice, cook, 118 Cumberland av

....Asheville Cleaning and Pressing Club....
Tailoring That Satisfies and Prices That Please
Steam and French Dry Cleaning of all delicate and fine wearing apparel for ladies and gentlemen. MESSENGER SERVICE IN THE CITY.
J. C. WILBAR, Prop. 4. N. Pack Square **PHONE 389**

Hunter Belle Miss, h W Asheville
*Hunter Clara, cook, h 76 Gudger
Hunter Cora Lee Miss, emp Hackney & Moale Co, h W Asheville
*Hunter Dilcy, laund, h 14 Ingle
Hunter Ethel Miss, clk Langren Hotel
*Hunter Jno (Jessie), porter Ashev Club, h 11 Black
Hunter Jno C (Guelda), lab, h 373 Southside av
Hunter Louis E (Estelle T), lumber, h 372 Montford av
Hunter Mary E, wid N B, h 39 n Ann
*Hunter Moses S (Nellie), lab, h 36 Ridge
Hunter Thos F, h 40 s French Broad av
*Hunter Wm (Clara), cook, h 39 Buttrick
Hunter Wm H (Mattie), carp, h 57 Hall
Huntington Elizabeth A, wid Albert W, h 149 Hillside
Huntington Sara W Miss, h 149 Hillside
Huntress Arthur G, clk Baltimore Cafe, rms Highland Hotel
*Hurd Barney (Fannie), lab, h 244 Southside av
Hursey Jno S, mngr Ray-Campbell Co, h 208 Pearson Drive
*Hurst Marshall, lab, h 61 Black
Hurst W Walter, stengr agt Land & Ind Dept Sou Ry, h 25 Asheland av
Hurt Jno H (Henrietta), agt Met Life Ins Co, h 100 Clingman av
Huskey Jas (Elizabeth), driver Beaumont Furn Co, h 5 Hall
Huskey Jane, wid David, h 49 Spring
Huskey Wm, driver, h 49 Spring
Huston Estelle Mrs, tchr Murray Schl, h 58 Arlington
HUSTON JNO W (Estelle), physician 2 Medical Bldg, office hours 11 to 1 and 4 to 5 p m—phone 1956, h 58 Arlington—phone 1956
Huston Josephine Miss, director of music Normal & Collegiate Inst, rms same
Huston Phoebe R Miss, clk Dr C P Ambler, h 58 Arlington
☞Huston see also Houston
*Hutcheson Andrew, elev opr Legal Bldg, h 117 Southside
HUTCHESON JNO R, collr Piedmont Directory Co, Amer Natl Bank Bldg
Hutchison Jno J, harness mkr Ashev Harness Co, h 261 s Main
Huxter J F, emp Piedmont Directory Co, rms 17 s Spruce
HYAMS MORD (Lillian V), family grocer and fresh meats, 130 n Main—phones 243 and 49, h 23 Orange (see back cover)

Asheville Dray, Fuel and Construction Co.

Heavy Hauling of all kinds — WE FURNISH BUILDING STONE — Moving Furniture a Specialty

61-2 South Main   PHONE - 223

DYNAMOS & MOTORS

Piedmont Electric Co.

64 Patton Av.
ASHEVILLE, N.C.

ASHEVILLE [1913] DIRECTORY

Hyams Washington S (Harriet L), dep clk U S Courts, Government Bldg, h 46 Charlotte
Hyatt Mary, dom, 71 Magnolia av
Hyatt Monroe, lab, h 188 Southside av
Hyatt Nancy J, wid Jas M, h Penna av, W Ashev
*Hyatt Robt L (Marie), butler, h 19 Short
Hyatt Wm R (Annie P), gro 188 Southside av, h same
Hyder Ada Miss, clk J H Law, h 11 Pearl
Hyder H Solan, slsmn T S Morrison & Co, h Emma N C
HYMAN NELLIE W, wid W R, propr Belvedere (formerly Ravenscroft), 95 Church, h same (see p 18)
Hyndman Cora E Miss, clk, h 32 Centre
Hyndman Jas F, tinner, h 32 Centre
Hyndman Thos L (Josephine C), shoe repr 47 Patton av, h 32 Centre

I

I X L Department Store (The), 22 Patton av, S H Michalov propr
Ideal Pressing Club, 5½ s w Pack Sq, F J Williams mngr
*Idson Douglas, watchman N & C Institute, h Livingston st
Illinois Surety Co, Court House (2d flr), R R Reynolds agt
Imperial Hotel, 24 w College, Louis Blomberg propr
IMPERIAL MUTUAL LIFE AND HEALTH INS CO (Inc), 31-32 Amer Natl Bank Bldg; Gay Green pres, J N Jarrett v-pres, W B Starnes treas, A W Ek sec, J P Starnes genl mngr (see side lines)
Independent Scale Co (W M Jones, L H Jones, C F Christopher), 21 Electrical Bldg
Ingle Andrew F (Hannah), lab, h 477 w Haywood
Ingle Carrie M Miss, h 36 Seney
Ingle Clarence J, police, h 115 Seney
Ingle Daisy Miss, h 477 w Haywood
Ingle Edwd J, clk J B Ingle, h W Asheville
Ingle Elmer, driver, h 330 s Main
Ingle Erastus E (Lillie C), carp, h nr Haywood rd, W Ashev
Ingle Eugene N (Mary C), motorman, h 2d av, W Ashev
Ingle F Bert (Maggie), real estate, h Allen st, W Ashev
Ingle Frank P (Mary), real estate 9 Revell Bldg, h 36 Seney
Ingle Fredk C, clk, h 3d, W Ashev
Ingle Henry (Ollie), carp, h 330 w Haywood
Ingle J H, lab, bds 8 North
Ingle J Vernon (Lottie), mtrmn, h 65 Seney

J. C. McPHERSON
SLATE AND TIN ROOFING
Galvanized Iron Work   Hot Air Furnaces
35-37 EAST COLLEGE STREET

PLUMBING STEAM AND HOT WATER **HEATING**
PHONE 133

Ingle Jas B (Sarah A), gro 47-49 n Main, h W Ashev
Ingle Jas F (Nannie), h Bingham Hghts
Ingle Jas M (Lorena), h 186 Haywood
Ingle Jas W (Yeauneta), lab, h Haywood rd, W Ashev
Ingle Jno E (Mary), carp, h W Asheville
Ingle Jno E (Florence), lab, h 330 s Main
Ingle Lelia Miss, laund, h 12 s Spruce
Ingle Leona Miss, h Haywood rd, W Ashev
Ingle Leslie, clk W U Tel Co, h 330 Montford av
Ingle Mack M (Ollie J), switchman, h Haywood rd, W Asheville
Ingle Mary, wid Lemuel, h 23 William
Ingle Mitchell A (Claudia), slsmn H J Olive, h W Asheville
Ingle Mollie Miss, housekpr, h Haywood rd, W Ashev
Ingle N Alex (Rosella), bricklyr, h 285½ College
Ingle Ollie Miss, laund, h 12 s Spruce
Ingle Robt (Kittie), h Bingham Hghts
Ingle T Clingman (Dorothy), driver, h 32 Catawba
Ingle T P (Ethel), plmbr J R Rich Co, h 174 Grove
Ingle Walter F (Corrie), clk Citizens Transfer Co, h 36 Seney
Ingram Carrie B Mrs, dressmkr 165 s Main, h same
Ingram Currie Miss, nurse Highland Hosp, h same
Ingram E Gray Miss, nurse Highland Hosp, h same
Ingram J Malcolm (Mamie E), prin Johnson School, h W Ashev (R F D 3)
Ingram Lovick F (Carrie B), paper hngr 165 s Main, h same
Ingram Millard F (Dollie), lab, h 112 Biltmore rd, S Biltmore
Inland Press (The), (B Geo and F A Barber), printers, 78 Patton av
INTERSTATE DEVELOPMENT CO, real estate 35-36 American Natl Bank Bldg—phone 108, Baxter Shemwell pres
INTERSTATE RAILWAY SWITCH & FROG CO, 35-36 American Natl Bank Bldg—phone 108, Baxter Shemwell pres
Investors Land Co, 2 Electrical Bldg, G S Powell sec-mngr
Iovine Geo T (Elizabeth), tailor, h 28 s Ann
Iovine Ralph R, presser, h 28 s Ann
Iovine Thos (Elizabeth), tailor S T Logan, h 71 Starnes av
Irick Olive M Miss, tchr Park av Schl, bds 111 Montford av
Irons Willis H (Mamie), driver Sou Exp Co, h 14 Chunn
☞ Irving see also Erwin

Candy Kitchen and Club Cafe
"A GOOD PLACE FOR REFRESHMENT"

Hot drinks on cold days. Cold drinks on hot days. The best drinks every day. Pure fruits and syrups blended "just right," served daintily. Our Ice Cream and Soda Water Department, Restaurant and Candy Departments are always kept up to the standard of nearest perfection. Phones 110 and 111. 19 and 21 Haywood St.

---

214 ASHEVILLE [1913] DIRECTORY

Isaac Freda L Miss, clk Peerless Dept Store, h 280 Southside av
Isaac Mabel Miss, clk Peerless Dept Store, h 280 Southside av
Isaac Tilford L (Margaret), gro 292 Southside av, h 280 same
Isenhour N Lee, rms Y M C A
Isom Jas D (Marinda N), clk P O, h 81 Josephine
Isom Martha C, wid Thos, h 240 College
Israel Andrew, warper, h 25 Roberts
Israel Aveline E, wid Augustus, h 324 s Main
Israel Chester W (Nora), plmbr G L Guischard, h 46 Vance
Israel E Wexley (Alice), propr Marquette Hotel, h 102 Patton av
Israel Ernest M (Ora G), sanitary plumbing inspr, 103 City Hall, h 82 Woodfin
Israel Eva E Miss, h 102 Patton av
Israel Everett I, warper, h 25 Roberts
Israel Frank R (Julia), plasterer, h 326 s Main
Israel G Meyers, ship clk, h 102 Patton av
Israel Josie E Miss, h 102 Patton av
Israel Lucinda Miss, h 9 Park pl
Israel Mamie B Miss, clk Ashev Dry Gds Co, h 102 Patton
Israel Norma L Miss, student, h 103 Blanton
Israel Otto L, county surveyor, h Candler N C
Israel Robt S (Lou), h W Asheville
Israel Zenas W (Zora), condr Sou Ry, h 103 Blanton
Ivey Jas T, foreman, rms 16½ n Pack Sq
Ivy Levi, gro 1 Hazard, h 58 Ashland av

J

Jackson Adrian C (Florence E), gro nr Smith's Bridge, W Ashev, h 146 Bartlett
*Jackson Anderson, lab, h 16 Hazzard
*JACKSON BENJ J (Lula), vegetables, fruits, country produce, etc, City Market, h 26 Magnolia (see side lines)
*Jackson Benj J Jr, clk B J Jackson, h 26 Magnolia
Jackson Blaine, carp, bds 323 s Main
Jackson Boney A, foremn, h Biltmore rd, S Biltmore
*Jackson Brady, lab, h 21 Latta
Jackson Branch M (Lola), caretkr, h "Hillcote" Victoria rd
Jackson Burt, driver Brown's Creamery, h 67 n Spruce
*Jackson Chas (Mary), lab, h 56 Pine

Brown's Undertaking Parlors

S. H. BROWN

50 Patton Avenue
ASHEVILLE, N. C.

Lady Assistant When Desired

Phone 193-2 Rings

THE MOORE Plumbing Company

16 N. Pack Square

PHONE 1025

Sanitary Plumbing, General Tin and Metal Work, Hot Air Furnaces

---

The Battery Park Bank

Capital - - $100,000.00
Surplus and Profits, $110,000.00

ASHEVILLE, N.C.   City, County and State Depositary

J. A. TILLMAN   **Jeweler**   I carry a nice line of Watches, Clocks and Jewelry, and make a specialty of repair work. Satisfaction guaranteed   **17 N. Main St.**

*Jackson Christopher E, slsmn B J Jackson, h 26 Magnolia
*JACKSON DAISY M, trained nurse, 39½ s Main—phone 1883, h same (see opp bus dept)
Jackson David L (Minnie L), propr Yuneda Dairy Lunch, h 46 Cumberland Circle
*Jackson Eva, dom, h W Asheville
*Jackson Fred L, clk B J Jackson, h 26 Magnolia
*Jackson Geo (Maggie), lab, h 12 Catholic av
*Jackson Geo (Novella), waiter, h 86 Pine
Jackson Grover C (Leona), fireman, h 455 Depot
*Jackson Hattie, cook, h 25 Ridge
*Jackson Hattie F, bkkpr B J Jackson, h 26 Magnolia
*Jackson Jas (Jane), lab 25 Orange
Jackson Jeffrey D (Hettie), lab, h 34 Spring
Jackson Jno F (Mary M), gro 170 Southside av, h 172 same
Jackson Lonnie B (Elsie), freezer Brown's Creamery, h 67 n Spruce
Jackson Lumber Co, h 203-205 Oates Bldg
Jackson M Louise Miss, h 46 Cumberland Circle
*Jackson Maria, laund, h 93 Pine
*Jackson Martha, laund, h 62 Poplar
*Jackson Minnie, laund, h 21 Latta
*Jackson Sarah, laund, h 29 Hill
*Jackson Sylvia, housekpr J E Joyner, W Ashev
*Jackson Wallace (Pearl), lab, h 19 Frederick
*Jackson Wm (Lizzie), lab, h 31 Aston pl
Jackson Wm M (Demia), pool 16 w College, h 28 Spring
Jacokes Jas W (Florence G), propr Glen Rock Barber Shop, h 23 Phifer
*James Amanda, h 5 Short Valley
James Bascom W, student, h 157 Blanton
James Claude N, clk, h 147 Patton av
James Claybrook (Eliza D), trav slsmn, h 43 Chestnut
*James Columbus (Jessie), cook, h 5 Atkin
*James Edwd (Mary), driver, h 10 New
James Floyd E (Mary J), carp, h 157 Blanton
James Grover C (Eva M), clk The Manor, h Hollyhock Cottage, Albemarle Park
James Harley B (Addie), lab, h 15 Coleman av
James Hubert, student, h 50 Hiawassee
James J Morrison, chf clk Sou Exp Co, h 147 Patton av
James Jno S (M Blanche), truck gardener, h 90 Cherry
JAMES JNO T (Helen T), agt Sou Express, h 147 Patton
James Julia, wid Dr M L, h 43 Chestnut
James R L, engnr, bds 102 Ralph

INSURANCE
Insure Your Salary With Us
Never Carry Your Own Risk
Safety Is The Best Policy
Unless You Are A Capitalist
Rest Easy If You Have
An Accident We Will
Not Keep You Waiting To
Collect Your Claim
Every Claim Promptly Paid

Imperial Mutual Life & Health Insurance Co.

Home Office:
ASHEVILLE, N. C.

Phone 495

HOTEL OXFORD   Redecorated and Refitted throughout. Recently enlarged to 60 rooms. Centrally located Depot cars stop at entrance. Long distance telephone office upstairs. American and European plan. Rates 50c, 75c and $1 per day; special rates by week or month. C. H. Branson & Sons, Proprietors. Phone 1887. 50-54 South Main St. **Asheville, N. C.**

Williams-Brownell Planing Mill Company — **Hardwoods**

Lumber---Rough and Dressed   Flooring a Specialty   Moulding, Interior Finish, Etc.
Office, Plant and Yards on Southern Railway, Near Biltmore Station
WHITE PINE   Phone 729   YELLOW PINE

James Rona Miss, h Woolsey
James Wm A Jr (Mary E), justice of the peace, and notary, 10½ n Pack Sq, h 50 Hiawassee
*Jamison Alice, laund, h 76 Market
Jamison Andrew J (Annie), emp Tannery, h 219 Asheland
Jamison Enna Miss, dom, h 324 s Main
*Jamison Thos, lab, bds 488 s Frenche Broad av
Jarrett David T (Daisy), bindery foreman Hackney & Moale Co, h W Asheville (R F D 3)
Jarrett Edwin C (Margaret E), gro 12 n Pack Sq and vegetables City Mkt, h 146 Asheland av
Jarrett Elbert M (Bertha), mngr Southside Furniture Co, h 22 Olive
JARRETT JAS N, v-pres Imperial Mut L & H Ins Co, Inc, h Winston-Salem N C
Jarrett Jas N (Sadie), bkkpr Coca-Cola Bottling Co, h W Asheville
Jarrett Jno W (Ida), painter, h W Ashev (R F D 3)
Jarrett Katherine B, wid Thos C, h Jarrett av, W Ashev
Jarrett Lela Miss, nurse Whitmore Sanitarium, rms same
Jarrett Lois E (Ethel), (Frady & Garrett), h Waynesville N C
Jarrett Otto (Bessie), carp, h 18 Olive
Jarrett Ralph C, emp W M Jones, h Jarrett av, W Ashev
Jarvis Albert K (Cora), collr, h 39 North
Jarvis Cora E Miss, h 67 n Spruce
Jarvis Creed F (Phinettie), mtrmn, h 70 Seney
Jarvis Florence Miss, h 14 Phifer
Jarvis Hubert C, clk, h 39 North
Jarvis Jno A, lab, h 14 Phifer
Jarvis Jno B (Maggie), condr St Ry, h 53 North
Jarvis Lena Miss, h 14 Phifer
Jarvis Mabel C Miss, student, h 39 North
Jarvis Thula Mrs, wks Ashev Mica Co, h 511 n Main
Jarvis W Milton, clk, h 67 n Spruce
Jay Guy V, emp Langren Bowling & Pool Room, h 458 w Haywood
Jay Mallie, wid Jas V, h 458 w Haywood
Jeanneret Louis W (Sarah E), watchmkr 22 s Pack Sq, h 216 College
JEFFERSON STANDARD LIFE INS CO, of Greensboro N C, 4 Paragon Bldg, Albert B Smith genl agt
*Jefferson Tina, cook, h Brevard rd, W Ashev
*Jeffrey Julia, cook, h 20 Dundee
*Jeffries Alice, dom, h 234 Flint

Asheville Electrical Co. Electrical Contractors
HEADQUARTERS 74 CENTRAL AVENUE
W. Mansfield Booze, Manager
PHONE 377

Asheville Dry Cleaning Co.
Telephones 835-836, All Dep't
MAIN, N. E. COR. COLLEGE

THE CLEANERS
Our Department for Oriental Rugs and Carpet Cleaning is prepared to serve you in all its branches.
E. S. Paine   O. E. Hansen

FOR BOX SHOOKS | **Call English Lumber Co.** **PHONE 321**

*Jeffries Anna, laund, h 180 Hill
*Jeffries Eugenia, laund, h 180 Hill
*Jeffries Robt O (Zenobia), barber J W Bowman, h 165 College
*Jeffries Wm (Catherine), porter, h 103 Market
Jellard Ella Mrs, mngr Viavi Co, h 108 Haywood
Jellard Meta B Miss, h 108 Haywood
Jellard Robt H (Ella), h 108 Haywood
Jellard Stanley T, h 108 Haywood
*Jenkins Belle, h 147 Valley
Jenkins Bertha M, wid G F, h (r) 79 Border
Jenkins Clara Miss, h Woolsey (R F D 1)
Jenkins D, engnr, h 99 Clingman av
Jenkins Edna Miss, h 166 s Main
Jenkins Fredk, slsmn Villa Heights Co, h 93 Church
Jenkins Gardiner, pressman Hackney & Moale Co, h 93 Church
Jenkins Garfield, cabt mkr, h 166 s Main
Jenkins Geo W (Corrie), dry goods 18 s Main, h 31 North View
Jenkins Grace E Miss, h 211 Merrimon av
Jenkins Jas T (Jennie), lab, h Woolsey (R F D 1)
Jenkins Jno H (Rachel), gro 32 n Main, h 211 Merrimon av
JENKINS LABAN L (Kate), pres American National Bank, h Edgemont Park
Jenkins Levada Miss, h 7½ s Main
Jenkins Mary T Miss, boarding 228 Cumberland av, h same
Jenkins Melvin W (Grace), farmer, h W Asheville
Jenkins Nancy M, wid A J, h 211 Merrimon av
Jenkins Robt B, h 82 Brick
Jenkins Robt L (Hattie), coach clnr, h Haywood rd, W Ashev
*Jenkins Susan E, laund, h 117 Ora
Jenkins Theodore M, tchr, h 166 s Main
*Jenkins Vera, cook, h 82 Brick
Jenkins Vinson J (Lola), mchst, h Broadway av, W Ashev
JENKINS WALTER J, sec-treas Asheville Sign Co, h 20 Central av
Jensen Jno L (Lucy E), h 15 Blake
Jervey Ida Mrs, h Forest Hill
*Jeter Lizzie, cook, h 60 Eagle
Jeter Susie B Miss, rms 74 Hillside
*Jeter Wm (Kate), lab, h 13 Madison
Johanneman Catherine Miss, h 415 Merrimon av
Johnigean Wm (Ida), bag mstr Sou Ry, h 136 Asheland av

Biggest Busiest Best Asheville Steam Laundry

Phones: 1936 and 1937

43 to 47 W. College Street

CHARLES H. HONESS OPTOMETRIST AND OPTICIAN

Exclusive maker of ATLAS SHUR-ON EYE GLASSES

THE Home of Ce-Rite Toric Lenses

We make a specialty of correcting optical defects with properly fitted glasses.

54 Patton Avenue Opposite Postoffice

Carolina Machinery Co. Founders, Machinists and Jobbers of Mill Supplies. We make all kinds of Castings in Iron, Brass or Aluminum.

WE ALSO FURNISH SKILLED MECHANICS FOR BOILER REPAIRS —— **PHONE 590**

LIFE INSURANCE COMPANY OF VA.
ORGANIZED 187
Richmond -:- Virginia
J. V MOON, Superintendent
Rooms 3-4-5- Maxwelton Bldg., Asheville, N. C.

All claims paid IMMEDIATELY upon receipt of satisfactory proofs of Death. Total payment to policyholders since organization, over $12,000,-000.00. Is paying its Policyholders over $1,000,000.00 annually.

T. P. JOHNSON & CO.

SHEET METAL WORKERS

All Kinds of Roofing Guttering and Conductor Work Metal Ceilings, Skylights and Galvanized Iron Cornices

OFFICE and SHOP:
69-71 S. MAIN
Phone 325

DR. C. H. MILLER

Mechano-Therapist

14 N. Spruce Street
ASHEVILLE, N. C.

PHONE 979

Hours by Engagement

DRUGLESS HEALING OF DISEASE

---

218 ASHEVILLE [1913] DIRECTORY

Johns Bayard (Grace), chffr, h 296 College
Johns Wm W (Edena), foreman, h 440 Depot
Johnson A Eugene Dr (Bessie L), h 204 College
*Johnson A Pauline, tchr Catholic Hill Schl, h 4 Haid
Johnson A R & Co, gro's 458 s Main, A R Johnson mngr
Johnson Ada, wid Wm E, dress mkr 308 Depot, h same
Johnson Albert R, mngr A R Johnson & Co, h 397 s Main
*Johnson Andrew (Nannie), lab, h 52 Black
*Johnson Andrew (Harriet), lab, h 47 Cole
*Johnson Anna B, laundress, h 17 Wallach
*Johnson Arthur (Lillie), clk Y M I Drug Store, h 8 Bay
Johnson B Lorena Miss, student, h 204 College
*Johnson Beatrice, dom, h 19 Wallach
*Johnson Belle, cook Western Hotel, h 4 Valley
Johnson Beulah E Miss, smstrs, h 60 Summit, S Biltmore
Johnson Bertram W, bkkpr Wachovia B & T Co, bds Cherokee Inn
Johnson Caroline, wid Josiah, h 28 Clingman av
*Johnson Chas (Lucy), lab, h 34 Black
JOHNSON CHAS E, pres Asheville Power & Light Co, h Raleigh N C
Johnson Chas M (Sarah S), mngr Excelsior P & P House, h W Asheville
Johnson David W (Edith), care taker Dr S E Winters, h Brevard rd, W Asheville
*Johnson Durant, lab, h 2 Madison
*Johnson Elbert (Mary), driver, h 154 Livingston
*Johnson Ellen, h 120 Roberts
*Johnson Emma, laund, h 40 Poplar
Johnson Eugene A (Hester), timber inspr, h 20 Turner
*Johnson Fannie, cook, h 36 Maiden la
*Johnson Fannie, dress mkr 134 Livingston, h same
Johnson Fannie Miss, dress mkr Mrs C B Harville, h 356 w Haywood
Johnson Frank E (Belle G), mngr Natl Casket Co, h 36 Cumberland Circle
Johnson Frank J (Annie), carp, h W Asheville
Johnson Frank M (Mollie), propr Excelior P & P House, h 14 Central av
Johnson Frank O, h Cherokee Inn
Johnson Fred'k L (Addie), paper hngr Excelior P & P House, h 79 Woodfin
*Johnson Geo W (Mary), waiter, h 44 Davidson
Johnson Geo W (Ida E), fruits 266 Depot, h 25 Rector
*Johnson Geo W (A Pauline), barber Oates Bldg, h 4 Haid

ASHEVILLE CLEANING and PRESSING CLUB

TAILORING THAT SATISFIES and PRICES THAT PLEASE

Hats cleaned, banded and bound. Silk hats ironed. Buttons made to order in all sizes. Plain or with rims. PHONE 389

DYEING IN ALL SHADES Cleaned. Messenger Service.

Kid Gloves, Slippers and Plumes. Fancy Jabots and Ties. French Dry Cleaned. Ladies' and Gentlemen's suits Steam

J. C. Wilbar, Prop. 4 NORTH PACK SQ.

*Johnson Gertrude, cook, h 16 Valley
Johnson Grace Miss, tchr, bds 20 s Ann
*Johnson Gus, porter, bds 16 Valley
Johnson H Ivey (Addie), condr Sou Ry, h 3 Oak, Biltmore
*Johnson Hampton, lab, h 34 Black
Johnson Harriett E Miss, student, h 123 Montford av
*Johnson Harvey (Jane), lab, h 14 Madison
*Johnson Hattie, laund, h 9 Greers Row
Johnson Herbert, appr D A Lashley, h W Asheville
Johnson Herbert H (Anna), foreman Excelior P & P House h 31 West
Johnson Horace, painter T J Perkinson, h 33 Victoria rd
JOHNSON HUGH C (Margaret C), propr Asheville Grocery Co (whol), h 123 Montford av—phone 988
Johnson J Watts (Sarah E), mill opr, h 42 Avery
Johnson Jacob, emp City, bds 306 n Main
Johnson Jas E (Olivia), h 291 Merrimon av
*Johnson Jno W (Mattie), lab, h 16 Valley
Johnson Jos E (Margaret), gro Grace, h same
Johnson Jos E (Cora), trav slsmn, bds 94 e College
*Johnson Julia, laund, h 152 Church
Johnson Kate Mrs, h 40 McDowell
Johnson Lawrence, fireman, bds Highland Hotel
*Johnson Lawrence (Mattie), porter, h 32 Hildebrand
*Johnson Lee (Annie), lab, h S Asheville
Johnson M Alonzo (May), carp, h 61 Summit, S Biltmore
Johnson M Drayton (Estelle), condr, h 117 s French Broad
Johnson M Taylor (Laura A), surveyor, h 60 Summit, S Biltmore
Johnson Malissa Miss, smstrs, h 60 Summit, S Biltmore
*Johnson Malvina, cook The Henrietta
*Johnson Mamie, student, h 34 Black
Johnson Margaret Miss, h Grace
*Johnson Martha A, boarding 32 Davidson, h same
Johnson Mary A Miss, h Grace
*Johnson Mary, dom, h 13 Lincoln av
Johnson Mary T, wid Capt Jas F, h 193 Montford av
*Johnson Mattie, laund, h S Asheville
Johnson May Miss, tchr, bds 20 s Ann
*Johnson Melvina, h 94 Grove
*Johnson Minnie, h 45 Brick
Johnson Mollie Mrs, canary birds 14 Central av, h same
Johnson Nellie L Miss, h 89 St Dunstan's rd
Johnson Omega, wid J C, dress mkr, h "Aiken Cottage", North st

*Johnson Ossie, laundress, h 36 Smith
Johnson P W, clk Wachovia Bank & Trust Co, bds Cherokee Inn
Johnson Paul J (Grace), linotype opr Ashe Gazette-News, h 42 Walnut
*Johnson Perry (Bell), driver, h 4 Valley
*Johnson Philip, waiter Sou Ry Dining Room
Johnson Pinckney G (Agnes B), slsmn Ashev Gro Co, h 11 Blake
Johnson Randolph R, gro Eagle cor Valley, h same
Johnson Robt, emp J M Hearn & Co, h Grace
Johnson Ruth C Miss, h Grace
Johnson Saml A (Carrie), electrn, h Grace
*Johnson Sarah, h 7 Velvet
*Johnson Sarah A, h nr Hazel Mill rd, W Ashev
Johnson Sarah L Miss, h 123 Montford av
Johnson School, W Ashev, J M Ingram prin
JOHNSON T P & CO (T Pinkney Johnson), tinners and metal workers, 69-71 s Main—phone 325 (see side lines)
Johnson Tessie Miss, h 23 Factory Hill
*Johnson Thos (Rebecca), lab, h 139 Weaver
Johnson Thos A (Tinie), tanner, h 33 Victoria rd
Johnson Thos F, h 60 Summit, S Biltmore
JOHNSON THOS PINKNEY (T P Johnson & Co), h 59 Woodfin
Johnson Thurlow, student, h Grace
*Johnson Tony (Rosa L), driver, h 101 Market
*Johnson Viola, cook, h 152 Church
*Johnson Walker, porter St Charles Barber Shop, bds 159 College
*Johnson Walter (Mary), hostler, h 52 Davidson
*Johnson Wheaton, lab, h 14 Madison
*Johnson Wm, lab, h 14 Madison
*Johnson Wm (Mary), cleaning, h 121 Clemmons
Johnson Wm C (Mae), lamp trimmer Ashev P & L Co, h 167 s Main
Johnson Wm E (Hattie), h 89 St Dunstan's rd
Johnston A T, rms 38 Temple Ct
Johnston Building (offices), 1½ s Main
Johnston Dana W (Mary W), chf dispr Sou Ry, h 197 Cumberland av
Johnston Emma C Miss, h 199 Montford av
Johnston Fannie L Miss, h 357 w Haywood
Johnston Harold E, real estate 20 Temple Court, rms 38 same

Johnston Herman, call boy, h 24 Turner
Johnston J Bergen (Ella), lineman, h 8 Spring
*Johnston J Parker, lab, h 13 Lincoln av
Johnston J Van (Louise), gro 325 w Haywood, h 24 Turner
Johnston R B (estate of), 20 Temple Court
Johnston Robbie Miss, tchr Murray Schl
Johnston Robt P (Alexandria), real estate 20 Temple Court, h 44 Grove
Johnston S Eugenia Miss, h 55 Grove
Johnston Wm (estate of), 20 Temple Court
Johnston Wm Jr (Sadie), real estate 20 Temple Court, h Edgemont
Johnstone Wm (Jeanet F), asst observer U S Weather Bureau, h 11 Cornelia
*Jolley Geo, cook N Murrough, h 1 Catholic av
*Jolly Lester (Reatha), lab, h 56 Ridge
Jones Abram V, condr Sou Ry, h 21 Blake
*Jones Adam, lab, h 54 Wallach
*Jones Adam, butler, h 5 Ingle
Jones Agnes Mrs, h 315 Pearson Drive
Jones Almond H, bkkpr Biltmore Estate, h S Biltmore
*Jones Andrew, lab, h 11 Wallach
Jones Annie, wid Patrick, h Main st, W Ashev
Jones Augustus (Lula), mill opr, h 50 Avery
Jones Awyer C, laundryman, bds 120 Clingman av
Jones B Daniel Miss, clk cir dept Ashev Gazette-News, h 21 Blake
Jones Bailey B (Ida V), farmer, h Haywood rd, W Ashev
Jones Belle D, wid Dr Alex S, h 21 Blake
Jones Belle D Miss, bkkpr, h 21 Blake
JONES BENJ M, asst cashr Ashev P & L Co, h 315 Pearson Drive
Jones Bessie Miss, dom, 21 Starnes av
Jones Campbell I Miss, h 377 Montford av
Jones Carl, lather, h 87 Park av
Jones Chas (Ethel), lab, h Lyman nr Depot
Jones Chas B (Sarah J), lather, h 87 Park av
Jones Chas E (Jones & Jones), h 377 Montford av
Jones Chas M, 263 Montford av
Jones Chas N, driver Ashev Ice Co, h 88 s French Broad av
Jones Chester A, lab, h Edgemont
Jones Daniel A (Nellie), genl mdse Chunn's Cove, h same
Jones Daisy L Miss, h 87 Park av
*Jones Duffy (Mattie), lab, h 2 Catholic av
Jones Edwd (Esther), h Chunn's Cove

Candy Kitchen and Club Cafe
"A GOOD PLACE FOR REFRESHMENT"

The very best ingredients with sanitary conditions in our Candy Manufacturing Department make possible the dainty, crisp confections sold here.

Bon Bons and Chocolates made every day, put up in neat, attractive boxes. Phones 110 and 111. 19 and 21 Haywood St.

Brown's Undertaking Parlors

S. H. BROWN

Lady Assistant When Desired

Phone 193-2 Rings

50 Patton Avenue
Asheville, N. C.

Established 1894

B. J. JACKSON

Carefully Selected Fruits and Vegetables

Stall No. 11, City Market

BUSINESS PHONES:
86 and 101

RESIDENCE PHONE
1596

Jones Edwd, mill opr, h 64 Avery
Jones Edwd F, student, h 258 n Main
Jones Edwd J (Lillian), bag mstr Sou Ry, h 25 Silver
*Jones Elias, lab, h 209 Clingman av
Jones Elizabeth E Miss, h 377 Montford av
Jones Emma Miss, smstrs, h Ashev av, W Ashev
Jones F Mack, constable, 8 s Pack Sq (basement), bds 34½ n Main
Jones Fred (Maude V), police, h 100 Cherry
Jones Geo H (Nannie), mch opr, h W Asheville
Jones Geo N (Luanne), driver Ashev Ice Co, h 25 Louie
Jones Geo (Nora), plstr, h 55 Furman av
Jones Geo W (Zora), driver, h 38 View
JONES GRACE McH MISS, librarian Pack Memorial Library, h 26 Clayton
Jones Hattie Miss, h 64 Avery
***JONES HENRY E** (Maggie), pharmacist Y M I Drug Co, h 7 Knob
Jones Hope E Miss, dom, h 38 View
Jones Horace E (Sallie), driver, h 15 Fagg
Jones Hortense H Miss, h 223 Haywood
Jones I LeRoy, pressman, h 258 n Main
Jones Isabel R Miss, tchr Allen Industrial Home & School, h 241 College
Jones J B, clk dep County Register of Deeds, bds Church st
Jones J Edwd (Katie), carp, h (r) 134 Poplar
***JONES J EUGENE** (Forney & Jones), rms 35½ e College
Jones J Harvey (Sarah A), h Ashev av, W Ashev
Jones J Herbert (Dollie), del clk Sou Exp Co, h Haywood rd, W Asheville
Jones J Ray (Nancy), bagmstr Sou Ry, h 63 Asheland av
Jones J Robt, clk Biltmore P O, h 4 Brook, Biltmore
Jones Jane Miss, student, h 263 Montford av
Jones Jno (Martha), weaver, h 1 Factory Hill
Jones Jno, presser, Ideal Pressing Club, h 74 Eagle
Jones Jno W (Gena R), bkkpr, h 20 Girdwood
Jones Josiah M (Patsey), h 464 s Main
Jones Julia Miss, dom, h 58 Vance
*Jones Julius, pressing club, h 78 Mountain
Jones Julius E (Jennie), mchst, h 325 College
Jones Karl L (Nina), agt Life Ins Co of Va, h 39 n Ann
*Jones Kate, dom, h 21 Catholic av
*Jones Kenneth, porter, rms 74 Eagle
JONES LAWRENCE H, with Wm M Jones, h 223 Haywood—phone 905

Yᵉ OLD BOOK SHOP

114 Patton Ave.   Phone 1674

BOOKS BOUGHT, SOLD OR EXCHANGED

Jones Lee W, lab, h nr Hazel Mill rd, W Asheville
*Jones Lewis, lab, h 11 Wallach
Jones Lillian W, wid B M, h 26 Clayton
Jones Lola, fireman, bds 308 Depot
*Jones Lollie, laund, h 20 Dundee
*Jones Lula, dom, h 54 Wallach
Jones Manning (Florence), carp, h 245 Hillside
Jones Martha N Miss, h 258 n Main
*Jones Mary, cook 194 Montford av
Jones Mattie B Miss, student, h Haywood rd, W Asheville
Jones May Miss, nurse 200 Montford av
Jones May F Miss, h 377 Montford av
Jones Minnie L Miss, tchr West Asheville School, h Haywood rd, W Asheville
Jones Moody (Bessie), clk, h 39 East
*Jones Oliver, lab, h 6 Cole
Jones Oscar, mill opr, h 64 Avery
Jones Otis, rms 19 Maxwelton Bldg
Jones Pinkney (Harriet L), watchman The Manor, h 258 n Main
Jones Rachel, wid Wm, h 25 Louie
*Jones Reuben J (Hattie), lab, h nr Hazel Mill rd, W Ashe
*Jones Rich'd P, propr The Big 400 Pressing Club and Beaumont Hotel, h 77 Mountain
Jones Robt B (Josephine), lab, h 10 Fagg
Jones Robt L (Josephine), carp, h Asheville av, W Ashe
JONES ROBERT S, business mngr The Asheville Citizen and pres-treas The Citizen Co, rms Asheville Club—phone 492
*Jones Rosa, laund, h 82 Hazzard
Jones Roxie Miss, h 174 Avery
Jones Roy, pressman H & M Co, h 285 n Main
Jones S Harley (Matilda M), mill opr, h 64 Avery
Jones Sarah H Miss, h 223 Haywood
Jones Stover (Kittie), driver, h Broadway av, W Asheville
*Jones Susie, laundress, h 54 Wallach
Jones T Wm (Callie), barkman, h 317 s Main
Jones Terrell B (Gertrude), boiler mkr, h 140 Park av
Jones Theodore E (Maggie), switchman, h Haywood rd, W Asheville
Jones Thos (Harriet), helper, h W Asheville
Jones Thos A (Josephine M) (Jones & Williams), h 263 Montford av
Jones Thos A Jr, asst mngr Haines, Jones & Cadbury Co, h 263 Montford av

Mrs. Wilder's SANITARY HOME LAUNDRY turns out first class work in Laundering and Dry Cleaning. No. 7 Montford Ave., Phone 1354

Jones Thos M (Hattie J), lab, h nr Hazel Mill rd, W Ashe
*Jones Virginia, dom, h 82 Hazzard
*Jones Wm (Jane), lab, h Dewey nr Hazzard
*Jones Wm (Leanna), keeper, h 17 Ridge
Jones Wm C, cigars, tobacco and fruits 43 s Main h same
Jones Wm C, clk Biltmore Estate, rms "Overbrook", Summit st, S Biltmore
*Jones Wm G, lab, h 21 Gudger
Jones Wm H (Rosa), driver Citizen Lbr Co, h 245 Hillside
Jones Wm J (Sallie), car repr Sou Ry, h 221 Pearl
Jones Wm L (Sallie), foreman, h 174 Avery
JONES WM M (Lily H), lumber, building material, planing mill, interior wood work, sash, doors, blinds, etc, 557 w Haywood—office phone 205, h 223 Haywood—phone 905 (see page 3)
Jones Wm M (Mollie), car inspr, h 98 Livingston
Jones Wm M (Dessie), clk Peerless Dept Store, h 39 East
Jones Wm W (Jones & Jones), h 377 Montford av
Jones Zebulon F (M Etta), brick lyr, h Hazel Mill rd, W Asheville
Jones & Jones (Wm W and Chas E), attys at law, 7-9 Library Bldg
Jones & Williams (Thos A Jones, Robt R Williams), attys at law, 417-421 Legal Bldg
*Jordan Alfred, waiter, h 17 Jordan
Jordan Alma L Miss, clk Palais Royal, h 30 Chestnut
Jordan Aloah W (Laura), h 133 Broad
*Jordan Armistead (Jane), butler, h 57 Eagle
Jordan Benj, emp Langren Bowling & Pool Room, h Grove Park
Jordan Chas S (Harriet B), phys 20 Battery Park pl, h 296 Montford av
Jordan Dyer (Hettie), carp, h 34 Spring
*Jordan Ernest (Sylvia), lab, h 118 Pine
Jordan Frank M (Nannie), ins inspr, h 30 Chestnut
*Jordan Geo (Irene), lab, h 93 Black
*Jordan Georgia, dom, h 17 Jordan
Jordan J Chas, firemn Sou Ry, bds 87 Ora
Jordan Jno W, gro 317½ w Haywood, h same
Jordan Jno Y (Meena S), trav slsmn, h 56 Cumberland av
Jordan Julius B (Sinda), dep sheriff County Jail, h Marjorie nr Eagle
*Jordan Louisa, laund, h 17 Jordan
*Jordan McGee (Kate), butler, h 49 Max
*Jordan O Martin, lab, h 17 Jordan

BUICK OLDSMOBILE
ARBOGAST MOTOR COMPANY
ACCESSORIES AND SUPPLIES
52-60 N. Main   Phones 302 and 1728
MAXWELLS DETROIT ELECTRIC

Asheville Dry Cleaning Co.
Telephones 835-836, All Dep't
MAIN, N. E. COR. COLLEGE

THE CLEANERS
Our Department for Oriental Rugs and Carpet Cleaning is prepared to serve you in all its branches.
E. S. Paine   O. E. Hansen

Jordan Pearle Mrs, h 25 Atkinson
Jordan Roy P, student, h 30 Chestnut
Jordan Thos W Prof (Florence), h Edgemont
Jordan W Claude, mchst Ashev Auto Co, h 30 Chestnut
*Jordan Wm (Pearl), bellmn, h 17 Jordan
Joyner Alfred, carp, rms 17½ n Main
Joyner Chas (Nina), deputy sheriff, h W Ashevill
Joyner J E & Son (Jas E and Jas E Jr), contrs, W Asheville
Joyner Jas E (Rose) (J E Joyner & Son), h W Asheville
Joyner Jas E Jr (Bessie) (J E Joyner & Son), h W Asheville
Joyner Lucy M, wid Jno N, h 128 Cumberland av
Joyner Marvin, mchst Asheville Auto Co
Jump Centennial B (Dora), switchman, h 9 Connolly's Ridge
Justice Bertha E Miss, h 3 Biltmore rd, S Biltmore
*Justice Clarence H, lab, h Haywood rd, W Asheville
Justice Clarence M (Leola), depty clk Internal Revenue, h 50 Oragne
Justice Claude B (Maude), civil engnr, h 102 s French Broad av
Justice Clyde N (Irene), trav slsmn, h 40 Vance
*Justice Geneva Miss, cook L H White W Asheville
*Justice Hattie, laund, h 122 Church
Justice Hattie M, wid G M, h 240 e Chestnut
Justice J Ernest, fireman, h 3 Biltmore rd, S Biltmore
Justice J Terrell (Eloise A), lab, h 62 Clayton
*Justice Jas H, farmer, h Haywood rd, W Asheville
*Justice Jno C, shoe mkr 155½ Patton av, h W Asheville
Justice Nancy E, wid Jas W, h 3 Biltmore rd, S Biltmore
Justice Saml, engnr Langren Hotel
Justice Wm S (Julia A), h 134 Poplar
Justice Wm T (Naomi), h 70 McDowell

K

Kaelin Frances, wid Jos J, h 30 Cumberland av
Kakor Gus, emp N S Trakas & Co, h 31 s Main
Kakor Jas, emp N S Trakas & Co, h 31 s Main
Kale Preston T (Cora), condr Sou Ry, h 25 Adams
Kale R Coach, clk The Union Store, h 25 Adams
"Kalmia Cottage", Albemarle Park
Kantsios Arthur J, mngr Baltimore Cafe, h 36 s Main
Kantsios Augustus, clk Baltimore Cafe, rms Highland Hotel
Kantsios Harry J, clk Baltimore Cafe, rms Highland Hotel
Karres Bros (Nicholas and Peter), confrs 11 n Main

The Life Insurance Co. of Virginia
ORGANIZED 1871 RICHMOND, VA.

ISSUES ALL THE MOST APPROVED FORMS OF LIFE INSURANCE CONTRACTS from $500.00 to $25,000.00, with premiums payable quarterly, semi-annually and annually

J. V. Moon, Superintendent, Rooms 3-4-5 Maxwelton Bldg., Asheville, N. C.

D. TREXLER TIN SHOP

All Kinds of Roofing, Gutter and Conductor Work.

Phone 862

159 South Main St.

DR. C. H. MILLER

MECHANO-THERAPIST

14 N. Spruce St.
Phone 979
ASHEVILLE, N. C.

Hours by engagement

Drugless Healing of Disease

Karres Nicholas (Karres Bros), rms 11½ n Main
Karres Peter (Karres Bros), rms 11½ n Main
Katz Alex H (Bessie), trav slsmn, h 37 s Liberty
Katz Hyman, clk M S Schas, h 24 Technical Bldg
Katz Meyer, Clk The Racket Store, h 37 s Liberty
☞ Kea see Key
*Kearney Augusta, laund, h 55 Mountain
Keber Lee, clk A W Lanning, h Biltmore
*Keebler Edwd (Maggie), porter Sou Ry, h S Asheville
☞ Keebler see also Kiibler
Keeler Irving P (Grace), supt, h 74 Cumberland av
Keeling Edwin D (Margaret C), bkkpr McConnell Bros, h 111 Montford av
Keen Buena V Miss, stewardress, h 75 Tiernan
Keen Chas (Dorothy), clk Glen Rock Hotel, h same
Keenan J T (Bertha), h Chunns Cove
*Keenan Jno, porter Ashev Club, h 60 Eagle
Keenan Mary Miss, house kpr The Avonmore, rms 107 Haywood
Keener Jno F (Minnie), condr Sou Ry, h 164 Bartlett
Keener Luther C (Daisy), clk, h 164 Bartlett
Keener Wm T, student, h 164 Bartlett
Keeter Merrimon G (Emma), carp, h 18 Crescent
Keever Carl E (Julia), flgmn, h 479 Depot
Keever Danl P, engnr, bds 426 Depot
Keever R Leslie, call boy, h 444 Depot
Keever Wm T (Mattie), h 147 Grove
Keith Anna Miss, h 176 Chestnut
Keith Guy W, cleaner Ideal Pressing Club, rms Morsell Bldg
Keith J H Mrs, h 176 Chestnut
KEITH JAMES F (Clara), sec-treas Asheville Dray, Fuel & Construction Co, h 32 s Liberty
Keith Lucile E Miss, cashr Princess Theatre, rms 36 Philip
Keith Nina L, wid Dr H H, h 3 Brook, Biltmore
Keith Omer R (Myrtle), emp Carolina Creamery Co
Keller Wilber F (Fannie), trav slsmn, h 68 Orange
Keller Wm A (Eleanor H), farmer, h 54 Fulton
Kelley Y O, collr Green Bros
Kelly Grace Miss, stengr, rms 356 Depot
Kelly Michael H (Mary L), sewer contr 16 Market, h 15 Vance
*Kelly Rose, nurse 230 Montford av
Kelly Tolliver B, engnr, bds 96 Bartlett
Kemp Elisha M (Ella), janitor P O, h 202 s Main

....Asheville Cleaning and Pressing Club....
Tailoring That Satisfies and Prices That Please
Steam and French Dry Cleaning of all delicate and fine wearing apparel for ladies and gentlemen. MESSENGER SERVICE IN THE CITY.

J. C. WILBAR, Prop.   4. N. Pack Square   PHONE 389

*Kemp Rebecca, laund, h 5 Ingle
*Kemp Wade (Elizabeth), lab, h S Asheville
Kendrick Edith Miss, nurse 84 s French Broad av, rms same
Kenerley Jno R (Emma), chffr, h 10 Central av
Kenerley Mollie Miss, dressmkr, h Biltmore rd, S Biltmore
Kenilworth Brick Works, Kenilworth Park
Kenilworth Co (The), land investments 15 Church; J G Mackenzie pres, J M Gazzam v-pres, J G Adams sec-treas
Kenilworth Hall (Misses A M Moore, I E Davies) (Swannanoa Hill), Biltmore rd
Kenilworth Lodge, boarding, Kenilworth Park
*Kennedy Addie, cook, h 121 Black
Kennedy Braxton, clk Smith's Drug Store
*Kennedy Chas (Ella), porter Sou Ry, h 86 Black
Kennedy Chas A (Minnie), barber 448 Depot, h same
Kennedy Eugenia, wid Sidney, bds 173 s Main
*Kennedy Hattie A, h Biltmore rd, S Biltmore
*Kennedy Henrietta, laund, h 34 Oakdale av
*Kennedy Jas T Rev (Florine R), rector St Matthias Episcopal Church and editor Weekly News, h 70 Beaumont
*Kennedy Jno L (Mary), gardener, h 232 Flint
Kennedy Robt V (Virginia), prin High Schl, h 27 Vance
Kennedy Saml (Katherine), mngr, h 423 s Main
Kennelly Mollie Miss, clk Palais Royal, h Biltmore
Kennerly Wm E (Asheville Steam Vulcanizing Co), rms Morsell Bldg
Kennett Frank S, sec-treas Amer Furn Mnfg Co, and mngr Amer Furn Buyers Assn, h 31 Bearden av
Kenny Fredk W (Amelia), bkkpr Biltmore Estate, h 7 All Souls Crescent, Biltmore
KENT FRED'K (Louise D), (Hoffman & Kent), (P W Lowe & Son), and mngr Storage Supply Co, h 173 Chestnut
Kepler Martha, wid Saml R, h 114 Montford av
Keplinger Hattie Miss, h 33 Clyde
Keplniger Mary A, wid C H, h 33 Clyde
*Kerns Beatrice, tchr, h 49 Atkinson
*Kerns Isaac W (Annie), propr Depot Pressing Club, h 49 Atkinson
*Kerns Mamie, nurse, h 49 Atkinson
*Kerns Wm (Bertha), driver, h 139 Clingman av
Kerr Anna P Miss, tchr, h 19 Vance
Kerr Augustus W (Arah A), bricklyr, h Haywood rd, W Ashev

Asheville Dray, Fuel & Construction Co. 6 1-2 South Main — **COAL** — Wood and Kindling, Stone and Sand **PHONE - 223**

EVER READY FLASHLIGHTS — Piedmont Electric Company, 64 Patton Avenue, ASHEVILLE, N. C.

Kerr Cordelia S Miss, h 19 Vance
Kerr Edith Miss, h Haywood rd, W Ashev
Kerr Estelle Miss, tchr, h Haywood rd, W Ashev
Kerr Geo D, carp, h 19 Vance
Kerr Harriett I Miss, h 19 Vance
Kerr Jno P, real est, h 19 Vance
Kerr Mabel Miss, tchr, h Haywood rd, W Ashev
Kerr Phoebe Miss, dressmkr, rms 224 Patton av
Kerr Susan E Miss, h 143 Montford av
Kerr ——, lumber, h 5 Oak, Biltmore
Kerr see also Carr
*Kesler Nellie A, smstrs, h 74 Mountain
Kesterson Avery (Temple), carp, h 22 Atkinson
Kesterson Howard, lab, h 22 Atkinson
Kesterson J Wm (Hattie), locksmith, h W Ashev
Kesterson Troy, h 22 Atkinson
*Keys M Theresa, laund, h 110 n Lexington av
Kibler A B Capt, tchr Bingham Schl, rms same
KIIBLER RICH'D E (Lena O), (Kiibler & Whitehead), h 59 Woodfin
KIIBLER & WHITEHEAD (R E Kiibler, L L Whitehead), meats City Market—phones 195-694 (see bottom lines)
Kilduff Wm J (Mary V), lumber, bds 141 Asheland av
*Kilgo Eugene, porter Supt Sou Ry, h 4 Max
*Kilgo Thos (Mattie), waiter, h 7 Dundee
*Kilgo Wm M (Rosa), porter Smith's Drug Store, h 22 Bay
Killian Calvin (Pearl), lather, h 11 Rector
Killian Frank M (Susie D), barber Ashev Barber Shop, h 77 n Spruce
Killian Frank M (Emma), condr Sou Ry, h 37 Adams
Killian Jno A (Elsie M), lather, h 11 Rector
*Killian Otis (Sallie), asst janitor Legal Bldg, h St Dunstan's rd
Kilpatrick Dewey W, clk W P Kilpatrick, h 19 Silver
Kilpatrick Dulcie Miss, clk W P Kilpatrick, h 19 Silver
Kilpatrick Elias M (Medora J), h 211 Patton av
Kilpatrick Medora J Mrs, propr The Waldheim, h 211 Patton av
Kilpatrick Raleigh W (Vashti), carp, h 14 Silver
Kilpatrick Waverly F, clk W P Kilpatrick, h 19 Silver
*Kilpatrick Wm, waiter, h 27 Max
Kilpatrick Wm P (Sallie C), gro and wood, 193 Asheland av h 19 Silver
Kimberly David (Elizabeth I), mchst, h 253 s French Broad

J. C. McPHERSON — SLATE AND TIN ROOFING — Galvanized Iron Work — Hot Air Furnaces — 35-37 EAST COLLEGE STREET

PLUMBING STEAM AND HOT WATER HEATING PHONE 133

Kimberly Fannie Miss, h Woolsey (R D 1)
Kimberly Jno, gro Riverside Drive, h Woolsey (R D 1)
Kimberly Mary Miss, tchr, h Woolsey (R D 1)
Kimberly Thos M (Janie), farmer, h Woolsey (R D 1)
Kimmons Mabel Miss, bkkpr J H Law, bds The Henrietta
Kincaid Clara M Miss, h 126 s French Broad av
Kincaid J Greer (Ollie), slsmn J L Smathers, h 134 s French Broad av
*Kincaid Maggie, laund, h 15 Haid
*Kincaid Sami (Zena), tanner, h 160 Livingston
*Kincaid Sarah, laund, h 91 Black
Kincaid Wm J, clk Sou Ry, h 126 s French Broad av
KINDEL W ALLEN (Lineta B), circulation mngr The Ashev Citizen, h 81 Chestnut
Kindergarten Public School, 94 East, Miss Ethel Ray and Miss Corrie Chambers tchrs
*King Addie, cook, h 20 Clemmons
King Albert H (Loula), prin Asheland av Schl, h 40 Flint
King Arlington (Lucy), fireman, h W Asheville
King Arthur, lab Water Dept
King B C (Ollie), farmer, h W Ashev (R F D 3)
King Bessie Miss, dom, h Woolsey (R F D 1)
King Chas G (Gertrude), train mstr Sou Ry, h 195 s French Broad av
King Eliza Miss, h 418 Southside av
King Genie, driver Ashe Ice Co, h Avery st
King Gus M, carp, bds 47 n Main
King Henry B (Elizabeth), h Merrimon av cor Hillside
King Horace L (Mattie), h Grace
King Ida Miss, h 96 Avery
King Jeannie Miss, h 96 Avery
*King Jerome, lab, h 26 Oakdale av
King Jesse (Augusta), driver, h 32 William
King Jno P, student, h Merrimon av cor Hillside
King Jno W (Nora B), lab, h Lester rd, W Ashev
King Jos, h 32 Clingman av
King Jos, painter R E Bowles, h Flat Rock N C
King Jos (Carrie), weaver, h 17 Brick
*King Martha, laund, h Haywood rd, W Ashev
King Matthew (Catherine), lab, h 32 Clingman av
King Matthew A (Catherine), lab, h 35 Turner
King Maude Miss, h 96 Avery
King Maurice E (Ora), painter 111 Broad, h same
King Monie, mill wkr, h 30 Short Roberts
King Nellie J Miss, housekpr, h W Asheville

Club Cafe and Candy Kitchen
"A GOOD PLACE FOR REFRESHMENT"

The standards we work to in our Restaurant Department are: Cooking, perfect; Service, prompt and cheerful; Prices, moderate; Menu, everything in season. Parties and Banquets, Teas and Dinners. 19 and 21 Haywood St. Phones 110 and 111.

Brown's Undertaking Parlors

S. H. BROWN

50 Patton Avenue
ASHEVILLE, N. C.

Lady Assistant When Desired

Phone 193-2 Rings

THE MOORE Plumbing Company

16 N. Pack Square
PHONE 1025

Sanitary Plumbing, General Tin and Metal Work, Hot Air Furnaces

---

230 ASHEVILLE [1913] DIRECTORY

King Perry L (Cornelia), lineman Ashev P & L Co, h 326 Pearson Drive
King Rachel, wid Geo W, h 96 Avery
King Robt P (Elizabeth), shoemkr 506 w Haywood, h 493 same
King Robt S (Mattie), trav slsmn, rms 18 Vance
King Rosa Miss, h 90 Avery
King T Monroe (Mary J), lab, h 94 Avery
King Wiley (Bessie), driver Ashev Ice Co, h 104 Avery
King Wm (Myrtle), driver, h 104 Avery
King Wilson T, reporter, bds 58 n Main
Kingsmore Leonard D (Lizzie E), condr, h 19 Hamilton
Kingsmore Ray L, news butcher, h 19 Hamilton
Kinsland Daisy Miss, nurse 18 Vance, rms same
Kintz Raymond E (Dovie), mchst, h 21 Phifer
Kirk Ester Miss, nurse Highland Hosp, rms same
*Kirk Walker (Eliza), porter Langren Barber Shop, h 28 Lincoln av
Kirkland Fredk E (Annie C), mngr Natl Biscuit Co, h 32 College Park pl
Kiser Amanda, wid Louis I, h Haywood rd, W Ashev
Kiser Connie L (Lillian), emp T S Morrison & Co, h W Asheville
Kiser J Ollie, uphr, h Haywood rd, W Ashev
Kiser McDonald C, clk J L Welch & Co, h Haywood rd, W Ashev
Kiser Mollie E Miss, h Haywood rd, W Ashev
Kiser Theo C, wood finisher, h Haywood rd, W Ashev
Kitchin Julian P (Hesta), sec Biltmore Farms, h 2 Oak, Biltmore
Kline Saml, driver, h 251 s Grove
"Klondyke," 440 Montford av, res of T C Coxe
Kluttz Chas A (Annie), condr Sou Ry, h 372 s French Broad av
Knapp Corrie Miss, h 3 New
Knapp Mack W (Charity), lab, h 3-4 New
KNICKERBOCKER (The), select boarding 77 College—phone 153, Mrs M H Harris propr (see page 15)
*Knight Bertha, hair dresser 18 Hilliard la, h same
Knight Nolan Mrs, stengr Martin, Rollins & Wright, h 324 s Main
Knight Sarah J, wid St Clair, h Haywood rd, W Ashev
Knight Thos B C (Nolan), engnr, h 324 s Main
KNIGHTS OF PYTHIAS HALL, (Pisgah Lodge), 1½ s Main

The Battery Park Bank
Capital - - $100,000.00
Surplus and Profits, $110,000.00
ASHEVILLE, N. C.   City, County and State Depositary

J. A. TILLMAN — Jeweler — 17 N. Main St.

I carry a nice line of Watches, Clocks and Jewelry, and make a specialty of repair work. Satisfaction guaranteed

*Knights of Pythias Hall, Masonic Temple, 44 Market
Knipe Jasper (Myrtle), mill hd, h 63 Roberts
Knoblauch G Henry (Ruth), trav buyer S Sternberg & Co, h W Asheville
Knott Dyonichus Miss, priv sec J C Arbogast, bds 1 Aston pl
Knott Frank E, mchst Western Carolina Auto Co, bds 51 Penland
Knott Nishia Miss, stengr, h 33 Aston
"Knowllacre," res of W S George, Victoria rd
*Knox Amanda, cook 192 Montford av
*Knox Fannie, laund, h 20 Ralph
*Knox Fannie, h 244 Southside av
*Knox Jack, porter baggage Sou Ry, h Ralph st
*Knox Mattie, h 43 Velvet
KNOXVILLE DIRECTORY CO, publishers 66 and L Amer Natl Bank Bldg, Ernest H Miller sec-treas
*Knuckles Chas W (Fannie), barber, h 24 Blanton
Kohn Adolf (Nannette), mngr, h 189 Chestnut
KOHN ADOLF (Nan), treas Peerless Fashion Stores Co and Peoples Department Store, h 189 Chestnut
Koon Ethen S, mchst, h 345 s Main
Koon J Hansell, A F D, h 345 s Main
Koon Job N (Ida V), emp Slayden, Fakes & Co, Inc, h 345 s Main
*Koon Julius (Malissa), lab, h 26 Gudger
*Koon Robt, driver Patton & Stikeleather
Koon Roy A, stage carp, h 345 s Main
Koonce Henry C (Nellie), photog Morsell Bldg (3d fl), h 35 Clayton
Koontz Ernest G (Celesta), car repr, bds 63 Ora
Koyle W C, trav slsmn, rms 24-25 Maxwelton Bldg
Kraft Annie L Miss, clk, h W Ashev
Kraft Mamie Miss, h W Asheville
Kraft Wilhelm F (Dora), concrete wkr, h W Ashev
Krause Frank (Lena), tailor H Petrie, h 46 West
KRESS S H & CO, five, ten and twenty-five cent store, 24-26 Patton av, L G Penland mngr
Krickhan Wm F (Myrtle), asst D B Burns, bds 180 Merrimon av
Kroger Wm, gro 240 Patton av, rms 17 Morsell Bldg
Kroman Esther Miss, with Paris Millinery Shop, h 20 Reed Bldg
Kroman Jennie Mrs, propr Paris Millinery Shop, h 20 Reed Bldg

INSURANCE
- **I**NSURE YOUR SALARY WITH US
- **N**EVER CARRY YOUR OWN RISK
- **S**AFETY IS THE BEST POLICY
- **U**NLESS YOU ARE A CAPITALIST
- **R**EST EASY IF YOU HAVE
- A**N** ACCIDENT WE WILL
- **N**OT KEEP YOU WAITING TO
- **C**OLLECT YOUR CLAIM
- **E**VERY CLAIM PROMPTLY PAID

Imperial Mutual Life & Health Insurance Co.

Home Office:
ASHEVILLE, N. C.

Phone 495

HOTEL OXFORD — Asheville, N. C.

Redecorated and Refitted throughout. Recently enlarged to 60 rooms. Centrally located. Depot cars stop at entrance. Long distance telephone office upstairs. American and European plan. Rates 50c, 75c and $1 per day; special rates by week or month. C. H. Branson & Sons, Proprietors. Phone 1887. 50-54 South Main St.

Williams-Brownell Planing Mill Company — *Hardwoods*

Lumber---Rough and Dressed Flooring a Specialty Moulding, Interior Finish, Etc.
Office, Plant and Yards on Southern Railway, Near Biltmore Station
WHITE PINE Phone 729 YELLOW PINE

Asheville Electrical Company
W. Mansfield Booze, Manager
74 CENTRAL AVE.
HEADQUARTERS
Phone 377

Kuchler Emeline S, wid J R, h 35 Vance
Kuykendall Alfred, lab, h Grace
Kurkendall Mabel Miss, h Grace
Kurkendall Wm A (Bonnie), driver, h Grace
Kuykendall Elijah L (Vinna), carp, h Haywood rd, W Ashev
Kuykendall Ellie Miss, h Grace
Kuykendall Flavius H (Ella), blksmith Grace, h R F D 1
Kuykendall J Angle (Cora L), lab, h nr Murphy Junc, W Ashev
Kuykendall Jas W (Hettie), lab, h Grace
Kuykendall Lydia Miss, mill wkr, h 8 Factory Hill
Kuykendall Mae L Miss, h 51 Penland
Kuykendall Mary Miss, h Grace
Kuykendall Wm H (Augusta), carp, h 56 Blanton
*Kyles Willis, cook Crescent Lunch Room, h 16 Eagle

L

LaBarbe Bettie Miss, h 202 Chestnut
LaBarbe Gertrude Miss, h 202 Chestnut
LaBarbe Hugh, real est, h 202 Chestnut
LaBarbe Margaret, wid Amos P, h 202 Chestnut
LaBarbe Nellie Miss, h 202 Chestnut
Lackman Fredk C (Hattie E), bkkpr Swannanoa Laundry, h 109 Biltmore rd, S Bilt
Lacy Clarence H, clk The Piedmont Electric Co, h 24 Cumberland av
Lacy J Milton (Mollie), cabt mkr, h 24 Cumberland av
Lacy Wm G (Elizabeth), rd mstr Sou Ry, h 99 Ora
LaDue Pomeroy (Emma B), h 38 Soco
LaDue Wm Mrs, bds 107 Haywood
Lail Ernest E, student, h Haywood rd, W Ashev
Lail Lee P (Cora B), carp, h Haywood rd, W Ashev
Lail Robt L, student, h Haywood rd, W Ashev
Lamb Edwd, clk frt office Sou Ry, h Southside av
Lamb Edwd (Esther), emp Sou Ry, h 11 Connolly's Ridge
Lamb Jacob B (Elsie), foreman, h W Asheville
Lamb Mary R Mrs, h 21 Washington rd
Lamb Robt S (Minnie A), inspr, h W Asheville
Lamb Thos A, car inspr, bds J A Ebbs, W Ashev
Lambert Agnes O Miss, bkkpr Ashev Gazette-News, h 12 Jefferson Drive
Lambert Bertha M Miss, stengr, h 12 Jefferson Drive
Lambert Geo H Dr (Maude), h 16 Cullowhee

Asheville Dry Cleaning Co.
Telephones 835-836, All Dep't
MAIN, N. E. COR. COLLEGE

THE CLEANERS
Our Department for Oriental Rugs and Carpet Cleaning is prepared to serve you in all its branches.

E. S. Paine   O. E. Hansen

Maple Flooring and Poplar Siding | **English Lumber Co.**
PHONE . . 321

Lambert Harriett A Mrs, dress mkr 12 Jefferson Drive, h same
Lambert Lucy, wid H S, h 166 e Chestnut
Lambert Moses (Nancy), butcher, h 55 North
Lambert Verg, helper Ashe Ice Co, h Hall st
Lambright Mohun M (Mattie), treas Boston Shoe Store, bds Western Hotel
Lancaster A Heenan, mchst Western Carolina Auto Co, bds 80 Penland
*Lancaster Emeline, h 20 Cole
Lance Dill F (Hattie), farm hd, h Bingham Hghts
Lance Ernest B (Nannie), blksmith, h Ashev av, W Ashev
Lance Hattie M Miss, bkkpr G F Stradley, h 194 Woodfin
*Lance J Edwd (Rachel), gro 17 Sorrell and wood, Eagle nr Valley, h 97 Beaumont
*Lance Jos (Mary), cook, h S Asheville
LANCE MARK W MRS, mngr The Henrietta and house sec Y W C A, h 78 s Main
Lance Sadie L Miss, h W Asheville
Lance Saml B (Angeline), farmer, h W Asheville
Lance Talmage S (Maud), gro 89 Clingman av, h same
*Land Broley (Rachel), lab, h 105 Roberts
Landreth Amos P (Lura), shoemkr 370 Southside av, h 399 same
Landreth Annie Miss, h 399 Southside av
Landreth Benj P (Nancy M), fruits 399 Southside av, h same
Landreth Chas E (Bessie), cashr Armour & Co, h 118 s French Broad av
Landreth Leola Miss, laund, h 399 Southside av
Landreth Monroe M (Emily), mailing clk Ashev Gazette-News, h 84 Starnes av
Lane Bertha Miss, wkr Ashev Mica Co, h W Asheville
Lane Jas (Lillie,) driver W M Jones, h nr Arlington st, W Ashev
Lane M B (Mary), banker, h "Columbus Cottage," Albemarle Park
*Lane Rachel, furn rooms, h 190 s Main
Lanening Floyd, helper, bds 443 s Main
Lanford Hubert C (Mary), painter, h 371 s Main
Lanford Stiles P (Lucinda), painter, h 371 s Main
Lange Chas, clk, rms 23 Meriwether Bldg
Lange Chas, bkkpr Glen Rock Hotel, rms Candy Kitchen
LANGE JNO H (Annie), pres Western Carolina Auto Co and propr Glen Rock Hotel, h same

BIGGEST
BUSIEST
BEST
Asheville Steam Laundry

Phones:
1936 and 1937

43 to 47
W. College Street

CHARLES H. HONESS
OPTOMETRIST
AND
OPTICIAN

Exclusive maker of
ATLAS SHUR-ON
EYE GLASSES

THE
Home of Ce-Rite
Toric Lenses

We make a specialty of correcting optical defects with properly fitted glasses.

54 Patton Avenue
Opposite Postoffice

in the market for a Gas Engine let us make you prices.
its heavy castings, such as columns or building plates, see us.
its a skilled mechanic for boiler work, see us.
you want machine work of any kind phone 590.
CAROLINA MACHINERY CO.

FOUNDERS
MACHINISTS and
Jobbers of Mill
Supplies

Life Insurance Company of Virginia
ORGANIZED 1871
Home Office - Richmond, Va.

Has won the hearty approval and active support of the people by its promptness and fair dealing during the FORTY-TWO YEARS of its operation

J. V. Moon, Superintendent, Rooms 3-4-5 Maxwelton Bldg., Asheville, N. C.

T. P. JOHNSON & CO.

SHEET METAL WORKERS

All Kinds of Roofing Guttering and Conductor Work Metal Ceilings, Skylights and Galvanized Iron Cornices

OFFICE and SHOP:
69-71 S. MAIN
Phone 325

DR. C. H. MILLER

Mechano-Therapist

14 N. Spruce Street
ASHEVILLE, N. C.

PHONE 979

Hours by Engagement

DRUGLESS HEALING OF DISEASE

Lange Jno H Jr, student, h Glen Rock Hotel
Lange Xavery B (Willie), propr Union Dairy Lunch, h 32 Soco
LANGEL HARRY L, mngr The Langren Hotel, h same—phone 605
Langford Bessie Miss, h 59 Clingman av
Langford Ella Miss, maid Cherokee Inn, h same
Langford J, h 59 Clingman av
Langford Jno (Sadie), carp, h (r) 326 s Main
Langford Lassie Mrs, wkr Ashev Mica Co, h 16 Spring
Langford Willard, driver, bds 52 Woodfin
Langley Wm P (Lula), mill wkr, h 22 Factory Hill
Langning Hillard, clk F S Foster, h McDowell st
LANGREN THE (Hotel), Main n e cor College—phone 9170, mngr's phone 605, H L Langel and J Baylis Rector mngrs
Langren Barber Shop (R C Parkins, C M Williams), 2 n Main
Langren Bowling & Pool Room, basement Langren Hotel, J E Moodie mngr
Langren Drug Store, 4 n Main, Asheville Paint & Glass Co, proprs
Langren Hotel Cigar Stand, Langren Hotel, E L Goldsmith mngr
*Lanham Lit (Lone), lab, h 18 Ingle
Lanier Mary Miss, tchr Orange St Schl
Lankford Hubert, painter R E Bowles
Lonkford Jas L (Lassie), carp, h 9 Spring
Lankford Nathan T (Bessie), carp, h 323½ s Main
Lankford Robt C (Mollie), lab, h 340 s Main
Lanneau Alexander C (Alice C), condr The Pullman Co, h 40 s French Broad av
Lanning Chas G (Tunie), police, h 24 s McDowell
Lanning Amos W (Dovie), gro 453 s Main, h Biltmore
Lanning Floyd, clk A W Lanning, rms 433 s Main
Lanning Lena Miss, clk H Redwood & Co, bds The Henrietta
Lanning May Miss, waitress Cherokee Inn, h same
Lanning W Harvey (Martha E), carp, h 131 Biltmore rd, S Biltmore
"Larkspur Cottage," Albemarle Park
Larson Helen Miss, maid "Oakwald," Forest Hill
Larson Jessie Mrs, bkkpr Bon Marche, h 38 Oak
Larson Jno J (Jessie), trav slsmn, bds 38 Oak
Lasater Wm H (Mary A), h 245 s Main

ASHEVILLE CLEANING and PRESSING CLUB

TAILORING THAT SATISFIES and PRICES THAT PLEASE

Hats cleaned, banded and bound. Silk hats ironed. Buttons made to order in all sizes. Plain or with rims. PHONE 389

DYEING IN ALL SHADES

Kid Gloves, Slippers and Plumes. Fancy Jabots and Ties. French Dry Cleaned. Ladies' and Gentlemen's suits Steam Cleaned. Messenger Service. **J. C. Wilbar, Prop.**

4 NORTH PACK SQ.

Lashley David A (Bessie G), florist Haywood rd, W Ashev, h same
*Latimer Jno S (Lizzie), waiter, h 104 Hazzard
*Latimer Texie, laundress, h 23 Aston pl
*Latimore Jos H (Mary), lab, h W Asheville
*Latta Fannie, dom, h Edgemont
*Latta Jane, laund, h 59 Clemmons
*Latta Thos, porter The Manor, h Sassafras nr Lincoln av
*Lattimore Jno (Martha), waiter, h 93 Pine
Lauchlin May C Miss, nurse 141 Asheland av, h same
Laughter Chas E (Mattie), weaver, h nr Murphy Junc, W Ashev
Laughter Columbus (Annie), florist, h 33 Fulton
Laughter Crawford, del boy V V Haynie, h 33 Fulton
Laughter J Fred (Electra), lab, h nr Murphy Junc W Ashev
Laufhter Jesse J, meat ctr Lutz Meat Co, h 33 Fulton
Laughter Jos B, lab, h Riverside Drive
Laughter Jos F (Lula), slsmn Citizens Lumber Co, h W Asheville
Laughter Lula V Miss, dressmkr 33 Fulton, h same
Laughter Raymond, lab, h 440 Depot
Laughter Winton, driver, h Riverside Drive nr n Main
Laughter Winton, driver Jno Kimberly, h Riverside Drive nr n Main
Laughter Zebulon (Lula), h Riverside Drive nr n Main
Laurel Springs Dairy, Chunn's Cove
LAW JESSE R, sec-treas Ashev Gazette-News, h 40 Cumberland Circle
LAW JOHN H, china, glass and silver, cutlery and house furnishing goods, 35 Patton av—phone 685, h same (2d fl)
Law Robt, rms Y M C A
Lawing Chas E (Olive), lab, h nr Arlington st, W Ashev
Lawing T Henry (Susan B), gro nr Smith's Bridge, W Ashev, h Emma N C
Lawless Frank S, harnessmkr Shope & Patton, h 40 East
Lawless Glenn W (Pearl), harnessmkr Shope & Patton, h 40 East
Lawrence Caroline C Dr, h Grove Park
Lawrence Edith C Miss, tchr, h Grove Park
Lawerence Edwd F, table turner, h Haywood rd, W Ashev
Lawrence Hattie M Miss, h Haywood rd, W Ashev
Lawrence Jas C (Lena), mchst Ashe Supply & Fdy Co, h W Asheville
Lawrence Louis H (Caroline), h 28 Soco

Lawrence Moses P (Ella), chf engnr Power Plant Ashev P & L Co, h 28 Soco
Lawrence Saml J (Josephine), clk Battery Park Hotel, rms same
*Lawrence Sarah, waitress, h 50 McDowell
Lawrence Susan A Mrs, h 23 Clingman av
Lawrence Thos Rev (Harriet), h Grove Park
Lawrence Thos J (Amanda A), pool room, h 484 w Haywood
Lawson Robt, lab French Broad Quarry, h Riverside Drive
Laxton Josephine Miss, tchr, h 36 College Park
Laxton Kate M Miss, music tchr 36 College Park, h same
Laxton Mary P Miss, nurse 36 College Park, h same
*Leach Amanda, laund, h 142 Livingston
*Leach Anderson, lab, h 142 Livingston
*Leach Grace, cook, h 24 Ralph
*Leach Jas, lab, bds 488 s French Broad av
*Leach Lola M, h 142 Livingston
*Leach Raymond, car clnr, h 142 Livingston
*Leaphart Walter (Amanda), painter, h 39 Buttrick
Leard Nannie S, wid A A, h 68 Grove
*Leatherwood Amanda, pressing 113 Cherry, h same
*Leatherwood Rosa, dom, h 113 Cherry
*Leazer Jas (Carrie), lab, h (r) 330 w Haywood
*Ledbetter Adeline, furn rooms, h 17 Atkin
Ledbetter Carroll, dairymn, h 331 College
Ledbetter Cleveland, carp, bds 12 Hilliard la
Ledbetter Cora, wid Richard O, h 8 View
Ledbetter Cora Miss, filler R I Smathers, h 20 View
Ledbetter Dock (Martha), dairyman, h 331 College
*Ledbetter Fannie, dom, h 55 Ridge
Ledbetter Geo W (Emma), automobile repr 8-10 e College h 23 Courtland av
Ledbetter L Calvin (Josephine), gro 60 Sycamore, h Valley cor Sycamore
*Ledbetter Martha, laund, h 55 Ridge
Ledbetter Sadie Miss, h 331 College
Ledbetter Vernon W, chauffeur, h 331 College
Ledbetter Zachary T (Martha A), truck farmer, h Haywood rd, W Ashev
Ledford Alice Miss, laund, h 110 Pearson Drive
Ledford Annie Miss, h 436 Pearson Drive
Ledford Benj, carp, h 436 Pearson Drive
LEDFORD D CLARENCE (Lizzie), supt English Lbr Co, h 44 Buxton

Yellow Pine	LUMBER	WOODWARD & SON
White Pine		Ninth and Arch Streets
Hardwoods	SASH, BLINDS, DOORS	RICHMOND - VIRGINIA
See bet. pgs. 188-189		

Ledford Ellen Miss, h 436 Pearson Drive
Ledford Edwd I, lab, h nr Smiths Bridge, W Ashev
Ledford Elva M, bkkpr, h 35 Buxton
Ledford Emanuel H, lab, h nr Smiths Bridge, W Ashev
Ledford Eugene (Ella), lab, h Hazel Mill rd, W Ashev
Ledford Isaac, driver Lutz Meat Co, h 436 Pearson Drive
Ledford Jas (Clara), engnr, bds 348½ Depot
Ledford Julius M (Naomi), gro 380 Depot, h 336 s French Broad
Ledford Lillian Miss, clk H Redwood & Co, h 306 Gaston st
Ledford Lucy A Miss, clk M V Moore & Co, h 35 Burton
Ledford Lula, h Edgemont
Ledford Mary E Miss, clk Peerless Dept Store, h 35 Buxton
Ledford Mary L, wid Milton M, h 35 Buxton
Ledford Sarah Mrs, attendant, h 5 Madison
Ledwell Kate, stengr, wid Jno, h Asheville av, W Ashev
Lee Annie G Miss, h 26 Flint
Lee Benj M (Winifred T), city engnr, office 206 City Hall, h 162 Flint
Lee C Elizabeth Miss, h 246 Cumberland av
Lee Chas E, clk Smith's Drug Store, h 73 Asheland av
Lee Chas G (Lavinia), (Lee & Ford), h 78 Asheland av
*Lee Choice C (Elmira), barber J A Wilson, h 124 Depot
Lee Claude F, student, h 111 Chestnut
Lee Eliza E, wid Robt H, h 73 Asheland av
*Lee Emma, cook, h 15 Short
Lee Emma A, wid D L, h 36 Madison av
Lee Eugenia, wid P H, bds The Henrietta
Lee Geo E (Lula), genl ins 5-6 Paragon Bldg, h 15 s French Broad av
*Lee H A, prin Southside av School
Lee Harry P (Margaret), trav slsmn, h 90 Asheland av
*Lee Hattie, laund, h 81 Valley
*Lee Henry (Julia), lab, h 11 Weaver
Lee J Hardy (Sallie A), cashr Biltmore Estate, h 246 Cumberland av
Lee Jas H Capt, clk frt office Sou Ry, h 30 Asheland av
Lee Jas Q, clk, h 73 Asheland av
Lee Jesse B (Ralla), clk frt office Sou Ry, h 165 Clingman
Lee Jno S Capt (Mattie P), clk Sou Ry frt depot, h 30 Asheland av
Lee Julia A, wid Chas E, boarding 26 Flint, h same
Lee L H, paperhngr R L Fitzpatrick & Son
Lee Lula Miss, h 36 Madison av
*Lee Lula B, h 64 Furman av

What Have You in Real Estate that You Don't Want?

What do You Want in Real Estate that You Haven't?

WESTERN CAROLINA REALTY CO.
J. W. Wolfe Sec. & Treas.

On the Square
PHONE 974
10 N. PACK SQ.

Brown-Carter Realty Co.
REAL ESTATE
23 TEMPLE COURT
PHONE 341
ASHEVILLE N. C.

FLORIDA SPECIALTIES
Grazing, Timbered, Farm Lands, Orange Groves, Turpentine Locations and Phosphate Lands.

NORTH CAROLINA SPECIALTIES
Orchard, Farm and Timbered Lands, City Property, Rent Collections.

Moale & Chiles Real Estate and Insurance 27 Patton Ave. (2d fl) Phone 661
General Agents United States Fidelity & Guaranty Co.

Club Cafe and Candy Kitchen
"A GOOD PLACE FOR REFRESHMENT"

Our Ice Cream manufacturing plant is absolutely clean and sanitary.
Prompt family delivery. Phones 110 and 111.
Catering for large parties and receptions. Special Creams.

Brown's Undertaking Parlors

S. H. BROWN

Lady Assistant When Desired

Phone 193-2 Rings

50 Patton Avenue
Asheville, N. C.

Established 1894

B. J. JACKSON

Carefully Selected Fruits and Vegetables

Stall No. 11, City Market

BUSINESS PHONES:
86 and 101

RESIDENCE PHONE
1596

Lee M, watchman Langren Hotel
Lee Mabel E Miss, h 15 s French Broad av
Lee Mary W Miss, h 75 Church
Lee Mattie P Mrs, artist 30 Asheland av, h same
Lee Niel (Anna B), carrier P O, h 66 Hillside
*Lee Nora, cook 276 Montford av
Lee Ralph E, ins with Waddell & Coxe, h 26 Flint
Lee Reuben F (Lillie), clk, h 111 Chestnut
Lee Richd C, clk, h 30 Asheland av
*Lee Robt J (Hester), tchr, h 167 College
*Lee Ruth, dom 276 Montford av
Lee Sarah H Miss, h 75 Church
*LEE WALTER S PROF (Hester), (Y M I Drug Store Co), and prin Catholic Hill Schl, h 159 e College—phone 1133
Lee & Ford (C G Lee, J F Ford), attys at law 13½ Patton
Leeper Hugh Y Rev (Mary), h 65 Hillside
Leeper Mary E Miss, tchr, h 65 Hillside
Lefevore Walter W, flgmn, bds 116 Clingman av
LEGAL BUILDING (offices), 10 s Pack Sq
LeHane M A Miss, nurse 225 Pearson Drive, rms same
Leidenger Henry H, h 78 s Liberty
Leidenger Katharine Miss, h 78 s Liberty
Leidenger Mary Miss, h 78 s Liberty
Leiman Henry (Margaret), box mnfr, h Edgemont
Leingerfeldt Mae Miss, nurse Biltmore Hosp, rms same
Leiphart Geo, baker Ashev Stm Bakery, h 50 Fulton
*Leister Jno (Emily), lab, h 119 Beaumont
*Lemond Earl W (Annie), porter, h 134 Livingston
*Lenoir Classie, laund, h 30 Oakdale av
*Lenoir Jno (Hattie), fireman, h 27 Buttrick
*Lenoir Mamie, clk, h 27 Buttrick
*Lenoir Martha, laund, h Haywood rd, W Ashev
*Lenoir Wesley H (Barbara E), lab, h 143 Livingston
Leonard Caleb B (Mamie), city building inspr, h 138 s French Broad av
Leonard E Frank, engnr Sou Ry, bds 87 Ora
*Leonard Jno (Mary), chffr, h 17 Eloise
*Leonard Nancy, cook, 266 Hillside
Leonardi Jno H (Rebecca), gro 155 s Main, h 156 same
Leslie Mary H, wid Alex, h 155 Charlotte
*Leslie Sophronia, dom Western Hotel, h 56 Mountain
Leverette Arthur, clk, h 24 Clingman av
Leverette Harvey, emp Ice plant, h 24 Clingman av
Leverette J Sebron (Tulon), police, h 24 Clingman av

Furniture and China Carefully Prepared for Shipment

Mahogany Furniture Hand Made & Carefully Reproduced | **E. E. GALER** 114 PATTON AVE. | Upholstering and Refinishing PHONE - 1674

Leverette Paul P (Bettie), yd clk spl agt Sou Ry, h 214 Patton av
Levitch Harry (Fannie), jeweler 29 College, h 51 Cumberland av
Levitt Morris (Nettie), 5-10 and 25 cent store, 3 s Main, h 31 s Liberty
Lewelwyn May Miss, tel opr, bds 58 East
*Lewis Ada, cook, h 63 Eagle
Lewis Amy K Miss, nurse 35 McAfee Bldg, h same
Lewis Carl, plmbr, h (r) 134 Poplar
Lewis Edgar G, flgmn, bds 96 Bartlett
Lewis Elda Miss, picker Ashev Mica Co, h 118 Short Roberts
*Lewis Elizabeth, cook, h 132 Hill
*Lewis Gertrude, maid, "Klondyke," Montford av
Lewis Henry, poultry, bds Riverside Drive nr Casket Co
Lewis Robt J (Agnes), sec-treas-mngr Red Cross Undertaking Co, Inc, h 18 College Park
Lewis Ruth, wid M A, h 300 Southside av
Lewis Susan, wid Jno, h W Asheville (R F D 3)
Lewis Walker, h W Asheville (R F D 3)
Library Building, offices 4 s Pack Sq
Lichtenfels Gustav (Edna L), (S Sternberg & Co), and (Ashev Pkg Co), h 49 n French Broad av
☞Lida see Lyda
Liephart Geo W (Bertha), baker, h 50 Fulton
LIFE INSURANCE COMPANY OF VA, rms 3-4-5 Maxwelton Bldg, J V Moon supt (see top lines)
*Lightner Jno, barber, h 165 College
*Liles Geo (Fannie), hostler, h 25 Haid
Lincoln Jno L (M), atty, h Grove Park
Lincoln Jno L Jr, student, h Grove Park
*Lincoln Jno P, driver Armour & Co, h W Asheville
*Lincoln Jos P (Emma E), lab, h Hazel Mill rd, W Ashev
Lindley Training School, W Asheville
*Lindsay Jas (Mayme), driver, h 18 Ralph
Lindsay Mary, wid Jas, h 15 Vance
Lindsay Roberta Miss, nurse 18 Vance, rms same
*Lindsey Bruce S, bellman, h 18 Cumberland av
LINDSEY FRANK A (Ann), sec-treas Carolina Machinery Co (Inc), h 153 Pearson Drive
Lindsey Frank A Jr, student, h 153 Pearson Drive
Lindsey Frank M (Eva J), plmbr J R Rich Co, h 34 n Ann
Lindsey Harry A (Mary A), mineralist, h 270 Cumberland
Lindsey Jno (Martha), h 53 East

Mrs. Wilder's SANITARY HOME LAUNDRY turns out first class work in Laundering and Dry Cleaning. No. 7 Montford Ave., Phone 1354

Lindsey Jno H (Vivia), tinner, h 97 Josephine
Lindsey Lloyd P, asst mngr S H Kress & Co, h 270 Cumberland av
Lindsey Martha Miss, h 57 East
Lindsey Martha J Mrs, weaver, h nr Smith Bridge W Ashev
*Lindsey Mary, h 18 Cumberland av
Lindsey Ralph B, asst foreman Western Carolina Auto Co, h 97 Josephine
Lindsey Thos A, bkkpr Ashev Carpet House, rms 30 Morsell Bldg
Lindsey Thos H (Catherine), photog, h Sunset Lodge
Lindsey Wm M (Katie), ins agt, h 20 Clyde
Lineberry Adam J (Addie), bill cutter W M Jones, h W Asheville
Lineberry Chas M (Cora), mchst, h Asheville av, W Ashev
Lineberry Elizabeth C, wid Jas, h Haywood rd, W Asheville
Liner Fred, lab, h Hazel Mill rd, W Asheville
Liner Fred, lab, Hazel Mill rd, W Asheville
Liner Lewis N (Lillie), farmer, h Hazel Mill rd, W Ashe
*Liney Frank, lab, h 40 Mountain
*Liney Henry, brkmn, rms 99 Black
*Liney Jno (Daisy), carp, h 22 Brick
*Liney Lula, laund, h 40 Mountain
*Liney Wm (Catherine), lab, h 40 Mountain
*Liney Wm (Lula), carp, h 22 Brick
Lingerfeldt Jno L (Alice), pressman Ashev Citizen, h 19 n Ann
Lingerfeldt Mary J, wid L M, h 19 n Ann
Lingerfeldt Wm, lineman, bds 49 n Main
Lingle Pinkney E (Lillie), carp, h 335 Hillside
☞**Linney see Liney**
Lipe Daniel B (Julia), propr Biltmore Shops, h 37 Summit, S Biltmore
Lipe Dean A, painter, h Biltmore rd, S Biltmore
Lipe Dudley (Katherine), painter, h Biltmore rd, S Biltmore
Lipe Edwin J, lab, h Biltmore rd, S Biltmore
Lipe Ethel Miss, wood carver, h 37 Summit, S Biltmore
Lipe Fred (Hattie), carp, h 334 w Haywood
Lipe Irene McK Miss, h 375 w Haywood
Lipe J Frank (Rowena), carp, h Biltmore Park
Lipe Jas C (Annabella), foreman, h 1 Biltmore rd, Biltmore
Lipe Jas C Jr, painter, h 1 Biltmore rd, Biltmore
Lipe Lucius A (Lee), fireman Sou Ry, h Biltmore rd, S Biltmore

BUICK — ARBOGAST MOTOR COMPANY — MAXWELLS
OLDSMOBILE — DETROIT ELECTRIC
ACCESSORIES AND SUPPLIES
52-60 N. Main — Phones 302 and 1728

Asheville Dry Cleaning Co.
Telephones 835-836, All Dep't
MAIN, N. E. COR. COLLEGE

THE CLEANERS
Our Department for Oriental Rugs and Carpet Cleaning is prepared to serve you in all its branches.
E. S. Paine   O. E. Hansen

For Kindling "What am Kindling" Call
ENGLISH LUMBER COMPANY Phone 321

Lipe May Miss, h Biltmore rd, S Biltmore
Lipe Nellie V Miss, wood carver, h 1 Biltmore rd, Biltmore
Lipe Oren H (Jennie), clk, h 3 Reed, S Biltmore
Lipe Rena B Miss, h 37 Summit, S Biltmore
Lipe Rufus P (Lucy E), engnr Sou Ry, h 375 w Haywood
Lipe Wallace D, student, h 37 Summit, S Biltmore
Lipinsky Clara Miss, cashr Bon Marche, h 156 Cumberland av
LIPINSKY LOUIS, with Bon Marche, h 156 Cumberland av
LIPINSKY MORRIS (Rae), genl mngr Bon Marche, h 41 Cumberland Circle
LIPINSKY S WHITLOCK, slsmn Bon Marche, h 156 Cumberland av
LIPINSKY SOLOMON (Eva), propr Bon Marche, h 156 Cumberland av
*Lipscombe Christopher C (Annie), v-pres Mtn City Mut Ins Co, h 96 Hill
Lipscombe Edwd H Jr (Ola), butler, h 131 Mountain
Lipscombe Lily B Mrs, h 127 Montford av
Little G Robt, drug clk Ashev P & G Co, h 127 Haywood
*Little Rutherford T (Lula), painter, h 318 Asheland av
LITTLE SMOKE HOUSE (The), 41½ Patton av, H G McFarland & Co proprs
Littlefield Andrew S (Blanche), Ry supplies, h "Ridgelawn" Vernon Hill
Littlefield Arthur S, h "Ridgelawn", Vernon Hill
Littlefield Calvin G, student, h "Ridgelawn", Vernon Hill
Littlefield Raymond S, student, h "Ridgelawn", Vernon Hill
Littleford Frank, h Hendersonville rd
*Littlejohn Alice, dom, h 22 Ridge
*Littlejohn Ellison (Cora), waiter, h 35 Ridge
*Littlejohn Essie, laund, h (r) 490 s French Broad av
*Littlejohn Geneva, laund, h 54 Short
*Littlejohn Hampton (Maggie), lab, h 104 n Lexington av
*Littlejohn Harriett, cook, h 2 Madison
*Littlejohn Susan, dom Kenilworth Hall
*Littlejohn Texanna, h 55 Cole
Littman Arthur, optometrist, h 98 e College
Littman E Estelle Miss, clk Bon Marche, h 98 e College
Littman Morris L, mngr suit dept Palais Royal, h 96 e College
Littman Rose Miss, h 98 e College
Littman Saml (Belle), trav slsmn, h 73 Orange
Littrell Howard H (Harriet), spl agt ins, h 5 Flint

BIGGEST **B**USIEST **B**EST

Phones 1936 and 1937
ASHEVILLE STEAM LAUNDRY
43 to 47 W. COLLEGE

S. D. HALL
REAL ESTATE AGENT
—
Money Loaned
—
Notary Public
—
32 PATTON AVENUE
—
Phone 91

Founders, Machinists and Jobbers of Mill Supplies
PHONE 590
When in the market for pipe and fittings, let us make you Prices.
Carolina Machinery Co.
PHONE 590
If it's a Gas Engine let us figure with you, also on other kinds of machinery

LIFE INSURANCE COMPANY OF VA. OLDEST, LARGEST STRONGEST Southern Life Insurance Co.

ORGANIZED 1871
RICHMOND, VIRGINIA

Issues Industrial Policies from $8.00 to $900.00, with Premiums Payable WEEKLY on persons from two to seventy years of age

J. V. Moon, Superintendent, Rooms 3-4-5 Maxwelton Bldg., Asheville, N. C.

D. TREXLER TIN SHOP

All Kinds of Roofing, Gutter and Conductor Work.

Phone 862

159 South Main St.

DR. C. H. MILLER

MECHANO-THERAPIST

14 N. Spruce St.
Phone 979
ASHEVILLE, N. C.

Hours by engagement

Drugless Healing of Disease

ASHEVILLE [1913] DIRECTORY

Littrell Jno T, lab, bds 265 s Main
Lively Verdie Miss, nurse Highland Hosp, h same
*Livingston Hampton (Anna), waiter, h 84 Hill
*Livingston Presbyterian Church, 72 Livingston, Rev Chas Dusenbury pastor
Livingston Sue, wid L L, seamstress M V Moore & Co, h Grace
*Lockman Jno, lab, h 60 Black
*Loder Reginald H (Georgia), (Greenlee & Loder), and (Wilson Undertaking Co), h 107 Broad
Loftain Blanche Miss, h 323 College
LOFTAIN CAROLINE S MRS, designer and maker fine dresses, 323 e College—phone 277, h same (see p 5)
Loftain Nancy R Miss, h 323 College
*Logan Annie, maid Sou Ry Depot, h 58 Black
Logan Annie L Miss, music tchr, h Haywood rd, W Ashev
*Logan Augustus (Mary), lab, h 43 Ocala
*Logan Benj, lab, h 13 Lincoln av
*Logan Eure (Ellen), lab, h 6 Short Pine
*Logan Hink, lab, h 27 Scott
*Logan Jennie, laundress, h 50 Smith
*Logan Jos (Nancy), lab, h 39 Ocala
*Logan Josephine, laund, h 15 Haid
*Logan Julia, h 245 Beaumont
*Logan Lula, cook, h S Asheville
*Logan Mamie, dom, h 91 Gibbons
*Logan Mattie, laund, h 84 Black
*Logan Minnie, dom, hd 9 Haid
Logan Myrtle L Miss, h Haywood rd, W Ashev
*Logan Saml, blksmith, h 60 Clemmons
Logan Saml T (Cora), mer tailor 12 s Pack Sq, h 124 Woodfin
*Logan Vernon (Alice), fireman, h 248 Southside av
Logan Wm E (Rose), U S Marshall, Government Bldg, h W Asheville
Lohman Carrie F Mrs, mlnr Sproat's, h 78 Cherry
Lohman Dennis F (Marie), artist, h "Edwin Pl," Grove Park
Lohman Lillian Mrs, bkkpr A L McLean & Co, h 78 Cherry
Lohman W Douglas (Lillian), tinner T P Johnson & Co, h 78 Cherry
Lominac Chas N (Bertha), police, h 36 Pearson Drive
Lominac Henry, bricklyr, bds 16 s Spruce
London Harvey R B (Martha A), lab, h Haywood rd, W Ashev

....Asheville Cleaning and Pressing Club....
Tailoring That Satisfies and Prices That Please
Steam and French Dry Cleaning of all delicate and fine wearing apparel for ladies and gentlemen. MESSENGER SERVICE IN THE CITY.

J. C. WILBAR, Prop.   4. N. Pack Square   PHONE 389

London Jettie, wid Lee, h Asheville av, W Ashev
London Kate G Miss, h Haywood rd, W Ashev
London Shop (The), art goods 8 s Park Sq, Mrs E C Dunn propr
Londow Dora Miss, bkkpr Crescent Jewelry Co, h 64 s Liberty
Londow Esther Miss, clk Bon Marche, h 64 s Liberty
Londow Ezekiel J, tchr High Schl, h 64 s Liberty
Londow Louis Rev (Bessie), gro 86 Eagle, h 64 s Liberty
Long Alfred A (Jessie), h Biltmore
Long Clyde (Allie), driver Felmet Bros, h 40 Atkinson
Long Dorothy Miss, h 50 Park av
*Long Ida, cook, h 156 Church
*Long Ila, dom, h 19 Wallach
*Long Lillie, cook, 167 Pearson Drive
Long Mary Miss, bds 94 e College
Long Mary Miss, bds The Henrietta
Long Mary E Miss, stengr Dr H H Briggs, bds 94 College
Long Moses D (Carrie), sec-treas Ashev Cotton Mills, h 50 Park av
*Long Nathan (Rosa E), porter Brown Hdw Co, h 28 Hildebrand
Long Robt A (Leonora), clk O Green Hdw Co, h Woolsey
*Long Stephen G (Beatrice), h 75 Ridge
Loomis Cornwell, asst collr Ashev Gazette-News, h 138 Charlotte
Loomis Geo C (Nannie), hardwood lumber, h 138 Charlotte
Loomis Helen Miss, h 138 Charlotte
Lonon W N, h Swannanoa rd
Lord Athalia Miss, nurse 63 Clayton, h same
Lord Bert, fireman, bds 308 Depot
*Lord Moses (Eliza), waiter, h 140 Pine
Lord Roberta Miss, h 63 Clayton
LORD WILLIAM H (Helen A), architect 17½ Church—phone 1006, h 267 Flint
Lorell Etta Mrs, h 23 Buxton
Lorick Jas M (Alice), mngr Citizens Transfer Co, h 35 Arlington
Lotspeich Orin P (Viola), broker 12 Harkins Bldg, h Weaverville N C
LOUGHRAN FRANK (S Adelaide), v-pres Beaumont Furn Co, and propr and owner Swannanoa-Berkeley Hotel, h 165 n Main—phone 1226
Loughran Geo B, student, h 165 n Main
Loughran Madeline Miss, h 165 n Main

Asheville Dray, Fuel and Construction Co.

Heavy Hauling of all kinds — **WE FURNISH BUILDING STONE** — Moving Furniture a Specialty

61-2 South Main   PHONE - 223

DYNAMOS & MOTORS

Piedmont Electric Co.

64 Patton Av.
ASHEVILLE, N.C.

Loughran Margaret J, wid Jas H, h 39 Charlotte
Loughran Richard B, cashr, h 165 n Main
LOUISIANA (The), private board, 51 College, Mrs Ida Ray propr—phone 1777 (see p 18)
*Love Addie, laund, h 16 Latta
*Love Annie, cook, h 4 Short Pine
Love Annie Miss, cashr Bon Marche, rms Y W C A
Love Bertha Mrs, clk Bon Marche, rms McAfee Bldg
LOVE F P & SON, DRS (F P and J M Love), veterinary surgeons, 9 w Walnut (see index for adv)
LOVE FRANKLIN P (Julia M), (Drs F P Love & Son), h 2½ miles from Biltmore
*Love Hattie, dom, h 31 Aston pl
Love Henry N (Bertha A), bkkpr Citizens Lumber Co, h 21 McAfee Bldg
LOVE JAS M (Annie), (Drs F P Love & Son), h Johnson S C
*Love Robt P (Martha), carp, h 87 Hazzard
*Love Sarah, dom, h 83 Hazzard
*Love Thos (Ella), lab, h 498 s French Broad av
LOVE WALTER W, sec Rogers Grocery Co, h Wilmington N C
Lovell Geo A (Margaret), saw filer, h 63 East
Lovey Louisa, wid Mosely, h 334 w Haywood
*Lovick Clarence (Emma), lab, h 25 Haid
Low Albert B, with Wachovia B & T Co, h 239 Haywood
Low Jessie V W, wid Jno G, h 137 Chestnut
Low Jno G, clk, h 137 Chestnut
Low Julia D W Miss, h 137 Chestnut
Low Mary L Miss, h 137 Chestnut
Low Wm V (Annie V), engnr, h 239 Haywood
Lowe Chas Spurgeon (W E Barnes & Co), h 190 Woodfin
Lowe Curtis (Mamie), mill wkr, h 14 Factory Hill
Lowe Georgia A Miss, h 190 Woodfin
Lowe Lina Miss, clk J A Guffey, bds The Henrietta
Lowe Mark, mill wkr, h 14 Factory Hill
Lowe Mollie Miss, h 25 Silver
Lowe P W & Son (Fred Kent, J A Nichols), produce, 16 e College
Lowe Pleasant W (Lena), h 190 Woodfin
LOWENBEIN JULIUS, sec The Peerless-Fashion Co, and Peoples Dept Store, 51 Patton av
LOWERY J A, v-pres Williams, Brownell Planing Mill Co, h Old Fort N C
Lowrie Queen, wid F H, h 56 Asheland av

J. C. McPHERSON
SLATE AND TIN ROOFING
Galvanized Iron Work   Hot Air Furnaces
35-37 EAST COLLEGE STREET

PLUMBING STEAM AND HOT WATER HEATING
PHONE 133

*Lowry Blanche, h 48 Gudger
*Lowry Jno W (Ida), helper D A Lashley, h Haywood rd, W Ashev
Lumpkin Chas (Amy), lab, h 47 Spring
Lumpkin Daniel (Ida), lab, h 47 Spring
Lumpkin Emery Miss, h 47 Spring
Lumpkin Josephine Miss, laund, h 47 Spring
*Lundy Jane, laundress, h 54 Southside av
Lunsford Albert L (Eva), driver T G Baird, h s Grove
Lunsford Anna Mrs, laund, h 32 View
Lunsford Arch, mason, bds 47 n Main
Lunsford Effie Miss, h 176 Grove
Lunsford Ethel L Miss, h 333 Southside av
Lunsford Frank (Bettie), hostler, h 34 Eloise
Lunsford J Woodfin (Ella M), driver, h Main st, W Ashev
Lunsford Jno C (Louise), boarding 333 Southside av h same
Lunsford Lloyd, lab, bds 51 Penland
Lunsford May Miss, dom Whitmore Sanitarium, h same
Lunsford Robt (Ellen), h Biltmore
Lunsford Robt F (Bettie), lab, h 42 Furman av
Lunsford Wm T (Lottie B), gro 88 Patton av, h same
LUSK V S COL (Mary J), atty at law 1 Library Bldg—phone 353, h 199 College
Luther Allen, mail clk Ashev Citizen, rms 12 Drhumor Bldg
Luther B J & Co (J D Stikeleather, B J Luther and W A Bostick), livery, 14 Brook, Biltmore
Luther Burgan F (Jennie E), farmer, h W Ashev (R F D 3)
Luther Byron J (B J Luther Co), and postmstr, Biltmore, h 1 Plaza, Biltmore
Luther C G & Bros (C G and Elmer Luther), gros 275 Asheland av
Luther Chesley G (Leah), (C G Luther & Bros), h 275 Asheland av
Luther Elmer (C G Luther & Bros), h 275 Asheland av
Luther Laura Mrs, wks Ashev Mica Co, h 47 Spring
Luther Melvin M, tinner A L McLean & Co, h 275 Asheland
Luther P Allen, stereotyper, rms 34 Meriwether Bldg
Luther Robt H (Estelle), clk G E Stradley, h 18 Vance
Lutz Meat Co (M Lutz, J H Manley), City Market
Lutz Michael (Eleanor B), (Lutz Meat Co), h 14 Orange
Lutz Walter L (Roma), undertaker, h 36 Pearl
Lyda Alex (Omie), tmstr, h 54 Pine Grove av
Lyda Althea R Miss, h 56 Hillside
*Lyda Arthur, cook, h 12 Latta
Lyda Augustus P (Nora), motorman, h 395 s French Broad

Candy Kitchen and Club Cafe
"A GOOD PLACE FOR REFRESHMENT"

Hot drinks on cold days. Cold drinks on hot days. The best drinks every day. Pure fruits and syrups blended "just right," served daintily. Our Ice Cream and Soda Water Department, Restaurant and Candy Departments are always kept up to the standard of nearest perfection. Phones 110 and 111. 19 and 21 Haywood St.

Brown's Undertaking Parlors

S. H. BROWN

50 Patton Avenue
ASHEVILLE, N. C.

Lady Assistant When Desired

Phone 193-2 Rings

THE MOORE Plumbing Company

16 N. Pack Square

PHONE 1025

Sanitary Plumbing, General Tin and Metal Work, Hot Air Furnaces

---

246 ASHEVILLE [1913] DIRECTORY

Lyda Benj (Mary), lab, h 10 Logan
LYDA EDGAR M (Fannie), county auditor, office Court House, h 56 Hillside
*Lyda Jackson (Lucy), lab, h 12 Latta
Lyda Minnie Miss, tchr Murray Schl
Lyda Wm C, clk, h 56 Hillside
LYERLY DAVID KELLY (Addie K), chf of police, office City Hall, h 28 McDowell
Lyerly Jesse L (Floyd), trav slsmn, h 84½ Starnes pl
Lyerly Jno A (Fidelia), h 15 Crescent
Lyerly Lillian Miss, h 15 Crescent
Lyerly Paul, clk, h 26 s McDowell
Lyerly Wm R (Laura A), blksmith, h 84½ Starnes pl
Lyerly Worth K, chauffeur, h 26 s McDowell
*Lyles Jno S (Mattie), barber P A Goins, h 93 Hazzard
Lyman A Julian (Julia E), atty at law 3 Paragon Bldg, h 126 Merrimon av
Lyman Chester Mrs, h Grace
Lynch Arthur R (Cora), asst mngr Princess Theatre, h 6 s Spruce
Lynch Eva Miss, clk, bds 12 Hilliard la
Lynch G Boyce, clk Grant's Pharmacy, h 155 Chestnut
*Lynch Ida, h 14 Sorrell
LYNCH JAS M (Anne I), physician 6-8 Drhumor Bldg, office hours 10 a m to 1 p m and 3 to 5 p m—phone 515, h 155 Chestnut—phone 1208
Lynch Jane S Mrs (Mrs Lynch & Son), h 6 s Spruce
*Lynch Janie, laund, h Dewey nr Hazzard
LYNCH JNO L, solr Piedmont Directory Co
*Lynch Jos (Etta), lab, h Haywood rd, W Ashev
*Lynch Mattie, cook, h 130 Church
*Lynch Maude, dom, h Dewey nr Hazzard
*Lynch Max, cook, h Dewey nr Hazzard
Lynch Mrs & Son (Mrs J S Lynch), fruits and vegetables, City Market
Lynch Stephen A (Flora), real estate and pres and genl mngr Carolina Amusement & Inv Co, Inc, h 89 n Liberty
Lynch Stephen S (Jane S), fruits, h 6 s Spruce
Lynn Elizabeth M Mrs, nurse 109 Cherry, h same
Lynn Robt, attendant Highland Hosp, h same
Lyons (The), boarding, 5 Starnes av, G W Trentham propr
*Lytle Deloin B, porter Langren Barber Shop, h 161 College
*Lytle Francis, bottler Haskell's Pepsi-Cola Wks, h 17½ Short Bailey

---

The Battery Park Bank

Capital - - $100,000.00
Surplus and Profits, $110,000.00

ASHEVILLE, N. C. City, County and State Depositary

J. A. TILLMAN Jeweler — I carry a nice line of Watches, Clocks and Jewelry, and make a specialty of repair work. Satisfaction guaranteed. **17 N. Main St.**

Lytle H Fred (Julia F), fireman, h 403 Southside av
*Lytle Hezil (Lillian), porter, h 77 Choctaw
*Lytle Jane, h S Asheville
Lytle Lola, wid W O, fitter M V Moore & Co, h 277 s Main
*Lytle Louise, dom, h 35 Valley
Lytle M Adelaide L Miss, h 44 John
*Lytle Robt (Hattie), hostler, h 221 s Main
Lytle Wm (Maude), carp, h 21 Courtland av
*Lytle Willie, h 35 Valley
*Lyttle Francis, lab, h 17½ Wallach
☞ Lytle see also Little

Mc

McAbee Geo W (Sidney), (West End Grocery), h 33 East
McAbee Jas V, clk West End Grocery, h 33 East
McAfee Building, offices 47-49 College
McAllister Wm (Ollie), lab, h Lester rd, W Ashev
☞ McAllister see also McCallister
McBee A Columbus (Alice), emp Wm L Moore, h W Asheville
McBee Ulysses (Vinie), painter, h Grace
*McBrayer Calvin, driver, h 16 Baxter al
McBrayer Jno, mldr, bds 348½ Depot
McBRAYER LEWIS B (L Cordie), physician 2 n Pack Sq (2d fl)—phone 390, h 33 Montford—phone 124
McBrayer Reuben, student, h 33 Montford av
McBrayer Sadie L Miss, student, h 33 Montford av
*McCaddick Lottie, car clnr, rms 73 Black
*McCain David (Stella), h 58 Eagle
McCain French M, tinner, h 39 Clingman av
McCain Henry D (Theresa), slsmn, h 39 Clingman av
McCain Theresa Mrs, propr Hill Cottage, h 39 Clingman av
☞ McCain see also McClain, McLain and McKain
McCall Alvin O, bkkpr, h 54 Vance
McCall Blanche Mrs, clk, bds 67 Ora
McCall Clifford C (Maud), carp, h 278 College
McCall Cora Miss, rms 11½ n Main
McCall Emma Miss, dom, 211 Montford av
McCall Jno F (Maude), blksmith 79 n Lexington av, h 64 Hillside
McCall Lennie M Miss, h 15 Carter
McCall Raymond A (Violet M), car inspr, h 15 John
McCall Robt S (Mary M), atty at law and U S Commissioner, 10½ n Pack Sq, h 54 Vance

INSURANCE
Insure Your Salary With Us
Never Carry Your Own Risk
Safety Is The Best Policy
Unless You Are A Capitalist
Rest Easy If You Have
An Accident We Will
Not Keep You Waiting To
Collect Your Claim
Every Claim Promptly Paid

Imperial Mutual Life & Health Insurance Co.
Home Office: ASHEVILLE, N. C.
Phone 495

HOTEL OXFORD — Redecorated and Refitted throughout. Recently enlarged to 60 rooms. Centrally located. Depot cars stop at entrance. Long distance telephone office upstairs. American and European plan. Rates 50c, 75c and $1 per day; special rates by week or month. C. H. Branson & Sons, Proprietors. Phone 1887. 50-54 South Main St. **Asheville, N. C.**

Williams-Brownell Planing Mill Company — *Hardwoods*

Lumber---Rough and Dressed — Flooring a Specialty — Moulding, Interior Finish, Etc.

Office, Plant and Yards on Southern Railway, Near Biltmore Station

WHITE PINE — Phone 729 — YELLOW PINE

Asheville Electrical Co. Electrical Contractors
HEADQUARTERS 74 CENTRAL AVENUE
W. Mansfield Booze, Manager
PHONE 377

McCall Thos D, carp, h 15 Carter
McCallister David M (Ann), lab, h 10 Logan
McCallister Raymond, engnr, bds 346 w Haywood
McCallister Wm P (E Henrietta), engnr Sou Ry, h 59 Ora
McCallope Cora Miss, h 131 Biltmore rd, S Biltmore
McCandless Clementine Miss, h 247 Montford av
McCanless Floyd V (Mary E), window trimmer Bon Marche, h 29 Cherry
McCanless Jas M (Lula E), photog 32 Patton av (3d fl), h 247 Montford av
McCanless Minnie B Mrs, agt, h 43 Clingman av
McCanless Wm J (Cora V), carp, h 127 Montford av
McCann Corrilla A, wid Wm D, h 135 Cumberland av
McCarroll Hugh T, emp Ashev Milling Co, h Haywood rd, W Ashev (R F D 3)
McCarroll Saml P (Sarah), tanner, h Haywood rd W Ashev
McCarson Bosher, lab, h 12 Roberts
McCarson J Edwd, lab, h W Ashev (R F D 3)
McCarson J Erastus (Hannah), farmer, h W Ashev (R D 3)
McCarson Monroe M (Julia), repr J L Smathers & Sons, h 18 Clingman av
McCarson R Benj (Elsie), carp, h Haywood rd, W Ashev
McCauley Cornelius, stengr div frt agt Sou Ry, h 3 Aston Pl
McClain Robt K (Elizabeth), dispr Sou Ry, h 130 s Main
☞ McClain see also McLain and McLean
McClammey Edwd L (Maude), genl foreman Sou Ry, h 164 Blanton
McCLOSKEY J J REALTY CO (J J McCloskey), real estate and insurance, 61-62 Amer Natl Bank Bldg—phone 771
McCLOSKEY JOSEPH J (J J McCloskey Realty Co), and notary, rms Asheville Club
McClure C Luther (Della), mchst, h 67 East
*McClure Irvin (Alice), lab, h 78 Market
McClure Oscar L (Sadie), stengr, h Maxwell nr Main
McCollum Edwd D (Martha), agt Met Life Ins Co, h W Asheville
McCollum Lillian Miss, h Haywood rd, W Ashev
*McComb Jno (Mary), lab, h 8 n Lexington av
McConkey Jasper N (Louise), h Grace
McConnell Bros (J H and W C), whol produce 38 n Main
McConnell Fred Y, mngr American Tailors, rms 25 Patton
McConnell Jas H (Ella), (McConnell Bros), h Woolsey (R F D 1)
McConnell Mollie, wid Edwd C, h 216 Haywood

Asheville Dry Cleaning Co. — **THE CLEANERS**
Telephones 835-836, All Dep't
MAIN, N. E. COR. COLLEGE
Our Department for Oriental Rugs and Carpet Cleaning is prepared to serve you in all its branches.
E. S. Paine — O. E. Hansen

McConnell Wm C (Abbie), (McConnell Bros), h 125 n Lexington av
*McCool Christopher H (Ethel), lab, h 14 Oakdale av
*McCorkle Brodie, cook, 287 Pearson Drive
McCorkle Harry F (Margaret), slsmn J L Smathers & Sons, h 235 s Grove
*McCorkle Judd, lab, h 3 Wallach
*McCorkle Love, dom, h 3 Wallach
*McCorkle Mack, lab, h 79 Roberts
*McCorkle Wm (Mary), lab, h 3 Wallach
McCORMICK ALEX H (Mary J), sec-treas Western Carolina Auto Co, h 319 Merrimon av
McCormick Alex L Jr, asst bkkpr Western Carolina Auto Co, h 319 Merrimon av
McCormick Alta, wid K R, h College pl
McCormick Eugene L, bkkpr Western Carolina Auto Co, h 319 Merrimon av
McCormick Lewis M, city bacteriologist, meat and milk inspr, 200 City Hall
McCoury Chas W (May), driver R E Bowles, h 62½ Penland
McCoy Adelaide M Mrs, boarding 346½ Depot, h same
*McCoy Alonzo, chauffeur C Sawyer, h 22 Lincoln av
McCoy DeEtta R Miss, clk, h 346½ Depot
McCoy Edgar, lab, h 458 Depot
McCoy Evelyn W Miss, h 50 Park av
McCoy Everett, slsmn J A Groves, bds 32 Ashland av
*McCoy Fannie, cook, 68 Park av
McCoy Fannie B Miss, stengr S Sternberg & Co, h 346½ Depot
McCoy Haliburton, student, h 68 Park av
McCoy Jas H (Adelaide M), real estate, h 346½ Depot
McCoy Lucille M Miss, h 346½ Depot
McCoy Naomi V, wid W H, clk Sou Ry Dining Room, h 454 Depot
McCoy Thos C (Sallie H), real est, h 68 Park av
McCoy W H Mrs, h 454 Depot
*McCoy Walter (Mary), lab, h 8 Richard
*McCrackin Frank, driver H B Brux, bds 128 Pearson Drive
*McCrackin King (Lola), waiter, h 128 Pearson Drive
McCrarey Chas T, pressmn Hackney & Moale Co, bds 96 Bartlett
McCrary Frank (Mary), h 103 Haywood
McCrary Mildred B Miss, h 103 Haywood
McCrumb Henry (Anna), lab, h (r) 334 w Haywood

LIFE INSURANCE COMPANY OF VA.

ORGANIZED 187

Richmond -:- Virginia

J. V MOON, Superintendent

Rooms 3-4-5- Maxweiton Bldg., Asheville, N. C.

All claims paid IMMEDIATELY upon receipt of satisfactory proofs of Death. Total payment to policyholders since organization, over $12,000,000.00. Is paying its Policyholders over $1,000,000.00 annually.

T. P. JOHNSON & CO.

SHEET METAL WORKERS

All Kinds of Roofing Guttering and Conductor Work Metal Ceilings, Skylights and Galvanized Iron Cornices

OFFICE and SHOP:
69-71 S. MAIN

Phone 325

DR. C. H. MILLER

Mechano-Therapist

14 N. Spruce Street
ASHEVILLE, N. C.

PHONE 979

Hours by Engagement

DRUGLESS HEALING OF DISEASE

---

250   ASHEVILLE [1913] DIRECTORY

McCulley Thos, painter, bds 49 n Main
*McCullough Berry (Myra), lab, h 9 Madison
*McCullough Squire (Julia), lab, h 2 Madison
McCurry Chas (Mary), motorman, h 32 Clingman av
McCurry J Saml (Nettie), farmer, h Haywood rd, W Ashev
*McCurry Jno, lab, bds 488 s French Broad av
McCurry Luther, lab, h 21 Lyman
McCurry Nelson E (Dora), lab, h 21 Lyman
*McDaniel Mitchell, hostler, h 21 Hildebrand
*McDaniel Saml, stone mason, h 21 Hildebrand
*McDaniel Walter (Ada), lab, h (r) 181 Beaumont
McDaris Bonnie Miss, weaver, h 140 Hall
McDaris Jos T (Nettie), driver, h 140 Hall
McDaris Loney P (Hannah), carp, bds 49 n Main
McDaris Stella Miss, weaver, h 140 Hall
McDarris Wm O, gro, 212 Livingston, h 204 same
*Mc David Jos (Luna), tailor, h 17 Hill
McDERMOTT WM R (Leslie), mngr H F Grant Realty Co and notary, h 14 Holland
McDivitt Anna C Miss, nurse 27 Border, bds same
McDivitt Jas A (Ethlene), blksmith, h 264 s French Broad
McDonald Allen C (Julia), h e 160 Chestnut
McDonald Annie Miss, housekpr, 316 w Haywood
*McDonald Cora, laund, h 10 Green's Row
McDonald Emma B, wid Eugene L, h 328 w Haywood
*McDonald Jefferson (Mary), lab, h 115 Grove
McDonald Jno, slsmn Villa Heights Co, bds 201 Merrimon
*McDonald Thos (Lizzie), barber 6 s Pack Sq, h 15 Sassafras
McDougle Aaron E (Artimecia), h 17 n Spruce
McDougle Artimecia Mrs, boarding 17 n Spruce, h same
McDowell A Kate Miss, clk A M Field Co, h 77 Victoria av
McDowell Anne G Miss, h 413 s Main
McDowell Annie E Miss, h 413 s Main
McDowell Annie K Miss, housekpr, h Jarrett av, W Ashev
McDowell Bessie L, wid Geo M, h 60 Livingston
McDowell Edwd E (Margaret), (McDowell & Patton), h 383 s Main
*McDowell Elijah (Lizzie), shoemkr (r) 14 n Spruce, h 41 Hildebrand
McDowell Ernest, plmbr Union Plumbing Co, h 77 Victoria av
*McDowell Fannie, laundress, h 272 Asheland av
McDowell Hamilton E, student, h 383 s Main
McDowell Harold C, plmbr, h 77 Victoria av

ASHEVILLE CLEANING and PRESSING CLUB

TAILORING THAT SATISFIES and PRICES THAT PLEASE

Hats cleaned, banded and bound. Silk hats ironed. Buttons made to order in all sizes. Plain or with rims. PHONE 389

DYEING IN ALL SHADES

Kid Gloves, Slippers and Plumes. Fancy Jabots and Ties. French Dry Cleaned. Ladies' and Gentlemen's suits Steam Cleaned. Messenger Service.

J. C. Wilbar, Prop.   4 NORTH PACK SQ.

McDowell Jessie H Miss, h 43 Chestnut
*McDowell L M (Dora), lab, h 394 Asheland av
*McDowell Lena, laund, h 12 McDowell
McDowell Marguerite S Miss, 383 s Main
*McDowell Mary, gro 80-82 Pine, h same
McDowell Mary B Miss, clk supt of schools, h 413 s Main
McDowell Mary C Miss, h 413 s Main
McDowell Mary M Miss, bkkpr Whitlock Clothing Co, h 77 Victoria av
McDowell Nannie L Miss, h 77 Victoria av
*McDowell Smiley, cook, h 15 Max
*McDowell Vance (Fannie), lab, h (r) 7 Depot
McDowell W Gaston (Martha A), sergt police, h 77 Victoria av
McDowell Wm (Alma), flgmn, bds 430 Depot
McDOWELL WM M, sec-treas Ashev Mercantile Agcy and ins agt, bds 23 Asheland av
McDowell Wm W (Emma L), carp, h 85 Victoria av
*McDowell Wilson, lab, h 12 McDowell
McDowell & Patton (E E McDowell, W H Patton), contrs, 34 College
*McElrath Amanda, cook 200 Montford av
McElrath Edwd (Hattie), lab, h 24 Miller
McElrath Jno W (Mary), emp Battery Park Hotel, h 68 Central av
*McElrath Mamie, waitress, 38 Sassafras
*McElrath Roberta, h 77 Choctaw
*McElrath Samantha, h 24 Miller
McElrath Virginia B Miss, h 68 Central av
McElrath W Jackson, fireman Sou Ry, h 68 Central av
*McElrath Wm (Esther), lab, h 14 Gaither
McElroy Jno W (Hannah), dep U S Marshall, h W Asheville
McElroy Lena Mrs, clk, h Asheville av, W Asheville
McEniry Eva Miss, h 118 Cumberland av
McEniry Jno E (Eva M), h 118 Cumberland av
McEntyre Lydia, wid Jas, h W Asheeville
☞ McEntyre see also McIntyre
McEwen Jno W (Margaret S), bkkpr J R Rich Co, h 62 Clayton
McEwen Lumber Co, Azalea N C, W B McEwen pres
McEWEN WOOSTER B (Caroline), v-pres Central Bank & Trust Co and pres McEwen Lumber Co, h 276 Chestnut
McFall Wm C (Martha), miller, h 85 Atkinson

McFarland Grover H (Pearle), emp Ashe P & L Co, h nr Haywood rd, W Asheville
McFARLAND H G & CO (H G McFarland), proprs The Little Smoke House, 41½ Patton av
McFARLAND HILDRETH G (H G McFarland & Co), h 95 Woodfin
McFarland Isabelle, wid Richard, h Main st, W Asheville
McFarland Jno W (Create), h Swannanoa av, W Asheville
McFarland Jos P (Annie), driver, h Woolsey
McFarland Robt M (Annie), watchman, bds 2 Fagg
McFee Fonella Miss, h Woolsey (R F D 1)
*McFee Mance (Fannie), driver, h (r) 350 w Haywood
McFerren Lily Miss, h 31 Panola
McFerren Pingree (Mary E), h 31 Panola
McGarry Jos (May M), photog 1½ n e Pack Sq, h 93 College
McGarry May M Mrs, propr The Traymore, h 93 College
McGee Brownlow (Gertrude), automobiles, bds 75 Penland
*McGee Wm (Mary), lab, h (r) 29 Clingman av
McGhee Kittie, wid Floyd, emp Ashev Mica Co, h 12 s Spruce
McGhee Wm B (Mary C), furn mkr, rms 161 Haywood
*McGinness Fred B, presser J H McGinness, h 44 Market
*McGinness Jno H (Carrie), pressing 44 Market, h 14 Haid
McGlamery Mack V, sub carrier P O, h Brevard rd, W Asheville
McGlamery S Annie Miss, dressmkr, h Brevard rd, W Asheville
McGlamery Wm A (Elvira), farmer, h Brevard rd, W Asheville
McGlone Frank H (Bertha), foreman, h 11 Brook, Biltmore
McGrath Thos H (Lulu), boiler mkr, h 196 Bartlett
McGraw Oscar P, trav slsmn, rms 23 Technical Bldg
McGuinn E May Miss, h 443 s Main
McGuinn Goldie Miss, h 443 s Main
McGuinn Jos A (Arkansas), emp A R Johnson, h 443 s Main
McGuinn Jos F, student, h 443 s Main
McGuire Edna, wid M L, h Woolsey (R F D 1)
McGuire Jno Q (C Estelle) (McGuire & Co), h 183 Woodfin
McGuire Max S, clk C E Henderson, h 183 Woodfin
McGuire Walter R (Grace M), (Yates & McGuire,) h 120 Flint
McGuire & Co (J Q McGuire, Geo Henderson), roots and herbs, 117 n Lexington av

☞McGuire see also MaGuire
McHardge Carl, condr Sou Ry, bds 29 Ora
McHarge Chas F (Bessie), condr Sou Ry, h 126 s French Broad av
McHodge Jno, condr, bds 102 Ralph
McHone Raymond M (Dervy), h 21 Atkinson
McInnis Henrietta C, wid Saml, h 188 Cumberland av
McIntire Alva J, clk frt office Sou Ry, h 157 Merrimon av
McINTIRE CARLIN R, cashr The Ashev Citizen, h 157 Merrimon av—phone 569
McIntire Filetus R (Jennie), contr, h 157 Merrimon av
McIntire Novella Miss, h 157 Merrimon av
*McIntire Thos (Bertha), lab, h 26½ Hildebrand
McIntosh Jas B, lineman Ashev P & L Co, bds 56 Penland
McIntosh Lizzie Miss, dressmkr, h 37 Orchard
McIntyre Annie L Miss, h Hazel Mill rd, W Ashev
McIntyre Building, 1-3 n e Pack Sq
*McIntyre Calvin, lab, h 109 Beaumont
McIntyre Cornelius B (Eugenia), h 103 Charlotte
*McIntyre Hattie, maid, rms 86 Eagle
McIntyre Jacob P (Angeline), carp, h Hazel Mill rd, W
McIntyre Jas A, justice of the peace 19 Paragon Bldg, h Chunn's Cove
*McIntyre Lula, cook, h 104 n Lexington av
McIntyre Major, fireman Ashev Pkg Co, h Emma N C
McIntyre Marguerite E Miss, h 174 Haywood
McIntyre Marion, lab, bds 135 n Main
McIntyre Patrick E (Mamie), propr The Cash Grocery, h 174 Haywood
McIntyre Roy B, woodwkr, h Hazel Mill rd, W Ashev
McKain Alice F Miss, wood carver, h 2 All Souls Crescent, Biltmore
McKain Annie, wid H F, h 4 All Soul's Crescent, Biltmore
McKain Claire M Miss, asst Dr F L Hunt, h 2 All Souls Crescent, Biltmore
McKain Clara A Miss, stengr, h 2 All Souls Crescent, Biltmore
McKain Lucy W, wid Winter, h 2 All Souls Crescent, Biltmore
☞McKain see also McLean
McKamey Geo E (Iva L), lino opr Ashev Citizen, h 330 w Haywood
☞McKay see also Mackay
McKay Edwin (Julia M), electrn 7 Technical Bldg, h 30 Vance

Candy Kitchen and Club Cafe
"A GOOD PLACE FOR REFRESHMENT"

The very best ingredients with sanitary conditions in our Candy Manufacturing Department make possible the dainty, crisp confections sold here.

Bon Bons and Chocolates made every day, put up in neat, attractive boxes. Phones 110 and 111. 19 and 21 Haywood St.

Brown's Undertaking Parlors

S. H. BROWN

Lady Assistant When Desired

Phone 193-2 Rings

50 Patton Avenue
Asheville, N. C.

Established 1894

B. J. JACKSON

Carefully Selected Fruits and Vegetables

Stall No. 11, City Market

BUSINESS PHONES:
86 and 101

RESIDENCE PHONE
1596

---

254 ASHEVILLE [1913] DIRECTORY

McKay Everett, clk, bds 34 Asheland av
McKAY'S PHARMACY (see MacKay)
McKee Andrew B (Lillian J), boarding 58 Haywood h same
*McKee Arthur (Gertrude), lab, h 11 Short
McKee Henrietta, wid M D, h Victoria rd
*McKee Homer, lab, h 113 Cherry
McKee Louis C, clk, h 58 Haywood
McKee S R Maj (Mary K), instr Bingham Schl, h Bingham Hghts
*McKee Thos (Tennie), lab, h 129 Southside av
McKee Wallace, lab, h 129 Southside av
McKenzie Clarence W (Callie F), foreman, h Arlington st, W Ashev
*McKenzie Henry, lab, rms 442 s French Broad av
McKenzie Henry G (Bonnie), propr City Fish Market, h 71 West
McKenzie Henry R, yd clk spl agt Sou Ry, h 101 Cumberland av
McKenzie Kate M Miss, stengr, h 101 Cumberland av
McKenzie Margaret C Miss, h 18 Flint
McKenzie Margaret E Miss, stengr, h 101 Cumberland av
McKenzie Minerva S Mrs, wid Donald, h 101 Cumberland
*McKenzie U C, cook, h 194 s Main
*McKesson Elsie, laund, h 11 Lincoln av
*McKesson Jeremiah (Jane), lab, h 189 Valley
McKibbon Geo, archt Grove Park Inn
McKinna Geo P (Lula), lab, h W Asheville
McKinney Lois Miss, tchr Normal & Collegiate Inst
McKinney Mack, driver, bds 52 Woodfin
McKinney Rufus, lab, bds 52 Woodfin
*McKinney Whit (Laura), lab, h 146 Livingston
McKinney Wm C (Alice), (Roberts & McKinney), and gro 21 Merrimon av, h 69 Penland
McKinnish Jno W (Sarah), h 12 Marjorie
McKinstry Elizabeth Miss, tchr Home Indus Schl rms same
*McKissick Ernest, porter Y M I Drug Store, h 81 Eagle
McLain Ella M Miss, student, h 128 Woodfin
McLain Jas P (Carrie), lumber, h 128 Woodfin
McLain Jessie G Miss, student, h 128 Wodfin
*McLain Orange (Etta), lab, h S Asheville
McLean A L & Co, sheet metal workers, 95-97 Patton av
McLean Augustus L (Olive), (A L McLean & Co), h 69 Furman av
McLean Beulah M Miss, h 75 Penland
McLean C Ross, tire repr W Caro Auto Co, h 75 Penland

Ye OLD BOOK SHOP
114 Patton Ave.   Phone 1674
BOOKS BOUGHT, SOLD OR EXCHANGED

ASHEVILLE [1913] DIRECTORY 255

*McLean Edwd (Mamie), brakeman Sou Ry, h (r) 29 Clingman av
McLean Frank L, buyer Hardwood Lbr Co, rms 31 Temple Court
McLean Fannie R Miss, h 92 Ora
McLean Ferry A, h 92 Ora
McLean Frank L, agt Hardwood Lumber Co, rms 31 Temple Ct
McLean Melvin G (Rebecca), fireman, h Riverside Drive nr Casket Factory
McLean Robt L (Johnnie), (McLean & Anders), h 75 Penland
McLean Wm H (Margaret N), engnr Sou Ry, h 92 Ora
McLean Wm P (Algeria), trav slsmn, h 38 n Ann
McLean Woodfin E (Florence), (Rhoads & McLean), h R F D 1
McLean & Anders (R L McLean, J B Anders), gros 100 Patton av
☞McLean see also McClain and McKain
McLoud Ella S, wid C M, h 34 Maxwell
McLoud Julia I Mrs, nurse Highland Hosp, rms same
McLurd Oscar L, stengr Carolina Amusement & Inv Co (Inc), h Maxwell st
McMahan Annie Mrs, spooler, h 25 Atkinson
McMahan Chas L, U S A, h 424 n Main
McMahan Jas R (Ellen), condr St Ry, h 32 Seney
McMahan Thos W (Leona), lmbr inspr, h 47 Gaston
McMahan Wm (Lou), drayman, h 424 n Main
McMenamin Patrick, nurse 71 Central av, rms same
*McMichael Henry (Sarah), baker, h 117 Grove
*McMickens Oscar E (Nettie), lab, h nr Hazel Mill rd, W Ashev
*McMickens Thos M (Jane), lab, h nr Hazel Mill rd, W Ashev
McMillan Owen F, h 270 Hillside
McMinn Carrie D, wid J T, tchr, rms 9 Grady
McMinn J Pierce (Maggie), clk T L Trantham, h S Biltmore
McMinn Robt L (Ida), painter Excelsior P & P Hse, h 14 Central av
McMinn Walter, carp, bds Hotel Warren
McMinn Wm J, druggist 313 w Haywood, h same
*McMullan Albert, h 113 Short Valley
McMurray Maggie E Miss, cook, h W Asheville
McNally Hugh, emp Grove Park Inn

Mrs. Wilder's SANITARY HOME LAUNDRY turns out first class work in Laundering and Dry Cleaning. No. 7 Montford Ave., Phone 1354

McNamara Thos J (Mary), wreck mstr Sou Ry, h 385 s French Broad av
McNeely Jane E, laund, h 57 Madison
McNeely Thos H (Ollie), flgmn Sou Ry, h 43 Bartlett
*McNeil Luetta, waitress, rms 39 Frederick
McNew Blanche B, wid Jno L, h 14 Blake
McPeeters Francis P (McPeeters & Mack), h 53 Victoria rd
McPeeters Thos C (Geneva), (McPeeters & Mack), h 53 Victoria rd
McPeeters & Mack (T C and F P McPeeters), gros 371 s Main
McPHERSON J C (Emma F), 35-37 e College—phone 133, h Burnsville Hill—phone 6602 (see bottom lines)
McQueen Hugh, driver, rms 12 n Pack Sq (3d fl)
McRae Jas P (Lillie), h 44 Watauga
McRary Elbert H (Hettie), plmbr, h Kenilworth Park
McRary J Walter, student, h Haywood rd, W Ashev
McRary M C, plmbr Union Plumbing Co, h Delaware av
McRary Walter S (Mary), foreman, h Haywood rd, W Ashev
McSherry Jas W (Mary), engnr Sou Ry, h 356 Depot
McVey B C, pres U S Furn Mnfg Co, h 5 Swan, Biltmore

M

Mac Donald Warren J (Louise), engnr, h 201 Merrimon av
Mac Ewen Jno W (Margaret S), bkkpr J R Rich Co, h 62 Clayton
MAC GREGOR JANET MISS, matron Faith Cottage Rescue Home, h same
Mace Chas E, spl del messgr, h 17 Morgan av
Mace Ernest L (Dora B), carrier P O, h 17 Morgan av
Mace Geo (Elizabeth), watchman, h Riverside Drive cor William
Mace Stella V Miss, h 17 Morgan av
*Macedonia Sanctified Church, 59 Max, Rev —— Bennett pastor
Machin Edgar, h W Asheville
Machin Jno (Sallie), pattern mkr, h Hazel Mill rd, W Ashev
Machin Stephen D, pressmn Hackney & Moale Co, rms 19 s Main
Mack Cleveland, lab, h nr Smiths Bridge, W Ashev
Mack Jacob A (Julia L), h nr Smiths Bridge, W Ashev
*Mack Leah, h 24 Richard
Mack Maude Miss, h W Asheville

MAC KAY DAN'L McN (Emma W), propr Mac Kay's Pharmacy, h Montford av cor Zillicoa
MAC KAY'S PHARMACY, 7 n w Pack Sq (next to Princess Theatre)—phone 1947, D McN Mac Kay propr
☞ Mac Kay see also McKay
*Mackey Geo R, lab, h Herren av, W Ashev
MACKEY JNO J, County Register of Deeds, office Court House—phone 907, h 153 Haywood
Mackey Lennie Miss, nurse Highland Hosp, rms same
*Mackey Maria, h Herren av, W Ashev
Mac Lauchlin A Muldrow Rev (Nettie P), pastor Ora St Presbyterian Church, h 83 Ora
Macon Lumber Co, 203-305 Oates Bldg
*Macon Martha, dom European Hotel, h 62 Ralph
*Madden Calvin D (Adah), lab, h 174 Beaumont
*Madden Jno, porter Wm W Young, h 174 Beaumont
*Madden Oliver, lab, h 174 Beaumont
*Maddox Newton (Josephine), driver, h 2 Greer's Row
*Madison Frank (Josie), bootblk, h 11 Hiawassee
Madison Gertrude Mrs, h 12 Elm
*Madison Jas A (Hattie), cook, h 62 Ridge
Madsen Christian (Augusta), carp, h 20 Spring
*Magee Anna, nurse 215 Clingman av, h same
*Magee Lois, nurse 215 Clingman av, h same
Magness Jake J, mngr Sou Ry Dining Room, rms Florence Hotel
MAGNOLIA COTTAGE, boarding 72 e College, Mrs K L Du Ren propr (see p 15)
Maguire Mary C Miss, housekpr The Avonmore, rms 107 Haywood
Maher Minnie E Miss, h 260 Haywood
Maher Wm P (Ina), frt agt Sou Ry, h 260 Haywood
Mahle G B Prof, tchr The Asheville Schl, rms same
Maines Rebecca D Mrs, h 55½ n Main
*Maie Geo W Rev (Mary), presiding elder Ashev Dist M E Church, h 265 Asheland av
Mallicote Lewis F (Lucy), (St Charles Barber Shop), h 149 Flint
MALONE ALBERT H (Irene), sec Albemarle Park Co, h The Manor
Malone Chas N (Joanna), atty at law and notary, 207 Oates Bldg, h 266 Hillside
Malone Chas W (Lela), magistrate, h 243 Hillside
*Mallory Aaron (Isabelle), lab, h S Asheville
*Mance Belle, dom, h 56 Clemmons

The Life Insurance Co. of Virginia
ORGANIZED 1871   RICHMOND, VA.

ISSUES ALL THE MOST APPROVED FORMS OF LIFE INSURANCE CONTRACTS from $500.00 to $25,000.00, with premiums payable quarterly, semi-annually and annually

J. V. Moon, Superintendent, Rooms 3-4-5 Maxwelton Bldg., Asheville, N. C.

D. TREXLER TIN SHOP

All Kinds of Roofing, Gutter and Conductor Work.

Phone 862

159 South Main St.

DR. C. H. MILLER

MECHANO-THERAPIST

14 N. Spruce St.
Phone 979
ASHEVILLE, N. C.

Hours by engagement

Drugless Healing of Disease

ASHEVILLE [1913] DIRECTORY

*Mance Edmund (Carrie), stone cutter, h 41 Fulton
*Mance Emma, cook, h 56 Clemmons
*Mance Solomon (Cora), lab, h 21 Latta
Maney Ella Miss, student, h 2 Church, S Biltmore
Maney Hugh, clk W D Maney, h Woolsey (R F D 1)
Maney Jefferson D (Rachel), farmer, h 2 Church S Biltmore
Maney Lorenzo D (Daisy), trav slsmn, h Woolsey (R D 1)
Maney Melvin M (Ava), h 116 Biltmore rd, S Biltmore
Maney W Harrey, mngr Biltmore Supply Co, h Biltmore rd, S Biltmore
Maney Wm D (Hattie), gro Woolsey (R F D 1), h same
Mangum Orrie M Miss, nurse 48 n Spruce
Manley Geo, iron wkr Ashev S & Fdy Co, rms 12 n Pack Sq
Manley Jno H (Emma), (Lutz Meat Co), h 41 Chestnut
Manley Patrick D, propr Haywood Street Market, h 41 Chestnut
Mann I Mitchell, dentist, 37 Patton av (2d fl) h 11½ Church
*Manning Elijah (Martha), driver, h (r) 350 w Haywood
*Manning Willis Rev (Sarah), h 23 Oliver
Mano Peter, waiter Central Cafe, rms Revell Bldg
MANOR (The), family hotel, Albemarle Park, A H Malone mngr (see p 17)
"Manzanita Cottage," Albemarle Park
Maple Leaf Dairy, Main st, W Ashev, T C Beacham propr
Marakas Paul, h 34 Atkin
Marandville Eva Miss, h 12 Connolly's Ridge
Marandville Wright (Susie), switchman, h 12 Connolly's Ridge
MARGO TERRACE, hotel, French Broad av s e cor Haywood P H Branch propr
"Marigold Cottage," Albemarle Park
Marion Pat'k F Rev, asst pastor St Lawrence's R C Church h 18 Flint
Marion Peter G Rev, pastor St Lawrence's R C Church, h 18 Flint
Marlow Briscoe M (Myrtle), (Marlow Bros), h 85 Central
Marlow Bros (W B and B M), meats City Market
*Marlow Curtis, lab, h Dewey nr Jordan
*Marlow Jos (Rachel), lab, h Dewey nr Jordan
*Marlow Lee, lab, h Dewey nr Jordan
*Marlow Minnie, cook, h Dewey nr Jordan
*Marlow Pender, lab, h Dewey nr Jordan
Marlow Roy, bkkpr Marlow Bros, h 26 Bearden av
Marlow Winslow B (Laura), (Marlow Bros), h 26 Bearden
Marmino Antonio (Mary), fruits 33 College, h 22 Philip

....Asheville Cleaning and Pressing Club....
Tailoring That Satisfies and Prices That Please

Steam and French Dry Cleaning of all delicate and fine wearing apparel for ladies and gentlemen. MESSENGER SERVICE IN THE CITY.

J. C. WILBAR, Prop.   4. N. Pack Square   **PHONE 389**

Marquardt Adolph E, meter reader Ashev P & L Co, h 3 Carroll av
Marquardt Jno A (Annie), tailor, h 3 Carroll av
Marquette Hotel, 102 Patton av, E W Israel propr
Marr Wm W Rev (Jeannette), pastor South Biltmore Bapt Church, h 44 Summit, S Biltmore
Marsh Adelbert H (Eda C), supt Amer Forest Co, h 45 Vance
Marsh Herbert N, student, h 45 Vance
Marsh Pearl A Miss, h 45 Vance
Marsh Ruby A Miss, tchr, h 45 Vance
Marshall Ercy C (Bertie), car inspr, h 8 Connolly's Ridge
MARSTELLER WYATT (Izella), mngr Marsteller & Co, h 142 s French Broad av
MARSTELLER & CO, real estate, 20 Haywood—phone 88 Wyatt Marsteller mngr
Martin Bess M Miss, tchr Home Indus Schl, rms same
*Martin Caleb (Mary), lab, h 56 Mountain
*Martin Carrie, laund, h 133 Roberts
Martin Claude (Vinnie), carp McDowell & Patton, bds 16 s Spruce
Martin Elizabeth Miss, h 36 Vivian
Martin Emma E, wid C M, h 106 Washington rd
*Martin Fredk P (Queenie), Eagle Street Pressing Club, h 78½ Mountain
Martin Harry A, student, h 19 n Liberty
*Martin Henry, lab, h 129 Poplar
*Martin Jas (Phoebe), waiter, h 129 Poplar
Martin Jas V (Florence C), mngr Met Life Ins Co, h 106 Washington rd
*Martin Janie, laund, h 12 Jordan
Martin Jno H (Effie), (Craig, Martin & Thomason), h 90 Liberty
*Martin Julia A, music tchr 74 Mountain, h same
MARTIN JULIUS C (Helen), (Martin, Rollins & Wright), and state senator, h 19 n Liberty
Martin K Richd (Nellie), (Frazier & Martin), h 26 Fulton
*Martin Lydia, laund, h 54 Sycamore
*Martin Mamie, tchr Catholic Hill Schl, h 71 Eagle
*Martin Nathaniel M (Anna P), genl sec Y M I, h 5 Haid
*Martin R J (Jennetta), barber W P Brooks, h 64 Hill
*Martin Roberta, cook, h 64 Hill
MARTIN, ROLLINS & WRIGHT (Julius C Martin, Thos S Rollins and Geo H Wright), attys at law, 308-314 Legal Bldg

Asheville Dray, Fuel & Construction Co.
6 1-2 South Main

COAL

Wood and Kindling
Stone and Sand
PHONE - 223

EVER READY FLASHLIGHTS
Piedmont Electric Company
ASHEVILLE, N. C.
64 PATTON AVENUE

Martin Saml (Bessie), fireman, bds 116 Bartlett
*Martin Thos (Nannie), hostler, h 122 Pine
Martin Wiley (Annie), gardener, h Jarrett av, W Ashev
Martindale Arthur H, helper, h 64 Roberts
Martindale Wm H (Emma), beamer, h 64 Roberts
Martorell Celestine L Miss, h 74½ Haywood
Martorell Gertrude H, h 74½ Haywood
Marvil Annie Miss, emp Dr T C Smith
Mascari Chas (Marie), fruits 58 Patton av, h same
Mason Burton C (Sarah S), whol lumber 9 Paragon Bldg, h 264 Montford av
Mason Harriet E, wid W D, dressmkr 357 s Main, h same
Mason Horace (Minnie), lumber, h 15 Chestnut
Mason Jas L, student, h 178 Montford av
Mason Jos Irving (G L), h 178 Montford av
Mason Katherine H Miss, h 178 Montford av
Mason Wm T (Elizabeth C), lumber, h 178 Montford av
Masonic Hall, Drhumor Bldg (3d fl)
*Masonic Temple, 44 Market
Massagee Chas A, carp A M Goodlake, h 25 Clyde
Massagee Sue S, wid J F, h 25 Clyde
Massagee Wm N, electrn, h 25 Clyde
Masters Ezra H (Eva,) mchst, h W Asheville
Masters Fred P (Burr), carrier R F D, h Woolsey (R D 1)
Mateny Annie B Miss, h 57 Cherry
Mateny Argus G, tchr, h 57 Cherry
Mateny Wm W (Sarah D), private school 57 Cherry, h same
Mathis Erskine, lab, bds 135 n Main
Mathis Governor M, clk frt office Sou Ry, h 17 Montford av
Mathis Maggie D, wid G M, h 17 Montford av
Matteson Geo W (Nora B), slsmn Singer Sewing Mch Co, h 32 Clingman av
Matthews Augustus (Ella), dentist 25-27 McAfee Bldg, h 60 Oak
Matthews Brayton, clk, h 60 Oak
*Matthews Geo (Clara), lab, h (r) 29 Hildebrand
Matthews Jack, elctrn, bds 34 Asheland av
*Matthews Lewis (Sallie), foreman, h 10 w Woodfin
*Matthews Mack (Mary), lab, h 42 Madison
Matthews Robt, electrn, bds 34 Asheland av
*Mattison Jane, cook, h 10 Bay
Mauck Geo W (Mollie), lab, h 125 Bartlett
Maupin Jas M (Lillie W), real estate, h 129 Charlotte
Maupin Jas M Jr, student, h 129 Charlotte

J. C. McPHERSON
SLATE AND TIN ROOFING
Galvanized Iron Work   Hot Air Furnaces
35-37 EAST COLLEGE STREET

PLUMBING
STEAM AND HOT WATER
HEATING
PHONE 133

Maupin Lillie V Miss, stengr, h 129 Charlotte
Maxwell Bessie A Miss, h 34 Buxton
*Maxwell Bettie, laund, h (r) 39 Clingman
*Maxwell Booker (Kate), cook, h (r) 57 Eagle
Maxwell Carrie E Miss, h 34 Buxton
Maxwell Chas (Penelope), h 21 East
Maxwell Clarence M (Wilsie J), bkkpr Lutz Meat Co, h 45 Seney
*Maxwell Ella, 62 Orange
*Maxwell Ella, cook, h 468 s French Broad av
Maxwell Geo, clk Ashev Candy Kitchen, rms 13 s Main
Maxwell Gertrude L Miss, h 34 Buxton
Maxwell Grace M Miss, tchr Home Industrial Schl, rms same
*Maxwell Hattie, h 39 Pearl
Maxwell J M, engraver A M Field Co, h 59 Haywood
Maxwell L Ottis (Emma), gro 50 East, h same
*Maxwell Mary, cook, h 97 Market
Maxwell Mattie C Miss, h 34 Buxton
*Maxwell Ora, laund, h 99 Market
Maxwell Robt H, mill wkr, h 34 Buxton
Maxwell Saml A (Sarah E), mill wkr, h 34 Buxton
Maxwelton Building, offices, 40-42 Patton av
*May Annie, dom, h 147 Valley
May Arthur, driver Ashev Packing Co, bds W Haywood st
May Donald R, lab, h 15 Girdwood
May Henry P (Sallie S), overseer, h 15 Girdwood
May Jno B, lab, h 15 Girdwood
May Rita S Miss, h 15 Girdwood
Mayes Marcus D (Roxie), lab, h nr Smiths Bridge, W
*Mayfield Hettie, h 6 Cole
*Mayfield Thos (Esther), lab, h 27 Max
MAYOR'S OFFICE, City Hall, J E Rankin mayor
*Mays Whitfield, lab, h 17 Miller
Meacham Edwd, mchst Asheville Auto Co, rms 17 s Lexington av
Meacham W Banks (Genevieve), (Meacham & Rockwell), h Ottari rd, Grace
Meacham Washington D (Connie), dispr Sou Ry, h 157 Park av
Meacham & Rockwell Drs (W Banks Meacham, Mrs L A Rockwell), osteopaths, 501-507 Legal Bldg
Meade Anne L Miss, h 311 Montford av
Meadows Lucy E, wid Chas, propr The Chatham, h 55 College

Club Cafe and Candy Kitchen
"A GOOD PLACE FOR REFRESHMENT"

The standards we work to in our Restaurant Department are: Cooking, perfect; Service, prompt and cheerful; Prices, moderate; Menu, everything in season. Parties and Banquets, Teas and Dinners. 19 and 21 Haywood St. Phones 110 and 111.

Brown's Undertaking Parlors

S. H. BROWN

50 Patton Avenue
ASHEVILLE, N. C.

Lady Assistant When Desired

Phone 193-2 Rings

THE MOORE Plumbing Company

16 N. Pack Square

PHONE 1025

Sanitary Plumbing, General Tin and Metal Work, Hot Air Furnaces

---

262 ASHEVILLE [1913] DIRECTORY

Meadows M R, blksmith Penland Bros, h Arlington st, W Asheville
Meadows Marshall E (Mamie D), barber St Charles Barber Shop, h 107 Church
Meadows Melvin, del clk The Cash Grocery, h W Asheville
Meadows Mitchell R (Delia V,) blksmith, h Arlington st, W Asheville
Meadows Otis F (Frances), tinner A L McLean & Co, h 140 Grove
Meadows Richmond A, helper, h 305 College
Meadows Solon A (Grace), carp, h 305 College
Meadows Ulysses S (Bettie), carp, h Haywood rd, W Ashev
Meadows Wm M, warehouseman Mustin-Robertson Co, h W Asheville
Meares F Exum Miss, student, h 39 Atkin
Meares Gaston (Helen), trav slsmn, h 39 Atkin
Meares Jos E (A Antoinette), trav slsmn, h 172 Cumberland av
Meares Laura E Miss, h 39 Atkin
Mears Frank A (Amy), mngr O K Auto Supply & Transit Co, rms 63½ s Main
Mears Geo A (Nancy), genl mdse 525 w Haywood, h 137 s Main
Mears Jay, h 137 s Main
Mears Patrick H Rev (Memphis), pastor Christian Church, h 241 Haywood
Mears S Parley (Ella M), mngr G A Mears, h 61 s French Broad av
Mears Wm C (Nina), clk G A Mears, h 100 Cherry
Mebane Benj F, mchst, bds 149 Park av
Medd Ernest, mch opr Princess Theatre
Medd Sarah J, wid Wm H, h 11 Pearl
Medd Thos (Mary), h 270 Patton av
Medical Building (offices), 16-18 Battery Park pl
Medical Society of Buncombe County, meets in City Hall
Meece Geo W, farmer, h Asheville av, W Asheville
Meeham Wm D (Marion), h "Edgemont"
Meehan Mary Miss, housekpr 28 Border
Meek Clarence A (Bertha), gro 266 n Main, h same
*Meekins Jas, lab, h 81 Wallach
Mehaffey C J, flgmn, bds 434 Depot
Mell Jas L, priv sec supt Sou Ry, h 117 s French Broad av
Melton Arthur L, clk, h 9 Pearson Drive
Melton Bryant, h 70 Blanton
Melton Elijah B (Mabel), condr St Ry, h 32 Spring

The Battery Park Bank

Capital - - $100,000.00
Surplus and Profits, $110,000.00

ASHEVILLE, N. C. City, County and State Depositary

J. A. TILLMAN — Jeweler — 17 N. Main St.

I carry a nice line of Watches, Clocks and Jewelry, and make a specialty of repair work. Satisfaction guaranteed

---

Melton Geo E (Lelia), plaster, h Grace
Melton Horace, waiter Windsor Cafe
Melton Jas C (Minnie), clk in charge Glen Rock Sta P O, h 23 Fagg
Melton Julius C (Zora), lab, h 39 East
Melton Louise Miss, h 9 Pearson Drive
Melton Ruth A, wid Jno W, h 403 Southside av
Mendel Lena Miss, propr The Caroleen, h same
Mercer Anne Mrs, h 40 Cherry
Merchant Luther L (Almeta H), contr 22 Livingston, h same
*Meredith Cornelia, dom, h 61 Madison av
*Meredith Oscar, lab, h Gram Creek
MERIWETHER FRANK T DR, propr The Meriwether Hospital and physician and surgeon, 24 Grove—phone 233, h 14 Grove—phone 1330 (see page 6)
MERIWETHER HOSPITAL (THE), 24 Grove—phone 233, Dr F T Meriwether propr, Miss N F Pitts supt (see page 6)
Meriwether Wm, h 14 Grove
Merrell Annie Laurie Miss, stengr J F Glenn, h 32 Furman
Merrell Benj F, keeper Home of the Aged and Infirm, 7 miles from city on Leicester rd, h same
Merrell G, clk W E Merrell, rms 311 w Haywood
Merrell Gertrude E Miss, clk, h 32 Furman av
Merrell Gladys W Miss, student, h 32 Furman av
Merrell Theodosia E, wid David L, h 32 Furman av
Merrell Wm E (Etta), genl mdse 311 w Haywood, h same
MERRICK DUFF (Charlotte W) (Merrick & Barnard), h 312 Montford av—phone 189
Merrick Wilbar K Mrs, house supt Ashev Schl for Girls, Woodfin cor Main
MERRICK & BARNARD (Duff Merrick and A S Barnard) attys at law, 315-319 Legal Bldg—phone 85
Merrill E Clifton (Alice W), foreman J M Hearn & Co, h 47 Clingman av
MERRIMON, ADAMS & ADAMS (J G Merrimon, J C Adams and J G Adams), attys at law, 15 Church—phone 987
Merrimon Emory H (R Augusta), atty, h 117 Chestnut
Merrimon Houston, bkkpr Battery Park Bank, h 288 s French Broad av
MERRIMON JAS G (Blanche S) (Merrimon, Adams & Adams) and v-pres Amer Natl Bank, h Haywood rd, W Asheville—phone 1361

INSURANCE

INSURE YOUR SALARY WITH US
NEVER CARRY YOUR OWN RISK
SAFETY IS THE BEST POLICY
UNLESS YOU ARE A CAPITALIST
REST EASY IF YOU HAVE
AN ACCIDENT WE WILL
NOT KEEP YOU WAITING TO
COLLECT YOUR CLAIM
EVERY CLAIM PROMPTLY PAID

Imperial Mutual Life & Health Insurance Co.

Home Office:
ASHEVILLE, N. C.
Phone 495

HOTEL OXFORD — Asheville, N. C.

Redecorated and Refitted throughout. Recently enlarged to 60 rooms. Centrally located. Depot cars stop at entrance. Long distance telephone office upstairs. American and European plan. Rates 50c, 75c and $1 per day; special rates by week or month. C. H. Branson & Sons, Proprietors. Phone 1887. 50-54 South Main St.

Williams-Brownell Planing Mill Company — **Hardwoods**

Lumber---Rough and Dressed Flooring a Specialty Moulding, Interior Finish, Etc.
Office, Plant and Yards on Southern Railway, Near Biltmore Station
WHITE PINE   Phone 729   YELLOW PINE

MERRIMON JAS H JUDGE, atty at law, 15 Church, h 288 s French Broad av
Merrimon Louise A Miss, phys 73 Haywood, h 117 Chestnut
Merrimon Mary A Miss,, h 112 Merrimon av
Merrimon Nan Miss, h 288 s French Broad av
Merritt Willie B, propr The Union Store, bds 418 Southside av
Messer Solomon M (Bertha), condr, h 286 Southside av
Messer Wm R (Lula), asst hotel steward, h 174 Asheland av
Messler Chas H, student, h 162 Charlotte
MESSLER FRED'K M (Mary E), real estate and insurance, 26 Amer Natl Bank Bldg—phone 682, h 162 Charlotte—phone 1019 (see back cover)
Metcalf Jno P (May), lab, h 493 w Haywood
*Metcalf Junita, laundr, h (r) 6 Clingman av
*Metcalf Peter, lab, h nr Hazel Mill rd, W Asheville
Methodist Protestant Church, Haywood nr Montford av, Rev W D Fogleman pastor
Metropolitan Life Ins Co, 223 Legal Bldg, J V Martin supt
Metting Margaret Miss, h Edgemont
Metz Jesse (Ella), plmbr, h 31 Ocala
Metz Jos (Rhoda), h Chunn's Cove
Metz Martha, wid T M, h Chunn's Cove
*Metz Olive, dom, h 31 Ocala
Meyer Catherine, wid B M, h 25 e Spears av
Meyer Wm, tchr High Schl
Meyers Morris (Belle), asst mngr Palais Royal, h Kenilworth
☞ Meyers see also Myers
MICHAEL FRANK A (Lena F), cashr Sou Exp Co, h 8 Baird
*Michael Jno H (Lelia), tchr Hill St Schl, h 22 Ridge
Michael Willard E (Alda), clk, h 29 Ora
Michaels Jas (P Elizabeth), carp, h W Ashev (R F D 3)
Michalov Gertrude R Miss, student, h 199 Asheland av
Michalov Isaac (Sarah), genl mdse, 203 Asheland av and 136-137 Valley, h 199 Asheland av
Michalov Louis (Annie), trav slsmn, h 68 Woodfin
Michalov Philip, student, h 199 Asheland av
Michalov Saml, clk The Gem Clothing Store, h 68 Woodfin
Michalov Solomon H (Jennie), propr I X L Dept Store, h 45 Montford av
Michalove Abraham (Jennie), gro 15 Furman av, h 67 same
Middleton Kinson, condr, bds 80 Penland

Asheville Electrical Company
W. Mansfield Booze, Manager
74 CENTRAL AVE.
HEADQUARTERS
Phone 377

Asheville Dry Cleaning Co.
Telephones 835-836, All Dep't
MAIN, N. E. COR. COLLEGE

THE CLEANERS
Our Department for Oriental Rugs and Carpet Cleaning is prepared to serve you in all its branches.

E. S. Paine   O. E. Hansen

Maple Flooring and Poplar Siding

English Lumber Co.
PHONE . . 321

Middleton Maude C Mrs, tchr, h 34 Cherry
Middleton Terrell F (Bonnie), mtrmn, h 31 Phifer
MILDRED E SHERWOOD HOME (The), (private sanitarium), 179 s French Broad av, Miss Mildred E Sherwood propr—phone 543 (see p 4)
"Milfoil Cottage," Albemarle Park
Milholland Lester A (Cornelia B), clk, h 1 Biltmore rd, Biltmore
Millard Charlton C (Grace), sec-treas The Millard Livery Co, Inc, h Edgemont Park
MILLARD D RALPH, L L B, atty at law, 16-17 New Sondley Bldg—phone 1302, h Battery Park Cottage—phone 1274
Millard Herbert R, pres The Millard Livery Co, h Battery Park Cottage
Millard Josephine, wid D T, h Battery Park Cottage
Millard Livery Co (Inc), (The), 33-35 n Main; H R Millard pres, C C Millard sec-treas
Millender Chas W, student, h 240 Pearson Drive
Millender Margaret Miss, h 240 Pearson Drive
MILLENDER MARION C (Mary W), physician 9-11 Drhumor Bldg, office hours 3-5 p m—phone 506, h 240 Pearson Drive, opp Watauga—phone 27
Miller Adele Miss, h 203 Merrimon av
*Miller Albert (Jessie), lab, h 27 Scott
*Miller Albert, coachman, h 28 Short McDowell
Miller Allen G (Georgia), emp Ashev Tel & Tel Co, h 26 Bennett
*Miller Alonzo (Mary), lab, h (r) 128 Cherry
Miller Annie Miss, h 203 Merrimon av
Miller Annie M Miss, dressmkr Miss E O'Rear, h W Asheville
*Miller Arthur, lab, h 45 Wallach
Miller C (Hester), lab, h 47 Spring
Miller C Frank (Bertha), appr, h W Asheville
Miller C Henry (Fannie), watchman, h West Chapel rd, Biltmore
Miller C P (Lucy), condr St Ry, h 59 Blanton
Miller Cagus H (Lula), mtrmn, h 51 Blanton
Miller Carrie V Miss, h 270 College
Miller Catherine L, wid Jacob, h 106 Biltmore rd, S Biltmore
Miller Chas, flgmn, bds 430 Depot
Miller Chas H (Rosa), clk, h 54 Chunn
Miller Chas M, steward Highland Hosp, rms same
Miller Clarence H, lab, h Haywood rd, W Ashev

Biggest Busiest Best
Asheville Steam Laundry
Phones: 1936 and 1937
43 to 47 W. College Street

CHARLES H. HONESS
OPTOMETRIST AND OPTICIAN
Exclusive maker of ATLAS SHUR-ON EYE GLASSES
THE Home of Ce-Rite Toric Lenses
We make a specialty of correcting optical defects with properly fitted glasses.
54 Patton Avenue
Opposite Postoffice

IF in the market for a Gas Engine let us make you prices.
its heavy castings, such as columns or building plates, see us.
its a skilled mechanic for boiler work, see us.
you want machine work of any kind phone 590.
CAROLINA MACHINERY CO.

FOUNDERS MACHINISTS and Jobbers of Mill Supplies

Life Insurance Company of Virginia
ORGANIZED 1871
Home Office - Richmond, Va.

Has won the hearty approval and active support of the people by its promptness and fair dealing during the FORTY-TWO YEARS of its operation

J. V. Moon, Superintendent, Rooms 3-4-5 Maxwelton Bldg., Asheville, N. C.

T. P. JOHNSON & CO.

SHEET METAL WORKERS

All Kinds of Roofing Guttering and Conductor Work Metal Ceilings, Skylights and Galvanized Iron Cornices

OFFICE and SHOP:
69-71 S. MAIN

Phone 325

DR. C. H. MILLER

Mechano-Therapist

14 N. Spruce Street
ASHEVILLE, N. C.

PHONE 979

Hours by Engagement

DRUGLESS HEALING OF DISEASE

Miller Clarissa E, wid Geo W, h Haywood rd, W Ashev
MILLER CLAUDIUS H DR (Lula R), physician 14 n Spruce—phone 979, h 24 same—phone 671 (see side cards and p 21)
Miller Clementine Miss, h 203 Merrimon av
*Miller Cleveland (Sarah), janitor, h 85 Choctaw
*Miller Cora, laund, h 131 Roberts
Miller Corlelia A Miss, mlnr M Webb Co, h 36 Vance
Miller Cozy Miss, tchr Allen Indus Home, h 241 College
Miller David U (Mary E), carp, h 103 Clingman av
Miller Doyce Z (Anna), gas mkr, h 15 Phifer
Miller E Hilliard, U S dep collr, h 24 n Spruce
*Miller Edna, laund, h 108 Eagle
*Miller Elias G, lab, h 18 Sassafras
MILLER ERNEST H (Carrie E), pres and genl mngr Piedmont Directory Co and sec-treas Knoxville Directory Co, office 66 and L Amer Natl Bank Bldg, h 90 Starnes av
Miller Eva M Miss, elecutionist, h 36 Vance
Miller Florence Miss, h 171 Montford av
Miller Francis M, gro 244 College, h 270 same
Miller Frank B (Emma V), painter 56 Hiawassee, h same
MILLER FRANK W, sec Greater Western N C Assn, h Waynesville N C
Miller Geo, brkmn, bds 430 Depot
Miller Grover, mchst, bds Riverside Drive nr Casket Co
Miller Hackney D (Lola), foreman Ashev Pkg Co, h nr Murphy Junc, W Ashev
Miller Harlie E (Della), carp, h 104 Clingman av
MILLER HARMON A (Florence G), treas and genl mngr Carolina Coal & Ice Co (Inc), pres Amer Furn Mnfg Co, h 171 Montford av—phone 430
Miller Hattie Miss, bds The Henrietta
Miller Herman, student, h 92 Church
Miller Hugh (Julie), slsmn McConnell Bros, h W Asheville
Miller Ike, clk The Gem Clothing Store, h 35 s Liberty
Miller Ina C, wid Henry L, h 8 Aston pl
Miller J Drayton (Maggie), clk frt office Sou Ry, h 91 Asheland av
Miller J Hardy (Lennie), painter, h 54 Summit, S Biltmore
Miller Jas A (Laura), carp, h 49 w Walnut
Miller Jas M (Sarah A), carp, h 49 Hall
Miller Jas R, student, h 24 n Spruce
Miller Jos P (Margaret), tel opr, h 65 Woodfin
Miller Kate Miss, h 30 Jefferson Drive

ASHEVILLE CLEANING and PRESSING CLUB

TAILORING THAT SATISFIES and PRICES THAT PLEASE

Hats cleaned, banded and bound. Silk hats ironed. Buttons made to order in all sizes. Plain or with rims. PHONE 389

DYEING IN ALL SHADES Cleaned. Messenger Service.

Kid Gloves, Slippers and Plumes. Fancy Jabots and Ties, French Dry Cleaned. Ladies' and Gentlemen's suits Steam

J. C. Wilbar, Prop. 4 NORTH PACK SQ.

Miller Lavada Mrs, cook A F Rees, Kenilworth
Miller Lawrence (Anna), carp, h Haywood rd, W Ashev
Miller Lawrence G (Lucy), foreman, h Haywood rd, W Ashev
*Miller Lawson M (Sarah), gro and shoemkr 29 Circle, h 81 Pine
*Miller Leila, dom, h 52 Davidson
Miller Lela E Miss, tchr, h W Ashev (R F D 3)
Miller Lila H Miss, smstrs, h Haywood rd, W Ashev
*Miller Lula, cook, 173 Chestnut
Miller Lula R Mrs, boarding, 24 n Spruce, h same
Miller Marcell L (Harriet), helper Ashev Pkg Co, h Murphy Junc, W Ashev
Miller Margaret Miss, stengr Zebulon Weaver
Miller Marion L (Mollie), driver, h W Asheville
*Miller Mary, domestic 56 Chestnut
Miller Mary E, wid Wm R, h Haywood rd, W Ashev
Miller Mary Ella, wid Chas A, h 36 Vance
Miller Mattie S Mrs, h 203 Merrimon av
Miller Minnie, wid Jno H, boarding 92 Church, h same
Miller Minnie Ida Miss, dressmkr, h Haywood rd, W Ashev
Miller Myrtle Miss, h 103 Clingman av
Miller Norma H Miss, clk Miss E J K Moore, h 56 Hiawassee
Miller Oscar O (Frieda), phys 5 Medical Bldg, h 104½ Haywood
Miller Otis A (Ellen P), artist, h 26 Bennett
Miller P Augustus (Ella M), tinner, h 145 Poplar
Miller Paul H, h 8 Aston pl
Miller Raymond U, helper Ashev Pkg Co, h Murphy Junc, W Ashev
Miller Rena Mrs, h 38 Short Roberts
*Miller Rena, dom, h 9 Haid
Miller Rex, clk Ashev Citizen, h 63 Cumberland av
*Miller Robt H (Daisy), tchr, h 151 College
MILLER ROBT M (Nellie), (Brown-Northup & Co), h Swannanoa av, W Ashev
*Miller Rosa L, dom, h 150 Church
Miller Roy P, student, h W Ashev (R F D 3)
Miller S Frank (Lillian), watchman, h 39 Rector
*Miller Schofield (Corrie), driver, h S Asheville
*Miller Spencer (Minnie), lab, h 16 McDowell
Miller Sylvester (Theodosia), supt Childrens Home, h Grace
Miller T Carlisle (Janie), ticket clk Sou Ry, h 136 Grove

WEAVERVILLE LINE NINE MILES BY TROLLEY FROM PACK SQUARE TO WEAVERVILLE

ASHEVILLE AND EAST TENNESSEE RAILROAD CO.

7 NORTH MAIN STREET — ASHEVILLE N. C.

ELECTRIC FIXTURES
Piedmont Electric Co.
64 PATTON AVE.
ASHEVILLE, N.C.

Miller Texas, wid Wm, smstrs, h 44 Clingman av
*Miller Thos (Hattie), driver, h 23 Gray
Miller Thos H (Martha E), glazier W H Westall & Co, h W Asheville
Miller Thos Q (I Saritta), clk Wachovia Bank & Trust Co, h 285 s Main
Miller Tindle, pressman Hackney & Moale Co, h W Asheville
MILLER ULYSSES S (Mollie E), v-pres Brown-Miller Shoe Co, h 63 Cumberland av
Miller Virginia Miss, h 171 Montford av
Miller W Mabelle V Miss, supervisor penmanship Ashev Public Schls, h 26 Bennett
Miller Waco, del boy Whitlock Clo Co, h 63 Cumberland av
Miller Walter, helper Western Carolina Auto Co, bds 56 Penland
Miller Wm (Nora), h Biltmore
Miller Wm D (Mary E), carp, h Haywood rd, W Ashev
*Miller Wm L (May), brick lyr, h Haywood rd, W Ashev
Millikan J M, clk U S Courts, h Greensboro N C
*Mills Andrew, lab, h S Asheville
*Mills B F, agt N C Mutual & Prov Assn, h Tryon N C
*Mills Birdo (Ora), brkmn, h 99 Black
Mills Columbus E (Frances), clk M V Moore & Co, h 106 Asheland av
Mills Columbus M (Celeste), real est, h 29 Cumberland av
*Mills Converse (Hattie), brkmn, h 25 Lyman
Mills E Maude Miss, manicurist, h 29 Cumberland av
*Mills Ellen, laund, h 60 Clemmons
Mills Harvey C, bkkpr J M Hearn & Co, rms 182 Patton av
Mills J Oscar, supt constr Grove Park Inn, h Sunset Drive
Mills Jesse R (Theodosia), trav buyer S Sternberg & Co, h W Asheville
Mills Jno C, trustee The Estate of Frank Coxe, Rutherfordton N C
*Mills Major, cook, h 194 s Main
*Mills Mira, dom 199 College
Mills Moses R, clk J M Ledford, h 511 w Haywood
Mills N Boylston (Pettis O), soda dispenser Allison's Drug Store, h 29 Cumberland av
Mills O Colatt, real est, h 29 Cumberland av
Mills Oakley C, electrn J M Hearn & Co, bds 39 Clingman
Mills R Jeffrey, condr Sou Ry, bds Glen Rock Hotel
*Mills Richard, lab, h 66 Clemmons
*Mills Richard (Estelle), plstr, h 346 n Main

CONTRACTOR and BUILDER
STEEL RANGES
J. C. McPHERSON
35-37 E COLLEGE ST.
PHONE 133
PLUMBING STEAM AND HOT WATER HEATING

Mills Roy C (Salena), beamer, h 65 Park Sq
*Mills Sallie, dom, h 17 Wallach
Mills Sarah A, wid Wm B, h nr Arlington st, W Ashev
*Mills Tony (Ellen), cook, h 177 Black
Mills Walter F (Maude A), miller, h 353 w Haywood
Mills Wm A (Rebecca), beamer, h Pennsylvania av, W Ashev
Mills Wm M (Elizabeth), boarding 511 w Haywood, h same
Milton Alice E, wid Theo, h 54 Asheland av
Milton Ernestine, student, h Grace
Milton Eugenia E Miss, h 54 Asheland av
Milton Irvine T, opr W U Tel Co, h 54 Asheland av
Milton Jas, student, h Grace
*Mims Danl (Ida), lab, h 15 Haid
Mims Leona A, wid O L, h 33 Orange
Mims Mabel, laundress, h 12 Aston pl
Mims Wm R (Ida), carp, h 14 Seney
*Mims Zachariah, lab, h 12 Aston pl
*Mince Nathaniel (Gertrude), porter, h (r) 5 Atkin
MINICK ALFRED A (Sarah), genl supt Hans Rees Sons (Inc), h 67 s French Broad av
Minick Larue Miss, student, h 67 s French Broad av
Minick Lillian Miss, student, h 67 s French Broad av
Minor Chas L (Mary V), phys Ashev Club Bldg, h 61 n French Broad av
Minor Jno, student, h 61 n French Broad av
Minor Lucy L Miss, h 61 n French Broad av
*Minson Henry (Vira), porter, h 124 Church
*Mintz Nathan, porter C A Walker
Minus Josiah P, bkkpr S Sternberg & Co, bds Florence Hotel
Minus M Stanley, clk Hotel Florence, rms same
MISENHEIMER DAVID W (Susie T), propr Cherokee Inn, h same (see p 19)
Misenheimer Geo W (Lulu), watchmn, h 18 Ora
Misenheimer Geo W (Susan), bds Cherokee Inn
Misenheimer Grover C, fireman, bds Cherokee Inn
Misenheimer Jay E (Kate), switchman, h Haywood rd, W Ashev
Misenheimer Ketner J (Dora), clk Cherokee Inn, h same
Misenheimer Locke, condr, bds Highland Hotel
Misenheimer Luther C, city slsmn Natl Biscuit Co, bds Cherokee Inn
Misenheimer Marshall S (Beulah), car repr, h 329 Southside
Miskelly Clara A Mrs, h 62 n Spruce

Club Cafe and Candy Kitchen
"A GOOD PLACE FOR REFRESHMENT"

Our Ice Cream manufacturing plant is absolutely clean and sanitary.
Prompt family delivery. Phones 110 and 111.
Catering for large parties and receptions. Special Creams.

ASHEVILLE [1913] DIRECTORY

Brown's Undertaking Parlors
S. H. BROWN

Lady Assistant When Desired

Phone 193-2 Rings

50 Patton Avenue
Asheville, N. C.

Established 1894
B. J. JACKSON
Carefully Selected Fruits and Vegetables

Stall No. 11, City Market

BUSINESS PHONES: 86 and 101

RESIDENCE PHONE 1596

Miskelly Elsie L Miss, clk Bon Marche, h 62 n Spruce
Miskelly Jno H (Clara A), civ engnr, h 62 n Spruce
Mission Hospital, Charlotte cor Woodfin
Mission of the Good Samaritan, Rev J S Williams in charge
Mitchell Allen E (Geneva), oiler Power Plant Ashev P & L Co, h W Asheville
Mitchell Bertha M Miss, student, h 106 Seney
Mitchell C C Mrs, boarding 37 Church, h same
Mitchell C A (Asheville School), h Haywood rd (5 miles w)
Mitchell David F (Annie), mill wright, h W Ashev (R F D 3)
*Mitchell David J (Matilda), lab, h 84 Baird
Mitchell Edwd W (Ida), painter, h 89 Grove
Mitchell Emory M (Cora E), dep sheriff, h 16 Marjorie
Mitchell Fredk E (Rachel), (Hodges, Mitchell & Reynolds), h 389 Montford av
Mitchell Fredk W, clk frt office Sou Ry, h W Ashev (R F D 3)
MITCHELL GEO E (Essie), pres and genl mngr Asheville Sign Co, h 110 East
*Mitchell Hagar, cook 265 Pearson Drive
Mitchell Hassie M Miss, h 62 Josephine
*Mitchell Hester, h 116 Eagle
Mitchell Jas A, h 389 Montford av
Mitchell Jimmie B Miss, bookbndr H & M Co, h W Asheville
Mitchell Jno W (Lula B), driver Swann Ldy, h 106 Seney
Mitchell Lelia E Miss, stengr Brown Hdw Co, h 115 Haywood
*Mitchell Mattie, dom, h 151 College
Mitchell Robt R, binder Hackney & Moale Co, h W Asheville (R F D 3)
MITCHELL STANLEY, city reporter Ashev Citizen, rms 15 s French Broad av
Mitchell Thos J (Ada A), engnr Power Plant Ashev P & L Co, h W Asheville
Mitchell Thos J, supt City Market, rms Library Bldg
Mitchell Thos L (Emma), carp, h 62 Josephine
Mitchell Willie E Miss, emp Hackney & Moale Co, h W Asheville
Mizales Mike N, eating hse Eagle nr Main, h 36 s Main
MOALE PHILIP R (Moale & Chiles), pres Hackney & Moale Co and v-pres Piedmont Directory Co and Birmingham Realty Co, h 28 Washington rd

---

Furniture and China Carefully Prepared for Shipment

Mahogany Furniture Hand Made & Carefully Reproduced
E. E. GALER
114 PATTON AVE.
Upholstering and Refinishing
PHONE - 1674

MOALE & CHILES (Philip R Moale, J Moore Chiles), real estate, insurance, loans and investments, timber and mineral lands, and genl agts U S Fidelity & Guaranty Co of Balto Md, office 27 Patton av (2d fl)—phone 661 (see p 8 and bottom lines)
Mobley Annie S Miss, tchr, h 24 Soco
Mobley Kate M, wid Geo, h 24 Soco
Moffat F Nora Mrs, h 131 Blanton
Moffitt Jos W (Theodosia), lab, h W Asheville
Mohler Margie Miss, musician, bds Cherokee Inn
Monday Benj U (Nellie), carp, h 76 Ralph
Monday Chas U (Nellie), barber 382 Depot and carrier R F D 3, h W Asheville
Monk Fred H (Emma), contr, h 28 Ralph
Monroe Geo A (Annie), car repr, h 150 Park av
Montague Loan Co, 12 n Pack Sq (2d fl), W P Brown atty
MONTAGUE MNFG CO, building material and planing mill, Richmond Va (see bet pages 188 and 189)
Monteath Arch D (Charlotte S), atty at law, 4-5 Temple Ct, h 33 Adams
Monteath Charlotte S, bkkpr C Sawyer, h 33 Adams
Monteath Jno H, clk, h 29 Blanton
Monteath Robt (Mary), chauffeur, h 285 College
Monteath Susan, wid Wm, h 29 Blanton
Monteeth Elisha (Ella J), fireman, h 47 n Main
Monteeth Ella J Mrs, boarding 47 n Main, h same
Monteeth Lawson, hackman, bds 47 n Main
Montford Avenue School, 80 Montford av, C T Carr prin
Montford Cottage, boarding 103 Montford av, Mrs M T Bertolett propr
Montford Dairy, Richmond Hill
Montgomery Geo W (Amanda), carp, h Woolsey (R F D 1)
Montgomery Richard, fireman, h 409 w Haywood
*Montgomery Saml B, waiter, rms 74 Eagle
MONTGOMERY STONEWALL R (Florence), h "Spurwood," Vernon Hill
Montgomery W Scott (Linna), engnr Sou Ry, h 409 w Haywood
Moodie Jno E (Effie M), mngr Langren Bowling & Pool Room, h 88 Central
Moody Benj F (Mary J), cattle dlr, h Main st, W Ashev
Moody Bessie E Miss, tchr Orange St Schl, h Chunn's Cove
Moody Chas (Bonnie), clk, h (r) 269 s Main
Moody Cornelius W, pressman Whiteside Ptg Co, h S Biltmore

Mrs. Wilder's SANITARY HOME LAUNDRY turns out first class work in Laundering and Dry Cleaning. No. 7 Montford Ave., Phone 1354

Moody David W (Lillie), brkmn, h 121 Bartlett
Moody Estelle Mrs, h 42 Pearson Drive
Moody H M Sales Co (H M Moody), scales and adding machines, 68 Patton av
Moody Harland M (Alice C), (H M Moody Sales Co), h 83 Elizabeth
Moody Jno W D, bds 173 s Main
Moody Jno W I, woodwkr, h nr Main st, W Ashev
Moody Wm C (Josephine), cattle dlr, h Main st, W Ashev
Mood Wm H, h Main st, W Ashev
*Moon Emma, laund, h 25 McDowell
MOON J VINCENT (Bettie J), supt Life Ins Co of Va, h 27 Clayton
*Moon Wm L (Lizzie), lab, h 10 Hibernia
Mooneyham Wm T (Mary), engnr, h 165 Clingman av
*Moore Ada, h 126 Eagle
*Moore Addie, dom 249 Cumberland av
Moore Albert H (Dora A), mldr, h Haywood rd, W Ashev
Moore Albert S (Sallie), engnr Sou Ry, h W Asheville
*Moore Alice, cook, h 23 Hill
Moore Alinda B Miss, demonstrator Singer Sewing Mch Co, h 182 s French Broad av
*Moore Allison (Peralle), lab, h 7 Ingle
MOORE AMY E MISS, propr Chapel Cottages, h 41 Victoria rd (see adv)
*Moore Anna, laund, h 23 Hill
Moore Annie Lee Miss, nurse Biltmore Hospital, rms same
Moore Annie M Miss (Kenilworth Hall), h same
*Moore Archibald, lab, h Louie nr Depot
Moore Arnold F (Carrie), pumper, h W Asheville
*Moore Arthur G (Emma), (West End Pressing Club), h 29 Turner
Moore Bettie H Miss, stengr, h 17 East
Moore Chas A (Lulu), atty, h 156 Merrimon av
Moore Chas R (Louise), mngr Sou Land Auction Co, h Weaverville N C
Moore Chas R Jr, slsmn Sou Land Auction Co, h Weaverville N C
*Moore Clement (Louvenia), elev opr Oates Bldg, h 64 Lincoln av
Moore Carroll B (Sallie), U S I R dep collr, h 468 n Main
*Moore David (Mary), lab, h 112 Black
*Moore Dennis, lab, h 9 Short Valley
Moore D C, painter, h 560 s Main
Moore E Drayton (Nannie A), ticket agt Sou Ry, h 6 Phifer

BUICK OLDSMOBILE
ARBOGAST MOTOR COMPANY
ACCESSORIES AND SUPPLIES
Phones 302 and 1728
52-60 N. Main
MAXWELLS DETROIT ELECTRIC

Asheville Dry Cleaning Co.
Telephones 835-836, All Dep't
MAIN, N. E. COR. COLLEGE

THE CLEANERS
Our Department for Oriental Rugs and Carpet Cleaning is prepared to serve you in all its branches.
E. S. Paine   O. E. Hansen

For Kindling "What am Kindling" Call
ENGLISH LUMBER COMPANY Phone 321

ASHEVILLE [1913] DIRECTORY

Moore Edwd B (Ella), mngr Wm L Moore, h 179 Woodfin
Moore Edwin W (Amanda V), barber, h 16 Clyde
Moore Elberta Miss, spooler, rms 327 w Haywood
Moore Eliza J, wid J L, h 141 Asheland av
Moore Elizabeth J Miss, h 25 n Liberty
MOORE ELIZABETH J K MISS, art goods and novelties, 52 Patton av—phone 638, h 27 Washington rd (see adv at Art Goods)
Moore Eugene A, h Bonnie Castle, Woolsey (R F D 1)
Moore Eunice L Miss, h 141 Asheland av
Moore Eva Miss, h 49 s French Broad av
Moore Fannie B, wid Jno W, h 9 Louie
*Moore Frank, lab, h 502 s French Broad av
Moore Fred M, slsmn Singer Sewing Mch Co, h Girdwood
*Moore Geo (Jane), plstr, h 25 Oakdale av
Moore Georgia Miss, clk Jno A Guffey, h Burnsville
Moore Helen Miss, h 25 n Liberty
Moore Helen C Miss, h Sand Hill rd, W Ashev
MOORE J WALTER (Minnie), (The Moore Plumbing Co), h 25 n Liberty
*Moore Jackson (Jane), lab, h 17 Knob
*Moore Jas, lab, h 7 Ingle
*Moore Jas, lab, h 47 Hazzard
*Moore Jas G (Ophelia), mngr Piedmont Shoe Co, h 63 Poplar
Moore Jas L (Margaret), lather, h W Asheville
Moore Jas R, spl del'y boy, h 468 n Main
Moore Jas W (Susan), clk, h 13 Buxton
*Moore Jane, cook, h 126 Eagle
*Moore Jane, laund, h 17 Knob
*Moore Jno, caretaker, 49 Zillicoa
Moore Jno C (Mattie), furniture 35 s Main, h Bonnie Castle Woolsey (R F D 1)
Moore Jno G (Julia A), ins, h 17 East
Moore Jno L (Sallie), engnr, h 560 s Main
Moore Jno T (Essie), carp, h 79 Washington rd
Moore Jos B, barber Wm W Young, h Asheville (R F D 5)
Moore Joyce D, clk, h 468 n Main
*Moore Katie, dom, 49 Zillicoa
*Moore Lane, helper, h Haywood rd, W Ashev
*Moore Lee (Lizzie), cook, h 304 Asheland av
Moore Lennie L, h 13 Buxton
*Moore Lewis, sexton, h 85 Circle
*Moore Lillie, cook, h 39 Gudger
Moore Lorenzo D (Lois), engine carp, h Main st, W Ashev

BIGGEST **B**USIEST **B**EST

ASHEVILLE STEAM LAUNDRY
Phones 1936 and 1937
43 to 47 W. COLLEGE

S. D. HALL
REAL ESTATE AGENT
—
Money Loaned
—
Notary Public
—
32 PATTON AVENUE
—
Phone 91

Founders, Machinists and Jobbers of Mill Supplies
PHONE 590 When in the market for pipe and fittings, let us make you Prices. **Carolina Machinery Co.** **PHONE 590** If it's a Gas Engine let us figure with you, also on other kinds of machinery

LIFE INSURANCE COMPANY OF VA. OLDEST, LARGEST, STRONGEST Southern Life Insurance Co.

ORGANIZED 1871
RICHMOND, VIRGINIA

Issues Industrial Policies from $8.00 to $900.00, with Premiums Payable WEEKLY on persons from two to seventy years of age

J. V. Moon, Superintendent, Rooms 3-4-5 Maxwelton Bldg., Asheville, N. C.

ASHEVILLE [1913] DIRECTORY

D. TREXLER TIN SHOP

All Kinds of Roofing, Gutter and Conductor Work.

Phone 862

159 South Main St.

DR. C. H. MILLER

MECHANO-THERAPIST

14 N. Spruce St.
Phone 979
ASHEVILLE, N. C.

Hours by engagement

Drugless Healing of Disease

Moore Lulu T Miss, h 156 Merrimon av
MOORE M V & CO (M V Moore, G J Williamson, W M Smathers), outfitters to men, women and children—phone 78, 11 Patton av
*Moore Maggie, laund, h 502 s French Broad av
Moore Mary C, wid Hiram, h 187 Charlotte
Moore Mary Davis Miss, h 141 Asheland av
Moore Mary J Miss, h 182 s French Broad av
MOORE MATTHEW V (Edith), (M V Moore & Co), and treas Ashev Ptg & Engrav Co, h 110 Cumberland av
*Moore Maude, bkkpr, h 63 Poplar
*Moore Ophelia, tchr Hill St Schl, h 63 Poplar
Moore Pinckney R (Lena R), mngr Yuneda Dairy Lunch, h 28½ Starnes pl
MOORE PLUMBING CO (The), (J Walter Moore), 15 e College—phone 1025 (see side lines)
Moore R Jos, stengr, h 182 s French Broad av
Moore Robt H (Julia), contr, h W Asheville
Moore Robt W (Mary E), engnr Sou Ry, h 182 s French Broad av
*Moore Sarah, cook, h 23 Hill
Moore Theodore V (Mary), fruit grower, h 138 Chestnut
Moore Thos F (Charity), mill wkr, h 55 Roberts
MOORE VERNON W, solr Piedmont Directory Co, 66 Amer Natl Bank Bldg
Moore W Josiah (Lucinda), farmer, h 458 Pearson Drive
Moore Wiley M, clk Yuneda Dairy Lunch, rms 19 Reed Bldg
Moore Wm C (Ella), engnr Sou Ry, h 329 Southside av
Moore Wm J (Allie), tailor S T Logan, h 56 Clayton av
Moore Wm J (Maude), painter, h Woolsey (R F D 1)
Moore Wm L (Madeline), furniture 27 n Main, h 49 s French Broad av
*Moore Zora, h 17 Atkin
Moorman Otway P (Lucy E), h 26 Starnes av
MORAN CHAS H E, v-pres-genl mngr Dixie Mutual Life Ins Co, bds The Knickerbocker
Morgan Avery, clk Ashev Grocery Co
Morgan Bessie Miss, tchr West Ashev Schl, h Fairview N C
Morgan C A, watchmkr A M Field Co, h 47 College
Morgan E Wm (Mary), driver, h 28 Silver
*Morgan Ellen, laundress, h 26 Smith
*Morgan Ellison, bleacher, h 27 Scott
*Morgan Ernest (Arcenna), lab, h 27 Frederick
Morgan Geo B (Rosa), condr St Ry, h 45 Highland

....Asheville Cleaning and Pressing Club....
Tailoring That Satisfies and Prices That Please

Steam and French Dry Cleaning of all delicate and fine wearing apparel for ladies and gentlemen. MESSENGER SERVICE IN THE CITY.

J. C. WILBAR, Prop.   4. N. Pack Square   **PHONE 389**

Morgan Grace Miss, wks Ashev Mica Co, h 60 Clingman av
*Morgan Hattie, cook, h 16 Short
*Morgan Hattie, cook, h 147 Southside av
Morgan Jas M, farmer, h Main st, W Asheville
Morgan Jno P (Cassie A), h 58 East
Morgan Jno W (Mabel), collr Green Bros, h 27 Atkinson
Morgan Jos P (Julina), collr, h 13 Buttrick
Morgan Mae Miss, clk The Peerless Store, h 68 Haywood
Morgan Manson McC, clk Ashev Gro Co, bds 56 Penland
Morgan Martha M Miss, slslady, bds 68 Haywood
Morgan Mattie Miss, emp Dr T C Smith, h 15 Buttrick
Morgan Minnie Miss, h 242 College
Morgan Ollie, wid N T, stengr Moale & Chiles, h 26 Patton
*Morgan Patrick, stone cutter, h 37 Seney
*Morgan Rose, dom, h 12 n Lexington av
*Morgan Rose, laund, h 12 Greer's Row
Morgan Russell, news butcher, bds 56 Penland
Morgan Ruth A Miss, h 28 Silver
Morgan Wade, supt Ashev Mica Co Warehouse, bds W Asheville
Morgan Wm (Maude), clk Dr T C Smith, h W Asheville
Morgan Wm R, student, h 28 Silver
Morgan Wm R (Maude L), lab, h Arlington st, W Ashev
Morgan Wilson A, clk, bds 56 Penland
Morley Willard A (Hattie), h 68 Penland
*Morris Barney (Lula), cook, h 166 Church
*Morris Chas, carp, h 8 Cole
*Morris Chas, driver, h 23 Hildebrand
Morris Clementine I, wid Ezra M, h 197 Cumberland av
Morris Edith Miss, tchr Normal & Collegiate Inst
Morris Emma M Mrs, h 72 Merrimon av
Morris Ernest C (Sarah L), phys 72 n Main, h 207 Haywood
Morris Eugene R, phys and coroner, 32 Patton av (2d fl)
Morris G Wilbur, fireman, h 25 Pearl
*Morris Geo W (Mattie), porter, h 23 Hildebrand
Morris Gilbert H (Delia), (W H Westall & Co), h 147 Asheland av
*Morris Harvey, waiter Crescent Lunch Room, h 16 Eagle
Morris Henry P (Martha), carp, h Haywood rd, W Ashev
Morris Hilliard L (Nellie V), clk Ry M S, h 59 Cumberland
*Morris Jas (Celia), janitor Catholic Hill Schl, h 123 Valley
Morris Jas L, mchst, h 25 Pearl
Morris Jno C, clk to chf dispr Sou Ry, h 197 Cumberland av
*Morris Jno P Rev (Mary E), pastor Berry Temple M E Church, h 250 College

Asheville Dray, Fuel and Construction Co.

Heavy Hauling of all kinds — **WE FURNISH BUILDING STONE** — **Moving Furniture a Specialty**

61-2 South Main   PHONE - 223

---

*Morris Jno W, driver 405 Charlotte
Morris L F, msgr Murphy Div Sou Exp
*Morris Lula, boarding 166 Church, h same
Morris M Evelyn Miss, student, h 147 Asheland av
Morris Nancy E, wid Jno F, h 25 Pearl
Morris Reynolds, rms 15 Technical Blydg
Morris Sarah R Miss, tchr Park av Achool
*Morris Thos, janitor, h 136 Pine
*Morris Walter, cabt mkr Ashev Cabinet Co, h 36 Short
*Morris Walter (Bertha), lab, h 12 Lincoln av
MORRISON ALLEN T (Bourne, Parker & Morrison) and notary nublic s Pack Sq cor Main, h 287 Pearson Drive
*Morrison Hattie, dom, h 79 Roberts
Morrison Mary, wid P S, propr The Elwood, h 119 Haywood
*Morrison Pinkney (Henrietta), driver, h 131 Roberts
Morrison S Ephraim (Mary), gro Haywood rd, W Asheville h same
Morrison Snell Miss, h 287 Pearson Drive
Morrison T S & Co (T S Morrison, H D Childs and T D Morrison), agricultural implts, 80-84 Patton av
Morrison Theo D (Nellie) (T S Morrison & Co), h 174 Montford av
MORRISON THEO S (Elenore) (T S Morrison & Co) and 2d v-pres Wachovia B & T Co, h 287 Pearson Drive
*Morrison Wm, lab, h 79 Roberts
Morrow B R (Mary), laundryman, h 11 Spring
Morrow Catherine P, wid Wm F, h 4 Starnes av
*Morrow Cornelius J (Psyche), meat cutter, h 41 Gudger
*Morrow Jos (Hattie), waiter, h 19 Gray
*Morrow Lemuel (Margaret), lab, h 19 Gray
Morrow May Miss, h 4 Starnes av
Morrow Polly E Miss, bkkpr Moale & Chiles, h 4 Starnes av
Morsell Building (The), offices, 110-112 Patton av
*Morton Jane, laund, h 280 Green's Row
*Morton Thos P (Maria), plstr, h (r) 18 Gudger
*Moseley Dora, laund, h 36 Short
Moseley Jas H (Florence), mtrmn, h 29 Seney
*Moseley Robt, gardner, h 101 Market
Moser Wm M (Lottie), driver, h 501 w Haywood
Moses Edwd A (Helen), mchst, h 66 Adams
Moses Larkin J (Laura), contr Sand Hill rd, W Asheville, h same
Moses Mamie V Miss, tchr, h Sand Hill rd, W Asheville

DYNAMOS & MOTORS

Piedmont Electric Co.

64 Patton Av.
ASHEVILLE, N.C.

J. C. McPHERSON
SLATE AND TIN ROOFING
Galvanized Iron Work   Hot Air Furnaces
35-37 EAST COLLEGE STREET

PLUMBING STEAM AND HOT WATER **HEATING**
PHONE 133

| Yellow Pine / White Pine / Hardwoods / See bet. pgs. 188-189 | **LUMBER** SASH, BLINDS, DOORS | **WOODWARD & SON** Ninth and Arch Streets RICHMOND - VIRGINIA |

Moses Rhea Dora Miss, h 66 Adams
Mosher Edwd A (Helen A) (removed from Starnes av)
*Moss Claude (Pearl), cook, h 28 Hill
*Moss Crockett (Eliza), lab, h 18 McDowell
Moss Eliza, wid Henry, h 16 Cumberland av
Moss Green (Rachel), lab, h 12 Bennett
*Moss Henry (Ella), stone mason, h 72 Clemmons
*Moss Jas (Jennie), janitor N & C Inst, h 86 Choctaw
Moss Jas D (Wilma H), dispr Sou Ry, h 122 s French Braod av
Moss Jessie M Miss, h 130 Poplar
Moss Saml (Ella), lab, h 303 s Main
Mosseller Annie J Miss, stengr Tonawanda White Pine Co, h 47 Cumberland av
Mosseller Danl F (Jno S Mosseller & Son), h 47 Cumberland av
Mosseller Jno S (Mary H) (Jno S Mosseller & Son), h 47 Cumberland av
Mosseller Jno S & Son (Jno S and Danl F), safe, gun and locksmiths, Main cor College
Mosseller Pearl A Miss, h 47 Cumberland av
☞ Mosseller see also Marsteller
Motley Jno R, lino opr Ashev Citizen, bds 42 Walnut
MOUNTAIN CITY LAUNDRY (INC), 30 n Lexington av—phones 426 and 429, E S Paine pres, J K Riggs sec-treas-mngr (see front and back covers)
*MOUNTAIN CITY MUTUAL INS CO (The) (Life), 29 Eagle—phone 762, J A Wilson pres, C C Lipscombe v-pres, L V Watson sec, Thos Oglesby genl mngr
Mountain Meadows Inn, Mountain Meadows
Mountain School Dept Home Mission Board, Sou Baptist Convention, 10 Library Bldg, Rev A E Brown supt
*Mountain Street School, 91 Mountain, Emma H Fenderson prin
*Mt Zion Baptist Church, 55 Eagle, Rev J R Nelson pastor
*Mouzon Chas C, barber Buckeye Parlor, h 167 E College
*Mouzon Jno D,, barber Buckeye Parlor, h 167 E College
*Muckelvene Sena, laund, h 43 Brick
Mudge Isaac R, h Van st, W Asheville
Mull Robt L (Callie), bkkpr, h 14 Ora
Muller Louise Miss, h 16 Charlotte
Muller Wm O, bkkpr J L Smathers & Son, h 16 Charlotte
☞ Muller see also Miller
*Mulligan Wm (Lucy), lab, h 61 Hill
Mullikin Robt R, dispr, bds 77 College

What Have You in Real Estate that You Don't Want?

What do You Want in Real Estate that You Haven't?

WESTERN CAROLINA REALTY CO.
J. W. Wolfe, Sec. & Treas.
On the Square
PHONE 974
10 N. PACK Sq.

H. A. BROWN & Co.
General Contractors
23 Temple Court Bldg.
Phone 341
—DEALERS IN—
Rough Building
and
all Kinds of Crushed Stone
—OUR SPECIALTIES—
STONE FOUNDATIONS CONCRETE WORK
and
EXCAVATING

Moale & Chiles Real Estate and Insurance
27 Patton Ave., [2d fl] Phone 661
City and Suburban Property FARMS and TIMBER LANDS

Candy Kitchen and Club Cafe "A GOOD PLACE FOR REFRESHMENT" Hot drinks on cold days. Cold drinks on hot days. The best drinks every day. Pure fruits and syrups blended "just right," served daintily. Our Ice Cream and Soda Water Department, Restaurant and Candy Departments are always kept up to the standard of nearest perfection. Phones 110 and 111. 19 and 21 Haywood St.

Brown's Undertaking Parlors

S. H. BROWN

50 Patton Avenue
ASHEVILLE, N. C.

Lady Assistant When Desired

Phone 193-2 Rings

THE MOORE Plumbing Company

16 N. Pack Square

PHONE 1025

Sanitary Plumbing, General Tin and Metal Work, Hot Air Furnaces

---

Mulwee Jno (Bertha), lab, h (r) 269 s Main
Mumpower Lillian Miss, h Woolsey
Mumpower Robt E (Ida Mae), dry goods 17 s Main, h Woolsey
Mumpower Robt E Jr, student, h Woolsey
Muncy Roy L (Myrtle L), barber Langren Barber Shop, h 15 Chestnut
Munsey Mary Miss, h 27 Brick
*Murdock Chas (Lucy), lab, h 225 Southside av
Murdock Clara, wid Robt, h 327 w Haywood
Murdock David S (Mamie), plmbr, h 335 Hillside
*Murdock Henritta, dom 179 Merrimon av
Murdock Jas E (Daisy), police, h 85 Asheland av
*Murdock Lizzie, h 133 Valley
Murdock Margaret Miss, h 327 w Haywood
*Murdock Sidney (Kate), watchmn, h 77 Beaumont
Murley Jno W (Emma), clk M F Farris, h 18 Clingman av
*Murphy Annie, laund, h 43 Circle
Murphy Division (Sou Ry), office Sou Ry Depot, T S Boswell supt
Murphy Elizabeth Miss, h 398 Montford av
Murphy Geo (Ellen), janitor, h 18 Gudger
Murphy Helen Miss, h Brevard rd, W Asheville
Murphy Jas D (Mary B), atty at law, 406-408 Oates Bldg, h 398 Montford av
Murphy Jas H (Icglenna), real estate, h 48 Courtland av
*Murphy Jno (Ellen), janitor Ashev Citizen, h 18 Gudger
Murphy Jos J (Mollie), janitor, h 560 s Main
Murphy Lee A, h Brevard rd, W Asheville
*Murphy Leola, cook, h 18 Gudger
*Murphy Mary, h 20 Magnolia
Murphy Ola Miss, h 37 s Liberty
Murray Addie Mrs, h 442 n Main
Murray Belle Miss, maid 40 Wautauga
Murray Bessie Miss, h 65 Clingman av
Murray Emma Mrs, maid A F Rees Kenilworth
Murray Florence Mrs, wks Ashev Mica Co, h 244 College
Murray Frances D Miss, student, h 65 Clingman av
MURRAY GEO A, pres-mngr The Murray Lbr Co and v-pres Citizens Bank, h 191 Cumberland av
Murray Hester, wid J M, dress mkr Mrs C B Harville, h 65 Clingman av
Murray Jas P (Gertrude), gardener, h 20 Ingle
Murray Jos W (Sarah), gardener, h 20 Ingle
Murray Lillian Miss, h 58 Avery

The Battery Park Bank Capital - - $100,000.00
Surplus and Profits, $110,000.00
ASHEVILLE, N. C.   City, County and State Depositary

J. A. TILLMAN   **Jeweler**   I carry a nice line of Watches, Clocks and Jewelry, and make a specialty of repair work. Satisfaction guaranteed   **17 N. Main St.**

Murray Lumber Co (The), whol and mnfrs, 68 Patton av, G A Murray pres-mngr, Geo Parnell v-pres, J E Fulgham sec-asst mngr
Murray Minnie Miss, dom, h 358 s Main
Murray Myra Miss, h 442 n Main
Murray Robt, mill opr, h 58 Avery
Murray School, 46 Tiernan, Mrs M W Williamson prin
Murray Sophie Miss, h 58 Avery
Murray Warren W (Harriet), gardener, h 19 Ingle
Murray Zant Miss, h 58 Avery
*Murrough Mary, h 19 Furman av
*Murrough Noah (Agnes), eating house Y M I Bldg and pres Peoples Undertaking Co, h 14 Philip
Muse Jas W (Minnie), switchmn, h 45 Tiernan
Musser Albert J, miller, h W Asheville
Mustin Albert R, asst sec-treas Mustin-Robertson Co, h 102 Merrimon av
Mustin Eli (Laura), v-pres-genl mngr Mustin-Robertson Co Inc, h 102 Merrimon av
Mustin-Robertson Co (Inc), whol gro's, 351 Depot, J D Robertson pres, Eli Mustin v-pres-genl mngr, R F Stevens sec-treas
MUTUAL LIFE INSURANCE CO OF N Y, 7-8 Paragon Bldg—phone 1236, R M Fitzpatrick div supt
Myers A C, barber Atiseptic Barber Shop, h 15 n Spruce
Myers Commie C, slsmn, bds 76 Starnes av
Myers Chas W (N L), carp, h Biltmore rd, S Biltmore
Myers Clarence C (Blanche), inspr Sou Ry, h 114 Montford av
Myers Cordelia Miss, h 56 Roberts
Myers Fred'k L, clk E C Jarrett, h 284 College
Myers Grover T (America), florist Woolsey Greenhouses, h Grace
Myers Jas F, wood wkr, h 56 Roberts
Myers Julia E Miss, student, h Biltmore rd, S Biltmore
Myers Kate S Miss, h 56 Roberts
Myers Marietta Miss, h Biltmore rd, S Biltmore
Myers Marion L (A Serena), carp, h 56 Roberts
Myers Thos B, paperhngr R L Fitzpatrick & Son
Myers Violet A Miss, h 56 Roberts
☞ Myers see also Meyers
Myrick Janie Miss, rms 327 w Haywood
Myrtle Bank Cottage, Haywood rd, W Asheville, residence of Mrs S J Knight

INSURANCE
Insure Your Salary With Us
Never Carry Your Own Risk
Safety Is The Best Policy
Unless You Are A Capitalist
Rest Easy If You Have
An Accident We Will
Not Keep You Waiting To
Collect Your Claim
Every Claim Promptly Paid

Imperial Mutual Life & Health Insurance Co.
Home Office:
ASHEVILLE, N. C.
Phone 495

HOTEL OXFORD   Redecorated and Refitted throughout. Recently enlarged to 60 rooms. Centrally located. Depot cars stop at entrance. Long distance telephone office upstairs. American and European plan. Rates 50c, 75c and $1 per day; special rates by week or month. C. H. Branson & Sons, Proprietors. Phone 1887. 50-54 South Main St.   **Asheville, N. C.**

N

*Nance Della, laund, h 43 Poplar
Nance Lucille Miss, h 16 Highland
Nance Saml S (Lena), trav slsmn, h 16 Highland
Nanney Robt C, solr Ashev Transfer & Storage Co, rms 394 Southside av
Nash Edmund L (Mary M), bkkpr Dr T C Smith, h 64 n Spruce
Nash Ella W Mrs, wid Ira W, h 76 Liberty
Nash Jno D (Paralee), foreman R L Fitzpatrick & Son, h 387 s French Broad av
Nash Mary W Miss, dress mkr 24 McAfee Bldg, h same
Nash Paralee Mrs, dep county register of deeds, h 387 s French Broad av
National Biscuit Co, 349 Depot, F E Kirkland mngr
National Cash Register Co, 78 Patton av, E O George sales agt
National Casket Co, mnfrs, Riverside Drive, F E Johnson mngr
National Special Sales Co, 17 Drhumor Bldg, A A Hall mngr
NATURAL METHOD SANITARIUM, 408 Haywood, Dr S L Whitmore physician in charge
*Neal Edna, laund, h (r) 29 Clingman av
Neale Philip (Florence), contr 76 Penland, h same
☞ Neal see also Neill and O'Neal and O'Neill
Neel Bessie Mrs, wid H B, h 124 Broad
*Neely Amelia, h 15 Sassafras
*Neely Ella, laund, h 124 Eagle
Neely Helen M Miss, student, h 175 Flint
Neely Jno W (Julia R) (H Redwood & Co), h 175 Flint
Neill Penelope Mrs, wid Robt, h 299 College
Neill Tryphenia Miss, h 306 Chestnut
Nelson Alice B, wid Napoleon B, h 11 Spring
*Nelson Dederick, porter Bon Marche, h 30 Ridge
*Nelson Jno, bellmn, h 30 Ridge
Nelson Jno D (Earle & Nelson), rms 25 Adelaide Bldg
*Nelson Jno R Rev (Emma) pastor Mt Zion Baptist Church h 30 Ridge
Nelson Lelia Miss, h 11 Spring
*Nelson Maggie, cook, h 20 Clemmons
*Nelson Maggie, laund, h 47 Brick
*Nelson Nea, laund, h 41 Madison

FOR BOX SHOOKS — Call English Lumber Co. PHONE 321

Nelson W Butler, brkmn, bds 96 Bartlett
*Nesbitt Jno, lab, h 231 Southside av
*Nesbitt Viola, maid, rms Louie nr Depot
*Nesbitt Wm (Florence), porter, h 2 Hibernia
Nettles Harry L (Margaret), mngr Brown's Creamery, h 44 Oak
NEVERCEL FRANK J (Ida H), bicycles, bicycle sundries and repairs, 47 w College—phone 1650, h 5 Kenilworth Park (see back fly A)
Neville Lucy Miss, h 173½ Patton av
Neville Olive L, wid Jno, propr The Colonial, h 58 n Main
New Sondley Building (offices), 15 Haywood
NEW SWANNANOA HOTEL (see Swannanoa Berkeley)
New York Fruit Stand, 404 Depot, Geo Daoulas mngr
New York Quick Lunch Restaurant, 11 s Main, S Papas propr
NEWELL WM A REV (Bertha), pastor Haywood St M E Church and pres Weaverville College, h 210 Patton av
Newkirk Guss R (Laura), slsmn W E Patterson & Co, h Woolsey av
Newman ———, ship clk, bds 56 Penland
Newton Academy Cemetery, Biltmore rd, J J Murphy supt
Newton C C Miss, bds 77 Montford av
Newton Laura A, wid Saml L, h 32 Soco
Newton Lula G Mrs, propr Park View, h Pearson Drive opp Riverside Park
Newton Minnie Lee Miss, stengr, h "Park View"
Newton Reuben T (Lula G), confr Riverside Bridge, h Pearson Drive opp Riverside Park
Newton Rockey T, clk Yuneda Dairy Lunch, h Riverside
Newton Ruby A Miss, manicurist, h Park View opp Riverside Park
Newton School, Biltmore rd, Mrs Mary C Pickens tchr
*Niblack Wm (Daisy(, tailor, h 13 Dundee
NICHOLS ARCHIBALD (Elizabeth), pres, treas-mngr Nichols Shoe Co (Inc), h 333 Montord av
Nichols Bert E, with Ashev Stm Ldy, h 85 n Liberty
NICHOLS CHAS (Cornelia), bkkpr Ashev Dray, Fuel & Constr Co, h 23 Ann st
Nichols Chas A, clk Ashev Stm Ldy, h 85 n Liberty
Nichols Helen Miss, h 85 n Liberty
Nichols Jas G, bkkpr Armour & Co, bds Western Hotel
Nichols Jas J (Mary G), foreman Ashev Stm Ldy, h 85 n Liberty

BIGGEST **B**USIEST **B**EST **Asheville Steam Laundry**
Phones: 1936 and 1937
43 to 47 W. College Street

CHARLES H. HONESS OPTOMETRIST AND OPTICIAN
Exclusive maker of ATLAS SHUR-ON EYE GLASSES
THE Home of Ce-Rite Toric Lenses
We make a specialty of correcting optical defects with properly fitted glasses.
54 Patton Avenue Opposite Postoffice

Carolina Machinery Co. Founders, Machinists and Jobbers of Mill Supplies. We make all kinds of Castings in Iron, Brass or Aluminum.
WE ALSO FURNISH SKILLED MECHANICS FOR BOILER REPAIRS — PHONE 590

LIFE INSURANCE COMPANY OF VA.
ORGANIZED 187
Richmond -:- Virginia
J. V MOON, Superintendent
Rooms 3-4-5- Maxweiton Bldg., Asheville, N. C.

All claims paid IMMEDIATELY upon receipt of satisfactory proofs of Death. Total payment to policyholders since organization, over $12,000,-000.00. Is paying its Policyholders over $1,000,000.00 annually.

T. P. JOHNSON & CO.

SHEET METAL WORKERS

All Kinds of Roofing Guttering and Conductor Work Metal Ceilings, Skylights and Galvanized Iron Cornices

OFFICE and SHOP:
69-71 S. MAIN

Phone 325

DR. C. H. MILLER

Mechano-Therapist

14 N. Spruce Street
ASHEVILLE, N. C.

PHONE 979

Hours by Engagement

DRUGLESS HEALING OF DISEASE

---

282 ASHEVILLE [1913] DIRECTORY

NICHOLS JNO A (Anna) (Ashev Ice Co) (P W Lowe & Son) and propr Asheville Steam Ldy, h 85 n Liberty
*Nichols Jos, cook, h 130 Pine
NICHOLS JOS W (Bess), v-pres-sec Nichols Shoe Co (Inc), h 210 Merrimon av
*Nichols Lee (Belle), porter, h 130 Pine
Nichols Leonidas W (Corrie), mngr Crescent Jewelery Co, h 10 s Ann
Nichols Lucy J Miss, h 276 Chestnut
Nichols Rena Miss, tchr Orange St Schl, h 210 Merrimon
*Nichols Richard, lab, h 30 Catholic av
Nichols Russel, barber Glen Rock Barber Shop, rms Halyburton House
NICHOLS SHOE CO (INC), 2 n Pack Sq—phone 299, Archibald Nichols pres, treas-mngr, J W Nichols v-pres sec
Nichols Vienna Miss, tchr Park av Schl, h 23 Ann st
Nicholson Agnes L Mrs, clk J H Nicholson, h Haywood rd, W Asheville
Nicholson Aurthur S (Rachel), farmer, h Pennsylvania av, W Asheville
Nicholson Burgan, student, h Pennsylvania av, W Ashev
Nicholson David M (Agnes L), condr, h Haywood rd, W Asheville
Nicholson Edgar L (Allie M), horse dlr, h Pennsylvania av, W Asheville
Nicholson Ernest J (Maggie A), farmer, h Haywood rd, W Asheville
Nicholson H Calloway, blksmith Ashev Power & Light Co, h Hillside
Nicholson Jas H (Delia), gro Haywood rd, W Asheville (R F D 3), h same
Nicholson Jas R (Effie), clk Sou Exp Co, h Haywood rd, W Asheville
Ninety Nine (The), boarding, 101 Haywood, Mrs Ora Cauble propr
*Nipson Jno J, bricklyr, h 202 s Main
*Nipson Jno W (Annie), emp Roger's Book Co, h 169 s Beaumont
Nitzer Wm A, real estate and notary, 15 Revell Bldg, h 88 Charlotte
Nix Adolphus, painter, bds 16 s Spruce
Nix Geo M (Brejettie), condr St Car, h 100 East
Nix Isabel Miss, h 19 n Liberty
Nix Thos F (Nettie), lab, h Haywood rd, W Asheville

ASHEVILLE CLEANING and PRESSING CLUB

TAILORING THAT SATISFIES and PRICES THAT PLEASE

Hats cleaned, banded and bound. Silk hats ironed. Buttons made to order in all sizes. Plain or with rims. PHONE 389

DYEING IN ALL SHADES

Kid Gloves, Slippers and Plumes. Fancy Jabots and Ties, French Dry Cleaned. Ladies' and Gentlemen's suits Steam Cleaned. Messenger Service. **J. C. Wilbar, Prop.**

4 NORTH PACK SQ.

Nixon Emma S Miss, h 50 Chestnut
Nixon Mamie C Miss, tchr Montford av Schl, h 50 Chestnut
Nixon Sarah L Miss, h 50 Chestnut
Nixon Walter B (Hattie S), gro 170-172 Charlotte, h 270 Hillside
Noble Mary L, wid C N, h 44 Panola
Noblitt Dorcas M Miss, h 180 Asheland av
Noblitt Martin W (Sophia A), jeweler 35 s Main, h 180 Asheland av
*Noblitt Nan, laund, h 73 Black
Noblitt Ossie B Miss, h 180 Asheland av
Noblitt Thos J (Fannie), shpping clk W H Westall & Co, h Haywood rd, W Asheville
Nolan Eleanor Miss, h 6 All Souls Crescent, Biltmore
Nolan Fannie Miss, h 6 All Souls Crescent, Biltmore
NOLAND, BOWN & CO (Inc), undertakers and embalmers, 16 Church—phone 65, D G Noland pres, C W Brown v-pres, E P Brownell Jr sec-treas, M C Noland genl mngr
Noland Burton M (Hattie M), ins agt, h 24 Oak
Noland D Govan, mdse broker, bds 140 Asheland av
NOLAND DOCTOR G (Louise) (Noland & McIntyre), pres Noland, Brown & Co, h 55 Vance—phone 1892
Noland Harry C, funeral directors, h 140 Asheland av
Noland Lawrence, student, h 140 Asheland av
NOLAND M CLIFTON (Georgia A), genl mngr Noland, Brown & Co, h 140 Asheland av—phone 561
Noland Massena C (Annie), funeral director, h 140 Asheland av
Norborn E L, news editor Ashev Gazette-News
NORMAL AND COLLEGIATE INSTITUTE, for Young Women, s Main cor Victoria rd—phone 2, Prof E P Childs pres (see inside back cover)
Norris Clyde O (Zola), painter R L Fitzpatrick & Son, h Haywood rd, W Asheville
*Norris Ida, cook, h 104 n Lexington av
Norris Jesse, lab W M Jones, h 431 Spring
Norris Otis V (Bertha), painter, h 273 s Main
North Asheville Methodist Church, 49-51 Chestnut, Rev W E Poovey pastor
North Asheville Grocery, 277 n Main, J F Hayes propr
North Carolina Mercantile Co, jobbers genl mdse, 200-202 Oates Bldg, J C Arbogast mngr
*North Carolina Mutual & Provident Assn of Durham N C, 44 Market, E Z Goodman supt

WEAVERVILLE LINE NINE MILES BY TROLLEY FROM PACK SQUARE TO WEAVERVILLE

ASHEVILLE AND EAST TENNESSEE RAILROAD CO.

7 NORTH MAIN STREET — ASHEVILLE N. C

Side ad: Electrical Supplies — PIEDMONT ELECTRIC COMPANY, ASHEVILLE, N. C., 64 PATTON AVE.

ASHEVILLE [1913] DIRECTORY

North Carolina Oil Co, Lyman cor Riverside, H A Wild mngr
North Carolina Power Co, 1-2 Maxwelton Bldg, W T Weaver pres, G S Powell v-pres, W E Reid sec-treas
North Carolina Trans-Continental Construction Co, 111-112-114 Citizen Bldg
NORTH STATE FITTING SCHOOL 157 Church—phone 1374, Prof J M Roberts principal (see p 12)
NORTH STATE LIFE INSURANCE CO OF KINSTON N C, 1 Harkins Bldg, Thos W Osteen mngr
NORTHROP S & W H LUMBER CO (INC), wholesalers and exporters of yellow pine lumber, 9th and Bragg, Richmond Va; Stewart M Woodward pres, Jos H Gordon sec (see top lines)
NORTHUP H KENDALL (Brown-Northup & Co), h 73 Merrimon av
NORTHUP WILLARD B (Fannie C) (Brown-Northup Hdw Co) and chmn School Committee, h 73 Merrimon av
Norton Jno R, clk M Hyams, bds Hotel Warren

When Writing to Advertisers Please Mention the City Directory

Norton Louie D Miss, nurse Highland Hosp, h same
Norvill Annie K Miss, clk, h 245 Asheland av
Norville Bessie Miss, h 245 Asheland av
Norville Thos W (Susan), shoemkr Boston Shoe Store, h 245 Asheland av
Norville Thos W Jr, pressman The Inland Press, h 245 Asheland av
Nottingham Edgar J (Cornelia), route agt Sou Exp Co, h 39 e Chestnut
Novich Bessie Miss, clk Bon Marche, h 70 College
Novich Harry, slsmn Bon Marche, h 70 College
Novich Saml (Jennie), slsmn, h 70 College
Nowell Chas E (Annie), police, h 265 s Main
Nowell Sylvester (Sue), gro 2 McDowell, h same
Nuckles Emmons L, carp, h Asheville av, W Asheville
Nuckles Geo C (Rosa B), carp, h Asheville av, W Ashev
*Nuckles Havon (Clara), driver Grove Park
*Nuckles Lyda, dom Grove Park
Nurses Home, Mission Hospital, 17 Charlotte
NYBERG AUTOMOBILE SALES CO OF N C, 17 s Main—phone 1386; R R Reynolds pres, J B Rumbough v-pres and genl mngr, Gilliland Stikeleather sec and treas

CONTRACTOR and BUILDER
STEEL RANGES — **J. C. McPHERSON** — 35-37 E COLLEGE ST. PHONE 133
PLUMBING STEAM AND HOT WATER HEATING

O

O K Auto Supply & Transit Co, 61-63 s Main, F A Mears mngr
"Oak Cottage," boarding, 115 Haywood, Mrs S H Brown propr
Oak Grove Cottage, Asheville av, W Asheville, residence of Mrs S D Patterson
Oak Grove Dairy, Chunns Cove
Oakes David E (Adelia), clk, h 46 Chestnut
Oakland Heights Presbyterian Church, s Main cor Victoria rd, Rev T A Cosgrove pastor
Oakley Annie Miss, h Edgemont
Oakley Jane Miss, h Edgemont
OATES BUILDING (Offices), 20-22 n Pack Sq
Oates Frances E Miss, h 56 College
OATES FRED B (Teague & Oates), h 56 College
OATES J RUSH (Dora), propr Legal and Oates Bldgs, office 210 Legal Bldg, h 56 College
Oates Luther, emp Cabt Shop, bds 34 Summit, S Biltmore
Oates W Robt (Emma), emp Green House, h 34 Summit, S Biltmore
O'Bannon J Bryant (Lillian), trav slsmn, bds 107 Haywood
O'Brien Annie Mrs, wid C A, h 70 Madison av
O'Brion Fannie Miss, tchr High School
Odd Fellows Hall, 18½ Church
Odd Fellow's Hall, Haywood rd, W Asheville
*Odd Fellow's Hall, 22 Eagle
*Odom Frank (Gertrude), lab, h 49 Black
O'Donnell Emma Mrs, housekpr 200 Montford av
O'Donnell Kate Mrs, h 36 n French Broad av
Ogden Annie S Miss, clk A M Field Co, h 31 w Chestnut
Ogden Daniel W (Mamie), clk L O Maxwell, h 38 East
Ogden Sarah J, wid Jno S, h 31 w Chestnut
***OGLESBY THOS** (Maria P), genl mngr Mtn City Mut Ins Co (Cannon & Oglesby), h 123 Mountain
*Ohanan Ernest, lab, h 27 Scott
*Ohanan Jacob (Elila), lab, h 79 Black
O'Kelley Alvin (Maude), engine clnr, h 492 w Haywood
O'Kelley B Zebulon (Laura), slsmn, h (r) 324 s Main
O'Kelley Robt G (Annie B), weaver, h 4 Factory Hill
O'Kelley Thos C (Martha E), farmer, h Broadway av, W Asheville
O'Kelley Thos L (Manning), flgmn, h 388 s French Broad

Candy Kitchen and Club Cafe
"A GOOD PLACE FOR REFRESHMENT"

The very best ingredients with sanitary conditions in our Candy Manufacturing Department make possible the dainty, crisp confections sold here. Bon Bons and Chocolates made every day, put up in neat, attractive boxes. Phones 110 and 111. 19 and 21 Haywood St.

Brown's Undertaking Parlors

S. H. BROWN

Lady Assistant When Desired

Phone 193-2 Rings

50 Patton Avenue
Asheville, N. C.

Established 1894

B. J. JACKSON

Carefully Selected Fruits and Vegetables

Stall No. 11, City Market

BUSINESS PHONES: 86 and 101

RESIDENCE PHONE 1596

O'Kelley Wiley (Margaret), slsmn, h (r) 326 s Main
Old Kentucky Home, boarding, 48 n Spruce, Mrs Julia Wolfe propr
Oliphant Edna Miss, piano tchr 35 Orange, h same
OLIVE HENRY J (Minnie), genl mdse, 547-548-550 and 551 w Haywood (Smiths Bridge)—phone 138 and W Asheville—phone 348, h 279 Haywood—phone 1004
Olive Kathleen Miss, h 279 Haywood
Ollis Fred (Nellie), lab, h 118 Ora
Ora Street Presbyterian Church, 96 Ora, Rev A M MacLauchlin pastor
*Orange Melissa, laundress, h 272 Asheland av
Orange Street School, 71 Orange, M K Weber prin
"Orchard Cottage," Albemarle Park
O'Rear Eva Miss, dressmkr 28 Amer Natl Bank Bldg, h W Asheville
O'Rear Jno C, h W Asheville
O'Rear Wm F (Minnie E), carrier P O, h W Ashev
Orpin Helen M Miss, h 372 s French Broad
Orpin Philander C (Rebecca), photog, h 372 s French Broad
Orr Andrew K (Elizabeth C), div frt agt Sou Ry, h 35 Bearden av
Orr Andrew K Jr, clk, h 35 Bearden av
Orr Barclay L (Louise), mchst, h 69 Victoria av
ORR CHAS C (Helen M), (Stevens & Orr), phys Adelaide Bldg, h 34 Courtland av—phone 1027
Orr E Marshall (Mary B), h 200 College
Orr Jno C (Sallie B), slsmn Ashev Gro Co, h 84 Starnes av
Orr Maggie, wid Marshall, h 40 Woodfin
Orr Mary D Miss, h 35 Bearden av
Orr Nora Miss, h 134 Flint
ORR PORTER BYNUM (Emma), physician 3 Drhumor Bldg, office hours 10 to 12 a m and 3 to 5 p m—phone 787-3, h W Asheville (R F D 3)—phone 787-2
Orr Robt (Florence), h 54 Madison
Orr Sarah L, wid Jno P, h Haywood rd, W Ashev
*Orr Thos (Mabel.) lab, h 5 Clemmons
Orr Thos F (Minnie), furn rooms, 426 Depot, h same
Orsi Geo, bkkpr Frank Greco, h 48 Philip
*Osborn Addie, laund, h 5 Clemmons
OSBORN GRACE L MISS, genl sec Y W C A, h 78 s Main
Osborne Alfred, slsmn, rms Franklin Hotel
Osborne Geo R, h 181 Merrimon av
Osborne Thos, proof reader Ashev Citizen, bds Montford av

Ye OLD BOOK SHOP
114 Patton Ave.   Phone 1674
BOOKS BOUGHT, SOLD OR EXCHANGED

ROUGH AND DRESSED LUMBER
WHITE PINE AND YELLOW PINE
FLOORING A SPECIALTY
Hardwoods

Williams-Brownell Planing Mill Company
Mouldings and Interior Finish
Office: Southern Railway Tracks, Near Biltmore Station
Phone 729 **Planing Mill**

OSTEEN THOS W (Minnie), mngr North State Life Ins Co of Kinston N C and agt coml dept Continental Casualty Co of Chicago Ill, office 1 Harkins Bldg, h 2 Fagg pl
Ottari Sanitarium, Grace, Dr W B Meacham propr
Ottinger McClung M (Nora), slsmn Mustin-Robertson Co, h 114 s French Broad av
Overcash Wm A (Irene E), slsmn Villa Heights Co, h 19 s French Broad av
Owen Altheae W, wid Wm E, inspr, h (r) 330 w Haywood
Owen Alva E, painter, h (r) 330 w Haywood
Owen Euphia Miss, nurse 18 Vance, rms same
Owen Jas E, student, h nr Haywood rd, W Ashev
Owen Jesse A (Ida), painter, h nr Arlington st, W Ashev
Owen Jno B, shoemkr, bds 50 Asheland av
Owen Jno S (Addie R), trav slsmn, h nr Haywood rd, W Ashev
Owen Lawrence E, repr A M Field Co, h nr Haywood rd, W Ashev
Owen Robt T, sign painter, h 53 North
Owen Wm T (Mary A), Chunn's Cove
Owen Zollie W (Etta), clk frt office Sou Ry, h Haywood rd W Asheville
Owenbey Delia Mrs, h 63 Park Sq
*Owens Alfred, lab, h 12 Green's Row
Owens Angie L Miss, h 382 Southside av
Owens Eugene, emp Amer Wagon Co, h w Haywood
Owens Eula M Miss, h 283 Southside av
*Owens Governor, lab, h 97 Market
Owens Jas H (Owens & Son), h 382 Southside av
Owens Jno (Bessie), shoemkr Champion Shoe Hospital, h 81 Penland
*Owens Jno (Minnie), hackman 84 Choctaw, h same
Owens Jno W (Henrietta), (Owens & Son), h 382 Southside av
Owens Jos L (Della E), clk, h 283 Southside av
Owens L LeRoy, student, h 283 Southside av
*Owens Lee, porter Allison's Drug Store, h 272 Asheland
*Owens Lillie, laund, h 12 Green's Row
Owens Pleasant M (Bertha), lab, h 22 Fagg
Owens Sarah, wid R A, h 323 Hillside
Owens Senith E Miss, h 382 Southside av
Owens Wm, driver Yates & McGuire, h 323 Hillside
*Owens Wm H (Mamie), waiter, h 97 Circle
Owens & Son (J W & J H), gros 382 Southside av

HUGHES
Transfer and Livery Co.

Automobiles for **HIRE**

TRUNKS 25c

Office:
401 Southside Avenue
PHONE 1405

Try our Hand Laundering. We strive to please in LAUNDERING and DRY CLEANING.

The Sanitary Home Laundry No. 7 MONTFORD AVE.
PHONE - 1354

Mrs. Wilder's SANITARY HOME LAUNDRY turns out first class work in Laundering and Dry Cleaning. No. 7 Montford Ave., Phone 1354

Ownbey Althea J, wid Wm, h 3 Merrimon pl
Ownbey Burt L (Camilla), mngr Pack Sq Book Co (Inc), h 31 w Chestnut
Ownbey Herbert W (Myrtle), condr Sou Ry, h 39 Bartlett
Ownbey Herman (Susan), chauffeur, h 63 Park Sq
Ownbey Lee (Ownbey & Son), h 42 Starnes av
Ownbey Parley A (R L Ownbey & Co), rms 14 e Pack Sq (3d fl)
Ownbey Paul L, clk McConnell Bros, rms 32 Patton av
Ownbey R L & Co (Reuben L and Parley A Ownbey), fruits and produce, whol and retail, 36 n Lexington av
Ownbey Reuben L (Ida M), (R L Ownbey & Co), h 83 Chestnut
Ownbey Sims (Caroline G), (Ownbey & Son), h 128 Cherry
Ownbey Viola I Miss, student, h 3 Merrimon pl
Ownbey Vivian A Miss, student, h 3 Merrimon pl
Ownbey & Son (Sims and Lee), gros 25 Montford
Ownsby Myra, wid Robt, h W Ashev
Ozark (The), boarding 76 n Main, Mrs L D Hammond prop

P

Pace B Harrison (Millard), bkkpr, h 83 Starnes av
Pace Benj H (Mildred), bkkpr J C Arbogast, h 83 Starnes
*Pace Georgia, maid Mrs E H Radeker, h same
Pack Frances, wid Geo W, h 140 Merrimon av
PACK MEMORIAL LIBRARY, 4 s Pack Sq; Miss Grace McH Jones librarian, Miss Ann T Erwin asst librarian
PACK MEMORIAL LIBRARY ASSN, 4 s Pack Sq; Donald Gillis pres, S P Ravanel v-pres, Mrs A M Field sec, W B Williamson treas
Pack Square Bakery, 6 n Pack Sq, O W Hawley mngr
Pack Square Book Co (Inc), 3 n w Pack Sq, B L Ownbey and R S Brown mngrs
Padgett Jas M (Sudie), condr, h 132 Asheland av
Padgett Marion D, sterotyper Ashev Citizen, h Woolsey
Padgett Robt F, embalmer Hare & Co, h Woolsey
Padgett Robt R (Irene), h Woolsey
Page Jno L (H Belle), propr Hotel Paxton, h 35 Clingman
Page O H, v-pres Ashev Ptg & Eng Co, h Jacksonville, Fla
Page S Elizabeth, wid Wm B, h 44 Clingman av
Pagett B Marion, clk Ry M S, rms 34 Meriwether Bldg
Paine Edna Lee Miss, h 58 Courtland av
PAINE EDWD S (Mary), propr Asheville Dry Cleaning Co, h 58 Courtland av

OLDSMOBILE — **DETROIT ELECTRIC**

ARBOGAST MOTOR COMPANY
ACCESSORIES AND SUPPLIES
Phones 302 and 1728
52-60 N. Main

BUICK — **MAXWELLS**

Asheville Dry Cleaning Co.
Telephones 835-836, All Dep't
MAIN, N. E. COR. COLLEGE

THE CLEANERS
Our Department for Oriental Rugs and Carpet Cleaning is prepared to serve you in all its branches.
E. S. Paine   O. E. Hansen

*Paine Rosa, h 138 Eagle
Paine Walter H, student, h 58 Courtland av
Painter Zeb V (Florence), motorman, h 42 Magnolia av
Palace Theatre, 76 Patton av
Palais Royal, dry goods 5-7 s Main, R G Fortune mngr
*Palmer Cecil (Motie), hostler, h 138 Weaver
Palmer Emilie I, wid Wm W, supt Woman's Exchange, h 98 Haywood
Palmer Jno L, condr, bds Highland Hotel
*Palmer Kay (Massie), porter, h 59 Curve
Palmer Nina Miss, student, h 98 Haywood
Pangle Chas M (Dora), carp, h 4 Gaston
Panzerbeiter Georgia, wid Herman C, rms 36½ s Main
Papas Gus, waiter, rms 11 s Main
Papas Symcon (Marie), propr N Y Quick Lunch Restaurant, h 11 s Main
PAQUIN PAUL DR (Hannah B), 217 Legal Bldg, office hours 10 to 12 a m, 3 to 4 p m and by appointment, h 45 Reed
Paquin Pauline E Miss, h 45 Reed
Paragon Building (offices), 55 Patton av
Parham Clarence W, carrier P O, h 23 Asheland av
Parham Dexter W (Leona V), clk P O, h 71 Starnes av
Parham Irma E Miss, h 77 Pine Grove av
Parham Oliver W (Geneva), flagman Sou Ry, h 77 Pine Grove av
Parham Wm F (Florence), foreman Sou Ry, h 77 Pine Grove av
Paris Millinery Shop, 78 Patton av, Mrs Jennie Kroman propr
Park Avenue School, Park av n w cor Haywood, Miss M Queen Carson prin
"Park View," boarding Pearson Drive opp Riverside Park, Mrs L G Newton propr
Parker Alex, tmstr, h 1 Wallach
Parker Anna F Miss, tchr, h 83 Arlington
PARKER ANTHONY L (Bettie R), sec Masonic Lodge, h 67 Chestnut
Parker Bessie M Miss, bkkpr, h 104 s French Broad av
Parker Caroline H, wid Jno M, h 83 Arlington
Parker Chas, lunchman, rms 64 Vance
Parker Chas N, dghtsman Smith & Carrier Co, h 83 Arlington
*Parker Dora, laund, h 67 Gudger
Parker Dorothy S Miss, h Edgemont

The Life Insurance Co. of Virginia
ORGANIZED 1871   RICHMOND, VA.

ISSUES ALL THE MOST APPROVED FORMS OF LIFE INSURANCE CONTRACTS from $500.00 to $25,000.00, with premiums payable quarterly, semi-annually and annually

J. V. Moon, Superintendent, Rooms 3-4-5 Maxwelton Bldg., Asheville, N. C.

D. TREXLER TIN SHOP

All Kinds of Roofing, Gutter and Conductor Work.

Phone 862

159 South Main St.

DR. C. H. MILLER

MECHANO-THERAPIST

14 N. Spruce St.
Phone 979
ASHEVILLE, N. C.

Hours by engagement

Drugless Healing of Disease

Parker E S Dr, h "Clematis Cottage," Albemarle Park
*Parker Edna, cook, h 67 Gudger
Parker Elretta Miss, cashr The Dreamland, h 68 Clingman
Parker Emily C Miss, tel opr, h 68 Clingman av
*Parker Ethel, laund, h 67 Gudger
Parker Gaither B, contr 3-4 Barnard Bldg, h same
Parker Geo F, student, h Edgemont
Parker Geo N, archt
Parker Gertrude B Miss, h 67 Chestnut
Parker Harry L, civil engnr 83 Arlington, h same
PARKER HAYWOOD (Josephine B), (Bourne, Parker & Morrison), and notary s Pack Sq cor Main, h 95 Charlotte
Parker Helen V Miss, tchr, h 67 Chestnut
Parker Jas D (Martha), driver, h 425 s Main
*Parker Jennie, laund, h 6 Sassafras
Parker Jno D, clk Yuneda Dairy Lunch, h 64 Vance
Parker Jno M (Mattie W), dentist 11-12 Paragon Bldg, h Edgemont Park
Parker Jno P (Nora), gardener, h W Asheville
Parker Lela Miss, h W Asheville
Parker Lucy J Mrs, h 104 s French Broad av
*Parker Lula, laund, h (r) 118 Church
Parker M Victoria, wid Geo G, h 68 Clingman av
Parker Mary M Miss, h 104 s French Broad av
Parker Nettie L Miss, tchr, h 67 Chestnut
Parker O Vernon (Florence), trav slsmn, rms 90 Asheland
Parker R Lee (Nancy), driver Swannanoa Laundry, h Jarrett av, W Ashev
Parker Ralph W, surveyor, h 67 Chestnut
*Parker Robt, barber, h 165 College
Parker Thos (Annie), h (r) 273 s Main
Parker Wm, lab, h 16 Bennett
Parkins Rich'd C (Antiseptic Barber Shop), bds 15 Spruce
*Parks Jas (Kate), lab, h 42 Ridge
*Parks Lida, dom, h 42 Ridge
*Parks Tench (Mary), waiter, h 97 n Main
Parnell Geo, v-pres The Murray Lbr Co, h Bee Log N C
Parris A Jackson (Levonia), car inspr, h Broadway av, W Ashev
Parris Annie C Miss, h 64 Park Sq
Parris Burnett (Lillie), lab, h 52 Maiden la
Parris Jno E, mill wkr, h 64 Park Sq
Parris Jos M, mill wkr, h 64 Park Sq
Parris Laura, h 52 Maiden la

....**Asheville Cleaning and Pressing Club**....
Tailoring That Satisfies and Prices That Please
Steam and French Dry Cleaning of all delicate and fine wearing apparel for ladies and gentlemen. MESSENGER SERVICE IN THE CITY.

J. C. WILBAR, Prop.   4. N. Pack Square   **PHONE 389**

CAROLINA "M & W" INDIAN — Prompt Delivery — **COAL** — **& ICE CO.** PHONE 130 — 50 PATTON AVE. — WEIGHTS ACCURATE

Parris Margaret A, wid Calvin, h 64 Park Sq
Parris Margaret M, wid Louis, h 52 Maiden la
Parris Noah F (Nannie), station mstr Sou Ry, h Louie nr Depot
Parris Robt E, painter R L Fitzpatrick & Son
*Pasour Bela (Ozella), lab, rms 92 Black
Pass Lucille R Miss, student, h 25 Highland
Pass Richard A (Bee), h 25 Highland
Passmore Catherine Miss, h Edgemont
Passmore Irene G, wid A F, h Edgemont
Passmore Kenneth A, student, h Edgemont
Pate Linda Miss, h 32 Carter
Pate Margaret Miss, h 32 Carter
Pate Texanna Mrs, h 32 Carter
*Patillo Wm (Maggie), lab, h (r) 48 Curve
Patterson Chas W (Jennie), clk E C Jarrett, h 59 Josephine
Patterson Ernest, emp lndry, rms 23 Maxwelton Bldg
Patterson Esther E Miss, h 93 Merrimon av
Patterson Hester A Miss, student, h Main st, W Ashev
PATTERSON J R & SON (Jas R and W R Patterson,) genl insurance, 1½ s Main (2d fl)
Patterson Jas M (Avalina), contr and bldr, Main st, W Ashev, h same
PATTERSON JAS R (J R Patterson & Son), h 28 College Park
*Patterson Jno (Ollie), lab, h 5 Short Valley
Patterson Jno C (Hattie), (A L McLean & Co), h 11 Clayton
Patterson Lottie L Miss, h 28 College Park
Patterson Mabel I Miss, asst, h Asheville av, W Ashev
Patterson Myrtle R Miss, tchr Carolina Commercial Schl, h 93 Merrimon av
Patterson Nathan R (W E Patterson & Co), h Indianapolis Ind
Patterson Robt O Lieut (Ada), h 254 n Main
*Patterson Rosa, dom, h 16 Bay
Patterson S Delano, wid Augustus C, h Asheville av, W Ashev
Patterson Sherman (Marguerite), foreman, h 5 Aston Park
Patterson Silas L (Mary J), lab, h 27 Aston pl
PATTERSON WM R (J R Patterson & Son), bds 28 College Park
Patterson W E & Co (W E and N R Patterson), furniture 57 n Main
PATTERSON WM R (J R Patterson & Son), bds 28 College Park

Asheville Power and Light Co. LIGHT and POWER PHONE 69

Poultry **Kiibler & Whitehead** CITY MARKET PHONES, 195 and 694

Asheville Dray, Fuel & Construction Co.
6 1-2 South Main

COAL

Wood and Kindling
Stone and Sand
PHONE - 223

Patterson Williard E (Nellie), (W E Patterson & Co), h 93 Merrimon av
PATTON BURGIN A (Lillie), (Shope & Patton), and County tax collr, h 23 Clayton
Patton Chas (Ida), painter, h 71 Livingston
Patton Clarence R, driver, h 23 Clayton
Patton Erwin W (Ellen A), (Patton & Stikeleather), and chmn County Board of Comrs, h Swannanoa Drive
Patton Etta Miss, h (r) 40 Maiden la
Patton Henry, collr clk Amer Natl Bank
Patton Hotel, 20 Patton av, W E Garrett propr
Patton J Erwin, clk Patton & Stikeleather, h Swannanoa Drive
Patton J Eugene, student, h 23 Clayton
Patton J Gaston (Ella), stone mason, h 240 College
Patton Jacob C (Gertrude E), prin Patton School, h 271 Haywood
*Patton Jas, porter, h S Asheville
Patton Jas (Ella), stone mason, h 27 Brick
Patton Jas P (Rebecca), armorer, h end of s McDowell
Patton Jean F Miss, h 39 Furman av
Patton Jno P (L Addie), driver, h 15 Hall
Patton Kinsey, barber, bds 434 Depot
Patton Mance C (Mary), lab, h 4 Richard
Patton Martha B, wid Thos W, h 95 Charlotte
*Patton Nora, laund, h 112 Church
Patton Pinkney, stone mason, h 27 Brick
*Patton Robt (Susan), driver Armour & Co, h (r) 58 Poplar
Patton Robt W (Georgia), trav slsmn, h 181 Charlotte
*Patton Saml (Daisy), driver C Sawyer, h S Asheville
Patton School for Boys, 271 Haywood, Jacob C Patton prin
Patton T Ernest (Bennie Mae), clk C Sawyer, h 109 Asheland av
Patton Tennie Mrs, wkr Ashev Mica Co, h 23 s Lexington
Patton Vina Mrs, h 27 Brick
*Patton Vinie, laundress, h 50 Smith
Patton Wm, collr, rms 12 n Pack Sq (3d fl)
Patton Wm H (Verna), (McDowell & Patton), h Bingham rd
Patton Wm K, barber Swannanoa-Berkeley Barber Shop, bds 11 Gaston
Patton & Stikeleather (E W Patton, J G Stikeleather), livery, 151-155 Patton av
Patty Jno H (Mary L), shoemkr 14 e College, rms 25 Willow

EVER READY FLASHLIGHTS
Piedmont Electric Company
ASHEVILLE, N. C.
64 PATTON AVENUE

J. C. McPHERSON
SLATE AND TIN ROOFING
Galvanized Iron Work   Hot Air Furnaces
35-37 EAST COLLEGE STREET

PLUMBING
STEAM
AND HOT WATER
HEATING
PHONE 133

Paul Alvin A (Frances E), pub stengr, bds Cherokee Inn
Paul Conrad C (Mary E), baker College Street Bakery, h 40 Hiawassee
Paulding Alfred F (Elizabeth R), mngr, h 59 Woodfin
Paxton Ernest Mrs, stengr Imp Mut L & H Ins Co
Payne Albert R (Lucy), collr Donald & Donald, h (r) 58 Pearson Drive
*Payne Annie, cook, h 14 Ingle
Payne Annie C Miss, h 4 Maple
Payne Collie L (Ethel), trav slsmn, h 215 s French Broad
Payne Harry C, flgmn, h 287 s French Broad av
Payne Jas H (Gertrude), condr Sou Ry, bds Cherokee Inn
*Payne Jno, cook H P Pearson, h 17 Pine
*Payne Mary, laund, h 48 Black
Payne Thrule T (Margaret), lab, h 39 Pearson Drive
*Payne Wm (Addie), lab, h S Asheville
*Payne Wm (Eldora), emp D B Lipe, h nr Shiloh Church
Payne Wm R (Mary), h 89 Grove
☞ Payne see also Paine
Peacock Henry F (Maude), mail clk, h 331 s French Broad
Pearce Bertha H Miss, boarding 46 n French Broad av, h same
Pearlman Barney (Hettie), gro 47 Hill, h same
*Pearson Abraham (Myra), lab, h Dewey nr Jordan
*Pearson Bettie, laund, h 117 Poplar
*Pearson Clementina, cook Mrs A T Connally, h same
*Pearson Edwd W (Clementine), genl organizer Royal Benefit Society of Washington D C, h 46 Short
Pearson Esther S Miss, h 67 Cumberland
*Pearson Henry P (Lula), eating hse 6 Eagle, h 64 Ridge
Pearson J Thos, h Richmond Hill
*Pearson Jno F (Emma), hd bellmn Battery Park Hotel, h 2 Ridge
*Pearson Malissa, h 5 s Grove
Pearson Marjorie H Miss, h Richmond Hill
*Pearson Moore (Lillie), lab, h 110 Madison
Pearson Richmond Hon (Gabrille), h Richmond Hill
Pearson Wm H Maj (Marietta A), h 67 Cumberland av
Pearson Wm L (Alice), woodwkr C L Brown, h 372 n Main
☞ Pearson see also Pierson
Pease Ann E, wid Louis M, chmn Allen Idus Home Committee, h Livingston nr Oliver
PEASE MEMORIAL HOUSE (Presbyterian School Compus), Biltmore rd, Victoria—phone 482, Miss Florence Stephenson prin

Club Cafe and Candy Kitchen
"A GOOD PLACE FOR REFRESHMENT"

The standards we work to in our Restaurant Department are: Cooking, perfect; Service, prompt and cheerful; Prices, moderate; Menu, everything in season. Parties and Banquets, Teas and Dinners. 19 and 21 Haywood St. Phones 110 and 111.

Brown's Undertaking Parlors

S. H. BROWN

50 Patton Avenue
ASHEVILLE, N. C.

Lady Assistant When Desired

Phone 193-2 Rings

THE MOORE Plumbing Company

16 N. Pack Square

PHONE 1025

Sanitary Plumbing, General Tin and Metal Work, Hot Air Furnaces

---

294 ASHEVILLE [1913] DIRECTORY

*Peck Simon, lab, h 25 Lyman
Peebles Atley L (Bessie), slsmn, h 160 s Main
Peebles Ernest A (May), condr Sou Ry, h 55 Bartlett
Peebles Floyd (Julia), slsmn Ashev Carpet House, h 10 Central av
Peebles Geo W (Rachel), slsmn Globe Furn Co, h 242 College
Peebles W Alex (Fuchsia), compositor Hackney & Moale Co, h 183 Asheland av
Peek Jane Miss, h Hazel Mill rd, W Asheville
PEERLESS-FASHION STORES CO (Inc), 51 Patton av—phone 336, operating Peoples Department Store 40-42 Patton av—phone 855; P H Thrash pres, Julius Lowenbein sec, Adolf Kohn treas
Pegas Jno D, cook D D Psychas, rms 36½ s Main
*Pegram Ritta, h 20 Ridge
Pegram Wm P, slsmn T S Morrison & Co, h Emma N C
*Pegram Wm T (Annie), butler, h 20 Ridge
Pegram Mary Miss, h 199 College
Pelham Chas P, poultry, W Asheville (R F D 3), h same
Pelham Saml D (Mary S), sec and mngr Depot Drug Co, h W Asheville
Peloubet Francis W (Rowena), piano tuner Dunham Music House, h Beaver Dam
Pelton Herbert W (Sarah B), photog 527-528 Legal Bldg, h 288 Charlotte
Pelzer Frank (Mattie), h "Rosebank Cottage", Albemarle Park
*Pendleton Alfred (Hattie), lab, h 45 Catholic av
Pendleton Fanny Miss, cook, rms 282 Patton av
*Pendleton Otis, driver, h 45 Catholic av
*Pendleton Sallie, laund, h 45 Catholic av
Pendleton Wert, brkmn, bds 308 Depot
Penland A Manly (Ruth), lab, h 23 Madison
Penland Annie L Miss, h Brevard rd, W Asheville
Penland Bertha Mrs, h Brevard rd, W Asheville
Penland Bromel, lab, h Haywood rd, W Asheville
Penland Bros (David A and Herbert E), blksmiths, Haywood rd, W Asheville
Penland Brownlow, driver Carolina C & I Co, h 30 Fagg
Penland Chas N (Bertha), meat ctr V V Haynie, h 292 n Main
Penland David A (Penland Bros), h Emma N C
Penland David E, bkkpr R B Johnston Estate, h 104 Asheland

The Battery Park Bank Capital - - $100,000.00
Surplus and Profits, $110,000.00
ASHEVILLE, N. C. **City, County and State Depositary**

J. A. TILLMAN — I carry a nice line of Watches, Clocks and Jewelry, and make a specialty of repair work. Satisfaction guaranteed. **Jeweler** **17 N. Main St.**

*Penland Dona, laund, h 40 Maiden la
Penland E Jane Miss, h 39 n Ann
Penland E M, clk, bds 76 Starnes av
Penland Elbert, clk Haywood Street Mkt, rms A F D
Penland Elizabeth, wid Wm, h 104 Asheland av
Penland Elmer, h Haywood rd, W Asheville
Penland Elwin M, clk T G Baird, h 29 Flint
Penland Emery, driver, h 30 Fagg
Penland G Christopher (Josephine), carp, h 30 Fagg
Penland Gage H, slsmn Smathers Wholesale Produce Co, 39 n Ann
Penland Gay H, chauffeur, bds 39 n Ann
Penland Gertrude Miss, emp Sou Mica Co, h W Asheville
Penland Herbert E (Penland Bros), h Emma N C
*Penland Hettie, laund, h 40 Maiden la
PENLAND J CLING (J D Penland & Son), h W Asheville
PENLAND J D & SON (J D and J C Penland), real estate, 11 Temple Court—phone 1183
Penland J Porter, clk Mrs Lynch & Son, h 30 Fagg
Penland Jas A (Addie), propr Globe Market, h 48 Walnut
*Penland Jenkins (Mattie), driver, h 135 Clingman av
PENLAND JESSE D (J D Penland & Son), h Brevard rd, W Asheville
*Penland Jno (Della), driver, h 22 Smith
Penland Jno (Mollie), public rd overseer, h Haywood rd, W Asheville
Penland Jno D (Susan), stone contr, h Pennsylvania av, W Asheville
PENLAND LEONARD G (Mattie C), mngr S H Kress & Co, h 158 Charlotte
Penland Luther J (Hattie L), car repr, h W Asheville
Penland Margaret J Miss, h 30 Fagg
Penland Marvin A (Maude), driver, h 54 Vance
Penland Oran W, driver Sou Exp Co, h Brevard rd, W Asheville
Penland Robt N (Delia), trav slsmn, h 181 Merrimon av
Penland W Crawford, farmer, h Brevard rd, W Asheville
Penland W Henry (Mollie), rms 18 Oak
Penland Weldon (Ida), chauffeur, h 180½ Asheland av
Penland Wm A (Ina), painter, h 51 Fulton
Penland Wm H, mason, h 6 Victoria av
Penland Wren C (Eliabeth), carp, h Jarrett av, W Ashev
Penley Chas (Hattie), drayman, bds 14 s Spruce
Penley J Everett, plmbr, rms 210 College
Penley Luther, lab, bds W G Ford, W Asheville

INSURANCE

Insure Your Salary With Us
Never Carry Your Own Risk
Safety Is The Best Policy
Unless You Are A Capitalist
Rest Easy If You Have
An Accident We Will
Not Keep You Waiting To
Collect Your Claim
Every Claim Promptly Paid

Imperial Mutual Life & Health Insurance Co.

Home Office:
ASHEVILLE, N. C.

Phone 495

HOTEL OXFORD — Redecorated and Refitted throughout. Recently enlarged to 60 rooms. Centrally located Depot cars stop at entrance. Long distance telephone office upstairs. American and European plan. Rates 50c, 75c and $1 per day; special rates by week or month. C. H. Branson & Sons, Proprietors. Phone 1887. 50-54 South Main St. **Asheville, N. C.**

Williams-Brownell Planing Mill Company — *Hardwoods*

Lumber---Rough and Dressed Flooring a Specialty Moulding, Interior Finish, Etc.
Office, Plant and Yards on Southern Railway, Near Biltmore Station
WHITE PINE Phone 729 YELLOW PINE

Penley Wm K (Julia), slsmn
Pennel Geo C, student, h 58 Jefferson Drive
Pennell J Burgin, clk Crystal Cafeterian, h 58 Jefferson Drive
PENNEL J CLINARD, slsmn S A Barbee, h 58 Jefferson Drive
Pennel Thos L, car inspr, h 58 Jefferson Drive
Pennel W Cloyd, slsmn Whitlock Clothing Co, h 58 Jefferson Drive
Penniman Anna W Miss, h 43 Chunn
Penniman Ellen B Miss, h 43 Chunn
Penniman Lucy Miss, student, h Forest Hill
Penniman Margaret Miss, h 192 Chestnut
Penniman Margaret A, wid W R, board 192 Chestnut, h same
Penniman Susan Miss, h Forest Hill
Penniman W Talbot Mrs, propr Forest Hill, h s Main extd
*Penson Jno (Lyda), lab, h 10 Ingle
PEOPLES DEPARTMENT STORE (Peerless-Fashion Stores Co), 40-42 Patton av—phone 855
*Peoples Undertaking Co, 29 Eagle, Noah Murrough pres
Peoples see also Peebles
Pepsi-Cola Bottling Co (see Haskell's Pepsi-Cola Bottling Co)
Perkins Aaron T (Mattie), fireman, h 17 Park av
Perkins Albert F (Florence), switchman, h Haywood rd, W Asheville
Perkins Fannie M Mrs, propr Fairview Cottage, h same
Perkins Fisher (Florence), switchman, h Sou Ry opp Rees Tannery
Perkinson Bessie M Miss, nurse 87 Woodfin, rms same
Perkinson Nettie J Miss, h 87 Woodfin
Perkinson Seth J, paperhngr T J Perkinson, 87 Woodfin
Perkinson Travis J (Emily H), paints and oils, 9 College, h 87 Woodfin
Peroulas Bros (Jno and Geo), propr Central Cafe, 5 s w Pack Sq
Peroulas Geo (Peroulas Bros), rms 2 Barnard Bldg
Peroulas Jno (Peroulas Bros), rms 2 Barnard Bldg
Peroulas Nick, cook Central Cafe, rms Barnard Bldg
*Perrin Alice, cook, h 59 Mountain
*Perrin Walter F (Rachel), barber J W Bowman, h 77 Eagle
Perry Chas R (Annie), ins agt, h 81 Blanton
*Perry Cyrus, driver, h 48 Mountain

Asheville Electrical Company
W. Mansfield Booze, Manager
74 CENTRAL AVE.
HEADQUARTERS
Phone 377

Asheville Dry Cleaning Co.
Telephones 835-836, All Dep't
MAIN, N. E. COR. COLLEGE

THE CLEANERS
Our Department for Oriental Rugs and Carpet Cleaning is prepared to serve you in all its branches.
E. S. Paine   O. E. Hansen

Maple Flooring and Poplar Siding

English Lumber Co.
PHONE . . 321

Perry Emma C Mrs, h 127 Montford av
Perry Jas M, wood turner, bds 346½ Depot
Perry Jno A Capt (Charlotte W,) h 62 Cumberland Circle
Perry Louis E (Lillie B), condr, h 127 Park av
Perry M Elizabeth, wid Claude, h 42 Highland
Perry Nelson R (Annie L), h Biltmore rd
Perry Pauline Miss, student, h 81 Blanton
Perry T Lockwood, h Biltmore rd
*Peters Henry (Lena), lab, h 42 Wallach
Peterson Albert R, appr, h Jarrett av, W Asheville
*Peterson Matthew (Ola), pipe wkr, h 76 Market
Peterson Maude Miss, clk Jno A Guffey, h W Asheville
Peterson Oscar (Selma), tanner, h 22 s French Broad av Asheville
Peterson Wm A (Allie), switchman, h Jarrett av, W Ashev
Peterson Wm R (Ella), shoemkr 39 College, h 33 Eugene av
Petrie Margaret Miss, student, h 77 Starnes av
Petrie Chas H (Eudora), carp, h Lyman nr St Car Line
Petrie Hugh P (Elizabeth), tailor 8 n Pack Sq (2d fl), h 77 Starnes av
Petteway G A, treas Blue Blue Ridge Development Co, h Tampa Fla
Pettit Laura, wid H B, h 391 w Haywood
*Petty Ernest (Kate), cook, h 43 Circle
*Petty Forest (Eular), h 55 Circle
*Pharr Isaac, lab, h 109 s Beaumont
☞ **Pharr see also Farr**
*Phelps Leana, dom, h Edgemont
*Phifer Cinda, cook North State Fitting School, rms same
*Phifer Lela, cook 49 Zillicoa
*Phifer Lillian, cook, h 233 Flint
*Phifer Wm, lab 49 Zillicoa
Phillips Brewster (Alice E), clk Biltmore Estate, h 147 Chestnut
Phillips Cornelia E, wid Damon, h 20 Spring
Phillips Dora B Mrs, boarding 29 Jefferson Drive, h same
Phillips Hettie Miss, h 20 Spring
*Phillips Isaac Z (Mary E), h (r) 27 Clingman av
*Phillips Jno H (Anna), h 28 Short McDowell
Phillips Mary Miss, h 20 Spring
Phillips Oscar, wood wkr, bds 470 w Haywood
Phillips Saml H (Dora B), air inspr, h 29 Jefferson Drive Sou Ry
*Phillips Wm (Ada), flgmn, h 28 Beach Hill

BIGGEST
BUSIEST
BEST

Asheville Steam Laundry

Phones:
1936 and 1937

43 to 47
W. College Street

CHARLES H. HONESS
OPTOMETRIST
AND
OPTICIAN

Exclusive maker of
ATLAS SHUR-ON
EYE GLASSES

THE
Home of Ce-Rite
Toric Lenses

We make a specialty of correcting optical defects with properly fitted glasses.

54 Patton Avenue
Opposite Postoffice

IF in the market for a Gas Engine let us make you prices.
its heavy castings, such as columns or building plates, see us.
its a skilled mechanic for boiler work, see us.
you want machine work of any kind phone 590.

CAROLINA MACHINERY CO.

FOUNDERS
MACHINISTS and
Jobbers of Mill
Supplies

Life Insurance Company of Virginia
ORGANIZED 1871
Home Office - Richmond, Va.

Has won the hearty approval and active support of the people by its promptness and fair dealing during the FORTY-TWO YEARS of its operation

J. V. Moon, Superintendent, Rooms 3-4-5 Maxwelton Bldg., Asheville, N. C.

T. P. JOHNSON & CO.

SHEET METAL WORKERS

All Kinds of Roofing Guttering and Conductor Work Metal Ceilings, Skylights and Galvanized Iron Cornices

OFFICE and SHOP:
69-71 S. MAIN

Phone 325

DR. C. H. MILLER

Mechano-Therapist

14 N. Spruce Street
ASHEVILLE, N. C.

PHONE 979

Hours by Engagement

DRUGLESS HEALING OF DISEASE

---

*Phinney Andrew (Julia), drayman, h 53 Hill
Phinney E G, h "Battle Bunglow", Beaumont Ridge
*Phinney Elmore (Nancy), lab, h 109 n Lexington av
Phipps Jno W (Effie J), eating house and furn rms, 18 n Lexington av, h same
Phipps Thos R, farmer, h W Asheville
Phoenix Hotel, 24 w College, L Blomberg propr
Pickelsimer J B, clk Carmichael's Pharmacy
Pickens Clarence W (Nannie), dentist, h 65 Starnes av
Pickens Janie Miss, bds 70 Seney
*Pickens Jno (Lucinda), farmer, h Haywood rd, W Ashev
*Pickens Leola, cook, h 22 Campbell
*Pickens Maria, h 48 Ralph
Pickens Mary C Mrs, tchr Newton Academy Schl
PIEDMONT DIRECTORY CO (Inc), publishers and owners the following city directories; Anderson S C, Albany Ga, Alexandria La, Asheville N C, Ashland-Catlettsburg Ky, Athens Ga, Bowling Green Ky, Biloxi Miss, Burlington, Haw River and Graham N C, Charlotte N C, Chester S C, Clarksville Tenn, Cleveland Tenn, Columbus Miss, Concord N C, Dalton Ga, Danville Va, Florence S C, Fredericksburg Va, Gastonia N C, Greenville S C, Greenwood S C, Gulfport Miss, Hickory N C, Hattriesburg Miss, Henderson-Oxford N C, High Point N C, Huntsville Ala, Jackson Tenn, Johnson City Tenn, Knoxville Tenn, Laurens-Clifton S C, Monroe La, Morristown Tenn, Natchez Miss, New Iberia La, Newberry S C, Rome Ga, Rock Hill and Yorkville S C, Salisbury N C, Spartanburg S C, Statesville N C, Suffolk Va, Union S C, Washington N C, Winchester Ky, Waynesville N C, Winchester Va, Winston-Salem N C: Ernest H Miller pres and mngr, Philip R Moale v-pres, A E Swayne sec-treas, office 66 & L Amer Nat'l Bank Bldg
PIEDMONT ELECTRIC CO (The), electrical supplies and contractors, 64 Patton av—phone 478, Wm Farr pres-mngr (see side lines)
*Piedmont Shoe Co, 26 Eagle, P L Hendricks pres, J G Moore mngr
*Piercey Abraham (Myra), lab, h 12 Madison
Piercy W Hicks (Mary J), carp, h 16 Starnes Pl
Pigeon River Ry Co, 200-202 Oates Bldg, J C Arbogast mngr
Pike J Baxter (Daisy,) h Bingham Hghts
Pike Sarah, wid Marion, h Bingham Hghts

ASHEVILLE CLEANING and PRESSING CLUB

TAILORING THAT SATISFIES and PRICES THAT PLEASE
Hats cleaned, banded and bound. Silk hats ironed. Buttons made to order in all sizes. Plain or with rims. **PHONE 389**

DYEING IN ALL SHADES Cleaned. Messenger Service.

Kid Gloves, Slippers and Plumes, Fancy Jabots and Ties, French Dry Cleaned. Ladies' and Gentlemen's suits Steam **J. C. Wilbar, Prop.**

4 NORTH PACK SQ

Pilalas Geo (Chakales & Pilalas), rms 5 s Main
Pines (The), boarding, 112 Pearson Drive
Pinkerton J Wannie, carp, bds 323½ s Main
Pinkerton Luther (Cora), emp J H Greenwood, h W Chapel rd, Biltmore
Pinkins July J, lab, h 64 Madison av
*Pinkins Presy (Maria), lab, h (r) 7 Depot
*Pinkston Jack, driver Ashev Gro Co, h Black st
Pinner Carroll A, clk, bds 89 Clingman av
Pinner Chas L (Nola), gas ftr, h 22 Asheland av
Pinner Geo W (Alice S), stone lyr, h Haywood rd, W Asheville
Pinner Jno D (Susan), stone contr, h W Asheville
Pinner J Robt, motorman, bds 22 Asheland av
Pinner Jos (Texanna), carp, h W Asheville
Pinner Martha C Miss, h Haywood rd, W Asheville
Piper Jennie Mrs, furnished rooms, 15 Woodfin, h same
Piper Jennie M Miss, nurse 15 Woodfin, h same
Piper Minnie L Miss, h 15 Woodfin
Piper Wesley (Jennie), engnr, h 15 Woodfin
Pirson Jacob G (Marie), mngr Union News Co, h 198 Bartlett
Pitman Stokes, hostler J H Wilson, h 69 Penland
Pittilla Kate, wid Robt A, asst matron Home Industrial School, h same
Pittillo Robt L (Ilah), meat ctr, h Swannanoa av, W Ashev
Pittillo W Lott (Ernestine), emp Tannery, h 28 Silver
Pittillo Wm L (Emeline M), tanner, h 470 w Haywood
Pitts Lee, mchst, bds 49 n Main
Pitts N Florence Miss, supt Meriwether Hosp, rms same
Pitts Wm W (Sallie), engnr Sou Ry, h 76 Park av
Pittsburg Life & Trust Co of Pa, 1 Electrical Bldg, Walter Toms Wray genl agt
Plemmons A Elbery (Maude E), driver, h Hazel Mill rd, W Asheville
Plemmons Caney (Rosanna), lab, h nr Smiths Bridge, W Asheville
Plemmons Chas C (Lulu F), rock mason, nr Smiths Bridge, W Asheville (R F D 3)
Plemmons Elberry, driver Rogers Gro Co, h W Asheville
Plemmons J Miles (Amanda), carp, h 38 Turner
Plemmons J Raymond (Verdie,) chauffeur, h 10 s Spruce
Plemmons June E, engnr Ashev L & P Co, h Hominy N C
Plemmons Lee (Margaret), quarrier, h Haywood rd, W Asheville

WEAVERVILLE LINE NINE MILES BY TROLLEY FROM PACK SQUARE TO WEAVERVILLE

ASHEVILLE AND EAST TENNESSEE RAILROAD CO.

7 NORTH MAIN STREET   ASHEVILLE N. C.

ELECTRIC FIXTURES

Piedmont Electric Co.

64 PATTON AVE.
ASHEVILLE, N.C.

300   ASHEVILLE [1913] DIRECTORY

Plemmons Neil S, auto mchst, h 16 s Spruce
Plemmons Rena Miss, h Haywood rd, W Asheville
Plemmons Robt L (Martha), boarding 16 s Spruce
Plemmons Wm B (Daisy), condr St Ry, h 18 Hamilton
Plemmons Zeb, h Haywood rd, W Asheville
Plemmons Zeb, emp Brown & Smith, h W Asheville
Pless Jno W, barber, bds 226 Asheland av
PLUMMER HARRY W, v-pres and genl mngr Asheville Power & Light Co, h 128 Flint
Poindexter Frank W (Irene), engnr Sou Ry, h 176 Park av
POLICE HEADQUARTERS, City Hall—phone 45, D K Lyerly chf
*Pollard Effie, cook, rms 442 s French Broad av
Pollock Benj, mngr Globe Sample Co, h 70 e College
Pollock Louis H, propr Globe Sample Co, h 70 e College
*Ponder Columbus (Belle), lab, h 8 Lincoln av
*Ponder Ella, dom, h 33 Wallach
Ponder Elva A (Addie), carp, h Biltmore rd, S Biltmore
*Ponder Geo (Mary), lab, h 41 Catholic av
*Ponder Jas, steward, h 33 Wallach
*Ponder Jas, bellmn Battery Park Hotel, h 2 Ridge
Pons Frank (Clementine), mngr Crystal Dairy Lunch, h 16 Buncombe
POOL O R SINGLETON (Nora), sec Ashev Paint & Glass Co, h 83 Josephine
Poole Bros (W G and G R Poole), cleaners and dyers, 43 w College and Woolsey
Poole Geo R (Lillian) (Poole Bros), h Woolsey (R F D 1)
*Poole Green (Nora), driver, h 11 Short
*Poole Jos (Janie), cook Sou Ry Dining Room, h 92 Black
Poole Lillian Mrs, emp Poole Bros, h Woolsey (R F D 1)
*Poole Lillie, laund, h 5 Brick
Poole Wm G (Wessie) (Poole Bros), h Woolsey (R F D 1)
Poor Geo F (Annie), mchst Ashev P & L Co, h 278 College
*Poor Henry, lab, rms 86 Eagle
Poor Lucy Miss, h 156 Hillside
*Poore Jas H, porter, h 152 Hill
Poore L Ellen Miss, h 293 Asheland av
Poore Wm H, farmer, h 293 Asheland av
Poovey W Edgar Rev (Mabel), pastor N Asheville Methodist Church, h 34 Chestnut
Pope Annie L Miss, clk The London Shop, bds The Henrietta
Pope W Allis, bkkpr Wachovia Bank & Trust Co, bds 94 College

CONTRACTOR and BUILDER
STEEL RANGES   **J. C. McPHERSON**   35-37 E COLLEGE ST.
                                            PHONE 133
PLUMBING STEAM AND HOT WATER HEATING

Porcher Wm B, adv solr Ashev Gazette-News, bds 112 Haywood
Porter Adelaide M Miss, student, h Biltmore rd, S Biltmore
Porter Anne W, wid H W, h 85 Merrimon av
*Porter Arthur C (Florence), bellman, h 25 Mountain
*Porter Caroline, dom, h 15 New
Porter Elizabeth Miss, music tchr, h 29 Adams
Porter J Alex (Carrie), real est, h Biltmore rd, S Biltmore
Porter Jesse B, trav slsmn, h 29 Adams
Porter Jno, carp, bds Hotel Warren
Porter O E Mrs, mlnr Sproat's, h 268 Chestnut
*Porter Peter (Frances), lab, h 47 West
Porter Robt R (Jennie), trav slsmn, h 29 Adams
Porter Roscoe F (Blanche), trav slsmn, h 36 Panola
*Porter Vina, laund, h 5 Sassafras
Portner Bessie Miss, h 86 Asheland av
Posey Campbell, student, rms 2 Angle, Biltmore
*Posey Greeva, h 19 Maiden la
Posey Horace G, atty, rms 2 Angle, Biltmore
*Posey Jas (Sallie), h 95 Black
*Posey Jas Jr (Florence), lab, h 95 Black
Posey Jas H, rms 15 Library Bldg
*Posey Mary, cook, h 27 Maiden la
Posey Robt E, student, rms 2 Angle, Biltmore
*Posey Wm (Lillie), lab, h 20 Oakdale av
POST OFFICE, Patton av cor Haywood, W W Rollins postmaster
Post Office, Biltmore, B J Luther postmaster
POST WM F (Anna), supt Carolina Machinery Co Inc, h 172 s French Broad av
POSTAL TELEGRAPH-CABLE CO, Haywood, Battery Park Hotel and Glen Rock Hotel, A K Akers mngr
*Postell Maude, h 13 Short Valley
☞ Potillo see Pittillo
*Poston Irene, cook, h 306 Asheland av
*Poston Lee (Sue), fireman, h 306 Asheland av
Potteat Benj F, clk frt office Sou Ry, h 346 Depot
Potter Ernestine Miss, tchr Normal & Collegiate Inst
Potts Arthur, auto repr Hollar Motor Co, h 390 Southside av
*Potts Chas, lab, h Haywood rd, W Asheville
*Potts Jas P, lab, h Haywood rd, W Asheville
Potts Jane Miss, boarding 390 Southside av, h same
Potts M L Mrs, h 37 Summit, S Biltmore
Potts Meta Miss, smstrs, bds 39 Clingman av

Club Cafe and Candy Kitchen
"A GOOD PLACE FOR REFRESHMENT"

Our Ice Cream manufacturing plant is absolutely clean and sanitary.
Prompt family delivery. Phones 110 and 111.
Catering for large parties and receptions. Special Creams.

Brown's Undertaking Parlors

S. H. BROWN

Lady Assistant When Desired

Phone 193-2 Rings

50 Patton Avenue
Asheville, N. C.

Established 1894

B. J. JACKSON

Carefully Selected Fruits and Vegetables

Stall No. 11, City Market

BUSINESS PHONES:
86 and 101

RESIDENCE PHONE
1596

Potts Rufus P (Lillian L), real estate, h Haywood rd, W Asheville
*Potts Wm C, lab, h Haywood rd, W Asheville
*Powell Allen (Ella), florist, h 31 McDowell
Powell Edwd B (Lizzie), produce, h 25 Asheland av
Powell Geo S (Alice), real estate, 2 Electrical Bldg, pres Carolina Vehicle Co, v-pres N C Power Co, sec Investors Land Co and treas Greater Western N C Assn, h Watauga Hill
Powell H Frank (Fannie), carp, h 12 s Ann
Powell Jno B (Daisy), watch mkr W H Shoffner, h 12 s Ann
Powell Jno H (Mary P), naval stores, h 188 Cumberland av
Powell Jos (Mary L), mngr drug dept P W Lowe & Son, h 94 Cherry
Powell Jos M (Laura), blksmith Amer Wagon Co, h 45 Seney
Powell Lizzie Mrs, boarding 25 Asheland av, h same
Powell McKinley, messgr W U Tel Co, h 45 Seney
Powell-Murray Land Co, 2 Electrical Bldg, G S Powell sec-mngr
Powell Ray V, actor, h 94 Cherry
Powell Viola E Miss, laund, h 45 Seney
POWELL W V (Drs Purefoy & Powell), h 236 Charlotte
Powell Walter A, driver, h 45 Seney
Powers C E, clk Yates & McGuire
*Powers Carl (Mollie), lab, h S Asheville
Powers F Gertrude Miss, h 131 Blanton
Powers Fleming W Miss, h 131 Blanton
Powers Jennie M, wid Joel, h 131 Blanton
Powers May A Mrs, h 36 Baird
Pratt M A Miss, tchr Orange St Schl
Praytor Edwd, yd condr Sou Ry, h 4 Swan, Biltmore
Praytor Laura Miss, public stengr 225 Legal Bldg, h W Asheville
Prescott Jas F (Annie), mldr, h 36 Philip
Presley Daniel (Dora), driver, h Biltmore Park
Presley Ervin F (Ethel), clk Biltmore Supply Co, h 4 Biltmore rd, S Biltmore
Presley Frank, lab, h 36 Short Roberts
Presley Jackson L (Hattie), engnr, h 41 Clyde
Presley Jas E (Mary), condr, h 44 Clyde
Presley Jas M (C May), shoe mkr 19 Paragon Bldg, h 15 Clingman av
Presley Jessie Miss, h 36 Short Roberts

Furniture and China Carefully Prepared for Shipment

Mahogany Furniture Hand Made & Carefully Reproduced **E. E. GALER** 114 PATTON AVE. Upholstering and Refinishing PHONE - 1674

ROUGH AND DRESSED LUMBER
WHITE PINE AND YELLOW PINE
FLOORING A SPECIALTY
Hardwoods

Williams-Brownell Planing Mill Company
Mouldings and Interior Finish
Office: Southern Railway Tracks, Near Biltmore Station
Phone 729   **Planing Mill**

Presley Martha E Miss, h 36 Short Roberts
Presley Melvin C, clk Biltmore Supply Co, h 4 Biltmore rd, S Biltmore
Presley Melvin H (Ella), gro 238 Southside av, h 240 same
Presley Nellie A Mrs stengr, h 211 Asheland av
Presley Robt, lab, bds 135 n Main
Presley Thos C (Bessie), gro Haywood rd, W Ashev (R F D 3), h same
Presley Wm H (Lillie), lab, h 80 Seney
Preston Saml S, trav slsmn, rms 54 Asheland av
Pretlow Chas F Mrs, h 111 Central av
Prett Jno S (Cerline), lab, h Lester rd, W Ashev
Price A L (Mamie), silk buyer Bon Marche, h 4 All Souls Crescent, Biltmore
Price Burt L (Josephine), vet surgeon, h 22 Montford av
Price Effie Miss, dom, h Hotel Warren
Price Ethel Miss, rms 18 n Lexington av
Price Hattie Miss, nurse 2 Lyman, h same
Price Jas R (Jane), blksmith Amer Wagon Co, h 2 Lyman
Price Josephine Mrs, dressmkr 22 Montford av, h same
Price Twitty, news boy, h 2 Lyman
*Price Walter, hostler, h 32 Davidson
*Priestly Lottie, h 26 Sorrell
*Priestly Minnie, dom, h Clayton Hill
*Prince Mary, cook, h 73 Ridge
Princess Theatre, 9 n w Pack Sq. Carolina Amusement & Inv Co, mngrs and proprs
Pritchard Mrs, nurse, 14 Grove, rms same
PRITCHARD ARTHUR T (Robin K), physician, rms 9-11 Drhumor Bldg, office hours 11 a m to 12 m and 3 to 4 p m—phone 506, h 31 Bearden av—phone 744
PRITCHARD JETER C HON (Lillian), judge U S Circuit Court, office Government Bldg—phone 287, h 223 Chestnut—phone 903
Pritchard McKinley, student, h 223 Chestnut
*Pritchett Albert (Mary), lab, h 111 n Main
Pritchett Savannah, wid Paul N, h 8 Redmon al
*Procter Aden K (Lottie), horseshoer Amer Wagon Co, h 15 Sorrell
*Proctor Elias (Annie), lab, h 26 Sorrell
*Proctor Jno (Laura), janitor, h 79 Roberts
Proctor P Levi, mill hd, h 64 Park Sq
Proffitt Ada L Miss, h 25 Orchard
Proffitt Howard B (Sallie C), bkkpr Ottis Green Hdw Co, h 25 Orchard

HUGHES

Transfer
and
Livery
Co.

Automobiles
for
HIRE

TRUNKS
25c

Office:
401 Southside Avenue
PHONE   1405

Try our Hand Laundering. We strive to please in LAUNDERING and DRY CLEANING.

The Sanitary Home Laundry   **No. 7 MONTFORD AVE.**
PHONE - 1354

Mrs. Wilder's SANITARY HOME LAUNDRY turns out first class work in Laundering and Dry Cleaning. No. 7 Montford Ave., Phone 1354

*Propes Laura, cook, h 18 Latta
Propst Edwd L (Mary), driver B W Warren, h 17½ n Main
Propst Robt W (M Lucile), ticket clk, Biltmore Station
*Provident Baptist Church, 109 Black, Rev J A Berry pastor
Prudential Insurance Co of America, The, 68 Patton av, Hodges, Mitchell & Reynolds mngrs
Pruett Clarence W (Ida), lab, h 23 Logan
Pruitt Arnold, helper Ashev Pkg Co, h W Asheville
*Pruitt Monroe (Lila), fireman, h 310 Asheland av
Pryor W Cecil (Lois), asst supt Williams Brownell Planing Mill Co, h 54 Gaston
*Prysoe Major (Ora), nurse, h 92 Curve
Psychas Demos D, eating house 36 s Main, rms 36½ s Main
Psychoghio Perikles D, cook D D Psychas, rms 36½ s Main
Public Service & Motor Co, 8-10 e College, F N Chalens propr
Puckett Wm L (Elizabeth), flgmn, h 20 Nelson av
Pugh Bert L (Minnie), fireman Sou Ry, h 7 Buxton
Pugh Chas S (Louzena), cigar mnfr 35 w Walnut, h 73 Hillside
Pugh Louis H (Mary), tel opr, h 138 s French Broad av
*Pullen Clarence (Essie), waiter, h 20 McDowell
Pulliam Amelia Miss, nurse 264 Haywood, h same
Pulliam Mary W Miss, h 264 Haywood
Pullman Co, agents office, Sou Ry Passngr Sta, J R Shearin agt
Purcell Bertha Miss, nurse Winyah Sanatorium
Purcell Eugene P, pharmacist Smith's Drug Store, rms Y M C A
Purcell Lucy Miss, h 36 n French Broad av
PUREFOY GEO W (Lizzie W), (Drs Purefoy & Powell), h 27 Charlotte—phone 94
Purefoy Heslope Miss, artist, h 27 Charlotte
Purefoy Jack, student, h 27 Charlotte
Purefoy Lucy Miss, student, h 27 Charlotte
PUREFOY & POWELL DRS (G W Purefoy, W V Powell), physicians, 325 Legal Bldg—phone 160
Purnell E S Mrs, stengr Amer Natl Bank
Pursley Edwd S (Mattie), glazier W H Westall & Co, h 69 Madison av
Putnam Van S (Kate), mchst Sky Cycle Co, h W Asheville

BUICK — OLDSMOBILE
ARBOGAST MOTOR COMPANY
ACCESSORIES AND SUPPLIES
52-60 N. Main Phones 302 and 1728
MAXWELLS — DETROIT ELECTRIC

Asheville Dry Cleaning Co.
Telephones 835-836, All Dep't
MAIN, N. E. COR. COLLEGE

THE CLEANERS
Our Department for Oriental Rugs and Carpet Cleaning is prepared to serve you in all its branches.
E. S. Paine   O. E. Hansen

For Kindling "What am Kindling" Call
ENGLISH LUMBER COMPANY Phone 321

Q

Queen Elizabeth, mad, h 18 Eagle Terrace
Quinton Jno R (Annie), plumber, h 26 Spring

R

Rabun Wiley T (Lucille C), mldr, h 57 John
Race Martha E Miss, bkkpr Coleman, Robinson & Co, bds 24 n Spruce
Racket Store (The), dry goods, 16 s Main, A Blomberg propr
Radeker Carrie E Miss, h "Sunnycrest," Vernon Hill
Radeker Evelyn H Mrs, h "Sunnycrest," Vernon Hill
Radeker Ruth Miss, h "Sunnycrest," Vernon Hill
Radeker W Scott, atty at law, h "Sunnycrest," Vernon Hill
Radford Henry (Fannie), mill wkr, h 21 Factory Hill
Radford Loran, mill wkr, bds 470 w Haywood
Radford Lula Miss, weaver, h 498 w Haywood
Radford Lulu Miss, weaver, h nr Smith's Bridge, W Ashev
Radford Saml W, with Southern Coal Co, and atty, rms 24 Meriwether Bldg
*Ragsdale Nola, dom, h S Asheville
*Ragsville Benj, h S Asheville
*Ragsville Ella, laund, h S Asheville
*Ragsville Lillian, laund, h S Asheville
*Ragsville Mahala, h 181 Beaumont
*Ragsville Nathaniel, lab, h S Asheville
*Railroad Men's Pressing Club, (r) 426 Depot, Clarence Brown propr
Ralston Carrie M Miss, bkkpr Donnahoe & Bledsoe, h Grace
Ralston Chas P, clk A Michalove, h Beaver Dam
Ralston Jos, emp Poole Bros, h Grace
"Ramoth Place," board, Woolsey, Mrs A C Ray propr
Ramsay Elizabeth H Miss, h 144 Cumberland av
Ramsay Jas F (Alice M), dentist 41-42 Amer Natl Bank Bldg, h 144 Cumberland av
☞ **Ramsay see also Ramsey**
*Ramseur Gertrude, dom, h Woolsey (R F D 1)
*Ramseur Jno (Minnie), porter Sou Ry, h S Asheville
*Ramseur Lewis, lab, h 54 Short
Ramsey Cyrus H, clk Sou Ry, h 141 Woodfin
Ramsey D Hiden, student, h 141 Woodfin
Ramsey D Hurt, clk Supt Sou Ry, h 141 Woodfin

BIGGEST BUSIEST BEST

Phones 1936 and 1937
ASHEVILLE STEAM LAUNDRY
43 to 47 W. COLLEGE

S. D. HALL
REAL ESTATE AGENT

Money Loaned

Notary Public

32 PATTON AVENUE

Phone 91

Founders, Machinists and Jobbers of Mill Supplies
PHONE 590 — When in the market for pipe and fittings, let us make you Prices.
Carolina Machinery Co.
PHONE 590 — If it's a Gas Engine let us figure with you, also on other kinds of machinery

LIFE INSURANCE COMPANY OF VA. OLDEST, LARGEST STRONGEST Southern Life Insurance Co.

ORGANIZED 1871
RICHMOND, VIRGINIA

Issues Industrial Policies from $8.00 to $900.00, with Premiums Payable WEEKLY on persons from two to seventy years of age

J. V. Moon, Superintendent, Rooms 3-4-5 Maxwelton Bldg., Asheville, N. C.

D. TREXLER TIN SHOP

All Kinds of Roofing, Gutter and Conductor Work.

Phone 862

159 South Main St.

DR. C. H. MILLER

MECHANO-THERAPIST

14 N. Spruce St.
Phone 979
ASHEVILLE, N. C.

Hours by engagement

Drugless Healing of Disease

Ramsey Daniel T (Susan A), mill wkr, h 470 w Haywood
Ramsey Henry, clk Harry Seigle, h 74 Central av
Ramsey Jacob L (Anna M), lab, h 16 View
Ramsey Jas, plmbr The Moore Plumbing Co
Ramsey Jessie L, wid Jno, h 17 n Spruce
*Ramsey Jno (Berna), driver, h (r) 11 Depot
Ramsey Jno W (Ellen L), mngr Globe Furn Co, h 31 Grove
Ramsey Leftwich P, clk Sou Ry, h 141 Woodfin
Ramsey McKinney H, clk, h 141 Woodfin
Ramsey Maxwell L, clk, bds 17 n Spruce
RAMSEY RILEY M, pres Asheville Dray, Fuel & Construction Co (Inc), h 32 s Liberty
Ramsey S Clay (Lucy M), rd mstr, h 141 Woodfin
Randall Alfred, h Chunns Cove
Randall Burton C, h Chunns Cove
Randall Chas R, h Chunns Cove
Randall Clyde C, h 23 Asheland av
Randall David E (Emma), h 3 s Liberty
Randall E Robt (Maggie), janitor P O, h 23 Asheland av
Randall Emma F Miss, h 3 s Liberty
Randall Hannah M Miss, clk, h 3 s Liberty
Randall Jno E (Sue), gro, Grace, h same
Randall Jos, lab, h Grace
Randall Lassie M Miss, bkkpr Bon Marche, h 23 Asheland
*Randall Lawson (Patience), brickylr, h 26 Jordan
Randall Maggie Mrs, propr The Trivola, h 23 Asheland av
Randall Nellie V Miss, student, h 23 Asheland av
Rando Dolph, hackman, bds 47 n Main
Randolph Donald W, asst foreman Grove Park h Edgemont
Randolph Dorothy Miss, h Edgemont
Randolph Eugene J (Anna C), atty at law 32 Patton av, h 36 s French Broad av
Randolph Mabel Miss, h Edgemont
Randolph Philip S, student, h Edgemont
Randolph R Bennett, paymstr Grove Park, h Edgemont
Randolph Virginia Miss, h Edgemont
Randolph Wm F (Eleanor), supt Grove Park, h Edgemont
Rankin Annie Miss, bkkpr Grove Park Inn, h 25 n Liberty
RANKIN ARTHUR E (Nancy), asst cashr Amer Natl Bank, h 25 Orange
RANKIN CLARENCE, asst cashr Battery Park Bank, h 63 Merrimon av
Rankin Eliabeth Miss, h 3 Swan, Biltmore
Rankin Georgia A Miss, h 3 Swan, Biltmore

....Asheville Cleaning and Pressing Club....
Tailoring That Satisfies and Prices That Please

Steam and French Dry Cleaning of all delicate and fine wearing apparel for ladies and gentlemen. MESSENGER SERVICE IN THE CITY.

J. C. WILBAR, Prop.   4. N. Pack Square   **PHONE 389**

RANKIN J EUGENE (Fannie), cashr Battery Park Bank, pres Blue Ridge B & L Assn and mayor of Asheville, h 63 Merrimon av
Rankin M Carrie, wid Alonzo, h 3 Swan, Biltmore
Rankin Minna, Miss, h 3 Swan, Biltmore
Ransom P A, clk Langren Hotel, rms same
Ranson Rosa J Miss, h 39 n French Broad av
RAOUL THOS W (Helen), pres Albemarle Park Co, h "Manzanita Cottage," Albemarle Park
Raper W Carlton (Grace M), rate clk div frt agt Sou Ry, h 55 w Chestnut
Rash Emma Mrs, dom, h 49 Gray
Ratcliff Jas (Laura), blksmith 25 Aston, h Main st, W Ashev
*Ravenel Rosa, cook, h 40 Poplar
Ravenel Saml P (Florence), atty at law, s Pack Sq cor Main h 2 Short, Biltmore
Rawls Annie B Miss, nurse, 57 Cherry, rms same
RAWLS CHAS T (Sarah), (Aston, Rawls & Co), h Woolsey (R F D 1)
Rawls Eric M, civ engnr, h 70 n Liberty
Rawls Reuben R (Alice), h 70 n Liberty
Raxter Emma Miss, h 117 Asheland av
*Ray Amanda, cook 228 Montford av
Ray Archibald F (Grace), condr Sou Ry, h 289 s French Broad av
Ray Avon O (Julia), collr Asheville Dray, Fuel & Construction Co, Inc, h 117 Hillside
Ray Belma L Miss, h 51 College
Ray Berry D, carp W M Jones, h Acton N C
Ray-Campbell Co, real estate and ins, 1 Haywood, J S Hursey mngr
*Ray Chas (Mary), weigher Sou Ry, h (r) 136 Asheland av
Ray Chas S (Callie), driver A F D, h 210 College
Ray Clarence F (Alice M), propr Ray's Studio, 2 n Pack Sq, h R F D 1
Ray Claude M, soda clk C A Raysor, h 51 College
Ray Danl O, watchman Riverside Park Ashev P & L Co, h 55 College
Ray Dock, chauffeur The Star Market, h 418 n Main
RAY EDWIN L, pres Citizens Bank and sec-treas Blue Ridge B & L Assn, h 83 Hillside
*Ray Elijah (Carrie), lab, h 8 Richard
Ray H Ethel Miss, tchr City Schls, h 83 Hillside
Ray Harris B (Mollie L), carrier P O, h 59 Montford av

Asheville Dray, Fuel and Construction Co.

Heavy Hauling of all kinds — WE FURNISH BUILDING STONE — Moving Furniture a Specialty
61-2 South Main — PHONE - 223

DYNAMOS & MOTORS

Piedmont Electric Co.

64 Patton Av.
ASHEVILLE, N.C.

Ray Hilda F Miss, h 51 College
RAY IDA, wid Danl O, propr The Louisiana, 51 College, h same (see p 18)
*Ray Isaac (Laura), carp, h 4 Short Pine
Ray J Hansel (Margaret), h 37 Summit, S Biltmore
Ray Jas M Col (Alice C), custodian Confederate Hall, h "Ramoth pl" (R F D 1)
Ray Jno (Susie), meat ctr Young & Robinson, bds 418 n Main
Ray Jno E R Capt (Mary), h 83 Hillside
Ray Lorena C Miss, nurse 141 Hillside, h same
Ray Robt R, boiler mkr, bds 87 Ora
Ray Robt W (Vestie), carp, h Haywood rd, W Ashev
Ray Saml L, clk P O, rms 25 Meriwether Bldg
Ray Saml W (Mary), sanitary inspr, h 141 Hillside
*Ray Sidney (Bessie), lab, h 10 Richard
Ray's Studio, photographer 2 n Pack Sq, C F Ray propr
Ray Susan Miss, dressmkr, 180 Livingston, h same
Ray Walter (Sallie), farmer, h 97 West
Ray Wayne S, livery 39 s Lexington av, h R F D 1
Ray Wm W (Carrie A), condr Sou Ry, h 287 s French Broad av
Ray see also Rea, Rhea and Wray
Rayfield Eveline, wid W R, h Woolsey (R F D 1)
Rayfield Thos C (Dora), driver, h Woolsey (R F D 1)
RAYMOND GEO H, pres Hans Rees Sons (Inc), h Brooklyn N Y
Raysor Cornelius A (Sara L), druggist 31 Patton av, h 68 Grove
Rea Sarah O, wid Thos S, h Sand Hill rd, W Ashev
Read Taft Mrs, h 192 Chestnut
Read see Reed and Reid
Reagan H Grady, slsmn Sou Land Auction Co, h Weaverville N C
REAGAN J ROY, city editor Ashev Gazette-News, h Weaverville N C
Reagan Jno, lab, bds 434 Depot
Rector Arthur, lab, h W Ashev (R F D 3)
Rector Etta Mrs, clk, bds 23 Asheland av
RECTOR J BAYLIS (Bessie F), mngr The Langren Hotel h same—phone 605
Rector Jas E, atty at law and sec Merchants Assn, 7 Temple Ct, h 25 Asheland av
Rector Jno G (Ollie), barber, h Haywood rd, W Ashev
Rector Julius (Roxie), h W Ashev (R F D 3)

J. C. McPHERSON
SLATE AND TIN ROOFING
Galvanized Iron Work — Hot Air Furnaces
35-37 EAST COLLEGE STREET

PLUMBING STEAM AND HOT WATER **HEATING**
PHONE 133

MAPLE FLOORING
HARDWOOD LUMBER OF ALL KINDS

WOODWARD & SON
9th and Arch Sts., Richmond, Va.
See Adv. Opposite Page 188

Rector Louie S, clk frt office Sou Ry, h W Asheville
Rector Louise B Miss, h 44 Clayton
Rector Margaret, clk The Peerless, h 20 Rector
Rector Robt, lab, h W Asheville
Rector Sallie H Miss, rms 242 Patton av
Rector Saml A (Constance), slsmn Donald & Donald, h 38 Charlotte
Rector Saml L (Annie S), emp frt office Sou Ry, h W Asheville
Rector Thos S (Lutie), h 44 Clayton
Rector Wiley G (Ruth), carp, h 20 Rector
Red Cross Undertaking Co (Inc), 49 College W R Whitson pres, R J Lewis sec-treas-mngr
Redden Jas, brick mkr, h Kenilworth
Redden Jno T (Etta), lab, h Kenilworth
Redden Robt (Blanche), h Kenilworth
Redfern Thos E (Gignellate), engnr Sou Ry, h 76 Park av
Redmon Beulah Miss, h 64 Seney
Redmon Chas, h 64 Seney
Redmon Etta Miss, h 76 Clingman av
Redmon H E, agt Ashev Transfer & Storage Co
Redmon J Seymour (Leona), driver Armour & Co, h 76 Clingman av
*Redmon Maria, h 78 Valley
Redmon Nebraska E, clk J H Young, h 357 n Main
Redmon Saml M (Mamie), gro 60 Seney, h 64 same
Redmon Viola Miss, clk, h 76 Clingman av
Redmond Ewart, checker, h 357 n Main
Redmond Frances B Miss, h 357 n Main
*Redmond Martha, cook, h 73 Gudger
Redmond Minnie L Miss, tchr, h 357 n Main
Redmond Thos B (Frances M), bricklyr, h 357 n Main
Red Shade Brick Co (J W Rutherford, W A Reynolds, J R Goode and J N Jarrett)
Redwine E M Miss, nurse Biltmore Hosp, rms same
Redwood H & Co (Henry, Harry W, and Wm M Redwood and Jno W Neely), dept store 7-9 Patton av
Redwood Harry W (H Redwood & Co), h 90 Cumberland
Redwood Henry (Susan T), (H Redwood & Co), and v-pres Amer Natl Bank, h 90 Cumberland av
Redwood Mary G Miss, h 90 Cumberland av
Redwood Robt L, clk Amer Natl Bank, h 90 Cumberland av
Redwood Wm M (Nina B), (H Redwood & Co), h 52 Cumberland Circle
*Reed Anna, dom, h 36 Madison

What Have You in Real Estate that You Don't Want?
What do You Want in Real Estate that You Haven't?

WESTERN CAROLINA REALTY CO.
J. W. Wolfe, Sec. & Treas.
On the Square
PHONE 974
10 N. PACK Sq.

H. A. BROWN & CO.
General Contractors
23 Temple Court Bldg.
Phone 341

—DEALERS IN—

Rough Building
and
all Kinds of
Crushed Stone

—OUR SPECIALTIES—

STONE
FOUNDATIONS
CONCRETE WORK
and
EXCAVATING

Moale & Chiles Real Estate and Insurance
27 Patton Ave., [2d fl], Phone 661
City and Suburban Property FARMS and TIMBER LANDS

Candy Kitchen and Club Cafe
"A GOOD PLACE FOR REFRESHMENT"

Hot drinks on cold days. Cold drinks on hot days. The best drinks every day. Pure fruits and syrups blended "just right," served daintily. Our Ice Cream and Soda Water Department, Restaurant and Candy Departments are always kept up to the standard of nearest perfection. Phones 110 and 111. 19 and 21 Haywood St.

---

310 ASHEVILLE [1913] DIRECTORY

Brown's Undertaking Parlors

S. H. BROWN

50 Patton Avenue
ASHEVILLE, N. C.

Lady Assistant When Desired

Phone 193-2 Rings

THE MOORE Plumbing Company

16 N. Pack Square
PHONE 1025

Sanitary Plumbing, General Tin and Metal Work, Hot Air Furnaces

---

Reed Benj (Malissa), lab, h 229 Asheland av
Reed Building (offices), 16-18 s Pack Sq
Reed Chas O, inspr Sou W & I Bureau, bds 29 Jefferson Drive
Reed Chas P, bricklyr, bds 51 Gaston
Reed Chas W (Annice W), h Reed's Hill, Biltmore
Reed Clyde S (Lucy), propr Biltmore Roller Mills, h Hickory Nut Gap rd, Biltmore
*Reed Dorcas, cook, h 122 Church
Reed F Julia, wid G W, h 2 Swan, Biltmore
Reed Farm Dairy, Biltmore, J H Greenwood propr
Reed Flora Miss, clk, h 229 Asheland av
Reed Harold M, stonemason, h 314 Asheland av
Reed J Henry (Sigourney), h 389 n Main
Reed Jas A (Ida), helper, h 322 Asheland av
*Reed Jas H, barber Buckeye Parlor, h 26 Sorrell
Reed Jno, lab, h Biltmore Park
Reed Myra W Miss, h 389 n Main
Reed Rossie B, student, h 389 n Main
Reed Saml A (Sallie), wood yard 314 Asheland av, h same
Reed Thos J (Mary A), carp, h 559 n Main
*Reed Victoria, laund, h 36 Madison
*Reed Wm, porter J L Smathers & Sons, h 166 Church
*Reed Wm (Ella), lab, h Chunns Cove
Reed Wm G (Ida), collr, h Biltmore rd, S Biltmore
Reed Wm R (Bertha E), tmstr, h 51 Gaston
Reed see also Reid
Reeder Julia A Miss, h 208 Haywood
Reel Claude N (Bonnie K), carp, h 63 Clingman av
Rees Arthur F (Martha B), h Kenilworth
Rees Arthur F Jr, student, h Kenilworth
REES HANS SONS (Inc), tanners, Sou Ry nr Passngr Sta—phone 73; Geo H Raymond pres, Chas E Rudd v-pres and genl mngr, H B Rees sec-treas, Geo E Eastmead asst sec-treas
REES HAROLD B (Elizabeth), sec-treas Hans Rees Sons (Inc), h 14 All Souls Crescent, Biltmore
Rees Louis D, student, h Kenilworth
*Rees Martha, laund, h 20 Mountain
Rees Reeda V Miss, h Kenilworth
Reese Alma Miss, h 147 Asheland av
Reese Belle H Miss, nurse 134½ s Main, h same
Reese Jas, h 134½ s Main
Reese Jos J (Ada), plstr, h 55 Furman av
Reese Minnie Miss, h 134½ s Main

The Battery Park Bank   Capital - - $100,000.00
Surplus and Profits, $110,000.00
ASHEVILLE, N. C.   City, County and State Depositary

A. W. DARDEN   O. N. DONNAHOE

Reliable Cleaning and Pressing Club

Cleaning :: Pressing :: Repairing

Prompt Service and Satisfactory Work

Place your order with us and become a satisfied customer   ::   ::   ::   ::

Reliable Cleaning & Pressing Club
We Are All That Our Name Implies

14 Church St.   -::-   Phone 445

J. A. TILLMAN — **Jeweler** — **17 N. Main St.**
I carry a nice line of Watches, Clocks and Jewelry, and make a specialty of repair work. Satisfaction guaranteed

Reese Myrtle Miss, h 134½ s Main
Reese Saml P (Mary), bkkpr, h 76 Woodfin
Reese Sue Miss, tchr Montford Schl, h 134½ s Main
REEVES ARTHUR F, physician and surgeon, 9 s w Pack Sq, office hours 11 to 12, 5 to 7—phone 1483, bds Langren Hotel
Reeves Awyer C (Maggie), carrier R F D 3, h 105 Biltmore rd, S Biltmore
Reeves Bessie E Miss, h 35 n Spruce
Reeves Bonnie L Miss, h 35 n Spruce
Reeves Chas H (Mary), fruit, 183 Patton av
Reeves Ethel Miss, h 35 n Spruce
Reeves Lester A, clk M T Rhinehart, bds 9 Montford av
Reeves Mattie Miss, clk Palais Royal, h W Asheville
Reeves Rufus H (Georgie), dentist 35 n Spruce, h same
Reeves Thos C, h 105 Biltmore rd, S Biltmore
Reeves Willie H Miss, h Edegmont
Reid C Albert (Sarah J), h 382 s French Broad av
Reid C Albert Jr, fireman Sou Ry, h 382 s French Broad av
Reid Nathaniel M, flgmn Sou Ry, h 382 s French Broad av
Reid W Ernest, sec-treas N C Electrical Power Co, rms Y M C A
Reid Winnie D Miss, tchr, h 382 s French Broad av
Reid Zebulon B, condr Sou Ry, h 382 s French Broad av
☞ Reid see also Reed
Reilly Jno J (Mattie), slsmn, h Lyman nr Depot
Reilly Michael J (Helen), mdse broker, h 171 Charlotte
Reis Edwd P (Mary L), lab, h Woolsey (R F D 1)
Reisecker Elbert A, drayman 34 s Lexington av
Reister Henry, lab, h 149 Park av
Reister Junius E, clk, h 149 Park av
Reister Wm W (Elva E), supervisor B & B Sou Ry, h 149 Park av
RELIABLE CLEANING & PRESSING CO (The), (A W Darden, O N Donnahoe), 14 Church
Rembert Christine E Mrs, boarding 153 n Main, h same
Renfro Doc C (Hettie), poultry Riverside Drive nr Natl Caket Co, h same
*Renwick Chavist, porter Asheville Paint & Glass Co, h 128 Pearson Drive
Restawyle (The), boarding 20 Oak, Mrs J L Ronci propr
Revell Building, offices, 3½ n w Pack Sq
Revell Nora, wid T J, h 47 Central av
Revell Oliver D (Caroline E), real est 15 Revell Bldg, h 88 Charlotte

INSURANCE
Insure your salary with us
Never carry your own risk
Safety is the best policy
Unless you are a capitalist
Rest easy if you have
An accident we will
Not keep you waiting to
Collect your claim
Every claim promptly paid

Imperial Mutual Life & Health Insurance Co.

Home Office:
ASHEVILLE, N. C.

Phone 495

HOTEL OXFORD — **Asheville, N. C.**
Redecorated and Refitted throughout. Recently enlarged to 60 rooms. Centrally located Depot cars stop at entrance. Long distance telephone office upstairs. American and European plan. Rates 50c, 75c and $1 per day; special rates by week or month. C. H. Branson & Sons, Proprietors. Phone 1887. 50-54 South Main St.

Williams-Brownell Planing Mill Company — *Hardwoods*

Lumber---Rough and Dressed Flooring a Specialty Moulding, Interior Finish, Etc.
Office, Plant and Yards on Southern Railway, Near Biltmore Station
WHITE PINE   Phone 729   YELLOW PINE

Asheville Electrical Co., Electrical Contractors
HEADQUARTERS 74 CENTRAL AVENUE
W. Mansfield Booze, Manager
PHONE 377

Revell Thos J, tel opr, h 47 Central av
Revis Anna May Miss, laund, h (r) 40 Maiden la
Revis Curtis (Harriet), helper, bds 46 Avery
Revis Dora Miss, waitress Cherokee Inn, h 49 Spring
Revis Elberta Miss, nurse Highland Hospital, rms same
Revis Eliza Miss, h Arlington st, W Asheville
Revis Etta Miss, waitress Cherokee Inn, h 49 Spring
Revis Geo (Margaret), h 35 Maiden la
Revis H Garfield (Mollie), carp, h Main st, W Asheville
Revis Henry C (Charlotte J), carp, h 12 Pearl
*Revis Ira L, porter Ashev Barber Shop, h 117 Poplar
Revis Jas (Lula), lab, h 445 w Haywood
Revis Jas H (Della), mchst, h 84 Clingman av
*Revis Jno, porter Ashev Barber Shop, h 117 Poplar
Revis Jos, emp Mustin-Robertson Co, h 49 Spring
Revis Jos, lab, h 16 Turner
Revis Jos B, lab W M Jones, h 49 Spring
Revis Jos V (Linda P), driver, h 25 Buttrick
Revis L Milton (Daisy E), carp, h Arlington st, W Ashev
Revis Loula Miss, dom, h Hotel Warren
Revis Lyda A (Josie), lab, h 83 Madison av
Revis Martha E, wid Thos, h 25 Buttrick
Revis S Chas (Sarah), lab, h 13 William
Revis Thos, driver, h 25 Buttrick
*Revis Thos (Rosaline), porter, h 117 Poplar
Revis W Thurman, clk Hollar & Co, h 25 Buttrick
REXFORD WM A, sec-treas H F Grant Realty Co, office Drhumor Bldg
Reynolds Alyne Miss, h Edgemont
Reynolds Blake O (Lottie P), asst foreman, h Haywood rd, W Asheville
Reynolds C Zebulon (Ida), mchst, h 41 Roberts
Reynolds Carl V (Edith R) (Reynolds & Cocke), h Edgemont Park
Reynolds Carolyne Miss, h Edgemont
*Reynolds Chas (Annie), carp, h 103 Pine
Reynolds Chas G (Ester), golf instr, h 407 Charlotte
Reynolds Cleveland (Lizzie), painter, h Haywood rd, W Asheville
Reynolds Dorcas M, wid Wm W, h Haywood rd, W Ashev
*Reynolds Effie, waitress, h 57 Short
Reynolds G S Mrs, h 22 Woodfin
Reynolds Geo S, atty at law 15½ Patton av, h 22 Woodfin
*Reynolds Jos (Lula), lab, h (r) 54 Asheland av
*Reynolds Jas B, butler, bds 93 Pine

Asheville Dry Cleaning Co.
Telephones 835-836, All Dep't
MAIN, N. E. COR. COLLEGE

THE CLEANERS
Our Department for Oriental Rugs and Carpet Cleaning is prepared to serve you in all its branches.
E. S. Paine   O. E. Hansen

Reynolds Jas R (Maude J), h Haywood rd, W Asheville
Reynolds Jos A (Minnie), clk H Redwood & Co, h 23 Crescent
Reynolds Lena P Miss, stengr Coca-Cola Bottling Co, h W Asheville
Reynolds Lewis S, h 22 Orchard
Reynolds Lillian Miss, h Edgemont
*Reynolds Lizzie, h 99 Eagle
*Reynolds Lott, barber, rms 74 Eagle
Reynolds Lucy B Miss, bkkpr, h 88 Hill
Reynolds Marie O Mrs, h 64 Bearden av
Reynolds Mary L Miss, h 22 Orchard
Reynolds N Augustus (Mamie S), h 22 Woodfin
Reynolds Nan E Miss, bkkpr Rogers Grocery Co, h 22 Orchard
Reynolds Nannie J, wid Henry, h 22 Orchard
REYNOLDS ROBT R (Fannie), atty at law, notary and solicitor 15th Judicial District and agt Illinois Surety Co, office Court House (2d fl), h Edgemont Park
Reynolds Thos P (Margaret) (Hodges, Mitchell & Reynolds), h 50 n French Broad av
Reynolds Wm A (Lillie), foreman, h Haywood rd, W Asheville
Reynolds Wm A (Mary), mchst, h 45 Roberts
Reynolds Wm V (Norma), contr, h 45 Chestnut
Reynolds & Cocke (C V Reynolds, J E Cocke), phys 11 Church
*Rhame Jno N (Rosa), barber J W Bowman, h 159 College
*Rhame Rosa M, tchr Catholic Hill Schl, h 159 College
Rhea Dora Mrs, h 71 Starnes av
Rhea see also Ray and Rea
*Rhine Jno, barber, h 159 College
Rhinehardt Annie May Miss, h 12 Grady
Rhinehardt Bros (I E and L F), plmbrs 91 Patton av
Rhinehardt Elmer T (Lillie L), contr, h 12 Grady
Rhinehardt Fannie Miss, h 9 Pearson Drive
Rhinehardt I Edgar (Daisy) (Rhinehardt Bros), h Cortland av nr Pearson Drive
Rhinehardt Leonidas F (Mary L) (Rhinehardt Bros), h 9 Pearson Drive
Rhinehardt Lucile Mrs, bkkpr, h 12 Grady
Rhinehardt Lucy B Miss, h 12 Grady
Rhinehardt Mark T, druggist 9 Montford av, h same
Rhinehardt Matilda H Miss, bkkpr Poole Bros, h 12 Grady
Rhoads Wm H (Josephine) (Rhoads & McLean), h R F D 4

LIFE INSURANCE COMPANY OF VA.
ORGANIZED 187
Richmond -:- Virginia
J. V. MOON, Superintendent
Rooms 3-4-5- Maxweiton Bldg., Asheville, N. C.

All claims paid IMMEDIATELY upon receipt of satisfactory proofs of Death. Total payment to policyholders since organization, over $12,000,000.00. Is paying its Policyholders over $1,000,000.00 annually.

T. P. JOHNSON & CO.

SHEET METAL WORKERS

All Kinds of Roofing Guttering and Conductor Work Metal Ceilings, Skylights and Galvanized Iron Cornices

OFFICE and SHOP:
69-71 S. MAIN

Phone 325

DR. C. H. MILLER

Mechano-Therapist

14 N. Spruce Street
ASHEVILLE, N. C.

PHONE 979

Hours by Engagement

DRUGLESS HEALING OF DISEASE

ASHEVILLE [1913] DIRECTORY

Rhoads & McLean (W H Rhoads, W E McLean), gro's Riverside Drive nr Casket Co
*Rhodes Albert (Lois), driver Ashev P & G Co, h 33 Catholic av
Rhodes Callie A, wid Abner, h 343 Southside av
Rhodes Geo W (Sarah), switchman, h nr Hazel Hill rd, W Asheville
*Rhodes Geo R (Lula), drayman 492 s French Broad av, h same
Rhodes Jas J (Eva), h 73 Magnolia av
Rhodes Lester (Dora), fireman, h Biltmore rd, S Biltmore
Rhodes Lewis L, driver A F D, h Biltmore rd, S Biltmore
Rhymer Floyd, carp, bds 135 n Main
Rhyne Wayne S, clk C A Walker, bds 23 Grove
Ribet Celestine Miss, dom, h 3 Aston Pl
Rice Algie Miss, weaver, h 118 Short Roberts
Rice Andrew, lab, bds 49 n Main
Rice Beulah Mrs, clk J H Law, h 299 College
Rice Elder Miss, weaver, h 118 Short Roberts
Rice Eliza J, wid Henry, h 118 Short Roberts
Rice Horace (Bertie), driver Jno Kimberly, h Riverside Drive nr n Main
Rice Jas (Belle), driver, h 26 Logan
Rice Jas A (Beulah), lab, h 299 College
Rice Jas O, clk H L Finklestein, rms 36 Temple Court
*Rice Kanzie, dom, rms 115 n Main
Rice Lillie Miss, dom, h Woolsey (R F D 1)
*Rice Margaret, laund, h 233 Flint
Rice Mary A, wid C A, h Woolsey (R F D 1)
*Rice Mary C, h 35 Clemmons
*Rice Mary H, cook, h 35 Clemmons
Rice Mary Webb Mrs, pres M Webb Co, h Candler N C
Rice Nancy R, wid Jno C, h 31 Reed, S Biltmore
Rice Noel, lab, h 118 Short Roberts
*Rice Rich'd, barber Windsor Hotel Barber Shop, h 165 McDowell
Rice Robt H (Georgia), weaver, h 11 Green
*Rice Theo (Alberta), lab, h 14 Smith
Rich A Dora, wid Jeremiah J, gro 38 Pearson Drive, h 42 same
Rich Araminta, wid Jno R, h 187 Haywood
Rich Claude E (Estella), barber Glen Rock Barber Shop, h W Asheville
Rich Conley J, h 2d av, W Asheville
Rich Elizabeth M Miss, tchr Home Indus Schl, rms same

ASHEVILLE CLEANING and PRESSING CLUB

TAILORING THAT SATISFIES and PRICES THAT PLEASE

Hats cleaned, banded and bound. Silk hats ironed. Buttons made to order in all sizes. Plain or with rims. PHONE 389

DYEING IN ALL SHADES

Kid Gloves, Slippers and Plumes. Fancy Jabots and Ties, French Dry Cleaned, Ladies' and Gentlemen's suits Steam Cleaned. Messenger Service. **J. C. Wilbar, Prop.**

4 NORTH PACK SQ.

Rich Etta Mrs, dom 134 Flint
RICH J R & CO (INC), plumbing and heating, 21 n Main —phone 364, T E Curtis pres, W M Hamrick sec-treas
Rich Jno O (Minnie), carp, h 2d av, W Asheville
Rich Texie C Miss, h 2d av, W Asheville
*Richards Cora, cook, h 20 Clemmons
Richards Wesley P (Elma), foreman, h 179 Flint
*Richardson Alvesta, dom Windsor Hotel
*Richardson Jas (Bertha), painter, h 18 Lincoln av
Richardson Jos H (Margaret), fireman Sou Ry, h 70 Bartlett
*Richardson Rosa, h S Asheville
Richelieu (The), boarding, 20 n French Broad av, Mrs S C Alley propr
Richard Jno J, lock and gunsmith 12 Smith and 195 Southside av
Richert Jas F (Ethel), condr Sou Ry, h 70 Asheland av
Rickman David (Ethel), driver M Hyams, bds 56 Penland
Rickman Edith Miss, maid 37 Wautauga
Rickman Howell R (Gertrude), clk Ashev Gro Co, h 21 Arlington
Rickman Thos J (Elizabeth), atty at law 5-6 Paragon Bldg, h 127 s French Broad av
*Ricks Jas (Henrietta), lab, h 17 Ridge
Riddick Chas O, student, h 125 Charlotte
Riddick Minnie Belle Miss, student, h 125 Charlotte
Riddick W Oscar (Minnie A), mngr Azalea Woodworking Co, h 125 Charlotte
Riddick Wm Allen, student, h 125 Charlotte
Riddle Guy, lab, h Grace
Riddle Romeo B (Bertha), tanner, h 320 Avery
Riddle Sidney, tanner, h 320 Avery
Riddle Thos (Martha), shoemkr, h 320 Avery
Ridgelawn, res A S Littlefield, Vernon Hill
*Ridley Jno (Anna), lab, h 153 Valley
 *Riggans Archie (Lillie), lab, h 117 Wallach
RIGGS JESSE K (Mamie O), sec-treas and mngr Mountain City Steam Laundry, h 121 Broad—phone 403
Rigsby Jesse J (Margaret), jeweler 12 n Pack Sq (2d fl), h same
Riley Wm C (Annie C), clk Augustus Hammett, h 488 w Haywood
☞Riley see also Reilly
*Rinehart Bessie, dom, h 4 Valley
Ringer Elizabeth Mrs, h 64 Merrimon av

WEAVERVILLE LINE NINE MILES BY TROLLEY FROM PACK SQUARE TO WEAVERVILLE

ASHEVILLE AND EAST TENNESSEE RAILROAD CO.

7 NORTH MAIN STREET   ASHEVILLE N. C.

Electrical Supplies
PIEDMONT ELECTRIC COMPANY
ASHEVILLE, N. C.
64 PATTON AVE.

Ringer Paul H, phys 1-2-3 Citizen Bldg, h 64 Merrimon av
Rinsland Lucinda, wid Louis, h 34 Fulton
Rinsland Lydia E Miss, music tchr 34 Fulton, h same
*Ritchie Jno (Rebecca), waiter Ashev Club, h 33 Max
Ritchie Walter (Matilda), car inspr, h 180 s Main
*Ritman Clara, cook 382 Montford av
Ritter W M Lumber Co, 301 Oates Bldg, S M Wolfe div supt
Riverside Base Ball Park, Riverside Drive
Riverside Cemetery (see Asheville Cemetery Co)
Riverside Park, Riverside Drive cor Pearson
Riverside Skating Rink Co, Riverside Park, Paul I Alexander mngr
Roach Flora C, wid E L, boarding 45 Charlotte, h same
Roath Warrington D Capt, h Woolsey (R F D 1)
Robbins Henry H Rev (Mary R), pastor Bethel M E Ch (South), h 32 Phifer
Roberson Frank D (Marietta), carp, h Woolsey (R F D 1)
Roberson Jackson A (Mary), carp, h Woolsey (R F D 1)
Roberson Lafayette W (Lillie), gro Riverside Drive nr Park, h 458 same
Roberson Ralph E, bkkpr, h Woolsey (R F D 1)
Roberson Rosa I Miss, artist H W Pelton, bds 100 Ashland av
Roberson Walter M, plstr, h Woolsey (R F D 1)
Roberson see also Robertson and Robinson
Roberts Alonzo L (Addie L), engnr Sou Ry, h 21 Girdwood
Roberts Arthur, lab, h 37 Catawba
*Roberts Arthur (Mary), coke wkr, h 23 Frederick
Roberts Beeler L Miss, h 132 Asheland av
Roberts Carl, clk V V Haynie, h 95 West
Roberts Chas, lab, h 37 Catawba
Roberts Chas Emmett (Roberts & McKinney), h 132 Asheland av
Roberts Chas W (Annie), clk Ashev Dry Gds Co, h 84 East
*Roberts Clement C, porter Zindel's Model Bakery, h 22 Weaver
Roberts Curtis J, trav slsmn Ashev Barber Supply Co, rms 8 Technical Bldg
Roberts D L, pressman The Inland Press, h Biltmore
Roberts David S (Emma), farmer, h Church cor Summit, S Biltmore
Roberts E Gallatin (Mary A) (Fortune & Roberts), notary public 11-12 Library Bldg and county representative, h W Asheville

CONTRACTOR and BUILDER
STEEL RANGES
J. C. McPHERSON
35-37 E COLLEGE ST. PHONE 133
PLUMBING STEAM AND HOT WATER HEATING

Roberts E Pearl Mrs, h 34 Flint
Roberts Edwd (Bessie), weaver, h 13 Factory Hill
Roberts Edwd G (Annie), mill hd, h 63 Roberts
Roberts Elizabeth S, wid J W, h 46 Summit, S Biltmore
Roberts Everett W (Hester), clk Ashev Dry Gds Co, h W Asheville
Roberts Frank V (Jessie), propr Franklin Hotel, h same
*Roberts Hattie, laundress, h 121 Southside av
Roberts J Carter (Nannie), dairyman, h 26 Vivian
Roberts J Paul, farmer, h Hazel Mill rd, W Asheville
Roberts J Wesley, stone setter, h 16 Ocala
Roberts Jacob C (Eliza J), mldr, h Haywood rd, W Ashev
Roberts Jas W, emp Nursery, h 46 Summit, S Biltmore
Roberts Jno A (Lottie C), lab, h Hazel Mill rd, W Ashev
Roberts Jno H, plumber, h 16 Ocala
ROBERTS JOHN M PROF A B AND A M (Margaret), prin North State Fitting School, 157 Church—phone 1374, h same (see page 12)
Roberts Jno R (Pattie R), h Hazel Mill rd, W Asheville
Roberts Julius (Martha), h Chunns Cove
Roberts M Duckworth (Melvina), lab, h 37 Catawba
*Roberts Mamie, h (r) 5 s Grove
*Roberts Marie, h 9 Short Valley
*Roberts Mary, h 113 Short Valley
Roberts Mary E, wid Jacob R, h Brevard rd, W Asheville
Roberts Maurice O (Roberts & Crook), h 21 Girdwood
Roberts Max, waiter U S Cafe, rms 11½ n Main
Roberts Mayme C Miss, h 21 Girdwood
Roberts Merritt N, farmer, h Hazel Mill rd, W Asheville
Roberts Moody, clk L W Roberson, h 458 Pearson Drive
Roberts Murat H, student, h 68 Flint
Roberts Nola M Miss, smstrs, h 16 Ocala
*Roberts Parker, barber J W Bowman, h 165 College
Roberts Pheltus N (Jennie), shoemkr 343 w Haywood, h (r) 65 Spring
Roberts Robt B (Sallie E), cashr, h 68 Flint
Roberts Robt C (Mary E), clk Ry M S, h Haywood rd, W Asheville
Roberts Robt W (Hester), clk Ashev P & G Co, h 106 East
Roberts Roy P, farmer, h Hazel Mill rd, W Asheville
Roberts Saml (Lillie), driver, h 212 Southside av
Roberts Stella Miss, h Chunns Cove
Roberts Susan E Miss, student, h 68 Flint
Roberts Sydna F Miss, clk Ashev Dry Gds Co, h W Ashev
Roberts Thos, lab French Broad Quarry, h 40 View

Candy Kitchen and Club Cafe
"A GOOD PLACE FOR REFRESHMENT"

The very best ingredients with sanitary conditions in our Candy Manufacturing Department make possible the dainty, crisp confections sold here.
Bon Bons and Chocolates made every day, put up in neat, attractive boxes. Phones 110 and 111. 19 and 21 Haywood St.

Brown's Undertaking Parlors

S. H. BROWN

Lady Assistant When Desired

Phone 193-2 Rings

50 Patton Avenue
Asheville, N. C.

Established 1894

B. J. JACKSON

Carefully Selected Fruits and Vegetables

Stall No. 11, City Market

BUSINESS PHONES: 86 and 101

RESIDENCE PHONE 1596

Roberts Wm C (Sallie), atty, h 317 Cumberland av
Roberts & Crook (M O Roberts, R L Crook), confrs 334 w Haywood
Roberts & McKinney (C E Roberts, W C McKinney), gro's 20 w College
*Robertson Aaron M (Ora), waiter, h 39 Magnolia av
Robertson Allen H (Emily), shoemkr 439 s Main, h Livingston st
*Robertson Barbara, h 104 Grove
Robertson Bessie Miss, h Grace
Robertson D W, carp, h Grace
Robertson Elizabeth Miss, h 40 n Liberty
*Robertson Emma, h 177 Hill
Robertson Glenn (Lola), mill wkr, h 478 w Haywood
*Robertson Grover, presser West End Club, h (r) 131 Clingman av
Robertson Helen Mrs, h 21 Washington rd
*Robertson Jas M (Lela), clk, h (r) 31 Clingman av
Robertson Jno D, pres Mustin-Robertson Co Inc, h 102 Merrimon av
*Robertson Karl, lab, h 139 Weaver
Robertson Lee M (Nora), tanner, h 82 East
Robertson Marcus W, bkkpr Battery Park Bank, h 40 n Liberty
*Robertson Milton (Etta), cook, h 177 Hill
*Robertson Norman, driver Wm Kroger, h Clingman av
Robertson Pearl Mrs, h 289 College
Robertson Reuben B (Hope T), mngr Champion Fiber Co, h Grove Park
Robertson Ruby B Miss, stengr Estate Frank Coxe, h 40 n Liberty
Robertson Sarah L, wid M W, h 40 n Liberty
Robertson Sylvester V (May), carp, h Grace
Robertson Walter, driver, bds 52 Woodfin
☞ Robertson see also Roberson and Robinson
Robey —— Miss, clk Bon Marche, h 163 Asheland av
Robey Paul C (Eunice), engnr Sou Ry, h 163 Asheland av
Robichaus Eugene G (Bridgett), planter, h 382 Montford av
*Robinson Alvin (Mary), bellman, h 35 Magnolia av
*Robinson Andrew, waiter Gladstone Hotel Cafe h 92 Black
*Robinson Arthur, porter, h 166 Church
Robinson Caroline Mrs, h 231 Haywood
*Robinson Carrie, h Haywood rd, W Asheville
Robinson Chas K (Agnes M), (Coleman, Robinsfon & Co), h 32 n French Broad av

---

Furniture and China Carefully Prepared for Shipment

Mahogany Furniture Hand Made & Carefully Reproduced

E. E. GALER
114 PATTON AVE.

Upholstering and Refinishing
PHONE -- 1674

*Robinson Chester (Janie), porter Whitlock's, h 77 Eagle
Robinson Claud, helper Western Carolina Auto Co, h 62 Penland
*Robinson Edwd (Jane), lab, h 154 Beaumont
*Robinson Ella, cook, rms 88 Eagle
Robinson Emma J Mrs, h 153 Haywood
*Robinson Essie, dom, h 36½ Mountain
Robinson Gaither S, condr St Ry, rms 31 Meriwether Bldg
*Robinson Geneva, cook, h 10 Magnolia av
*Robinson Henry (Daisy), lab, h 31 Oakdale av
Robinson Isaac R (Lula), trav slsmn, h 251 Haywood
Robinson Jas (Ella), car clnr, h 477 w Haywood
Robinson Jas B (Loretta), weaver, h 514 w Haywood
Robinson E (Margaret S), cutter Ashev Mica Co, rms 72 Ralph
Robinson Jennie K Miss, h 51 Penland
Robinson Jeremiah H, flgmn Sou Ry, bds 29 Jefferson Drive
*Robinson Jessie, laundress, h 85 Wallach
*Robinson Jno (Sallie), lab, h (r) 492 s French Broad av
Robinson Jno G (Sarah), kodaks and supplies, 3 Haywood h 74 same
Robinson L Carey (Clara), bag mstr Sou Ry, h 8 Silver
Robinson Lewis B (Dora M), tanner, h nr Smith Bridge, W Asheville
*Robinson Lillie, cook, h 24 Gibbons
*Robinson Louisa, laund, h 3 w Woodfin
*Robinson Lucy, dom, h 52 Hill
Robinson Margaret Mrs, wks Ashev Mica Co, h 72 Ralph
*Robinson Mattie, cook 41 Starnes av
Robinson Maude Miss, h 62 Penland
Robinson Miller M (Sallie), carp, h 125 Hall
*Robinson Phylis, laundress, h 85 Wallach
Robinson S Lucylle Miss, stengr The Piedmont Electric Co, h 119 Haywood
Robinson Saml D (Lorrie) (Young & Robinson) and livery 61 n Lexington av, h 62 Penland
Robinson Sarah V Miss, with Jno G Robinson, h 153 Haywood
Robinson T C (Lola), lab, h 514 w Haywood
*Robinson Wm (Belle), porter, h 163 Hill
Robinson Wm H (Frances E), baker, h 514 w Haywood
Robinson see also Roberson and Robertson
Rochester Wm, lab, h 13 William
Rock Ledge (The), board, 68 Haywood, Mrs M J Corcoran propr

Mrs. Wilder's SANITARY HOME LAUNDRY turns out first class work in Laundering and Dry Cleaning. No. 7 Montford Ave., Phone 1354

ROCKETT OSCAR N (Lovency), watchmaker, jeweler and restaurant, 29 n Main, h same (see p 22)
Rockholdt Jas, lab, h 560 s Main
Rockwell Agnes Miss, h 142 Hillside
Rockwell Kiffin Y, h 77 Montford av
Rockwell Loula A, wid J C (Meacham & Rockwell), h 142 Hillside
ROCKWELL PAUL A, adv solr Piedmont Directory Co, h 142 Hillside
Rodgers Attlee G, clk, h 115 Park av
Rodgers Benj (Ethel), h Richmond Hill
Rodgers Clarence (Rosa), lab French Broad Quarry, h Richmond Hill
Rodgers Cleveland, painter, h (r) 79 Border
Rodgers Geo, carp, h (r) 79 Border
Rodgers Jno F (Betsie), gro 56 Eagle, h W Asheville
Rodgers Phoebe E, wid Henry, h 115 Park av
Rodgers Wiley R (Mary), carp, h (r) 79 Border
*Roderick Jas, lab, h 113 n Lexington av
*Roderick Mary, laund, h 113 n Lexington av
Roesel Paul, barber St Charles Barber Shop, bds 79 Woodfin
Rogers Bertie Miss, stengr, bds 174 Asheland av
Rogers Bessie L Miss, weaver, h 4 Short Roberts
Rogers Chas H (Josephine), trav slsmn, h Woolsey
Rogers Clayton T, elec engnr, h 43 Grove
ROGERS GROCERY CO (Inc), whol gro's, 365-369 Depot, L B Rogers pres and treas, W W Love sec
Rogers H Taylor (Mary E), book seller, 39 Patton av, h 43 Grove
Rogers Hilliary J, tanner, h 9 Park Pl
Rogers Jacob A (Mary), saw filer, h 10 Biltmore rd, S Biltmore
Rogers Jas J (Annie), foreman P H Henry, h "Zealandia"
Rogers Jas L (Emma D), engnr, bds 29 Jefferson Drive
Rogers Jno, emp Allisons Drug Store, res Pisgah Mtn
Rogers LeRoy B (Blanch), pres and treas Rogers Grocery Co, h 179 Montford av
*Rogers Lillie, laund, h 107 Clingman av
Rogers Lyda Miss, cook, h Livingston nr Oliver
Rogers Mary M Miss, h 43 Grove
*Rogers Mollie, h 22 Weaver
Rogers Nancy, wid Newton A, h 9 Park Pl
Rogers Robt B (Frances), carp, h 431 w Haywood
Rogers Sarah J, wid Jesse, h 4 Short Roberts

OLDSMOBILE — ARBOGAST MOTOR COMPANY — DETROIT ELECTRIC
ACCESSORIES AND SUPPLIES
52-60 N. Main   Phones 302 and 1728
BUICK — MAXWELLS

Asheville Dry Cleaning Co.
Telephones 835-836, All Dep't
MAIN, N. E. COR. COLLEGE

THE CLEANERS
Our Department for Oriental Rugs and Carpet Cleaning is prepared to serve you in all its branches.
E. S. Paine   O. E. Hansen

ALL KINDS
Hardwood Lumber

ENGLISH LUMBER CO.

Phone - - 321

Rogers Sarah T Miss, student, h 43 Grove
Rogers Thos (Allie), lab, h Arlington st, W Asheville
Rogers Thos, gluer, bds 34½ n Main
Rogers Thos B, weaver, bds J R Teague, W Asheville
Rogers W Frank, fertilizer, 527 w Haywood, h 44 View
Rogers Wiley E (Sallie), condr Sou Ry, h 106 Bartlett
Rogers Wm A (Daisy), stengr Harris-Barnett Dry Goods Co, h 17 Highland
Rohde Edwd J, h 72 Haywood
Rohde Henry J (Mary), h 72 Haywood
Roland Augusta S Mrs, h 306 Chestnut
Roland Mary F Miss, h 40 Bartlett
Roland Richard L, h 40 Bartlett
Roland Ruby Miss, h 40 Bartlett
Roland T Fulton (Mary J), dep U S Marshall, h 40 Bartlett
Rollins Hattie D Miss, clk P O, h 26 Blake
Rollins Hester J Mrs, wid Pinckney, h 26 Blake
Rollins Katherine C Miss, clk P O, h 209 Chestnut
Rollins Myrtle J Miss, h 209 Chestnut
Rollins Sadie M Miss, h 209 Chestnut
ROLLINS THOS S (Ida P) (Martin, Rollins & Wright), h 224 Chestnut
ROLLINS WM W MAJ, U S postmaster, h 209 Chestnut
Ronci A Humbert, student, h 20 Oak
Ronci Adele M Miss, h 20 Oak
Ronci Eleanora T Miss, cashr Bon Marche, h 20 Oak
Ronci Johanna L, wid J B, propr The Restawyle, h 20 Oak
*Rook Henry D, barber G W Johnson
Roper Bessie C Miss, h 506 Depot
Roper Cora A, wid A N, h 502 Depot
Roper Della L Miss, h 502 Depot
Roper Jas J, furn mkr, h 502 Depot
Roper Lollie E Miss, clk Jno A Guffey, h 502 Depot
Roper Ottis, barber Ashev Barber Shop
Rorison Elizabeth S, wid Jno L, h 65 Montford av
Rorison Minnie Miss, dep clk U S Courts, h 65 Montford av
"Rosebank Cottage", Albemarle Park
*Roseborough Annie, laundress, h 54 Wallach
*Roseborough Benj, lab, h 54 Wallach
*Roseborough Wm, porter Sou Exp Co
Roseland Dairy (B C Randall and A C Smith), Chunns Cove
Roselawn (The), boarding, 52 Merrimon av, E E Collister propr
*Roseman Jas (Maria), lab, h 40 Maiden la

BIGGEST BUSIEST BEST

Phones 1936 and 1937
ASHEVILLE STEAM LAUNDRY
43 to 47 W. COLLEGE

S. D. HALL
REAL ESTATE AGENT
—
Money Loaned
—
Notary Public
—
32 PATTON AVENUE
Phone 91

CAROLINA MACHINERY CO.
—US when you want machine work of any kind . . .

Founders Machinists and Jobbers of Mill Supplies
When in the market for heavy castings such as columns or building plates get our prices. **Phone 590**

The Life Insurance Co. of Virginia
ORGANIZED 1871   RICHMOND, VA.

ISSUES ALL THE MOST APPROVED FORMS OF LIFE INSURANCE CONTRACTS from $500.00 to $25,000.00, with premiums payable quarterly, semi-annually and annually

J. V. Moon, Superintendent, Rooms 3-4-5 Maxwelton Bldg., Asheville, N. C.

D. TREXLER TIN SHOP

All Kinds of Roofing, Gutter and Conductor Work.

Phone 862

159 South Main St.

DR. C. H. MILLER

MECHANO-THERAPIST

14 N. Spruce St.
Phone 979
ASHEVILLE, N. C.

Hours by engagement

Drugless Healing of Disease

---

322   ASHEVILLE [1913] DIRECTORY

Rosen Max (Annie), coppersmith, 59 n Lexington, produce 82 same, h 251 s Grove
*Rosenborough Jas (Isabel), lab, h 32 Grail
Rosenfeld Chas, clk, h 32 Clayton
Rosenfeld Morris (Rebecca), tailor S T Logan, h 32 Clayton av
Rosenfeld Nathan I (Sara), repr A M Field Co, h 59 Starnes av
Rosenfeld Rosa Miss, clk, h 32 Clayton
Ross Annie Mrs, h 191 Cumberland av
*Ross Grace, cook, h 11 Haid
Ross L S Mrs, h 260 Montford
*Ross Wm (Ella), coachman, h 11 Haid
Roth Clara R Miss, h 205 Merrimon av
Roth Lewis F, clk H L Finklestein, h 40 Merrimon av
Roth Moritz L, mngr Guarantee Shoe Store, h 578 Montford av
Roth Richard H (Clara), druggist, h 205 Merrimon
Rouse Jno A Rev (Cora), h 334 w Haywood
Rowe D Guy (Christine), engnr Sou Ry, h 139 Park av
Rowe Eugenia Miss, tchr Murray Schl
*Rowe Harold (Willie), lab, h 20 Weaver
Rowe S Nixon (Annie), clk Brown Book Co, h 40 Holland
Rowe Thos (Hattie), furn mkr, h Church cor Reed, S Biltmore
*Royal Fraternal Assn of Charlotte N C (branch), 26 Eagle C B Bailey genl agt, J G Moore supt
RUDD CHAS E (Emma), v-pres and genl mngr Hans Rees Sons (Inc), h 276 Montford av—phone 1839
Rudolph Jno G (Irene), lab, h 78 East
Rumbough Della Miss, cook, h 390 w Haywood
RUMBOUGH JAMES E (Martha E) (Enterprise Machine Co) and v-pres and genl mngr Nyberg Auto Sales Co, h 49 Zillicoa
RUMBOUGH JOHN B (Mayme G) (Enterprise Machine Co), h Watauga st
*Rumley Danl (Cecelia), lab, h 1 Greer's Row
*Rumley Harrison (Mamie), lab, h 103 Market
*Rumley Jos (Ophelia), cook, h 119 Mountain
Rumple Ida B Miss, bkkpr The Inland Press, h 36 Haywood
Runnion Robt S (W), ship clk, h 44 Charlotte
Runyon Lillian R, wid Richard, phone opr, h 60 s Liberty
*Rush Hattie, h 22 Lincoln av
Russell A Cicero (Carrie), mldr, h 139 Grove
*Russell Alberta, dom, h 190 Grove av

....Asheville Cleaning and Pressing Club....
Tailoring That Satisfies and Prices That Please
Steam and French Dry Cleaning of all delicate and fine wearing apparel for ladies and gentlemen. MESSENGER SERVICE IN THE CITY.

J. C. WILBAR, Prop.   4. N. Pack Square   PHONE 389

St. Genevieve's College

is both a Boarding and Day School and within easy access of the car line though sufficiently removed from the city to prevent the college work being disturbed by the noise of traffic. A private bus (free of charge) conducts the day scholars to and from the college.

The faculty is a body of experienced teachers, each holding one or more degrees in European universities, several from Oxford as well as from the continent, with their Ph. D., B. A., M. A., etc. degrees from Vassar. German and French are taught by thoroughly qualified native sisters, and the same might be very significantly said of the English language as well.

From music and mathematics to household economics and sewing, the ground is well covered. Unlike many other schools no extra charge is made for French, German, Needlework and Physical Culture. There is also a Commercial Department in connection with the college. Basket Ball and Tennis Courts are laid out in the spacious grounds.

St. Genevieve's is divided into three distinct departments:

THE PREPARATORY—
Which covers the program of regular grammar schools. Boys are admitted up to the age of thirteen.

THE ACADEMIC—
Which corresponds to the High School.

THE COLLEGE—
Which leads to Degrees.

These two last cover four years each.

Young children are also received as boarders and have their special quarters.

For both catalogues, address,

MOTHER DEPLANCK
St. Genevieve's College   Asheville, N. C.

St. Genevieve's College

Select Home College for the Higher Educacation of Young Ladies

SEE OTHER SIDE

Russell Arsenith S, wid Wm T, h Van st, W Asheville
Russell C Eugene, carp, h Van st, W Asheville
*Russell Carrie, waitress, h 44 Max
Russell Delia Miss, bds 340 w Haywood
Russell E Reid (Fannie M), phys 303-307 Legal Bldg, h 159 s French Broad av
Russell Eustice F Miss, nurse 37 Chestnut, rms same
Russell Jno Z (Elsie), farmer, h Brevard rd, W Asheville
*Russell Louisa, dom, h 44 Max
*Rutherford Geo (Rena), lab, h (r) 288 s French Broad av
*Rutherford Jas (Jessie), foreman Water Wks, Biltmore Estate, h 317 Asheland av
*Rutherford Jno, lab, h 305 Asheland av
Rutledge Fred'k (Mabel R) (Fred'k Rutledge & Co), genl ins agt, Girard F & M Ins Co, h 209 Cumberland av
Rutledge Fred'k & Co (Fred'k Rutledge, L F Hartsell), genl ins, 31 Patton av (2d fl)
Rutledge Fred'k, student, h 209 Cumberland av
Rutledge Jas (Cresey), lab, h 450 n Main
*Ryder Cora B, laund, h 4 Ingle
Rymer Chas (Belle), h Richmond Hill
Rymer Ella, wid Wm, h 22 Grady
Rymer Frank, tel opr, bds Haywood rd, W Asheville
Rymer Furman, appr, bds Haywood rd, W Asheville
Rymer Leona Mrs, clk The Peerless, h 25 Pearl
Rymer Oscar, lab, h 180 s Main

S

St Charles Barber Shop (L F Mallicotte), 7 Haywood
ST GENEVIEVE COLLEGE (school for young ladies), Victoria rd, Mother Deplanck in charge (see opp)
*St James A M E Church, 40 Hildebrand, Rev J R Barnum pastor
St Joseph Sanitorium, 428 s Main, Sisters of Mercy in charge
St Lawrence Roman Catholic Church, 95-97 Haywood, Rev P G Marion pastor
*St Matthias Episcopal Church, Valley cor Beaumont, Rev J T Kennedy rector
*Saboid Jas, plumber, h 45 Wallach
Sadler Henley M, agt Dixie Mut Life Ins Co, bds 16 Spruce
Sage Harry J, designer A M Field Co, rms 195 s French Broad av
Sales Annie Miss, h 35 Clayton
Salinas Mai H Miss, h 208 Pearson Drive

Salinas Sue K Miss, h 208 Pearson Drive
Salisbury J Harris (Mary), condr Sou Ry, h 136 s Main
Salisbury Jno F (Sarah J), bricklyr, h 155 Flint
Salley Hannah J, wid Jno J, h 35 Grove
Salley Hannah R Miss, stengr Ashev P & L Co, h 35 Grove
Salley Lottie L Miss, cashr Ashev Tel & Tel Co, h 35 Grove
Salomons Frieda Miss, dom S Sternberg, h same
*Salone Horace, lab, h 143 Pine
*Salone Mary, laund, h 143 Pine
Salter Annie L, wid J H, h 166 Chestnut
Salvation Army Hall, 38½ s Main and 504 w Haywood, Adjutant Jno Bouters in charge
*Sample Alice, dom, h 84 Valley
Sams Alfred, helper Ashe Ice Co, h W Asheville
Sams B Frank (Sarah), lab, h 495 w Haywood
Sams Daisy L Miss, h 462 w Haywood
Sams Elsie Mrs, bds W G Ford, W Asheville
Sams Geo (Sallie), lab, h 9 Buxton
Sams Horace W, clk M Hyams, bds 23 Orange
Sams Irving (Kate), janitor, h 504 w Haywood
Sams J Leroy (Gertrude), spl agt N S Int Rev, h 100 Asheland av
Sams J Riley, clk, h 462 w Haywood
Sams J Robt (Cora), lab, h 419 w Haywood
Sams Jack B (Bernice), contr, h 80 Avery
Sams Lattie T (Minnie), lab, h 433 w Haywood
Sams Lucy E Miss, stengr, h 462 w Haywood
Sams Margaret S, wid J B, rms 92 East
Sams Rebecca J Miss, dressmkr 70 Seney, h same
SAMS REUBEN B (Maggie), agt U S Internal Revenue, office Government Bldg—phone 1221, h 48 Starnes av —phone 1111
Sams Robt B (Sue), lab, h Haywood rd, W Asheville
Sams Sarah Miss, spinner, h Haywood rd, W Asheville
Sams Stephen J (Mary E), carp, h 462 w Haywood
Sams T Abigail, wid A B, h 70 Seney
Sams Thaddeus W (Omie), lab, h Haywood rd, W Ashev
Samson Gertrude E Miss, h 76 Liberty
Samson Lewis N, h 76 Liberty
Samuel Frank (Lydia), driver, h 59 Madison av
Samuel L Ray, clk P O, rms 25 Meriwether Bldg
Samuels Aaron, student, h 254 Cumberland av
Samuels Abraham (Rosa), h 254 Cumberland av
*Sanders Amanda, cook, h 17 Short Valley
Sanders Judas M (Alva), gro 510 w Haywood, h 481 same

Sanders Junius P (Della M), fireman Sou Ry, h 181 Bartlett
*Sanders Mamie, eating house 125 Southside av, h same
*Sanders Mattie, h 19 Short Valley
*Sanders Richard (Lavenia), janitor, h 33 Hildebrand
Sanders Rosa L Miss, bkkpr M Hyams, h 207 Haywood
*Sanders Sarah, laund, h 65 Hazzard
Sanders Thos R (Rosa L), trav slsmn, h 30 Starnes av
Sanders Victor A (Mary), h 29 Reed, S Biltmore
☞Sanders see also Saunders
Sandlin Geo, train dispr, bds Glen Rock Hotel
Sands Ada Miss, h (r) 35 Hall
Sands Edwd L (Mary), h Woolsey (R F D 1)
Sands Golden Miss, h Woolsey (R F D 1)
Sands Harvey S (Elizabeth), lab, h (r) 35 Hall
*Sanford Geo H (Sarah), presser J C Wilbar, h 31 Max
Sanford —— Rev, pastor Seventh Day Adventists, h 238 Haywood
SANITARY HOME LAUNDRY, 7 Montford av—phone 1354, Mrs E Wilder propr (see top and bottom lines)
Sarafian La Von G, clk J H Law, h 171 Woodfin
Sarafian Nevart Miss, stengr Balfour Quarry Co, h 171 Woodfin
Sarasfield Mayme Mrs, h 75 Starnes av
*Sartor Arthur (Hattie), lab, h 134 Pine
*Sartor Bertha, laund, h 109 n Lexington av
***SARTOR J R** (Julia), cleaning and pressing, 39 s Main—phone 1461, h 27 McDowell (see opp business dept)
*Sartor Jessie, cook, h 109 n Lexington av
*Sasportas Walter (Maria), bellman, h 26 Sassafras
Saumenig Harry F Rev, h Montford Cottage
Saunders Berry G (Victoria), foreman, h 233 s Grove
Saunders Lottie M Miss, h 233 s Grove
☞Saunders see also Sanders
Sawyer Clarence R (Carrie H), gro 53 Patton av, h 123 s Main
Sawyer Cleveland, driver Wm L Moore, h W Asheville
Sawyer Cora B, wid Marshall, h 18 Morgan av
Sawyer Ethel L Miss, bds A P Davis, W Asheville
Sawyer Eugene C, propr Asheville Auto Co, h 214 Montford av
Sawyer Grover C (Sadie), car repr Sou Ry, h 10 Connolly's Ridge
Sawyer J P, student, h 123 s Main
Sawyer Jas P Capt (Nancy C), chairman Board of directors Battery Park Bank, h 214 Montford av

Club Cafe and Candy Kitchen
"A GOOD PLACE FOR REFRESHMENT"

The standards we work to in our Restaurant Department are: Cooking, perfect; Service, prompt and cheerful; Prices, moderate; Menu, everything in season. Parties and Banquets, Teas and Dinners. 19 and 21 Haywood St. Phones 110 and 111.

Brown's Undertaking Parlors

S. H. BROWN

50 Patton Avenue
ASHEVILLE, N. C.

Lady Assistant When Desired

Phone 193-2 Rings

THE MOORE Plumbing Company

16 N. Pack Square

PHONE 1025

Sanitary Plumbing, General Tin and Metal Work, Hot Air Furnaces

---

Sawyer Jno Y (Nancy), driver, h 50 Seney
Sawyer R Holmes, student, h 123 s Main
*Sawyer Sidney (Flora), lab, h 32 Brick
Sax Saml, barber Antiseptic Barber Shop, h 560 Montford
*Saxton Hugh (Eva), lab, h 47 Short
Sayles Paul, peanuts, bds 49 n Main
Sayre Helen Miss, h Woolsey (R F D 1)
Sayre Martha E, wid Wm A, h Woolsey (R F D 1)
Scaffe Jno T (Rose), slsmn J A Groves, h 340 w Haywood
Scism Iona Miss, h 68 Church
*Schaeffer Chas T (Mayme), dentist 16 Eagle, h 13 Ridge
Schaffe Jno T (Rose), trav slsmn, h 169 Patton av
Scharlotte Carrie M Miss, tchr, h 36 Orange
Schartle D Norman, stengr Dr T C Smith, h 36 Orange
Schartle Dorothy Miss, tchr, h 36 Orange
Schartle Helen Miss, tchr Asheland av Schl, h 36 Orange
Schartle Jno W (Julia), tailor R B Zageir, h 36 Orange
Schartle Linda N Miss, organist, h 36 Orange
Schartle Wilhelmina F Miss, h 36 Orange
Schas Annie Miss, clk S I Blomberg, h 52 Central av
Schas Benj, clk M S Schas, h 53 Vance
Schas Harris, clg S I Blomberg, h 51 Central av
Schas Harry (Fannie), clk, h 51 Central av
Schas Lewis, mngr M S Schas, h 51 Central av
Schas Morris S, cigars 6 s Main, h 51 Central av
Schas Tillie Miss, clk, h 55 Vance
Scherlock Madam, trimmer and designer Sproat's, h 77 Spruce
Schmidt Edwd A, h 15 Phifer
SCHMINKE GUS (Zoe A), linotype opr Hackney & Moale Co and musician, h 184 w Chestnut
Schochet Jas B (Jennie B), clk, h 66 n Spruce
Schochet Jennie B Mrs, dry gds 9 n Main, h 66 n Spruce
Schoenheit Edwd W, student, h Dortch av cor East
SCHOENHEIT WM (Grace), business mngr Winyah Sanatorium and notary, h Dortch av cor East
Schoepf Burton H (Mary), slsmn Villa Heights Co, h 83 Montford av
Schoepf Jos H (Carrie A), h 83 Montford av
Schofield Mary Mrs, nurse 47 Central av, h same
School Committe, 208 City Hall, Wm Jones chmn, W B Northup chmn, R J Tighe sec
Schreyer Roy (Vennetta), carrier R F D No 5, h 16 Centre
Schuessler Christine R, wid Calhoun, boarding 107 Merrimon av, h same

---

The Battery Park Bank

Capital - - $100,000.00
Surplus and Profits, $110,000.00

ASHEVILLE, N. C.   City, County and State Depositary

J. A. TILLMAN — Jeweler — **17 N. Main St.**
I carry a nice line of Watches, Clocks and Jewelry, and make a specialty of repair work. Satisfaction guaranteed

Schuessler Harry H, clk Supt Sou Ry, h 107 Merrmon av
Schuessler Irma E Miss, h 107 Merrimon av
Schuessler S Paul, student, h 107 Merrimon av
*Scott Alonzo (Sallie), driver C Sawyer, h S Asheville
Scott Anna L, wid G F, h 200 Haywood
Scott Cyrus E (Mabel S), chemist, h 17 Panola
Scott Edwd F (Celia), lbr inspr W H Westall & Co yards, h 29 Orchard
Scott Ethel D Miss, student, h 268 Chestnut
Scott F W Rev, h Lyman nr st car line
*Scott Geo, lab, h 36 Maiden la
Scott Hattie M Miss, tchr, h 200 Haywood
*Scott Hester, h (r) 167 Beaumont
Scott Lucy E Miss, stengr Grove Park Inn, h 268 Chestnut
Scott Marjore A Miss, h 268 Chestnut
*Scott Martha, h (r) 167 Beaumont
Scott Mayme Miss, h 143 Montford av
SCOTT SIDNEY A (Lula) dist mngr Continental Casualty Co of Chicago Ill, office 8 Harkins Bldg, h W Asheville
Scott Wm A (Clara), boarding 268 Chestnut, h same
Screamer Manus (Nannie), printer Ashev Ptg & Engrav Co, h 56 Blanton
Searcy Dock V, foreman, bds W P Ford, W Asheville
Searcy J Boyd (May), kpr West Asheville Cemetery, h Jarret av, W Asheville
Searcy Thurman, foreman, bds W P Ford, W Asheville
Searcy Wm G (Tina), switchman, h Haywood rd, W Ashev
Seawell Chas C, rms 16½ n Pack Sq
Seay Jas D (Margaret), condr, h 71 Ora
Seay Jno, chauffeur Hollar Motor Co, bds 418 Southside av
Seay Jonah (Nellie), condr, h 207 s French Broad av
Seay Jos B, clk Gladstone Hotel Cafe, h 346½ Depot
Seay Marilla Miss, dress mkr, bds 25 Pearl
*Sebron Jno, lab, h 261 Asheland av
Seigal Benj, clk Louis Blomberg, rms Phoenix Hotel
Seigle Harry (Bessie), gro 54 Woodfin, h 43 s Liberty
Seigler Hilliard B, clk Carolina I & C Co, h 56 Penland
Seigler Jas B (Cordelia), collr Carolina I & C Co, h 56 Penland
Seigler Jas M, h 56 Penland
Selby Jos (Lucy), h 39 Josephine
Self Carroll, locksmith J M Hearn & Co, h Elk Mtn
Self Geo Lyda (Minnie), typewriter repr J M Hearn & Co, h Woolsey

INSURANCE
- **I**NSURE YOUR SALARY WITH US
- **N**EVER CARRY YOUR OWN RISK
- **S**AFETY IS THE BEST POLICY
- **U**NLESS YOU ARE A CAPITALIST
- **R**EST EASY IF YOU HAVE
- **A**N ACCIDENT WE WILL
- **N**OT KEEP YOU WAITING TO
- **C**OLLECT YOUR CLAIM
- **E**VERY CLAIM PROMPTLY PAID

Imperial Mutual Life & Health Insurance Co.
Home Office:
ASHEVILLE, N. C.
Phone 495

HOTEL OXFORD — Redecorated and Refitted throughout. Recently enlarged to 60 rooms. Centrally located. Depot cars stop at entrance. Long distance telephone office upstairs. American and European plan. Rates 50c, 75c and $1 per day; special rates by week or month. C. H. Branson & Sons, Proprietors. Phone 1887. 50-54 South Main St. **Asheville, N. C.**

Self Jas C (Gertha), locksmith, h Grace
Sellers Jno H (Minnie H), sign painter 7 Aston, h 59 Clayton
Sellers Nettie E Miss, student, h 59 Clayton
Semple Johanna M Miss, h 16 Bearden av
Settle Thos (Eliza P), atty at law Temple Ct, h 435 Pearson Drive
Seventh Day Adventist Church, Haywood nr Ann, Rev Sanford pastor
*Seventh Day Adventist Church, 37½ Sycamore
Severson Bertha C Mrs, h 43 Clingman av
Severson Carl P (Bertha), bkkpr Ashe Supply & Fdy Co, h 43 Clingman av
Sevier Chas C, clk Battery Park Hotel News and Cigar Stand, h Montrealla Farm N C
Sevier D E & J T (Danl E and Jos T), phys 6½ s Main
Sevier Danl E (Lutie) (Drs D E & J T Sevier) and county supt of Health, h 56 Oak
Sevier Jas V Jr, propr Battery Park Hotel News and Cigar Stand, h Montrealla Farm N C
Sevier Jos D, carp, h 85 Hill
Sevier Jos T (Carolina R) (D E & J T Sevier), h 40 Clayton Cigar Stand, h Montrealla Farm N C
Sevier Mary E Mrs, h 188 Charlotte
Sevier Sarah E Miss, h 85 Hill
*Sewell Ellen, dressmkr, h 18 Eagle
Sewell Jas J, pres Tonawanda White Pine Co, Temple Ct
*Sewell Lucy, dressmkr 18 Eagle, h same
Sexton Elizabeth Miss, h 19 William
Sexton Jno H (Mattie A), driver, h Hazel Mill rd, W Asheville
*Sexton Lillie, cook, h 40 Madison
Shackelton O G, bkkpr Ashev P & G Co, h Fairview Cottage
*Shade Alice, cook, h 20 Jordan
*Shade Isaac A, propr Shades Pharmacy, h 20 Jordan
*Shade's Pharmacy, 24 Eagle, I A Shade propr
Shaft Albert (Laura), h Chunns Cove
Shaft Alvers (Josie), h Chunns Cove
Shaft Elizabeth Mrs, h Chunns Cove
Shank Robt H (Emma), h 34 Asheland av
Sharp Anna Miss, emp Cherokee Inn, h same
Sharp D Harrison, chauffeur, bds 16 Hilliard la
Sharp Pack, chauffeur The Star Market, h 171 Haywood
Sharp Robt, tinner, h 182 s Main

Maple Flooring and Poplar Siding

English Lumber Co.
PHONE . . 321

*Sharp Adeline, h 195 Beaumont
Sharpe Burgin A, lab, h 13 Biltmore rd, S Biltmore
Sharpe Elizabeth Miss, h 454 Depot
*Sharpe Esther, laund, h 33 Buttrick
Sharpe F Lee (Jennie), police, h 2 Brook, Biltmore
Sharpe J Alex (Mollie), lab, h 13 Biltmore rd, S Biltmore
Sharpe Wm K, lab, h 13 Biltmore rd, S Biltmore
Shas Benj, clk, h 53 Vance
Shas Mich'l (Eva), peddler, h 53 Vance
Shas Tillie Miss, h 53 Vance
Shas see also Schas
Shaw Carl D (Edna), clk W H Westall & Co, h 109 Pearson Drive
*Shaw Jno, helper, h 15 Mountain
*Shaw Jno, butler Whitmore Sanitarium, rms same
*Shaw Lang (Martha), lab, h 15 Mountain
*Shaw Saml, lab, h 113 Short Valley
Sheak Mary Miss, tchr Normal & Collegiate Inst, rms same
Shearin Jno R, agt The Pullman Co, bds Gladstone Hotel
Shearin T S, supt, bds Gladstone Hotel
Shehan Geo C, propr Kenilworth Brick Wks, h 401 s Main
*Shell Wm (Jane), lab, h 27 Maiden la
Shell see also Schell
Shelton Bailey, clk frt office Sou Ry, bds 418 Southside av
Shelton Benj, foreman, h 418 Southside av
helton Jno F (Sarah A), farmer, h Haywood rd, W Ashev
Shelton Saml, lab, bds 135 n Main
Shelton Theo D (Georgia), dep collr Int Rev, h W Asheville
SHEMWELL BAXTER (Susan), pres Interstate Development Co and Interstate Railway Switch & Frog Co, 35 Amer Natl Bank Bldg—phone 108, h 90 Merrimon av—phone 811
*Shepard Lottie, cook, h 205 Clingman av
Shepard Mary H, wid Geo J, h 169 Charlotte
Shepherd Baxter M (Octavia), gro 45 College, h 41 Central
Shepherd Frank, h 11 Blair
Shepherd Luther V, driver Brown's Creamery, h 41 Central
Shepherd Thaddeus, mill wkr, bds 470 w Haywood
*Sheppard Carrie, maid, h 22 Davidson
*Sheppard Chas (Emma), waiter, h 17 Weaver
*Sheppard Emma, dom, h 57 Fulton
Sheppard Frank (Zealie), farmer, h nr Hazel Mill rd, W Ashev
*Sheppard Newton E (Lucinda), janitor, h 172 Hill
*Sheppard Otis, waiter, h 57 Fulton

ASHEVILLE [1913] DIRECTORY 329

BIGGEST
BUSIEST
BEST

Asheville Steam Laundry

Phones:
1936 and 1937

43 to 47
W. College Street

CHARLES H. HONESS
OPTOMETRIST
AND
OPTICIAN

Exclusive maker of
ATLAS SHUR-ON
EYE GLASSES

THE
Home of Ce-Rite
Toric Lenses

We make a specialty of correcting optical defects with properly fitted glasses.

54 Patton Avenue
Opposite Postoffice

in the market for a Gas Engine let us make you prices.
its heavy castings, such as columns or building plates, see us.
its a skilled mechanic for boiler work, see us.
you want machine work of any kind phone 590.

CAROLINA MACHINERY CO.

FOUNDERS
MACHINISTS and
Jobbers of Mill
Supplies

ife Insurance Company of Virginia
ORGANIZED 1871
lome Office - Richmond, Va.

Has won the hearty approval and active support of the people by its promptness and fair dealing during the FORTY-TWO YEARS of its operation

. V. Moon, Superintendent, Rooms 3-4-5 Maxwelton Bldg., Asheville, N. C.

T. P. IOHNSON & CO.

SHEET METAL WORKERS

All Kinds of Roofing Guttering and Conductor Work Metal Ceilings, Skylights and Galvanized Iron Cornices

OFFICE and SHOP: 69-71 S. MAIN

Phone 325

DR. C. H. MILLER

Mechano-Therapist

14 N. Spruce Street
ASHEVILLE, N. C.

PHONE 979

Hours by Engagement

DRUGLESS HEALING OF DISEASE

ASHEVILLE [1913] DIRECTORY

*Sheppard Rufus (Ola), lab, h 22 Davidson
*Sheppard Saml, janitor, h 172 Hill
*Sheppard Wm A (Chaney), janitor, h Haywood rd, W Ashev
*Sheppard Willie G, dom, h 172 Hill
Sherbune C L Prof, tchr The Asheville Schl, rms same
Sherlin David, carp, h 270 Southside av
Shirlin Geo (Mary), lab, h Broadway av, W Ashev
Sherlin Harrison B (Maude), tanner, h Broadway av, W Ashev
Sherlin Hattie Miss, dom, h 415 n Main
Sherlin J Luther (May), lab, h 415 n Main
Sherlin Jno, lab, bds 49 n Main
Sherlin Jno (Kittie), tmstr, h 270 Southside av
Sherlin Jonas (Clara), tanner, h 270 Southside av
Sherlin Maroney Miss, h 415 n Main
Sherlin Wesley (Allie), lab, h 36 Catawba
Sherrill Emma C Mrs, bkkpr Amer Furn Buyers Assn, h 6 Aston pl
Sherrill Frank H, mchst, Western Carolina Auto Co, h 42 Highland
Sherrill J L, firemn, bds 102 Ralph
Sherrill Jas B, farmer, h Hazel Mill rd, W Ashev
Sherrill Lee M (Janee), blksmith Amer Wagon Co, bds 135 n Main
Sherrill Margaret C, wid C L, h 42 Highland
Sherrill Mollie L Miss, h Hazel Mill rd, W Ashev
Sherrill Oscar H, painter, h 42 Highland
*Sherrill Otha (May), lab, h 26 Bay
Sherrill Rufus J (Anna J), h 208 Montford av
Sherrill Wm H, farmer, h Hazel Mill rd, W Ashev
SHERWOOD MILDRED E MISS, propr Mildred E Sherwood Home, h 179 s French Broad av
SHERWOOD MILDRED E HOME (private sanitarium), 179 s French Broad av, Miss Mildred E Sherwood propr —phone 543 (see p 4)
Shipley Bardie H (Debbie), coach clnr, h Haywood rd, W Ashev
Shipley Jno (Essie), helper, h Main st, W Ashev
Shipman Domer, lab, h 22 Atkinson
*Shipman Frank, lab, h (r) 33 Clingman av
*Shipman Hampton, lab French Broad Quarry, h (r) 33 Clingman av
Shipman Jas S (Cordie), plstr, h 15 Silver
Shipman Moses S (Mary J), plstr, h 10 Blanton

ASHEVILLE CLEANING and PRESSING CLUB

TAILORING THAT SATISFIES and PRICES THAT PLEASE

Hats cleaned, banded and bound. Silk hats ironed. Buttons made to order in all sizes. Plain or with rims. PHONE 389

DYEING IN ALL SHADES Cleaned. Messenger Service.

Kid Gloves, Slippers and Plumes. Fancy Jabots and Ties. French Dry Cleaned. Ladies' and Gentlemen's suits Steam

J. C. Wilbar, Prop. 4 NORTH PACK SQ.

*Shippey Wm (Florence), waiter, h 235 Flint
Shirlin see Sherlin
Shob Sophie Miss, bds 107 Haywood
SHOCKLEY HENRY S (Martha P), prin Asheville Business College, h 84 Asheland av
Shockley Vernon P, student, h 84 Asheland av
*Shoffner A Osborne (Eliza), driver J R Rich Co, h 352 Hill
Shoffner Wm H (Alice), jeweler 27 Patton av, h 257 Montford av
Shook Benj F (Josephine), foreman Ashev Gazette-News, h 64 Woodfin
Shook Irene Mrs, h nr Arlington st, W Ashev
Shook J Warner (Anna), h "Clover Cottage," Albemarle Park
Shook Jos B (Ceneth), carp, h 60 Highland
Shook Maurice P (Mabel), (J L Welch & Co), h W Asheville
Shook Oscar S (Minnie), lab J M Westall & Co, h W Asheville
Shope Jno B (Mary), (Shope & Patton), h 39 s French Broad av
Shope Lena K Miss, nurse 37 Chestnut, h same
Shope Leona Miss, h (r) 40 Maiden la
Shope M Love Miss, h 39 s French Broad av
Shope Pearl C Miss, h 39 s French Broad av
Shope Walter, car coupler, bds Miss Belle Hunter, W Ashev
Shope & Patton (J B Shope, B A Patton), harness and saddlery, 30 n Main
Shroat Arthur (Pollie), painter, h 66 Summit, S Biltmore
Shroat J Gordon (Bertha), carp, h 62 Summit, S Biltmore
Shroat L Vernon, firemn, bds 102 Ralph
*Shuford Claud (Sallie), brkmn, h 184 Livingston
Shuford Edgar B (Sallie), slsmn, h 375 s Main
Shuford Frank A (Laura), emp T L Hyndman, h 169 Bartlett
Shuford Frank L (R L), bricklyr, h 14 Crescent
SHUFORD GEO A JUDGE (Julia D), atty at law 2 Library Bldg—phone 353, h 50 Orange
Shuford Geo A Jr, student, h 50 Orange
Shuford Robt E (Eliza), timekpr Biltmore Estate, h Biltmore Park
Shuford Susan, wid P H, h 14 Crescent
Shuford Wm E (Cora J), atty at law and notary, 24 Temple ct, h 134 Flint
Shultz Giles F (Carrie), lab, h W Asheville

*Shumate Nannie, dom, h 17½ Wallach
Shytle Columbus L (Zyra), carp, h 118 Seney
Shytle J H (May), carp, h 374 s Main
Shytle Lillie Mrs, dom, h 374 s Main
Sicard Alma Miss, h 118 Cumberland av
Sierp W E Mrs, h "Edwin Place," Grove Park
Sigel see Seigal
Sigman Geo, fireman, bds 418 Southside av
*Siler Dollie, waitress, h 50 McDowell
*Siler Hattie, cook, h 18 Gudger
Siler Thos, flgmn, bds 9 Louie
*Silver Jno, driver Kiibler & Whitehead
Silverman Sadie Miss, clk Bon Marche
Simmons Honora M, wid Hamilton F, h 83 Ora
Simons Lula Mrs, bds Cherokee Inn
Simmons T Park, clk M V Moore & Co, h 69 Park av
Simmons Wm G (Jennie), trav slsmn, h 69 Park av
*Simons Mary C, hair dresser 38 Hill, h same
*Simonton Amos (Maggie), lab, h (r) 176 Woodfin
*Simonton Wm M (Theresa), janitor, h 5 Mountain
Simpkins Jno, condr, bds 430 Depot
*Simpkins Leila, cook 112 College, rms same
*Simpson Allen (Mattie), lab, h 128 Choctaw
*Simpson Carrie M, h 128 Choctaw
*Simpson Casper (Lillian), lab, h 39 Max
*Simpson Chas, driver, h 128 Choctaw
*Simpson Chas (Ida), lab, h 53 Gudger
*Simpson Chas (Iowa), driver, h 129 Southside av
Simpson David M (Lucia), trav slsmn, h 30 Spring
Simpson Jas B (Jessie C), carrier P O, h 10 Locust
*Simpson Lake (Marie), porter, h 62 Ralph
Simpson Nicholas (Lena), h 27 s Liberty
Simpson Robt J (Claudia), condr Sou Ry, h 199 s French Broad av
Sims Ethel O Miss, h 7 Panola pl
*Sims Jas (Cicily), porter, h 76 Ridge
Sims Jennie A, wid Walter, h 7 Panola pl
*Sims Jesse (Nora), lab, porter Sou Ry, h 58 Ralph
Sims Jno F (Hannah B), gro 168 Patton av, h 182 same
*Sims Thompson (Jeannette), porter Berkeeley Pool Room, h Pine cor Gaither
Sinclair Jas A (Eva S), dentist 206-209 Legal Bldg, h 197 Chestnut
Sinclair Peter D (Mary S), dentist 206-209 Legal Bldg, h 18 Holland

MAPLE FLOORING
HARDWOOD LUMBER OF ALL KINDS

WOODWARD & SON
9th and Arch Sts., Richmond, Va.
See Adv. Opposite Page 188

*Sinclair Rachel, h 109 Valley
*Sinclair Thos, mchst helper Ashev P & L Co, h Asheland
Singer Sewing Machine Co, 18 n Pack Sq, C D Thorpe mngr
*Singleton Saml L (Ida), sanitarium helper, h 216 Asheland
Sircy Dock, foreman, bds 2 Lyman
Sircy J Henry (Nancy), weaver, h 488 w Haywood
Sircy Sarah Miss, h 488 w Haywood
Sircy Thermol, lab, bds 2 Lyman
Sircy W Riley, clk, h 488 w Haywood
☞**Sircy see also Searcy**
*Sisley Chas (Lydia), porter, h (r) 35 Clingman av
SISTERS OF CHRISTIAN EDUCATION, in charge Hillside Convent, Victoria rd
Sisters of Mercy, in charge St Joseph's Sanitarium, 428 s Main
Sites Abraham B (Kate L), bkkpr Green Bros, h 97 College
Sites Bettie A Miss, h 97 College
Sites Kate L Mrs, boarding 97 College, h same
Sitton Hurst E (Essie), clk Brown Hdw Co, h 24 Clingman
Skinner Addie Miss, cashr Life Ins Co of Va, h 66 s Main
Skinner Mattie Miss, bkpr, bds 85 Central av
Sky Cycle Co, 28 w College, L C Wilson propr
Slack Saml H (Emma), blockman, h 105 College
*Slade Mayfield Rev (Rena), h 127 Valley
Slagle David (Ethel), driver Ashev Pkg Co, h Lyman nr Depot
Slagle Jacob, watchman, h Lyman nr Depot
Slagle Jno, bds 46 Haywood
Slagle Mary Miss, h Lyman nr Depot
Slayden, Fakes & Co (Inc), whol gros 27-33 s Lexington av; W J Slayden pres, B R Fakes v-pres-treas, C S Davis sec
Slayden Wm J, pres Slayden, Fakes & Co, Inc, res New York City
Sloan Alberta B Mrs, clk Bon Marche, h 299 s Main
Sloan Jno B (Alberta B), h 299 s Main
*Sloane Jas, blksmith Ashe Supply & Fdy Co
Sloatermen Alfred F (Eula L), carp, rms 146 Asheland av
Sloop Elizabeth Miss, h Hazel Mill rd, W Ashev
Sloop L Aubrey (Elizabeth), fireman, h 87 Park av
Sloop Wm J, fireman, h Hazel Mill rd, W Asheville
Sloop Wm R (Nannie E), mngr Standard Oil Co, h W Asheville
Sluder Aubrey, clk Storage Supply Co, h W Asheville (R F D 3)

What Have You in Real Estate that You Don't Want?

What do You Want in Real Estate that You Haven't?

WESTERN CAROLINA REALTY CO.
J. W. Wolfe Sec. & Treas.

On the Square
PHONE 974
10 N. PACK SQ.

Brown-Carter Realty Co.
REAL ESTATE
23 TEMPLE COURT
PHONE 341
ASHEVILLE N. C.

FLORIDA SPECIALTIES
Grazing, Timbered, Farm Lands, Orange Groves, Turpentine Locations and Phosphate Lands.

NORTH CAROLINA SPECIALTIES
Orchard, Farm and Timbered Lands, City Property, Rent Collections.

Moale & Chiles Real Estate and Insurance
27 Patton Ave., (2d fl) Phone 661
General Agents United States Fidelity & Guaranty Co.

Club Cafe and Candy Kitchen
"A GOOD PLACE FOR REFRESHMENT"

Our Ice Cream manufacturing plant is absolutely clean and sanitary.
Prompt family delivery. Phones 110 and 111.
Catering for large parties and receptions. Special Creams.

Brown's Undertaking Parlors

S. H. BROWN

Lady Assistant When Desired

Phone 193-2 Rings

50 Patton Avenue
Asheville, N. C.

Established 1894

B. J. JACKSON

Carefully Selected Fruits and Vegetables

Stall No. 11, City Market

BUSINESS PHONES:
86 and 101

RESIDENCE PHONE
1596

Sluder Chas L (Annie), furniture 20 s Pack Sq, h 64 Vance
Sluder E Huston (M Etta), blksmith, h W Asheville
SLUDER ERWIN C (Cora D), v-pres Battery Park Bank, h 192 Montford av
Sluder Fletcher S (Maude), plmbr J R Rich Co, h 26 Woodfin
Sluder Frances W Miss, h Hill st, W Asheville
Sluder Hiram S (Sallie), clk T L Trantham, h Robert's Town
Sluder J Arthur (Addie), mtrmn, h 71 East
Sluder Jos L (Mollie), ice puller, h Haywood rd, W Ashev
Sluder Josiah W, mngr Waddell & Coxe and notary, 16 Patton av, h 192 Montford av
Sluder Lawrence C (Lena), plmbr J R Rich, h 41 Woodfin
Sluder Lester, helper Western Carolina Auto Co, rms 71 East
Sluder Minnie Miss, mill wkr, h 38 Short Roberts
Sluder Randie Miss, h Haywood rd, W Ashev
Sluder Thos J (Deliah), carp, h Hill st, W Ashev
Sluder Wm R (Savannah), clk G W Jenkins, h 58 s Liberty
*Small Bessie, laund, h (r) 39 Clingman av
Smarageles Gus, waiter Central Cafe, rms Revell Bldg
Smart Callie Miss, h 445 w Haywood
Smart Elizabeth Mrs, boarding 33 Starnes av, h same
Smart Leander P, driver, h 445 w Haywood
*Smathers Chas (Daisy), lab, h S Asheville
Smathers Coyl, edger, bds 56 Penland
Smathers Earl H, h Biltmore Park
Smathers Fred I (J L Smathers & Sons), h 316 w Haywood
Smathers Fred L, switchman, 373 w Haywood
Smathers Gettie R, opr Postal Tel-Cable Co, h 25 Roberts
Smathers Isabelle Miss, maid 312 Montford av
Smathers J L & Sons (J L, F I and R I), furniture, 15-17 n Main
Smathers Jasper L (J L Smathers & Sons), h 316 w Haywood
Smathers Jno E (Mary E), clk Green Bros, h 71 Asheland
Smathers Jno W (Mabel L), trav slsmn, h 6 Charlotte
Smathers Maggie, wid E V, h 373 w Haywood
Smathers Marie E Miss, artist, h Biltmore Park
Smathers Paul P, h Biltmore Park
Smathers Pearl Miss, h 13 Roberts
Smathers Pearle Miss, h Biltmore Park
Smathers Philip A (Dora), agt, h 25 Roberts
Smathers Rhet T, clk Sou Exp Co, h 373 w Haywood

Furniture and China Carefully Prepared for Shipment

Mahogany Furniture Hand Made & Carefully Reproduced | **E. E. GALER** 114 PATTON AVE. | Upholstering and Refinishing PHONE - 1674

Smathers Richd I (Margaret), (J L Smathers & Sons), and mattress mnfr 172 Clingman av, h 316 w Haywood
Smathers Rosa Miss, h 373 w Haywood
Smathers Spurgeon, tel opr, h 25 Roberts
Smathers Thelma V Miss, student, h 71 Asheland av
*Smathers Thos (Delia), lab, h S Asheville
SMATHERS WEXLER (Maggie E), dentist (finished from schools—dental dept Tennessee Medical, Chicago of Dental Surgery, John H Myer's, Post Graduate of New York and Philadelphia Dental), rms 14-16 Paragon Bldg—phone 219, h Biltmore Park
Smathers Wholesale Produce Co, 184 Clingman av, R I Smathers propr
SMATHERS WM M (M V Moore & Co), h 16 Charlotte
*Smile Earle, h 81 Eagle
*Smith Abraham L (Alice), coachman, h 82 Brick
Smith Addie Mrs, h 38 East
SMITH ALBERT B (Kate M), genl agt Jefferson Standard Life Ins Co of Greensboro N C, h 58 Vance
Smith Alfred (Emma), h Chunn's Cove
Smith Alice A Miss, h 184 Chestnut
*Smith Andrew (Cora), lab, h 209 Clingman av
Smith Andrew J (Mary E), attendant Highland Hosp, h 50 Panola
*Smith Anna, h 211 Beaumont
*Smith Anna, cook, h 150 Church
Smith Audrey Miss, dom 167 n Main
Smith Augustus R (Julia), painter, h 30 Blake
Smith Benj M (Lucy E), track supervisor Sou Ry, h 16 John
Smith Bessie Miss, clk Peerless Dept Store, h 15 North View
Smith Bessie A Miss, student, h 15 North View
Smith Bonnie Miss, h 2 Avery
Smith's Bridge (across the French Broad river), end of w Haywood
*Smith Brooks, lab, h 19 Baxter al
Smith C Furman (Kathryn L), farmer, h W Asheville
Smith Carl E, painter, h 15 North View
*Smith Carrie, maid, h 17 Short Valley
*Smith Carrie, cook, h 39 Gudger
Smith Celia E Miss, clk Peoples Dept Store, h 15 North View
Smith Chas J (Alice), carp, h Richmond Hill
*Smith Clarence, lab, h 11 Baxter al

Mrs. Wilder's SANITARY HOME LAUNDRY turns out first class work in Laundering and Dry Cleaning. No. 7 Montford Ave., Phone 1354

Smith Claude A (Ila), ins agt, bds 93 College
Smith Daisy M Miss, organist, h 184 Chestnut
Smith Delia E, wid Edwin S, h 38 e Spears av
Smith Douglas (Rebecca), mill wkr, h 41 Roberts
SMITH'S DRUG STORE, 1 s Main, F S Smith mngr
Smith Earle N (Lillie), painter, h (r) 166 s Main
*Smith Edwd (Alice), butler, h 42 Davidson
*Smith Edwd (Vinie), mldr, h 158 Livingston
Smith Elizabeth A Miss, h 24 n Spruce
Smith Elsie Miss, dressmkr Mrs C B Harville, h 281 s Main
*Smith Emma, laund, h 11 Baxter al
Smith Etta M, wid F P, h 156 Blanton
Smith F Loving (Laura E), contr, h 35 Turner
Smith Flossie Miss, h 59 Asheland av
SMITH FRANK S (Beatrice), mngr Smith's Drug Store, h 150 Hillside
Smith Gay, clk C S Hayes, h 281 s Main
*Smith Geo (Nellie), driver Rogers Gro Co, h 140 Church
Smith Geo R (Lizzie), lab, h Hazel Mill rd, W Ashev
Smith Geo W (Roxanna), gro Haywood rd, W Ashev, h same
Smith Grace F Miss, student, h 156 Blanton
Smith Gussie Miss, tchr Orange St Kindergarten, h 184 Chestnut
*Smith Henry (Dora), lab, h 205 Clingman
Smith Hubert V (Kittie), lineman Ashev P & L Co, h Grace
Smith Irvin D, horseshoer C L Brown, bds 511 w Haywood
*Smith Isaiah (Ruth), waiter, h 102 Hazzard
Smith J Ray, driver Ashe Ice Co, h 1 Marjorie
Smith J Wm (Ida L), carp, h 15 North View
Smith Jacob (Minnie), attendant Highland Hosp, h 373 Cumberland av
*Smith Jas (Leila), lab, h Louie nr Depot
*Smith Jas (Martha), presser, h 12 Cumberland av
*Smith Jane, laund, h 23 Hill
*Smith Jane, cook, h 83 Valley
Smith Jno, carp, h 173 Asheland av
*Smith Jno (Clara), cook, h 53 Gudger
*Smith Jno (Dorothy), lab, h 70 Gudger
*Smith Jno H (Fannie), driver I R Coffey, h 107 Valley
*Smith Jno H (Eveline), porter, h 9 Knob
Smith Jos (Mary J), contr, h 52 Cumberland av
Smith Jos E (Uriah S), lab, h 12 Roberts
Smith Jos F, printer Ashev Gazette-News, h 42 Walnut
Smith Jos R (Nannie), driver, h 12 Marjorie

OLDSMOBILE — **DETROIT ELECTRIC**

ARBOGAST MOTOR COMPANY
ACCESSORIES AND SUPPLIES
Phones 302 and 1728
52-60 N. Main

BUICK — **MAXWELLS**

Asheville Dry Cleaning Co.
Telephones 835-836, All Dep't
MAIN, N. E. COR. COLLEGE

THE CLEANERS
Our Department for Oriental Rugs and Carpet Cleaning is prepared to serve you in all its branches.
E. S. Paine   O. E. Hansen

Smith Josephine Mrs, h 46 Velvet
Smith Kate Miss, bds 55 College
Smith King D (Sarah), lab, h Hazel Mill rd, W Asheville
Smith Lamar G (Bertha), foreman, h 2 Avery
Smith Leona Mrs, h 9 Buxton
Smith Lillian Miss, clk H T Rogers, h Woolsey (R F D 1)
*Smith Lonnie, fireman, h (r) 19 Mountain
*Smith Lonnie, lab, h 48 Davidson
Smith Lonnie F, motorman, rms 26 Meriwether Bldg
Smith Louis F (Leona), carp, h 22 Atkinson
*Smith Louisa, laundress, h 83 Valley
Smith M Julia Miss, tchr, h 117 Asheland av
*Smith Mack (Alice), waiter The Winyah, h 156 Church
Smith Maggie Miss, h 9 Buxton
Smith Mamie Miss, h 2 Avery
Smith Mark, clk J E Johnson, h Grace
*Smith Martha, cook, h 139 Eagle
Smith Mary Mrs, h Chunns Cove
*Smith Mattie, maid, h 23 Hill
*Smith Michl D Rev (Mamie E), pastor Southside A M E Zion Church, h 58 McDowell
*Smith Monroe, lab, h 209 Clingman av
*Smith Myra, laund, h 80 Brick
Smith Myrtle A Miss, h Haywood rd, W Ashev
Smith Nellie E Miss, nurse 44 Atkin, h same
Smith Nola Miss, bds Hotel Warren
Smith Norman H (Annie), loom fxr, h 492 w Haywood
*Smith Oliver (Anna), carp, h nr Hazel Mill rd, W Ashev
*Smith O'Neil, lab, h 39 Gudger
Smith Ora D Mrs, h Brevard rd, W Ashev
Smith Othabelle Miss, musician, h 52 Cumberland av
SMITH OWEN (Avonia), physician 78 Patton av—phone 346, office hours 11 a m to 1 p m and 3 to 5 p m, h 44 Montford av—phone 631
*Smith Palmer, coachman, 68 Park av
*Smith Perry (Cora), driver, h 137 Clingman av
Smith R Oscar (Pearle), clk Crystal Dairy Lunch, h 36 Furman av
SMITH R SHARP (Isabelle C), (Smith & Carrier Company), h 51 Arlington
*Smith Rebecca, nurse, h 36 Hill
Smith Rhoda E, wid S W, h 58 Vance
*Smith Robt (Annie), lab, h 138 Eagle
Smith Robt P Rev (Ella R), supt Presby Synodical Home Missions, h 117 Asheland av

LIFE INSURANCE COMPANY OF VA. OLDEST, LARGEST STRONGEST Southern Life Insurance Co.

ORGANIZED 1871
RICHMOND, VIRGINIA

Issues Industrial Policies from $8.00 to $900.00, with Premiums Payable WEEKLY on persons from two to seventy years of age

J. V. Moon, Superintendent, Rooms 3-4-5 Maxwelton Bldg., Asheville, N. C.

D. TREXLER TIN SHOP

All Kinds of Roofing, Gutter and Conductor Work.

Phone 862

159 South Main St.

DR. C. H. MILLER

MECHANO-THERAPIST

14 N. Spruce St.
Phone 979
ASHEVILLE, N. C.

Hours by engagement

Drugless Healing of Disease

ASHEVILLE [1913] DIRECTORY

Smith Robt W (Fannie L), condr Sou Ry, h 281 s Main
Smith Ross (Cordelia), mill wkr, h 8 Logan
Smith Roy, helper, h 281 s Main
Smith S Kate Miss, tailoress S T Logan, h 55 College
Smith S Montgomery (Mary K), lumber 425-428 Legal Bldg, h 43 Oak
Smith S O Capt, rms Y M C A
Smith Silas S (Myrtis), attendant Highland Hosp, h 50 Panola
Smith Thos C Dr (Annie E), propr Biltmore Drug Co, and whol drugs, 14-16 s Lexington av, h 184 Chestnut
Smith Thos C Jr (Madge), mngr Dr T C Smith, h 156 Chestnut
SMITH THOMAS W (Mattie R), (H A Brown & Co), and (Brown-Carter Realty Co), h W Asheville
*Smith Thurman (Eugenia), lab, h 18 Brick
Smith W G Mrs, mngr Womens Dept M V Moore & Co, h 18 Bearden av
*Smith Wm (Fannie), lab, h 90 Mountain
Smith Wm B (Frances A), h 9 Buxton
Smith Wm H, well digger, h Brevard rd, W Ashev
Smith Wm H (Corrie), carp, h 37 Hall
Smith Wm M (Laura), boarding 98 Patton av, h same
Smith Zebulon, mill wkr, bds 8 Logan
SMITH & CARRIER COMPANY (R S Smith and A H Carrier), architects Carrier Bldg, College cor Market—phone 283
Smitherman Louise Miss, matron Allen Indus Home & School, h 241 College
Smyer Arthur L, flgmn Sou Ry, h 167 Blanton
Sneed Chas T (Mollie), farmer, h 173 s Main
Sneed Kate, mad, h 14 Eagle Terrace
Sneed Mollie Mrs, boarding 173 s Main, h same
Snelson Ferdinand R, brkmn, bds 96 Bartlett
Snider Alley M (Minnie), farmer, h Asheville av, W Ashev
Snider Lawrence M, lab, h Asheville av, W Ashev
*Snider Mary, laund, h 11 Greer's Row
*Snider Mattie, laund, h 11 Greer's Row
Snipes Elisha L, supervisor Sou Ry, rms 331 Southside av
*Snow Laura, maid Wm S George, h same
Snowden Clarence, barber Ashev Barber Shop, bds Patton
Snowden Jocelyn Miss, nurse 71 Central av, rms same
Snyder Amy B, wid Frank N, dressmkr 75 Seney, h same
Snyder Curtis H (Marie), police, h 7 Merrimon av
Snyder Emanual, emp D A Lashley, h W Asheville

....Asheville Cleaning and Pressing Club....
Tailoring That Satisfies and Prices That Please
Steam and French Dry Cleaning of all delicate and fine wearing apparel for ladies and gentlemen. MESSENGER SERVICE IN THE CITY.

J. C. WILBAR, Prop. 4. N. Pack Square PHONE 389

Snyder Frances Miss, stengr, h 75 Seney
Snyder Madge Miss, student, h 7 Merrimon av
Socialist Reading Room, 15 Drhumor Bldg
Society for Prevention of Cruelty to Animals, J C Orr sec
Solesbee Jno W (Lula), miller, h nr Haywood rd, W Ashev
Solesbee Marion G (Lizzie), fireman The Winyah, h 27 Dortch av
Solerwitz Israel, watchmkr 39 College, h W Asheville
Solomon Nat E, musical director The Dreamland, rms 30 Technical Bldg
Solsbee Grover W (Annie), foreman R I Smathers, h 495 w Haywood
*Somers Jno K (Rosalie L), draymn 16 Dundee, h same
Soncrant Emmon R (Pearl), foreman Western Carolina Auto Co, h 43 Highland
SONDLEY F A, L L D, atty at law, 4-5-6 New Sondley Bldg—phone 1304, h "Angkosia," Country
Sorrell Flora McD, wid M W, boarding 100 s Main, h same
Sorrell L Frank, h 23 Sorrell
Sorrell Pinckney D, carp, h 23 Sorrell
Sorrells Jas T (Lena), driver Coca-Cola Bottling Co, h 63 Phifer
Sorrels Chas E, del boy, h 161 Charlotte
Sorrels Chas E (Dora), propr Asheville Fish Co, h 35 West
Sorrels Earle L, lab, h 23 North View
Sorrels Geo A (Mary), gro 13½ n Main, h 161 Charlotte
Sorrels Mamie A Miss, h 161 Charlotte
Sorrels Rufus Z (Ida), truck gardener, h 23 North View
Sorrels Sallie, wid L F, dressmkr 53½ Orange
*South Asheville A M E Zion Church, S Asheville
South Asheville Cemetery, S Asheville, Geo Avery and Benj Ragsville trustees
*South Asheville School (Dist 14), S Asheville
South Atlantic Trans-Continental R R Co, 111-112-114 Citizen Bldg
South Biltmore Baptist Church, 18 Summit, S Biltmore, Rev W W Marr pastor
South Biltmore Graded School, Biltmore rd, S Biltmore
Souther Chas E (Ella J), condr Sou Ry, h (r) 326 s Main
*Souther Furman (Josephine), brkmn, h (r) 88 Black
Souther Grace I Miss, student, h 45 Clayton
*Souther Morris (Louise), lab, h S Asheville
Souther W Hix (Georgia), h 45 Clayton
Southerland Cecil P (Mary E), stengr div frt agt Sou Ry and mngr General Supply Co, h 51 Asheland av

Asheville Dray, Fuel and Construction Co.

Heavy Hauling of all kinds — 61-2 South Main — **WE FURNISH BUILDING STONE** — Moving Furniture a Specialty — PHONE - 223

ASHEVILLE [1913] DIRECTORY

SOUTHERN COAL COMPANY, domestic and steam coal 10 n Pack Sq—phones, office 114, yard 662, F C Todd genl mngr (see insert with index tab)
Southern Dray, Riverside Drive, J H Allport propr
SOUTHERN EXPRESS CO, 99-103 Patton av—phone 83 and Ry Station—phone 598, J T James agt
Southern Hotel (The), 12-14 s Main, Mrs W A Webb propr
Southern Land Auction Co, 225 Legal Bldg, C R Moore mngr
Southern Mica Co (see Ashev Mica Co)
Southern Railway Dining Room, Sou Ry Passngr Sta, Gresham & Fogus proprs
Southern Railway District Passenger Agent, 60 Patton av, J H Wood agt
Southern Railway Division Freight Agent, 60 Patton av (2d fl), A K Orr agt
Southern Railway Freight Depot, Depot cor Avery, W P Maher agt
Southern Railway Land & Industrial Department, 60 Patton av (2d fl), T G Wood agt
Southern Railway Passenger Station, Depot nr Southside
Southern Railway Passenger and Freight Depot, Biltmore, Geo A Digges agt
Southern Railway Ticket Office, 60 Patton av, O'Connor Wilson agt
Southern Railway Offices, Sou Ry Passngr Station
    Baggage Agent—W B Weaver
    Chief Clerk to Supt—Wm E Clarke
    Claim Agents—A S Guerard and Jno M Acee
    Dispatcher—D W Johnston
    General Foreman—E L McClammey
    Roadmaster—W G Lacy
    Special Agent—W B Thomas
    Station Masters—C D Clarke and N F Parris
    Superintendent (Ashev Div)—C C Hodges
    Superintendent (Murphy Div)—T S Boswell
    Ticket Agent—E D Moore
    Time Keepers—R R Dufour and Wm M Clarke
    Trainmaster—C G King
    Yard Masters—W W Hannah and J M Weaver
Southers see Souther
Southern Weighing & Inspection Bureau, Sou Ry Frt Depot
Southside A M E Zion Church, Southside av nr Choctaw, Rev M D Smith pastor

---

DYNAMOS & MOTORS

Piedmont Electric Co.

64 Patton Av.
ASHEVILLE, N.C.

J. C. McPHERSON
SLATE AND TIN ROOFING
Galvanized Iron Work — Hot Air Furnaces
35-37 EAST COLLEGE STREET

PLUMBING STEAM AND HOT WATER **HEATING**

PHONE 133

MONARCH COAL

The Coal With the Quality That Makes Friends of all Who Use it :: :: :: ::

MONARCH COAL

FOR STOVE and GRATE

We Handle Monarch Coal Exclusively in Asheville

Southern Coal Co.

Phone 114   10 North Pack Sq.   Asheville, N. C.

PHONE 114 FOR

MONARCH COAL

COAL that gives Satisfaction
in Stove and Grate :: ::

CLINCHFIELD COAL

The Acknowledged Leader
in Coals for use in Furnace

Monarch and Clinchfield Coal

HANDLED EXCLUSIVELY BY US IN ASHEVILLE

Southern Coal Co.

Phone 114   10 North Pack Sq.   Asheville, N. C.

Southside Furniture Co, 372 Southside av, S T Early pres, E M Jarrett mngr
Southside Hall, 372 Southside av
*Southside School, Southside av nr Choctaw, H A Lee prin
Southwick Chas H (Debby J), h Haywood rd, W Ashev
Southwick Margaret C Miss, h Haywood rd, W Ashev
Spann Mary E Miss, tchr Montford Av Schl, boarding 2 Angle, Biltmore, h same
Spanner Alma Miss, student, h 372 Montford av
Spanner Margaret, wid Henry, h 372 Montford av
Sparks Carter D, lab, bds J W Gentry, W Ashev
Sparks Hiram G (Lennie M), tanner, h Haywood rd, W Ashev
Sparks Wm G (Lillian), h 171 Patton av
*Sparrow Louise, cook Forest Hill
Spear Elwin W (Sadie E), music tchr 9 Maxwelton Bldg, bds 200 Haywood
Spears Jas W (Irene), contr, h 12 Edgehill av
Spears Jane C, wid Geo T, h 22 Woodfin
*Spears Sonnie, driver Patton & Stikeleather, h 129 Beaumont
Speer Janie D Miss, tchr Allen Indus Home, h 241 College
*Spencer W R, paver, h 80 Valley
Spirella Corset Agency, 21 s Main, Mrs B F Gruner agt
Spivey Clyde (Jessie A), lab, h 69 Atkinson
Spivey Fred A (Zora), carp, h 28 Turner
Spivey J C, lab W M Jones, h 69 Atkin
Spivey Jas T (Arrie), driver, h 38 William
Spivey Jerome (Josie), carp, h 3d av, W Asheville
Spivey Oscar J, agt Dixie Mutual Life Ins Co, bds 16 Spruce
Spivey Robt L (Ina), mchst, h Swannanoa av, W Ashev
*Springs Lee (Maggie), baker, h 26 Gibbons
Sprinkle Alfred P (Mary), laund, h 353 Hillside
Sprinkle Ida L Miss, phone opr, h 11 Buttrick
Sprinkle Jno R, clk Yates & McGuire, h 11 Buttrick
Sprinkle Marion C (Bertie), marker, h Jarrett av, W Ashev
Sprinkle Nancy A, wid Wm N, h 11 Buttrick
Sproat Anna D Mrs, millinery 20 n Pack Sq, bds 107 Haywood
Sproles Wm J (Dora C), pres Virginia-Carolina Coal Co, and Fork Ridge Coal Co, h 21 Orange
Sprouse Effie Miss, h 81 Tiernan
Sprouse Hosea M (Priscilla), gro 59 Black, h 295 Asheland
Sprouse Jno (Amanda), driver, h 2 Fagg
Sprouse Jos (Zennie), clk, h 2 Fagg

Candy Kitchen and Club Cafe — "A GOOD PLACE FOR REFRESHMENT" — Hot drinks on cold days. Cold drinks on hot days. The best drinks every day. Pure fruits and syrups blended "just right," served daintily. Our Ice Cream and Soda Water Department, Restaurant and Candy Departments are always kept up to the standard of nearest perfection. Phones 110 and 111. 19 and 21 Haywood St.

Brown's Undertaking Parlors

S. H. BROWN

50 Patton Avenue
ASHEVILLE, N. C.

Lady Assistant When Desired

Phone 193-2 Rings

THE MOORE Plumbing Company

16 N. Pack Square

PHONE 1025

Sanitary Plumbing, General Tin and Metal Work, Hot Air Furnaces

---

ASHEVILLE [1913] DIRECTORY — 342

Sprouse Max L (Della), capt police, h 81 Tiernan
Sprouse Nellie, wid Wiley, h 299 Asheland av
Sprouse Stuart (Lillie), carp, h 297 Asheland av
*Spurgeon Anna, h 215 College
*Spurgeon Saml J Rev (Caroline), pastor Hopkins Chapel A M E Zion Church, h 215 College
Spurlin Jane K, wid Wm, h 233 s Grove
Spurlin Jno M (Mary P), cabtmkr W M Jones, h 359 s French Broad av
"SPURWOOD," res S R Montgomery, Vernon Hill
Staffon Jno B (Vera E), emp Sou Ry, h Hazel Mill rd, W Ashev
Staffon Nicholas S (Laura), shoemkr T G Bowden, h Bingham Hghts
*Staggs Jno S (Mary J), barber C T Howell, h 63 Ridge
*Staley Jas, washer Western Carolina Auto Co, h 159 College
Stamey Claude C (Elsie R), flgmn Sou Ry, h 116 Bartlett
Stamey Reuben, brkmn Sou Ry, h 116 Bartlett
*Stanard Wm, porter Buckeye Parlor, h 216 Asheland av
*Stanback Jas (Cora), shoemkr 178 Livingston, h same
*Stanback Lottie, laundress, h 45 Wallach
Stanberry Edgar E (Laura), barber Langren Barber Shop, h 29 Vance
Stanberry J Pierce, fireman, bds 286 Southside av
Stancill Alice, wid David, dressmkr 114 Poplar, h same
Stancill Florence A Miss, h 5 Furman av
Standard Mining Co, 15 Church, J G Adams sec-treas
Standard Oil Co, 171 Avery, W R Sloop mngr
Stanley Nancy A, wid W H, bds 172 Southside av
Staples Alfred F (Anna L), h 72 Merrimon av
STAR MARKET (The), meats City Market—phones 1917-1918-1919, Hoffman & Kent proprs (see front cover)
Starnes Alfred N, surveyor, h Acton N C
Starnes Geo H (Theresa E), farmer, h Haywood rd, W Ashev
Starnes Gonano Miss, nurse 18 Grady, h same
STARNES J PINK (Lillie E), genl mngr Imperial L & H Ins Co (Inc), h 21 Green—phone 1619
Starnes J Pink Jr, emp Imp Mut L & H Ins Co, h 21 Green
Starnes Jesse R (Margaretha), atty, h 143 n Main
Starnes Jno H (Eliza N), slsmn, h 78 West
Starnes Jno W, piano tchr Ashev Schl of Musical Art, h 33 Hiawassee
Starnes Mabel Miss, student, h Haywood rd, W Ashev

The Battery Park Bank

Capital - - $100,000.00
Surplus and Profits, $110,000.00

ASHEVILLE, N. C.   City, County and State Depositary

J. A. TILLMAN — Jeweler — 17 N. Main St. I carry a nice line of Watches, Clocks and Jewelry, and make a specialty of repair work. Satisfaction guaranteed

Starnes Margaret E Miss, furn rooms, 18 Grady, h same
Starnes Mary J, wid Jno W, h 33 Hiawassee
Starnes Melvin R, clk, h 78 West
Starnes O Edwin, agt Imp Mut L & H Ins Co, h 21 Green
STARNES WALTER B, treas Imperial Mut L & H Ins Co (Inc), h Charlotte N C
Starnes Zona Miss, dress mkr 18 Grady, h same
Steadman Lena A Miss, dressmkr 83 Washington rd h same
*Stelle Alice, laund, h 28 Sassafras
*Steele Bruce (Effie), janitor Ashev Club, h 26 Hildebrand
*Steele Cora, cook, h 6 Knob
Steele Dora Miss, cashr Bon Marche, h 153 Haywood
Steele Dora E, wid Robt L, h 153 Haywood
Steele Ella F, wid J W, h 250 Chestnut
Steele Eloise Miss, h 250 Chestnut
Steele Emma, wid Daniel, h 7 Baird
Steele Harold M, h 197½ Asheland av
Steele Martin T (Nora), engnr Sou Ry, h 381 s French Broad av
Steele Pearl L Miss, h 7 Baird
Steele Samantha C, wid Jno M, h 197½ Asheland av
Steele Walter A (Mary), asst mngr Ashev Ptg & Engrav Co h 7 Silver
Steelman Jno A (Blanche), trav auditor Sou Ry, h 42 Starnes av
*Stelle Jesse (Sophia), cook, h 118 Hill
Stelling Jacob H (Katharine), h 141 Chestnut
Stelling Jas H (Stella), slsmn, h 11 Highland
Stelling Julia T Miss, h 141 Chestnut
*Stephens Jacob, waiter, h 27 Circle
*Stephens Jas, waiter The Winyah, h 120 Pine
Stephens Victor F (Nannie), clk T L Trantham, h 1 Irwin, S Biltmore
☞ Stephens see also Stevens
STEPHENSON FLORENCE MISS, prin Home Industrial School and Pease Memorial House, h Biltmore rd (Victoria)—phone 482
☞ Stephenson see also Stevenson
*Stepp Alice W, h 111 Blanton
*Stepp Burgin, driver Asheville Grocery Co
Stepp Eugene H, fireman, h 67 Clingman av
Stepp Geo B (Sara J), carp, h (r) 269 s Main
Stepp J Robt (Ella), lumber inspr, h 67 Clingman av
*Stepp Martin (Lula), lab, h 115 Black
Stepp W Lucius (Nola), watchman, h 42 Jefferson Drive

INSURANCE
Insure your salary with us
Never carry your own risk
Safety is the best policy
Unless you are a capitalist
Rest easy if you have
An accident we will
Not keep you waiting to
Collect your claim
Every claim promptly paid

Imperial Mutual Life & Health Insurance Co.
Home Office:
ASHEVILLE, N. C.
Phone 495

HOTEL OXFORD — Redecorated and Refitted throughout. Recently enlarged to 60 rooms. Centrally located Depot cars stop at entrance. Long distance telephone office upstairs. American and European plan. Rates 50c, 75c and $1 per day; special rates by week or month. C. H. Branson & Sons, Proprietors. Phone 1887. 50-54 South Main St. **Asheville, N. C.**

Williams-Brownell Planing Mill Company — **Hardwoods**
Lumber---Rough and Dressed   Flooring a Specialty   Moulding, Interior Finish, Etc.
Office, Plant and Yards on Southern Railway, Near Biltmore Station
WHITE PINE   Phone 729   YELLOW PINE

Stern Jos (Eva), auctioneer, h 11 Cumberland Circle
Stern Saml, cashr Bon Marche, h 41 Cumberland Circle
Stern Victor (Louise H), jeweler 17 Haywood, h 239 Montford av
Sternberg S & Co (Seigfried Sternberg, Gustav Lichtenfels), junk, 353-359 Depot, and 84 n Lexington av
STERNBERG SIEGFRIED (Anna), (S Sternberg & Co), (Asheville Ptg Co), and v-pres Carolina Machinery Co, h Victoria rd
Stevens B Lealand Miss, stengr frt office Sou Ry, h 49 Hiawassee
Stevens Elizabeth C Miss (The Misses Stevens), h 15 Bearden av
Stevens Francis M (Fannie J), medicine, 49 Hiawassee, h same
Stevens Fred'k G (Mabel), clk Brown Book Co, h 32 Clyde
Stevens Geo W (Emma), carp, h (r) 386 n Main
Stevens Henry B Judge (Katie M) (Stevens & Anderson), h 300 Montford av
Stevens Jesse S, bds Western Hotel
Stevens Jewell F (Carrie), clk frt office Sou Ry, h 78 Cherry

---
Always mention the Directory when writing to advertisers

SEVENS MARTIN L (M Lula) (Stevens & Orr), phys Adelaide Bldg, h 133 w Chestnut—phone 990
Stevens Mary E Miss, student, h 14 s Main
Stevens Misses (The) (Misses Nannie B and Elizabeth C), School 15 Bearden av
Stevens Nannie B Miss (The Misses Stevens), h 15 Bearden
Stevens Ralph F (Mayme), sec-treas Mustin-Robertson Co Inc and notary, h 19 Blake
Stevens Richard, clk R W Harkins, h 100 Cherry
Stevens Susan J, wid Jos M, h 15 Bearden av
Stevens Vinnie Leah Miss, h 49 Hiawassee
Stevens Wm H (Mamie), foreman Ashev Mica Co, h Biltmore rd, S Biltmore
Stevens & Anderson (H B Stevens, J B Anderson), attys at law, 203-205 Oates Bldg
STEVENS & ORR (Drs M L Stevens and C C Orr), physicians, 1-2-3-5-6 Adelaide Bldg—phone 186, office hours 10 a m to 1 p m and by appointment

Asheville Electrical Co. — Electrical Contractors
HEADQUARTERS 74 CENTRAL AVENUE
W. Mansfield Booze, Manager
PHONE 377

Asheville Dry Cleaning Co.
Telephones 835-836, All Dep't
MAIN, N. E. COR. COLLEGE

THE CLEANERS
Our Department for Oriental Rugs and Carpet Cleaning is prepared to serve you in all its branches.
E. S. Paine   O. E. Hansen

FOR BOX SHOOKS — **Call English Lumber Co. PHONE 321**

STEVENS SAMUEL M (Annie B), licensed plumber and sanitary engineer, 95 Cumberland av—phone 1314, h same

Telephone 1314   "The Best is Cheapest"

S. M. STEVENS

Licensed Plumber and Sanitary Engineer

Steam Vacuum, Vapor and Water Heating of All Kinds Put in Your Home

95 CUMBERLAND AVENUE

Stevens see also Stephens
Stevenson Albert, wood wkr, h Haywood rd, W Asheville
Stevenson Oscar A (May), engnr, h 168 Bartlett
Stevenson see also Stephenson
Stewart Amanda I, wid Wm A, gro 93 Livingston, h 95 same
Stewart Augustus (Cora), h Chunns Cove
*Stewart Cora, cook, h 14 McDowell
Stewart Daniel W, lineman, h Grace
Stewart Edwd D (Lottie), h Chunns Cove
Stewart Elijah, lineman, bds 80 Penland
Stewart Geo W, lab, h Grace
*Stewart Jas (Annie), shoemkr, h 7 Brick
Stewart Jno M, h Chunns Cove
Stewart Jno P, piano tuner Falk's Music House
Stewart Mary A Miss, nurse 71 Central av, rms same
Stewart Newton H (Mary), lab, h Grace
Stewart Wm (Rosa), h Chunns Cove
STIKELEATHER FERGUS (Mary) (Aston, Rawls & Co), h 45 Church
Stikeleather Fergus Jr (Harriet N V), carrier P O, h 79 w Chestnut
STIKELEATHER GILLILAND (Aileen), sec-treas Nubery Auto Sales Co of N C, h 134 s Main
Stieleather Jas G (Nancy) (Patton & Stikeleather) and treas Brown Book Co, h 63 Church
Stikeleather Mary Miss, h 45 Church

BIGGEST **B**USIEST **B**EST

Asheville Steam Laundry

Phones: 1936 and 1937

43 to 47 W. College Street

CHARLES H. HONESS

OPTOMETRIST AND OPTICIAN

Exclusive maker of ATLAS SHUR-ON EYE GLASSES

THE Home of Ce-Rite Toric Lenses

We make a specialty of correcting optical defects with properly fitted glasses.

54 Patton Avenue
Opposite Postoffice

Carolina Machinery Co. Founders, Machinists and Jobbers of Mill Supplies. We make all kinds of Castings in Iron, Brass or Aluminum.

WE ALSO FURNISH SKILLED MECHANICS FOR BOILER REPAIRS —— **PHONE 590**

LIFE INSURANCE COMPANY OF VA.
ORGANIZED 187
Richmond -:- Virginia
J. V MOON, Superintendent
Rooms 3-4-5- Maxweiton Bldg., Asheville, N. C.

All claims paid IMMEDIATELY upon receipt of satisfactory proofs of Death. Total payment to policyholders since organization, over $12,000,000.00. Is paying its Policyholders over $1,000,000.00 annually.

T. P. JOHNSON & CO.

SHEET METAL WORKERS

All Kinds of Roofing Guttering and Conductor Work Metal Ceilings, Skylights and Galvanized Iron Cornices

OFFICE and SHOP:
69-71 S. MAIN
Phone 325

DR. C. H. MILLER

Mechano-Therapist

14 N. Spruce Street
ASHEVILLE, N. C.
PHONE 979

Hours by Engagement

DRUGLESS HEALING OF DISEASE

Stiles Harper (Julia), confrs 420 Depot, h 436 s French Broad av
Stimson Erasmus B, music tchr, h 70 Bartlett
Stines Maggie D Miss, nurse 63 Asheland av, rms same
Stinnette Chas R (Grace), foreman J C Wilbar, h 69 Blanton
*Stinson Green A (Berta), draymn 18 Knob, h same
*Stinson Wm M (Blanche), eating house 417 Depot, h 2 Max
Stirewalt Adolphus D (Lula), mchst, h 99 Clingman av
Stirewalt C Chester, mchst, h 99 Clingman av
Stirewalt Emmett H, lab, h 99 Clingman av
Stitton Hurst E (Essie), mtrmn, h 24 Clingman av
Stockinger Hedwig Miss, h 125 Broad
Stockinger Johanna Miss, dressmkr Mrs J Price, h 125 Broad
*Stocks Lewis, lab, h 105 Roberts
Stockton Alice Miss, tchr Murry Schl, h 348 Merrimon av
Stockton Cora Miss, tchr Montford Av Schl, h 348 Merrimon av
Stockton Martha C, wid Alex H, h 348 Merrimon av
Stockton May E Miss, nurse Winyah Sanatorium, rms same
Stokely Lilla E Miss, h 21 Orange
Stokely Mabel Miss, tchr, h 21 Orange
Stokely Royal J (M Dora), county auditor, h 21 Orange
Stokely Royal J Jr, student, h 21 Orange
Stone Harry L, electrn, h 39 n French Broad av
Stone Herbert R, clk, h 39 n French Broad av
Stone Mabelle Miss, h 39 n French Broad av
Stone Moses A (Carrie P), h 126 w Chestnut
Stone Peyton L (Cora B), police, h 160 s Main
Stone Rudolph B (Nancy), dispr Sou Ry, h 39 n French Broad av
Stone Victor L (Estella), lumber inspr, h 68 Asheland av
Stoner Aurelius D, genl mdse 25 Plaza, Biltmore, h 2 Brook same
Stoner Jno M, pres Birmingham Realty Co and broker, 18 s Main
*Stoner Wm (Della), lab, h 62 Black
Storage Supply Co, cold Storage 91-99 Avery, Fred'k Kent mngr
*Stover Martha, h 30 Davidson
Stowe H R, drug clk C A Raysor, bds Cherokee Inn
Stowe Lucy V Mrs, dressmkr 20 n French Broad av, h same

ASHEVILLE CLEANING and PRESSING CLUB

TAILORING THAT SATISFIES and PRICES THAT PLEASE
Hats cleaned, banded and bound. Silk hats ironed. Buttons made to order in all sizes. Plain or with rims. PHONE 389

DYEING IN ALL SHADES
Kid Gloves, Slippers and Plumes, Fancy Jabots and Ties, French Dry Cleaned. Ladies' and Gentlemen's suits Steam Cleaned. Messenger Service. **J. C. Wilbar, Prop.**

4 NORTH PACK SQ.

Stowe Wm W (Bertha), carp, h Woolsey (R F D 1)
*Strachan Maude, nurse 17 Hill, h same
Stradley Edwin P (Bertha), sec-treas Farmers Union, h R F D No 1
Stradley Gedwin F (Neola), gro 3 n e Pack Sq, h 194 Woodfin
Stradley J Lionel, bkkpr Fred'k Rutledge & Co, h 102½ Haywood
Stradley Margaret, wid Chas, mlnr H B Hood, 102½ Haywood
Stradley Marie E Miss, h 102½ Haywood
Stradley Ruth Miss, h 60 Starnes av
Strebig Jane W Miss, cashr Langren Hotel, h 36 Haywood
*Street Chas (Rosa), driver C Sawyer, h 22 Baxter al
Street Jas R (Junia B), engnr Sou Ry, h 145 Park av
*Streetor Harriett, cook, h 154 Hill
*Stribling Saml (Lula), cook, h 259 Beaumont
Stricker Louis R (Margaret J), h 42 College Park
Stricklin Chas A (Lida E), mstr mech, h 9 Louie
Stricklin Lida E Mrs, boarding, 9 Louie, h same
Strong Wm S (Ramelle), merchant, h Edgemont
Stroud Celia J Mrs, h 88 Haywood
*Stroud Jno, lab, h Blanton
*Stroud Rhoda, laundress, h 87 Wallach
Stroup S C, painter, bds 16 Hilliard la
Stuart Danl W, clk J B Hermann, h Grace
☞ **Stuart see also Stewart**
Stubbs Alfred H Rev, h "Schoenberger Hall," 135 Church
*Studman Chas (Julia), hostler, bds 88 Eagle
Stuman Ernest, clk 7½ s Main
Stuman Jno (Nannie), bricklyr, h 39 East
Stuman Jos W (Sallie E), h 7½ s Main
Styles J Scroop (Eloise M), atty at law and notary, 409-410 Oates Bldg, h W Asheville
☞ **Styles see Stiles**
Suber Annie, wid Presley, nurse 176 Woodfin, h same
Suber Wm P, plmbr, h 176 Woodfin
Sudderth Curran B, bds Cherokee Inn
Sudderth Geo (Rosa), carp, h W Asheville
Sudderth Jno S (Minnie), foreman Sou Ry, h 16 Green
Sudderth Martha C, wid Wm P, h 41 Montford av
Sugarman Harry L, clk Ashev Dry Gds Co, h 30 Montford
Sugarman Jacob (Rebecca), tailor 4 n Lexington av, h 30 Montford av
Sugarman Minnie Miss, h 30 Montford av

WEAVERVILLE LINE NINE MILES BY TROLLEY FROM PACK SQUARE TO WEAVERVILLE

ASHEVILLE AND EAST TENNESSEE RAILROAD CO.

NORTH MAIN STREET　　　　　　　　　　　　　　　　　　　　　ASHEVILLE N. C.

Electrical Supplies
PIEDMONT ELECTRIC COMPANY
ASHEVILLE, N. C.
64 PATTON AVE.

SUGG J LEO (Union Plumbing Co), bds 237 s Main
Sugg Jno E (Winnie), with I W Glazier, bds 46 Haywood
Sugg Jno K (Cornelia), carp, h 237 s Main
Sugg Robt, clk Union Plumbing Co, h 237 s Main
*Sullivan Eli (Lula), driver J H Creasman, h n Lexington
Sullivan Hezekiah H (Ada Lee), engnr Sou Ry, h 275 Haywood
Sullivan Joel H (Corinne), engnr Sou Ry, h 218 s French Broad av
Sullivan M M, propr Crystal Cafeterian and Crystal Dairy Lunch, rms 21 Library Bldg
Sullivan Mittie E Miss, nurse 36 Haywood, h same
Sullivan Nim B (Lila), h 18 n Liberty
*Sullivan P Albert (Sudie), eating hse 98 Eagle, h same
Sullivan Saml, h 18 n Liberty
*Sullivan Wm M, barber J W Bowman, h 167 College
*Summey Belle, cook, h 144 Pearson Drive
*Summey Florence, dom, h 144 Pearson Drive
*Summey Harriet, laund, h 18 Clemmons
*Summey Hattie, dom, h 144 Pearson Drive
Summey Junius H, clk Brown Hdw Co, rms Temple Court
Summey Wm C (Ruth), cabt mkr E E Galer, h 24 Spring
Sumner Alma Miss, emp Ashev Mica Co, h 24 Roberts
Sumner Bynum H (Annie M), trav slsmn, h 215 n Main
Sumner Chas E (Alma), lab, h 24 Short Roberts
Sumner Conrad (Sallie), car repr, h Penna av, W Ashev
Sumner Edwd M (Lillie), emp Sou Ry, h Swannanoa av, W Ashev
Sumner Francis, slsmn, h Swannanoa av, W Ashev
Sumner Frances A Miss, student, h 381 Sumner
Sumner Frank A (Florence), real est, h 381 Montford av
Sumner Jesse H (Elizabeth), slsmn, h Swannanoa av, W Ashev
Sumner Lonnie (Eva), dispr Sou Ry, h W Asheville
Sumner Lula Miss, nurse Highland Hosp, rms same
*Sumner Minnie, cook, h 130 Short McDowell
Sumner Sallie E, wid T J, h Church cor Summit, S Biltmore
Sumner Theodore B, student, h 215 n Main
Sumner Wilbur C, student, h 381 Montford av
SUNDAY CITIZEN (The), Citizen Bldg, Battery Park pl
"Sunniside Cottage," Sunset Drive
"Sunnycrest," res Mrs E H Radeker, Vernon Hill
Sunny Smoke Shop, 3 Haywood, David H Fater propr
"Sunset Lodge," Sunset Drive
Superior Court, Court Hse, Marcus Erwin clk

CONTRACTOR and BUILDER
STEEL RANGES | **J. C. McPHERSON** | 35-37 E COLLEGE ST. PHONE 133
PLUMBING STEAM AND HOT WATER HEATING

Sutherland Wm H (Alice), emp Creamery, h 16 Orchard
☞ Sutherland see also Southerland
*Sutton Willis (Gussie), butler Dr A W Calloway, h 122 Church
Suttle C Pinckney, h 68 e College
Suttle Claud (Jessie M), engnr Sou Ry, h 410 Southside av
Suttle Drury D (Jane), real est, h 68 College
Suttle G Emma Miss, h 68 College
Suttle Jos B, clk, h 68 College
Suttle S Frances Miss, tchr Murray Schl, h 68 e College
*Sutton Willis (Augusta), porter, h 122 Church
Swain A B, painter, bds 16 Hilliard la
Swain Cornelia Miss, h Grace
Swain Harriet E, wid J L, h Grace
SWAIN J EDWARD (Wells & Swain), and notary, h Grace—phone 1109
☞ Swain see also Swayne
Swaney Florence E Miss, h 28 Spring
Swaney Harriett, wid J H, h 28 Spring
Swaney Jas H, car inspr, h 28 Spring
Swaney Minnie Mrs, h 4 Richard
Swangum Emma, wid B S, h Woolsey (R F D 1)
Swangum Rhoda Mrs, h 22 Central av
Swann Chas McK, mill wkr, h 19 Factory Hill
Swann Eliza H Miss, stengr McConnell Bros, bds 125 n Lexington
Swann Grace L Miss, emp Ashev Stm Ldy, h 19 Factory Hill
*Swann Hattie V, tchr Hill St Schl, h 139 Poplar
*Swann Irving Rev (Hattie V), h 139 Poplar
Swann Jno R (Rena), produce, h 418 n Main
Swann Lattie W (May), lab, h Woolsey (R F D 1)
Swann Lena Miss, dom Whitmore Sanitarium, rms same
Swann Minnie E Miss, laund, h 19 Factory Hill
Swann R Benj (Addie), h 19 Factory Hill
Swann Suetta Miss, emp Ashev Stm Ldy, h 19 Factory Hill
SWANNANOA-BERKELEY HOTEL (The), leading family and commercial hotel, 45-57 s Main, Frank Loughran owner and propr (see backbone and p 16)
Swannanoa-Berkeley Hotel Barber Shop, 53 s Main, T L Cline mngr
Swannanoa-Berkeley Hotel Pool Room, 55 s Main
SWANNANOA DRUG CO (Inc), 45 s Main—phone 201; R L Boyd pres-treas, J A Ridley v-pres, S O Bradley sec

Candy Kitchen and Club Cafe
"A GOOD PLACE FOR REFRESHMENT"

The very best ingredients with sanitary conditions in our Candy Manufacturing Department make possible the dainty, crisp confections sold here. Bon Bons and Chocolates made every day, put up in neat, attractive boxes. Phones 110 and 111. 19 and 21 Haywood St.

Brown's Undertaking Parlors

S. H. BROWN

Lady Assistant When Desired

Phone 193-2 Rings

50 Patton Avenue
Asheville, N. C.

Established 1894

B. J. JACKSON

Carefully Selected Fruits and Vegetables

Stall No. 11, City Market

BUSINESS PHONES:
86 and 101

RESIDENCE PHONE
1596

ASHEVILLE [1913] DIRECTORY

Swannanoa Hill, sanitorium, Biltmore rd
SWANNANOA LAUNDRY, 22-24 Church—phone 70; Canie N Brown propr (see back cover)
Swartzberg Ike (Annie), propr The Gem Clothing Store, 6 Patton av, h 35 s Liberty
Swartzberg Leo, clk, h 1 Merrimon av
Swartzberg Maurice, trav slsmn, h 25 s Liberty
Swartzberg Moses (Henrietta), (Asheville Dry Goods Co), h 1 Merrimon av
Swartzberg Roy E, bkkpr Ashev Dry Goods Co, h 1 Merrimon av
SWAYNE A E (Lou M), v-pres Hackney & Moale Co, and sec-treas Piedmont Directory Co, office 10-12 s Lexington av, h 1 Merrimon pl
Swayngim Mamie Miss, wrapper Peerless Dept Store, h 410½ Southside av
Swayngim S Pinkney (Addie), fireman, h 410½ Southside
Swearngan M Arthur (Jessie), bkkpr Ashev P & L Co, h 132½ s Main
*Swepson Dorothy, h (r) 70 Hill
*Swepson Ernest W, cleaning and pressing 7½ n w Pack Sq, h 70 Hill
*SWEPSON PINKNEY J (Edmonia), real estate, loans, collections, insurance and notary 29 Eagle—phone 762, h 70 Hill—phone 1690
*Swepson Wm (Beulah), janitor genl office Biltmore Estate, h Biltmore rd, S Biltmore
Swicegood D Lindsay (Mary), h 165 s Main
Swicegood Wm Y (Cornelia), clk, h 199 Woodfin
Swiggett Walter F (Edna M), h 144 Montford av
Swink Archie F, auto repr, h 176 s Main
Swink Carl, painter R L Fitzpatrick & Son
Swink Ella, wid LeRoy, h 166 s Main
Swink Fred (Mary L), (Swink & Co), h 157 s Main
Swink Jas C (Jane E), mngr city stables, h 180 s Main
Swink Jno J (Hattie), clk W M Jackson, h 184 s Main
Swink Jno L (Susan), paperhngr, h 184 s Main
Swink Lula, wid Wm, smstrs, h 27 Brick
Swink Mamie E Miss, h 176 s Main
Swink Robt (Susan), (Swink & Co), and gro 178 s Main, h 176 same
Swink Susan Mrs, mngr, h 176 s Main
Swink Wm, painter, h 176 s Main
Swink & Co (Robt and Fred Swink), carriage painters, 9 Aston

Ye OLD BOOK SHOP
114 Patton Ave.   Phone 1674
BOOKS BOUGHT, SOLD OR EXCHANGED

Swope Mary L Miss, h 16 All Souls Crescent, Biltmore
Swope Rodney R Rev, rector All Souls Episcopal Church, h 16 All Souls Crescent, Biltmore
Sykes Chas E, atty at law, 34 Amer Natl Bank Bldg, rms 61 s French Broad av
*Sylvas Mary, cook, h 48 Hill
*Sylvas Rachel, laund, h 44 Gudger

T

Taft G W, clk Langren Hotel, rms 6 Technical Bldg
Taft T R Mrs, h 192 Chestnut
Talbert May Miss, housekpr, h Asheville av, W Ashev
Talbot O Roland, lab R I Smathers, h 32 Eugene av
Tallant David (Mary A), h Valley cor Eagle
Talley Alex N (Annie), h 459 Depot
Tallulah (The), boarding, 100 e College, Miss K C Brandl propr
Tannahill Louise Miss, h 35 Panola
Tannahill Saml J (Laura M), clk O Green Hdw Co, h 33 Panola
*Tanner Cleveland, porter, h 77 Eagle
Tarpley Hugh M, clk frt office Sou Ry, bds 149 Park av
Tate Albert A (Carrie), flgmn, h 88 Ora
Tate Danl M, condr, h 88 Ora
Tate Helen, wid Thos, h 14 Factory Hill
*Tate Jas (Emma), lab, h (r) 32 Clingman av
Tate Jos B (Mae L), mngr Ashev Club, h 166 Montford av
*Tate Napoleon, lab, rms 442 s French Broad av
*Tatum Benj (Margaret), waiter, h (r) Forest Hill
*Tatum Clayton, lab, h S Asheville
*Tatum Lewis (Malissa), brkmn, h 77 Black
*Tatum Maggie, dom, h (r) Forest Hill
*Tatum Wm (Alice), lab, h S Asheville
*Taylor Addie, laund, h 37 Catholic av
Taylor Arthur T (Carrie), trav slsmn, h 48 Hillside
Taylor Briscoe, driver, bds R T Hendley, W Ashev
TAYLOR CHAS A JR, pay teller Battery Park Bank, h 1 Aston Pl
Taylor Carl, engnr, h 15 Roberts
Taylor D Sylvester (Julia), carp, h 28 Oak
Taylor Elizabeth, wid J W, h 48 Hillside
Taylor Elizabeth I Miss, h 320 Montford av
Taylor Emma C, wid Wm, h 179 Merrimon av
*Taylor Eva, cook, 231 Haywood

Mrs. Wilder's SANITARY HOME LAUNDRY turns out first class work in Laundering and Dry Cleaning. No. 7 Montford Ave., Phone 1354

Taylor Frank D (Harriett), h Woolsey
Taylor Harrell, mill opr, h 70 Avery
Taylor Helen Miss, h 320 Montford av
Taylor Henry G (Leona), emp Sou Ry Shops, h 85 Blanton
Taylor Jas, farmer, h W Chapel rd, Biltmore
Taylor Jas B, clk Pack Sq Book Co, h 320 Montford av
Taylor Jas M, carp, h 371 n Main
Taylor Jas R (Zora E), metal wkr, h 48 Central av
Taylor Jeter G (Osa E), mchst, h nr Arlington st, W Ashev
Taylor Jno (Mary), carp, h 13 Gray
Taylor Jno G (Alice), painter R L Fitzpatrick & Son, h 182 s Main
Taylor Jno S, pres Blue Ridge Development Co, h Largo, Fla
Taylor Lillian Miss, bkkpr, rms 1 Starnes av
*Taylor Lottie, cook, h 37 Catholic av
*Taylor Mary, cook 30 Bearden av
Taylor Mary A, wid Wallace B, h 242 Patton av
Taylor Minnie Miss, h 70 Avery
Taylor Minnie Miss, laund, h 15 Roberts
Taylor Mitchell B (Lillie J), carp, h Arlington st, W Ashev
Taylor Morgan L, farmer, h 371 n Main
Taylor Norman, lab, h 70 Avery
Taylor Oscar C (Nicha), leather ctr, h Haywood rd, W Ashev
Taylor Owens, brkmn, bds 30 Jefferson Drive
Taylor R Eugene, student, h 48 Central av
Taylor Ralph T (Ethel), boilermkr, h 150 Park av
*Taylor Robt (Nellie), presser, h 142 s French Broad av
Taylor Robt C (Jessie), chauffeur, h nr Haywood rd, W Ashev
*Taylor Saml F (Effie), waiter, h 35 Hill
Taylor Saml J (Isabelle), h 371 n Main
Taylor Sue W Miss, student, h 48 Central av
Taylor Thos R (Geneva), observer in charge U S Weather Bureau, h 107 Merrimon av
Taylor Vernon C, painter, h 371 n Main
Taylor Virgil (Algy), driver, h 97 William
Taylor W Granville, h 44 Panola
Taylor W Latimer (Laura), lab, h 11 Redmon's al
Taylor Walter G, blksmith, h 8 Biltmore rd, S Biltmore
TAYLOR WALTER P (Mary K), sec-treas Citizens Lumber Co, h 48 Grove
Taylor Wm B (Jennie), sec-treas-mngr Beaumont Furn Co, h 320 Montford av

OLDSMOBILE
ARBOGAST MOTOR COMPANY
ACCESSORIES AND SUPPLIES
Phones 302 and 1728
52-60 N. Main
DETROIT ELECTRIC
BUICK **MAXWELLS**

Asheville Dry Cleaning Co.
Telephones 835-836, All Dep't
MAIN, N. E. COR. COLLEGE

THE CLEANERS
Our Department for Oriental Rugs and Carpet Cleaning is prepared to serve you in all its branches.
E. S. Paine   O. E. Hansen

ALL KINDS
Hardwood Lumber

ENGLISH LUMBER CO.

Phone - - 321

Taylor Wm D (Bessie), spl officer Sou Ry, h 40 Magnolia
Taylor Wm H (Loduska E), driver, h 70 Avery
Teague Isaac M (Ollie), meat ctr Haywood Mkt, h Haywood rd, W Ashev
Teague Jas R (Hattie), driver H J Olive, h Broadway av, W Ashev
TEAGUE M F (Beatryce V), (Teague & Oates), bds The Knickerbocker
*Teague Minnie, laund, h 180 Hill
*Teague Richard (Addie), lab, h 116 Pine
TEAGUE & OATES (M F Teague, F B Oates), druggists, 22 n Pack Sq—phone 260
Teasley Thos E (Rosa E), gro 41 College, h 27 s Liberty
Teasley Wm L, agt Life Ins Co of Va, h College st
Technical Building, offices 18-22 College
Teehan Maida A Miss, h 5 Swan, Biltmore
Telfer Ralph, dom, h Edgemont
Temple Court (offices), 47-53 Patton av
Templeton Saml A Rev, missionary, h 2 Reed Bldg
Templeton Wm C (Cornelia), contr 5 Aston, h 35 s French Broad av
Tennent Annie Miss, student, h 22 Blake
Tennent Annie, wid Jas E, h 22 Blake
Tennent Chas E, carp, h 22 Blake
Tennent Chas G, student, h 22 Blake
Tennent Gailliard S Dr (Mary L), oculist 10-24 Electrical Bldg, h 207 Pearson Drive
Tennent J Albert (Elizabeth), architect 16 Patton av, h 102 Montford av
Tennent Julia Miss, boarding 111 Montford av, h same
Tennent Laura Miss, h 111 Montford av
Tennent Marie L Mrs, wood carvers 10-24 Electrical Bldg, h 207 Pearson Drive
Tennent Mary A Miss, student, h 22 Blake
Tennent Raby, student, h 22 Blake
Tennent Walter D (Minnie J), clk, h 37 Ora
Tennessee & North Carolina R R Co, 200-202 Oates Bldg, J C Arbogast mngr
Terhune Chas G, printer The Inland Press, h 122 Seney
Terhune Hattie G, wid Jas H, h 122 Seney
Terhune Hattie L Miss, h 122 Seney
Terrell Jas A, trav slsmn Natl Biscuit Co, rms 32 College Park pl
Terry Eleanor V Mrs, bds 68 e College
Terry Philip R, phys 221 Legal Bldg, bds 68 w College

BIGGEST
BUSIEST
BEST

ASHEVILLE STEAM LAUNDRY
Phones 1936 and 1937
43 to 47 W. COLLEGE

S. D. HALL
REAL ESTATE AGENT

Money Loaned

Notary Public

32 PATTON AVENUE

Phone 91

CAROLINA MACHINERY CO.
—US when you want machine work of any kind . . .

Founders Machinists and Jobbers of Mill Supplies
When in the market for heavy castings such as columns or building plates get our prices. **Phone 590**

The Life Insurance Co. of Virginia
ORGANIZED 1871 — RICHMOND, VA.

ISSUES ALL THE MOST APPROVED FORMS OF LIFE INSURANCE CONTRACTS from $500.00 to $25,000.00, with premiums payable quarterly, semi-annually and annually

J. V. Moon, Superintendent, Rooms 3-4-5 Maxwelton Bldg., Asheville, N. C.

D. TREXLER TIN SHOP

All Kinds of Roofing, Gutter and Conductor Work.

Phone 862

159 South Main St.

DR. C. H. MILLER

MECHANO-THERAPIST

14 N. Spruce St.
Phone 979
ASHEVILLE, N. C.

Hours by engagement

Drugless Healing of Disease

---

354 ASHEVILLE [1913] DIRECTORY

Test Hannah M Miss, stewardess, tchr, rms Margo Terrace
Theobold Genevieve L Miss, h 166 w Chestnut
THEOBOLD HARRY C, with Club Cafe & Candy Kitchen h 166 w Chestnut
THEOBOLD LOUISE M MRS (Theobold & Brandl), h 166 w Chestnut
THEOBOLD & BRANDL (Mrs Louise M Theobold, A C Brandl), proprs Club Cafe & Candy Kitchen, 19-21 Haywood (see top lines)
Theodore Andrew (Winona), h 34 Atkin
Theodore Geo, h 34 Atkin
*Thomas Annie, h 29 Poplar
*Thomas Arthur (Siscily), porter Y M C A, h 148 Hill
Thomas Belle Miss, housekpr D A Lashley, W Ashev
*Thomas Benj (Nora), lab, h (r) 33 Clingman av
*Thomas Blanche, dressmkr 136 Pine, h same
Thomas Chas (Carrie B), electrn, bds 346½ Depot
*Thomas David (Mary), baker Zindel's Model Bakery, h 29 Poplar
Thomas DeWitt T, h Pennsylvania av, W Ashev
THOMAS FRED'K W (Lillian), atty at law 33 Amer Natl Bank Bldg and sec Elks Home Co, h 69 Charlotte
Thomas Geo, painter R E Bowles, bds 34 Asheland av
Thomas Herman, emp H Leonardi, h Chunn's Cove
*Thomas Jas (Emma), presser, h 231 Flint
*Thomas Jno, baker, h 29 Poplar
Thomas Julian W (Harriet L), plant chf Ashev Tel & Tel Co, h 11 Locust
*Thomas Margaret, nurse 37 Magnolia av, h same
*Thomas Rachel, laund, h Haywood rd, W Ashev
*Thomas Sallie, dom, h 29 Poplar
*Thomas Savannah, laund, h 27 Circle
*Thomas Susie, cook, h 36 Short
Thomas Wm B (Minnie), spl agt Sou Ry, h 211 s French Broad av
Thomason Garland A (Craig, Martin & Thomason), rms 32 Temple Ct
Thomason Grace M Mrs, h 36 Short Roberts
*Thompson Annie, laund, h 99 Mountain
*Thompson Annie B, dom, h 90 Southside av
*Thompson Blossom, dom, h S Asheville
Thompson Chas H (Pearl L), (H P Devine Furn Co), h 319 w Haywood
Thompson Chas W, bds Cherokee Inn
Thompson Clarence, driver A R Johnson, h 460 s Main

....Asheville Cleaning and Pressing Club....
Tailoring That Satisfies and Prices That Please

Steam and French Dry Cleaning of all delicate and fine wearing apparel for ladies and gentlemen. MESSENGER SERVICE IN THE CITY.

J. C. WILBAR, Prop.   4. N. Pack Square   PHONE 389

Thompson Claud M (Mamie), mchst, h Asheville av, W Ashev
*Thompson Elizabeth, laundress, h 90 Southside av
*Thompson Ella, laund, h 240 Asheland av
*Thompson Ella, laund, h 2 Catholic av
Thompson Emma L, wid Clifford H, stengr Mtn School Dept Home Mission Board Sou Baptist Convention, h 18 Josephine
*Thompson Frances, cook, h 104 n Lexington av
Thompson Frank T, student, h 68½ Orange
*Thompson Gabriel (Eliza), lab, h 60 Max
Thompson Grace M Miss, h 44 Charlotte
Thompson Hannah Mrs, cook Cherokee Inn, rms same
Thompson Harley (Hannah), motorman, bds Cherokee Inn
Thompson Henry E (Annie Gibson), mtrmn, h 212 s French Broad av
Thompson Holt C (Roberta), condr Sou Ry, h 330 s French Broad av
*Thompson Ida, laund, h 99 Mountain
Thompson Jas M (Sallie), lab, h 35 Clyde
*Thompson Jno, cook 174 Montford av
*Thompson Jno (Addie), porter, h 96 Mountain
Thompson Louisa J, wid J C, baker, h 68½ Orange
*Thompson Lucinda, laund, h 138 Choctaw
*Thompson Mary, dom, h 12 Aston Pl
Thompson Mattie, h 181 Beaumont
*Thompson Myra, laund, h 22 Ingle
*Thompson Nannie, laund, h 17 Sassafras
*Thompson Reuben, lab, h 96 Mountain
*Thompson Solomon T (Rosa), lab, h 123 Roberts
Thompson Tinnie Mrs, h 84 Avery
*Thompson Virginia, h 9 w Woodfin
Thompson Walter E (Lucy), driver Natl Biscuit Co, h 12 s Spruce
Thornton A A, h "Hillcote Cottage", Victoria
Thornton Austell (Robert), h "Orchard Cottage", Albemarle Park
Thorpe Claude D (Carrie F), mngr Singer Sewing Mch Co, bds Cherokee Inn
Thorpe Edith Miss, matron Pease Memorial House, rms same
THRASH PATRICK H (Olive B), pres Peerless Fashion Stores Co and Peoples Dept Store, h 343 Southside av
Tiddy Elizabeth Miss, bkkpr M V Moore & Co, h 47 Clingman av

Tiddy Jno, clk, h 47 Clingman av
Tiddy Nannie S, wid Robt C, h 47 Clingman av
Tiddy Robt, cashr M V Moore & Co, h 47 Clingman av
Tiddy Rosamond L Miss, h 47 Clingman av
Tigar Wm (May), contr, h 411 Merrimon av
Tighe J Reginald, clk, h 62 Orange
Tighe Rich'd J (Emeline), supt Ashev City Schools, office 207 City Hall, h 62 Orange
TILLER BENJ T (Lora D) pres Asheville Barber's Supply Co, h 81 Penland
Tiller Clair T, clk Ashev Tel & Tel Co, h 81 Penland
TILLER JNO T, sec Asheville Barber's Supply Co, h 23 n Main
Tillinghast Emily, wid Crawford, h 21 Blake
TILLMAN JAS A (Daisy), jeweler and watchmaker— watch repairing a specialty—phone 226, 17 n Main, h 9 Furman av (see top lines)
Tilson Ina Miss, phone opr, bds 56 Penland
Tilson Jas H (Amanda), shoe mkr 309 w Haywood, h 20 Short Spring
Tilson Melvin B, clk M Hyams, h 201 Chestnut
Tilson Pasco G, electrn J M Hearn & Co, h 20 Spring
Tilson Saml (Celie), lab, h 36 Bennett
Tilton Jennie, wid Harry D, h nr Main st, W Asheville
Tilton Laura P Miss, stengr, h nr Main st, W Asheville
Tinnemeyer Henry (Lula), supt Natl Casket Co, h 118 Cherry
Tinnemeyer Josephine Miss, stengr, h 118 Cherry
Tinsley S Jefferson (Cordelia), wood wkr, h Haywood rd, W Asheville
Tinsley Telisa Miss, dressmkr, h Haywood rd, W Asheville
*Tinsley Thos C, phys 22 Eagle, h same
Tipping Renolds, ship clk J L Smathers & Sons, h 35 Vance
Tipton Fred T (Fannie), ticket tkr, h 334½ w Haywood
Tipton Maria T Mrs, h 334½ w Haywood
Tipton Rennie Miss, emp Ashev Mica Co, h 15 Short East
Tipton Wm M (Alice), vulcanizer Ashev Stm Vulcanizing Co, h 44 Asheland av
TODD FRED'K C (Helen L), genl mngr Southern Coal Co and sec Fork Ridge Co and Va-Carolina Coal Co, h 244 Chestnut—phone 1340
*Todd Jno, lab, h 14 Smith
Todd Jno, lab, h 8 Haid
Tolley Dulcie Mrs, h 97 West
Tolley W Dock (May), tinner, h (r) 323 s Main

*Tolliver Earle, switchboard opr, rms 74 Eagle
Tomberlin Grover G (Bessie), motorman, h 195 Patton av
Tomberlin Wm (Ann Eliza), lab, h 26 Morgan avv
*Tomlin Alvin, horse trader, h 115 Poplar
*Tomlin Belle, cook 133 Montford av
*Tomlin Clinton (Sarah), car clnr, h 37 Oaksdale
Tomlin Henry L (Mayme L), condr, h 123 Park av
Tomlin Perry, clk E S Galyean
Tomlinson Peter, h 98 n Holland
*Tompkins Thos (Emma), lab, h 123½ Clingman av
Toms Chas F (Ethel), atty at law 1-2 Temple Court, h 227 Cumberland av
*Toms Everett, cook, h 135 Clingman
Toms Hortense P Miss, student, h 227 Cumberland av
Tonawanda White Pine Co, J J Sewell pres
Toomer Frank G (Lillian), h 63 Clayton
Toomer Lillian G Miss, nurse 63 Clayton, h same
Torence Jno W (Mamie), blksmith, h Biltmore rd, S Biltmore
*Torrence Saml (Pearl), lab, h 22 Campbell
*Torrence Wm G (Eleanor), phys Y M I Bldg, h 95 Hill
Tow Carl F (Della), painter, h W Asheville
Tow Chas S, clk spl agt Sou Ry, bds 14 s Spruce
Tow Jno F (Nora), foreman, h 111 Biltmore rd, S Biltmore
Tow Saml M (Elizabeth J), h W Asheville
Tow Wm P (Elizabeth), clk The Racket Store, h 149 s Main
Towe C Elma Miss, h (r) 149 s Main
Towe Hattie Miss, h Eagle cor Valley
Towe Jesse L (Lucretia), driver Pepsi-Cola Wks, h 170½ Southside av
Towe W Pinkney (Elizabeth), clk, h (r) 149 s Main
*Townes Annie, h 20 Cumberland av
*Townes Lula, dom 42 n Liberty
Townsend Frank (Nellie), brkmn, h 3 Gaston
Townsend Harold N, printer, h 14 Crescent
Townsend Jno, lab, h (r) 328 w Haywood
Townsend Luther F (Mollie), lab, h 108 Centre
Townsend Wm L (Annie), lab, h (r) 328 w Haywood
Tracey Wm D (Lida), real est, h 40 Highland
*Trail Amanda, laund, h 42 Brick
*Trail Jno, driver, h 42 Brick
TRAKAS N S & CO, fruits and produce, wholesale, 31 s Main—phone 271, Ernest G Copses mngr (see p 5)
Trantham Bertha Miss, smstrs, rms 153 s Main
Trantham Rosa Miss, rms 153 s Main

ub Cafe and Candy Kitchen
"GOOD PLACE FOR REFRESHMENT"

The standards we work to in our Restaurant Department are: Cooking, perfect; Service, prompt and cheerful; Prices, moderate; Menu, everything in season. Parties and Banquets, Teas and Dinners. 19 and 21 Haywood St. Phones 110 and 111.

Brown's Undertaking Parlors

. H. BROWN

Patton Avenue
ASHEVILLE, N. C.

Lady Assistant When Desired

Phone 193-2 Rings

THE MOORE Plumbing Company

N. Pack Square

PHONE 1025

Sanitary Plumbing, General Tin and Metal Work, Hot Air Furnaces

358 ASHEVILLE [1913] DIRECTORY

Trantham Thos L (Leona), gro Brook cor Reed, h Biltmore rd, S Biltmore
Trantham Wm I (Annie E), paperhngr, h 26 Charlotte
Traymore (The), boarding, 93 College, Mrs M M Traymore propr
Treadway Jno R (Marguerite R), h 18 Pearl
Trentham Chas M, painter R L Fitzpatrick & Son
Trentham F Elmer, clk, rms A F D
Trentham Geo W (Hannah L), propr The Lyons, h 5 Starnes av
Trentham Jas M (Belle), trav slsmn, h 5 Starnes av
TREXLER DAVID (Mollie), tin and sheet metal worker, 159 s Main—phone 286, h 166 same (see side lines)
Trexler Walter (Lizzie), tinner David Trexler, h 166 s Main
*Tribble Elmira, dom, h 98 Eagle
Trinity Episcopal Church, Church cor Aston
Trist M H Miss, supt Biltmore Hospital, Biltmore Hospital, Biltmore, rms same
Trivola (The), boarding 23 Asheland av, Mrs Maggie Randall propr
*Trotter Alex (Bettie), lab, h 152 Eagle
Troy Hillard P, student, h 77 Pine Grove av
Truitt Edith W Miss, supervisor vocal music Ashev Public Schools, bds 62 Orange
Trull Chas M (Susan L), trav slsmn, h 84 s French Broad av
Trull Katharine E Miss, student, h 84 s French Broad av
Trumbo A Louise D Miss, bds 5 Flint
Trumbo Augustus S (Anna), spl agt U S Int Rev, bds 5 Flint
Trumbo Leila Miss, bds 5 Flint
*Tucker Amanda, dom, h Edgemont
*Tucker Grant, presser The Reliable Cleaning & Pressing Co, h 58 Poplar
*Tucker Jno (Bessie), lab, h 17 Turner
*Tucker Jno P (Bessie), tanner, h (r) 62 Clingman av
*Tucker Zela, hair dresser 58 Poplar, h same
Tumblin Arthur, painter, h 19 Courtland av
Tumblin Geo B (Rachel C), carp, h 19 Courtland av
Turbyfill Newton H (Elizabeth), h Bingham Heights
*Turl Augustus (Lou), lab, h 251 Beaumont
Turnbull Annie L, wid Robt T, h Woolsey
*Turnbull Helen, dom, h 78 Phifer
Turnbull Jno J, rodman City Engnr, h 215 s French Broad
Turnbull Nora L, wid Jas N, h 215 s French Broad av
Turnbull R T, student, h Woolsey

The Battery Park Bank   Capital - - $100,000.00
                             Surplus and Profits, $110,000.00
ASHEVILLE, N. C.   City, County and State Depositary

J. A. TILLMAN — **Jeweler** — **17 N. Main St.**

I carry a nice line of Watches, Clocks and Jewelry, and make a specialty of repair work. Satisfaction guaranteed

ASHEVILLE [1913] DIRECTORY

Turner Edna J, wid W T, h 188 Charlotte
Turner Elizabeth, wid Wm, h 69 Charlotte
Turner Emma Miss, h 64 Livingston
TURNER FRANK, linotype opr Hackney & Moale Co, h 69 Charlotte
Turner Giles B (Delia), shoemkr 160 Southside av, h 323 s Main
Turner Jno, carp, h 64 Livingston
*Turner Martha, h 9 Blanton
Turner Martha L, wid Wilson, h 64 Livingston
*Turner Perry (Anna), butler, h 64 Hill
Turner Roscoe F, plstr, h 64 Livingston
Turner Saml F, carp, h 64 Livingston
Turner Tessie Miss, propr Union Art Studio, h 323 s Main
Turner Whitt W, carp, h 323 s Main
Tuttle Allen A, vet surg, 58-60 s Main, h same
Tuttle Jos B (Anna), trav slsmn, bds Cherokee Inn
Tweed Ethel Miss, h 58 Park Sq
Tweed Everett R (Buena), lab, h 13 Catawba
Tweed Fred A, driver Yates & McGuire, h 59 Montford av
Tweed Lorraine, slsmn, h 59 Montford av
Tweed Marshall N (Nancy A), h 58 Park Sq
Tweed Minnie Miss, h 58 Park Sq
Tweed R Hayes (Leona), plstr, h nr Hazel Mill rd, W Ashev
Tweed T Rankin, slsmn, h 59 Montford av
Tweed Valentine T (Annie), coach clnr, h nr Haywood rd, W Ashev
*Tyson Presley, fireman, h (r) 12 Sorrell

U

Uleeta (The), boarding 5 Flint
Ulmer N W, v-pres Blue Ridge Development Co, h Largo, Fla
*Underwood Ervin, baker Zindel's Model Bakery
*Underwood Fritz (Esther), lab, h Beaumont nr College
Underwood Jane Mrs, h 55 Lincoln av
*Underwood Mary, h Biltmore rd, S Biltmore
UNDERWOOD TYPEWRITER CO, typewriters and typewriter supplies, 9 Temple Ct—phone 1726, Chas J Elliott mngr
Union Art Studio, 16½ n Pack Sq, Miss Tessie Turner prop
Union Dairy Lunch, 414 Depot, X B Lange propr
Union News Co, 373 Depot, J G Pirson mngr

INSURANCE

INSURE YOUR SALARY WITH US
NEVER CARRY YOUR OWN RISK
SAFETY IS THE BEST POLICY
UNLESS YOU ARE A CAPITALIST
REST EASY IF YOU HAVE
AN ACCIDENT WE WILL
NOT KEEP YOU WAITING TO
COLLECT YOUR CLAIM
EVERY CLAIM PROMPTLY PAID

Imperial Mutual Life & Health Insurance Co.

Home Office:
ASHEVILLE, N. C.

Phone 495

HOTEL OXFORD — Redecorated and Refitted throughout. Recently enlarged to 60 rooms. Centrally located. Depot cars stop at entrance. Long distance telephone office upstairs. American and European plan. Rates 50c, 75c and $1 per day; special rates by week or month. C. H. Branson & Sons, Proprietors. Phone 1887. 50-54 South Main St. **Asheville, N. C.**

Williams-Brownell Planing Mill Company — *Hardwoods*
Lumber---Rough and Dressed Flooring a Specialty Moulding, Interior Finish, Etc.
Office, Plant and Yards on Southern Railway, Near Biltmore Station
WHITE PINE **Phone 729** **YELLOW PINE**

Asheville Electrical Company, W. Mansfield Booze, Manager, 74 Central Ave. Headquarters, Phone 377

Union News Co, Sou Ry Passenger Depot, J H Walker clk
UNION PLUMBING CO (J C Cauble, J L Sugg), plumbing, steam and hot water heating 23 n Main—phone 432
Union Store (The), 420 Southside av, W B Merritt propr
United States Army Recruiting Station, 1½ s Main, Sergt E W Bonney in charge
Union States Cafe, 7 n Main, Chas Valeams propr
United States Commissioner, McCall R S, 10½ n Pack Sq
UNITED STATES COURTS, Government Bldg (2d fl); Jeter C Pritchard judge, W S Hyams dep clk
UNITED STATES FIDELITY & GUARANTY CO of Balto Md, 27 Patton av (2d fl), Moale & Chiles, genl agts
United States Furniture Mnfg Co, Sou Ry nr Biltmore Sta, B C McVey pres, C A Hoitt sec-treas
UNITED STATES GOVERNMENT BUILDING, Patton av and Haywood, J C Bradford custodian
United States Health & Accident Ins Co of Saginaw Mich, 13½ Patton av, C G Ward state agt
UNITED STATES INTERNAL REVENUE AGENT, Government Bldg—phone 1221, R B Sams agt
United States Marshal's Office, Government Bldg, Wm E Logan marshall
UNITED STATES POST OFFICE, Patton av n w cor Haywood—phone 74; W W Rollins postmaster, J C Bradford asst
United States Post Office (Glen Rock Station), 376 Depot
United States Weather Bureau, 512-514-515 Legal Bldg, T R Taylor, observer in charge

V

Valeams Chas, propr U S Cafe, rms 11½ n Main
Valentine Jno C M (Isabel M), county road engnr, h Weaverville N C
Valentine W Basil (Jessie), sec-treas Balfour Quarry Co, h 36 Bearden av
Van Hoy Jno W, clk, Martin, Rollins & Wright, rms Y M C A
Van Valkenburg J Frank (Annie), kpr boat house Riverside Park, Ashev Power & Light Co, h W Asheville
VAN WINKLE KINGSLAND (Harkins & Van Winkle), bds 95 Church
Vance Alice C, wid David, furnished rooms 147 Haywood, h same

Asheville Dry Cleaning Co.
Telephones 835-836, All Dep't
MAIN, N. E. COR. COLLEGE

THE CLEANERS
Our Department for Oriental Rugs and Carpet Cleaning is prepared to serve you in all its branches.
E. S. Paine O. E. Hansen

Maple Flooring and Poplar Siding

English Lumber Co
PHONE . . 32

Vance C Thos (Dora), section foreman Sou Ry, h Sou Ry nr Biltmore
Vance Eleanor P Miss, mngr Biltmore Estate Industries, h 9 Plaza, Biltmore
Vance Ella R, wid Jno P, h 9 Plaza, Biltmore
*Vance Furman (Louise), emp Kenilworth Hall, rms same
*Vance Hattie, laund, h 31 Hildebrand
*Vance Jas (Ida), janitor Central M E Ch, h 31 Hildebrand
*Vance Jas Jr, lab, h 31 Hildebrand
*Vance Jno, butler, h 31 Hildebrand
Vance Jno C, plmbr Union Plumbing Co, h 147 Haywood
Vance Lucy M Miss, h 147 Haywood
*Vance Mark (Jane), gro 317 w Haywood, h 23 Turner
*Vance Wm M (Rebecca), gro 38 Mountain, h 19 Latta
Vanstory Jas C, clk Battery Park Hotel, bds same
Varnon Martha Miss, h 111 Chestnut
Varnon Realty Co (W E Varnon), 45 Amer Natl Bank Bldg
Varnon Thos W, atty at law 2 Library Bldg, h 111 Chestnut
Varnon Wallace E (Sallie), (Varnon Realty Co), h 111 Chestnut
VAUGHAN FRANK M, sec Dixie Mutual Life Ins Co, h Norfolk Va
Vaughan Hardy L (Maude), weaver, h 19 Factory Hill
Vaughan Henry A (Cora), helper, h Haywood rd, W Ashev
*Vaughan Herbert (Louvenia), lab, h (r) 57 Eagle
Vaughan Margaret, wid Wm, h Haywood rd, W Ashev
Vaughan Matthew L (Mary), helper, h Haywood rd, W Ashev
Vaughn Annie Miss, waitress Cherokee Inn, rms same
*Vaughn Lee (Belle), presser, h 177 Clingman av
*Vaughn Wister (Freelove), lab, h 6 Short Pine
Veley Alice L, wid W M, stengr, h 102 Broad
*Vernon Elias (Harriet), shoemkr 11 Eagle, h 173 Clingman
*Vernon Fannie, laundress, h 16 Smith
*Vernon Lizzie, dom, h 38 Smith
Vess Florence G Miss, clk, h 12 Redmon's al
Vess Mary A, wid Jasper M, h 12 Redmon's al
Vess Robt A (Carrie), painter, h 112 Seney
Viavi Co, 210-211 Legal Bldg, Mrs Janie Haverson local mngr
Vick Cecelia L Miss, h 12 Blair
Vick S Inez, wid S L, h 12 Blair
Vickers Eddie Miss, h 1 Wallach
Vicks Elias J, mngr, rms 331 Southside av

BIGGEST
BUSIEST
BEST

Asheville Steam Laundry

Phones:
1936 and 193

43 to 47
W. College Stree

CHARLES H. HONESS

OPTOMETRIST
AND
OPTICIAN

Exclusive maker
ATLAS SHUR-O
EYE GLASSES

THE
Home of Ce-Rit
Toric Lenses

We make a special
of correcting optical d
fects with properly fi
ted glasses.

54 Patton Avenu
Opposite Postoffice

IF in the market for a Gas Engine let us make you prices.
its heavy castings, such as columns or building plates, see us.
its a skilled mechanic for boiler work, see us.
you want machine work of any kind phone 590.

CAROLINA MACHINERY CO.

FOUNDE
MACHINISTS a
Jobbers of M
Suppli

Insurance Company of Virginia
ORGANIZED 1871
Home Office - Richmond, Va.

Has won the hearty approval and active support of the people by its promptness and fair dealing during the FORTY-TWO YEARS of its operation

_. Moon, Superintendent, Rooms 3-4-5 Maxwelton Bldg., Asheville, N. C.

T. P. HNSON & CO.

EET METAL WORKERS

Kinds of Roofing uttering and nductor Work al Ceilings, Sky-lights and alvanized Iron Cornices

CE and SHOP: -71 S. MAIN

one 325

DR. H. MILLER

chano-Therapist

. Spruce Street EVILLE, N. C.

'HONE 979

Hours by Engagement

GLESS HEALING OF DISEASE

---

362 ASHEVILLE [1913] DIRECTORY

Villa Heights Company, real est, 52 Amer Natl Bank Bldg; L B Whatley pres, F M Messler sec, W R Whatley treas
Ville Roye Cottage, Sunset Drive, Miss K E Doughty propr
VINIARSKI BARLOLMINY A (Kate), propr Champion Shoe Repair Shop, h 30 Jefferson Drive (see p 22)
Virginia-Carolina Coal Co, 25 Amer Natl Bank Bldg; W J Sproles pres, F C Todd sec, D S Elias treas
von Ruck Dairy, 556 n Main
von **RUCK KARL DR** (Delia), consultant Winyah Sanatorium, h 50 Reed—phone 304
von **RUCK SILVIO DR** (Hurley), medical director Winyah Sanatorium, h Spears av—phone 329
von **TOBEL ALBERT E DR** (Edith), bacteriologist Bacterio Therapeutic Laboratory, h 85 Chestnut
Voorhies Florence Miss, h 252 Hillside
VOORHIES HARRY B (Margaret), sec Brown-Miller Shoe Co, h 212 n Main
Voorhies Jessamine Miss, h 252 Hillside
Voorhies Martha E, wid J B, h 252 Hillside
Vowell Elizabeth Miss, h 239 Montford av

W

WACHOVIA BANK & TRUST CO, 34 Patton av; H Fries pres, Henry F Shaffner v-pres and treas, Theodore S Morrison 2d v-pres, James A Gray sec and asst treas, W B Williamson cashr, S M Hanes asst cashr (see stencils and p 8)
WACHOVIA BANK & TRUST CO, Insurance Department, 34 Patton av, P R Allen mngr

---

Representing a Strong Line of Companies

Courteous Treatment, Prompt Service

—AND—

Absolute Protection OUR BOAST

Waddell Chas E (Eleanor), consulting engnr 78 Patton av, h 20 Biltmore rd, Biltmore
Waddell Chas E Jr, h 20 Biltmore rd, Biltmore
Waddell Duncan C Jr (Lelia J), (Waddell & Coxe), h 55 Grove
Waddell Frank B (Julia), painter, h 28 Clingman av

SHEVILLE CLEANING and PRESSING CLUB

ORING THAT SATISFIES PRICES THAT PLEASE nd. Silk hats ironed. r in all sizes. Plain or with rims. **PHONE 389**

Hats cleaned, banded and Buttons made to

DYEING IN ALL SHADES Cleaned. Messenger Service.

Kid Gloves, Slippers and Plumes Fancy Jabots and Ties. French Dry Cleaned. Ladies' and Gentlemen's suits Steam **J. C. Wilbar, Prop.** **4 NORTH PACK SQ.**

Waddell Frank N (Anna I), justice of the peace, Library Bldg (basement), h 6 Oak, Biltmore
WADDELL MAUDE MISS, society editor Ashev Gazette-News, h 6 Oak, Biltmore
Waddell Saml C (Lillian), brake inspr Sou Ry, h 37 Louie
Waddell Sidney M (Allie), air brake inspr Sou Ry, h 441 s French Broad av
Waddell Wm D (Margaret), tel opr Sou Ry, h 7 Reed, S Biltmore
Waddell & Coxe (D C Waddell Jr), genl ins 16 Patton av
*Wade Hattie, dom, h 33 Catholic av
Wadsworth Margaret Miss, h 19 Orange
Wadsworth Mollie C, wid W D, h 19 Orange
Wadsworth Wm C, emp Sou Ry, h 19 Orange
Wagner Arthur W (Marguerite B), condr Sou Ry, h 39 s French Broad av
Wagner Carrie L Miss, tchr, h 143 Pearson Drive
Wagner Jno A Capt, contr, h 143 Pearson Drive
Wagner Roy B (Helen Y), h 143 Pearson's Drive
Wagner W L, electrn, rms A F D
Wagoner Frank M, h 18 Silver
Wagoner J Davis (Julia), carp, h 18 Silver
Wainscott Laura L, wid J A, dressmkr 24 Cherry, h same
Wainscott Lawrence A, collr, h 24 Cherry
Wainscott Ogdon K (Mary), slsmn, h 36 s Spruce
Wakefield Thos A (Maude), condr Sou Ry, h 196 s French Broad
Walden Laura Miss, nurse, Winyah Sanatorium, rms same
Walden Walter W (Cora), U S Army, h 176 Grove
Walden Winston, trav auditor Sou Ry, h 285 Merrimon av
Waldheim (The), furnished rooms, 211 Patton av, Mrs M J Kilpatrick propr
Waldo Minnie Miss, mlnr H B Hood, h 124 Patton av
Waldrop Ethan A, printer, h 40 Woodfin
Waldrop Fred'k, printer, h 40 Woodfin
Waldrop Geo I, printer, h 40 Woodfin
Waldrop H C, rms Y M C A
Waldrop Saml (Loula), plstr, h 40 Woodfin
Waldrop Saml W, slsmn C M Cohen, bds 98 Patton av
Walker Albert E, publr office 10 Paragon Bldg, h 108 Merrimon av
*Walker Alice, laund, h 41 Tuskee
*Walker Amanda, cook, h 174 Beaumont
*Walker Augustus (Hannah), driver, h 129 Eagle
*Walker Beulah, cook, h 22 Hill

Walker C A Mrs, h 181 Merrimon av
WALKER CALVIN A (Hettie), druggist Haywood n e cor College—phones 132 and 183, h 23 Grove—phone 1474
Walker Charlotte M Miss, nurse 37 Chestnut, rms same
Walker Charlotte P Miss, h 86 Asheland av
*Walker Eliza, h 306 Charlotte
*Walker Emma, laundress, h 36 Smith
*Walker Emma, cook, h 39 Sycamore
*Walker Gilbert, flagman, h 468 s French Broad av
*Walker Henry (Hester), lab, h 29 Gray
Walker J Harry, clk Union News Co, rms 117 s French Broad av
*Walker J Monroe, driver, h 14 Latta
*Walker Jno, cook, h 154 Hill
*Walker Jno (Hattie), lab, h (r) 413 s Main
*Walker Jno W (Eleanor) (Y M I Drug Co) and phys Y M I Bldg, h 44 Circle Terrace
*Walker Johnson, lab, h 159 College
*Walker King, lab, h 144 Hill
*Walker Lizzie, cook, h 6 Greer's Row
Walker Love I Miss, h 181 Merrimon av
*Walker Lucy, h 14 Latta
Walker Osborne J, trav slsmn, h 181 Merrimon av
*Walker Saml W (Fannie), barber J A Wilson and eating hse 419 Depot, h same
*Walker Thos (Beulah), waiter, h 22 Hill
*Walker Walter (Carrie), butler, h 25 Seney
Wall B Percy, condr, bds Cherokee Inn
*Wall J Watt (Esther), chauffeur, h 176 Hill
*Wallace Casper, stone mason, h 29 Circle
Wallace Clara Miss, h 75 Phifer
*Wallace Daisy, laund, h 116 Eagle
*Wallace David (Ella), lab, h 29 Circle
*Wallace Frank (Mattie), lab, h 108 Eagle
Wallace Georgia Miss, nurse Biltmore Hosp, rms same
Wallace Jas C (Carrie) (American Wagon Co), h W Ashev
Wallace Jas S (Martha), mining engnr, h 75 Phifer
*Wallace Jos B (Sarah), gro 183 Beaumont, h 34 Miller
Wallace Louise Miss, clk Bon Marche, bds 5 Starnes av
Wallace Olive Miss, housekpr, h Hazel Mill rd, W Asheville
*Wallace Viola, dom, h 159 College
*Wallace Wm, driver, h 9 w Woodfin
Wallen Emory J (Vira), motorman St Ry, h 32 Spring
Wallen Fuchsia A, mica splitter, h 83 Clingman av

Wallen Henry K, clk O N Rockett, h 29 n Main
Wallen Jno T (Myra), driver, h 29 Clingman av
Wallen Lillian Miss, emp Ashev Mica Co, h 83 Clingman av
Wallen R Fulton (Lydia), emp Burton & Holt, h W Ashev
Wallen Stephen, lab, bds 49 n Main
Wallen W Frank (Julia), carp, h 83 Clingman av
Waller Calvin B Rev (Lela), pastor First Baptist Church, h 225 Chestnut
Wallis Geo M, student, h 118 Chestnut
Wallis Margaret S, wid T J, h 118 Chestnut
*Walls Hattie, h 59 Fulton
*Walls Lucy, cook, h (r) 140 Pine
Walser Fred T Jr (Bruce), farmer, h Woolsey (R F D 1)
Walsh Agatha G, wid Robt E, clk Marsteller & Co, h 63 Church
Walsh Dorcas, wid P F, h 19 Buxton
WALSH GEO F, solr Piedmont Directory Co, res St Louis Mo
Walsh Juna P (Ovalena), mchst, h Swannanoa av, W Ashev
Walters Allie W, wid Augustus F, h 1 Zillicoa
Walters Howard E (Elizabeth), district deputy, h 20 s Ann
Walton Blanche L Miss, stengr Carolina Hardwood Lbr Co, h 54 Oak
Walton F Arthur (Hattie), real estate 21 s Main, h 36 Summit, S Biltmore
Walton Gertrude M Miss, bkkpr Union Plumbing Co, h 54 Oak
Walton Grace W Miss, student, h 36 Summit, S Biltmore
Walton Harry L, tinner, h 54 Oak
Walton Henry S (Laura), collr, h 54 Oak
Walton Ida Miss, h 71½ Magnolia av
Walton Jessie E Miss, clk Jno A Guffey, h 65 Summit, S Biltmore
Walton Myra M, wid A F, h 65 Summit, S Biltmore
Walton Nancy I, wid T M, h 91 Asheland av
Wamboldt Miles M Rev (Mary B), h Asheville av, W Asheville
Ward C G (Carrie), state agt U S Health & Accident Ins Co of Saginaw Mich, office 13½ Patton av, h 104 s French Broad av
Ward Collie, lab, h 32 Clingman av
Ward Ecton W (Anna), lab, h 32 Clingman av
*Ward Edwd, driver, bds 458 Pearson Drive
Ward Geo (Rhoda), lab, h Riverside Drive
Ward Geo C, tel opr, bds 15 s French Broad av

lub Cafe and Candy Kitchen "A GOOD PLACE FOR REFRESHMENT"

Our Ice Cream manufacturing plant is absolutely clean and sanitary.
Prompt family delivery. Phones 110 and 111.
tering for large parties and receptions. Special Creams.

Brown's Undertaking Parlors

. H. BROWN

Lady Assistant When Desired

hone 193-2 Rings

0 Patton Avenue
sheville, N. C.

Established 1894

B. J. JACKSON

arefullySelected Fruits and Vegetables

tall No. 11, City Market

USINESS PHONES:
86 and 101

ESIDENCE PHONE
1596

Ward Jas M (Georgia), lab, h 32 Clingman av
Ward Jennie Mrs, emp Ashev Mica Co, h 71 Grove av
Ward Lizzie, wid W W, h 44 Clyde
Ward Lizzie, wid C A, h 79 Merrimon av
Ward Mary Miss, clk Jno A Guffey, h 44 Clyde
Ward Mary Neal Miss, h 79 Merrimon av
Ward P W (Jennie), carp, h 71 Livingston
Ward Percy L (Ella), claim agt Sou Ry, h 126 Woodfin
Ward Robt E, asst cashr Armour & Co, bds Holland House
Ward Saml E (Annie), fireman, h 179 Bartlett
Ward Sandy (Rachel), lab, h 23 Madison
Ward Thos (Nannie), (r) 4 Hunt Hill
Ward Wm, carp, bds 34½ n Main
Ward Wm A (Martha), electrn 12 Church, h 182 Haywood
Ware Albert B (Esther), dentist 11 n w Pack Sq (2d fl), h 47 Orange
Ware Jas A, carrier P O, h 47 Orange
Ware Kathleen D Miss, tchr High Schl, h 47 Orange
Ware Margaret L Miss, tchr Orange St Schl, h 47 Orange
Warford see Wofford
Waring Archibald H (Ellen S), trav slsmn, h 114 Cumberland av
WARLICK JASPER W (Zetta M), cashr Imp Mut L & H Ins Co, bds 98 Patton av
Warlick Zetta M Mrs, stengr L C Bell, h 98 Patton av
Warn Eula Miss, bds 98 Patton av
*Warner Jos (Kate), presser, h 228 Beaumont
*Warner Jos Jr, presser, h 228 Beaumont
Warner Norman J (Amy B), sou mngr Carolina Hardwood Lbr Co, rms 159 Woodfin
Warner Belle Miss, housekpr, h Haywood rd, W Asheville
Warren Benj W (Ella), livery 5 e Walnut and propr Hotel Warren and real estate 39 n Main, h same
Warren Carl M, electrn, rms 36 Temple Court
Warren Columbus W (Johannah), lab, h Arlington st, W Asheville
Warren Daisy Miss, cutter, h 60 Clingman av
Warren Dessie E Miss, h 48 Buxton
Warren Emma Miss, h 21 Green
Warren Floyd, driver, h 17½ n Main
Warren Fred H (Ella), farmer, h W Asheville (R F D 3)
Warren Henry H (Martha J), hostler B W Warren, h 17½ n Main
Warren Hilliard M (Laura), restaurant 386 Depot, h 55 Clingman av

---

'urniture and China Carefully Prepared for Shipment

ahogany Furniture Hand ade & Carefully Reproduced

E. E. GALER
114 PATTON AVE.

Upholstering and Refinishing
PHONE - 1674

Warren Laura, wid Frank, h 55 Clingman av
Warren Lizzie Miss, emp Ashev Mica Co, h 60 Clingman av
Warren Lucas D (Addie M), condr St Ry, h 11 Park av
Warren McElroy, mill wkr, h 48 Buxton
Warren Maggie Miss, h 48 Buxton
Warren Oscar (Stella), tanner, h 17½ n Main
Warren Saml T (Bertha), tel opr Sou Ry, h 10 Brook, Biltmore
Warren Selia A, wid David, h 48 Buxton
*Warren Silas, porter Falk's Music House, h 71 Wallach
Warren Whitfield W (Violet), barber Ashev Barber Shop, h 77 n Spruce
*Washburn Flossie, h 150 Livingston
*Washburn Louise, laund, h 150 Livingston
*Washburn Marcus, lab, h 150 Livingston
*Washington Annabelle, h 190 s Main
*Washington Carol E, dom, h 28 Davidson
*Washington Dora E, boarding 28 Davidson, h same
*Washington Lottie, dom 224 Chestnut
*Washington Wm, barber J A Wilson
Waters Anne F Miss, stengr, h 132 Charlotte
Waters Christine M Miss, h 132 Charlotte
Waters Donald, electrn, h 132 Chestnut
Waters Fannie B, wid W J, h 421 s Main
Waters Jno (Annie), farmer, h 132 Charlotte
Waters Jno, plmbr J R Rich Co, h 132 Charlotte
Waters Maxwell G, h 421 s Main
Waters Walter E, h 421 s Main
Waters Wm, farmer, h 132 Chestnut
Waters Willie M Miss, tchr Asheland av Schl, h 421 s Main
☞Waters see also Walters
Watkins Angelina, wid Wm M, h nr Arlington st, W Asheville
Watkins Broaddus (Bessie), lab, h Riverside Drive nr n Main
Watkins Chas R (Sallie N), h 45 n Spruce
Watkins J Dickson, flgmn, bds 96 Bartlett
Watkins Jno C (Ida L), gro, h nr Arlington st, W Ashev
Watkins Jos E, driver H J Olive, h W Asheville
Watkins Mary Miss, h Riverside Drive nr n Main
Watkins Nora B Mrs, bds 357 s Main
Watkins Peter J (Hester), trav slsmn, h 46 Fulton
WATKINS SALLIS N MRS, propr The Elton, h 45 n Spruce—phone 958
Watkins Thos, lab, h Riverside Drive nr n Main

Mrs. Wilder's **SANITARY HOME LAUNDRY** turns out first class work in Laundering and Dry Cleaning. **No. 7 Montford Ave., Phone 1354**

Watson Arabella T, wid Dr J A, h 13 Grove
*Watson Benj S E, gro 190 Southside av, h 29 McDowell
Watson D S & Co (D S Watson and Matt Forestburg), real estate, Library Bldg (basement)
Watson David S (Sylvia H) (D S Watson & Co), h 13 Grove
Watson Estelle Mrs, h 12 Elm
*Watson Howard, lab, h S Asheville
*Watson Jno, lab, h S Asheville
*Watson L B, sec Mtn City Mut Ins Co, h 29 McDowell
*Watson Lizzie, laund, rms 12 McDowell
*Watson Maria, cook, h 25 Haid
Watson Nettie M, wid E W, h Edgemont
*Watson Rosa, laund, h 24 Gudger
Watson Roy G, student, h Edgemont
*Watson Silas (Mary), lab, h 57 Black
Watts Leander C (Addie), drayman, h 3d av, W Asheville
*Watts Mattie, h 5 Sorrell
*Watts Nannie, dom, h 159 College
Watts Ruth E Miss, tchr Orange St Schl, h 27 Washington rd
Watts Walter M, plmbr Moore Plumbing Co, h 27 Washington rd
*Watts Wm (Maggie), lab, h 5 Sorrell
Way Eugene, atty at law 10½ n Pack Sq, h Grace (R F D 1)
Way Martha J, wid C B, propr Del Rosa Farm, h Grace (R F D 1)
Way S H Mrs, mngr Y W C A Lunch Room, h Biltmore
*Weathers Sallie, cook, h 124 Church
Weaver Bessie Miss, h 91 Wallach
Weaver Blanche Mrs, h 83 Starnes av
Weaver C Guy, atty at law and notary, 306 Oates Bldg, bds 22 Courtland av
WEAVER DICK (Carrye L) (Chambers & Weaver), h 147 Charlotte
Weaver Eugene M, bkkpr, h Jarrett av, W Asheville
*Weaver Forrest (Hattie), lab, h 45 Wallach
WEAVER FRANK M (Cornelia), pres Carolina Coal & Ice Co, Brown Hdw Co and mngr Asheville Coal Co, office 6 n Pack Sq—phone 40, h 82 Merrimon av—phone 190
Weaver Fred, lab, h 91 Wallach
Weaver Henry B (Hattie), phys 405-407 Legal Bldg, h 201 Chestnut

ARBOGAST MOTOR COMPANY
ACCESSORIES AND SUPPLIES
Phones 302 and 1728
52-60 N. Main
DETROIT ELECTRIC
MAXWELLS

Asheville **Dry Cleaning Co.**
Telephones 835-836, All Dep't
MAIN, N. E. COR. COLLEGE

THE CLEANERS
Our Department for Oriental Rugs and Carpet Cleaning is prepared to serve you in all its branches.
E. S. Paine   O. E. Hansen

For Kindling "What am Kindling" Call
ENGLISH LUMBER COMPANY Phone 321

Weaver J Marvin (Minnie), yd mstr Sou Ry, h 58 Bartlett
*Weaver Jas (Carrie), lab, h 17 Turner
Weaver Jno H (Carrie Lee) (American Wagon Co), h 119 Cumberland av
Weaver Kelcey V, asst baggage agt Sou Ry, h Weaverville N C
Weaver Lillian R Miss, h 201 Chestnut
Weaver Lucius E, bds 58 Bartlett
Weaver Margaret Miss, missionary Faith Cottage Rescue Home, rms same
Weaver Marie A, wid Wm B, h 175 s Main
Weaver Mattie Miss, clk Bon Marche, rms Y W C A
*Weaver Rufus (Sallie), lab, h S Asheville
Weaver Sallie, wid W M, h Eagle cor Valley
*Weaver Vivian, lab, h S Asheville
Weaver W T Power Co, 1-2 Maxwelton Bldg
Weaver Wayne B (Lucile), baggage agt Sou Ry, h 70 Adams
Weaver Wm P (Bettie), locksmith, h 91 Wallach
Weaver Wm T (Annie L), pres N C Electrical Power Co, h Woolsey (R F D 1)
Weaver Zebulon (Anna H), atty at law, 406-408 Oates Bldg, h 46 Baird
WEAVERVILLE COLLEGE, Weaverville N C—phone 33 Wm Allen Newell pres, Walter B West v-pres, Marion A Yost sec
WEAVERVILLE ELECTRIC CO, telephone and lighting, 7 n Main, Stanley Howland pres, R S Howland v-pres, Reginald Howland treas, G W Epps sec
WEAVERVILLE LINE (see Ashev & East Tenn R R Co)
Webb Andrew J (Bessie), painter, h Haywood rd, W Asheville
Webb C May Miss, spinner, h Haywood rd, W Asheville
Webb Chas A (Bruce), atty at law, 302-303 Oates Bldg, h Beaver Dam
Webb Clara G Miss, sec-treas M Webb Co, h 25 n French Broad av
Webb Clarence F (Clota), car cleaner, h 483 w Haywood
Webb Clayton, driver Ashev Ice Co, h W Asheville
Webb David H (Wilhelmina), gro 425 s Main, h 77 Victoria rd
*Webb Edwd V (Hattie), waiter, h 105 Mountain
*Webb Ella, dom, h 76 Ridge
Webb Emma Miss, h 51 n Main

Biggest Busiest Best

ASHEVILLE STEAM LAUNDRY
Phones 1936 and 1937
43 to 47 W. COLLEGE

S. D. HALL REAL ESTATE AGENT

Money Loaned

Notary Public

32 PATTON AVENUE

Phone 91

Founders, Machinists and Jobbers of Mill Supplies

PHONE 590
When in the market for pipe and fittings, let us make you Prices.

Carolina Machinery Co.

PHONE 590
If It's a Gas Engine let us figure with you, also on other kinds of machinery

LIFE INSURANCE COMPANY OF VA. OLDEST, LARGEST STRONGEST Southern Life Insurance Co.
ORGANIZED 1871
RICHMOND, VIRGINIA
Issues Industrial Policies from $8.00 to $900.00, with Premiums Payable WEEKLY on persons from two to seventy years of age
J. V. Moon, Superintendent, Rooms 3-4-5 Maxwelton Bldg., Asheville, N. C.

D. TREXLER TIN SHOP

All Kinds of Roofing, Gutter and Conductor Work.

Phone 862

159 South Main St.

DR. C. H. MILLER

MECHANO-THERAPIST

14 N. Spruce St.
Phone 979
ASHEVILLE, N. C.

Hours by engagement

Drugless Healing of Disease

---

370 ASHEVILLE [1913] DIRECTORY

Webb Ernest H, clk, h 77 Victoria rd
Webb Estelle C Miss, clk Jno A Guffey, h 25 n French Broad av
Webb Harley T (Lessie), helper, h Haywood rd, W Ashev
Webb J Albert, clk, h 77 Victoria rd
*Webb Jas, butler 23 Woodfln
Webb L Leona Miss, spinner, h Haywood rd, W Asheville
Webb Lutie E Miss, h 25 n French Broad av
Webb M Co, milliners, Haywood cor Battery Park Pl, Mrs Mary Webb Rice pres, Miss Grace Fanning 1st v-pres, Miss Jessie Wright 2d v-pres, Miss Clara Webb sec-treas
Webb Mary E, wid J A, boarding 25 n French Broad av, h same
Webb Minnie V Miss, clk Mrs M C Denoon, h 25 n French Broad
Webb Nora B Miss, spinner, h Haywood rd, W Asheville
Webb Porter A, with W A Webb, h 25 n French Broad av
Webb R Susan, wid M C, h Haywood rd, W Asheville
Webb Romulus M (Florence), h 470 w Haywood
Webb Wm, surveyor, bds 62 Penland
Webb Wm A (Maggie W), livery 9 s Lexington av, h 12½ s Main
Weber M K, prin Orange Street School
Webster Calvin N (Eleanor), sec-treas Ashev Harness Co, h 128 s Main
Webster Emma Miss, foreman, bds 34 Asheland av
Webster Mary E Miss, h 128 s Main
Webster W L Capt, tchr Bingham Schl, rms same
Weddle Wm S (Nannie), engnr, h 67 Ora
*Weekly News, Beaumont cor Valley, Rev T Kennedy prop
Weeks Elizabeth S Miss, h 144 Flint
Weeks Horace S, h 144 Flint
Weems Lacy (Emma), trav slsmn, h 106½ Haywood
Weidler E Penrose (Sadie), farmer, h Haywood rd, W Ashev (R F D 3)
Weiler Cora L, wid Fred, h 308 Depot
Weinberger M, slsmn Bon Marche, h w Chestnut
Weinberger Max (Ida), mngr Bon Marche, h 136 w Chestnut
Weir H M, collr J L Smathers & Sons, h 10 West
Welborn Chas W (Lyda), lino opr Ashev Gazette-News, h Woolsey (R F D 1)
Welborn Jas L (Bertha), flgmn, h 479 Depot
Welborn Jno M (Cynthia), h Woolsey (R F D 1)

....Asheville Cleaning and Pressing Club....
Tailoring That Satisfies and Prices That Please
Steam and French Dry Cleaning of all delicate and fine wearing apparel for ladies and gentlemen. MESSENGER SERVICE IN THE CITY.
J. C. WILBAR, Prop. 4. N. Pack Square **PHONE 389**

Welch Daisy Miss, h Woolsey (R F D 1)
Welch Gilmer (Ninon), atty at law 7-8-9 Library Bldg, h 106 Cumberland av
Welch J L & Co (J L Welch and M P Shook), gros 549 w Haywood
*Welch John, emp Y M C A, h 140 Hill
Welch Jno L (Julia), (J L Welch & Co), h W Asheville
Welch Nellie L Miss, bds 29 Jefferson Drive
Weldon R L, clk W U Tel Co, h 107 Haywood
Weldon Robt Mrs, clk Bon Marche, h 107 Haywood
Weldon Saml G (Hattie A), tel opr Sou Ry, h 4 Oak, Biltmore
Welfare Cottage (Club), 9 Factory Hill
Welfley Blanche Miss, h 397 s Main
Welfley Katie Miss, h 397 s Main
Welfley Martin L (Bertha), atty, h 397 s Main
Welfley Vidie Miss, h 397 s Main
Wellborn Thos M (Aimee J), lab, h 463 Depot
Wellman Edwd F (Harriette), supt French Broad Mnfg Co, h Elk Mountain
*Wells Alice, laund, h 93 Pine
*Wells Alice, maid, rms 86 Eagle
Wells C Mitchell (Nettie), agt Imp Mut L & H Ins Co, h 42 Roberts
Wells C N Mrs, clk H Redwood & Co, h Grace
*Wells Clarence, chauffeur, 41 Starnes av
Wells Cora W Mrs, propr The Wentworth, h same
*Wells Frank (Viola), lab, h 29 Haid
*Wells Geo (Martha), brkmn, h 4 Hibernia
Wells Horace A (Lura), contr, h Haywood rd, W Ashev (R F D 3)
Wells Jos B (Cora W), trav slsmn, h 38 Oak
Wells Robt (Tinie), slsmn Beaumont Furn Co, h 49 Spring
WELLS ROBT M (Annie M), (Wells & Swain), h W Asheville (R F D 3)—phone 1545
Wells Rose Miss, with Miss B H Pearce, h 46 n French Broad av
*Wells Saml (Cora), lab, h 42 Davidson
Wells Vance L (Ann Lee), bkkpr Glen Rock Hotel, h 32 Soco
WELLS & SWAIN (R M Wells, J E Swain), attys at law, 400-402 Oates Bldg—phone 589
Welsh Jas A (Lizzie), mchst, h 455 Depot
Wentworth (The), boarding 38 Oak, Mrs Cora W Wells, propr

Asheville Dray, Fuel and Construction Co.

Heavy Hauling of all kinds — 1-2 South Main — WE FURNISH BUILDING STONE — Moving Furniture a Specialty — PHONE - 223

DYNAMOS & MOTORS

Piedmont Electric Co.

64 Patton Av.
ASHEVILLE, N.C.

*Wesley Susie, h 176 Hill
*West Asheville A M E Zion Church, Haywood rd, W Ashev, Rev Jas W Henderson pastor
West Asheville Baptist Church, W Asheville, Rev R D Cross pastor
West Asheville Cemetery, W Asheville, J B Searcy keeper
West Asheville Graded School, Haywood rd, W Ashev, J W Bradley prin
*West Asheville M E Church, Haywood rd, W Ashev, Rev Gilbert Caldwell pastor
*West Asheville Public School, W Asheville, T M Elrod, prin
West Bertha E Miss, h 277 s Main
West Chas H, slsmn Ashev Carpet House, h Beaver Dam
West Chas W, phys, h 306 Chestnut
West Claude C (Rose P), condr, h 394 Southside av
West Edwd S, lmbr, h 306 Chestnut
West Elmer M (Rachel), hostler Sou Ry, h 40 Buxton
West End Baptist Church, Buxton nr Roberts, Rev G P Hamrick pastor
West End Drug Store, 270 Patton av, C A Walker propr
West End Grocery (Geo W McAbee), 344 w Haywood
*West End Pressing Club (Arthur G Moore), 342 w Haywood
West Fred, pressmn Hackney & Moale Co, h W Asheville
West Harry M (Maud), condr, bds 418 Southside av
West Jas S (Sarah T), standard keeper, bds 111 Montford
West Sarah S Miss, h 306 Chestnut
West Shippen D, h 306 Chestnut
West Virginia (The), boarding, 88 Penland, Mrs O J Hall propr
West Wm G, clk, bds 101 Haywood
West Wm W (Sarah), U S A, h 306 Chestnut
West Z Caroline, wid Henry, h 111 Chestnut
Westall Annie Miss, h Woolsey
Westall Chas, student, h 4 Clayton
Westall Elmer C (Grace), trav slsmn, rms 18 Oak
Westall Grace Mrs, voice tchr Ashev Schl of Musical Art, bds 18 Oak
WESTALL J M & CO (J M and James Westall), dealers in lumber, laths, shingles, glass, doors, sash, mouldings, hair, lime and cement, office 17 Walnut—phone 954, yard Old Depot—phone 253
Westall Jack F, lumberman, h Woolsey
Westall Jas M (Minnie), (J M Westall & Co), h Woolsey

J. C. McPHERSON
SLATE AND TIN ROOFING
Galvanized Iron Work — Hot Air Furnaces
35-37 EAST COLLEGE STREET

PLUMBING
STEAM AND HOT WATER
HEATING
PHONE 133

Westall Mary Miss, h Woolsey
Westall Minnie L Miss, piano tchr Ashev Schl of Musical Art, h Woolsey
Westall T Crockett (Una), bkkpr W H Westall & Co, h 41 Clayton
Westall W H & Co (W H Westall, G H Morris,) lumber and building material, 22 Spruce
Westall Wm B (Lula), yd mngr J M Westall & Co, h 543 w Haywood
Westall Wm H (Emily), (W H Westall & Co), h Chestnut nr Charlotte
Westdale Cottage, Victoria
Westerlund Alva M (May), compositor Hackney & Moale Co, h 3 s Liberty
Western Carolina Auto Co, Walnut cor n Lexington av; J H Lange pres, A H McCormick sec-treas
WESTERN CAROLINA REALTY CO, real estate and investments, 10 n Pack Sq—phone 974, J W Wolfe sec-treas (see side lines)
Western Hotel, 11½ s w Pack Sq, Mrs Anna Cowgill propr
WESTERN UNION TELEGRAPH CO, 62 Patton av—phones 1930 and 1931, E N Williams mngr
Western Union Telegraph Co, Battery Park Hotel, C G Blankenship opr
Western Union Telegraph Co, Sou Ry Passenger Depot
Westmoreland Benj F (Lillian C), gro 10 Roberts, h same
*Westmoreland Maria, cook, h 97 n Main
*Weston Arthur (Bessie), driver, h (r) 9 Depot
Weston Delia B Miss, tchr High Schl
*Weston Jeremiah (Hattie), farmer, h 1 Catholic av
*Weston Jos, shoemkr 39 s Main, rms 16 Eagle
*Weston Laura, dom, h 110 Madison
Whaley Eliabeth S Miss, tchr, h Sand Hill rd, W Ashev (R F D 3)
Whatley Louis B, pres Villa Heights Company, bds 197 Cumberland av
Whatley Wm R, treas Villa Heights Company
Wheeler A S Dr, mngr Biltmore Dairy, h Biltmore Estate
Wheeler Druid E, student, h 109 Chestnut
Wheeler Geo W (Cora), clk V V Haynie, h 394 n Main
Wheeler Jessie L Miss, h 109 Chestnut
Wheeler Louis B (Cora), trav slsmn, h 109 Chestnut
*Wheeler Mack (Amelia), lab, h 18 Brick
Wheeler Merrit S (Lillie), driver, h W Ashev (R F D 3)
Wheeler Thurman C (Lillie), chffr, bds 320 n Main

Candy Kitchen and Club Cafe
"A GOOD PLACE FOR REFRESHMENT"

Hot drinks on cold days. Cold drinks on hot days. The best drinks every day. Pure fruits and syrups blended "just right," served daintily. Our Ice Cream and Soda Water Department, Restaurant and Candy Departments are always kept up to the standard of nearest perfection. Phones 110 and 111. 19 and 21 Haywood St.

Brown's Undertaking Parlors
S. H. BROWN

50 Patton Avenue
ASHEVILLE, N. C.

Lady Assistant When Desired

Phone 193-2 Rings

THE MOORE Plumbing Company
16 N. Pack Square
PHONE 1025

Sanitary Plumbing, General Tin and Metal Work, Hot Air Furnaces

---

ASHEVILLE [1913] DIRECTORY

Wheeling Louisa Miss, laund, h 9 Brick
Whelchel Jefferson, barber Antiseptic Barber Shop, rms 20 Patton av
Whisnant Ashbury (Ella), condr St Ry, h 44 s French Broad av
Whisnant Marvin, mchst Western Carolina Auto Co, bds 80 Penland
Whitaker A May Miss, h 72 Adams
Whitaker Jno B (Kate), foreman, h Haywood rd, W Ashev
Whitaker M Seth (Ada), lab, h 1 Reed, S Biltmore
Whitaker Mary Miss, cook O N Rockett, rms 10½ n Pack Sq
Whitaker Mary Mrs, bds 10½ n Pack Sq
Whitaker May Miss, clk Palais Royal, h Allen
Whitaker Susan C, wid Dr A S, h 102 Biltmore rd, S Biltmore
Whitaker Wm B (Myrtle), flgmn Sou Ry, h 72 Adams
☞Whitaker see also Whittaker
White Alice Miss, clk Bon Marche, h Aston Park
White Annie M, wid J J, dressmkr 138 Poplar, h same
*White Arthur (Lulu), lab, h 36 Ocala
White Bertha Miss, h 455 Depot
White Bertha A Miss, h 35 Gaston
White C Herbert, mngr Smathers Wholesale Produce Co, h Aston Park
White Chas, carp, rms 1 Barnard Bldg
White Chas P, carp, h Woolsey
White Edith Miss, clk The Racket Store, h Poplar
White Edna Miss, tchr, Normal & Collegiate Inst
White Edwd L (Allie), clk Zimmerman & Son, h 24 Phifer
White Edwd P (Jeannie C), supt, h 76 Woodfin
*White Eli (Emma), janitor, h 223 s Beaumont
White Garland B, h Brevard rd, W Ashev (R F D 3)
*White Hattie, cook, h 205 Clingman av
*White Herbert H, shoe mkr, h 306 Charlotte
*White Herbert N, student, h 306 Charlotte
White Hiram G (Dora), barber H B Black, h 35 Gaston
White Howard (Amelia), brick lyr, h 138 Poplar
White Hubert Y (Florence), plstr, h 382 n Main
White J A, propr European Hotel, h 418½ Depot
White J Oscar (Lily V), mngr lamp dept Ashev Power & Light Co, h 138 Cherry
*White Jas, porter W E Patterson & Co, h 93 Merrimon av
*White Jno, porter, h 160 Hill
*White Jno, driver Ashev Ice Co, h Brick

The Battery Park Bank
Capital - - $100,000.00
Surplus and Profits, $110,000.00
ASHEVILLE, N. C.   City, County and State Depositary

We Want Your Printing and

If giving you the best work at the lowest possible price, prompt service and courteous treatment "cut any figure"

We Are Going to Have It

Whiteside Printing Co.
Opposite City Hall

We Want Your Printing and

If giving you the best work at the lowest possible price, prompt service and courteous treatment "cut any figure"

We Are Going to Have It

Whiteside Printing Co.
Opposite City Hall

J. A. TILLMAN I carry a nice line of Watches, Clocks and Jewelry, and make a specialty of repair work. Satisfaction guaranteed **Jeweler** **17 N. Main St.**

*White Jno (Hattie), driver, h 127 Eagle
White Jno M (Emma), motorman, h Riverside Drive nr Park
White Lettie C Miss, stengr Asheville Lbr Co h 40 s French Broad av
*White Lillian, h 306 Charlotte
White Lucius H (Mollie B), engnr, h Brevard rd, W Ashev
White Marintha E, wid J A, h Woolsey
*White Marshall (Mottie), porter, h 3 Short Valley
White Nellie J Miss, steno S M Smith, bds 43 Oak
White Oak Cottage, Asheville av, W Ashev, residence of C M Hamilton
White Phoebe A, wid Wm, h 84 Avery
*White Virgil (Laura), h S Asheville
White Wm, condr, bds Highland Hotel
Whitehead Hermus V (Dora), U S N, h 85 Asheland av
Whitehead Kathleen R Miss, student, h 85 Asheland av
Whitehead Leonidas L (Kübler & Whitehead), h 85 Asheland av
Whitehead Rex O, opr W U Tel Co, h 85 Asheland av
Whiteside Chas M (Louise), carp, h 282 Cumberland av
*Whiteside Dock M (Myra W), lumber inspr, h Hazel Mill rd, W Asheville
Whiteside Dudley B, plbr, h 46 Panola
WHITESIDE EDWD W (Whiteside Printing Co), h 22 s Pack Sq
Whiteside Frank, appr Hackney & Moale Co, bds 34½ n Main st
*Whiteside Jno (Martha), lab, h 101 Roberts
Whiteside Jno B (Mary C), contr, 46 Panola, h same
Whiteside Jno K (Jennie), carp, h 36 Josephine
*Whiteside Lucy, laund, h 4 Greer's Row
WHITESIDE PRINTING CO (E W Whiteside), job printing, 22 s Pack Sq (see opp p)
*Whiteside Wm M, lab, h Hazel Mill rd, W Asheville
Whiting Wm S (Carrie), wholesale lumber, 56-59 Amer Nat'l Bank Bldg, h 211 Montford av
Whitlock Bernard, pres Whitlock Clo Co, res New York City
Whitlock Carrie E Miss, h 278 Haywood
Whitlock Clothing Co (Inc), 41 Patton av, Bernard Whitlock pres, Mrs S K Whitlock v-pres, J L Whitlock sec-treas
Whitlock J Leon, sec-treas Whitlock Clo Co, h 278 Haywood

INSURANCE
Insure your salary with us
Never carry your own risk
Safety is the best policy
Unless you are a capitalist
Rest easy if you have
An accident we will
Not keep you waiting to
Collect your claim
Every claim promptly paid

Imperial Mutual Life & Health Insurance Co.

Home Office: ASHEVILLE, N. C.

Phone 495

HOTEL OXFORD Redecorated and Refitted throughout. Recently enlarged to 60 rooms. Centrally located Depot cars stop at entrance. Long distance telephone office upstairs. American and European plan. Rates 50c, 75c and $1 per day; special rates by week or month. C. H. Branson & Sons, Proprietors. Phone 1887. 50-54 South Main St. **Asheville, N. C.**

Whitlock Sarah K Mrs, v-pres Whitlock Clo Co, h 278 Haywood
*Whitmire Edwd, lab, h 36 Hill
WHITMORE SAMUEL L DR, physician in charge Whitmore Sanitarium, 408 w Haywood—phone 1020, h same (see page 11)
WHITMORE SANITARIUM, Dr Samuel L Whitmore physician in charge, 408 w Haywood—phone 1020 (see page 11)
Whitner Ethel, wid Philip, housekpr, h 4 Factory Hill
Whitner J Wilfred (Mayme), flgmn, h 385 Southside av
Whitney Arthur C (Irma), florist, h Asheville av W Asheville (R F D 3)
*Whitney Jos (Ola), lab, h 108 Eagle
*Whitson Addie, laund, h 70 Gudger
*Whitson Annie, cook 214 Montford av
Whitson Geo M (Minnie), h Chunns Cove
*Whitson Jas (Annie), lab, h 170 Beaumont
Whitson Jennie Miss, tchr West Ashev School, h Swannanoa N C
*Whitson Jno, gardener 214 Montford av
*Whitson Jno H (Annie), butler, h 228 Beaumont
*Whitson Jno N, lab, h 192 Beaumont
*Whitson Kate, laund, h 118 Church
*Whitson Martha, h 70 Gudger
Whitson Maud Miss, h 176 e Chestnut
Whitson Max E, student, h 176 e Chestnut
Whitson Sallie Miss, stengr, h 176 e Chestnut
*Whitson Wm (Clarissa), lab, h 40 Maiden la
*Whitson Wm (Eula), h (r) 28 Depot
Whitson Wm K, student, h 176 e Chestnut
WHITSON WM R, atty at law, 6 n Pack Sq, h 176 Chestnut
Whitt Merritt, lab, bds 49 n Main
Whitt Reuben Y (Nancy E), boarding 49 n Main, h same
Whittaker Erwin, foreman Ashev Mica Co, h Fairview rd
Whittaker Frank, exp msgr, bds 29 Jefferson Drive
Whittaker J Emory (Essie), carp, h 21 Central av
Whittaker Solomon (Anna M), carp, h 8 View
Whittaker W F, msgr Sou Exp
☞ Whittaker see also Whitaker
*Whitted Hart, cook 103 Montford av
Whitted J Olin (Gertrude), h 204 Livingston
Whitted Ruston A (Lizzie), coach clnr, h Haywood rd, W Asheville (R F D 3)

FOR BOX SHOOKS — **Call English Lumber Co.** PHONE 321

Whittemore Geo W (Ettie), driver, h 22 Central av
Whittemore Le Roy, lab, h 22 Central av
Whittemore Martin A (Margaret), clk Ry M S, h 76 Blanton
Whittemore Matthew S, h 22 Central av
Whittemore Sue Miss, wks Ashev Mica Co, h 8 North
Whittington Clara E Miss, h 25 Vance
Whittington Mamie W Miss, h 25 Vance
Whittington Robt B, student, h 25 Vance
Whittington Willard P, phys 2 n Pack Sq (2d fl), h 25 Vance
Whittmore Clarindy J, wid Jas B, h 8 North
Whittmore Lona Miss, waitress, h 16 Cumberland av
Whyte Alex (Mattie), florist, h 292 n Main
Wicker Alexander C, trav slsmn, h 201 Merrimon av
Wight Anna H, wid Grant, dressmkr 28 Philip, h same
Wight Grant, h 28 Philip
*Wike Jno (Bessie), helper Ashev Supply & Fdy Co, h 33 Catholic av
Wilbar Dovie Miss, h 644 s Main
WILBAR JOSEPH C, propr Asheville Cleaning & Pressing Club and merchant tailor, 4 n Pack Sq—phone 389, h 644 s Main—phone 1030
*Wilbar Mary, laund, h 468 s French Broad av
Wilbar Mary E Miss, h Biltmore rd
*Wilber Etta, dom, 55 Grove
*Wilburn Olivia, cook, h 33 Circle
Wild Fannie P, wid Wm B, genl sec Flower Mission and Associated Charities and Free Medical Dispensary, h 247 s Grove
Wild Henry A, mngr North Carolina Oil Co, h 264 Patton
Wild J Celia Miss, phone opr, h 204 Patton av
Wild Jesse A, gro 470 w Haywood, h 264 Patton av
Wild Ralph, warehouseman North Carolina Oil Co, h 264 Patton av
WILDER E MRS, propr Sanitary Home Laundry, h 11 Montford av
WILDER EUGENE DR (Josephine D), h 11 Montford av
WILDER'S SANITARY HOME LAUNDRY, 7 Montford av—phone 1354 (see top and bottom lines)
Wiley Arthur L (Emma), slsmn Rogers Gro Co, h 216 Patton av
*Wiley Geo (Anna), cabt mkr, h 64 Clemmons
*Wiley Jos (Nancy), lab, h 33 Buttrick
Wiley Laura Miss, tchr Normal & Collegiate Inst

Biggest Busiest Best Asheville Steam Laundry
Phones: 1936 and 1937
43 to 47 W. College Street

CHARLES H. HONESS
OPTOMETRIST AND OPTICIAN
Exclusive maker of ATLAS SHUR-ON EYE GLASSES
THE Home of Ce-Rite Toric Lenses
We make a specialty of correcting optical defects with properly fitted glasses.
54 Patton Avenue
Opposite Postoffice

Carolina Machinery Co. Founders, Machinists and Jobbers of Mill Supplies. We make all kinds of Castings in Iron, Brass or Aluminum.
WE ALSO FURNISH SKILLED MECHANICS FOR BOILER REPAIRS —— PHONE 590

LIFE INSURANCE COMPANY OF VA.
ORGANIZED 187
Richmond -:- Virginia
J. V MOON, Superintendent
Rooms 3-4-5- Maxwelton Bldg., Asheville, N. C.

All claims paid IMMEDIATELY upon receipt of satisfactory proofs of Death. Total payment to policyholders since organization, over $12,000,000.00. Is paying its Policyholders over $1,000,000.00 annually.

T. P. JOHNSON & CO.

SHEET METAL WORKERS

All Kinds of Roofing Guttering and Conductor Work Metal Ceilings, Skylights and Galvanized Iron Cornices

OFFICE and SHOP:
69-71 S. MAIN
Phone 325

DR. C. H. MILLER

Mechano-Therapist

14 N. Spruce Street
ASHEVILLE, N. C.

PHONE 979

Hours by Engagement

DRUGLESS HEALING OF DISEASE

---

378   ASHEVILLE [1913] DIRECTORY

Wiley Marguerite Miss, student, h 216 Patton av
Wiley Ruth Miss, h 216 Patton av
Wiley Sarah Miss, clk Bon Marche, h 23 Asheland av
*Wiley Wm Rev, h 188 Livingston
Wilfong Christina, wid J T, housekpr, h 18 Flint
*Wilfong Jno (Jessie B), lab, h 81 Wallach
WILFORD ISAAC B (Baird-Wilford Realty Co), h 73 Cumberland av—phone 1308
Wilhelm Geo (Johantges), furn finisher, h 17 s Ann
Wilhelm May Miss, matron Home Industrial School h same
WILKIE HARRIET C MISS, mngr Allanstand Cottage Industries, h 118 Woodfin
*Wilkins Edwd (Della), brkmn, h 64 Ralph
*Wilkins Jno J, janitor, rms 16 Eagle
*Wilkins Millard (Anna), fireman, h 499 Depot
*Wilkins Roland, lab, h Sou Ry opp Tannery
Wilkinson A Shuford (Annie L), harness mkr Ashev Harness Co, h 39½ n French Broad av
Wilkinson Clara B, wid Marvin B, h 135 Cumberland av
Willard (The), boarding 112 Haywood, C E Smart propr
Willer Nonia Miss, stengr Asheville Paint & Glass Co, h 25 Asheland
Willey Herbert B, with Fred'k Rutledge & Co and asst genl agt Girard F & M Ins and City of New York Ins Co, h 77 e College
Williams A Conrad (Mary), plumber, h 239 s Grove
Williams Anna Miss, dom, h Hotel Warren
Williams Annie C Miss, h 43 Watauga
*Williams Arthur, cook Sou Ry Dining Room, h 88 Black
*Williams Bessie, laund, h 25 Short Valley
Williams Bonnie Miss, student, h 180 Merrimon av
Williams Branch H (Salina), police capt, h 180 Merrimon
WILLIAMS, BROWNELL PLANING MILL CO (Inc), Sou Ry nr Biltmore—phone 729; E P Brownell Jr pres, J A Lowery v-pres, Edwin L Gaston sec-treas (see top and bottom lines)
*Williams Calvin, bootblk, h 26 Frederick
Williams Caroline A, wid Mahon, h 10 Clayton
*Williams Caroline L, h 159 College
*Williams Catherine T, h 40 Davidson
*Williams Charity, dom, Merrimon av cor Hillside
*Williams Charlotte, laund, h 38 Bay
Williams Chas F, county sheriff office Court House, h 1½ mile south of Weaverville N C
Williams Chas M (Lillie), tax collr, h 29 Central av

ASHEVILLE CLEANING and PRESSING CLUB

TAILORING THAT SATISFIES and PRICES THAT PLEASE

Hats cleaned, banded and bound. Silk hats ironed. Buttons made to order in all sizes. Plain or with rims. PHONE 389

DYEING IN ALL SHADES Cleaned. Messenger Service.

Kid Gloves, Slippers and Plumes. Fancy Jabots and Ties. French Dry Cleaned. Ladies' and Gentlemen's suits Steam Cleaned.

J. C. Wilbar, Prop.   4 NORTH PACK SQ.

Williams Chas M (Antiseptic Barber Shop), h 50 Asheland
*Williams Claude, porter, h 174 Beaumont
Williams Clo E, wid A F, h 59 Charlotte
Williams Clyde, driver W L Barrett, h 52 Woodfin
*Williams Coleman (Viola), lab, h 318 Asheland av
Williams Connie, plmbr J R Rich Co, h s Grove
Williams D Elbert B (Sallie), tchr, h 38 Clingman av
Williams D McGregor, engnr N C Electrical Co, office 78 Patton av, rms Y M C A
*Williams Edwd (Maggie), porter, h Sou Ry opp Rees' Tannery
Williams Edwd, lab, h 11 Biltmore rd, S Biltmore
WILLIAMS EDWD N, mngr W U Tel Co, h 10 Clayton
*Williams Elizabeth, cook, h Louis nr Depot
*Williams Ellen, laund, h Valley nr College
*Williams Elliott (Mary), lab, h 7 Ridge
*Williams Emma, h 99 s Beaumont
*Williams Ernest (Elizabeth), lab, h 99 Roberts
*Williams Eugene, lab, h 105 Gudger
*Williams Eugenia, dom 405 Charlotte
Williams Fannie C Miss, h 50 Asheland av
*Williams Fleming (Mamie), lab, h 42 Wallach
Williams Florence, wid Jno A, h 79 Furman av
Williams Francis M (Loduska), h 50 Asheland av
*Williams Frank, lab, h 121 Black
*Williams Frank, porter, rms 74 Eagle
*Williams Frank, whseman Armour & Co, h 7 Ridge
*Williams Fred (Lucy), driver Carolina Coal & Ice Co, h 26 Frederick
Williams Fred J, mngr Ideal Pressing Club, h Cherokee Inn
Williams G W Kirk (Elizabeth), candy mnfr, h 207 Asheland av
Williams Garnette Miss, music tchr, h 180 Merrimon av
Williams Geneva Miss, laund, h 38 Clingman av
*Williams Geo (Lily), brick lyr, h 105 Gudger
Williams Geo P, emp Tannery, h 147 Grove
Williams Georgia Miss, dressmkr 10 Orchard, h same
*Williams Henry (Amanda), lab, h Biltmore rd, S Biltmore
*Williams Henry (Georgia), blksmith, h 20 Weaver
*Williams Henry (Lizzie), butcher, h 135 Pine
Williams Horace, plumber Union Plumbing Co, h 107 Blanton
*Williams Horace, h 34 Ridge
*Williams Irene, cook, h (r) 26 Gudger
*Williams Israel (Mollie), waiter, h 30 Magnolia av

Williams J Calvin, janitor, City Hall, h 52 Woodfin
Williams J Hamilton (Carrie), porter, h 134 Choctaw
Williams J McFarland (Pattie), rms 147 Haywood
Williams Jas M (Lillian), lumber 423-424 Legal Bldg, h 50 Chunn
Williams Jas S Rev, h 297 Merrimon av
Williams Jas W, shoemkr J C Henninger, h 34 Blanton
Williams Janie Miss, cashr Peerless Fashion Store, h 10 Philip
Williams Jessie Miss, h 297 Merrimon av
*Williams Jno (Dora), lab, h 10 Cole
*Williams Jno (Mary), lab, h nr Hael Mill rd, W Ashev
*Williams Jno H, driver, h 25 Short Valley
WILLIAMS JOHN HEY (Margaret), physician 20 Battery Park pl—phone 46, h 43 Watauga
Williams Jno L, student, h 50 Chunn
*Williams Jos, porter Antiseptic Barber Shop, h 57 Eagle
Williams Jos M (Louise), bricklyr, h 107 Blanton
Williams Laura D Mrs, matron Normal & Collegiate Inst, rms same
*Williams Lawrence (Marie), driver, h (r) 7 Depot
Williams Leonore Miss, h 21 n Liberty
*Williams Lillian, dom, Manzanita Cottage Albemarle Park
*Williams Lizzie, cook, 55 Grove
Williams Loduska Mrs, boarding 50 Asheland av, h same
*Williams Lula, laund, h 35 Short Valley
Williams Luther J (Mollie), lab, h 11 Biltmore rd, S Biltmore
*Williams Marshall (Minnie), janitor, h 19 Lincoln av
*Williams Mary, cook, h 15 Short
*Williams Mary, laund, h 98 Hazzard
*Williams Matilda, laund, h 99 Eagle
Williams Minnie E, wid Claudius C, bds 68 Church
Williams Nannie, wid Noah A, h Haywood rd, W Ashev, R F D 3
*Williams Nellie, h 8 Sorrell
Williams Nellie C Miss, h 50 Asheland av
Williams Ocie L Miss, h 50 Asheland av
*Williams Olivette, dress mkr, h 128 Pearson Drive
Williams Pascal U (Sarah), bricklyr, h 93 Victoria av
Williams Pattie Mrs, musician, rms 147 Haywood
Williams Paul C, boiler mkr Sou Ry, h 50 Asheland av
*Williams Peter W (Margaret), janitor, h 20 Curve
Williams R Jefferson (Mary), electrn, h Haywood rd, W Ashev (R F D 3)

Williams Robt, appr Ashev Ptg & Engrav Co, h 207 Asheland av
*Williams Robt (Lillian), hallman, h 39 Frederick
*Williams Robt (Mary), lab, h 118 Church
*Williams Robt, lab, h 159 College
Williams Robt L (Sarah), condr, h Woolsey (R F D 1)
Williams Robt R (Jones & Williams), rms 18 Vance
Williams S Elizabeth Miss, h 58 East
*Williams Seymour, lab, h 26 Frederick
Williams Sidney, h 400 Pearson Drive
*Williams Susan, maid, h 13 Short Valley
Williams T Frederick, emp auto shop, h 107 Blanton
Williams Thelma Miss, student, h 180 Merrimon av
*Williams Thos, janitor Phoenix Hotel
*Williams Thos G (Ashev Cabinet Co), h 68 Clemmons
Williams Virginia M Miss, h 50 Asheland av
*Williams W Henry, meat ctr The Star Market h 135 s Pine
Williams W Robt, mill wkr, bds 470 w Haywood
*Williams Walter, emp Cafe, h 15 New
Williams Walter J (Susie E), poultry Haywood rd, W Ashev, h same (R F D 3)
Williams Wilburn, emp W Union, bds 52 Woodfin
Williams Wm, condr, bds 308 Depot
Williams Wm B (Iney M), lab, h 119 Park av
*Williams Wm M (Mary), janitor, h 15 Latta
Williams Wm R (Mollie E), driver, h 340 w Haywood
Williamson Elizabeth A Miss, h 301 Pearson Drive
Williamson Frances Miss, rms 14 Grove
Williamson Geo J (Katherine), (M V Moore & Co), h Margo Terrace
Williamson Jas A (Nettie), propr Battery Park Hotel Barber Shop, h same
Williamson Jean Miss, clk Bon Marche, h 14 Grove
Williamson Louisa G Miss, asst to city clk, h 285 Merrimon
Williamson Mary V Miss, h 301 Pearson Drive
Williamson Mary W, wid Jno A G, prin Murray School, h 285 Merrimon av
WILLIAMSON WM B (Addie), cashr Wachovia Bank & Trust Co, treas Pack Memorial Library Assn, h 301 Pearson Drive
Williamson Nettie Mrs, manicure Battery Park Hotel, h same
Willis Adelaide Miss, h 122 w Chestnut
Willis Beatrice Miss, h 122 w Chestnut
Willis Chas C (Ada), h 117 Broad

Candy Kitchen and Club Cafe
"A GOOD PLACE FOR REFRESHMENT"

The very best ingredients with sanitary conditions in our Candy Manufacturing Department make possible the dainty, crisp confections sold here.

Bon Bons and Chocolates made every day, put up in neat, attractive boxes. Phones 110 and 111. 19 and 21 Haywood St.

Brown's Undertaking Parlors

S. H. BROWN

Lady Assistant When Desired

Phone 193-2 Rings

50 Patton Avenue
Asheville, N. C.

Established 1894

B. J. JACKSON

Carefully Selected Fruits and Vegetables

Stall No. 11, City Market

BUSINESS PHONES:
86 and 101

RESIDENCE PHONE
1596

Willis Chas P (Sarena), blksmith, h 16 Bennett
Willis E Frank (C Julius), clk, h 114 Bartlett
Willis Frances M Miss, nurse 14 Blake, h same
Willis Jas (Cynthia), h Grace
Willis Jas W (Ellen), colr Globe Furn Co, h 35 Blanton
Willis Jno (Mary), blksmith, h 36 Bennett
Willis Maggie Mrs, wkr Ashev Mica Co, h 244 College
Willis Montez Miss, clk Palais Royal, h 22 Buttrick
Willis Ollie M Miss, clk, h 22 Buttrick
Willis Piety Miss, phone opr, h 16 Bennett
*Willis Priscilla, cook, h 16 Hazzard
Willis R Nelson (Alice), blksmith Western Carolina Auto Co, h 82 n Lexington
Willis Rebecca Miss, h 16 Bennett
Willis S Dora Miss, clk Palais Royal, h 22 Buttrick
Willis Sallie T, wid Milton, propr The Bon Air, h 66 Asheland av
Willis Virginia Miss, clk Palais Royal, h 12 Hilliard pl
Willis Wilborne E (Maude), lab, h 36 Bennett
Willis Wm A (Mary A), gro 65 Spring, h 22 Buttrick
Willow Nona Miss, stengr Ashev P & G Co, h 25 Asheland
*Wills Lawrence A, clk, h Herren av, W Ashev (R F D 3)
*Wills Robt E (Sophia), lab, h S Asheville
*Wills Rufus (Kate), truant officer, h Herren av, W Ashev (R F D 3)
Wilson Agnes R Mrs, dressmkr 40 Carter, h same
Wilson Alfred I, h 477 w Haywood
*Wilson Alonzo (Lucy), lab, h nr Hazel Mill rd, W Ashev
Wilson Annie Miss, h 20 Marjorie
Wilson Annie Miss, student, rms 70 Adams
Wilson Annie Miss, student, h 49 Bartlett
Wilson Archer D (Myrtle), clk Sunny Smoke Shop, h 284 College
Wilson Arthur E (Dora), engnr, h 35 Ora
Wilson Arthur M (Emma), mtrmn St Car, h 93 East
Wilson Avery H (Mattie), firemn, h 25 Ora
Wilson B Rankin Miss, asst supt Highland Hospital, h same
*Wilson Bessie, laund, h 8 Ingle
Wilson C Bessie, wid N B, h 40 s French Broad
Wilson C H, rms Y M C A
*Wilson Catherine, laund, h 19 Tuskee
Wilson Chas, wkr Ashev Mica Co, h Biltmore
*Wilson Chas (Annie), lab, h 8 Madison
*Wilson Chas (Bertha), lab Sou Coal Co, h 9 Depot

Yᵉ OLD BOOK SHOP

114 Patton Ave.   Phone 1674

BOOKS BOUGHT, SOLD OR EXCHANGED

Wilson Connie H, pharmacist Smith Drug Store, rms Y M C A
*Wilson David J (Ethel), mngr N Murrough, h 74 Hill
Wilson Dexter, laundrymn, h 20 Marjorie
Wilson Dora M Miss, h 95 East
WILSON EDGAR F, livery and sale stable, 58 s Main—phone 709, h same (see page 24)
*Wilson Edna, dom, h 42 Ridge
Wilson Emmaline, wid Wm, h 125 Bartlett
Wilson Ethel Miss, stengr Supt Sou Ry, h 169 Cumberland
Wilson Everett, student, h 169 Cumberland av
*Wilson Florence, h 27 Turner
*Wilson Frank (Fannie), cook, h 516 s French Broad av
Wilson Frank A, h 156 Asheland av
*Wilson Geo, porter Hotel Oxford
*Wilson Harrison (Mary), plstr, h 40 Madison
Wilson Harry W, plstr, h 109 Biltmore rd, S Biltmore
Wilson Hattie E, wid Wm H, h 169 Cumberland av
Wilson Henry (Bonnie), switchman, h 321 s Main
Wilson Herman C, attendant Highland Hosp, h same
Wilson Hester A, wid Geo S, h 20 Marjorie
Wilson Ida Miss, nurse Highland Hospital, h same
Wilson J Alfred (Wilson Undertaking Co), pres Mtn City Mut Ins Co and barber, 39 s Main, h 269 s Beaumont
Wilson J C Mrs, tchr High Schl
Wilson J Elma Miss, student, h 40 s French Broad av
Wilson J Robt (Laura), driver, h 450 n Main
Wilson Jas, well digger, bds 14 Sassafras
*Wilson Jas (Lenora), presser, h 48 Max
Wilson Jas H (Minnie H), stable, 82 n Lexington av, h 69 Penland
Wilson Jas L (M Catherine), carp, h Arlington st, W Ashev (R F D 3)
*Wilson Jeremiah (Essie), cook, h 23 Max
Wilson Jesse B (Marguerite), contr, h 260 Hillside
Wilson Jesse F, mchst Sky Cycle Co, h 93 East
Wilson Jno, clk, h 93 East
*Wilson Jno (Rosa), lab, h (r) 36 Clingman av
Wilson Jno B (Carrie), emp Ideal Pressing Club, h 59 Woodfin
Wilson Jno B (Agnes R), trav slsmn, h 40 Carter
*Wilson Laura, laund, h 16 Hazzard
*Wilson Leola, dom, h 18 Clemmons
Wilson Lucius C (Maude), propr Sky Cycle Co, h 82 Starnes Pl

Mrs. Wilder's SANITARY HOME LAUNDRY turns out first class work in Laundering and Dry Cleaning. No. 7 Montford Ave., Phone 1354

Wilson Luther, clk Carmichael's Pharmacy, h W Asheville
*Wilson Maggie, laund, h 41 Lincoln av
Wilson Margaret Mrs, h Haywood rd, W Asheville (R F D 3)
Wilson Mary H, wid J B, h 210 Merrimon av
*Wilson Miles (Laura), lab, h 89 Circle
Wilson Nellie Miss, clk Brown Book Co Inc, bds 139 Montford av
*Wilson Nellie, dom, h 14 Aston Pl
Wilson O'Connor C (Fleta), ticket agt Sou Ry, h 251 s French Broad av
Wilson Oscar, painter, bds 34½ n Main
Wilson Oscar C, driver Ashev P & G Co, h 12 Bennett
Wilson Pollie, wid Wm, h 12 Bennett
Wilson Rachel M, wid Jno T, h 95 East
Wilson Roland A (Martha W), box mnfgr, h Edgemont
Wilson Roland A Jr, student, h Edgemont
Wilson Romulus (Mamie), lab, h 242 College
*Wilson Rosa L, cook 124 Montford av
Wilson S Austin Miss, supt Highland Hospital, h same
*Wilson Saml (Carrie), lab, h Haywood rd, W Asheville (R F D 3)
*Wilson Tandy (Alice), lab, h 22 Bay
Wilson Theo, barber Ashev Barber Shop, h 38 Asheland av
Wilson Theron (Lillie), carp, h 293 s Main
*Wilson Thos (Fannie), lab, h W Asheville
Wilson Thos E (Lillie), dep sheriff, h 156 Asheland av
*Wilson Undertaking Co (J A Wilson, G L Greenlea and R H Loder), 18 Eagle
Wilson W Lane Miss, nurse Highland Hospital, h same
Wilson Watson A (Aurelia), bldg contr 331 n Main, h same
Wilson Weaver V (Lula), asst supt Water Dept, h 24 College Park
Wilson Wm, blksmith, bds 348½ Depot
*Wilson Wm, lab, h 9 Madison
Wilson Wm A (Hattie), foreman, h Arlington st, W Ashev (R F D 3)
Wilson Wm E, bicycle repr J M Hearn & Co, bds 39 Clingman av
Wilson Wm M, slsmn Harris-Barnett Dry Goods Co (Inc), h 56 Orchard
Wilson Wm P (Mary), carp, rms 379 w Haywood
*Wilson Willis (Margaret), driver Owenbey & Son, h 21 Gudger

BUICK OLDSMOBILE ARBOGAST MOTOR COMPANY ACCESSORIES AND SUPPLIES 52-60 N. Main Phones 302 and 1728 MAXWELLS DETROIT ELECTRIC

Asheville Dry Cleaning Co.
Telephones 835-836, All Dep't
MAIN, N. E. COR. COLLEGE

THE CLEANERS
Our Department for Oriental Rugs and Carpet Cleaning is prepared to serve you in all its branches.
E. S. Paine   O. E. Hansen

ALL KINDS
Hardwood Lumber

ENGLISH LUMBER CO.

Phone - - 321

Winans Fenton J (Minnette), mnfr, h 42 Madison av
Winchester Frank L, lumberman, rms 14-15 Medical Bldg
Windsor Hotel & Cafe, 48-50 s Main, W P Black propr
Windsor Hotel Barber Shop, 46 s Main, W P Black propr
*Wingate Marion (Emma), cook, h 139 Pine
Wingo Hugh, flgmn, bds 418 Southside av
Wingo Isham, fireman, bds 418 Southside av
Wingren Pauline Miss, h 201 Cumberland av
Wingren Richard (Estella), h 201 Cumberland av
*Winkler Rufus (Maria), lab, h 108 Livingston
Winn Earl, bkkpr Natl Casket Co, bds 58 Orange
Winn Jas A (Elizabeth C), prin The Winn School for Boys, h 135 Merrimon av
Winn Paul P Rev, asst prin The Winn School for Boys, h 135 Merrimon av
Winn School For Boys (The), 135 Merrimon av, Jas A Winn prin
Winslow Edwd L (Ida), engnr, h W Asheville (R F D 3)
Winston Geo T (Carolin T), h Edgemont
Winston R W Capt, tchr Bingham School, h Bingham Heights
Winters Marcus R, motorman, rms 20 Meriwether Bldg
WINYAH SANATORIUM (The) (Drs Karl and Silvio von Ruck), East cor Spears av—phone 84
*Wise Geo W, lab, h (r) 246 College
"Witchwood", res Mrs A S Woolsey, East cor Hillside
Withers Jane Miss, h 403 Merrimon av
*Withers Sherman (Linda), coachmn, h (r) 166 Chestnut
*Witherspoon Emma, cook 16 Hilliard la
*Witherspoon Preston (Emma), cook, h 60 n Lexington av
Witz Jos (Laura C), slsmn H B Brux, h 115 Montford av
*Wofford Frank (Emma), lab, h 8 Short McDowell
*Wofford Henry, bricklyr, h 97 n Main
Wohlforth Justine Dr (Catherine), h Pearson Drive
Wolf P Wetherly, motorman, rms 27 Meriwether Bldg
WOLFE BENJ, adv collr Ashev Citizen, h 48 n Spruce—phone 769
Wolfe Building, 22 s Pack Sq
Wolfe Carl, lab, bds 306 n Main
Wolfe Frank W, photogr, h 48 n Spruce
Wolfe Frederick W, chffr, h 92 Woodfin
Wolfe Jas J (Josephine), h Haywood rd, W Ashev (R D 3)
WOLFE JAS W (Genevieve M), sec-treas Western Carolina Realty Co and notary public, h 64 n Spruce—phone 831

BIGGEST
BUSIEST
BEST

Phones 1936 and 1937
ASHEVILLE STEAM LAUNDRY
43 to 47 W. COLLEGE

S. D. HALL
REAL ESTATE AGENT

Money Loaned

Notary Public

32 PATTON AVENUE

Phone 91

CAROLINA MACHINERY CO.
—US when you want machine work of any kind . . .

Founders Machinists and Jobbers of Mill Supplies
When in the market for heavy castings such as columns or building plates get our prices. Phone 590

The Life Insurance Co. of Virginia
ORGANIZED 1871   RICHMOND, VA.

ISSUES ALL THE MOST APPROVED FORMS OF LIFE INSURANCE CONTRACTS from $500.00 to $25,000.00, with premiums payable quarterly, semi-annually and annually

J. V. Moon, Superintendent, Rooms 3-4-5 Maxwelton Bldg., Asheville, N. C.

D. TREXLER TIN SHOP

All Kinds of Roofing, Gutter and Conductor Work.

Phone 862

159 South Main St.

DR. C. H. MILLER

MECHANO-THERAPIST

14 N. Spruce St.
Phone 979
ASHEVILLE, N. C.

Hours by engagement

Drugless Healing of Disease

Wolfe Julia E Mrs, propr Old Kentucky Home, h 48 n Spruce
Wolfe Kate Miss, maid "Klondyke," Montford av
Wolfe Lillie Miss, dressmkr, rms 118 Woodfin
Wolfe Mabel E Miss, h 92 Woodfin
Wolfe Saml M (Katie), div supt W M Ritter Lbr Co, h 54 Courtland av
Wolfe W Frank (Carrie), h Biltmore rd, S Biltmore
Wolfe Wm O (Julia E), marble wks 22 s Pack Sq, h 92 Woodfin
Wolfram Harry F, student, h 202 e Chestnut
Wolfram Sally S (Fannie), jeweler, h 202 e Chestnut
Woman's Exchange, 36 Haywood; Mrs C E Gibbs sec, Mrs E I Palmer supt
Woman's Exchange Tea Room, 36 Haywood, Miss Jessie Woodfin mngr
Woman's Social and Study Club, Morsell Bldg
Womble Jno A, painter R L Fitzpatrick & Son, bds Hotel Warren
Womble Carrie V Mrs, boarding 96 Bartlett, h same
Wood Albert C, student, h 84 Bartlett
Wood Clyde F (Laura S), clk Ry M S, h 23 n Ann
Wood Garfield F, lineman Ashev Power & Light Co, h 120 Biltmore rd, S Biltmore
WOOD JAS H (Blanche), dist passngr agt Sou Ry and chf A F D, h 84 Bartlett
Wood Jas H Jr, student, h 84 Bartlett
Wood Julia, wid Robt, h 120 Biltmore rd, S Biltmore
*Wood Lee (Lillian), driver, h 24 Silver
Wood Samantha Miss, h 120 Biltmore rd, S Biltmore
Wood Sibler E, wid Rolly, h 218 s French Broad av
Wood T Gilbert, agt Land & Ind Dept Sou Ry, rms Y M C A
Wood Winnie M Miss, h 218 s French Broad av
☞ Wood see also Woods
Woodard Alice, wid W R, h 39 Furman av
Woodard Edwd (Myrtelle), bkkpr Ashev Harness Co, Inc, h 234 n Main
Woodard Hugh M, clk frt office Sou Ry, h 39 Furman av
Woodard Jas W, inspctr, h 39 Furman av
Woodard Jno, clk, h 39 Furman av
Woodard Wm T, clk frt office Sou Ry, h 39 Furman av
☞ Woodard see also Woodward
Woodbury Frank P (Edith H), cashr The Piedmont Electric Co, h 19 Chunn

---

....Asheville Cleaning and Pressing Club....
Tailoring That Satisfies and Prices That Please
Steam and French Dry Cleaning of all delicate and fine wearing apparel for ladies and gentlemen. MESSENGER SERVICE IN THE CITY.
J. C. WILBAR, Prop.   4 N. Pack Square   PHONE 389

Woodbury Grace Miss, h 72 n Main
Woodbury Wm H (Gertrude), lumber office Ambler Bldg, h 72 n Main
Woodcock Julia E, wid Julian, h 199 Montford av
Woodcock Julian A (Blanche), propr Citizens Transfer Co, h 255 Haywood
Woodcock Rufus J (Blanche), (Woodcock & Gillis), h 228 Montford av
Woodcock Sidney J, phys, h 199 Montford av
Woodcock & Gillis (R J Woodcock, Donald Gillis), real estate, 21 Amer Natl Bank Bldg
Woodfin Anna M Miss, h 26 Clayton
Woodfin Bascomb A, mngr Corner Pool Room, h 84 Penland
Woodfin Benj H, clk, h 84 Penland
Woodfin Jessie Miss, mngr Woman's Exchange Tea Room, h 36 Hiawassee
Woodfin Myra Miss, rms 36 Hiawassee
*Woodford Fred, yd boy 287 Pearson Drive
*Woodford Hattie, dom 315 Pearson
Woodmen of the World Hall, Haywood rd, W Ashev
*Woodruff Jno, lab, h (r) 26 Depot
*Woods Alice, laund, h 30 Catholic av
*Woods Clarence W (Janie), porter, h 43 Circle
*Woods Claude, car clnr, h 43 Circle
Woods F T H (Julia E), real estate and notary public, 14½ s Main, h 128 Charlotte
Woods Sim F (Bertha), gro 44 s Main, h 172 Asheland av
☞ Woods see also Wood
*Woodside Jas A (Minnie), bellmn, h 12 Jordan
*Woodside Wm (Lily), janitor Amer Natl Bank, h 27 Short
*Woodson Frank (Minnie), waiter, h 81 Pine
WOODWARD STEWART M (Woodward & Son), and pres S & W H Northrop Lbr Co (Inc), res Richmond Va
WOODWARD & SON, lumber, building material and hardwoods, 9th and Arch, Richmond Va (see top lines and bet pages 188 and 189)
☞ Woodward see also Woodard
Woody Amelia I, wid Jno H, h 18 Starnes av
Woody Bertha L Miss, h Hazel Mill rd, W Ashev (R F D 3)
Woody Chas J (Laura E), slsmn Rogers Grocery Co, h W Asheville (R F D 3)
Woody Claude (Jettie), clk J F Sims, h W Asheville
Woody Cole, baker, h Hazel Mill rd, W Ashev (R F D 3)

Asheville Dray, Fuel & Construction Co.
9 1-2 South Main

COAL

Wood and Kindling
Stone and Sand
PHONE - 223

Woody Colen, baker Zindel's Model Bakery, h Emma
Woody Eleanor G Miss, clk Amer Natl Bank, h 18 Starnes
Woody Floyd, clk Ownbey & Son, h W Asheville
*Woody Grant (Mary), lab, h (r) 40 Clingman av
*Woody Jas (Annie), cook, h 111 Clingman av
*Woody Jas, waiter Sou Ry Dining Room
Woody Pink M (Althea), carp McDowell & Patton, h Hazel Mill rd, W Asheville (R F D 3)
Woody Russell C, mchst, h 18 Starnes av
Wooldridge Thos J (Mary M), bkkpr Ashev Power & Light Co, h 114 Montford av
Woolsey Alice S, wid Chas, h "Witchwood," East cor Hillside
Woolsey Greenhouse, Woolsey (R F D 1), E C Dickinson propr
Woolsey Hall, R F D 1
Wooten Addie L Miss, h 153½ Grove
Wooten Ellen Miss, dom, 40 Magnolia av
Wooten Geo W, emp Steam Dye Wks, h 159 Grove
Wooten Lester H (Susan), painter, h 153 Grove
Wooten Luther, switchmn, bds 60 Clingman av
Wooten Marion J (Laura), carp, h 159 Grove
*Worford Jno (Carrie), lab, h 374 Magnolia av
*Workman Fannie, cook, h 18 Clemmons
Worley Berley M Miss, wkr Ashev Mica Co, h 60 Clingman
Worley Chas McC, student, h Hazel Mill rd, W Asheville (R F D 3)
Worley Etta L Miss, wks Ashev Mica Co, h 60 Clingman av
Worley Geo W (Laura), carp, h 60 Clingman av
Worley Horace B (Rena), car repr, h Swannanoa av, W Ashev (R F D 3)
Worley Jesse H, switchmn, h 60 Clingman av
Worley Major Clingman (Cordelia), switchmn, h 60 Clingman av
Worley Mark W, student, h Hazel Mill rd, W Ashev (R F D 3)
Worley Rachel M, wid Wiley J, h Arlington st, W Ashev (R F D 3)
Worley Robt L (Fannie), motorman, h 43 w Chestnut
Worley Wm W (Ella L), tobacco dlr, h Hazel Mill rd, W Ashev (R F D 3)
Worrell Clarence A (Annabell), artist 76 Flint, h same
Worsley J Mrs, clk Bon Marche
Worsley Jno J (Nova), painter Excelsior P & P House, h 49 w Walnut

EVER READY FLASHLIGHTS
Piedmont Electric Company
ASHEVILLE, N. C.
64 PATTON AVENUE

J. C. McPHERSON
SLATE AND TIN ROOFING
Galvanized Iron Work   Hot Air Furnaces
35-37 EAST COLLEGE STREET

PLUMBING
STEAM AND HOT WATER
HEATING
PHONE 133

Wortham Irene Mc, wid J T, tchr Park av School, h 34 Maxwell
Wray David (Josephine), plmbr G L Guischard, h 85 Asheland av
Wray Julius A (Sue P), farmer, h 96 e College
Wray Mary S Miss, h 96 e College
Wray Walter Toms, genl agt Pittsburg Life & Trust Co of Pa, h 96 College
Wray see also Ray and Rhea
Wrenn Geo W (Florence), (Wrenn & Garland) h 150 Asheland av
Wrenn Mildred M Miss, bkkpr Wrenn & Garland, h 150 Asheland av
Wrenn & Garland (G W Wrenn and G E Garland), contrs 69-71 s Main
Wrenwood (The), boarding 61 s French Broad av, Mrs Ella M Mears propr
Wright Alma Miss, bds 173 s Main
*Wright Babe, emp Lutz Meat Co
Wright Bessie Miss, h 67½ Avery
Wright Edwd B (Maggie), plmbr, h Brevard rd, W Ashev (R F D 3)
Wright Edwd N, student, h 68 College
Wright Eula S Miss, music tchr 68 e College, h same
*Wright Fannie, dom, h 52 Davidson
Wright Frances M Miss, h Victoria rd
WRIGHT GEO H (Irene G), (Martin, Rollins & Wright), and sec-treas Carolina Abstract & Title Co, h 175 Merrimon av
Wright Horace (Doshia), section hnd Sou Ry, h Sou Ry nr Biltmore
Wright Jennie L Miss, h 331 s French Broad av
Wright Jessie Miss, 2d v-pres M Webb Co, h Chattanooga, Tenn
*Wright Jno C (Carrie), waiter, rms 74 Eagle
Wright Jno P (Maggie), blksmith Amer Wagon Co, h w Haywood
*Wright Julius (Abbie), waiter, h 2 Dundee
Wright Kate H Miss, h Marigold Cottage, Albemarle Park
Wright Lee, driver, h W Ashev (R F D 3)
Wright Maggie D, wid Edwd H, boarding 68 e College, h same
Wright Mamie B Miss, tchr Orange St School, h 68 e College
*Wright Nancy, tchr Catholic Hill Schl, h 22 Ridge

Club Cafe and Candy Kitchen
"A GOOD PLACE FOR REFRESHMENT"

The standards we work to in our Restaurant Department are: Cooking, perfect; Service, prompt and cheerful; Prices, moderate; Menu, everything in season. Parties and Banquets, Teas and Dinners. 19 and 21 Haywood St. Phones 110 and 111.

Brown's Undertaking Parlors

S. H. BROWN

50 Patton Avenue
ASHEVILLE, N. C.

Lady Assistant When Desired

Phone 193-2 Rings

THE MOORE Plumbing Company

16 N. Pack Square

PHONE 1025

Sanitary Plumbing, General Tin and Metal Work, Hot Air Furnaces

---

Wright Nora L Miss, smstrs, h Haywood rd, W Ashev (R F D 3)
Wright Rowland (Sallie), h Richmond Hill
Wright Roy M, driver Sou Exp Co, h W Asheville
*Wright Saml (Amelia), lab, h 34 Campbell
Wright Sarah, wid Jno (Bowman & Wright), h 21-25 Reed Bldg
Wright Wallace B, student, h 68 e College
Wright Wm (Minnie), h 67½ Avery
Wright Wm A (Martha), h 111 Montford av
Wright Wm H, emp W M Jones, h W Asheville (R F D 3)
Wyatt Bertha Miss, wkr Ashev Mica Co, h 41 Spring
Wyatt Wm H (Clara), police and genl mdse, 99 Roberts, h 13 same
Wyatt S Woodward (Mattie E), lab, h 41 Spring
Wyness Annie Mrs, mngr corset dept M V Moore & Co, h 33 Aston
Wynn see also Winn
Wynne E L, bkkpr, rms 34 Temple Ct

Y

Y M C A BUILDING, 27 Haywood
Y M I Building (offices), Eagle cor Market
*Y M I DRUG STORE, Eagle s e cor Market—phone 538, H E Jones pharmacist
*Y M I DRUG STORE CO (A Blackwell, Walter S Lee, and J W Walker), proprs Y M I Drug Store
*Y M I Pressing Club, Y M I Bldg, S A Asbury propr
Y W C A Gymnasium, 21 s Main (3d fl)
Y W C A Lunch Room, 11½ Church
Yale Charlotte L Miss, mngr Biltmore Estate Industries, h 9 Plaza, Biltmore
Yarberry Cleveland (Lou), h 114 Biltmore rd, S Biltmore
Yarborough H Taylor (Pinkney), butcher, h Hazel Mill rd, W Ashev (R F D 3)
Yarborough Lon F (Florence), painter, h W Ashev (R D 3)
Yarborough Mary, wid Thos, laund, h (r) 40 Maiden la
Yarborough Wm (Narcissus), lab, h (r) 40 Maiden la
Yarbrough Fred, weaver, h 493 w Haywood
Yates Jesse J (Elizabeth G), (Yates & McGuire), h 97 Flint
Yates Roselyn Miss, clk H Redwood & Co, h The Henrietta
Yates Wm B, carp, bds 47 n Main
Yates & McGuire (J J Yates, W R McGuire), grocers 35 Haywood

The Battery Park Bank

Capital - - $100,000.00
Surplus and Profits, $110,000.00

ASHEVILLE, N. C.   City, County and State Depositary

J. A. TILLMAN — Jeweler — 17 N. Main St.
I carry a nice line of Watches, Clocks and Jewelry, and make a specialty of repair work. Satisfaction guaranteed

YE OLD BOOK STORE, 114 Patton av, E E Galer propr
Yeatman Susan Miss, tchr Orange St Schl
*Yellock Elwood, porter J A Wilson, h 433 Depot
*Yellock Hattie, boarding 433 Depot, h same
Yelton Jas, h Swannanoa av, W Ashev (R F D 3)
Yoder Lola M Miss, student, h 102 Patton av
Yonge Karyll M (Clara L), meat ctr The Star Market, h 75 Starnes av
*Young Ada E, tchr, h Haywood rd, W Ashev (R F D 3)
Young Allie M Miss, h 54 Gaston
Young Annie, wid L R, h 25 Southside av
Young Anthony M (Florence), gro Asheville av, W Ashev, R F D 3
*Young Beatrice, waitress Windsor Cafe, h 12 Lincoln al
Young Benj B, driver, bds Mrs Eva L Edwards, W Ashev
*Young Bessie, h 151 College
*Young Blaine, lab, h 221 Southside av
Young Carmen W, student, h 61 Josephine
Young Clarence A, clk, h 61 Josephine
*Young Edwd (Alice), lab, h 9 Short Valley
*Young Edwd F, barber J W Bowman, h 35 w Chestnut
Young Eva E, wid Jas H, h 166 s French Broad av
Young Fannie, wid Lynch, h 134 Poplar
Young Fredk, condr Sou Ry, h 166 s French Broad av
Young Fredk R (Allie), driver M Hyams, h 242 n Main
Young Georgia Miss, h 40 Holland
Young Georgia Miss, clk Bon Marche
Young H L, rms Y M C A
Young Harmen G, student, h 61 Josephine
Young Helen E Miss, h 459 Depot
Young J W, appr J R Rich Co
Young J Henry (Carrie), gro 418 n Main, h 372 same
Young J Talmage, condr, bds 32 n Ann
Young Jabe T (Mary E), h 87 Starnes av
Young Jas M (Martha L), carp, h 459 Depot
*Young James W (Cora), driver, h nr Hazel Mill rd, W Ashev (R F D 3)
Young Jeptha W (Lurie), plmbr, h 109 Asheland av
*Young Jno (Julia), driver, h 5 Greer's Row
*Young Jno (Sarah), janitor, h 81 Valley
*Young Jno, lab, h (r) 39 Clingman av
*Young Jno, lab, h 36 Maiden la
Young Jno, lab, bds 39 Pearl
Young Jos A, butcher Ownbey & Son, h 60 s Liberty
Young Jos G (Nellie R), meat ctr Lutz Meat Co, h 9 Short

INSURANCE
Insure Your Salary With Us
Never Carry Your Own Risk
Safety Is The Best Policy
Unless You Are A Capitalist
Rest Easy If You Have
An Accident We Will
Not Keep You Waiting To
Collect Your Claim
Every Claim Promptly Paid

Imperial Mutual Life & Health Insurance Co.
Home Office: ASHEVILLE, N. C.
Phone 495

HOTEL OXFORD — Redecorated and Refitted throughout. Recently enlarged to 60 rooms. Centrally located. Depot cars stop at entrance. Long distance telephone office upstairs. American and European plan. Rates 50c, 75c and $1 per day; special rates by week or month. C. H. Branson & Sons, Proprietors. Phone 1887. 50-54 South Main St. **Asheville, N. C.**

Williams-Brownell Planing Mill Company — *Hardwoods*
Lumber---Rough and Dressed Flooring a Specialty Moulding, Interior Finish, Etc.
Office, Plant and Yards on Southern Railway, Near Biltmore Station
WHITE PINE Phone 729 YELLOW PINE

Young Jos M, barber St Charles Barber Shop, h 45 Gaston
Young Katherine Miss, chiropodist, h 6 Battery Park pl
YOUNG LAURENCE W (Hessie U), city clk, office 202 City Hall, h 94 Starnes av
Young Lela M Miss, clk Peoples Department Store, h 54 Gaston
Young Leona Miss, music tchr 23 Adelaide Bldg, h same
*Young Lewis, driver, h 166 Church
*Young Lucy, dom, h 26 Smith
Young McFarland, barber, h 54 Gaston
Young M Abeline, wid Z T, h 60 s Liberty
*Young Mary, cook, h 20 Clemmons
YOUNG MEN'S CHRISTIAN ASSOCIATION, 27 Haywood, Edwd B Brown sec
*Young Men's Institute, Y M I Bldg
*Young Men's Institute Building, Market cor Eagle
*Young Pinkie, cook Windsor Cafe, h 12 Lincoln al
Young Pinkney, mason, h 1 Black
Young R Ganey (Clora), tanner, h 17 Green
Young Robt C, driver Coca-Cola Bottling Co, h 40 Holland
Young Rodman A, engraver C E Henderson, h 75 Starnes
Young Roy, clk Citizens Transfer Co, h 60 s Liberty
Young S Kelse (Lizzie), (Young & Robinson), h New Bridge Station
Young Thos M (Cammie), supt Coca-Cola Bottling Co, h 380 s Main
Young T Perry (Stella), propr Ashev Barber Shop, h 60 s Liberty
*Young Violet, cook, h 17 Wallach
Young W Biss (Myrtle), condr, h 32 n Ann
*Young Walter L (Carrie), porter Ashev Club, h Haywood rd, W Ashev (R F D 3)
*Young Wm (Sarah J), h Haywood rd, W Ashev (R F D 3)
Young Wm W (Emma), barber 6 n Pack Sq, h 61 Josephine
*Young Willie D, music tchr, h Haywood rd, W Ashev (R F D 3)
YOUNG WOMEN'S CHRISTIAN ASSN, 78 s Main, Miss Grace L Osborn genl sec
Young Women's Christian Association, lunch room, 11½ Church, Mrs S H Way mngr
Young & Robinson (S K Young, S D Robinson), gros 93 n Lexington av
Youngblood Thos R (Mattie), harness mkr Ashev Harness Co, h 261 s Main
Younginer Glenn P (Sophia), clk, h 176 Flint

Asheville Electrical Company
W. Mansfield Booze, Manager
74 CENTRAL AVE.
HEADQUARTERS
Phone 377

Asheville Dry Cleaning Co.
Telephones 835-836, All Dep't
MAIN, N. E. COR. COLLEGE

THE CLEANERS
Our Department for Oriental Rugs and Carpet Cleaning is prepared to serve you in all its branches.
E. S. Paine   O. E. Hansen

Maple Flooring and Poplar Siding

English Lumber Co.
PHONE . . 321

Yount Adrian A, slsmn H Redwood & Co, bds 94 e College
Yount Max A, flgmn, bds 96 Bartlett
Yuneeda Dairy Lunch, 32 Patton av, D L Jackson propr

Z

Zazeir Colman, clk, h 51 Vance
Zageir Frances B, wid Moses, h 51 Vance
Zageir Israel, clk R B Zageir, h 51 Vance
Zageir Philip, clk R B Zageir, h 51 Vance
ZAGEIR ROB'T B, clothing and men's furnishings, 8 s Main—phone 1228, h 51 Vance
Zageir Sallie Miss, cashr R B Zageir, h 51 Vance
Zaharopoulos Nick, cook Central Cafe, rms Revell Bldg
Zealandia Cottage, nr end of College
Zealandia Lodge, Town Mountain
Ziegler Emma P, wid A A, h 127 Hillside
Zimmerman Chas L, clk, h 26 Arlington
Zimmerman Chas St V (Lucy), phys 15-16 New Sondley Bldg, h 26 Arlington
ZIMERMAN FRED (Bertha), (Zimmerman & Son), (Ashev Packing Co), h W Asheville—phone 748
ZIMMERMAN FRED W (Zimmerman & Son), h W Asheville
Zimmerman Johanna Miss, bkkpr Zimmerman & Son, h W Asheville
Zimmerman Johannah O Miss, bkkpr, h Murphy Junct, W Ashev
Zimmerman Lily Miss, bkkpr, h 3 Cumberland pl
Zimmerman Nellie Miss, student, h 26 Arlington
Zimmerman Salome Miss, dressmkr Mrs Josephine Price, h 30 Montford av
ZIMMERMAN WM H (Florence), bkkpr Estate Frank Coxe, h 3 Cumberland pl
ZIMMERMAN & SON (Fred and Fred W Zimmerman), grocers, meats and provisions, 428 Depot—phone 565
Zindel Mac K (Minnie), propr Zindel's Model Bakery, h 90 Patton av
Zindel's Model Bakery, 90 Patton av, M K Zindel propr
Zurburg Wm H, mngr Berkeley Pool Room, h 30 Cumberland av

When writing to advertisers please mention the City Directory

BIGGEST
BUSIEST
BEST

Asheville Steam Laundry

Phones:
1936 and 1937

43 to 47
W. College Street

CHARLES H. HONESS
OPTOMETRIST
AND
OPTICIAN

Exclusive maker of
ATLAS SHUR-ON EYE GLASSES

THE
Home of Ce-Rite Toric Lenses

We make a specialty of correcting optical defects with properly fitted glasses.

54 Patton Avenue
Opposite Postoffice

IF in the market for a Gas Engine let us make you prices.
its heavy castings, such as columns or building plates, see us.
its a skilled mechanic for boiler work, see us.
you want machine work of any kind phone 590.

CAROLINA MACHINERY CO.

FOUNDERS MACHINISTS and Jobbers of Mill Supplies

Life Insurance Company of Virginia
ORGANIZED 1871
Home Office - Richmond, Va.

Has won the hearty approval and active support of the people by its promptness and fair dealing during the FORTY-TWO YEARS of its operation

J. V. Moon, Superintendent, Rooms 3-4-5 Maxwelton Bldg., Asheville, N. C.

MEMBERS OF THE ASSOCIATION OF AMERICAN DIRECTORY PUBLISHERS

ATKINSON-ERIE DIRECTORY CO., Erie, Pa.
ATLANTA CITY DIRECTORY CO., 65 E. Alabama St., Atlanta, Ga.
BALLENGER & RICHARDS, 28-29 Good Block, Denver, Colo.
BOYD, W. H. CO., 1411 Perkiomen Av., Reading, Pa.
BURCH DIRECTORY CO., Akron, Ohio.
CARON DIRECTORY CO., 311 W. Jefferson St., Louisville, Ky.
CHICAGO DIRECTORY CO., Plymouth Court, Chicago, Ill.
CLEVELAND DIRECTORY PUB. CO., The Arcade, Cleveland, Ohio.
COURIER CO., 197 Main St., Buffalo, N. Y.
DREW ALLIS COMPANY, 452 Main St., Worcester, Mass.
DUNHAM DIRECTORY CO., Springfield, Mo.
FITZGERALD, THOMAS F., Trenton, N. J.
GATE CITY DIRECTORY CO., 304 10th St., Kansas City, Mo.
GOULD DIRECTORY CO., 316 North 8th St., St. Louis, Mo.
HARTFORD PRINTING CO., 16 State St., Hartford, Conn.
HENDERSON PUBLISHING CO., Winnipeg, Manitoba.
HILL DIRECTORY CO., 1111 E. Main St., Richmond, Va.
HOWE, C. E., CO., 208 S. 4th St., Philadelphia, Pa.
KIMBALL DIRECTORY PUB. CO., Watertown, N. Y.
LOS ANGELES CITY DIRECTORY CO., 122 W. 3d St., Los Angeles, Cal.
MEEK, HENRY W., PUBLISHING CO., Salem, Mass.
MIGHT DIRECTORIES, LIMITED, 74 Church St., Toronto, Ont., Can.
MINNEAPOLIS DIRECTORY CO., 216 National German Bank Building, St. Paul, Minn.
PIEDMONT DIRECTORY CO., Asheville, N. C.
POLK, R. L. & CO., 68 Griswold St., Detroit, Mich.
POLK-HUSTED CO., Oakland, Cal.
POLK-McAVOY CO., Omaha, Neb.
POLK-SOUTHERN DIRECTORY CO., Little Rock, Ark.
PORTLAND DIRECTORY CO., 92 Exchange St., Portland, Me.
PRICE & LEE CO., 206 Meadow St., New Haven, Conn.
RICHMOND, W. L., 45 Warburton Av., Yonkers, N. Y.
SAMPSON, MURDOCK & CO., 246 Summer St., Boston, Mass.
SOARDS DIRECTORY CO, 606 Commercial Place, New Orleans, La.
TROW DIRECTORY, PRINTING & BOOKBINDING CO., 89 3d Av., N. Y. City.
UPINGTON, GEORGE, 317 Washington St., Brooklyn, N. Y.
UTICA DIRECTORY PUBLISHING CO., 47 Arcade Bldg., Utica, N. Y.
WILLIAMS DIRECTORY CO., 208 Post Square, Cincinnati, O.
WORLEY, JOHN F., DIRECTORY CO., 373 Commerce St., Dallas, Tex.
WRIGHT DIRECTORY CO., 107 Wisconsin St., Milwaukee, Wis.

T. P. JOHNSON & CO.
SHEET METAL WORKERS
All Kinds of Roofing Guttering and Conductor Work Metal Ceilings, Skylights and Galvanized Iron Cornices
OFFICE and SHOP:
69-71 S. MAIN
Phone 325

DR. C. H. MILLER
Mechano-Therapist
14 N. Spruce Street
ASHEVILLE, N. C.
PHONE 979
Hours by Engagement
DRUGLESS HEALING OF DISEASE

ASHEVILLE CLEANING and PRESSING CLUB
TAILORING THAT SATISFIES and PRICES THAT PLEASE
Hats cleaned, banded and bound. Silk hats ironed. Buttons made to order in all sizes. Plain or with rims. PHONE 389
DYEING IN ALL SHADES
Kid Gloves, Slippers and Plumes Fancy Jabots and Ties, French Dry Cleaned. Ladies' and Gentlemen's suits Steam Cleaned. Messenger Service.
J. C. Wilbar, Prop.
4 NORTH PACK SQ.

Cook by Electricity!

Only a few minutes current from any electric light socket—then the imprisoned heat cooks the food. You can roast, bake, boil or stew perfectly in a

Detroit Fireless Electric Stove

We also make "Detroit Fireless Cookers" with indestructible metal alloy radiators.

SIX SIZES EACH

Save Fuel—
Save Time—
Save Heat—
Save Work—
Save Grocery and Meat Bills.

Sold on 30 days' Trial

Our famous Water Seal keeps in the heat and steam—retains the flavor. Try one at our risk. Write for catalog mailed free, and our TRIAL OFFER.

Detroit Fireless Stove Co 10 Jefferson Ave. DETROIT, MICH.

DEALERS: We have a splendid offer for YOU. WRITE us

NOTICE— When answering an advertisement, mention the Directory in which you saw the ad as we guarantee you against loss or mis-representation.

**Piedmont Directory Co.
Asheville, N. C.**

Dr. F. P. Love & Son
Veterinary Surgeons

PERMANENT HEADQUARTERS
9 W. Walnut St., Asheville, N. C.

Stock Treated for all Diseases

Ring Bones, Spavins and Weak Eyes a Specialty
Can give the best of References

PRICES REASONABLE

North Carolina—Buncombe County:
ASHEVILLE, N. C., June 22, 1908.

To Whom it May Concern:—

This is to Certify, that F. P. Love has, in all respects, complied with the Laws relative to qualification of Veterinary Practitioners in the State of North Carolina, and is duly registered as a Practitioner in Veterinary Medicine and Surgery in Buncombe County.

In Testimony Whereof, I have hereunto set my hand and affixed the seal of the Superior Court of Buncombe County, N. C.

MARCUS ERWIN,
Clerk of Superior Court, Buncombe County, N. C.

Mrs. B. P. Faulkner	Daisy M. Jackson
MASSUESE	Trained Nurse
Hair Weaving, Braids and Switches Made From Combings	Seven Years Experience Terms Reasonable
39 1-2 S. Main, (2 fl)	:: Phone 1883

W. G. FORNEY   J. EUGENE JONES

College St. Dye Works & Merchant Tailors
FORNEY & JONES, Proprs.

Cleaning, Pressing and Repairing

35 ½ East College St.   Asheville, N. C.   Telephone 981

JOHN R. SARTOR
39 SOUTH MAIN

Cleaning, Pressing and Repairing

TAILORING

Prompt Service and Satisfaction Guaranteed

JOSEPH CARTER

Blacksmith and Horseshoer		Repair Work a Specialty

All Work Guaranteed   4 Penland Street

ASHEVILLE COAL CO.
6 North Pack Sq.   Phone 40

M. & W. COAL

Classified Business Directory
OF
Asheville, N. C.

Vol. XII   THE PIEDMONT SERIES   1913

NOTE—Patronize those whose names are in large type, for they are the progressive ones and generally leaders in their line.

☞ Index appears in front of special business headings only, for which an extra charge is made.

*Star in front of name generally means that such person is colored.

ABATTOIRS   395   ART GOODS

Abattoirs

Asheville Packing Co, Murphy junc, W Asheville

Abstract Title Companies

CAROLINA ABSTRACT & TITLE CO, 312 Legal Bldg

Adding Machines

Moody H M Sales Co, 68 Patton av

☞ Addressing and Mailing

PIEDMONT DIRECTORY CO, 66 Amer Natl Bank Bldg

Agricultural Implements

Morrison T S & Co, 80-84 Patton av

Apartments

Hull's Flats, 80-82½ Cumberland av

Architects

Carrier A H, Carrier Bldg
Chunn Chas H, 32 Patton av
Davis T E, 20½ Spruce
LORD W H, 17½ Church
Smith R S, Carrier Bldg
SMITH & CARRIER CO, Carrier Bldg, College cor Market

Tennent J A, 16 Patton av

Art Goods

ALLANSTAND COTTAGE INDUSTRIES, 33 Haywood (see adv in genl dept)
Denoon M C Mrs, 17 Haywood
London Shop (The), 8 s Pack Sq
MOORE E J K MISS, 52 Patton av

IMPORTED ART MATERIALS

COLUMBIA WOOLS
IRISH CROCHET AND SPANISH LACES.
STAMPING to ORDER.
NEW DESIGNS in ALL LINES
ROYAL SOCIETY GOODS.
POST CARDS

MISS E. J. R. MOORE
52 PATTON AVE.

Gas Ranges   PHONE 69   **Asheville Power and Light Co.**

Meats   Kiibler & Whitehead
CITY MARKET   PHONES, 195 and 694

WEAVERVILLE LINE
NINE MILES BY TROLLEY FROM PACK SQUARE TO WEAVERVILLE
ASHEVILLE AND EAST TENNESSEE RAILROAD CO.
7 NORTH MAIN STREET — ASHEVILLE N. C.

ELECTRIC FIXTURES
Piedmont Electric Co.
64 PATTON AVE.
ASHEVILLE, N.C.

ART CRAFTS 396 ATTORNEYS

Art Crafts

ALLANSTAND COTTAGE INDUSTRIES, 33 Haywood (see adv in genl dept)

Artists

Lee Mattie P Mrs, 30 Asheland av
Worrell C A, 76 Flint

Attorneys at Law

Arthur J P, 29 Morsell Bldg
Bell L C, 308-309 Oates Bldg
Bennett O K, 10½ n Pack Sq
BERNARD S G, 201-202 Legal Bldg
BOURNE, PARKER & MORRISON, s Pack Sq cor Main
Brown M W, 4 s Temple Court
Brown W P, 208 Oates Bldg
Carter H B, 10½ n Pack Sq
Chedester H C, 412-415 Legal Bldg
Cocke P C, 212 Legal Bldg
Cocke Wm J, 212-214 Legal Bldg
Craig, Martin & Thomason, 403-405 Oates Bldg
CURTIS Z F, 3-4 Library Bldg
Daniel W H, 3 Temple Court
Davidson T F (retired), 61 n Liberty
Davies W M, 17 Library Bldg
Diggs A L, 13½ Patton av
Fortune & Roberts, 11-12 Library Bldg
Gillis Donald, 21 Amer Natl Bank Bldg
GLENN J FRAZIER, 215 Legal Bldg
Goldstein R C, 10 Temple Ct
Gudger H A, 307 Oates Bldg
Gudger J M, 8 Short
Gudger J M Jr, Oates Bldg
GUDGER V L, 1-3 Brown-Gudger Bldg
Gudger W R, 8 s Pack Sq
HARKINS & VAN WINKLE, 9-10-11 Harkins Bldg
HAYNES & GUDGER, 18-19 Temple Ct
Jones & Jones, 7-9 Library Bldg
Jones & Williams, 417-421 Legal Bldg
Lee & Ford, 13½ Patton av
LUSK V S COL, 1 Library Bldg
Lyman A J, 3 Paragon Bldg
Malone C N, 207 Oates Bldg
MARTIN, ROLLINS & WRIGHT, 308-314 Legal Bldg
McCall Robt S, 10½ n Pack Sq
MERRICK & BARNARD, 315-319 Legal Bldg
MERRIMON, ADAMS & ADAMS, 15 Church
MERRIMON JAS H, 15 Church
MILLARD D RALPH, 16-17 New Sondley Bldg
Monteath A D, 4-5 Temple Ct
Moore C A, 156 Merrimon av
Murphy J D, 406-408 Oates Bldg
PRITCHARD J C (Judge) Government Bldg
Randolph E J, 64 Patton av
Rankin Clarence, 15 Patton av
Ravenel S P, s Pack Sq cor Main
Rector J E, 6-8 Temple Ct
Reynolds G S, 13½ Patton av
REYNOLDS R R, Court House (2d fl)
Rickman T J, 5-6 Paragon Bldg
Settle Thos, Temple Ct
SHUFORD G A (Judge), 2 Library Bldg
Shuford W E, 24 Temple Ct
SONDLEY F A, LL D, 4-5-6 New Sondley Bldg
Starnes J R, 143 n Main
Stevens & Anderson, 203-205 Oates Bldg
Styles J S, 409 Oates Bldg
Sykes C E, 34 Amer Natl Bank Bldg
Thomas F W, 33 Amer Natl Bank Bldg
Toms C F, 1-2 Temple Ct
Varnon T W, 2 Library Bldg
Way Eugene, 10½ n Pack Sq
Weaver Guy, 306 Oates Bldg
Weaver Zebulon, 406-408 Oates Bldg
Webb C A, 302-303 Oates Bldg
Welch Gilmer, 7-8-9 Library Bldg
WELLS & SWAIN, 400-402 Oates Bldg
WHITSON W R, 6 n Pack Sq

CONTRACTOR and BUILDER
STEEL RANGES
J. C. McPHERSON
35-37 E COLLEGE ST.
PHONE 133
PLUMBING STEAM AND HOT WATER HEATING

Yellow Pine / White Pine / Hardwoods
See bet. pgs. 188-189

LUMBER
SASH, BLINDS, DOORS

WOODWARD & SON
Ninth and Arch Streets
RICHMOND - VIRGINIA

AUCTIONEERS 397 BARBERS

Auctioneers

Moore C R, 225 Legal Bldg

Automobiles

(Dealers and Repairers)
ARBOGAST MOTOR CO, 52-60 n Main (see side lines)
Asheville Auto Co, 15-17 s Lexington av
ENTERPRISE MACHINE CO, 67-71 n Main (see p 14)
HOLLAR MOTOR CO, 56 s Main
Ledbetter Geo, 8-10 e College
NYBERG AUTOMOBILE SALES CO OF N C, 17 s Main
O K Auto Supply & Transit Co, 61-63 s Main
Western Carolina Auto Co, Walnut cor Lexington av

(For Hire)
HUGHES TRANSFER & LIVERY CO, 401 Southside av (see side lines)

(Supplies)
ARBOGAST MOTOR CO, 52-60 n Main
ENTERPRISE MCH CO, 67-71 n Main
NYBERG AUTOMOBILE SALES CO, 17 s Main

Bakers

Asheville Steam Bakery, 110-112 Patton av
College Street Bakery, 37 e College
Pack Square Bakery, 6 n Pack Sq
Zindel's Model Bakery, 90 Patton av

Bands and Orchestras

First Regiment Band, New Sondley Bldg

Banks

AMERICAN NATIONAL BANK (The), 44 Patton av (see front cover)
BATTERY PARK BANK (The), 15 Patton av (see front cover and bot lines)
CENTRAL BANK & TRUST CO, Legal Bldg, s Pack Sq (see front cover)
CITIZENS BANK, 55 Patton av (see front cover)
WACHOVIA BANK & TRUST CO, 34 Patton av (see stencils and p 8)

Bank Examiners

Hull F A, 9 Medical Bldg

Barbers

Antiseptic Barber Shop, 1 Patton av
Ashev Barber Shop, 14 Patton av
Ball E G, 8 Roberts
Battery Park Hotel Barber Shop, Battery Park Hotel
Black H B, 418 Depot
*Bowman J W, 5 n w Pack Sq
*Brooks Wm P, 8 Eagle
*Buckeye Sanitary Shaving Parlor, 11½ s Main
*Conley Lee, 13 n Main
*Conley W T, 8 w College
Creasman L W, W Asheville
Crook J E, 513 w Haywood
Crook R L, 342 w Haywood
Glen Rock Barber Shop, 402 Depot
*Goins P A, 11 Eagle
*Howell C T, 2 Eagle
*Johnson G W, Oates Bldg (basement)
Kennedy C A, 448 Depot
Langren Barber Shop, 2 n Main
*McDonald Thos, 6 s Pack Sq
Monday C U, 382 Depot
St Charles Barber Shop, 7 Haywood
Swannanoa - Berkeley Hotel Barber Shop, 53 s Main
*Wilson J A, 39 s Main
Windsor Hotel Barber Shop, 46 s Main
Young W W, 6 n Pack Sq

Barbers Supplies

ASHEVILLE BARBERS' SUPPLY CO, 23 n Main

What Have You in Real Estate that You Don't Want?

What do You Want in Real Estate that You Haven't?

WESTERN CAROLINA REALTY CO.
J. W. Wolfe Sec. & Treas.

On the Square
PHONE 974
10 N. PACK SQ.

Brown-Carter Realty Co.
REAL ESTATE
23 TEMPLE COURT
PHONE 341
ASHEVILLE N. C.

FLORIDA SPECIALTIES
Grazing, Timbered, Farm Lands, Orange Groves, Turpentine Locations and Phosphate Lands.

NORTH CAROLINA SPECIALTIES
Orchard Farm and Timbered Lands, City Property, Rent Collections.

Moale & Chiles Real Estate and Insurance
27 Patton Ave. (2d fl) Phone 661
General Agents United States Fidelity & Guaranty Co.

Club Cafe and Candy Kitchen
"A GOOD PLACE FOR REFRESHMENT"

Our Ice Cream manufacturing plant is absolutely clean and sanitary.
Prompt family delivery. Phones 110 and 111.
Catering for large parties and receptions. Special Creams.

BATHS   398   BOARDING

Brown's Undertaking Parlors

S. H. BROWN

Lady Assistant When Desired

Phone 193-2 Rings

50 Patton Avenue
Asheville, N. C.

Established 1894

B. J. JACKSON

Carefully Selected Fruits and Vegetables

Stall No. 11, City Market

BUSINESS PHONES:
86 and 101

RESIDENCE PHONE
1596

Baths

GRUNER SANITARIUM (The), 29-31 Haywood

The Gruner Sanitarium
PHONE 684
29-31 Haywood St., Asheville, N. C.
Hydro-Thermo-Electro and Mechano-Therapy-Dietics

Devoted to the thorough and scientific treatment for selected cases of Nervousness, Paralysis, Hayfever, Malaria, Asthma, Habit, Stomach, Rheumatism, Diseases of Women, and other chronic Diseases.

THE BATHS AND MASSAGE
Department of the Sanitarium is open to the public. Skillful attendants for both LADIES and GENTLEMEN will administer Turkish, Russian, Cabinet, Betz Hot-Air, Electric Light, Tub, Sitz, Foot, Shower and Needle Baths, Galvanic and Faradic Treatments. Electric Vibrating, Swedish Massage and Movements. Thure Brandt Massage for diseases of women. Douche, Lavage.

OPEN DAY AND NIGHT
THE GRUNER SANITARIUM
29-31 Haywood St., Asheville, N. C.

Bicycle Dealers and Repairers

Hearn J M & Co, 4 Battery Park Pl
NEVERCEL F J, 47 w College (see adv)
Sky Cycle Co, 28 w College

Billiard and Pool Rooms

Battery Park Hotel Billiard & Pool Room, Battery Park Hotel
Berkeley Pool Room, 17 n Lexington av
Chakales & Pilalas, 4 Patton av
Corner Pool Room (The), Patton av cor Pack Sq
Estes P D, 416½ Depot
*Greenlee & Loder, 4 Eagle and 40 s Main
*Haynes Jonas, 10 Eagle
Hermann J B, 9 s w Pack Sq
Jackson W M, 10 w College

Langren Bowling & Pool Room Langren Hotel (basement)
Marmino Antonio, 33 College
SWANNANOA BERKELEY HOTEL POOL ROOM, 55 s Main

Blacksmiths, Horseshoers and Wheelwrights

AMERICAN WAGON CO, 67 s Main
Biltmore Shops, Biltmore rd and Sou Ry
Bishop A B, W Asheville
BROWN C L, 21-27 n Lexington av (see p 21)
Calloway W E, Riverside Drive nr Quarry
*CARTER JOS, 4 Penland (see adv)
Cauble D W, 425 n Main
Coffey I R, 28-30 College
*Hopkins J W & Son, 7 w Walnut
Kuykendall F H, Grace
McCall J F, 79 n Lexington av
Penland Bros, W Asheville
Ratcliff J I, 25 Aston
Webb D H, 441 s Main

Boarding Houses

Alabama (The), 127 Haywood
Allen Jas, 51 Penland
Allen M A Mrs, 135 n Main
Anderson S J Mrs, 655 Oakland av
Avanmore (The), 107 Haywood
Ball V J Mrs, 10½ n Pack Sq
Baumberger Margaret Mrs, 102 Ralph
"BELVEDERE" (formerly Ravenscroft), 95 Church (see p 18)
"Billows Rest," Grace
Bird L A Mrs, 60 Central av
Bishop G A Mrs, 348½ Depot
Blair M E Mrs, 418 Southside av
Bon Air (The), 66 Asheland av
"BONNIVIEW" (Mrs J Taylor Amiss), 128 Haywood (see p 20)
Brigmon E B Mrs, 16 Hilliard la
"Buxton Place," 157 Church

Furniture and China Carefully Prepared for Shipment

Mahogany Furniture Hand Made & Carefully Reproduced   **E. E. GALER**   Upholstering and Refinishing
114 PATTON AVE.   PHONE - 1674

ROUGH AND DRESSED LUMBER
WHITE PINE AND YELLOW PINE
FLOORING A SPECIALTY
Hardwoods

Williams-Brownell Planing Mill Company
Mouldings and Interior Finish
Office: Southern Railway Tracks, Near Biltmore Station
Phone 729   **Planing Mill**

BOARDING 309 BOARDING

Bryson Cora Mrs, 34½ n Main
Buchanan Bessie Mrs, 34 Asheland av
Buckner E I Mrs, 41 Oak
Burnette C B Miss, 157 Patton av
CANSLER P U MRS, 76 College (see p 20)
Caroleen (The), 94 s College
Cassada Maggie Mrs, 14 s Spruce
Chance E L Mrs, 68 Church
Chandler T C Mrs, 346 w Haywood
"**CHAPEL COTTAGES**," 41 Victoria rd (see p 20)
Chatham (The), 55 College
Cheek A E Mrs, 87 Ora
Colonial (The), 58 and 70 n Main
Davis S R Mrs, 80 Penland
*Davis Sisley, 74 Eagle
"Del Rosa Farm," Grace
Dillingham (The), 55 Penland
Dixie (The), 15 n Spruce
Dugan J S, 434 Depot
"Edgewood Cottage," Sunset Drive
Elm (The), 42 w Walnut
ELTON (The), 45 n Spruce (see p 16)
Elwood (The), 119 Haywood
Eureka (The), 153 n Main
Featherston C M Mrs, 23 Woodfin
*Flack A J, 16 Davidson
"Forest Hill," s Main extd
Franklin Hotel, s Pack Sq
Geiger E E Mrs, 18 College pl
*Glascow Mary, 194 s Main
Gross Nola Mrs, 51 n Main
Halyburton House, 430 Depot
Harris Mattie Miss, 53 Church
Hawes K R Mrs, 23 Flint
HENRIETTA (The), (Y W C A), 78 s Main
"Hill Cottage," 39 Clingman av
"Hillside Cottage," Sunset Drive
Hughey R W C, 46 w Walnut
Jenkins M T Miss, 228 Cumberland av
*Johnson M A, 32 Davidson
"Kenilworth Hall," Biltmore rd
KNICKERBOCKER (The), 77 College (see p 15)

Lee Julia A Mrs, 26 Flint
LOUISIANA (The), 51 College (see p 18)
"Lyons" (The), 5 Starnes av
McCoy A M Mrs, 346½ Depot
McDougle Artimecia Mrs, 17 n Spruce
McKee A B, 58 Haywood
"Magnolia Cottage," 72 e College (see p 15)
Marquette Hotel, 102 Patton av
Miller L R Mrs, 24 n Spruce
Miller Minnie Mrs, 92 Church
Mills W M, 311 w Haywood
Mitchell C C Mrs, 37 Church
Monteeth E J Mrs, 47 n Main
"Montford Cottage," 103 Montford av
*Morris Lula, 166 Church
Ninety Nine (The), 101 Haywood
"Oak Cottage," 115 Haywood
"Old Kentucky Home," 48 n Spruce
Ozark (The), 76 n Main
"Park View," Pearson Drive opp Riverside Park
Pearce B H Miss, 46 n French Broad av
Penniman Ridgely Mrs, 192 Chestnut
Phillips D B Mrs, 29 Jefferson Drive
Pines (The), 112 Pearson Drive
Pitillo Kate Mrs, 12 Hilliard la
Plemmons R L, 16 s Spruce
Potts Jane Miss, 390 Southside av
Powell E B Mrs, 25 Asheland av
Rembert Christine Mrs, 153 n Main
Restawyle (The), 20 Oak
Richelieu (The), 20 n French Broad av
Roach F C Mrs, 45 Charlotte
Rock Ledge (The), 68 Haywood
Roselawn (The), 52 Merrimon av
Schuessler C R Mrs, 107 Merrimon av
Scott W A, 263 Chestnut
Sites Kate L Mrs, 97 College
Smart C E Mrs, 33 Starnes av
Smith Wm M, 98 Patton av
Sneed Mollie Mrs, 173 s Main

HUGHES

Transfer and Livery Co.

Automobiles for HIRE

TRUNKS 25c

Office:
401 Southside Avenue
PHONE 1405

Try our Hand Laundering. We strive to please in LAUNDERING and DRY CLEANING.

The Sanitary Home Laundry   No. 7 MONTFORD AVE.
PHONE - 1354

Mrs. Wilder's SANITARY HOME LAUNDRY turns out first class work in Laundering and Dry Cleaning. No. 7 Montford Ave., Phone 1354

BOARDING 400 BUILDING

Sorrell F McD Mrs, 100 s Main
Spann M E Miss, 2 Angle, Biltmore
Southern Hotel (The), 12-14 s Main
Starnes M E Miss, 18 Grady
Stricklin L E Mrs, 9 Louie
Tallulah (The), 100 e College
Tennent Julia Miss, 111 Montford av
Traymore (The), 93 College
Trivola (The), 23 Asheland av
Uleeta (The), 5 Flint
*Washington D E, 28 Davidson
Webb M E Mrs, 25 n French Broad av
Weiler C L Mrs, 308 Depot
Wentworth (The), 38 Oak
West Virginia (The), 88 Penland
Whitt R Y, 49 n Main
Willard (The), 112 Haywood
Williams Loduska Mrs, 50 Asheland av
Womble C V Mrs, 96 Bartlett
Wrenwood (The), 61 s French Broad av
Wright Maggie D Mrs, 68 e College
*Yellock Hattie, 433 Depot

Bookbinders

HACKNEY & MOALE CO, 10-12 s Lexington av

Books and Stationery

Brown Book Co, 66 Patton av
Pack Square Book Co, 3 n w Pack Sq
Rogers H T, 39 Patton av
YE OLD BOOK STORE (second hand), 114 Patton av

Bootblacks

Chakalas & Philalas, 4 and 56½ Patton av

☞Bottlers—Ginger Ale

HASKELL'S PEPSI - COLA BOTTLING WORKS, 217 Haywood

☞Bottlers—Pepsi-Cola

HASKELL'S PEPSI - COLA BOTTLING WORKS, 217 Haywood (see p 12)

Bottlers—Soft Drinks

Coca-Cola Bottling Co, 90-92 s Main
HASKELL'S PEPSI - COLA BOTTLING WORKS, 217 Haywood (see p 12)

Bowling Alleys

Hampton F B, 12 w College
Langren Bowling & Pool Room Langren Hotel (basement)
Y M C A Alleys, Y M C A (basement)

Box Manufacturers

Biltmore Box Factory, Sou Ry nr Biltmore

Brick Manufacturers

Beaverdam Brick Co, New Bridge Sta
Kenilworth Brick Works, Kenilworth Park

Brokers

Baird J T, 2 Morsell Bldg
Earle & Nelson, Depot cor Roberts
Lotspeich O P, 12 Harkins Bldg
Stoner J M, 18 s Main

Building and Loan Associations

BLUE RIDGE B & L ASSN, 1 Haywood (see fly A)
Home B & L Assn, 2 Drhumor Bldg

Building Material

CITIZENS LUMBER CO, 20-24 College
ENGLISH LBR CO, Avery and Sou Ry (see top lines)
JONES W M, 557 w Haywood (see p 3)

BUICK OLDSMOBILE
ARBOGAST MOTOR COMPANY
ACCESSORIES AND SUPPLIES
52-60 N. Main Phones 302 and 1728
MAXWELLS DETROIT ELECTRIC

Asheville Dry Cleaning Co.
Telephones 835-836, All Dep't
MAIN, N. E. COR. COLLEGE

THE CLEANERS
Our Department for Oriental Rugs and Carpet Cleaning is prepared to serve you in all its branches.
E. S. Paine   O. E. Hansen

For Kindling "What am Kindling" Call
ENGLISH LUMBER COMPANY   Phone 321

BUILDING   401   CEMETERY

MONTAGUE MNFG CO, Richmond Va (see top lines)
NORTHROP S & W H LBR CO (Inc), Richmond Va
WESTALL J M & CO, 17 Walnut
Westall W H & Co, 22 s Spruce
WILLIAMS - BROWNELL PLANING MILL CO, Biltmore
WOODWARD & SON, Richmond Va (see top lines)

Buildings

(See also Office Buildings)
Asheville Club Bldg, 24 Battery Park pl
CITY HALL, e Pack Sq
COUNTY COURT HOUSE, 57-71 College
County Jail, Marjorie nr Spruce
GOVERNMENT BLDG, Patton av cor Haywood
Library Bldg, s Pack Sq
Reed Bldg, 16-18 s Pack Sq
Wolfe Bldg, 22 s Pack Sq
Y M C A BLDG, 27 Haywood
*Y M I Bldg, Eagle cor Market

Business Colleges

ASHEVILLE BUSINESS COLLEGE, 8 n Pack Sq (3d fl)
Carolina Commercial School, Legal Bldg
EMANUEL SCHOOL OF STENOGRAPHY AND TYPEWRITING, 16 Drhumor Bldg

Butchers

(See also Meat Markets)
HILL'S MARKET, City Mkt (see front cover)
KIIBLER & WHITEHEAD, City Mkt (see bot lines)
STAR MARKET, City Mkt (see front cover)

Cabinet Makers

Asheville Cabinet Co, 17½ Church

GALER E E, 114 Patton av (see bot lines)

Cakes and Crackers

National Biscuit Co, 349 Depot

Candies

LITTLE SMOKE HOUSE (The), 41½ Patton av

Carpenters and Builders
(See Contractors)

Carpets, Mattings and Rugs

Asheville Carpet House, 18-20 Church
Ashev Carpet House, 18-20 Church

Carriage and Wagon

(Builders)
American Wagon Co, 65-67 s Main
BROWN C L, 21-27 n Lexington (see p 21)

(Dealers)
Morrison T S & Co, 80-84 Patton av

(Painters)
BRADFORD J M, 25-27 n Lexington av (see p 21)

Cash Registers

Natl Cash Register Co, 78 Patton av

☞ Caterers

THEOBOLD & BRANDL, 19-21 Haywood

Cement
(See Lime, Plaster and Cement)

Cemetery Companies

Ashev Cemetery Co, s Pack Sq
W Ashev Cemetery Co, W Ashev

BIGGEST **B**USIEST **B**EST

Phones 1936 and 1937

ASHEVILLE STEAM LAUNDRY

43 to 47 W. COLLEGE

S. D. HALL
REAL ESTATE AGENT

Money Loaned

Notary Public

32 PATTON AVENUE

Phone 91

Founders, Machinists and Jobbers of Mill Supplies

PHONE 590
When in the market for pipe and fittings, let us make you Prices.

Carolina Machinery Co.

PHONE 590
If it's a Gas Engine let us figure with you, also on other kinds of machinery

LIFE INSURANCE COMPANY OF VA. OLDEST, LARGEST STRONGEST Southern Life Insurance Co.

ORGANIZED 1871
RICHMOND, VIRGINIA

Issues Industrial Policies from $8.00 to $900.00, with Premiums Payable WEEKLY on persons from two to seventy years of age

J. V. Moon, Superintendent, Rooms 3-4-5 Maxwelton Bldg., Asheville, N. C.

CENSUS 402 CLERGYMEN

D. TREXLER TIN SHOP

All Kinds of Roofing, Gutter and Conductor Work.

Phone 862

159 South Main St.

DR. C. H. MILLER

MECHANO-THERAPIST

14 N. Spruce St.
Phone 979
ASHEVILLE, N. C.

Hours by engagement

Drugless Healing of Disease

Census Takers

PIEDMONT DIRECTORY CO, 66 Amer Natl Bank Bldg

China Decorators

Atkins M M Miss, 136½ s Main
Swayne Lou M Mrs, 1 Merrimon Place

China, Glass and Earthenware

KRESS S H & CO, 24-28 Patton av
LAW J H, 35 Patton av

Cider and Vinegar

Casler Sol, Sycamore cor Market

Cigar Manufacturers

Pugh C S, 35 w Walnut

Cigars and Tobacco

BARBEE S A, 14 Patton av (see back cover)
Battery Park Hotel News and Cigar Stand, Battery Park Hotel
Blomberg Louis, 15 Patton av
Jones Wm C, 43 s Main
Langren Hotel Cigar Stand, Langren Hotel
LITTLE SMOKE HOUSE (The), 41½ Patton av
Schas Morris S, 6 s Main
Sunny Smoke Shop, 3 Haywood
Union News Co, Sou Ry Passngr Sta

Civil Engineers

(See Engineers)

Cleaning and Pressing

(See also Pressing Clubs)
ASHEVILLE CLEANING & PRESSING CLUB, 4 n Pack Sq (see bottom lines)
ASHEVILLE DRY CLEANING CO, Main n e cor College (see bottom lines)
*Big Four Pressing Club (The), Oates Bldg (basement)
*Bryant & Clarke, 94 Haywood
*COLLEGE STREET DYE WORKS AND MERCHANT TAILORS, 35½ e College (see adv)
Ideal Pressing Club, 5 s w Pack Sq
*McGinness Jno H, 44 Market
*Railroad Men's Pressing Club, (r) 426 Depot
RELIABLE CLEANING & PRESSING CO, 14 Church (see insert)
SANITARY HOME LAUNDRY, 7 Montford av (see lines)
*SARTOR J R, 39 s Main (see adv)
*Swepson E W, 7½ n w Pack Sq
*Y M I Pressing Club, Y M I Bldg

Clergymen

*Anderson W M (A M E), 27 Furman av
*Ashe H L (Meth), 20 Hildebrand
Barker J J (Meth), S Biltmore
Barnhardt Z E (Meth), W Asheville
*Barnum J R (A M E), 42 Hildebrand
*Beatty J W (Bapt), 21 Black
Bernhard C H (Luth), 44 Philip
*Bennett Geo (Holiness), Pine cor Hazzard
*Berry J Alex (Bapt), 23 Ingle
Brown A E (Bapt), 10 Library Bldg
Byrd Chas W (Meth), 35 Church
Cain W S (Episco), 36 Watauga
*Caldwell G H (Meth), W Asheville
*Caldwell Gilbert (Meth), W Asheville
Campbell R F (Presby), 6 Pearson Drive
Carver Jno (Meth), Factory Hill
Clapp E B (Meth), S Biltmore
Cole T M (Bapt), W Asheville

....Asheville Cleaning and Pressing Club....
Tailoring That Satisfies and Prices That Please
Steam and French Dry Cleaning of all delicate and fine wearing apparel for ladies and gentlemen. MESSENGER SERVICE IN THE CITY.

J. C. WILBAR, Prop.   4. N. Pack Square   **PHONE 389**

CAROLINA "M & W" INDIAN COAL & ICE CO.
Prompt Delivery
PHONE 130
50 PATTON AVE.
WEIGHTS ACCURATE

CLERGYMEN 403 CLUBS

Collins Lewis (Presby), 42 Chunn
COMPTON L B (Holiness), 53 Atkinson
Cosgrove T A (Presby), 515 s Main
*Cowans E O (A M E Zion), 9 Maiden la
Cross R D (Bapt), Haywood rd, W Asheville
*Dusenbury C B (Presby), 71 Eagle
Fogleman W D (M P), 176 Flint
*Fortune Giles (Meth), 9 Chestnut
Fox Ellis (Hebrew), Central av nr Woodfin
*Hadden T G (A M E), 80 Valley
*Hairston R P (Episco), 57 Short
Hamrick G P (Bapt), 51 Buxton
Harris C F (Bapt), 9 Grady
*Harshaw Lee (Bapt), Black st
Haynes Washington (Bapt), Grace R F D 1
*Henderson J W (A M E Zion), Haywood rd, W Ashev
Horner J M Bishop (Episco), 135 Church
Hoyle E M (Meth), 58 Fulton
*Hughes J F (Bapt), 25 Ridge
*Kennedy J T (Episco), 70 Beaumont
Lawrence Thos, Grove Park
Leeper H Y (Presby), 65 Hillside
Londow Louis (Hebrew), 64 s Liberty
MacLauchlin A M (Presby), 83 Ora
*Maize G W (Meth), 265 Asheland av
*Manning Willis (Bapt), 23 Oliver
Marion P G (Catho), 18 Flint
Marion P F (Catho), 18 Flint
Marr W W (Bapt), S Biltmore
Mears P H (Christian), 241 Haywood
*Morris J P (Meth), 250 College
*Nelson J R (Bapt), 30 Ridge
NEWELL W A (Meth), 210 Patton av
Poovey W E (Meth), 34 Chestnut
Robbins H H (Meth), 32 Phifer
Rouse J A (Wesleyan Meth), 334 w Haywood
Sanford — — (Adventist), 238 Haywood
Saumenig H F (Episco), 260 Montford av
Scott F W (Holiness), Lyman nr st car line
*Slade Mayfield (A M E Zion), 127 Valley
*Smith M D (Meth), 58 McDowell
Smith R P (Presby), 117 Asheland av
*Spurgeon S J (A M E Z), 215 College
Stubbs A H (Episco), 135 Church
*Swann Irving (Meth), 139 Poplar
Swope R R (Episco), Biltmore
Templeton S A (Missionary), 2 Reed Bldg
Waller C B (Bapt), 225 Chestnut
*Watson L V (Meth), 29 McDowell
*Wiley Wm (Bapt), 188 Livingston
Williams J S (Meth P), 297 Merrimon av
Winn P P (Presby), 135 Merrimon av

Clothing

Diamond Morris, 14 Eagle
Finestein S, 12 n Main
Gem Clothing Store (The), 6 Patton av
Glaser I W, 18 Patton av
MOORE M V & CO, 11 Patton av
Redwood H & Co, 7-9 Patton av
Union Store (The), 420 Southside av
Whitlock Clothing Co, 41 Patton av
ZAGEIR R B, 8 s Main

Clubs

Albemarle Club, Albemarle Park

St. Rw'y — Electric Light and Power — Gas

ASHEVILLE POWER AND LIGHT COMPANY
PHONE 69

Poultry Kiibler & Whitehead
CITY MARKET PHONES, 195 and 694

Asheville Dray, Fuel and Construction Co.

Heavy Hauling of all kinds
61-2 South Main

WE FURNISH BUILDING STONE

Moving Furniture a Specialty
PHONE - 223

CLUBS 404 CONTRACTORS

DYNAMOS & MOTORS

Piedmont Electric Co.

64 Patton Av.
ASHEVILLE, N.C.

Asheville Base Ball Club, Legal Bldg
Asheville Club, Haywood cor Battery Park Pl
Asheville Country Club, Charlotte bey city limits
ELKS' CLUB, 53 Haywood
Welfare Cottage, 9 Factory Hill

Coal and Fuel

(Retail)

ASHEVILLE COAL CO, 6 n Pack Sq (see top lines)
ASHEVILLE DRAY, FUEL & CONSTRUCTION CO, 6½ s Main (see top lines)
CAROLINA COAL & ICE CO, 50 Patton av (see top lines)
SOUTHERN COAL CO, 10 n Pack Sq (see insert with index tab)

(Wholesale)

ASHEVILLE COAL CO, 6 n Pack Sq
CAROLINA COAL & ICE CO, 50 Patton av
SOUTHERN COAL CO, 10 n Pack Sq

(Miners and Shippers)

Fork Ridge Coal Co, 24 Amer Natl Bank Bldg
Virginia-Carolina Coal Co, 25 Amer Natl Bank Bldg

Coffin Manufacturers

National Casket Co, Riverside Drive

Cold Storage

Storage Supply Co, 91-99 Avery

Collection Agencies

ASHEVILLE MERCANTILE AGENCY, 27 Amer Natl Bank Bldg

Colleges

NORMAL & COLLEGIATE INSTITUTE, s Main cor Victoria rd (see inside back cover)
ST GENEVIEVE COLLEGE, Victoria rd (see insert)
WEAVERVILLE COLLEGE, Weaverville N C

Confectioners

*Alexander Frank, 12 Eagle
Asheville Candy Kitchen, 13 s Main
CLUB CAFE & CANDY KITCHEN, 19-21 Haywood (see top lines)
Dew Drop Candy Parlor, 32 Patton av
Fisher H L, 9 s Main
Galyean E S, 405 Depot
Green P F, 246 Patton av
Johnson G W, 266 Depot
Karres Bros, 11 n Main
KRESS S H & CO, 26-28 Patton av
Lunsford W T, 88 Patton av
Marmino Antonio, 33 College
Mascari Chas, 58 Patton av
Newton R T, Riverside Bridge
Roberts & Crook, 334 w Haywood
Stiles Harper, 420 Depot

Contractors

(Builders)

Belote E T, 188 Flint
BROWN H A & CO, 23 Temple Ct (see side lines)
Colvin & Davidson, 95 Woodfin
Cowan I W, W Asheville
Dalton T S, 167 s Main
Duckett I W, W Asheville
Glenn O T, Woolsey (R F D 1)
Goodlake A M, 22 s Pack Sq (see card at name)
Hamilton W R B, 31 Tiernan
Henderson R H, 151 Woodfin
Joyner J E & Son, W Asheville
Leonard Caleb, City Hall
McDowell E E, 383 s Main
McDowell & Patton, 34 e College
McIntire F R, 157 Merrimon av
Merchant L L, 22 Livingston
Moore R H, W Asheville
Moses L J, W Asheville
Patterson J M, W Asheville

J. C. McPHERSON
SLATE AND TIN ROOFING
Galvanized Iron Work   Hot Air Furnaces
35-37 EAST COLLEGE STREET

PLUMBING STEAM AND HOT WATER HEATING
PHONE 133

MAPLE FLOORING
HARDWOOD LUMBER OF ALL KINDS

WOODWARD & SON
9th and Arch Sts., Richmond, Va.
See Adv. Opposite Page 188

CONTRACTORS 405 CREAMERIES

Taylor D S, 28 Oak
Templeton W C, 5 Aston
Tigar Wm, 411 Merrimon av
Wells H A, W Asheville
Whiteside J B, 46 Panola
Wilson J B, 260 Hillside
Wilson W A, 331 n Main

(Concrete and Cement)
BROWN H A & CO, 23 Temple Court
GOODLAKE A M, 22 s Pack Sq
Neale Philip, 76 Penland

(Excavating)
ASHEVILLE DRAY, FUEL & CONSTRUCTION CO, 6½ s Main
BROWN H A & CO, 23 Temple Ct

(General)
ASHEVILLE DRAY, FUEL & CONSTRUCTION CO, 6½ s Main (see top lines)
BROWN H A & CO, 23 Temple Ct (see side lines)
GOODLAKE A M, 22 s Pack Sq
Wren & Garland, 69 s Main

(Metal Workers)
JOHNSON T P & CO, 69 s Main
McPHERSON J C, 35 College

(Painting)
BOWLES R E, 1 e Pack Sq (see p 5)

(Plumbing)
McPHERSON J C, 35 College
MOORE PLUMBING CO, College nr Market
Rich J R Co, 21 n Main
STEVENS S M, 95 Cumberland av (see card at name)

(Railroad)
ASHEVILLE DRAY, FUEL & CONSTRUCTION CO, 6½ s Main
Davidson G H, 147 Woodfin
Greco Frank, 209 Oates Bldg

South Atlantic Trans-Continental R R Co, 111-114 Citizen Bldg

(Sewer)
Kelly M H, 16 Market

(Stone)
BROWN H A & CO, 23 Temple Ct

Constables

Jones F M, Library Bldg

Construction Companies

ASHEVILLE DRAY, FUEL & CONSTRUCTION CO, 6½ s Main
North Carolina Trans-Continental Construction Co, 111-114 Citizen Bldg

Coppersmiths

Rosen Max, 59 n Lexington av

Corsets

Spirella Corset Co, Agency, 21 s Main

☞Cottage Industries

ALLANSTAND COTTAGE INDUSTRIES, 33 Haywood

Cotton Mills

Asheville Cotton Mills, w Haywood and Sou Ry
Elk Mtn Cotton Mill, Ownbey Sta

☞Country Produce

*JACKSON B J, City Mkt

☞Creameries

CAROLINA CREAMERY, 252-258 Patton av

What Have You in Real Estate that You Don't Want?

What do You Want in Real Estate that You Haven't?

WESTERN CAROLINA REALTY CO.
J. W. Wolfe, Sec. & Treas.
On the Square
PHONE 974
10 N. PACK Sq.

H. A. BROWN & Co.
General Contractors
23 Temple Court Bldg.
Phone 341

—DEALERS IN—

Rough Building
and
all Kinds of Crushed Stone

—OUR SPECIALTIES—

STONE FOUNDATIONS
CONCRETE WORK
and
EXCAVATING

Moale & Chiles Real Estate and Insurance
27 Patton Ave. [2d fl] Phone 661
City and Suburban Property FARMS and TIMBER LANDS

Candy Kitchen and Club Cafe
"A GOOD PLACE FOR REFRESHMENT"

Hot drinks on cold days. Cold drinks on hot days. The best drinks every day. Pure fruits and syrups blended "just right," served daintily. Our Ice Cream and Soda Water Department, Restaurant and Candy Departments are always kept up to the standard of nearest perfection. Phones 110 and 111. 19 and 21 Haywood St.

CRUSHED STONE 406 DRAYAGE

Brown's Undertaking Parlors

S. H. BROWN

50 Patton Avenue
ASHEVILLE, N. C.

Lady Assistant When Desired

Phone 193-2 Rings

THE MOORE Plumbing Company

16 N. Pack Square

PHONE 1025

Sanitary Plumbing, General Tin and Metal Work, Hot Air Furnaces

---

☞ Crushed Stone and Rough Building Rock

BROWN H A & CO, 23 Temple Ct

☞ Cut Flowers

BROWNHURST GREENHOUSES, Murdock av opp Grove Park

Dairies

Anandale Purity Dairy, W Asheville
CAROLINA CREAMERY, 252-258 Patton av
CAROLINA DAIRY, Weaverville rd nr New Bridge
Biltmore Dairy, Biltmore Estate
Gash's Creek Dairy, nr Biltmore
Laurel Springs Dairy, Chunn's Cove
Maple Leaf Dairy, W Asheville
Middlebrook Dairy, County
Montford Dairy, Richmond Hill
Mountain Range Dairy, County
Reed Farm Dairy, Biltmore
Roseland Dairy, Chunn's Cove
Sunset Dairy, R F D 1

☞ Decorators—Interior

BOWLES R E, 1 e Pack Sq

Dental Supplies

Hagan H J, 63 B Amer Natl Bank Bldg

Dentists

Brooks Alfred, 42 Atkinson
Chambers E O, 4-6 Harkins Bldg
Durham B J, 10-11 Medical Bldg
EVANS EDWD, 3 s w Pack Sq
Faucette J W, 16-17 Electrical Bldg
Foreman J W Dr, 17½ Church
GLENN C F, 9-11 New Sondley Bldg
HALL B F, 48-49 Amer Natl Bank Bldg

Hunt F L, 510 Legal Bldg
Mann I M, 37 Patton av (2d fl)
Matthews Augustus, 25-27 Oak
Parker J M, 11-12 Paragon Bldg
Ramsay J F, 41-42 Amer Natl Bank Bldg
Reeves R H, 35 n Spruce
*Schaeffer C T, 16 Eagle
Sinclair J A, 206-209 Legal Bldg
Sinclair P D, 206-209 Legal Bldg
SMATHERS WEXLER, 14-16 Paragon Bldg
Ware A B, 11 n w Pack Sq (2d fl)

Department Stores

Asheville Dry Goods Co, 10-12 Patton av
BON MARCHE, 19-23 Patton av
I X L Dept Store, 22 Patton av
PEOPLE'S DEPT STORE, 40-42 Patton av
Redwood H & Co, 7-9 Patton av

Development and Industrial Companies

ASHEVILLE BOARD OF TRADE, Temple Ct
GREATER WESTERN N C ASSN, 3-4 Electrical Bldg

Directory Publishers

KNOXVILLE DIRECTORY CO, 66 Amer Natl Bank Bldg
MILLER ERNEST H, 66 Amer Natl Bank Bldg
PIEDMONT DIRECTORY CO, 66 Amer Natl Bank Bldg

Drayage

ASHEVILLE DRAY, FUEL & CONSTRUCTION CO, 6½ s Main
Reisecker E A, 34 s Lexington av
Southern Dray, Riverside Drive
*Rhodes G R, 492 s French Broad av
*Somers J K, 16 Dundee
*Stinson G A, 18 Knob

The Battery Park Bank

ASHEVILLE, N. C.   City, County and State Depositary

Capital - - $100,000.00
Surplus and Profits, $110,000.00

J. A. TILLMAN — Jeweler — 17 N. Main St.

I carry a nice line of Watches, Clocks and Jewelry, and make a specialty of repair work. Satisfaction guaranteed

Dressmakers

Atkin S G Mrs, 34 Monroe pl
Barton Jennie Mrs, 167 Patton av
Bernecker Frieda Miss, 60 n Spruce
Bowman & Wright, 21-25 Reed Bldg
Briggs Harriet Miss, 17 Merrimon av
Campbell M E Mrs, 114 Poplar
Campbell N P Miss, 153 s Main
Clapp L M Miss, S Biltmore
Crompton Betty Mrs, 16 Jefferson Drive
Donnan M O Mrs, 6 Battery Park Pl
Farmer Elsie L Mrs, 10 s Main
Feezer Hepsie B Mrs, 18 s Main
*Fredwell Mary, 73 Eagle
Gideon N J Mrs, 57 East
Gudger L M Mrs, 145 s Main
Hannon L R Mrs, 6 Central av
Hardin Sallie Miss, W Asheville
*Hartman Alice, 78 Valley
HARVILLE C B MRS, 172 Haywood (see p 24)
Hatcher K S Mrs, 64 n French Broad av
Hays L E Mrs, 102 Haywood
Hipp E L Mrs, 64 Phifer
Hughey Loretta Miss 46 w Walnut
Ingram C B Mrs, 165 s Main
Johnson Ada Mrs, 308 Depot
*Johnson Fannie, 134 Livingston
Lambert H A Mrs, 12 Jefferson Drive
Laughter Lula V Miss, 33 Fulton
LOFTAIN C S MRS, 323 e College (see p 5)
McGlamery S A Miss, Brevard rd, W Ashev
Mason H E Mrs, 357 s Main
Miller M I Miss, W Asheville
Murray Hester Mrs, 65 Clingman av
Nash M W Miss, 24 McAfee Bldg
O'Rear Eva Miss, 28 Amer Natl Bank Bldg
Price Josephine Mrs, 22 Montford av
Ray Susan Miss, 180 Livingston
Sams R J Miss, 70 Seney
*Sewell Lucy, 18 Eagle
Snyder A B Mrs, 75 Seney
Sorrels Sallie Mrs, 53½ Orange
Stancill Alice Mrs, 114 Poplar
Starnes Zona Miss, 18 Grady
Steadman L A Miss, 83 Washington rd
Stowe L V Mrs, 20 n French Broad av
*Thomas Blanche, 136 Pine
Wainscott L L Mrs, 24 Cherry
White A M Mrs, 138 Poplar
Wight A H Mrs, 28 Philip
Williams Georgia Miss, 10 Orchard
Wilson A R Mrs, 40 Carter

Druggists

(Retail)

ALLISON'S DRUG STORE, 43 Patton av
Biltmore Drug Store, 10 Plaza, Biltmore
CARMICHAEL'S PHARMACY, 1 n w Pack Sq
Finley R S, 408 Depot
GRANT'S PHARMACY, 10 s Main
Depot Drug Co, 400 Depot
Langren Drug Store, 4 n Main
MAC KAY'S PHARMACY, 7 n w Pack Sq
McMinn W J, 313 w Haywood
Pelham S D, 411 Depot
Raysor C A, 31 Patton av
Rhinehart M T, 9 Montford av
*Shades Pharmacy, 24 Eagle
SMITH'S DRUG STORE, 1 s Main
SWANNANOA DRUG CO, 45 s Main
TEAGUE & OATES, 22 n Pack Sq
WALKER C A, 15 Haywood
WEST END DRUG STORE, 270 Patton av
*Y M I DRUG STORE, 29 Eagle

(Wholesale)

Smith T C Dr, 14-16 s Lexington av

INSURANCE

INSURE YOUR SALARY WITH US
NEVER CARRY YOUR OWN RISK
SAFETY IS THE BEST POLICY
UNLESS YOU ARE A CAPITALIST
REST EASY IF YOU HAVE
AN ACCIDENT WE WILL
NOT KEEP YOU WAITING TO
COLLECT YOUR CLAIM
EVERY CLAIM PROMPTLY PAID

Imperial Mutual Life & Health Insurance Co.

Home Office: ASHEVILLE, N. C.

Phone 495

HOTEL OXFORD — Asheville, N. C.

Redecorated and Refitted throughout. Recently enlarged to 60 rooms. Centrally located. Depot cars stop at entrance. Long distance telephone office upstairs. American and European plan. Rates 50c, 75c and $1 per day; special rates by week or month. C. H. Branson & Sons, Proprietors. Phone 1887. 50-54 South Main St.

Williams-Brownell Planing Mill Company — *Hardwoods*

Lu..ber---Rough and Dressed Flooring a Specialty Moulding, Interior Finish, Etc.
Office, Plant and Yards on Southern Railway, Near Biltmore Station
WHITE PINE Phone 729 YELLOW PINE

DRY CLEANING 408 ELECTRIC

☞ Dry Cleaning

ASHEVILLE DRY CLEANING CO, Main n e cor College (see bottom lines)

Dry Goods

(Retail)

Asheville Dry Goods Co, 10-12 Patton av
Blomberg S I, 13 n w Pack Sq
BON MARCHE, 19-23 Patton av
Gentry J C, 22 s Main
GUFFEY J A, 9 s w Pack Sq

JOHN A. GUFFEY

DRY GOODS
AND NOTIONS

Phone 471   9 W. Pack sq., ASHEVILLE, N. C

Jenkins G W, 18 s Main
Mumpower R E, 17 s Main
OLIVE H J, 547-551 w Haywood
Palais Royal, 5-7 s Main
PEERLESS (The), 42-44 Patton av
PEOPLES DEPT STORE, 40-42 Patton av
Racket Store (The), 16 s Main
Redwood H & Co, 7-9 Patton av
Schochet J B Mrs, 9 n Main

(Wholesale)

Harris-Barnett Dry Goods Co, 36 n Main

☞ Dry Kilns

ENGLISH LBR CO, Avery and Sou Ry tracks
JONES WM M, 557 w Haywood

Dye Works

ASHEVILLE CLEANING & PRESSING CLUB, 4 n Pack Sq

ASHEVILLE DRY CLEANING CO, Main n e cor College
Poole Bros, College and Penland
RELIABLE CLEANING & PRESSING CO, 14 Church (see insert)
*SARTOR J R, 39 s Main

Eating Houses

(See also Restaurants)

*Alexander Geo, 17 Eagle
*Alexander S E, 103 Pine
Boyd W H, 515 w Haywood
Bradley N B, 523 w Haywood
Ducker Z T, 16-18 w College
*Farr Josephine, 86 Pine
*Floyd Theresa, 88 Eagle
*Franklin Jno, 227 Clingman av
*Gray Porter, 40 Mountain
*Hampton Laura, 140 Valley
*Hellams M C, 5 w Walnut
Mizales Mike N, Eagle nr Main
*Murrough Noah, Y M I Bldg
*Pearson H P, 6 Eagle
Phipps J W, 18 n Lexington av
*Sanders Mamie, 125 Southside av
*Stinson W M, 417 and 420 Depot
*Sullivan P A, 98 Eagle
*Walker S W, 419 Depot

Electric Light and Power Co's

ASHEVILLE POWER AND LIGHT CO, Patton av n e cor Asheland av (see side lines)
North Carolina Electrical Power Co, 1-2 Maxwelton Bldg
WEAVERVILLE ELECTRIC CO, 7 n Main

Electric Railways

ASHEVILLE POWER AND LIGHT CO, Patton av n e cor Asheland av
ASHEVILLE & EAST TENN R R, 7 n Main (see front cover and top lines)

Asheville Electrical Co. Electrical Contractors
PHONE 377 — HEADQUARTERS 74 CENTRAL AVENUE
W. Manstield Booze, Manager

Asheville Dry Cleaning Co.
Telephones 835-836, All Dep't
MAIN, N. E. COR. COLLEGE

THE CLEANERS
Our Department for Oriental Rugs and Carpet Cleaning is prepared to serve you in all its branches.   :-:   :-:   :-:
E. S. Paine O. E. Hansen

FOR BOX SHOOKS | **Call English Lumber Co.** PHONE 321

ELECTRIC 409 FEED

Electric Vehicles

Carolina Electric Vehicle Co, 2 Electrical Bldg

Electrical Contractors

ASHEVILLE ELECTRICAL CO, 74 Central av (see side lines)
McKay Edwin, 7 Technical Bldg
PIEDMONT ELECTRIC CO, 64 Patton av (see side lines)
Ward W A, 12 Church

☞ Electrical Fixtures and Supplies

PIEDMONT ELECTRIC CO 64 Patton av

☞ Electrical Power Machinery

ENTERPRISE MACHINE CO, 67-71 n Main (see back cover)

☞ Embalmers

NOLAND, BROWN & CO, 16 Church

☞ Embroidery and Stamping

MOORE E J K MISS, 52 Patton av

Engines and Boilers

ASHEVILLE SUPPLY & FDY CO, 18-22 Market

Engineers

(Civil, Mining, Mechanical and Consulting)

Burns D B, 321 Legal Bldg
Carrier R A, Carrier Bldg
Case B H, 5 Edgehill av
Fanning F J, 106 Citizens Bldg
Folsom Chas, 14 Clayton
Hamlet A A, Court House
Justice C B, 102 s French Broad av
Lee B M, City Hall
Parker H T, 83 Arlington
Waddell C E, 78 Patton av

Engravers

Ashev Ptg & Engraving Co, 15 Church

Estates

BILTMORE ESTATE (genl office), Plaza cor Lodge, Biltmore
COXE FRANK, 10 Battery Park Pl
Johnston Mattie A Miss, Temple Ct
Johnston R B, Temple Ct
Johnston Thos D, Temple Ct
Johnston Wm, Temple Ct
Smith Estate, n Pack Sq

Exchanges

Woman's Exchange, 36 Haywood

☞ Export Lumber

NORTHROP S & W H LBR CO (Inc), 9th and Bragg Sts, Richmond Va

Express Companies

SOUTHERN EXPRESS CO, 99-103 Patton av and Sou Ry Sta

☞ Fancy Work

MOORE E J K MISS, 52 Patton av

☞ Farm and Orchard Lands

BROWN CARTER REALTY CO, 23 Temple Ct
WESTERN CAROLINA REALTY CO, 10 n Pack Sq

Feed Dealers

ASHEVILLE GRAIN & HAY CO, Depot cor Roberts
ASHEVILLE GROCERY CO (whol), 385 Depot
OLIVE H J, 551 w Haywood

BIGGEST BUSIEST BEST

Asheville Steam Laundry

Phones: 1936 and 1937

43 to 47 W. College Street

CHARLES H. HONESS

OPTOMETRIST AND OPTICIAN

Exclusive maker of ATLAS SHUR-ON EYE GLASSES

THE Home of Ce-Rite Toric Lenses

We make a specialty of correcting optical defects with properly fitted glasses.

54 Patton Avenue
Opposite Postoffice

Carolina Machinery Co. Founders, Machinists and Jobbers of Mill Supplies. We make all kinds of Castings in Iron, Brass or Aluminum.

WE ALSO FURNISH SKILLED MECHANICS FOR BOILER REPAIRS —— PHONE 590

LIFE INSURANCE COMPANY OF VA.
ORGANIZED 187
Richmond -:- Virginia
J. V MOON, Superintendent
Rooms 3-4-5- Maxwelton Bldg., Asheville, N. C.

All claims paid IMMEDIATELY upon receipt of satisfactory proofs of Death. Total payment to policyholders since organization, over $12,000,000.00. Is paying its Policyholders over $1,000,000.00 annually.

FERTILIZERS 410 FUNERAL

T. P. JOHNSON & CO.
SHEET METAL WORKERS

All Kinds of Roofing Guttering and Conductor Work Metal Ceilings, Skylights and Galvanized Iron Cornices

OFFICE and SHOP:
69-71 S. MAIN
Phone 325

DR. C. H. MILLER
Mechano-Therapist

14 N. Spruce Street
ASHEVILLE, N. C.
PHONE 979

Hours by Engagement

DRUGLESS HEALING OF DISEASE

Fertilizers
Asheville Packing Co, office 353 Depot
Rogers W F, 527 w Haywood

Fish, Oysters and Game
Asheville Fish Co, City Market
City Fish Market, City Market

Five and Ten Cent Stores
Levitt Morris, 3 s Main
KRESS S H & CO, 24-26 Patton av

Flavoring Extracts—Mnfrs
DeVault C W, 70 Patton av

Flooring
ENGLISH LUMBER CO, Avery and Sou Ry
JONES WM M, 557 w Haywood
WILLIAMS - BROWNELL PLANING MILL CO, Sou Ry nr Biltmore
WOODWARD & SON, Richmond Va (see top lines)

Florists
BROWNHURST GREENHOUSES, Murdock av opp Grove Park
Lashley D A, W Asheville
Woolsey Greenhouse, Woolsey (R F D 1)

Flour Mills
(See Mills—Flour and Grist)

Fresh Meats
HILL'S MARKET, City Market
HYAMS MORD, Main and Merrimon av
KIIBLER & WHITEHEAD, City Market
STAR MARKET, City Market

Founders and Machinists
ASHEVILLE SUPPLY & FDY CO, 18-22 Market

G. W. DONNAN, Gen. Mgr.
D. S. HILDEBRAND, Pres.
W. C. BRITT, Secretary and Treasurer

Asheville Supply & Foundry Company
— DEALERS IN —

Machinery, Repairs, Shafting, Pulleys and Appurtenances. Belting a Specialty. Pipe-valves and Fittings :: :: :: ::

GENERAL MILL SUPPLIES

CAROLINA MACHINERY CO, Avery and Sou Ry (see bottom lines)

Fruits
(See also Confectioners)
*JACKSON B J, City Mkt
Landreth B P, 399 Southside av
New York Fruit Stand, 404 Depot
TRAKAS N S & CO (whol), 31 s Main (see p 5)

Funeral Directors
(See also Undertakers)
BROWN'S UNDERTAKING PARLORS, 50 Patton av (see right side lines)
NOLAND, BROWN & CO, 16 Church

ASHEVILLE CLEANING and PRESSING CLUB

TAILORING THAT SATISFIES and PRICES THAT PLEASE
Hats cleaned, banded and bound. Silk hats ironed. Buttons made to order in all sizes. Plain or with rims. PHONE 389

DYEING IN ALL SHADES Cleaned. Messenger Service.

Kid Gloves, Slippers and Plumes. Fancy Jabots and Ties. French Dry Cleaned. Ladies' and Gentlemen's suits Steam

J. C. Wilbar, Prop.
4 NORTH PACK SQ.

ASHEVILLE COAL CO. 6 North Pack Sq. Phone 40

M. & W. COAL

Asheville Power and Light Co. Electric Flat Irons — Phone 69

FURNISHED ROOMS 411 GAS FITTERS

Furnished Rooms

Allport F D Mrs, 18 Oak
Baker Addie Mrs, 71 Woodfin
Brookshire J A Mrs, 39 s French Broad av
Cabe M C Mrs, 72 Ralph
Coffey Z Mrs, 11½ n Main
Drhumor Bldg, 48 Patton av
Florida House (The), 41½ s Main
Freck Carrie Mrs, 153 s Main
Library Bldg, s Pack Sq
Maxwelton Bldg, 40 Patton av
Orr T F, 426 Depot
Phipps J W, 18 n Lexington av
Piper Jennie Mrs, 15 Woodfin
Technical Bldg, 18-20 e College
Temple Court, 47-53 Patton av
Vance A C Mrs, 147 Haywood
Waldheim (The), 211 Patton av
Warren B W, 17½ n Main
Y M C A, 27 Haywood

Furniture

(Buyers)

Amer Furn Buyers Assn, 37-38-39 Amer Natl Bank Bldg

(Dealers)

Asheville Furn Co, 29 s Main
Beaumont Furn Co, 27 s Main
BURTON & HOLT, 2 s Main cor Pack Sq
DAVIS J R, 37 s Main
Devine H P Furn Co, 315 w Haywood
Donald & Donald, 14 s Main
Globe Furn Co, 52 s Main
Golightly L O, 16 n Pack Sq
GREEN BROS, 45 Patton av
Moore J C, 35 s Main
Moore W L, 27 n Main
Patterson W E & Co, 57 n Main
Smathers J L & Sons, 15-17 n Main
Southside Furn Co, 372 Southside av

(Manufacturers)

American Furn Mnfg Co, office 37-39 Amer Natl Bank Bldg, plant Riverside Drive
United States Furn Mnfg Co, Sou Ry, nr Biltmore

(Packers for Shipment)

GALER E E, 114 Patton av (see bottom lines)

(Repairers)

Asheville Cabinet Co, 17½ Church
GALER E E, 114 Patton av (see bottom lines)
*Gray Henry, 101 n Lexington av
Havner R A, 57 n Main

Fuel

ASHEVILLE DRAY, FUEL & CONSTRUCTION CO, 6½ s Main
CAROLINA COAL & ICE CO, 50 Patton av
SOUTHERN COAL CO, 10 n Pack Sq

Galvanized Iron Cornices

McPHERSON J C, 35-37 College

Garage—Automobile

ARBOGAST MOTOR CO, 52-60 n Main (see side lines)
Asheville Auto Co, 15-17 s Lexington av
O K Auto Supply & Transit Co, 61-63 s Main
Public Service & Motor Co, 8-10 e College
Western Carolina Auto Co, Walnut cor Lexington av

Gas Making Machines

Asheville "F P" Gas Machine Co, 62 s Main

Gas and Steam Fitters

McPHERSON J C, 35-37 College
MOORE PLUMBING CO, 15 College
STEVENS S M, 95 Cumberland av

Meats — Kiibler & Whitehead — CITY MARKET — PHONES, 195 and 694

WEAVERVILLE LINE — NINE MILES BY TROLLEY FROM PACK SQUARE TO WEAVERVILLE

ASHEVILLE AND EAST TENNESSEE RAILROAD CO.
7 NORTH MAIN STREET — ASHEVILLE N. C.

GENL MDSE — 412 — GROCERS

General Merchandise

Bright A L, W Asheville
Carolina Supply Co, office 200-202 Oates Bldg
Farmers Union, 55 n Main
Mears G A, 525 w Haywood
Merrell W E, 311 Haywood
Michalov Isaac, 203 Asheland av
North Carolina Mercantile Co, office 200-202 Oates Bldg
OLIVE H J, 547-548-550 and 551 w Haywood and W Asheville
Stoner A D, 2-5 Plaza, Biltmore
Wyatt W H, 9 Roberts

☞ General Outfitters

MOORE M V & CO, 11 Patton av

☞ Ginger Ale—Bottlers

HASKELL H S, 217 Haywood

Glass
(See Paints, Oil and Glass)

☞ Glassware

KRESS S H & CO, 24-26 Patton av

Greenhouses

BROWNHURST GREENHOUSES, Murdock av—opp Grove Park
Lasley D A, W Asheville
Woolsey Greenhouses, Woolsey (R F D1)

Grocers
(Retail)

*Alexander W M, Max cor Haid
Allison G D, 225 Merrimon av
*Anthony Jos, 23 Hazzard
BAIRD T G, 152 Montford av
Barnett W L, 37 n Main
Black J M, 337 w Haywood
Bradburn J H, W Asheville
Bradley J N, 527 w Haywood
Bright A L, W Asheville
Bryce S P, 34 Roberts
*Campbell F S, Eagle cor Valley
Cannon & Haynes, 467 n Main
Carter W R, WAsheville
Cash Grocery (The), 1 s w Pack Sq
*Castion Eugene, 67 Hill
*Colley Henry, 1 Mountain
Cornell H A Mrs, W Asheville
CRISP N L, 305 w Haywood

N. L. CRISP
Staple and Fancy
GROCERIES
COUNTRY PRODUCE
305 West Haywood Street

Davis W A, 41 s Main
*Doster Henry, 104 Pine
Ducker Z T, 16-18 w College
Fagan Max, 36 Mountain
Fairchild G W, W Asheville
Farris M F, 250 Patton av
Featherston A A, 19 n Main
Felmet Bros, 349 w Haywood
Ford W P & Son, 348 Depot
Foster F S, 356 Depot
Foster J S, 162 Southside and 262 Depot
Gibson J A, W Asheville
Goodis Nathan, 80 Poplar
Green P J, 246 Patton av
*Green Theodore, 160 Beaumont
Groves J A Grocery Co, 116 Patton av
Hammett Augustus, 502 w Haywood
Hamrick G P, 70 Charlotte
Harkins R W, 268 Patton av
Hawkins A N Mrs, 326 s Main
Hayes C S, 161 s Main
Haynie V V, East cor Main

Electrical Supplies
PIEDMONT ELECTRIC COMPANY
ASHEVILLE, N. C.
64 PATTON AVE.

CONTRACTOR and BUILDER
STEEL RANGES
J. C. McPHERSON
35-37 E COLLEGE ST. PHONE 133
PLUMBING STEAM AND HOT WATER **HEATING**

GROCERS — 413 — GROCERS

Haywood Street Market, 336 w Haywood
Henson Lillie Mrs, 86 Avery
Hill J B, W Asheville
Hill J F, 545 w Haywood
Hollar & Co, 414 Southside av
Hughes W H, W Asheville
Hunt J T, 418 Depot
HYAMS MORD, 130 n Main (see back cover)
Ingle J B, 47-49 n Main
Isaac T L, 292 Southside av
Ivy Levi, 1 Hazzard
Jackson, A. C., W Asheville
Jackson J F, 170 Southside av
Jarrett E C, 12 n Pack Sq
Jenkins J H, 32 n Main
Johnson A R, 458 s Main
Johnson J E, Grace
Johnson R R, Eagle cor Valley
Johnston I V, 325 w Haywood
Jordan J W, 317½ w Haywood
Kilpatrick W P, 193 Asheland av
Kimberly Jno, Riverside Drive nr n Main
Kroger Wm, 240 Patton av
*Lance J E, 17 Sorrell
Lance T S, 89 Clingman av
Lanning A W, 453 s Main
Lawing T H, W Asheville
Ledbetter L C, 60 Sycamore
Ledford J M, 380 Depot
Leonardi J H, 155 s Main
London Louis, 86 Eagle
Lunsford W T, 88 Patton av
Luther C G & Bros, 275 Asheland av
McDarris Wm O, 212 Livingston
*McDowell Mary, 80-82 Pine
McKinney W C, 21 Merrimon av
McLean & Anders, 100 Patton av
McPeeters & Mack, 371 s Main
Maney W D, Woolsey (R F D 1)
Maxwell L O, 50 East
Meek C A, 266 n Main
Michalove Abraham, 15 Furman av
Miller F M, 244 College
*Miller L M, 29 Circle
*Miller Lawson, 39 Mountain
Morrison S E, W Asheville
Nicholson J H, W Asheville
Nixon W B, 170-172 Charlotte
North Asheville Grocery, 277 n Main
Nowell Sylvester, 2 McDowell
OLIVE H J, 547-551 w Haywood and W Asheville
Ownbey & Son, 25 Montford av
Owens & Son, 382 Southside av
Pearlman B, 47 Hill
Presley M H, 238 Southside av
Presley T C, W Asheville
Randall J E, Grace
Redmon S M, 64 Seney
Rhoads & McLean, Riverside Drive nr Casket Co
Rich A D Mrs, 38 Pearson Drive
Roberson L W, Riverside Drive nr Park
Roberts & McKinney, 20 w College
Rodgers J F, 56 Eagle
Saunders J M, 510 w Haywood
Sawyer C R, 53 Patton av
Shepherd B M, 45 College
Shepherd B M, 45 College
Sims J F, 168 Patton av
Smith G W, W Asheville
Sorrels G A, 13½ n Main
Sprouse H M, 59 Black
Stewart A I Mrs, 93 Livingston
Stradley G F, 3 n e Pack Sq
Swink Robt, 178 s Main
Teasley T E, 41 College
Trantham T L, Brook cor Reed Biltmore
*Vance Mark, 317 w Haywood
*Vance W M, 38 Mountain
*Wallace J B, 183 Beaumont
*Watson B S E, 190 Southside
Webb D H, 425 s Main
Welch J L & Co, 549 w Haywood
Werthes P D, 453 s Main
West End Grocery, 344 w Haywood
Westmoreland B F, 10 Roberts
Wild J A, 470 w Haywood
Willis W A, 65 Spring
Woods S F, 44 s Main
Yates & McGuire, 35 Haywood
Young A M, W Asheville
Young J H, 418 n Main
Young & Robinson, 93 n Lexington av

Candy Kitchen and Club Cafe
"A GOOD PLACE FOR REFRESHMENT"

The very best ingredients with sanitary conditions in our Candy Manufacturing Department make possible the dainty, crisp confections sold here. Bon Bons and Chocolates made every day, put up in neat, attractive boxes. Phones 110 and 111. 19 and 21 Haywood St.

GROCERS　　　　414　　　　HARNESS

Brown's Undertaking Parlors

S. H. BROWN

Lady Assistant When Desired

Phone 193-2 Rings

50 Patton Avenue
Asheville, N. C.

Established 1894

B. J. JACKSON

Carefully Selected Fruits and Vegetables

Stall No. 11, City Market

BUSINESS PHONES:
86 and 101

RESIDENCE PHONE
1596

ZIMMERMAN & SON, 428 Depot

(Wholesale)
ASHEVILLE GROCERY CO, 385 Depot
Mustin-Robertson Co, 351 Depot
Rogers Grocery Co, 365-369 Depot
Slayden, Fakes & Co, 27-33 s Lexington av

Gun and Locksmiths

Mosseller J S & Son, Main cor College
Rickard J J, 195 Southside av

☞Gymnasiums

Y W C A, 21 s Main

Hackmen

*Bridges G C, 104 Choctaw
Brown C B, 293 s Main
Bryson U S, 34½ n Main
*DOBBINS JAMES, 56-64 Valley
*Owens Jno, 84 Choctaw

Hair Dressers

Cruise J B Miss, 25 Haywood
*FAULKNER BENNIE P, 39½ s Main
*Foster Ethel, 272 Asheland av
*Knight Bertha, 18 Hilliard la
*Simons Mary C, 38 Hill
*Tucker Zela, 58 Poplar

☞Hair Goods

*FAULKNER B P MRS, 39½ s Main (see opp bus)

Halls

Armory Hall, e s Penland nr Walnut
Central Labor Union Hall, 39 Patton av (3d fl)
Confederate Veterans, Court House (2d fl)
Eagles Hall, 33½ s Main
ELKS—Haywood cor Walnut

First Regiment Band Hall, 37 s Main
Hilliard Hall, 37 s Main
K OF P HALLS, 1 s Main and Paragon Bldg (3d fl)
Masonic Temple, Drhumor Bldg
*Masonic Hall, 44 Market
New Sondley Hall, Haywood n e cor w College (3d fl)
Odd Fellows' Hall, 18½ Church, Plaza, Biltmore, and W Asheville
*Odd Fellows' Hall, 22 Eagle
Salvation Army Halls, 38½ s Main and 504 w Haywood
Woolsey Hall, Woolsey av
Y M C A Hall, Y M C A Bldg
*Y M I Hall, Eagle cor Market

☞Handiwork

ALLANSTAND COTTAGE INDUSTRIES, 33 Haywood

Hardware

BROWN HDW CO, 25 n Main
BROWN-NORTHUP & CO, 33 Patton av
Green Ottis Hdw Co, 11 s w Pack Sq

Hardwoods

Greenwood & Blackstock, 305 Oates Bldg
Coleman, Robinson & Co, Morsell Bldg
ENGLISH LUMBER CO, Avery and Sou Ry
Hardwood Lumber Co, Temple Ct
WILLIAMS, BROWNELL PLANING MILL CO, Sou Ry nr Biltmore
WOODWARD & SON, Richmond Va (see bet pages 188 and 189)

Harness and Saddlery

Asheville Harness Co (Inc), 33 s Main
Shope & Patton, 30 n Main

Yᵉ OLD BOOK SHOP
114 Patton Ave.　　　　Phone 1674
BOOKS BOUGHT, SOLD OR EXCHANGED

ROUGH AND DRESSED LUMBER
WHITE PINE AND YELLOW PINE
FLOORING A SPECIALTY
Hardwoods

Williams-Brownell Planing Mill Company
Mouldings and Interior Finish
Office: Southern Railway Tracks, Near Biltmore Station
Phone 729 — *Planing Mill*

HATS 415 INSURANCE

Hat Blockers and Renovators

Chakales & Pilalos, 4 Patton av

☞Hats and Caps

Moore M V & Co, 11 Patton av
Zageir R B, 8 s Main

Hides and Pelts

Sternberg S & Co, 353 Depot

☞Horseshoers

(See also Blacksmtihs)
American Wagon Co, 65 s Main
BROWN C L, 21-27 n Lexington av (see p 21)

Hospitals

Asheville Mission Hospital, Charlotte cor Woodfin
Clarence Barker Memorial Hospital, Biltmore
HIGHLAND HOSPITAL, Cumberland av and Zillicoa
MERIWETHER HOSPITAL (The), 24 Grove (see p 6)
WHITMORE SANITARIUM, 408 w Haywood (see p 11)

☞Hot Water Heating

McPHERSON J C, 37 College

Hotels

BATTERY PARK HOTEL, Patton av and Haywood
*Beaumont Hotel, 77 Mountain
CHEROKEE INN, Oak n e cor Woodfin (see p 19)
European Hotel, 418½ Depot
Florence Hotel, 436 Depot
Franklin Hotel, s Pack Sq, cor Main
Gladstone Hotel, 409 Depot
GLEN ROCK HOTEL, 400 Depot, opp Sou Ry Depot
Grove Park Inn, Grove Park (Sunset Mtn)
HIGHLAND HOTEL, 368 Depot (see p 18)
HOTEL OXFORD, 50-54 s Main (see side lines)
Hotel Paxton, 26-28 s Main
Hotel Warren, 39 n Main
LANGREN (The), Main n e cor College
MANOR (The), Albemarle Park, Charlotte extd (see p 17)
MARGO TERRACE, French Broad av, s e cor Haywood
Mountain Meadows Inn, 7 miles n e of city
Patton Hotel, 20 Patton av
Phoenix Hotel, 24 w College
Southern Hotel, 12-14 s Main
SWANNANOA - BERKELEY HOTEL, 47-57 s Main (see backbone and p 16)
Western Hotel, 11½ s w Pack Sq
Windsor Hotel & Cafe, 48-50 s Main

☞House Furnishing Goods

BURTON & HOLT, 2 s Main
Green Bros, 45 Patton av
LAW J H, 35 Patton av

Ice Cream Manufacturers

CAROLINA CREAMERY, 252-258 Patton av
CLUB CAFE & CANDY KITCHEN, 19-21 Haywood

Ice Manufacturers and Dealers

ASHEVILLE ICE CO, 8 Market
CAROLINA CREAMERY, 252-258 Patton av
Storage Supply Co, 91-99 Avery

☞Instruments—Scientific

ENTERPRISE MACHINE CO 67-71 n Main

Insurance—General Agents

ALLEN P R, 34 Patton av
ASTON, RAWLS & CO, 22-23 Amer Natl Bank Bldg
BAIRD-WILFORD REALTY CO, 206 Oates Bldg (see p 24)
FITZPATRICK R M, 7-8 Paragon Bldg

HUGHES
Transfer and Livery Co.

Automobiles for **HIRE**

TRUNKS 25c

Office:
401 Southside Avenue
PHONE 1405

Try our Hand Laundering. We strive to please in LAUNDERING and DRY CLEANING.

The Sanitary Home Laundry
No. 7 MONTFORD AVE.
PHONE - 1354

Mrs. Wilder's SANITARY HOME LAUNDRY turns out first class work in Laundering and Dry Cleaning. No. 7 Montford Ave., Phone 1354

INSURANCE 416 INSURANCE

GREENE & GOODMAN, 1½ s Main
Hodges, Mitchell & Reynolds, Electrical Bldg
Lee G E, 5-6 Paragon Bldg
McCLOSKEY J J REALTY CO, 61-62 Amer Natl Bank Bldg
MESSLER F M, 26 Amer Natl Bank Bldg (see back cover)
MOALE & CHILES, 27 Patton av (2d fl), (see bottom lines)
*OGLESBY THOS, 29 Eagle
OSTEEN T W, 1 Harkins Bldg
PATTERSON J R & SON, 1½ s Main
Ray-Campbell Co, 1 Haywood
Rutledge, Fredk & Co, 31 Patton av (2d fl)
SCOTT S A, 3 Harkins Bldg
SMITH A B (life), 4 Paragon Bldg
*Swepson P J, 29 Eagle
WACHOVIA BANK & TRUST CO, 34 Patton av
Waddell & Cox, 16 Patton av
Ward C G, 13½ Patton av
Wray Walter Toms, 1 Electrical Bldg

Insurance Companies

(Accident)

CONTINENTAL CASUALTY OF CHICAGO ILL (Com'l Dept), Harkins Bldg, T W Osteen agt
EMPLOYER'S ..LIABILITY ASSURANCE CORP of London Eng, 43 Patton av, Wachovia B & T Co agts
Fidelity & Casualty of N Y, 22-23 Amer Nat'l Bank Bldg, Aston, Rawls & Co, agts
IMPERIAL MUTUAL LIFE & HEALTH OF ASHEVILLE, 31-32 Amer Natl Bank Bldg, J P Starnes mngr (see side lines)
Maryland Casualty of Balto Md, 61-62 Amer Natl Bank Bldg, J J McCloskey agt
NEW ENGLAND CASUALTY OF BOSTON MASS, 26 Amer Natl Bank Bldg, F M Messler agt
PENNSYLVANIA CASUALTY, 26 Amer Natl Bank Bldg, F M Messler agt
PROVIDENCE INS CO of Chattanooga Tenn, 1½ s Main, Greene & Goodman agts
ROYAL INDEMNITY, 26 Amer Natl Bank Bldg, F M Messler agt
U S Health & Accident of Saginaw Mich, 13½ Patton av

(Automobile)

EMPLOYERS' LIABILITY ASSURANCE CORP of London Eng, 34 Patton av, Wachovia B & T Co agts
NEW ENGLAND CASUALTY OF BOSTON MASS, 26 Amer Natl Bank Bldg, F M Messler agt
PENNSYLVANIA CASUALTY, 26 Amer Natl Bank Bldg, F M Messler agt
*Mtn City Mutual, 29 Eagle
*North Carolina Mutual & Prov Assn of Durham N C, 44 Market
*Royal Fraternal Assn of Charlotte N C, 26 Eagle

(Bonding)

AMERICAN BONDING CO of Balto Md, 34 Patton av, Wachovia B & T Co agts
American Surety Co of New York, 1 Haywood, Ray-Campbell Co agts
Illinois Surety Co, Court House (2d fl), R R Reynolds agt
ROYAL INDEMNITY, 26 Amer Natl Bank Bldg, F M Messler agt
TITLE GUARANTY & SURETY of Scranton Pa, 34 Patton av, Wachovia B & T Co agts
U S FIDELITY & GUARANTY CO of Balto Md, 27 Patton av (2d fl), Moale & Chiles agts

(Burglary)

AMERICAN BONDING CO of

BUICK OLDSMOBILE
ARBOGAST MOTOR COMPANY
MAXWELLS ACCESSORIES AND SUPPLIES DETROIT ELECTRIC
52-60 N. Main Phones 302 and 1728

Asheville Dry Cleaning Co.
Telephones 835-836, All Dep't
MAIN, N. E. COR. COLLEGE

THE CLEANERS
Our Department for Oriental Rugs and Carpet Cleaning is prepared to serve you in all its branches.
E. S. Paine   O. E. Hansen

ALL KINDS — Hardwood Lumber

ENGLISH LUMBER CO.
Phone - - 321

| INSURANCE | 417 | INSURANCE |

Balto Md, 34 Patton av, Wachovia B & T Co agts
Fidelity & Casualty of N Y, 22-23 Amer Natl Bank Bldg, Aston, Rawls & Co agts
ROYAL INDEMNITY, 26 Amer Natl Bank Bldg, F M Messler agt
UNITED STATES FIDELITY & GUARANTY CO, 27 Patton av (2d fl), Moale & Chiles agts

(Casualty)
CONTINENTAL CASUALTY of Chicago Ill, 3 Harkins Bldg, S A Scott dist mngr
CONTINENTAL CASUALTY of Chicago Ill (coml dept), 1 Harkins Bldg, T W Osteen agt
Maryland Casualty of Balto Md, 61-62 Amer Natl Bank Bldg, J J McCloskey Realty Co agts
PENNSYLVANIA CASUALTY, 26 Amer Natl Bank Bldg, F M Messler agt
Royal Indemnity, 26 Amer Natl Bank Bldg, F M Messler agt
U S FIDELITY & GUARANTY CO, 27 Patton av, Moale & Chiles genl agts

(Elevator)
Employers Liability Assurance Corp of London Eng, 34 Patton av, Wachovia B & T Co agts
Fidelity & Casualty of N Y, 22-23 Amer Natl Bank Bldg, Aston, Rawls & Co agts
ROYAL INDEMNITY, 26 Amer Natl Bank Bldg, F M Messler agt

(Employers Liability)
Fidelity & Casualty of N Y, 22-23 Amer Natl Bank Bldg, Aston, Rawls & Co agts
PENNSYLVANIA CASUALTY, 26 Amer Natl Bank Bldg, F M Messler agt
ROYAL INDEMNITY, 26 Amer Natl Bank Bldg, F M Messler agt

U S FIDELITY & GUARANTY CO of Balto Md, 27 Patton av, Moale & Chiles genl agts

(Fire)
AACHEN & MUNICH of Germany, 34 Patton, Wachovia B & T Co agts
Aetna of Hartford Conn, 5 Paragon Bldg
AGRICULTURAL OF WATERTOWN N Y, 34 Patton av, Wachovia B & T Co agts
ALLIANCE OF PHILA PA, 34 Patton av, Wachovia B & T Co agts
American Central of St Louis, 16 Patton av
AMERICAN HOME of Greenville S C, 1½ s Main, J R Patterson & Son agts
AMERICAN OF NEWARK N J, 34 Patton av, Wachovia B & T Co, agts
American-Union of Phila, 31 Patton av
ATLANTA HOME OF GA, 27 Patton av (2d fl), Moale & Chiles agts
Atlantic, 22-23 Amer Natl Bank Bldg, Aston, Rawls & Co agts
ATLANTIC NATIONAL of Macon Ga, 61-62 Amer Natl Bank Bldg, J J McCloskey Realty Co agts
Atlas Assurance Co of London Eng, 1½ s Main, J R Patterson & Son agts
BRITISH-AMERICAN of Toronto Canada, 27 Patton av, Moale & Chiles agts
Carolina of Wilmington N C, 16 Patton av, Waddell & Coxe agts
CITIZENS OF CHARLESTON W VA, 27 Patton av, Moale & Chiles agts
Citizens of Missouri, 16 Patton av, Waddell & Coxe agts
CITY OF NEW YORK, 27 Patton av, Moale & Chiles agts
Columbia of Jersey City N J, 61-62 Amer Natl Bank Bldg, J J McCloskey Realty Co

BIGGEST BUSIEST BEST

ASHEVILLE STEAM LAUNDRY
Phones 1936 and 1937
43 to 47 W. COLLEGE

S. D. HALL
REAL ESTATE AGENT
—
Money Loaned
—
Notary Public
—
32 PATTON AVENUE
—
Phone 91

CAROLINA MACHINERY CO.
—US when you want machine work of any kind . . .

Founders Machinists and Jobbers of Mill Supplies
When in the market for heavy castings such as columns or building plates get our prices. **Phone 590**

The Life Insurance Co. of Virginia

ORGANIZED 1871   RICHMOND, VA.

ISSUES ALL THE MOST APPROVED FORMS OF LIFE INSURANCE CONTRACTS from $500.00 to $25,000.00, with premiums payable quarterly, semi-annually and annually

J. V. Moon, Superintendent, Rooms 3-4-5 Maxwelton Bldg., Asheville, N. C.

INSURANCE   418   INSURANCE

D. TREXLER TIN SHOP

All Kinds of Roofing, Gutter and Conductor Work.

Phone 862

159 South Main St.

DR. C. H. MILLER

MECHANO-THERAPIST

14 N. Spruce St.
Phone 979
ASHEVILLE, N. C.

Hours by engagement

Drugless Healing of Disease

COMMERCIAL UNION ASSURANCE OF ENG, 22-23 Amer Natl Bank Bldg, Aston, Rawls & Co agts
Continental of N Y, 1½ s Main, J R Patterson & Son agts
DELAWARE OF PHILA PA, 34 Patton av, W B & T Co agts
DIXIE FIRE OF GREENSBORO N C, 27 Patton av, Moale & Chiles agts
Exchange Underwriters, 16 Patton av, Waddell & Coxe agts
FIDELITY UNDERWRITERS OF NEW YORK, 27 Patton av, Moale & Chiles agts
FIRE ASSOCIATION OF PHILA PA, 22-23 Amer Natl Bank Bldg, Aston, Rawls & Co agts
Firemans Fund of Cal, 16 Patton av, Waddell & Coxe agts
Firemen's of Newark N J, 34 Patton av, W B & T Co agts
FRANKLIN, 26 Amer Natl Bank Bldg, F M Messler agt
Georgia Home of Columbus Ga, 16 Patton av
Germania of N Y, 22-23 Amer Natl Bank Bldg, Aston, Rawls & Co agts
GIRARD OF PHILA PA, 26 Amer Natl Bank Bldg, F M Messler agt
GERMAN ALLIANCE OF N Y, 34 Patton av, W B & T Co agts
Globe & Rutgers of N Y, 22-23 Amer Natl Bank Bldg, Aston, Rawls & Co agts
Hanover of N Y, 16 Patton av
Hartford of Hartford Conn, 22-23 Amer Natl Bank Bldg, Aston, Rawls & Co agts
Home of N Y, 22-23 Amer Natl Bank Bldg, Aston, Rawls & Co agts
Insurance Co of N A, 22-23 Amer Natl Bank Bldg, Aston, Rawls & Co agts
LONDON ASSURANCE CORP of London Eng, 34 Patton av, W B & T Co agts

Milwaukee Mechanics of Wis, 27 Patton av, Moale & Chiles agts
National of Hartford Conn, 22-23 Amer Natl Bank Bldg, Aston, Rawls & Co agts
National Union of Pittsburg Pa, 34 Patton av, W B & T Co agts
NEW HAMPSHIRE OF MANCHESTER N H, 26 Amer Natl Bank Bldg, F M Messler agt
New York Underwriters of N Y, 16 Patton av
Niagara of N Y, 34 Patton av, W B & T Co agts
North British & Mercantile of Eng, 22-23 Amer Natl Bank Bldg, Aston, Rawls & Co agts
North Carolina Home of Raleigh N C, 16 Patton av
North River, 22-23 Amer Natl Bank Bldg, Aston, Rawls & Co agts
NORTHERN OF LONDON, ENG, 27 Patton av, Moale & Chiles agts
Norwich-Union, 16 Patton av
Orient of Hartford Conn, 16 Patton av
Palatine of Eng, 16 Patton av
Peoples Natl of Phila Pa, 16 Patton av
PETERSBURG SAVINGS & INS OF VA, 34 Patton av, W B & T Co agts
Philadelphia Underwriters of Phila Pa, 16 Patton av
Phoenix Assurance of London Eng, 16 Patton av
Phoenix of Hartford Conn, 34 Patton av, Wachovia B & T Co agts
Piedmont of Charlotte N C, 16 Patton av, Waddell & Coxe agts
Providence-Washington, 1½ s Main, J R Patterson & Son agts
RUSSIAN NATIONAL OF GERMANY, 27 Patton av, Moale & Chiles agts
Queen of America, 22-23 Amer Natl Bank Bldg, Aston, Rawls & Co agts

---

....Asheville Cleaning and Pressing Club....

Tailoring That Satisfies and Prices That Please

J. C. WILBAR, Prop.

Steam and French Dry Cleaning of all delicate and fine wearing apparel for ladies and gentlemen. MESSENGER SERVICE IN THE CITY.

4. N. Pack Square   PHONE 389

CAROLINA "M & W" INDIAN — Prompt Delivery

COAL & ICE CO. PHONE 130 50 PATTON AVE. WEIGHTS ACCURATE

INSURANCE 419 INSURANCE

Queen of America, 34 Patton av, Wachovia B & T Co agts
Rhode Island of Providence R I, 61-62 Amer Natl Bank Bldg, J J McCloskey Realty Co agts
Rochester German Underwriters of Rochester N Y, 16 Patton av
ROYAL EXCHANGE ASSURANCE, 22-23 Amer Natl Bank Bldg, Aston, Rawls & Co agts
Royal of Liverpool Eng, 16 Patton av
Scottish Union & National of Scotland, 1½ s Main, J R Patterson & Son agts
Security of Hartford Conn, 1½ s Main, J R Patterson & Son agts
Southern Stock of Greensboro N C, 22-23 Amer Natl Bank Bldg, Aston, Rawls & Co agts
SOUTHERN UNDERWRITERS OF GREENSBORO N C, 27 Patton av, Moale & Chiles agts
Spring Garden of Phila Pa, 22-23 Amer Natl Bank Bldg, Aston, Rawls & Co agts
Springfield Fire & Marine of Springfield Mass, 22-23 Amer Natl Bank Bldg, Aston, Rawls & Co agts
Sterling of Ind, 27 Patton av, Moale & Chiles agts
Stuyvesant of N Y, 1½ s Main, Greene & Goodman agts
Teutonia of New Orleans La, 22-23 Amer Natl Bank Bldg, Aston, Rawls & Co agts
Underwriters of Greensboro N C, 34 Patton av, W B & T Co agts
Underwriters of Rocky Mount N C, 61-62 Amer Natl Bank Bldg, J J McCloskey Realty Co agts
UNITED FIREMEN'S, 26 Amer Natl Bank Bldg, F M Messler agt
Virginia Fire & Marine of Richmond Va, 16 Patton av
Virginia State of Richmond Va, 1½ s Main, J R Patterson & Son agts
Western of Pittsburg Pa, 26 Amer Natl Bank Bldg, F M Messler agt
Western of Toronto Can, 1½ s Main, J R Patterson & Son agts
WILLIAMSBURG CITY OF N Y, 26 Amer Natl Bank Bldg, F M Messler agt

(Fly Wheel)

Fidelity & Casualty of N Y, 22-23 Amer Natl Bank Bldg, Aston, Rawls & Co agts

(Fraternal)

*Royal Fraternal Assn of Charlotte N C, 26 Eagle

(Health)

CONTINENTAL CASUALTY OF CHICAGO ILL (coml dept), 1 Harkins Bldg, T W Osteen agt
Fidelity & Casualty of N Y, 22-23 Amer Natl Bank Bldg, Aston, Rawls & Co agts
IMPERIAL MUTUAL LIFE & HEALTH OF ASHEVILLE, 31-32 Amer Natl Bank Bldg, J P Starnes mngr (see side lines)
NEW ENGLAND CASUALTY OF BOSTON MASS, 26 Amer Natl Bank Bldg, F M Messler agt
ROYAL INDEMNITY, 26 Amer Natl Bank Bldg, F M Messler agt
U S FIDELITY & GUARANTY CO, 27 Patton av, Moale & Chiles, genl agts

(Industrial)

IMPERIAL MUTUAL LIFE & HEALTH OF ASHEVILLE, 31-32 Amer Natl Bank Bldg, J P Starnes mngr (see side lines)
LIFE INSURANCE CO OF VA, 3-4-5 Maxwelton Bldg, J V Moon supt (see top lines)

LIGHT and POWER — Asheville Power and Light Co. PHONE 69

Poultry — **Kiibler & Whitehead** — CITY MARKET — PHONES, 195 and 694

Asheville Dray, Fuel & Construction Co.
6 1-2 South Main

COAL

Wood and Kindling
Stone and Sand
PHONE - 223

EVER READY FLASHLIGHTS
Piedmont Electric Company
64 PATTON AVENUE — **ASHEVILLE, N. C.**

INSURANCE 420 JEWELERS

(Life)

DIXIE MUTUAL LIFE INSURANCE CO of Asheville N C, 408-414 Legal Bldg
EQUITABLE LIFE OF N Y, 26 Amer Natl Bank Bldg, F M Messler agt
IMPERIAL MUTUAL LIFE & HEALTH OF ASHEVILLE, 31-32 Amer Natl Bank Bldg, J P Starnes mngr (see side lines)
JEFFERSON STANDARD LIFE INS CO of Greensboro N C, 4 Paragon Bldg, A B Smith agt
LIFE INSURANCE CO OF VA, 3-4-5 Maxwelton Bldg, J V Moon supt (see top lines)
Metropolitan Life of N Y, 223 Legal Bldg
*MOUNTAIN CITY MUTUAL of Asheville, 29 Eagle
MUTUAL LIFE INS CO OF N Y, 7-8 Citizens Bank Bldg, R M Fitzpatrick div supt
Mutual of N Y, 22-23 Amer Natl Bank Bldg, Aston, Rawls & Co agts
NORTH STATE OF KINSTON N C, 1 Harkins Bldg, T W Osteen agt
Phoenix Mutual of Hartford Conn, 1½ s Main, Greene & Goodman agts
Pittsburg Life & Trust Co of Pa, 1 Electrical Bldg, W T Wray genl agt
Prudential of America (The), 68 Patton av, Hodges, Mitchell & Reynolds agts

(Plate Glass)

Fidelity & Casualty of N Y, 22-23 Amer Natl Bank Bldg, Aston, Rawls & Co agts
Lloyds of N Y, 1½ s Main, J R Patterson & Son agts
NEW YORK, 26 Amer Natl Bank Bldg, F M Messler agt
PENNSYLVANIA CASUALTY, 26 Amer Natl Bank Bldg, F M Messler agt
ROYAL INDEMNITY, 26 Amer Natl Bank Bldg, F M Messler agt
U S FIDELITY & GUARANTY CO, 27 Patton av, Moale & Chiles agts

(Registered Mail)

LLOYDS OF LONDON ENG, 34 Patton av, W B & T Co agts

(Steam Boiler)

Fidelity & Casualty of N Y, 22-23 Amer Natl Bank Bldg, Aston, Rawls & Co agts
NEW ENGLAND CASUALTY 26 Amer Natl Bank Bldg, F M Messler agt
ROYAL INDEMNITY, 26 Amer Natl Bank Bldg, F M Messler agt
UNITED STATES FIDELITY & GUARANTY of Balto Md, 27 Patton av, Moale & Chiles, agts

(Surety)

NEW ENGLAND CASUALTY, 26 Amer Natl Bank Bldg, F M Messler agt
ROYAL INDEMNITY, 26 Amer Natl Bank Bldg, F M Messler agt
U S FIDELITY & GUARANTY CO, 27 Patton av, Moale & Chiles agts

(Tornado)

Girard of Phila Pa, 26 Amer Natl Bank Bldg, F M Messler agt

Investments

HALL S D, 32 Patton av
MOALE & CHILES, 27 Patton av (2d fl)
WESTERN CAROLINA REALTY CO, 10 n Pack Sq

Jewelers and Watchmakers

Alexander Gustave, 33 Patton av
CARPENTER JAS E, 8 n Pack Sq
Cosby B H, 70 Patton av

J. C. McPHERSON
SLATE AND TIN ROOFING
Galvanized Iron Work   Hot Air Furnaces
35-37 EAST COLLEGE STREET

PLUMBING
STEAM AND HOT WATER
HEATING
PHONE 133

Yellow Pine / White Pine / Hardwoods — See bet. pgs. 188-189

LUMBER — SASH, BLINDS, DOORS

WOODWARD & SON — Ninth and Arch Streets, RICHMOND - VIRGINIA

JEWELERS   421   LEATHER

Crescent Jewelry Co, 16 Patton av
Field A M Co, Patton av cor Church
Frost H M, 15 Church
Goldsmith W W & Son, 10 n Pack Sq
Henderson C E, 52 Patton av
Levitch Harry, 29 College
Rigsby J J, 12 n Pack Sq (2d fl)
ROCKETT O N, 29 n Main (see p 22)
Shoffner W H, 27 Patton av
Stern Victor, 17 Haywood
TILLMAN J A, 17 n Main (see top lines)

☞ Jewelry

FINKELSTEIN H L, 23-25 s Main (see back cover)

Junk Dealers

Sternberg S & Co, 353-359 Depot

Justices of the Peace

Creasman M A, Oates Bldg (basement)
Gudger W R, 8 s Pack Sq
James W A Jr, 10½ n Pack Sq
McIntyre J A, 19-20 Paragon Bldg
Waddell F N, Library Bldg (basement)

☞ Kindling

ASHEVILLE DRAY, FUEL & CONSTRUCTION CO, 6½ s Main
ENGLISH LUMBER CO, Avery and Sou Ry

Kodaks and Kodak Supplies

LITTLE SMOKE HOUSE (The), 41½ Patton av
Robinson J G, 3 Haywood

Laboratories

BACTERIO-THERAPEUTIC LABORATORY, Winyah Sanatorium
CITY LABORATORY, City Hall

☞ Ladies Ready to Wear

Argintarter Bros, 43 College
PEERLESS FASHION STORES CO, 51 Patton av

Land Companies

ALBEMARLE PARK CO, Charlotte extd (see p 17)
Blue Ridge Development Co, 201-202 Legal Bldg
Chestnut Ridge Park Co, Electrical Bldg
Grove Park Co, Charlotte extd
Investors Land Co, 2 Electrical Bldg
Kenilworth Land Co, 15 Church
Powell-Murray Land Co, 2 Electrical Bldg
Villa Heights Co, Amer Natl Bank Bldg
WESTERN CAROLINA REALTY CO, 10 n Pack Sq

☞ Laths and Shingles

ENGLISH LUMBER CO, Avery nr Sou Ry
WOODWARD & SON, Richmond Va (see top lines)

Laundries

ASHEVILLE STEAM LAUNDRY, 43 w College (see side lines)
MOUNTAIN CITY LAUNDRY (Inc), 30 n Lexington av (see front and back cover)
SANITARY HOME LAUNDRY, 7 Montford av (see top and bottom lines)
SWANNANOA LAUNDRY, 22-24 Church (see back cover)

Lawyers
(See Attys at Law)

Leather Mnfrs

HANS REES SONS (Inc), Sou Ry s of Passngr Sta

What Have You in Real Estate that You Don't Want?

What do You Want in Real Estate that You Haven't?

WESTERN CAROLINA REALTY CO.
J. W. Wolfe, Sec. & Treas.
On the Square
PHONE 974
10 N. PACK Sq.

H. A. BROWN & Co.
General Contractors
23 Temple Court Bldg.
Phone 341

—DEALERS IN—

Rough Building and all Kinds of Crushed Stone

—OUR SPECIALTIES—

STONE FOUNDATIONS
CONCRETE WORK
and EXCAVATING

Moale & Chiles — Real Estate and Insurance
City and Suburban Property — FARMS and TIMBER LANDS
27 Patton Ave., [2d fl] Phone 661

Club Cafe and Candy Kitchen
"A GOOD PLACE FOR REFRESHMENT"

The standards we work to in our Restaurant Department are: Cooking, perfect; Service, prompt and cheerful; Prices, moderate; Menu, everything in season. Parties and Banquets, Teas and Dinners. 19 and 21 Haywood St. Phones 110 and 111.

LIBRARIES   422   LUMBER

Brown's Undertaking Parlors

S. H. BROWN

50 Patton Avenue
ASHEVILLE, N. C.

Lady Assistant When Desired

Phone 193-2 Rings

THE MOORE Plumbing Company

16 N. Pack Square

PHONE 1025

Sanitary Plumbing, General Tin and Metal Work, Hot Air Furnaces

---

Libraries

DIRECTORY LIBRARY, 66 Amer Natl Bank Bldg
PACK MEMORIAL LIBRARY, 4 s Pack Sq
Y M C A LIBRARY, Y M C A Bldg

Light and Power Companies

ASHEVILLE POWER & LIGHT CO, Patton av s e cor Asheland av (see side lines)
North Carolina Electrical Power Co, 1-2 Maxwelton Bldg
WEAVERVILLE ELECTRIC CO, 7 n Main

☞Lime, Plaster and Cement

JONES WM M, 557 w Haywood
Westall J M & Co, 17 Walnut

Live Stock

BROWN W P, 11 s Lexington av

☞Livery

(see also Stables)
Chambers J K, 39-41 n Lexington av
CHAMBERS & WEAVER, Aston (Willow), s e cor Lexington
HUGHES TRANSFER & LIVERY CO, 401 Southside av (see side lines)
WEBB W A, 9 s Lexington av
WILSON E F, 58 s Main (see p 24)

☞Loan Office

FINKELSTEIN H L, 23-25 s Main (see back cover)

Loans and Investments

BAIRD-WILFORD REALTY CO, 206 Oates Bldg (see p 24)
Grant H F Realty Co, 48 Patton av
HALL S D, 32 Patton av (2d fl)
Marsteller & Co, 20 Haywood
MESSLER F M, 26 Amer Natl Bank Bldg
MOALE & CHILES, 27 Patton av (2d fl)
Montague Loan Co, 12 n Pack Sq (2d fl)
Penland J D & Son, Temple Ct
*SWEPSON P J, 29 Eagle
WACHOVIA BANK & TRUST CO, 34 Patton av
WESTERN CAROLINA REALTY CO, 10 n Pack Sq

Lumber Dealers and Manufacturers

Asheville Lumber Co, 14 Temple Ct
Carolina Hardwood Lbr Co, 12 Temple Ct
Champion Lbr Co, 200-202 Oates Bldg
CHAPMAN S F, 3-5 Technical Bldg
CITIZENS LUMBER CO, 20-24 e College
Coleman, Robinson & Co, 4 Morsell Bldg
English J M & Co, 16-17 Temple Ct
ENGLISH LUMBER CO, Avery and Sou Ry (see top lines)
Fulgham J E, 423-424 Legal Bldg
Hardwood Lumber Co, 31 Temple Ct
Jackson Lbr Co, 203-205 Oates Bldg
JONES WM M, 557 w Haywood (see p 3)
Macon Lbr Co, 203-205 Oates Bldg
Mason B C, 9 Paragon Bldg
McEwen Lbr Co, Azalea N C
MONTAGUE MNFG CO, Richmond Va (see top lines and bet pages 188 and 189)
Murray G A, 68 Patton av
Murray Lumber Co (The), 68 Patton av
NORTHROP S & W H LBR CO (Inc), Richmond Va

The Battery Park Bank

ASHEVILLE, N. C.   City, County and State Depositary

Capital - - $100,000.00
Surplus and Profits, $110,000.00

J. A. TILLMAN — I carry a nice line of Watches, Clocks and Jewelry, and make a specialty of repair work. Satisfaction guaranteed. **Jeweler — 17 N. Main St.**

LUMBER

Ritter W M Lbr Co, 301 Oates Bldg
Smith S M, 425-428 Legal Bldg
Tonawanda White Pine Co, 15 Temple Ct
WESTALL J M & CO, 17 Walnut, yard Old Depot
Westall W H & Co, 22 s Spruce
Whiting W S, 56-59 Amer Natl Bank Bldg
WILLIAMS, BROWNELL PLANING MILL CO, Sou Ry nr Biltmore (see top lines)
Williams J M, 423-424 Legal Bldg
Woodbury W H, 72 n Main
WOODWARD & SON, Richmond Va (see top lines and bet pages 188 and 189)

Machinery—Electrical Power

ENTERPRISE MACHINE CO 67-71 n Main (see back cover)

Machinery — Metal Working

ENTERPRISE MACHINE CO 67-71 n Main (see p 14)

Machinists

(See also Founders and Machinists)
ASHEVILLE SUPPLY & FDY CO (Inc), 18-22 Market
CAROLINA MACHINERY CO, Avery and Sou Ry (see lines)

Manicurists

Cruise J B Miss, 23 Haywood
Williamson Nettie Mrs, Battery Park Hotel

Mantels, Tiles and Grates

JONES WM M, 557 w Haywood

Manufacturers Agents

General Supply Co, 51 Asheland

Moody H M Sales Co, 68 Patton av

Marble and Granite Works

Asheville Marble Works, 170 Patton av
BEAN S I & CO, 94 Patton av
Wolfe W O, 22 s Pack Sq

Markets

City Market, e Pack Sq

Massage

*Clemmons Otis, 18 Hilliard la
*FAULKNER B P MRS, 39½ s Main (see adv)
GRUNER SANITARIUM (The), 29-31 Haywood

Mattress Manufacturers

Smathers R I, 172 Clingman av

Meat Markets

Bishop A B, W Asheville
Dodd T L, 4 Plaza, Biltmore
Faulkner Bros, City Market
Globe Market, City Market
Haynie V V, East cor Main
HILL'S MARKET, City Market (see bottom line front cover)
HYAMS MORD, 130 n Main (see back cover)
KIIBLER & WHITEHEAD, City Market (see bot lines)
Lanning A W, 453 s Main
Luther C G & Bros, 275 Asheland av
Lutz Meat Co, City Market
Marlow Bros, City Market
STAR MARKET (The), City Market (see front cover)
ZIMMERMAN & SON, 428 Depot

Medicines

Stevens F M, 49 Hiawassee
Viavi Co, 210-211 Legal Bldg

INSURANCE

- **I**NSURE YOUR SALARY WITH US
- **N**EVER CARRY YOUR OWN RISK
- **S**AFETY IS THE BEST POLICY
- **U**NLESS YOU ARE A CAPITALIST
- **R**EST EASY IF YOU HAVE
- **A**N ACCIDENT WE WILL
- **N**OT KEEP YOU WAITING TO
- **C**OLLECT YOUR CLAIM
- **E**VERY CLAIM PROMPTLY PAID

Imperial Mutual Life & Health Insurance Co.

Home Office: ASHEVILLE, N. C.

Phone 495

HOTEL OXFORD — Redecorated and Refitted throughout. Recently enlarged to 60 rooms. Centrally located. Depot cars stop at entrance. Long distance telephone office upstairs. American and European plan. Rates 50c, 75c and $1 per day; special rates by week or month. C. H. Branson & Sons, Proprietors. Phone 1887. 50-54 South Main St. **Asheville, N. C.**

Williams-Brownell Planing Mill Company — *Hardwoods*

Lumber---Rough and Dressed   Flooring a Specialty   Moulding, Interior Finish, Etc.
Office, Plant and Yards on Southern Railway, Near Biltmore Station
WHITE PINE   Phone 729   YELLOW PINE

Asheville Electrical Company
W. Mansfield Booze, Manager
74 CENTRAL AVE.
HEADQUARTERS
Phone 377

MENS FURNISHINGS   424   MUSICAL

Men's Furnishings

MOORE M V & CO, 11 Patton av
ZAGEIR R B, 8 s Main

Merchant Tailors

(See also Tailors)
ELIAS & HOPSON, 68 Patton av
WILBAR J C, 4 n Pack Sq (see bottom lines)

Metal Working Machinery

ENTERPRISE MACHINE CO 67-71 n Main (see p 14)

Mica Manufacturers

Asheville Mica Co, 26-28 Market

Milliners

BON MARCHE, 21-23 Patton av
Burns Millinery Store, 10 Church
Hood H B, 5 Haywood
Paris Millinery Shop, 78 Patton av
Sproat A D Mrs, 20 n Pack Sq
Webb M Co, Ashev Club Bldg

Mill Machinery—Supplies

CAROLINA MACHINERY CO Avery and Sou Ry

Mills

(Cotton, see Cotton Mills)
(Flour)
Asheville Milling Co, 530 w Haywood
Biltmore Roller Mills, Hickory Nut Gap rd
(Grist)
Weaverville Milling Co, W'ville
(Saw and Planing)
ENGLISH LUMBER CO, Avery opp Sou Ry frt Depot
JONES WM M, 557 w Haywood (see page 3)

MONTAGUE MNFG CO, Richmond Va (see 188 and 189)
WILLIAMS - BROWNELL PLANING MILL CO, Biltmore (see top lines)
WOODWARD & SON, Richmond Va (see opp 188 and 189)

Mineral Water Bottlers

HASKELL H S, 217 Haywood

Mirrors Resilvered

Hall E S, 57 n Main

Mission Furniture

GALER E E, 114 Patton av

Modistes

BERNECKER FRIEDA MISS, 60 n Spruce
HARVILLE C BELLE MRS, 172 Haywood (see p 24)

Monuments

BEAN S I & CO, 94 Patton av

Music Teachers

Asheville School of Musical Art, Auditorium Bldg
Atkins E F Miss, 136½ s Main
Cole Fulton, 51 n Main
DAY MARY FRANCES, 157 Church (see p 12)
Florio Caryl, 37 Patton av
Laxton K M Miss, 36 College Park
Logan A L Miss, W Asheville
*Martin Julia A, 74 Mountain
Oliphant Edna Miss, 35 Orange
Rinsland L E Miss, 34 Fulton
Spears E W, 9 Maxwelton Bldg
Wright Eula S Miss, 68 e College
Young Leoni Miss, 23 Adelaide Bldg

Musical Merchandise

DUNHAM'S MUSIC HOUSE, 14 n Pack Sq

Asheville Dry Cleaning Co.
Telephones 835-836, All Dep't
MAIN, N. E. COR. COLLEGE

THE CLEANERS
Our Department for Oriental Rugs and Carpet Cleaning is prepared to serve you in all its branches.
E. S. Paine   O. E. Hansen

Maple Flooring and Poplar Siding

English Lumber Co.
PHONE . . 321

MUSICAL 425 NOVELTIES

FALK'S MUSIC HOUSE, 21 s Main
Finkelstein H L, 23 s Main

☞ Needle Work

MOORE E J K MISS, 52 Patton av

Newsdealers

BARBEE S A, 14 Patton av (see back cover)
LITTLE SMOKE HOUSE, 41½ Patton av
Union News Co, 373 Depot

Newspapers and Periodicals

ASHEVILLE CITIZEN (The), (daily, Sunday and weekly), 8 Battery Park Pl
ASHEVILLE CITY DIRECTORY, 66 Amer Natl Bank Bldg
ASHEVILLE GAZETTE-NEWS (daily ex Sunday), 4 n Pack Sq
*Weekly News, Beaumont cor Valley

Notaries Public

Anderson J B, 203-205 Oates Bldg
Bledsoe J T, s Pack Sq and Main
BOSTICK V BUREN, 10 Battery Park Pl
Brown C E G, 15 Patton av
Brown P P, Amer Natl Bank
Buckner Neptune, 7 Temple Ct
Chedester H C, 412-415 Legal Bldg
Cocke P C, 212 Legal Bldg
Creasman M A, Oates Bldg
CURTIS Z F, 3-4 Library Bldg
Daniel W H, 3 Temple Court
DAVIS W B, Central Bank & Trust Co
GLENN J FRAZIER, 215 Legal Bldg
GUDGER V L, 1-3 Brown-Gudger Bldg
Gudger W R, 8 s Pack Sq
HALL S D, 32 Patton av
HANES S M, 34 Patton av
HARKINS T J, 9-11 Harkins Bldg
James W A Jr, 10½ n Pack Sq
Jones T A, 417-421 Legal Bldg
Lee C G, 11½ Patton av
Lyman A J, 3 Paragon Bldg
McCLOSKEY J J, 61-62 Amer Natl Bank Bldg
McDERMOTT W R, 48 Patton
Malone C N, 207 Oates Bldg
MARSTELLER WYATT, 20 Haywood
MESSLER F M, 26 Amer Natl Bank
MILLARD D RALPH, 16-17 New Sondley Bldg
MOALE P R, 27 Patton av
Morrison A T, s Pack Sq cor Main
Nitzer W A, 15 Revell Bldg
PARKER HAYWOOD, s Pack Sq cor Main
Penland J C, Temple Ct
RAY E L, Citizens Bank
Reynolds G S, 13½ Patton av
REYNOLDS R R, Court House (2d fl)
Roberts E G, 11-12 Library Bldg
Shuford W E, 24 Temple Ct
Sluder J W, 16 Patton av
Stevens R F, 351 Depot
Styles J S, 409-410 Oates Bldg
SWAIN J E, 400-402 Oates Bldg
SWEPSON P J, 29 Eagle
Thomason G A, 403-405 Oates Bldg
Way Eugene, 10½ n Pack Sq
Welch Gilmer, 7-9 Library Bldg
WILLIAMSON W B, 34 Patton
WOLFE J W, 10 n Pack Sq
Woods F T H, 14½ s Main
Wright G H, 308-314 Legal Bldg

Notions and Smallwares

BON MARCHE, 21 23 Patton av
Davis G W, 426 Depot
KRESS S H & CO, 24-26 Patton av
Mumpower R E, 17 s Main

☞ Novelties

ALLANSTAND COTTAGE INDUSTRIES, 33 Haywood

BIGGEST BUSIEST BEST

Asheville Steam Laundry

Phones:
1936 and 1937

---

43 to 47
W. College Street

CHARLES H. HONESS
OPTOMETRIST
AND
OPTICIAN

Exclusive maker of
ATLAS SHUR-ON EYE GLASSES

THE
Home of Ce-Rite
Toric Lenses

We make a specialty of correcting optical defects with properly fitted glasses.

54 Patton Avenue
Opposite Postoffice

in the market for a Gas Engine let us make you prices.
its heavy castings, such as columns or building plates, see us.
its a skilled mechanic for boiler work, see us.
you want machine work of any kind phone 590.

CAROLINA MACHINERY CO.

FOUNDERS MACHINISTS and Jobbers of Mill Supplies

Life Insurance Company of Virginia
ORGANIZED 1871
Home Office - Richmond, Va.

Has won the hearty approval and active support of the people by its promptness and fair dealing during the FORTY-TWO YEARS of its operation

J. V. Moon, Superintendent, Rooms 3-4-5 Maxwelton Bldg., Asheville, N. C.

NOVELTIES 426 NURSES

T. P. JOHNSON & CO.

SHEET METAL WORKERS

All Kinds of Roofing Guttering and Conductor Work Metal Ceilings, Skylights and Galvanized Iron Cornices

OFFICE and SHOP:
69-71 S. MAIN

Phone 325

DR. C. H. MILLER

Mechano-Therapist

14 N. Spruce Street
ASHEVILLE, N. C.

PHONE 979

Hours by Engagement

DRUGLESS HEALING OF DISEASE

MOORE E J K MISS, 52 Patton av

Nurses—Trained

Adams Georgia Miss, 36 Haywood
Aikens Marguerite Miss, Aiken Cottage
Bradfield Annie Miss, 5 Charlotte
Bright Annie Mrs, 176 Woodfin
Brown H E Mrs, Main st, W Ashev
*Burgess Jennie L, 13 Ridge
Cameron Mary Miss, 179 s French Broad av
Campbell Belle Miss, 63 Clayton
Carriker Susanna Miss, Highland Hospital
Case E A Miss, 6 Battery Park Pl
Clement B C Miss, 16 s French Broad av
Corland Beulah Miss, Biltmore Hospital
*Creasman Kate, 60 n Lexington av
Dobson Lula R Miss, 84 s French Broad av
Evans Hester Miss, 21 Jefferson Drive
Evers Mattie Miss, Winyah Sanatorium
Fisher Anna Miss, 287 Chestnut
Fisher Janet L Miss, 287 Chestnut
Fitzpatrick M L Miss, 28 Orange
Foister Mabel Miss, 23 Park av
Ford Laura Miss, 84 s French Broad av
Foster M A Mrs, 29 Clingman av
Gaines Emma Miss, Highland Hosp
Galloway L E Miss, 31 Gaston
Gibbs Minnie Miss, 71 Central av
Grove Mary Miss, Biltmore Hosp
Hern N B Miss, 135 Asheland av
Hirst Lillie Miss, 109 Biltmore rd, S Biltmore
Hughes A J Miss, Brevard rd, W Asheville
Hunt M E Miss, 36 College Park
Ingram Currie Miss, Highland Hosp
Ingram E G Miss, Highland Hosp
*JACKSON DAISY M, 39½ s Main (see adv)
Jarrett Lela Miss, 408 w Haywood
Kendrick Edith Miss, 84 s French Broad av
Kinsland Daisy Miss, 18 Vance
Kirk Ester Miss, Highland Hosp
Laxton M P Miss, 36 College Park
Lingerfeldt Mae Miss, Biltmore Hosp
Lewis Amy K Miss, 35 McAfee Bldg
Lindsay Roberta Miss, 18 Vance
Lively Verdie Miss, Highland Hosp
Lord Athalia Miss, 63 Clayton
Lynn E M Mrs, 109 Cherry
McDivitt A C Miss, 27 Washington rd
McLoud J I Mrs, Highland Hospital
McMenamin Patrick, 71 Central av
Mackey Lennie Miss, Highland Hosp
*Magee Anna, 215 Clingman av
*Magee Lois, 215 Clingman av
Mangum Orrie M Miss, 48 n Spruce
Moore A L Miss, Biltmore Hosp
Norton Louie Miss, Highland Hosp
Owen Euphia Miss, 18 Vance
Perkinson B M Miss, 87 Woodfin
Piper J M Miss, 15 Woodfin
Price Hattie Miss, 2 Lyman
Pritchard Mrs, 14 Grove
Pulliam Amelia Miss, 264 Haywood
Purcell Bertha Miss, Winyah Sanatorium
Rawls Annie B Miss, 57 Cherry
Ray Lorena C Miss, 141 Hillside
Redwine E M Miss, Biltmore Hosp

ASHEVILLE CLEANING and PRESSING CLUB

TAILORING THAT SATISFIES and PRICES THAT PLEASE

Hats cleaned, banded and bound. Silk hats ironed. Buttons made to order in all sizes. Plain or with rims. PHONE 389

DYEING IN ALL SHADES Cleaned. Messenger Service.

Kid Gloves, Slippers and Plumes. Fancy Jabots and Ties. French Dry Cleaned. Ladies' and Gentlemen's suits Steam

J. C. Wilbar, Prop. 4 NORTH PACK SQ.

ASHEVILLE COAL CO. — 6 North Pack Sq. — Phone 40

M. & W. COAL

| NURSES | 427 | OSTEOPATHS |

Reese B H Miss, 134½ s Main
Revis Elberta Miss, Highland Hosp
Russell E F Miss, 37 Chestnut
Schofield Mary Mrs, 47 Central av
Shope Lena K Miss, 37 Chestnut
Smith Jacob, Highland Hosp
Smith Nellie E Miss, 44 Atkin
Snowden Jocelyn Miss, 71 Central av
Starnes Gonano Miss, 18 Grady
Stewart Mary A Miss, 71 Central av
Stines Maggie D Miss, 63 Asheland av
Stockton May Miss, Winyah Sanatorium
*Strachen Maude, 17 Hill
Sullivan M E Miss, 36 Haywood
Sumner Lula Miss, Highland Hosp
*Thomas Margaret, h 37 Magnolia av
Toomer L G Miss, 63 Clayton
*Tucker Zela, 58 Poplar
Walden Laura Miss, Winyah Sanatorium
Walker C M Miss, 37 Chestnut
Wallace Georgia Miss, Biltmore Hosp
Willis F M Miss, 14 Blake
Wilson B R Miss, Highland Hosp
Wilson Ida Miss, Highland Hosp
Wilson S Austin Miss, Highland Hosp
Wilson W L Miss, Highland Hosp

Oculists

Tennent G S Dr, 10-24 Electrical Bldg

Office Buildings

Adelaide Bldg, 33-35 Haywood
Ambler Bldg, 72 n Main
AMER NATL BANK BLDG, 44 Patton av
Ashev Club Bldg, 24 Battery Park Pl
Barnard Bldg, 1 Patton av
Brown Bldg, 10½ n Pack Sq
Brown-Gudger Bldg, 33 Patton
Carrier Bldg, College n e cor Market
CITIZENS BLDG, 8-14 Battery Park Pl
Coxe Bldg, 4-6 Battery Park Pl
Drhumor Bldg, 48-50 Patton av
Electrical Bldg, 64 Patton av
Fountain Bldg, 16½ n Pack Sq
Halthenon Bldg, 29-31 Haywood
Harkins Bldg, 26 Patton av
Johnston Bldg, 1½ s Main
LEGAL BLDG, 10 s Pack Sq
LIBRARY BLDG, 4 s Pack Sq
Maxwelton Bldg, 40 Patton av
McAfee Bldg, 47-49 College
McIntyre Bldg, 1-3 n e Pack Sq
Medical Bldg, Battery Park Pl
Meriwether Bldg, 19-23 Haywood
Morsell Bldg, Patton av
New Sondley Bldg, 15 Haywood
OATES BLDG, 20-22 n Pack Sq
Paragon Bldg, 55 Patton av
Revell Bldg, 3½ n w Pack Sq
Technical Bldg, 18-22 e College
Temple Court, 47-53 Patton av
Wolfe Bldg, 22 s Pack Sq
*Y M I Bldg, Market cor Eagle

Office Supplies

UNDERWOOD TYPEWRITER CO, 9 Temple Ct

Oil

North Carolina Oil Co, Lyman cor Riverside
Standard Oil Co, 171 Avery

Opticians

ALEXANDER L I, 78 Patton av
Gardner F D, 43 s Main
Highsmith Z F, 9 Grady
HONESS C H, 54 Patton av (see side lines)

Osteopaths

Meacham & Rockwell, 501-507 Legal Bldg

Asheville Power and Light Co. — Gas Ranges — PHONE 69

Meats — Kiibler & Whitehead — CITY MARKET — PHONES, 195 and 694

WEAVERVILLE LINE — NINE MILES BY TROLLEY FROM PACK SQUARE TO WEAVERVILLE

ASHEVILLE AND EAST TENNESSEE RAILROAD CO.
7 NORTH MAIN STREET — ASHEVILLE N. C.

OPTOMETRISTS — PHYSICIANS

Optometrists

ALEXANDER L I, 78 Patton av

> We can fit you with a pair of glasses that will give you satisfaction
>
> We do Optical Repair Work, and can Duplicate your Broken Lenses without the Prescription
>
> **ALEXANDER,**
> Optometrist and Optician
>
> 78 PATTON AVENUE
> Next to Palace Theatre

HONESS C H, 54 Patton av (see side lines)

Paint Manufacturers

ASHEVILLE PAINT & GLASS CO, 4-6 n Main

Painters—House and Sign

ASHEVILLE SIGN CO, (signs), 25-27 n Lexington av (see adv)
BRADFORD J M, 25-27 n Lexington av (carraige) (see p 21)
Brown Alex, 32 McDowell
Brown G H, 7 Park Pl
*Dalrymple Larkin (r) 14 n Spruce
Fitzpatrick R L & Son, 20 n Main
Huff J H & Son, 7 Aston
King M E, 111 Broad
Miller F B, 56 Hiawassee
Swink & Co, 9 Aston

Painters Supplies

BOWLES R E, e Pack Sq

Paints, Oils and Glass

ASHEVILLE PAINT & GLASS CO, 4-6 n Main (see back cover)
BOWLES R E, 1 e Pack Sq (see p 5)
Excelsior Paint & Paper House, 34 n Main
Fitzpatrick R L & Son, 53 n Main
Perkinson T J, 9 College

Paper and Twine

Brux H B, 57 s Main

Paperhangers

Fitzpatrick R L & Son, 53 n Main
Ingram L F, 165 s Main
Parker G B, 3-4 Barnard Bldg

Pawnbrokers

Crescent Jewelry Co, 16 Patton av
FINKELSTEIN'S PAWN SHOP, 23-25 s Main (see back cover)

Photographers

Brock N, Morsell Bldg (3d fl)
Higgason Studio, 18 n Pack Sq (2d fl)
Koonce H C, Morsell Bldg
McCanless J M, 32 Patton av (3d fl)
McGarry Jos, 1½ n e Pack Sq
Pelton H W, 527-528 Legal Bldg
Ray's Studio, 2 n Pack Sq
Union Art Studio, 16½ n Pack Sq

Physicians (Regular) Licensed by N C State Board of Medical Examiners

AMBLER C P, 72 n Main

ELECTRIC FIXTURES
Piedmont Electric Co.
64 PATTON AVE.
ASHEVILLE, N.C.

CONTRACTOR and BUILDER
— STEEL RANGES —
J. C. McPHERSON
35-37 E COLLEGE ST.
PHONE 133
PLUMBING STEAM AND HOT WATER **HEATING**

MAPLE FLOORING
HARDWOOD LUMBER OF ALL KINDS

WOODWARD & SON
9th and Arch Sts., Richmond, Va.
See Adv. Opposite Page 188

PHYSICIANS   429   PIANOS

ANDERSON JAS G, 14-15 Morsell Bldg
Battle S W, Halthenon Bldg
Briggs H H, 73 Haywood
BROWNSON W C, 1-2 Medical Bldg
*Bryant R H, 18 Eagle
BUCKNER R G (eye, ear, nose and throat), 7-8 Medical Bldg
CALLOWAY A W, 16 Medical Bldg
Carroll J L, 11 Church
CARROLL R S, Highland Hospital
Cheesborough T P, 107-108 Citizen Bldg
Clemenger F J, Halthenon Bldg
Cocke C H, 216 Pearson Drive
COLBY C D W, 18 Battery Park Pl
DUNN WM L, Medical Bldg
Eckel O F, 17 Church
ELIAS L W, 19-20 Morsell Bldg
Fletcher M H, 17 Church
Frazer Thompson, 6-7 Citizen Bldg
GARDNER G D, 266½ Patton
GLENN E B, 1-2-3 New Sondley Bldg
GREENE J B (ear, nose and throat), 20 Battery Park pl
Griffith F W, 20 Battery Park pl
Herbert Wm P, 16 Battery Park pl
HUNNICUTT W J, 19-20 Morsell Bldg
HUSTON J W, 2 Medical Bldg
Jordan C S, 20 Battery Park pl
LYNCH JAS M, 6-8 Drhumor Bldg
McBRAYER L B, 2 n Pack Sq (2d fl)
MERIWETHER F T, 24 Grove
Merrimon L A Miss, 73 Haywood
MILLENDER M C, 9-11 Drhumor Bldg
Miller O O, 5 Medical Bldg
Minor C L, 24 Battery Park pl
Morris E C, 72 n Main
Morris E R, 32 Patton av
ORR P B, 3 Drhumor Bldg
PAQUIN PAUL, 217 Legal Bldg
PRITCHARD A T, 9-11 Drhumor Bldg
PUREFOY & POWELL, 325 Legal Bldg
REEVES A F, 9 s w Pack Sq
Reynolds & Cocke, 11 Church
Ringer P H, 1-3 Citizen Bldg
Russell E R, 303-307 Legal Bldg
Sevier D E & J T, 6½ s Main
SMITH OWEN, 78 Patton av
STEVENS & ORR, 1 to 6 Adelaide Bldg
Terry P R, 221 Legal Bldg
*Tinsley T C, 22 Eagle
*Torrence W G, Y M I Bldg
von RUCK KARL, Winyah Sanatorium
von RUCK SILVIO, Winyah Sanatorium
von Tobel A E, Winyah Sanatorium
*Walker J W, Y M I Bldg
Weaver H B, 405-407 Legal Bldg
Whittington W P, 2 n Pack Sq
WILLIAMS JNO HEY, 20 Battery Park pl
Zimmerman C St V, 15-16 New Sondley Bldg

Physicians

Ballard A M, 208 Haywood
BIGGS A C, 104 Woodfin
Costello M J, 74 e College
GRUNER E P (Natureopathic) 29-31 Haywood
Meacham & Rockwell, 501-507 Legal Bldg
MILLER C H, 14 n Spruce (see side cards and p 21)
WHITMORE S L, 408 w Haywood (see p 11)
Wilder Eugene, 11 Montford av

Physicians—Mecano-Therapy

MILLER C H, 14 n Spruce (see side cards and p 21)

Pianos and Organs
(Dealers)

DUNHAM'S MUSIC HOUSE, 14 n Pack Sq
FALK'S MUSIC HOUSE, 21 s Main

What Have You in Real Estate that You Don't Want?

What do You Want in Real Estate that You Haven't?

WESTERN CAROLINA REALTY CO.

J. W. Wolfe Sec. & Treas.

On the Square
PHONE 974
10 N. PACK SQ.

Brown-Carter Realty Co.
REAL ESTATE
23 TEMPLE COURT
PHONE 341
ASHEVILLE   N. C.

FLORIDA SPECIALTIES

Grazing, Timbered, Farm Lands, Orange Groves, Turpentine Locations and Phosphate Lands.

NORTH CAROLINA SPECIALTIES

Orchard Farm and Timbered Lands, City Property, Rent Collections.

Moale & Chiles Real Estate and Insurance
27 Patton Ave., (2d fl)   Phone 661
General Agents United States Fidelity & Guaranty Co.

Club Cafe and Candy Kitchen
"A GOOD PLACE FOR REFRESHMENT"

Our Ice Cream manufacturing plant is absolutely clean and sanitary.
Prompt family delivery. Phones 110 and 111.
Catering for large parties and receptions. Special Creams.

PIANOS 430 PRODUCE

Brown's Undertaking Parlors
S. H. BROWN
Lady Assistant When Desired
Phone 193-2 Rings
50 Patton Avenue Asheville, N. C.

Established 1894
B. J. JACKSON
Carefully Selected Fruits and Vegetables
Stall No. 11, City Market
BUSINESS PHONES: 86 and 101
RESIDENCE PHONE 1596

(Repairers)
Davis J W, 118 Patton av

Planing Mills
ENGLISH LUMBER CO, Avery and Sou Ry
JONES WM M, 557 w Haywood
WILLIAMS, BROWNELL PLANING MILL CO, Sou Ry nr Biltmore
WOODWARD & SON, Richmond Va

Plasterers
(See Contrs—Plasterers)

Plumbers, Steam and Gas Fitters
Felthaus Anton, 36 Clayton
Guischard G L, 22 s Pack Sq
McPHERSON J C, 35 College (see bottom lines)
MOORE PLUMBING CO (The), 15 College (see side lines)
Rhinehardt Bros, 91 Patton av
RICH J R CO (Inc), 21 n Main
STEVENS S M, 95 Cumberland (see adv)
UNION PLUMBING CO, 23 n Main

Plumbing Supplies
Haines, Jones & Cadbury Co, 1 Technical Bldg
McPHERSON J C, 35 College
RICH J R CO (Inc), 21 n Main
MOORE PLUMBING CO (The), 15 College

Post Cards
BARBEE S A, 14 Patton av
MOORE E J K MISS, 52 Patton av

Poultry
KIIBLER & WHITEHEAD, City Mkt (see bottom lines)

Poultry Farms
Brown Paul, Chunn's Cove
Pelham C P, W Asheville
Renfro D C, Riverside Drive nr Casket Co
Williams W J, W Asheville

Power Companies
(See Light and Power Co's)

Pressing Clubs
(See also Cleaning and Pressing)
ASHEVILLE CLEANING & PRESSING CLUB, 4 n Pack Sq (see bottom lines)
ASHEVILLE DRY CLEANING CO, Main n e cor College (see left bottom lines)
*Depot Pressing Club, 424 Depot
*Eagle Street Pressing Club, 28 Eagle
Ideal Pressing Club, 5½ s w Pack Sq
RELIABLE CLEANING & PRESSING CO (The), 14 Church (see insert)
*SARTOR J R, 39 s Main
*West End Pressing Club, 342 w Haywood

Printers—Book and Job
Asheville Ptg & Engraving Co, 15 Church
HACKNEY & MOALE CO, 10-12 s Lexington av
Inland Press (The), 78 Patton av
Rogers H T, 39 Patton av
WHITESIDE PRINTING CO, 22 s Pack Sq (see insert)

Produce
Barnes W E & Co, 34 n Lexington av
Lowe P W & Son, 16 e College
McConnell Bros, 38 n Main
Ownbey R L & Co, 36 n Lexington av
Smathers Wholesale Produce Co, 184 Clingman av

Furniture and China Carefully Prepared for Shipment

Mahogany Furniture Hand Made & Carefully Reproduced — **E. E. GALER** 114 PATTON AVE. — Upholstering and Refinishing PHONE - 1674

ROUGH AND DRESSED LUMBER
WHITE PINE AND YELLOW PINE
FLOORING A SPECIALTY
Hardwoods

Williams-Brownell Planing Mill Company
Mouldings and Interior Finish
Office: Southern Railway Tracks, Near Biltmore Station
Phone 729   *Planing Mill*

PRODUCE   431   REAL ESTATE

TRAKAS N S & CO, 31 s Main (see p 5)
Young S K, 59 n Lexington av

Promoters

Shemwell Baxter, 35 Amer Natl Bank Bldg

Provisions

Armour & Co, 375 Depot
BAIRD T G, 152 Montford av
ZIMMERMAN & SON, 428 Depot

Publishers

Walker A E, 16 Paragon Bldg
CITIZEN CO (The), 8 Battery Park pl
EVENING NEWS PUB CO, 4 n Pack Sq
KNOXVILLE DIRECTORY CO, 66 Amer Natl Bank Bldg
MILLER E H, 66 Amer Natl Bank Bldg
PIEDMONT DIRECTORY CO, 66 Amer Natl Bank Bldg

Quarries

Balfour Quarry Co, 7-8 Electrical Bldg
French Broad Quarry Building & Material Co, Riverside Drive

Railroads

ASHEVILLE & EAST TENN R R, 7 n Main (see front cover)
Pigeon River Railway Co, 200-202 Oates Bldg
Southern Railway Ticket Office, 60 Patton av, Passngr Sta and offices Depot nr S'side av
Tenn & N C R R Co, 200-202 Oates Bldg

Railway Supplies

INTERSTATE RAILWAY SWITCH & FROG CO, 35-36 Amer Natl Bank Bldg

Real Estate

ASTON, RAWLS & CO, 22-23 Amer Natl Bank Bldg
Atkinson Natt Sons Co, 5 w Pack Sq
BAIRD-WILFORD REALTY CO, 206 Oates Bldg (see p 24)
Batterham Harry, Library Bldg (basement)
Birmingham Realty Co (Inc), 27 Patton av
BROWN-CARTER REALTY CO, 23 Temple Ct (see side lines)
Campbell J M, 212 Legal Bldg
*Cannon & Oglesby, 44 Market
Donnahoe & Bledsoe, s Pack Sq cor Main
Edwards Gwyn, 11 Temple Ct
Forbes & Campbell, 2 Drhumor Bldg
Garrett R U, 9 Electrical Bldg
GRANT H F REALTY CO, 48 Patton av
GREENE & GOODMAN, 1½ s Main
HALL S D, 32 Patton av (see side lines)
Ingle F P, 9 Revell Bldg
INTERSTATE DEVELOPMENT CO, 35-36 Amer Natl Bank Bldg
Johnston Wm Jr, 20 Temple Ct
Lyman A J, 3 Paragon Bldg
Lynch S A, 11 n w Pack Sq (2d fl)
McCLOSKEY J J REALTY CO, 61-62 Amer Natl Bank Bldg
MARSTELLER & CO, 20 Haywood
MESSLER F M, 26 Amer Natl Bank Bldg (see back cover)
MOALE & CHILES, 27 Patton av (2d fl) (see bottom lines)
Nitzer W A, 15 Revell Bldg
PENLAND J D & SON, 11 Temple Ct
Powell G S, 2 Electrical Bldg
Ray-Campbell Co, 1 Haywood
Revell O D, 15 Revell Bldg
Southern Land Auction Co, 225 Legal Bldg
*SWEPSON P J, 29 Eagle

HUGHES
Transfer and Livery Co.

Automobiles for HIRE

TRUNKS 25c

Office:
401 Southside Avenue
PHONE   1405

Try our Hand Laundering. We strive to please in LAUNDERING and DRY CLEANING.

The Sanitary Home Laundry
No. 7 MONTFORD AVE.
PHONE - 1354

Mrs. Wilder's SANITARY HOME LAUNDRY turns out first class work in Laundering and Dry Cleaning. No. 7 Montford Ave., Phone 1354

REAL ESTATE 432 SAW MILLS

Varnon Realty Co, 45 Amer Natl Bank Bldg
Villa Heights Co, 52 Amer Natl Bank Bldg
Walton F A, 21 s Main
Warren B W, 39 n Main
Watson D S & Co, Library Bldg (basement)
WESTERN CAROLINA REALTY CO, 10 n Pack Sq (see side lines)
Woodcock & Gillis, 21 Amer Natl Bank Bldg
Woods F T H, 14½ s Main

Rental Agents

ALBEMARLE PARK CO, Charlotte nr city limits
BROWN-CARTER REALTY CO, 23 Temple Ct
GREENE & GOODMAN, 1½ s Main
HALL S D, 10 n Pack Sq
Marsteller & Co, 20 Haywood
MESSLER F M, 26 Amer Natl Bank Bldg
MOALE & CHILES, 27 Patton av
WESTERN CAROLINA REALTY CO, 10 n Pack Sq

Restaurants

(See also Eating Houses)
American Dairy Lunch Restaurant, 1½ s w Pack Sq
Baltimore Cafe, 412 Depot
Central Cafe, 5 s w Pack Sq
CLUB CAFE & CANDY KITCHEN, 19-21 Haywood (see top lines)
*Crescent Lunch Room, 16 Eagle
Crystal Cafeterian, 8 n Pack Sq
Crystal Dairy Lunch, 56 Patton av
Gem Lunch Room, 388 Depot
Gladstone Hotel Cafe, 407 Depot
New York Quick Lunch Restaurant, 11 s Main
ROCKETT O N, 29 n Main
Southern Railway Dining Room, Sou Ry Passngr Station
Union Dairy Lunch, 314 Depot

United States Cafe, 7 n Main
Warren H M, 386 Depot
Windsor Cafe, 48-50 s Main
Woman's Exchange Tea Room, 36 Haywood
Young Women's Christian Assn, 11½ Church
Yuneda Dairy Lunch, 32 Patton av

Roofers—Slate and Metal

JOHNSON T P & CO, 69 s Main
TREXLER DAVID, 159 s Main

Roofing Material

ASHEVILLE PAINT & GLASS CO, 4-6 n Main
BOWLES R E, e Pack Sq

Roots and Herbs

McGuire & Co, 117 n Lexington av

Safe Deposit Boxes

AMERICAN NATL BANK, Patton av cor Church
BATTERY PARK BANK, 13-15 Patton av
CENTRAL BANK & TRUST CO, s Pack Sq
CITIZENS BANK, Patton av cor Haywood
WACHOVIA BANK & TRUST CO, 34 Patton av

Sash, Doors and Blinds

ENGLISH LUMBER CO, Avery and Sou Ry
JONES W M, 557 w Haywood (see p 3)
MONTAGUE MNFG CO, Richmond Va
WOODWARD & SON, Richmond Va

Saw Mills

(See Mills, Saw and Planing)

BUICK — OLDSMOBILE

ARBOGAST MOTOR COMPANY

ACCESSORIES AND SUPPLIES
Phones 302 and 1728
52-60 N. Main

MAXWELLS — DETROIT ELECTRIC

Asheville Dry Cleaning Co.
Telephones 835-836, All Dep't
MAIN, N. E. COR. COLLEGE

THE CLEANERS
Our Department for Oriental Rugs and Carpet Cleaning is prepared to serve you in all its branches.
E. S. Paine   O. E. Hansen

For Kindling "What am Kindling" Call
ENGLISH LUMBER COMPANY Phone 321

SANITARIUMS   433   SEWER PIPE

Sanitariums

(See also Hospitals)
BIGGS SANITARIUM, 104 Woodfin
GRUNER SANITARIUM (The), 29-31 Haywood

The Gruner Sanitarium
PHONE 684
29-31 Haywood St., Asheville, N. C.
Hydro-Thermo-Electro and Mechano-Therapy-Dietics

Devoted to the thorough and scientific treatment for selected cases of Nervousness, Paralysis, Hayfever, Malaria, Asthma, Habit, Stomach, Rheumatism, Diseases of Women, and other chronic Diseases.

THE BATHS AND MASSAGE
Department of the Sanitarium is open to the public. Skillful attendants for both LADIES and GENTLEMEN will administer Turkish Russian, Cabinet, Betz Hot-Air, Electric Light, Tub, Sitz, Foot, Shower and Needle Baths, Galvanic and Farradic Treatments. Electric Vibrating, Swedish Massage and Movements. Thure Brandt Massage for diseases of women. Douche, Lavage.

OPEN DAY AND NIGHT
THE GRUNER SANITARIUM
29-31 Haywood St., Asheville, N. C.

MERIWETHER HOSPITAL, 24 Grove (see p 6)
MILDRED E SHERWOOD HOME, 179 s French Broad av (see p 4)
Ottare Sanitarium, Grace
St Joseph's Sanitarium, 428 s Main
WHITMORE SANITARIUM, 408 w Haywood (see p 11)
WINYAH SANATORIUM (The), East cor Spears av

Scales

Independent Scale Co, 21 Electrical Bldg
Moody H M Sales Co, 68 Patton av

Schools and Colleges

ALLEN INDUSTRIAL HOME AND ASHEVILLE ACADEMY, 241 College (see p 23)
ASHEVILLE ACADEMY, 241 College
ASHEVILLE BUSINESS COLLEGE, n Pack Sq
Asheville School (The), Haywood rd
Asheville School for Girls, 2 Woodfin
Asheville School of Music, Auditorium Bldg
BINGHAM SCHOOL (The), Bingham Heights (see p 2)
Carolina Commercial School, 301 Legal Bldg
EMANUEL SCHOOL OF STENOGRAPHY AND TYPEWRITING, 16 Drhumor Bldg (see card at name)
HOME INDUSTRIAL SCHOOL, Biltmore rd, Victoria
Matney W W, Cherry cor Flint
NORMAL & COLLEGIATE INSTITUTE, s Main cor Victoria rd (see inside back cover)
NORTH STATE FITTING SCHOOL, 157 Church (see p 12)
Patton School for Boys, 271 Haywood
PEASE MEMORIAL HOUSE, Biltmore rd, Victoria
ST GENEVIEVE COLLEGE, Victoria rd (see insert)
Stevens Misses (The) 15 Pearden
WEAVERVILLE COLLEGE, Weaverville N C
Winn School for Boys (The), 135 Merrimon av
ENTERPRISE MACHINE CO 67-71 n Main

☞ Second Hand Books

YE OLD BOOK STORE, 114 Patton av

Sewer Pipe Mnfrs

Asheville Concrete Pipe & Block Co, 6½ s Main

BIGGEST **B**USIEST **B**EST

ASHEVILLE STEAM LAUNDRY
Phones 1936 and 1937
43 to 47 W. COLLEGE

S. D. HALL
REAL ESTATE AGENT
—
Money Loaned
—
Notary Public
—
32 PATTON AVENUE
Phone 91

Founders, Machinists and Jobbers of Mill Supplies

PHONE 590
When in the market for pipe and fittings, let us make you Prices.

Carolina Machinery Co.

PHONE 590
If it's a Gas Engine let us figure with you, also on other kinds of machinery

LIFE INSURANCE COMPANY OF VA. OLDEST, LARGEST STRONGEST Southern Life Insurance Co.

ORGANIZED 1871
RICHMOND, VIRGINIA

Issues Industrial Policies from $8.00 to $900.00, with Premiums Payable WEEKLY on persons from two to seventy years of age

J. V. Moon, Superintendent, Rooms 3-4-5 Maxwelton Bldg., Asheville, N. C.

SEWING MCHNS 434 STABLES

D. TREXLER TIN SHOP

All Kinds of Roofing, Gutter and Conductor Work.

Phone 862

159 South Main St.

DR. C. H. MILLER

MECHANO-THERAPIST

14 N. Spruce St.
Phone 979
ASHEVILLE, N. C.

Hours by engagement

Drugless Healing of Disease

Sewing Machines

Singer Sewing Machine Co, 18 n Pack Sq

☞ Sheet Iron Metal Workers

JOHNSON T P & CO, 69 s Main (see side lines)
McLean A L & Co, 95-97 Patton av

☞ Sheet Music

KRESS S H & CO, 24-26 Patton av

☞ Shingle Stains

BOWLES R E, 1 e Pack Sq

Shirt Manufacturers

ELIAS & HOPSON, 68 Patton av

Shoe Stores

Boston Shoe Store, 30 Patton av
BROWN-MILLER SHOE CO, 47 Patton av
Globe Sample Co, 32 s Main
Guarantee Shoe Store, 4 s Main
NICHOLS SHOE CO (Inc), 2 n Pack Sq
*Piedmont Shoe Co, 26 Eagle

Shoemakers and Repairers

Bowden T G, 26 e College
*Brown J B, 60 Sycamore
Champion Shoe Hospital, 42 s Main
CHAMPION SHOE REPAIR SHOP, 30 w College (see p 22)
Henninger Jos C, 100 Patton av
*Hill C D, 8 Eagle
Hollingsworth S O, 303 s Main
Hoskovitz B H, 2 Eagle
Hyndman T L, 47 Patton av
*Justice J C, 155½ Patton av
King R P, 506 w Haywood
Landreth A P, 370 Southside av
*McDowell Elijah, (r) 14 n Spruce

*Miller L M, 29 Circle
*Miller Lawson, 39 Mountain
Patty J H, 14 e College
Peterson Wm R, 39 College
Presley J M, 19-20 Paragon Bldg
Roberts P N, 343 w Haywood
Robertson A H, 439 s Main
*Stanback Jas, 178 Livingston
Tilson J H, 309 w Haywood
Turner G B, 160 Southside av
*Vernon Elias, 11 Eagle
VINIARSKI B A, 30 w College (see p 22)
*Weston Jos, 39 s Main

Sign Painters

(See also Painters)
ASHEVILLE SIGN CO, 25-27 n Lexington av
Bard C J, 23 Arlington
Sellers J H, 7 Aston

☞ Soda and Mineral Waters

(Dealers)
CLUB CAFE & CANDY KITCHEN, 19-21 Haywood

(Manufacturers)
HASKELL'S PEPSI-COLA BOTTLING WORKS, (r) 217 Haywood

☞ Souvenirs

KRESS S H & CO, 24-26 Patton av
MOORE E J K MISS, 52 Patton av

☞ Specialists

GREENE J B, (eye, ear, nose and throat), Medical Bldg

Sporting Goods

Blomberg Louis, 15 Patton av
Crescent Jewelry Co, 16 Patton av
FINKELSTEIN H L, 23-25 s Main

Stables

(Livery, Feed, Hitch and Sale)

....Asheville Cleaning and Pressing Club....
Tailoring That Satisfies and Prices That Please
Steam and French Dry Cleaning of all delicate and fine wearing apparel for ladies and gentlemen. MESSENGER SERVICE IN THE CITY.

J. C. WILBAR, Prop. 4. N. Pack Square **PHONE 389**

CAROLINA "M & W" INDIAN — Prompt Delivery
COAL & ICE CO.
PHONE 130
50 PATTON AVE.
WEIGHTS ACCURATE

STABLES 435 TAILORS

Britt W E & Co, 32 w College
Chambers J K, 39-41 n Lexington av
CHAMBERS & WEAVER, Aston (Willow), s e cor Lexington av
Coffey I R, 28-30 College
Creasman J H, 9 Walnut
Millard Livery Co (The), 33-35 n Main
Patton & Stikeleather, 151-155 av
Ray W S, 39 s Lexington av
Robinson S D, 61 n Lexington av
Warren B W, 5 e Walnut
WEBB W A, 9 s Lexington av
WILSON E F, 58-60 s Main (see p 24)
Wilson J H, 82 n Lexington av

Steam Laundries

ASHEVILLE STEAM LAUNDRY, 34 w College (see side lines)
MOUNTAIN CITY LAUNDRY (Inc), 30 n Lexington av (see front and back covers)
SANITARY HOME LAUNDRY, 7 Montford av (see top and bottom lines)
SWANNANOA LAUNDRY, 22-24 Church (see back cover)

Steam and Hot Water Heating

McPHERSON J C, 35-37 College
STEVENS S M, 95 Cumberland av

Stenographers—Public

Bayless Rebecca Miss, 301 Legal Bldg
Daniel W H, 3 Temple Ct
Devenish A G Miss, 8 Paragon Bldg
EMANUEL SADIE MISS, 16 Drhumor Bldg
Goode Frances A Miss, 35 Amer Natl Bank Bldg
Holman Pearl L Miss, 301 Legal Bldg
Praytor Laura Miss, 225 Legal Bldg

Storage

ASHEVILLE DRAY, FUEL & CONSTRUCTION CO, 6½ s Main
Asheville Transfer & Storage Co, Main cor Atkin

☞ Stoves and Ranges
(See also Hardware)

☞ Surgeons

Street Railways

ASHEVILLE POWER & LIGHT CO, Patton av s e cor Asheland av
ASHEVILLE & EAST TENN R R CO, 7 n Main
GARDNER G D, 266½ Patton av
MERIWETHER F T, 24 Grove
REEVES A F, 9 s w Pack Sq

Surveyors
(See Engineers, Civil)

Tailors

American Tailors, 25 Patton av
British Woolen Mills, 28 s Main
Burrows H S, 1-2 Paragon Bldg
*****COLLEGE STREET DYE WORKS AND MERCHANT TAILORS**, 35½ e College (see adv)
ELIAS & HOPSON, 68 Patton av
Foller J J, 32 Patton av
Logan S T, 12 s Pack Sq
Petrie H P, 8 n Pack Sq
RELIABLE CLEANING & PRESSING CO, 14 Church (see insert)
*****SARTOR J R**, 39 s Main
Sugarman Jacob, 4 n Lexington av
WILBAR J C, 4 n Pack Sq (see bottom lines)

St. Rw'y — Electric Light and Power — Gas
ASHEVILLE POWER AND LIGHT COMPANY — PHONE 69

Poultry — **Kiibler & Whitehead**
CITY MARKET PHONES, 195 and 684

Asheville Dray, Fuel and Construction Co.

Heavy Hauling of all kinds — WE FURNISH BUILDING STONE — Moving Furniture a Specialty

61-2 South Main   PHONE - 223

TALC MINERS   **436**   TYPEWRITERS

Talc Miners

GEORGIA TALC CO (Inc), 215 Legal Bldg

Tanners

REES HANS SONS (Inc), Sou Ry nr Passngr Sta

Tea and Coffee

Great Atlantic & Pacific Tea Co, 36 Oak

Telephone and Telegraph Co's

ASHEVILLE TEL & TEL CO, 32 w Walnut
POSTAL TELEGRAPH-CABLE CO, 1 Haywood
Tri-County Public Service Co, 7 n Main
Weaverville Electric Co, 7 n Main
WESTERN UNION TELEGRAPH CO, 62 Patton av

Theatres and Places of Amusement

Asheville Auditorium (The), Haywood at junc of Flint
Dreamland (The), 81 Patton av
Palace Theatre, 76 Patton av
Princess Air Dome, 86 Patton av
Princess Theatre, 9 n w Pack Sq
Riverside Park, Riverside Park

☞ Timber Lands

BROWN-CARTER REALTY CO, 23 Temple Ct
CHAPMAN S F, 3-5 Technical Bldg
Hall S D, 32 Patton av (2d fl)
MOALE & CHILES, 27 Patton av (2d fl)
WESTERN CAROLINA REALTY CO, 10 n Pack Sq

Tinners

JOHNSON T P & CO, 69 s Main (see side lines)

McLean A L & Co, 95-97 Patton av
McPHERSON J C, 35-37 e College
TREXLER DAVID, 159 s Main (see side lines)

☞ Tinware

RICH J R & CO, 21 n Main

Tire Repairers

Asheville Steam Vulcanizing Co, 7 College

Title Examiners

Carolina Abstract & Title Co, Legal Bldg

☞ Trade Lists

PIEDMONT DIRECTORY CO, 66 Amer Natl Bank Bldg

Tobacco Manufacturers

Asheville Tobacco Co, 35 w Walnut

☞ Trunks, Bags and Valises

BROWN-MILLER SHOE CO, 47 Patton av
FINKELSTEIN H L, 23-25 s Main

Trust Companies

CENTRAL BANK & TRUST CO, Legal Bldg, s Pack Sq (see front cover)
WACHOVIA BANK & TRUST CO, 34 Patton av (see stencils)

Typewriters

UNDERWOOD TYPEWRITER CO, 9 Temple Ct

DYNAMOS & MOTORS

Piedmont Electric Co.

64 Patton Av.
ASHEVILLE, N.C.

J. C. McPHERSON
SLATE AND TIN ROOFING
Galvanized Iron Work   Hot Air Furnaces
35-37 EAST COLLEGE STREET

PLUMBING STEAM AND HOT WATER **HEATING**
PHONE 133

Yellow Pine / White Pine / Hardwoods
See bet. pgs. 188-189

LUMBER
SASH, BLINDS, DOORS

WOODWARD & SON
Ninth and Arch Streets
RICHMOND - VIRGINIA

TRANSFER COS 437 WHEELWRIGHTS

Transfer Companies

ASHEVILLE DRAY, FUEL & CONSTRUCTION CO (Inc), 6½ s Main (see top lines)
Asheville Transfer & Storage Co, 60 Patton av
Citizens Transfer Co, 48 Patton
HUGHES TRANSFER & LIVERY CO, 401 Southside av (see side lines)

HUGHE'S Transfer & Livery

Trunks: 25c

PHONE - 1405

Undertakers

(See also Funeral Directors)
BROWN'S UNDERTAKING PARLORS, 50 Patton av
Hare & Co, 21 s Main
NOLAND, BROWN & CO, 16 Church
*Peoples Undertaking Co, 29 Eagle
Red Cross Undertaking Co, 49 College
*Wilson Undertaking Co, 18 Eagle

Upholsterers

Asheville Cabinet Co, 17½ Church
GALER E E, 114 Patton av (see bottom lines)

☞ Varnish

ASHEVILLE PAINT & GLASS CO, 6 n Main

BOWLES R E, 1 e Pack Sq

Vegetables

Goff W A, City Market
*JACKSON B J, City Market
Jarrett E C, City Market
Lynch Mrs & Son, City Market

Veterinarians

LOVE F P & SON DRS, 9 w Walnut (see adv)
Price B L, 22 Montford av
Tuttle A A, 60 s Main

Wagon and Carriage Makers

AMERICAN WAGON CO, 65-67 s Main

Wall Paper

BOWLES R E, 1 e Pack Sq (see p 5)
Excelsior P & P House, 34 n Main
Fitzpatrick R L & Son, 53 n Main

Warehouses

(See Storage)

Watchmakers

(See also Jewelers)
CARPENTER J E, 8 n Pack Sq
Goldsmith W W Jr, 37 s Main
Jeanneret L W, 22 s Pack Sq
Noblitt M W, 35 s Main
ROCKETT O N, 29 n Main
Solerwitz Israel, 39 College
TILLMAN J A, 15 n Main

Water Companies

Buckeye Water Co, Haywood rd, W Asheville
MUNICIPAL WATER DEPT, City Hall (1st fl)

☞ Well Pumps

RICH J R CO, 21 n Main

Wheelwrights

(See Blacksmiths)

What Have You in Real Estate that You Don't Want?

What do You Want in Real Estate that You Haven't?

WESTERN CAROLINA REALTY CO.
J. W. Wolfe, Sec. & Treas.
On the Square
PHONE 974
10 N. PACK Sq.

H. A. BROWN & Co.
General Contractors
23 Temple Court Bldg.
Phone 341

—DEALERS IN—

Rough Building and **all Kinds of Crushed Stone**

—OUR SPECIALTIES—

STONE FOUNDATIONS CONCRETE WORK and **EXCAVATING**

Moale & Chiles — Real Estate and Insurance
27 Patton Ave., (2d fl) Phone 661
City and Suburban Property FARMS and TIMBER LANDS

Candy Kitchen and Club Cafe
"A GOOD PLACE FOR REFRESHMENT"

Hot drinks on cold days. Cold drinks on hot days. The best drinks every day. Pure fruits and syrups blended "just right," served daintily. Our Ice Cream and Soda Water Department, Restaurant and Candy Departments are always kept up to the standard of nearest perfection. Phones 110 and 111. 19 and 21 Haywood St.

WOOD CARVERS 438 YELLOW PINE

Brown's Undertaking Parlors

S. H. BROWN

50 Patton Avenue
ASHEVILLE, N. C.

Lady Assistant When Desired

Phone 193-2 Rings

Wood Carvers

Tennent M L Mrs, 10-24 Electrical Bldg

Wood Dealers

CAROLINA COAL & ICE CO, 50 Patton av
*Crosby Isaac, 99 Market
Kilpatrick W P, 193 Asheland av
*Lance J E, Eagle nr Valley
Reed S A, 314 Asheland av

SOUTHERN COAL CO, 10 n Pack Sq

Yeast

Fleischmann Co (The)

Yellow Pine Lumber

NORTHROP S & W H LBR CO (Inc), Richmond Va
WILLIAMS-BROWNELL PLANING MILL CO, Sou Ry nr Biltmore

THE MOORE Plumbing Company

16 N. Pack Square

PHONE 1025

Sanitary Plumbing, General Tin and Metal Work, Hot Air Furnaces

The Battery Park Bank

Capital - - $100,000.00
Surplus and Profits, $110,000.00

ASHEVILLE, N. C. City, County and State Depositary

J. A. TILLMAN — I carry a nice line of Watches, Clocks and Jewelry, and make a specialty of repair work. Satisfaction guaranteed. **Jeweler — 17 N. Main St.**

Asheville, N. C., Street Directory

Giving Name of Householders and Denoting Business Places

Vol. XII   THE PIEDMONT SERIES   1913

Note—All streets and avenues are arranged in alphabetical order; the house numbers are arranged in numerical order, with names of occupants after each number.

Dash (———) before names denotes that the number is wanting.

*Star before names generally means that such persons are colored

The location of the Suburbs of Asheville may be found at the end of this department.

ADAMS   439   ASHELAND AV

ADAMS—South from 54 Bartlett to Southside av
- 20 Hines H E
- 25 Kale P T
- 29 Forter R R
- 33 Monteath A D
- 37 Killian F M
- 66 Moses E A
- 70 Weaver W B
- 72 Whitaker W B

ALBEMARLE PARK — (See Charlotte street)

ALL SOULS' CRESCENT— (See Biltmore)

ALLEN—West Asheville

ANN—North and south from Patton av, 2 w of French Broad av

    Going North
- 19 Lingerfeldt J L
- 23 Wood C F
- 28 Dermid J W
- 32 Clouse J H
-    Young W B
- 34 Lindsey F M
- 38 McLean W P
- 39 Hunter M E Mrs

    Going South
- 10 Nichols L W
- 12 Powell H F
- 16 Briggs C O
- 17 Wilhelm Geo
- 20 Walters H E
- 21 Baldwin P L
- 28 Iovine G T

ARLINGTON — East from 59 Charlotte
- 21 Rickman H R
- 23 Bard C I
- 26 Zimmerman C St V Dr
- 35 Lorick J M
- 37 Dunn C W
- 38 Claverie J S
- 40 Boardman Hattie Miss
- 43 Clayton T E
- 46 Ford J F

   (Furman av intersects)
- 51 Smith R S
- 52 Gee H M
- 58 Huston J W
- 60 Vacant
- 80 Craddock T E Dr
- 83 Parker G N

ARLINGTON—West Asheville

ASHELAND AVENUE—south from 100 Patton av to Southside av
- 18 Brookshire T J
- 22 Pinner C L
- 23 Randall E R
-    Trivola (The)
- 25 Powell E B
- 29 Vacant
- 30 Lee J S Capt
- 33 Boling E J Mrs
- 34 Buchanan Bessie Mrs, boarding
-    Buchanan J F
- 42 Vacant
- 44 Tipton W M
- 50 Williams F M
-    Williams Loduska Mrs
- 51 Southerland C P
- 54 Milton A E Mrs

INSURANCE
- **I**nsure your salary with us
- **N**ever carry your own risk
- **S**afety is the best policy
- **U**nless you are a capitalist
- **R**est easy if you have
- a**N** accident we will
- **N**ot keep you waiting to
- **C**ollect your claim
- **E**very claim promptly paid

Imperial Mutual Life & Health Insurance Co.

Home Office:
ASHEVILLE, N. C.

Phone 495

HOTEL OXFORD — Redecorated and Refitted throughout. Recently enlarged to 60 rooms. Centrally located. Depot cars stop at entrance. Long distance telephone office upstairs. American and European plan. Rates 50c, 75c and $1 per day; special rates by week or month. C. H. Branson & Sons, Proprietors. Phone 1887. 50-54 South Main St. **Asheville, N. C.**

Williams-Brownell Planing Mill Company — *Hardwoods*

Lumber---Rough and Dressed Flooring a Specialty Moulding, Interior Finish, Etc.
Office, Plant and Yards on Southern Railway, Near Biltmore Station
WHITE PINE Phone 729 YELLOW PINE

ASHELAND AV 440 ASTON

Asheville Electrical Co. Electrical Contractors
HEADQUARTERS 74 CENTRAL AVENUE
PHONE 377
W. Mansfield Booze, Manager

- 56 Lowrie Queen Mrs
- Blackwood Martha Mrs
- 58 Ivey Levi
- 59 Buchanan I B
- 62 Vacant
- 63 Jones J R
- 66 Bon Air (The), boarding
- 68 Stone V L
- 70 Rickert J F
- 71 Smathers J E
- 73 Lee E E Mrs
- 78 Lee C G
- 79 Vacant
- 84 Shockley H S

(Philip intersects)

- 85 Whitehead R O
- Whitehead L L
- Wray David
- 86 Walker C P Miss
- 90 Lee H P
- 91 Miller J D
- 98 Clarke C D
- 99 Green Gay
- 100 Sams J L
- 104 Hayes B G
- 105 Arthur J W L
- 106 Mills C E
- 109 Patton T E
- Young J W
- 111 Murdock J E
- 113 Cliff H G
- 117 Smith R P Rev
- 123 Chambers E C
- 131 Clarke J J
- 132 Padgett J M
- 135 Baird S L Mrs
- 136 Cherry P B Mrs
- Johnigean Wm
- 136 (r) Ray Chas

(Wallach intersects)

- 140 Noland M C
- 141 Moore E J Mrs
- 146 Jarrett E C
- 147 Morris G H
- 150 Wrenn G W
- 156 Wilson T E

(Morgan av intersects)

- 157 Donnan G W
- 163 Robey P C
- 165 Cooper O W
- 167 Clark D C
- 169 Bishop W B
- 172 Woods S F
- 173 Davis J W
- Smith Jno
- 174 Messer W R
- 180 Noblitt M W
- 180½ Penland Weldon
- 181 Eller B L
- 181½ Debruhl G W
- 183 Peebles W A
- Hayes C S
- 186 Hayes W V
- 189 Blalock W C
- 190-214 Asheland Avenue Schl

(Silver Begins)

- 193 Kilpatrick W P, gro
- 197½ Steele S C Mrs
- 199 Michalov Isaac
- 203 Michalov Isaac, genl mdse
- 207 Williams G W K
- 211 Presley N A Mrs
- 216 *Singleton S L
- 219 Barber Warren
- 226 Christopher C F
- 229 Clarke D V Mrs
- Reed Benj
- 238 *Brown Wm
- 240 *Thompson Ella
- *Harrington Estelle
- 245 Norville T W
- 249 *Conley Douglas
- 261 *Sebron Jno
- 265 *Maize G W Rev
- 272 *Foster H C
- 275 Luther C G & Bros, gros
- 293 Poore W H
- Brittner R B
- 295 Sprouse H M
- 297 Sprouse Stuart
- 299 Sprouse Nellie Mrs
- 302 *Fisher Tina
- 303 *Brewton Jno
- 304 *Moore Lee
- 305 *Rutherford Jno
- 306 *Poston Lee
- 310 *Pruitt Monroe
- 314 Reed S A
- 317 *Rutherford Jas
- 318 *Williams Coleman
- 321 *Hudson I S
- 322 Reed J A
- 326 *Candy Isaac
- 393 *Hopkins Isaac
- 394 *McDowell L

ASHEVILLE AVENUE— W Asheville

ASTON—W from 43 s Main
- 5 Templeton W C, painter
- 7 Sellers J H, sign painter
- 7 (r) Huff J H & Son, painters

Asheville Dry Cleaning Co.
Telephones 835-836, All Dep't
MAIN, N. E. COR. COLLEGE

THE CLEANERS
Our Department for Oriental Rugs and Carpet Cleaning is prepared to serve you in all its branches.
E. S. Paine O. E. Hansen

FOR BOX SHOOKS — **Call English Lumber Co.** **PHONE 321**

ASTON 441 BAIRD

9 Swink & Co, painters
11-15 Chambers & Weaver, livery
18 Vacant
(Lexington av ends)
24 Vacant
25 Ratcliff J I, blksmith
33 Guffey J A
ASTON PARK—West from 129 s French Broad av
1 Baxter Jos
5 King M A
— Boyd E A
3 Bouters Jno
ASTON PLACE — W from Church, s of Main
5-6 Vacant
7 Buckner Neptune
8 Gardner F K Dr
10 *Duncan Fred
12 *Nims Zachariah
12½ *Cash Isabella
14 *Green Mary
23 *Latimer Texie
27 *Patterson S L
31 *Jackson Wm
ATKIN—East from 140 s Main
5 *James Columbus
5 (r) *Mince Nathaniel
7 *Hall Cornelius
*Burgin Luther
17 *Ledbetter Adeline
34 Theodore Andrew
39 Meares Gaston
40 Vacant
41 Braman H O
44 Fulton R W Mrs
46 Vacant
51 Bowden T G
ATKINSON—Northwest from junc of Haywood and Hill
13 Chambers C J
21 Guthrie O M
McHone R M
22 Smith L F
Kesterson Avery
Davis Claude
25 Fisher J E
McMahan Annie Mrs
27 Morgan J W
Bradley S W
38 Anderson Margaret Mrs
40 Long Clyde
42 Brooks Alfred
49 *Kerns I W
53 Faith Cottage Rescue Home

Compton L B Rev
69 Spivey Clyde
75 Vacant
78 Beck W S
85 Dayton T L
McFalls Wm
89 Vacant
AUGUSTA—n e from Murdock 1 n of Hillside
AVERY — South from 548 w Haywood
2 Smith L G
40 Callaway Wm
42 Johnson J W
46 Burrell Milford
50 Jones Augustus
54 Burrell P D
58 Murray Robt
59 Vacant
59½ Barnes Reed
61 to 67 Vacant
64 Jones S H
67½ Wright Wm
68 Vacant
70 Taylor W H
72 Henson Lizzie Miss
73 Vacant
78 Garrison H H
80 Sams J B
84 White P A Mrs
85 Avery St M E Church
86 Henson Lillie Mrs, gro
90 Brooks Geo
91-99 Storage Supply Co
94 King T M
96 King Rachel Mrs
100 Archer Chas
104 King Wiley
King Wm
108 Atkins Laura Mrs
131-151 Ashev Power & Light Co
171 Standard Oil Co
174 Jones W L
— Scott Lbr Co's yards
— English Lbr Co
— Westall W H & Co yards
— Carolina Machinery Co
— Rees Hans Sons tanners
320 Riddle Thos
BAIRD—E from 135 Charlotte
3 Rickard — —
7 Steele Emma Mrs
15 Bragg W M
20 Acee J M
24 Michael F A

BIGGEST BUSIEST BEST Asheville Steam Laundry

Phones: 1936 and 1937

43 to 47 W. College Street

CHARLES H. HONESS OPTOMETRIST AND OPTICIAN

Exclusive maker of ATLAS SHUR-ON EYE GLASSES

THE Home of Ce-Rite Toric Lenses

We make a specialty of correcting optical defects with properly fitted glasses.

54 Patton Avenue
Opposite Postoffice

Carolina Machinery Co. Founders, Machinists and Jobbers of Mill Supplies. We make all kinds of Castings in Iron, Brass or Aluminum.

WE ALSO FURNISH SKILLED MECHANICS FOR BOILER REPAIRS —— **PHONE 590**

LIFE INSURANCE COMPANY OF VA.
ORGANIZED 187
Richmond -:- Virginia
J. V MOON, Superintendent
Rooms 3-4-5- Maxwelton Bldg., Asheville, N. C.

All claims paid IMMEDIATELY upon receipt of satisfactory proofs of Death. Total payment to policyholders since organization, over $12,000,000.00. Is paying its Policyholders over $1,000,000.00 annually.

BAIRD 442 BATTERY PARK PL

T. P. JOHNSON & CO.

SHEET METAL WORKERS

All Kinds of Roofing Guttering and Conductor Work Metal Ceilings, Skylights and Galvanized Iron Cornices

OFFICE and SHOP:
69-71 S. MAIN
Phone 325

DR. C. H. MILLER

Mechano-Therapist

14 N. Spruce Street
ASHEVILLE, N. C.
PHONE 979

Hours by Engagement

DRUGLESS HEALING OF DISEASE

(Chunn intersects)
36 Powers May A Mrs
46 Weaver Zebulon
(Reed intersects)
60 Holmes J C Mrs
72 Holmes E I
80 *Goodman Sallie
84 *Mitchell D J
BAPTIST HILL—Pine St between Eagle and Hazzard
BARTLETT—Northwest from 326 Asheland av
30 Harmon R T
39 Ownbey H W
40 Roland T F
43 McNeely T H
45 Fortune W G
51 Burnett T R
54 Harris Dell
55 Peebles E A
58 Weaver J M
59 Allison Irvin
70 Richardson J H
(French Broad av intersects)
84 Wood J H
96 Womble C V Mrs, boarding
100 Rogers W E
104 Gudger C H
  Abernathy R S
105 Vacant
(Ora intersects)
114 Willis E F
115 Adams E T
116 Stamey C C
121 Moody D W
  Hawkins A D Mrs
125 Mauck G W
  Franklin M W
146 Jackson A C
148 Vacant
149 Shuford F A
  Brown P B
(John intersects)
164 Keener J F
168 Stevenson O A
169 Bishop J L
175 Howell T N
177 Vacant
179 Ward S E
181 Sanders J P
195 Holcombe E S
196 McGrath T H
198 Pirson J G
BATTERY PARK HILL—Patton av and Haywood
— Battery Park Hotel

Battery Park Barber Shop
Battery Park Hotel Billiard & Pool Room
Battery Park News and Cigar Stand

BATTERY PARK PLACE
(Government St)—northeast from Patton av to Haywood
2 Dreamland Theatre
4 Hearn J M & Co, bicycles
4-6 Coxe Bldg
  Donnan F W
  Cunningham H O Mrs
  Case Ella Miss, nurse
8-14 Citizen Bldg (The)
  Citizen Co (The)
  Asheville Citizen (The)
  Ringer P H, phys
  Frazer Thompson, phys
8-14 Cheesborough T P, phys
  Fanning F J, civ engnr
  North Carolina Trans-Continental Constrn Co
  South Atlantic Trans-Continental R R Co
10 Coxe Frank (Estate of)
12-14 Vacant (stores)
16-18 Medical Bldg (offices)
Ground Floor—
  Dunn W L, phys
  Colby C D W, phys
  Calloway A W, phys
  Herbert W P, phys
Rooms—
1-2 Brownson W C, phys
2-3 Huston J W, phys
5 Miller O O, phys
7-8 Buckner R G, phys
9 Hull F A, natl bank exmnr
10-11 Durham B J, dentist
14-15 Winchester F L
16 Donald J C
17 Ball W A
18 Elias Bernard
19 Evans Solomon
20-21 Bostick V B
(Battery Park Pl Continued)
20 Greene J B, phys
  Griffith F W, phys
  Williams J H, phys
  Jordan C S, phys
24 Asheville Club Bldg
  Asheville Club
  Webb M Co, millinery
  Minor C L, phys

ASHEVILLE CLEANING and PRESSING CLUB

TAILORING THAT SATISFIES and PRICES THAT PLEASE

Hats cleaned, banded and bound. Silk hats ironed. Buttons made to order in all sizes. Plain or with rims. PHONE 389

DYEING IN ALL SHADES Cleaned. Messenger Service.

Kid Gloves, Slippers and Plumes. Fancy Jabots and Ties, French Dry Cleaned. Ladies' and Gentlemen's suits Steam J. C. Wilbar, Prop. 4 NORTH PACK SQ.

ASHEVILLE COAL CO. 6 North Pack Sq. Phone 40 — **M. & W. COAL**

Electric Flat Irons — Asheville Power and Light Co. Phone 69

BAXTER ALLEY—West from Blackwell's Alley
- 11 *Smith Emma
- 12 *Alexander Frank
- 16 *McBrayer Calvin
- 19 *Smith Brooks
- 22 *Street Chas

BAY—North from 53 Hill
- 8 *Harris Irvin
- 10 *Mattison Jane
- 15 *Scott Ellen
- 16 *Patterson Rosa
- 19 *Armstrong J C
- 21 *Gibbs Wm
- 22 *Wilson Tandy
- — *Kilgo W M
- 26 *Anderson Sandy
- — *Sherrell Other
- 38 *Williams Charlotte
- 55 *Chaney Ida

BEACH HILL—s from South side av opp n French Broad

BEARDEN AVENUE — East from 89 Montford av
- 12 Vacant
- 15 Stevens S J Mrs
- — Stevens Misses (The), schl
- 16 Bourne L M
- 21 Ferguson K G

(Short Ends)
- 22 Hackney W N
- 25 Brauns H E
- 30 Hatcher R W
- 31 Kennett F S
- 35 Orr A K
- 36 Valentine W B

(Cumberland av intersects)
- 41-43 Barger Taylor

BEAUMONT—East from Valley, 1 s of Eagle
- 70 *Kennedy J T Rev
- — *St Matthias Episcopal Ch
- 77 *Murdock Sidney
- 97 *Lance Edwd
- 99 *Williams Emma

(Sorrell intersects)
- 105 *Neal Mary
- 109 *Austin Louvinia
- 115 *Howard Agnes
- 119 *Leister Jno
- 125 *Hunt Perry
- 129 *Smith Maggie
- 137 *Vacant
- 154 *Robinson Edwd
- 158 *Harris Abbie
- 160 *Green Theodore, gro
- — *Cannon R B
- 166 *Abbott Lewis
- 167 *Vacant
- 167 (r) *Scott Hester
- 169 *Nipson Jno W
- 170 *Whitson Jas
- 174 *Madden C D
- 175 *Carter Jos
- 180 *Bradshaw Green
- 181 Ragsville Mahala
- 181 (r) *McDaniel Walter
- 183 *Wallace J B, gro
- 187 *Bohannon Jas
- 192 *Hatten G A
- — *Whitson J N
- 195 *Sharpe Adeline
- 211 *Smith Anna
- 214 *Forney Thos
- 216 *Vacant
- 223 *White Eli
- — *Harris Felix
- 226 *Evans Edwd
- 228 *Warner Jos
- 241 *Goins P A
- 242 *Brooks W P
- 245 *Logan Julia
- 249 *Byers Jno
- 251 *Turl Augustus
- 259 *Stribling Saml
- 264 *Coachman Chas
- 269 *Wilson J A
- — *Underwood Fritz

BEECH—South from Southside av, 1 e of Depot

BENNETT—east from 1 Merrimon av to Liberty
- 12 Moss Green
- 16 Hensley Isaac
- 26 Miller O A
- 36 Willis Wilborne

BILTMORE (see Suburbs)

BILTMORE ROAD—Continuation of s Main from Victoria

BIRD'S ALLEY—West from 269 s Main

BLACK—From 492 s French Broad av
- 1 Young Pinkney
- 2 *Vacant
- 11 *Hunter Jno
- 21 *Beatty J W
- 29 *Vacant
- 33 *Coleman Thos
- 34 *Johnson Chas
- 37 *Greer Barney
- 42 *Haden Rome

Meats — Kiibler & Whitehead
CITY MARKET — PHONES, 195 and 694

WEAVERVILLE LINE NINE MILES BY TROLLEY FROM PACK SQUARE TO WEAVERVILLE

ASHEVILLE AND EAST TENNESSEE RAILROAD CO.

7 NORTH MAIN STREET — ASHEVILLE N. C.

Electrical Supplies — **PIEDMONT ELECTRIC COMPANY**, ASHEVILLE, N. C., 64 PATTON AVE.

| BLACK | 444 | BRICK |

- 46-50 *Vacant
- 47 *Bradley Mollie
- 48 *Payne Mary
- 49 *Odom Frank
- 52 *Johnson Andrew
- 53 *Vacant
- 54 *Haynes Tolbert
- 57 *Hicks Minnie
- 58 *Conley Harriet
- 59 Sprouse H M, gro
- 60 *Lockman Jno
- 61 *Hurst Marshall
- 62 *Stoner Wm
- 71 *Carson Alfred
- 73 *Noblett Nan
- 77 *Tatum Lewis
- 79 *Ohanan Jacob
- 84 *Logan Mattie
- 86 *Kennedy Chas
- 88 *Williams Arthur
- 88 (r) *Southers Furman
- 89 *Cureton Jas
- 91 *Kincaid Sarah
- 92 *Poole Jos
- 93 *Jordan Geo
- 95 *Posey Jas Jr
- 99 *Mills Birdo
- 109 *Provident Baptist Ch
- 112 *Moore David
- 113 *Banks Alice
- 115 *Stepp Martin
- 117 *Dobbins Jno
- 121 *Williams Frank
- 177 *Figgins Wm

BLACKWELL'S ALLEY —
  (see Lincoln av)

BLAIR—E from 171 Charlotte
- 11 Shepherd Frank
- 12 Guy J L
- 16 Cathey J H

BLAKE—E from 114 Montford
- 11 Johnson P G
- 14 Beck A M Mrs
  Willis F M Miss, nurse
- 15 Jensen J L
- 18 Fater D H
- 19 Stevens R F
- 21 Jones B D Mrs
  Tillinghast Emily Mrs
- 22 Tennent Annie Mrs
- 26 Rollins H J Mrs
- 27 Bosse J H
- 28 Howell C R
- 30 Smith H A

BLANTON—South from Silver, 1 w of Asheland av

- 9 *Turner Martha
- 10 Shipman M S
- 12 *Anderson Jno
- 15 *Forney Stanley
- 20 *Grey Augustus
- 24 *Knuckles C W
- 29 Monteath Susan Mrs
- 34 Williams J W
- 35 Willis J W
- 45 Folk Casimir
- 51 Miller C H
- 56 Kuykendall W H
  Scremer Manus
- 58 Bean A J
- 59 Miller C P
- 60 Britt H C
- 63 Beck G W
- 69 Grant W B
  Stinnette C R
- 69½ Bell O B
- 70 Melton E B
- 76 Whittemore M A
  (Phifer intersects)
- — Bethel M E Church (South)
- 81 Perry C R
- 85 Taylor H G
- 97 Divelbiss J E
- 102 Bryson W C
- 103 Israel Z W
- 107 Williams J M
- 111 *Stepp A W
- 131 Braman H O Jr
  (Bethel intersects)
- 153 Goodman L V
  Bell J A
- 156 Smith E M Mrs
- 157 James F E
- 158 Arthur W H
- 163 Efird W A
- 164 McClammy E L
- 165 Bean J C
- 167 Smyer A L

BORDER — (see Washington Road)

BREVARD ROAD—W Asheville

BRICK—South from 30 Poplar
- 4 *Harris Saml
- 5 *Poole Lillie
- 7 *Stewart Jas
- 9 Wheelan Louisa Miss
- 13 Bishop Eliza Mrs
- 17 King Jos
- 18 *Wheeler M R
- 22 *Linney Jno
- 27 Patton Jas

CONTRACTOR and BUILDER — **J. C. McPHERSON** — STEEL RANGES — 35-37 E COLLEGE ST. PHONE 133

PLUMBING STEAM AND HOT WATER HEATING

| 400 South 9th St Richmond, Va. See Bet. Pages 188-189 | **Montague Mfg. Co.** Rough and Dressed Lumber | Sash, Blinds, Doors Frames, Columns Brackets, Mantels Porch Work, Etc. |

BRICK 445 CARTER

- 27 (15) Munsey Mary Miss
- — Gryder W M
- 32 *Sawyer Sidney
- 40 *Chavis J C
- 42 *Trail Amanda
- 43 *Muckelvene Sena
- 45 *Johnson Minnie
- 47 *Nelson Maggie
- 80 *Smith Myra
- 82 *Jenkins Vera
-    *Smith A L

BROAD—East from Merrimon av to Charlotte, 1 n of Chestnut
- — Grace J T Mrs
- 25 Carrier A H
  (Liberty intersects)
- 49 Cefalu J B
  (Border intersects)
- 87 Eller Y D Mrs
- 91 Blackwelder J M
- 97 Argoe R T
- 98 Harmon C W
- 102 Veley A L Mrs
- 106 Forester J H
- 107 *Loder R H
- 111 King M E, painter
  (Madison av intersects)
- 117 Willis C C
- 120 Braswell A F
  Braswell L F
- 121 Riggs J K
- 124 Neel Bessie Mrs
- 125 Stockinger Johanna Miss
- 126 Evans A J Dr
  (Cresent intersects)
- 129 Goldsmith W W
- 133 Jordan A W
- 143 Shytle J H

BROADWAY AVENUE — W Asheville

BROOK—(see Biltmore)

BROOKLYN ALLEY—S from Haywood, 1 e of Rector

BUCHANAN'S ROAD—East from s Main

BUNCOMBE—South from rear of 17 Church
- 16 Cochrane Girdwood
  Pons Frank
- 17 Holder C B
- 18 Dewey E C

BUTTRICK—N from Junction of Patton av and w Haywood
- 11 Sprinkle J R
- 13 Morgan J P

- 16 Frady H M
- 19 Hawkins R M
- 22 Willis W A
- 25 Revis M E Mrs
- 26 Austin H A Mrs
- 27 *Lenoir Jno
- 27 (r) *Clayburn Isabelle
- 32 Ingram M F
- 33 *Hopkins J W
- 35 *Hall Wm
- 39 *Leaphart Walter

BUXTON—S w from w Haywood
- 1 Elmore J M
- 7 Pugh B L
- 9 Smith W B
  (Park av intersects)
- 13 Moore J W
- 19 Edwards Susan Mrs
- 23 Black Jos
- 24 Holiness Church
- 31 Haney G W
- 33 Bryce S P
- 34 Maxwell S A
- 35 Ledford M L Mrs
- 40 West E M
- 44 Ledford D C
- 48 Warren S A Mrs
  Harbin Jas
- 51 Hamrick G P Rev
- — West End Baptist Church
- 54 Carver J W
  Gillispie G R

CAMERON—N from 306 College
- 3 Bell M C

CAMPBELL—N from 95 Hill
- 22 *Torrence Saml
- 28 *Harrison Sarah
- 34 *Wright Saml

CARROL AVENUE—Northeast from Edgehill av, a Continuation of Atkin
- 1 Clarke M F
- 2 Fruchey F J
- 3 Marquardt J A
- 4 Carpenter J E
- 5 Vacant
- — Hamilton O C

CARTER—N from 182 Patton av
- 15 McCall T D
- 32 Pate Texanna Mrs
- 34 Darby J A
- 36 Braun Adam
- 38 Brannon C R

What Have You in Real Estate that You Don't Want?

What do You Want in Real Estate that You Haven't?

WESTERN CAROLINA REALTY CO.

J. W. Wolfe Sec. & Treas.

On the Square
PHONE 974
10 N. PACK SQ.

Brown-Carter Realty Co.

REAL ESTATE
23 TEMPLE COURT
PHONE 341
ASHEVILLE   N. C.

FLORIDA SPECIALTIES

Grazing, Timbered, Farm Lands, Orange Groves, Turpentine Locations and Phosphate Lands.

NORTH CAROLINA SPECIALTIES

Orchard Farm and Timbered Lands, City Property, Rent Collections.

Moale & Chiles Real Estate and Insurance
27 Patton Ave., (2d fl)   Phone 661
General Agents United States Fidelity & Guaranty Co.

Candy Kitchen and Club Cafe
"A GOOD PLACE FOR REFRESHMENT"

The very best ingredients with sanitary conditions in our Candy Manufacturing Department make possible the dainty, crisp confections sold here.
Bon Bons and Chocolates made every day, put up in neat, attractive boxes. Phones 110 and 111. 19 and 21 Haywood St.

CARTER 446 CHARLOTTE

Brown's Undertaking Parlors

S. H. BROWN

Lady Assistant When Desired

Phone 193-2 Rings

50 Patton Avenue
Asheville, N. C.

Established 1894

B. J. JACKSON

Carefully Selected Fruits and Vegetables

Stall No. 11, City Market

BUSINESS PHONES:
86 and 101

RESIDENCE PHONE
1596

---

40 Wilson J B
  Wilson A R Mrs, dressmkr
44-48 Vacant
CATAWBA—W from Main to Panola, 2 n of Magnolia av
13 Tweed E R
23 Fair J R
32 Ingle T C
33 Fair J O
35 Fox J M
  (Cumberland av intersects)
36 Sherlin Wesley
37 Roberts M D
40 *Alexander J A
41 Brown I B
CATHOLIC AVENUE—northeast from Valley, 1 n of Beaumont
1 *Weston Jeremiah
2 *Thompson Ella
  *Jones Duffy
11 *Catholic Hill School
12 *Ford Eugene
17 *Alexander Peter
19 *Alexander Amos
21 *Jones Kate
23 *Alexander W M
30 *Woods Alice
32 *Birchett J F
  *Forney Luther
33 *Roberts David
  *Rhodes Albert
37 *Taylor Addie
41 *Ponder Geo
45 *Pendleton Alfred
47 *Colter G W
  (Haid intersects)
52 *Friday Jno
59 *Vacant
CAVASSA ALLEY—from 410 Depot to 72 Ralph
CEMETERY DRIVE—W from Pearson Drive to Cemetery
— Asheville Cemetery
— Hebrew Cemetery
CENTRAL AVENUE—N from 644 Woodfin to Chestnut
6 Hannon L R Mrs
8 Vacant
9 Goldberg Max
  Hensley T M
10 Peebles Floyd
  Kenerly J R
14 Johnson F M
18 Rawls D D
20 Barnes W E

21 Whittaker J E
22 Whittemore G W
  Braswell L F
23 Capehart Ivy
  Hensley M E
29 Williams C M
33 Buckner W G
34 Vacant
41 Shepherd B M
47 Revell Nora M Mrs
48 Taylor J R
51 Schas Harry
  (Orchard intersects)
54 Baird H L Mrs
57 Vacant
60 Bird L A Mrs, board
63 Vacant
68 McElreath J W
71 Bostick J T
74 Booze W M
  Ashev Elec Co
79 Dean C H
  (Orange intersects)
80 Baumgardner H L Mrs
83 Gelula Max
85 Marlow B M
88 Vacant
  (Clayton intersects)
92 Under Constr
96-100 Vacant
104 Brown W P
108 Egerton J A
111 Pretlow C F Mrs
CENTRE—N from 18 Seney
15 Charles J A
16 Schreyer Roy
19 Guffin Martha J Mrs
20 North Asheville Bapt Mission
32 Hyndman T L
  (Hillside intersects)
52 Garren A G
108 Townsend L F
  Church W F
  Church J L
CHARLOTTE—north from 128 Woodfin to City Limits
2 Golightly L O
5 Mission Hospital
6 Smathers J W
16 Muller W O
17 Nurses Home
26 Trantham W I
27 Purefoy G W Dr
30 Blomberg Aaron
  (Orchard Ends)

Yᵉ OLD BOOK SHOP
114 Patton Ave.   Phone 1674
BOOKS BOUGHT, SOLD OR EXCHANGED

ROUGH AND DRESSED LUMBER
WHITE PINE AND YELLOW PINE
FLOORING A SPECIALTY
Hardwoods

Williams-Brownell Planing Mill Company
Mouldings and Interior Finish
Office: Southern Railway Tracks, Near Biltmore Station
Phone 729   *Planing Mill*

CHARLOTTE   447   CHESTNUT

35 Banks Annette Mrs
35 (r) Hawley M F Miss
38 Rector S A
39 Fitzgerald O L
44 Runnion R S
45 Roach F C Mrs
46 Hyams W S
54 Blomberg S I
   (Arlington begins)
57 Vacant
59 Williams C E Mrs
62 Clevenger E H
65 Bradley J S
69 Turner Frank
   Thomas F W
   (Clayton Begins)
70 Griset E J
74 Hamrick G P, gro
80 Hamrick G P
81 Dickerson J E
88 Revell O D
95 Patton M B Mrs
   (Chestnut intersects)
103 McIntyre C B
109 Vacant
114 Burt Aden
120 Dufour A R Mrs
124 Cauble J C
125 Riddick W O
128 Woods F T H
129 Maupin J M
132 Waters Jno
   (Broad intersects)
135 Harris M A Mrs
138 Loomis G C
   (Baird intersects)
146 Beadles R M
147 Brister S L Dr
148 Devenish D G
155 Burke Helen L Mrs
158 Penland L G
161 Sorrels G A
162 Messler F M
169 Shepard M H Mrs
170-172 Nixon W B, gro
171 Reilly M J
   (Blair intersects)
174 Davis J R
179 Barnett A G
180 Featherstone Mamie Miss
181 Patton R W
187 Guischard G L
188 Sevier M E Mrs
   (Clyde intersects)
194 Cox Rosa N Miss
202 Burbanks E W Mrs

236 Vacant
288 Elliott C J
   Pelton H W
289 Bennett B F
— Albemarle Park Co
   Manor (The)
   (Caroline intersects)
306 *White H H
— Grove Park
   Grove Park Co
392 Chapman S F
405 Frazer Thompson Dr
407 Reynolds C G
— Lawrence Thos Dr
— Asheville Country Club
CHATHAM (Woolsey)
CHERRY — W from Main to Montford av, 4 n of Patton
24 Wainscott L L Mrs, dressmkr
   (Grady Begins)
25 W L Schooler
29 McCanless F V
34 Middleton M C Mrs
40 Frost T V
48 Brandle A C
57 Mateny W W, school
58 Davis C S
   (Flint intersects)
76 Bagwell I G
78 Lohman Douglas
90 James J S
94 Powell Jos
98 Bagwell E G Mrs
100 Mears W C
   (Cumberland av Begins)
109 Jones Fred
   Lynn E M Mrs, nurse
113 *Leatherwood Amanda
117 *Crawford W L
118 Tinnemeyer Henry
125 Brunner F L
126 Brunner E H
128 Ownbey Sims
128 ((r) *Miller Alozno
134 Vacant
138 White J O
CHESTNUT — E from 270 n Main
15 Mason Horace
26 Brown C L
   (Fulton Begins)
30 Jordan F M
34 Poovey W E Rev
   (Highland av intersects)
37 Shope L K Miss

HUGHES

Transfer
and
Livery
Co.

Automo-
biles
for
HIRE

TRUNKS
25c

Office:
401 Southside
Avenue

PHONE   1405

Try our Hand Laundering. We strive to please in LAUNDERING and DRY CLEANING.

The Sanitary Home Laundry
No. 7 MONTFORD AVE.
PHONE - 1354

Mrs. Wilder's SANITARY HOME LAUNDRY turns out first class work in Laundering and Dry Cleaning. No. 7 Montford Ave., Phone 1354

| CHESTNUT | 443 | CHOCTAW |

OLDSMOBILE — ARBOGAST MOTOR COMPANY — ACCESSORIES AND SUPPLIES — 52-60 N. Main — Phones 302 and 1728 — DETROIT ELECTRIC — BUICK — MAXWELLS

39 Nottingham E J
41 Manley J H
43 Curry S J
45 Reynolds W V
46 Oakes D E
49-51 North Asheville M E Ch
   (Monroe Place Begins)
50 Nixon M C Miss
56 Carland Eugene
   (Holland intersects)
67 Parker A L
81 Kindel W A
83 Ownbey R L
85 Von Tobel A E Dr
   (Merrimon av intersects)
109 Wheeler L B
111 Varnon W E
117 Merrimon E H
118 Wallis M S
122 Vacant
127 Blake Blanche Miss
   (Liberty Ends)
137 Low J V W Mrs
138 Moore T V
141 Stelling J H
144 Brown E L Jr
147 Phillips Brewster
150 Heidtman J D
155 Lynch J M Dr
156 Smith T C
160 McDonald A C
166 (r) *Withers Sherman
166 Lambert Lucy Mrs
   (Border Ends)
167 Barnard W W
173 Kent Fred'k
176 Whitson W R
184 Smith T C Dr
   (Central av Ends)
189 Kohn Adolf
191 Bivings M A Mrs
192 Penniman M A Mrs
197 Sinclair J A Dr
   (Madison av intersects)
201 Weaver H B Dr
202 LaBarbe Margaret Mrs
206 English J M
209 Rollins W W Maj
212 Curtis Z F
218 Currier W M
223 Pritchard J C Hon
224 Rollins T S
225 Waller C B Rev
226 Westall W H
235 Hines C A
240 Justice H M Mrs

243 Carroll J L Dr
244 Hudson W C
   Todd F C
250 Steele E F Mrs
   (Charlotte intersects)
268 Oakwood Cottage (The)
   Scott W A, boarding
276 McEwen W B
281 Vacant
287 Fisher S J
306 West W W Capt

CHESTNUT — WEST — West from 270 n Main
19 *Collins Selina
31 Ownbey B L
35 *Fletcher Edwd
43 Worley R L
   (Flint intersects)
49 Galer E E
55 Raper W C
79 Strikeleather F C Jr
83 Davis B K Mrs
   (Cumberland av intersects)
122 Willis Adelaide Miss
123 Bartlett C C Mrs
126 Stone M A
128 Glass F J
130 Glass F S
132 Bartlett C C Mrs, boarding
133 Stevens M L Dr
136 Alexander L I
   Weinberger Max
   (Montford av intersects)
162 Holt S D
16 Theobold H C
   Theobold L M Mrs
170 Brown G A
174 Ewrin J B
175 Vacant
178 Brown W M
179 Vacant
182 Holcombe J B
184 Schminke Gus
186 *Haynes J S

CHOCTAW — South from 328 Southside av
7 Israel E W
9 *Fortune Giles Rev
77 *Lytle Hezil
84 *Owens Jno
85 *Miller Cleveland
86 *Moss Jas
89 *Hill Hoke
92 *Henderson Mattie
103 *Foster Chas
104 *Bridges G C, hackmn

Asheville Dry Cleaning Co.
Telephones 835-836, All Dep't
MAIN, N. E. COR. COLLEGE

THE CLEANERS
Our Department for Oriental Rugs and Carpet Cleaning is prepared to serve you in all its branches.
E. S. Paine   O. E. Hansen

ALL KINDS
Hardwood Lumber

ENGLISH LUMBER CO.
Phone - - 321

CHOCTAW 449 CIRCLE

128 *Simpson Allen
130 *Heard Emma
134 *Williams J H
138 *Thompson Lucinda

CHUNN—North from 36 Baird
10 Carpenter J L
14 Irons W H
19 Woodbury F P
27 Cooke Geo
  (Blair intersects)
42 Collins Lewis Rev
43 Penniman A W Miss
50 Williams J M
54 Miller C H
69 *Burgin Champ
73 *Burgin Jackson
76 *Bowman W J

CHURCH—S from 46 Patton av
10 Burns Millinery Shop
11 Carroll J L, phys
  Reynolds & Cocke, phys
11½ Y W C A Lunch Room
12 Ward W A, elec contr
14 Reliable Cleaning & Pressing Co (The)
15 Ashev Ptg & Engrav Co
  Merrimon J H, atty
  Merrimon, Adams & Adams, attys
  Frost H M, jeweler
16 Noland, Brown & Co, undertakers
17 Fletcher M H, phys
  Eckel O F, phys
17½ Foreman J W, dentist
  Lord W H, archt
— Ashe Cabinet Co, uphr's
18-20 Asheville Carpet House
18½ Odd Fellows Hall
22-24 Swannanoa Laundry
— Central M E Church (south)
— First Presby Church
  Presby Baraca Bldg
35 Byrd C W Rev
37 Aston Place No 1, boarding
  Mitchell C C Mrs
45 Aston Place No 2, boarding
  Stikeleather Fergus
53 Aston Place No 3, boarding
63 Aston Place No 4
  (Aston Ends)
— Trinity Episcopal Church
68 Chance E L Mrs, boarding
  Chance I C
75 Lee Mary W Miss
82 Batterham Harry

84 Green O L
90 Coston J P
90½ Vacant
92 Miller Minnie Mrs, boarding
93 Mitchell C C Mrs
95 "Belvedere"
  Hyman N W Mrs, boarding
107 Meadows M E
  Cochrane H G
112 *Crump Lizzie
112 (r) *Patton Nora
118 *DeLoach Moses
  *Williams Robt
  *Whitson Kate
118 (r) *Baxter Clinton
  *Parker Lula
  *Holden Wade
122 *Justice Hattie
  *Reed Dorcas
  *Sutton Willis
124 *Clement Janie
  *Cannon Alice
  *Minson Henry
130 *Lynch Mattie
135 "Shoenberger Hall"
  Horner J M Rev
  Stubbs A H Rev
140 *Smith Geo
150 *Smith Anna
  *Miller Rosa L
152 (148) *Johnson Julia
  *Henderson Fate
  *Bryson Mamie
156 *Smith Mack
  *Clark Jas
157 North State Fitting Schl
  Roberts J M
  Days M F Miss, music tchr
166 *Morris Barney
  *Morris Lula, boarding

CHURCH—(see also Biltmore)

CIRCLE — South from Eagle circling the hill between Eagle and Hazzard
27 *Thomas Savannah
29 *Miller L M, shoe mkr
  *Wallace David
33 *Wilburn Olivia
43 *Petty Ernest
47 *Dizer Geo
55 *Petty Forest
70 *Horshaw Arthur
  *Credle Green
74 *Brown Bettie
— *Walker J W Dr
85 *Elrod T M

BIGGEST BUSIEST BEST

ASHEVILLE STEAM LAUNDRY
Phones 1936 and 1937
43 to 47 W. COLLEGE

S. D. HALL
REAL ESTATE AGENT
—
Money Loaned
—
Notary Public
—
32 PATTON AVENUE
—
Phone 91

CAROLINA MACHINERY CO.
—US when you want machine work of any kind . . .

Founders Machinists and Jobbers of Mill Supplies
When in the market for heavy castings such as columns or building plates get our prices. **Phone 590**

The Life Insurance Co. of Virginia

ORGANIZED 1871 — RICHMOND, VA.

ISSUES ALL THE MOST APPROVED FORMS OF LIFE INSURANCE CONTRACTS from $500.00 to $25,000.00, with premiums payable quarterly, semi-annually and annually

J. V. Moon, Superintendent, Rooms 3-4-5 Maxwelton Bldg., Asheville, N. C.

CLAYTON   450   CLINGMAN AV

D. TREXLER TIN SHOP

All Kinds of Roofing, Gutter and Conductor Work.

Phone 862

159 South Main St.

DR. C. H. MILLER

MECHANO-THERAPIST

14 N. Spruce St.
Phone 979
ASHEVILLE, N. C.

Hours by engagement

Drugless Healing of Disease

---

89 *Wilson Miles
97 *Owens W H
CLAYTON—East from Central av to Charlotte
4 Vacant
10 Williams E M
11 Patterson J C
14 Folsom E E Mrs
15 Bunn Albert
20 "Clayton Heights", boarding
   Davie H B
23 Patton B A
26 Jones L W Mrs
27 Moon J V
30 Hilton L M
31 Carter H B
32 Rosenfeld Miles
35 Koonce H C
36 Felthaus Anton
40 Sevier J T Dr
41 Westall T C
44 Rector T S
45 Souther W H
49 Case J H
50 Vacant
53 Vacant
56 Moore W J
59 Sellers J H
62 Justice J T
   McEwen J W
63 Toomer F G
   Lord Athalia Miss
CLAYTON AL—from 94 Pine
CLEMMONS—Southeast from junction of Mountain and Pine
3 *Cook Della
5 *Osborn Addie
11 *Burton Harriet
18 *Summey Harriet
20 *Nelson Maggie
27 *Abernathy Julius
   (Latta intersects)
35 *Rice Mary C
43 *Butler J F
52 *Forney Julia
56 *Mance Emma
58 *Vacant
59 *Latta Jane
60 *Mills Ellen
63 *Hemphill Cecelia
64 *Wiley Geo
66 *Mills Richard
68 Williams Thos
72 *Moss Henry

79 *Clark Douglas
121 *Johnson Wm
125 *Higgins R H
CLINGMAN AVE—Southwest from 250 Patton av
15 Clarke J N
   Presley J M
18 Berry W L
   Farris M F
   McCarson M M
23 Clark Mitchel
   Lawernce S A Mrs
24 Leverette J S
27 (r) *Phillips I Z
28 Waddell F B
29 Wallen J T
   Hoyle Walter
   Foster M A Mrs, nurse
29(r) *McLean Edwd
   *McGee Wm
31 (r) *Robertson J M
32 Ward E W
   Ward J M
   King Matthew
   McCurry Chas
32 (r) *Tate Jas
33 (r) *Thomas Benj
   *Shipman Frank
35 Hawkins M L Mrs
35 (r) *Ferguson Florence
36 (r) *Wilson Jno
38 Corbin J T
   Gordon Edwd
   Williams D E B
38 (r) *Henderson May
39 McCain H D
39 (r) *Maxwell Bettie
40 (r) *Woody Grant
49 Severson B C Mrs
44 Brown J M
47 Tiddy N S Mrs
50 Vacant
51½ Goodlake A M, contr
54 Cosby B H
55 Bracket R B
59 Langford J
60 Worley G W
60 (r) *Gaither Jas
62 (r) *Tucker J P
63 Reel C N
65 Murray Hester Mrs, dress mkr
67 Stepp J R
68 Gilreath C H
72 Vacant
73 *Graham D J

....Asheville Cleaning and Pressing Club....
Tailoring That Satisfies and Prices That Please

Steam and French Dry Cleaning of all delicate and fine wearing apparel for ladies and gentlemen. MESSENGER SERVICE IN THE CITY.

J. C. WILBAR, Prop.   4. N. Pack Square   **PHONE 389**

CAROLINA "M & W" INDIAN — Prompt Delivery

COAL

& ICE CO.
PHONE 130
50 PATTON AVE.
WEIGHTS ACCURATE

CLINGMAN AV   451   COLLEGE

- 76 Redmon J S
- 80-81 Vacant
- 83 Wallen W F
- 84 Revis J H
- 88 Vacant
- 89 Lance T S, gro
- 91 Byerly Ephraim
- 94 Harris P A
  (Rector Ends)
- 99 Stirewalt A D
- 100 Hurt J H
- 103 Miller D V
  Branks E C
- 104 Miller H E
- 107 *Black Anderson
- 111 *Woody Jas
- 112 Fisher C C
- 114 Vacant
- 116 Brown J H
- 120 Green A W
- 123½ *Tompkins Thos
  *Franklin Jno
- 123½ (r) *Glymp Wm
- 127 *Anderson Jas
- 127 (r) *Gudger Wm
- 135 *Penland Jenkins
  *Toms Everett
- 135 (r) *Holly Alex
- 127 *Smith Perry
  *Gudger Chas
- 139 *Compton J L
- 143 Vacant
- 165 Mooneyham W T
  Lee J B
- 172 Smathers R I, mattress mnfr
- 173 *Varnon Elias
- 177 *Brooks Butler
- 184 Smathers Wholesale Produce Co
- 205 *Smith Henry
- 209 *Smith Andrew
- 213 Vacant
- 215 *Magee Grith
  *Magee Anna, nurse
  *Magee Lois, nurse
- 217 *Gudger Jas
- 227 *Franklin Jno, eating hse

CLYDE—Northwest from 188 Charlotte
- 16 Moore E W
- 17 Bagur P E
- 20 Lindsey W M
- 25 Massagee S S Mrs
- 26 Harding G W
- 32 Stevens F G
- 33 Keplinger M A Mrs

- 35 Thompson J M
- 41 Presley J L
- 43 Presley Jas
- 44 Byas W M
- 46 Dewese Elizabeth Mrs

COLE—North from 15 Turner
- 6 *Mayfield Hettie
- 8 *Morris Chas
- 10 *Williams Jno
- 19 *Greys Sallie
- 20 *Lancaster Emeline
- 29 *Baker Henry
- 31 *Baker Alfred
- 33 *Vacant
- 47 *Johnson Andrew
- 55 *Littejohn Texanna

COLE AVENUE — West from 403 Merrimon av
- 15 James H B
- 17 Hill J J

COLLEGE—East from Main, 1 n of Pack Square
- 7 Ashev Stm Vulcanizing Co
- — Ledbetter Geo, auto repr
  Public Service &Motor Co
- 10 Langren Cafe
- 9 Perkinson T J, paints
- 13 Vacant
- 14 Patty J H, shoe mkr
- 15 Moore Plumbing Co (The)
- 16 Lowe P W & Son, produce
- 17 Vacant
- 18-22 Technical Bldg (offices)

Rooms—
- 1 Haines, Jones & Cadbury Co
- 2 Hayes C L
- 3-5 Chapman S F, lumber
- 6 Taft G W
- 7 McKay Edwin, electn
- 9-13 Smith & Carrier Co, archts
- 8 Roberts C J
- 10 Emmons L E
  Caslar Sol
- 15 Morris Reynolds
- 16 Chilton Jos
- 19 Cherry C M
- 21 Borne W G
- 23 Grindstaff E C
- 24 Katz Hyman
- 25 Eaves Paul
- 28 Alberts Jos
- 29 Hall B F
- 30 Solomon N E

☞College Continued

Asheville Power and Light Co.
LIGHT and POWER
PHONE 69

Poultry
Kiibler & Whitehead
CITY MARKET   PHONES, 195 and 694

Asheville Dray, Fuel & Construction Co.
6 1-2 South Main

COAL

Wood and Kindling
Stone and Sand
PHONE - 223

COLLEGE 452 COLLEGE

20-24 Citizens Lumber Co
    Carrier Bldg
    (Market intersects)
26 Bowden T G, shoemkr
28-30 Coffey I R, stable
29 Levitch Harry, jeweler
33 Marmino Antonio, fruits
34 McDowell & Patton, contrs
35 McPherson J C, plmbr
35½ *College Street Dye Wks
    & Merchant Tailors
37 College Street Bakery
38 Webb W A & Son, stable
39 Solerwitz Israel, watch mkr
    Peterson W R, shoe mkr
40 Vacant
41 Teasley T E, gro
43 Argintarter Bros, ladies
    suits
    (Spruce intersects)
45 Shepherd B M, gro
— First Baptist Church
47-49 McAfee Bldg (offices)
Rooms—
21 Love H N
23 Eckel O F
24 Nash M W Mrs, dressmkr
25 Matthews Augustus, dentist
33 Gearhart P H
35 Lewis A K Miss, nurse
37 Gudger C S
☞College Continued
49 Red Cross Undertaking Co
51 Louisiana (The) board
    Ray Ida Mrs
55 Chatam (The), board
    Meadows L E Mrs
56 Oates J R
57-71 Court House (county)
    Confederate Hall
    County Officials
68 Wright M D Mrs, board
    Suttle D D
70 Novich Saml
72 Magnolia Cottage, boarding
    Du Ren K L Mrs
74 Costello M J
    (Vance intersects)
76 Vacant
77 Knickbocker (The), board
    Harris M H Mrs
    (Davidson Begins)
93 McGarry Jos
    Traymore (The), board
94 Caroleen (The), boarding
    Mendel Lena Miss

96 Wray J A
97 Sites A B
    Sites K L Mrs, board
98 Littman Arthur Dr
100 Tallulah (The), boarding
    Brandl K C Miss
105 Slack S H
111 Frances Wm
    Oak and Valley begin)
112 Faucette J W Dr
— High School
151 *Miller R H
159 *Williams C L
155 *Jeffers R O
167 *Lee R J
173 Vacant
    (Locust intersects)
194 Forster J P
199 Lusk V S Col
200 Orr E M
204 Johnson A E
210 Ray C S
215 *Spurgeon S J Rev
216 Jeanneret L W
    (Pine Ends, Furman av Begins)
217 *Hopkins Chapel
    A M E Zion Church
240 Patton J G
241 *Allen Industrial Home
    Asheville Academy
242 Peebles G W
    Wilson Romulus
244 Miller F M, gro
246 *Berry Temple M E Church
246 (r) *Wise G W
250 *Morris J P Rev
258 Gross David
    (Hollywood intersects)
263 *Howard Sim
270 Miller F M
275 Alexander J T
278 Poore G F
    McCall C C
279 Vacant
283 Easley J H
284 Bryson W A
    Wilson A D
285 Monteath Robt
285½ Ingle N A
    Creasman G W
289 Cathey B S
291 Vacant
296 Caddy J G
    Johns Bayard
299 Rice J A
304 Henderson J D

EVER READY FLASHLIGHTS
Piedmont Electric Company
ASHEVILLE, N. C.
64 PATTON AVENUE

J. C. McPHERSON
SLATE AND TIN ROOFING
Galvanized Iron Work   Hot Air Furnaces
35-37 EAST COLLEGE STREET

PLUMBING
STEAM AND HOT WATER
HEATING
PHONE 133

MAPLE FLOORING
HARDWOOD LUMBER OF ALL KINDS

WOODWARD & SON
9th and Arch Sts., Richmond, Va.
See Adv. Opposite Page 188

COLLEGE 453 CUMBERLAND AV

305 Meadows S A
323 Loftain C S Mrs, dress mkr
324 Arthur J P
325 (335) Jones J E
331 Ledbetter Dock
384 *Brown Anna
388 *Cline Walter
— City Reservoir
— Henry P H
COLLEGE WEST—West from Main to Haywood, 1 n of Patton av
 8 *Conley W T, barber
 9 Vacant
10 Jackson W M, pool
12 Hampton F B, bowling alley
14 Vacant
16-18 Ducker Z T, gro
   (Lexington av intersects)
20 Roberts & McKinney, gros
21 Berkeley Pool Room
22-24 Bloomberg Bldg
   Phoenix Hotel
26 Vacant
28 Sky Cycle & Repair Shop
30 Champion Shoe Repair Shop
   Viniarski B A, shoe repr
32 Britt W E & Co, livery
   (Penland begins)
43 Asheville Steam Ldy
   Pool Bros, dyers
47 Nevercel F J, bicycles
COLLEGE PARK—Near Oak
 8 Holman Pearl Miss
14 Geiger E E Mrs
18 Lewis R J
24 Wilson W V
28 Patterson J R
30 Akers Arthur
32 Kirkman F E
36 Laxton M P Miss, nurse
   Laxton K M Miss, music tchr
   Hunt M E Miss, nurse
42 Stricker L R
CONESTEE—Northwest from Spears av, 1 w of Merrimon av
60 Ballard J A
70 Chambers S G
71 Anders T C
CONNALLY'S RIDGE—South from Depot, 1 e of Sou Ry
 6 Goff Jno
 7 Hampton C G
 8 Marshall E C

 9 Jump C B
10 Sawyer G C
11 Lamb Edwd
12 Marandville Wright
13 Harris J P
CORNELIA—N from Hillside to Josephine, 7 e of Main
11 Johnstone Wm
COURTLAND AVE—Northwest from 80 Montford av
19 Tumblin G B
21 Lytle Wm
22 Blackstock T E
27 Cook W M
34 Orr C C Dr
48 Murphy J H
54 Wolfe S M
58 Payne E S
62 Erskine M A
70 Vacant
74 Cartwright Herbert
CRESCENT—North from 130 Broad
10 Vacant
14 Shuford F L
15 Lyerly J A
18 Keeter M G
23 Reynolds J A
25 Vacant
27 DeYoung J T
CULLOWHEE—East from 223 Montford av to Cumberland
11 Hazzard Elliott Mrs
16 Lambert G H Dr
17 Adams J G
35 Bryant C S
CUMBERLAND AVENUE—N from Cherry, 1 w of Flint
12 *Anderson Hettie
   *Smith Jas
16 Moss Eliza Mrs
18 *Battle Sarah
20 *Edgerton Fannie
21 *Greenlee Letitia
24 Lacy J M
29 Mills C M
30 Zurburg W H
36 Vacant
   (Starnes av Ends)
40 Gentry J C
42 Deal O H
47 Mosseller J S
50 Henderson C E
51 Levitch Harry
52 Smith J N
56 Jordan J Y

What Have You in Real Estate that You Don't Want?

What do You Want in Real Estate that You Haven't?

WESTERN CAROLINA REALTY CO.

J. W. Wolfe, Sec. & Treas.

On the Square
PHONE 974
10 N. PACK Sq.

H. A. BROWN & Co.

General Contractors
23 Temple Court Bldg.
Phone 341

—DEALERS IN—

Rough Building
and
all Kinds of
Crushed Stone

—OUR SPECIALTIES—

STONE
FOUNDATIONS
CONCRETE WORK
and
EXCAVATING

Moale & Chiles Real Estate and Insurance
27 Patton Ave., [2d fl] Phone 661
City and Suburban Property FARMS and TIMBER LANDS

Club Cafe and Candy Kitchen
"A GOOD PLACE FOR REFRESHMENT"

The standards we work to in our Restaurant Department are: Cooking, perfect; Service, prompt and cheerful; Prices, moderate; Menu, everything in season. Parties and Banquets, Teas and Dinners. 19 and 21 Haywood St. Phones 110 and 111.

CUMBERLAND AV 454 DEPOT

Brown's Undertaking Parlors

S. H. BROWN

50 Patton Avenue
ASHEVILLE, N. C.

Lady Assistant When Desired

Phone 193-2 Rings

THE MOORE Plumbing Company

16 N. Pack Square

PHONE 1025

Sanitary Plumbing, General Tin and Metal Work, Hot Air Furnaces

---

59 Morris H L
  (Bearden av Ends)
60 Albright F J
63 Miller U S
64 Hall E H
67 Pearson W H Maj
73 Baird C W
74 Keeler I P
79 Askew J M
80 Baird J T
80½ Vacant
82 Hendley J B
82½ Currence R E
90 Redwood Henry
95 Stevens S M, plmbr
96 Hartsell J M Mrs
  (Blake Ends)
101 McKenzie M S Mrs
102 Gorham J W Mrs
106 Welch Gilmer
110 Moore M V
  (West Chestnut intersects)
114 Waring A H
118 McEnery J E
119 Weaver J H
128 Davis E K Mrs
129 Vacant
135 Wilkinson Clara Mrs
144 Ramsay J F Dr
150 George E O
153 Vacant
156 Lipinsky Solomon
162 Gaston E L
  (Magnolia av intersects)
169 Wilson H E Mrs
170 Collins W E
172 Mears J E
175 Call J E
177 Brown W V
182 Brown S H
188 Powell J H
191 Murray Geo A
197 Johnston D W
  (Cullowhee intersects)
201 Wingren Richard
209 Rutledge Fred'k
218 Brown J J Mrs
227 Toms C F
228 Jenkins M T Miss, boarding
  (Soco intersects)
246 Lee J H
249 Cowley A Mrs
254 Samuels Abraham
  (Cumberland Circle begins)
255 Campbell J A
270 Lindsey H A

282 Whiteside C M
317 Roberts W C
373 Smith Jacob
387 Dalton G L
CUMBERLAND CIRCLE — N from 249 Cumberland av
3 Vacant
36 Johnson F E
40 Honess C H
41 Stern Jos
  Lipinsky Morris
46 Jackson D L
52 Redwood W M
62 Perry J A Capt
CUMBERLAND PLACE — W from Cumberland av opp Starnes
3 Zimmerman W H
CURVE—s e from Beaumont
20 *Williams P W
24 *Hendricks Jno
  *Durham Elmer
27 *Avery Jennie
35 *Downs J W
40 *Gibson W M
46 *Bryson Bessie
48 *Baird Jno
51 *Vacant
59 *Palmer Kay
63 *Bost M L
70 *Gibson Hardy
86 *Abbott Maggie
92 *Prysoe Major
DAVIDSON—S from 93 College
10 *Flack A J, board
22 *Sheppard Rufus
28 *Washington D E, bldg
30 *Stover Martha
32 *Johnson M A, board
38 *Helington Lucille
40 *Williams C T
42 *Wells Saml
44 *Johnson Geo
48 *Smith Lonnie
52 *Miller Leila
DEPOT—South from Lyman, a Continuation of Clingman av
— Ashev Grain & Hay Co
262 Foster J S, genl mdse
266 Johnson G W
286 Hunt Mary Mrs
308 Weiler C L Mrs
  Johnson Ada Mrs, dressmkr
— Sou Ry Freight Depot
341 Smith Whol Drug Co, whse

The Battery Park Bank

Capital - - $100,000.00
Surplus and Profits, $110,000.00

ASHEVILLE, N. C. City, County and State Depositary

J. A. TILLMAN — I carry a nice line of Watches, Clocks and Jewelry, and make a specialty of repair work. Satisfaction guaranteed. **Jeweler** — **17 N. Main St.**

DEPOT 455 DUNDEE

- 346½ McCoy J H
- McCoy A M Mrs, boarding
- 347 Green Otis Hdw Co, whse
- 348 Ford W P & Son, gro
- 348½ Bishop G A Mrs, boarding
- 349 Nat'l Biscuit Co
- 341 Mustin-Robertson Co, whol gro's
- 352-354 Vacant
- 353-359 Sternberg S & Co, junk
- Ashev Packing Co
- 356 Foster F S, gro
- McSherry J W
- (Bartlett intersects)
- 362-366 Vacant
- 363 Brown & Northup, whol
- 365-369 Rogers Grocery Co, whol
- 368-370 Highland Hotel, Else Emma Mrs
- 373 Union News Co
- McConnell Bros, whse
- 375 Armour & Co, provisions
- 376 Glen Rock Sta P O
- 378 Vacant
- 386 Warren H M, restaur
- 380 Ledford J M, gro
- 382 Monday C U
- 385 Asheville Gro Co, whol
- 388 Gem Lunch Room
- 390 *Stinson W M, eating hse
- 400 Glen Rock Hotel
- Postal Tel-Cable Co
- Lange J H
- Depot Drug Co
- 401 Sou Ry Passngr Sta and offices
- Sou Express Co
- Union News Co
- Gresham & Fogus restaur
- Pullman Co (The)
- Western Union Tel Co
- 402 Glen Rock Barber Shop
- 404 New York Fruit Stand
- 405 Galyean E S, confr
- 406 Vacant
- 407 Gladstone Hotel Cafe
- 408 Finley R S
- 409 Gladstone Hotel
- Blake Frank
- 411 Pelham S D, drugs
- 412 Baltimore Cafe
- 414 Union Dairy Lunch
- 416 Estes P D, pool
- 417 *Stinson Wm, eating hse
- 418 Hunt J T, gro
- — Black H B, barber
- 418½ European Hotel
- 419 *Walker S W, eating hse
- 420 Stiles Harper, confr
- 424 *Depot Pressing Club
- 426 Orr T F, furn rooms
- Davis G W, notions
- 426 (r) *Railroad Men's Pressing Club
- 428 Zimmerman & Son, gros
- 430 Halyburton House, board
- 433 *Yellock Hattie, board
- 434 Dugan J S, board
- 436 Florence Hotel (The)
- 440 Johns W W
- 444 Askew W A
- 446 Beaver C E
- 448 Kennedy C A, barber
- Hoskovitz Barnett, shoemkr
- 454 Sharpe Elizabeth Miss
- 455 Jackson G C
- Welsh J A
- 458 Hemphill J P
- 459 Young J M
- 463 Wellborn T J
- 479 Welborn J L
- 480 Click S M
- 492 Harrison T J
- 495 Green D B
- 499 *Wilkins Millard
- 502 Roper C A Mrs

DEWEY—n e from 104 Hazzard

- — *Jones Wm
- — *Lynch Janie
- — *Marlow Jos
- — *Corpening Harrison
- — *Pearson Abraham

DORTCH AVENUE — West from East av at "The Winyah"

- — Schoenheit Wm
- 25 Vacant
- 27 Solsbee M G
- 40 Claudius H F

DUNDEE—s e from Catholic av, 1 n of Beaumont

- 2 *Wright Julius
- 60 Vacant
- 7 *Kilgo Thos
- 12 *Dickson Silas
- 13 *Bogle M B
- 16 *Somers J K, draymn
- 20 *Jones Lollie

INSURANCE
- **I**NSURE YOUR SALARY WITH US
- **N**EVER CARRY YOUR OWN RISK
- **S**AFETY IS THE BEST POLICY
- **U**NLESS YOU ARE A CAPITALIST
- **R**EST EASY IF YOU HAVE
- A**N** ACCIDENT WE WILL
- **N**OT KEEP YOU WAITING TO
- **C**OLLECT YOUR CLAIM
- **E**VERY CLAIM PROMPTLY PAID

Imperial Mutual Life & Health Insurance Co.

Home Office:
ASHEVILLE, N. C.

Phone 495

HOTEL OXFORD — Redecorated and Refitted throughout. Recently enlarged to 60 rooms. Centrally located. Depot cars stop at entrance. Long distance telephone office upstairs. American and European plan. Rates 50c, 75c and $1 per day; special rates by week or month. C. H. Branson & Sons, Proprietors. Phone 1887. 50-54 South Main St. **Asheville, N. C.**

Williams-Brownell Planing Mill Company — *Hardwoods*

Lumber---Rough and Dressed   Flooring a Specialty   Moulding, Interior Finish, Etc.
Office, Plant and Yards on Southern Railway, Near Biltmore Station
WHITE PINE   Phone 729   YELLOW PINE

EAGLE 456 EAST

Asheville Electrical Company
W. Mansfield Booze, Manager
74 CENTRAL AVE.
HEADQUARTERS
Phone 377

EAGLE—East from 38 s Main
— Mizales M N, eating house
2 Hoskovitz B H, shoemkr
2 *Howell C T, barber
4 *Greenlee & Loder, pool
6 *Pearson H P, eating hse
8 *Brooks W P, barber
 *Hill C D, shoemkr
10 *Haynes Jonas, pool
11 *Goins P A, barber
 *Vernon Elias, shoemkr
12 *Alexander Frank, fruits
14 Diamond Morris, clothing
16 *Crescent Lunch Room
16 (2d fl) *Schaeffer C T, dentist
17 *Alexander Geo, eating hse
18 *Bryant R H, phys
18 *Wilson Undertaking Co
 *Sewell Lucy, dressmkr
22 *Tinsley T C, phys
 *Conley Lee
 *Dobbins J F
 *Odd Fellows Hall
24 *Shade's Pharmacy
26 *Piedmont Shoe Co
 *Royal Fraternal Assn
28 *Eagle Street Pressing Club
 (Market intersects)
29 *Y M I
 *Y M I Bldg
 *Y M I Drug Store
 *Swepson P J & Co, real est
 *Mtn City Mutual Ins Co
 *Oglesby Thos
 *Peoples Undertaking Co
— *Mt Zion Baptist Church
56 Rodgers J F, gro
57 *Jordan Armistead
57 (r) *Maxwell Booker
 *Vaughan Herbert
58 *McClain David
60 *Brown Eliza
63 *Crump Richard
 *Dellinger Chas
64 *Vacant
 (Velvet intersects)
— *Calvary Presbyterian Ch
71 *Dusenbury C B Rev
73 *Fredwell H B
 *Brown Ernest
 *Fredwell Mary, dressmkr
74 *Davis Sicily
77 *Perrin W F
 *Robinson Chester
81 *Hill Annie M

86 Londow Louis, gro
87 *Campbell F S, gro
88 *Floyd Theresa, eating hse
— Johnson R R, gro
 WeaverSallie Mrs
 (Valley intersects)
92 *Gaston Wm
— *Lance J E, wood
98 *Sullivan P A, eating hse
99 *Reynolds Lizzie
 *Williams Matilda
108 *Wallace Frank
 *Whitney Jos
110 *Baird Mary
116 *Mitchell Hester
124 *Neely Ella
126 *Avery Caroline
127 *White Jno
129 *Walker Augustus
138 *Smith Robt
139 *Smith Martha
152 *Trotter Alex
180 *Gardner Lillie

EAGLE TERRACE— s w from junc of Spruce and Eagle
14 Sneed Kate Mad
18 Queen Elizabeth Mad
22 Cooper Emma Mad
24 Cook Mollie Mad
27 Cook Roxie Mad

EAST—North from junc of Chestnut and Main
— Haynie V V, gro
15 Hare P E
17 Moore J G
21 Maxwell Chas
25 Haynie V V
33 Vacant
35 Boone Adolphus
38 Ogden D W
39 Stuman Jno
 Jones Moody
 Melton J C
40 Lawless G W
45 Cannon Thos
50 Maxwell L O, gro
51 *Baird G M
52 Vacant
53 Lindsey J D
56 Gibbs W A
57 Gideon N J Mrs
58 Morgan J P
 (Seney intersects)
63 Lovell G A
67 McClure C L
71 Sluder J A

Asheville Dry Cleaning Co.
Telephones 835-836, All Dep't
MAIN, N. E. COR. COLLEGE

THE CLEANERS
Our Department for Oriental Rugs and Carpet Cleaning is prepared to serve you in all its branches.
E. S. Paine   O. E. Hansen

Maple Flooring and Poplar Siding

English Lumber Co.
PHONE . . 321

EAST 457 FLINT

77 Corn N P
78 Rudolph J G
81 Briggs J W
82 Robertson L M
84 Roberts C W
87 Garren J H
   (Redmon's Alley Begins)
92 Henderson H A
93 Wilson A M
94 Vacant
95 Wilson R M Mrs
99 Bradshaw H R
100 Nix G M
106 Roberts R W
   (Hillside intersects)
— "Witchwood"
   Woolsey A S Mrs
110 Mitchell G E
— Winyah Sanitorium
   Von Ruck K & S Drs
144 Denton M K
EDGEHILL AV — S from 51 Atkin
5 Case B H
12 Spears J W
EDGEMONT — North end of Charlotte St
   Capps J A
   Forbes S L
   Goode A J
   Goodwill B C
   Harrison W H
   Hester E G
   Hildebrand W A
   Johnston Wm Jr
   Jordan T W
   Leinman Henry
   Meeham W D
   Millard C C
   Oakley Annie Miss
   Parker J M Dr
   Passmore I G wid A F
   Reynolds C V
   Reynolds R R
   Strong W S
   Watson N M Mrs
   Wilson R A
   Winston G T
EDWIN PLACE—Grove Park
ELECTRIC—W Asheville
ELIZABETH — West from Main to Cumberland av, 1 n of Starnes av
83 Moody H M
87 Caine J H
91 Fletcher F O'C

ELLA—From s French Broad
ELOISE—W from 180 Merrimon
17 *Leonard Jno
23 Brank A V
27 *Hendricks P L
34 Lunsford Frank
ERVIN—n w from 73 Gudger
ETOWAH AV—S Asheville
EUGENE—E from 172 Clingman av
EVELYN PL—Grove Park
FACTORY HILL—Mill settlement, w end of Patton av
1 Jones Jno
2 Coleman Saml
3 Banks J O
   Carver B J
4 O'Kelley R G
5 Barclay F W
6 Buckner Starling
7 Carver M H
8 Frasier D H
   Bugg David
9 Welfare Cottage (club)
10 Davis Merritt
11 Davis J P
12 Buckner C D
13 Roberts Edwd
14 Lowe Curtis
15 Ballard Robt
18 Fox J C
19 Vaughan H L
   Swann R B
20 Vacant
21 Radford Henry
22 Langley W P
23 Ball E G
FAGG—S from Bartlett
2 Sprouse Jno
10 Jones Robt B
15 Jones H E
20 Buckner J R
22 Owens P M
23 Melton J C
30 Penland G C
FAGG PLACE—East from 212 n Main
FAIRVIEW—See TUSKEE
FLINT—N from 93 Haywood
5 Ennes U R R Mrs
   Uleeta (The), board
11 Cline R F
18 Marion P G Rev
   (Hiawassee ends)
23 Hawes K R Mrs

BIGGEST BUSIEST BEST

Asheville Steam Laundry

Phones:
1936 and 1937

43 to 47
W. College Street

CHARLES H. HONESS

OPTOMETRIST AND OPTICIAN

Exclusive maker of
ATLAS SHUR-ON EYE GLASSES

THE
Home of Ce-Rite Toric Lenses

We make a specialty of correcting optical defects with properly fitted glasses.

54 Patton Avenue
Opposite Postoffice

IF in the market for a Gas Engine let us make you prices.
its heavy castings, such as columns or building plates, see us.
its a skilled mechanic for boiler work, see us.
you want machine work of any kind phone 590.

CAROLINA MACHINERY CO.

FOUNDERS MACHINISTS and Jobbers of Mill Supplies

Life Insurance Company of Virginia
ORGANIZED 1871
Home Office - Richmond, Va.

Has won the hearty approval and active support of the people by its promptness and fair dealing during the FORTY-TWO YEARS of its operation

J. V. Moon, Superintendent, Rooms 3-4-5 Maxwelton Bldg., Asheville, N. C.

FLINT 458 FRENCH BROAD AV

T. P. JOHNSON & CO.

SHEET METAL WORKERS

All Kinds of Roofing Guttering and Conductor Work Metal Ceilings, Skylights and Galvanized Iron Cornices

OFFICE and SHOP:
69-71 S. MAIN

Phone 325

DR. C. H. MILLER

Mechano-Therapist

14 N. Spruce Street
ASHEVILLE, N. C.

PHONE 979

Hours by Engagement

DRUGLESS HEALING OF DISEASE

---

26 Lee J A Mrs, board
29 Vacant
34 Vacant
40 Alexander Wm J
  (Cherry intersects)
68 Vacant
69 Curtis T E
76 Creasman M A
80 Harding Milton
  (Starnes av intersects)
97 Yates J J
98 Clark W C
  Coday P H
120 McGuire W R
121 Davis Linnie W Mrs
124 Bearden A R Mrs
128 Caldwell J D
134 Shuford W E
  (Elizabeth intersects)
141 Hamlet A A
144 Weeks H S
145 Hess E A
149 Mallicote L F
155 Holmes J C Mrs
  Salisbury J F
160 Buehrer A A
162 Lee B M
  (W Chestnut intersects)
175 Neely J W
176 Younginer G P
  Fogleman W D Rev
179 Richards W P
182 Bridges J M
188 Belote E T, contr
  (Magnolia intersects)
224 *Brown Mattie
  *Caldwell Ella
231 *Austin Henry
232 *Kennedy J L
233 *Rice Margaret
234 *Jeffries Alice
235 *Shippey Wm
  (Ocala intersects)
240 *Carson R C, vet surg
247 *Hudson Andrew
251 Askew Ira
267 Lord W H

FREDERICK—n e from McDowell
18 *Foreman Edna
19 *Jackson Wallace
23 *Roberts Arthur
27 *Morgan Ernest
26 *Williams Fred
39 *Holmes Addie
45 *Hill Henry

47 *Bailey Jas

FRENCH BROAD AVENUE
—North and south from Patton av, 1 w of Grove
☞Going North
20 Richelieu (The), boarding
  Alley C S
  Stowe L V Mrs, dressmkr
25 Webb M E Mrs, board
32 Carter S R Mrs
33 Vacant
36 O'Donnell Kate Mrs
39 Stone R B
39½ Wilkinson A S
40-42 Vacant
45 Vacant
45 (r) *Bacon Jas
46 Pearce B H Miss, boarding
48 Harris W R
49 Lichtenfels Gustav
50 Reynolds T P
61 Minor C L Dr
64 Davis G W
66 First Church Christ Scientist
70 Vacant
— Margo Terrace, hotel
  Branch P H
☞Going South
10 Greenwood Sallie Mrs
15 Lee G E
16 Clement G W
19 Overcash W A
22 Peterson Oscar
  Davidson Jno
23 Kimberly David
27 Templeton W C
31 Brown W C
32 Henderson S E
35 Brookshire J A Mrs, furn rooms
36 Randolph E J
39 Shope J B
  Wagner A W
40 Hunter T C
43 Fanning E H
44 Whisnant Ashbury
49 Moore W L
51 Chedester S H
61 "Wrenwood" (The)
  Mears S P
67 Minich A A
  (Philip ends)
— Aston Park (city)
— Emanuel Lutheran Church
80 Vacant

ASHEVILLE CLEANING and PRESSING CLUB

TAILORING THAT SATISFIES and PRICES THAT PLEASE

Hats cleaned, banded and bound. Silk hats ironed. Buttons made to order in all sizes. Plain or with rims. PHONE 389

DYEING IN ALL SHADES Cleaned. Messenger Service.

Kid Gloves, Slippers and Plumes. Fancy Jabots and Ties. French Dry Cleaned. Ladies' and Gentlemen's suits Steam

J. C. Wilbar, Prop. 4 NORTH PACK SQ.

ASHEVILLE COAL CO. — 6 North Pack Sq. — Phone 40

M. & W. COAL — Gas Ranges — Asheville Power and Light Co. — PHONE 69

FRENCH BROAD AV — 459 — FULTON

- 84 Trull C M
- 88 Duckett T M
- Jones C N
- 96 Vacant
- 102 Justice C B
- 104 Parker T J Mrs
- Ward C G
- 114 Ottinger M M
- Carmichael E R
- 117 Johnson M D
- 118 Drummond G C
- Landreth C E
- 122 Moss Jas
- 126 McHarge C F
- 127 Rickman T J
- 130 Brookshire L L
- 134 Kincaid J G
- 137 Gudger J M Jr Hon
- 138 Leonard C B
- Pugh L H
- 142 Marsteller Wyatt
- 146 Briggs Pierre, boarding
- 149 Cocke W J
- 159 Russell E R Dr
- 166 Young E E Mrs
- 172 Post W F
- 179 Sherwood Mildred E Home (sanitarium)
- Sherwood Mildred E Miss
- 182 Moore R W
- 193 Boone C A
- 195 King C G
- 196 Wakefield T A
- 199 Simpson R J
- 202 Donald J M
- 207 Chandley Everett
- 208 Cline J W
- 211 Thomas W B
- 212 Thompson H E
- 215 Payne C L
- 218 Sullivan J H
- 222 Burt C S
- (Street car tracks cross)
- 227 Black W L
- 244 Enloe A C
- 251 Wilson O C
- 252 Clarke W M
- (Phifer intersects)
- 264 McDevitt J A
- 275 Vacant
- 287 Ray W W
- 288 Merrimon J H Judge
- 289 Ray A F
- 295 Collins H T
- 302 Hunt J T
- Davis G W

- (Bartlett intersects)
- 328 Vacant
- 330 Thompson H C
- 331 Peacocke H F
- 336 Ledford J M
- 337 Ballard H D
- 342 Cuthbertson T W
- 359 Spurlin J M
- 361 Hill Margaret Mrs
- 372 Kluttz C A
- 373 Hollar H F
- 381 Steele M T
- 382 Reid Z B
- 385 McNamara T J
- 386 Chunn M L
- 387 Nash J D
- 388 O'Kelley T L
- 390 Hinton D S
- 391 Brendle D B
- 395 Lydia A P
- (Southside av intersects)
- 416 Vacant
- 436 Stiles Harper
- 441 Waddell S M
- 442 *Taylor Robt
- 450 Vacant
- (Livingston intersects)
- 468 *Walker Gilbert
- 472 Gasperson G B
- 474 Fagan Max
- 476 Vacant (store)
- 488 *Bruton Rena
- 490 (r) *Littlejohn Essie
- 492 *Rhodes G R
- 492 (r) *Robinson Jno
- 498 *Love Thos
- 502 *Moore Maggie
- 510 Vacant
- 512 (r) *Blackwell Henry
- 514 *Greenlee Jane
- 516 *Wilson Frank

FULTON—N from 30 Chestnut

- 18 Dillingham E C
- 26 *Martin R K
- 30 Vacant
- 33 Laughter Columbus
- 34 Rinsland Lucinda Mrs
- 41 *Mance Edmund
- 43 Vacant
- 46 Watkins P J
- 50 Liephart G W
- 51 Penland W A
- 54 Keller W A
- 57 *Sheppard Emma
- 58 Hoyle E M Rev
- 59 *Walls Hattie

Meats — **Kiibler & Whitehead** — CITY MARKET — PHONES, 195 and 694

WEAVERVILLE LINE
NINE MILES BY TROLLEY FROM PACK SQUARE TO WEAVERVILLE

ASHEVILLE AND EAST TENNESSEE RAILROAD CO.
7 NORTH MAIN STREET — ASHEVILLE N. C.

FURMAN AV 460 GROVE

ELECTRIC FIXTURES
Piedmont Electric Co.
64 PATTON AVE.
ASHEVILLE, N.C.

FURMAN AVENUE—N from College, 1 e of Charlotte
- 5 Hildebrand E G Mrs
- 9 Tillman J A
- 15 Carr J J
- 15 Michalove A, gro
- 19 *Murrough Mary
- 27 *Anderson W M Rev
- 32 Merrill T E Mrs
  (Woodfin intersects)
- 36 Smith R O
- 39 Woodard Alice Mrs
- 42 Lunsford R F
- 44 Vacant
- 51 Herron H M
  Herron Edwd
- 55 Jones G W
  Reese J J
- 64 *Lee Lula B
- 67 Michalove Abraham
- 69 McLean A L
- 79 Guerard A S
  (Arlington intersects)
- 101 Erwin Marcus
- 109 Vacant

GAITHER—Southwest from Pine, s of Ridge
- 14 *McElrath Wm
- 18 *Gaither Alfred
- 22 *Hamilton Henry
- 26 *Fuller Wm

GASTON—S from 292 S'side av
- 2 Vacant
- 3 Townsend Frank
- 4 Hollingworth H W
- 31 Galloway A M
- 35 White H G
- 47 McMahon T W
- 51 Reed W R
- 54 Pryor W C
- 56 Arthur J W
- 69 Blackwood W C

GAY—s w from Pearson Drive

GERTRUDE PLACE—Grove Park

GIBBONS—Catholic Hill
- 22 (92) *Floyd Theresa
- 24 *Carson Davis
- 26 *Springs Lee
- 29 *Cathey Jno

GIRDWOOD—W from 17 Park
- 15 May H P
- 17 Vacant
- 20 Jones J W
- 21 Roberts A L
- 34 Vacant

GRADY—N from 25 Cherry
- 8 Bollinger M E Mrs
- 9 Highsmith Z F Dr
- 11 Harris C F Rev
- 12 Rhinehardt E T
- 18 Starnes M E Miss, furn rooms
- 22 Fulbright A B Mrs

GRAIL—E from 130 Valley to Ridge, Catholic Hill
- 32 *Rosenborough Jas

GRAND AVENUE—Proximity Park

GRAY—s w fr Pearson Drive
- — Taylor Jno
- 13 Debrew Henrietta Mrs
- 19 *Morrow Lemuel
- 23 *Hamilton Julia
- 29 *Hicks Jno
- 29 *Walk Henry
- 49 Rash Emma Mrs

GREEN—South from Buxton
- 11 Rice R H
- 12 Corn Jas
- 15 Crompton W P
- 16 Sudderth J S
  Ellege Nellie Mrs
- 17 Young R G
- 21 Starnes J P
- 27 Bean H J

GREEN'S ROW—Depot section

GREER'S ROW—(see 81 to 93 n Lexington av)

GROVE—S from Patton av to Silver, 4 w of Main
- 13 Watson A T Mrs
- 14 Goodwin J W
- 16 Freeman J E Mrs
- 19 Brownell E P
- 23 Walker C A
- 24 Meriwether Hospital (The)
  Meriwether F T, phys
- 31 Ramsay J W
- 35 Salley H J Mrs
- 36 Hunt W L
- 39 Hood H B
- 43 Rogers H T
- 44 Johnston R P
- 48 Henderson Geo
- 55 Waddell D C Jr
- 58 Field A M
- 68 Raysor C A
  (Philip intersects)
- 89 Payne W R
- 93 Holcombe C A

CONTRACTOR and BUILDER
STEEL RANGES
J. C. McPHERSON
35-37 E COLLEGE ST.
PHONE 133
PLUMBING STEAM AND HOT WATER HEATING

Yellow Pine White Pine Hardwoods See bet. pgs. 188-189	**LUMBER** SASH, BLINDS, DOORS

WOODWARD & SON
Ninth and Arch Streets
RICHMOND - VIRGINIA

GROVE 461 HAYWOOD

94 *Johnson Melvina
100 *Conley W T
104 Robertson Barbara
115 *McDonald Jefferson
117 *McMichael Henry
122 *Ray Chas
132 Vacant
136 Miller T C
(Morgan av intersects)
137 Brookshire C W
139 Russell A C
140 Meadows O F
147 Chappell Viola Mrs
151 Cook T L
    Cook Daniel
153 Wooten L H
153½ Wooten A L Miss
159 Wooten M J
160 Bell J H
164-168 Vacant
165 Ballard H A
174 Ingle Ethel Mrs
175 Davis W M
176 Davis J P
233 Saunders B G
235 McCorkle H F
239 Williams A C
245 Dickinson C D
247 Edwards Eugene
251 Rosen Max

GROVE PARK—North end of Charlotte street

GUDGER—N from 207 Haywood
18 *Murphy Geo
18 (r) *Morton T P
20 Haskell's Pepsi-Cola Co
21 *Wilson Willis
23 *Vacant
24 *Watson Rosa
26 *Koon Julius
30 *Hargraves Malinda
   *Williams Irene
(Hill intersects)
36 *Bradley R C
39 *Moore Lillie
   *Smith Carrie
41 *Morrow C J
44 *Sylvas Rachel
48 *Crosby I T
53 *Smith Jno
— *Simpson Chas
67 *Bowman Robt
   *Gore Victor
68 *Carter Preston
70 *Smith Jno

   *Whitson Addie
(Erwin intersects)
76 *Hunter Clara
77 Hawkins Lucy
105 *Williams Geo

HAID—s e from 180 Valley
4 *Johnson G W
5 *Martin N M
8 *Todd Jno
9 *Miller Rena
11 (1) *Cross Lizzie
11 (2) *Ross Grace
12 *Harris Calvin
13 *Edgerton Julia
   *Funches Georgianna
14 *McGinness J H
15 *Logan Josephine
   *Mims Danl
21 *Harris Ina
25 *Liles Geo
29 *Wells Frank
31 *Forney Maria

HALL—n e from junc of Spring and Haywood
5 Huskie Jas
15 Patton J P
35 Vacant
37 Smith W H
39 Vacant
43 Coche E Z
49 Miller J M
57 Hunter W H
61 Vacant
62 Gentry Claude
68 Burrell D A
79 Anders L P
82 Andrews G W
83 Blanchard Lula Mrs
84 Vacant
85 Coche J J
125 Robinson M M
135 (r) Sands H S
140 McDaries J T
— Gentry W T
142 Gentry H C
144 Vacant
146 Evans L E

HAMILTON— s from 89 Chactaw
18 Plemmons W B
19 Kingsmore L D

HAYWOOD—North from Patton av at Post Office to Flint, thence w and s w to Patton av
— Government Bldg

What Have You in Real Estate that You Don't Want?

—

What do You Want in Real Estate that You Haven't?

—

WESTERN CAROLINA REALTY CO.

J. W. Wolfe Sec. & Treas.

On the Square
PHONE 974
10 N. PACK SQ.

Brown-Carter Realty Co.
REAL ESTATE
23 TEMPLE COURT
PHONE 341
ASHEVILLE   N. C.

FLORIDA SPECIALTIES

Grazing, Timbered, Farm Lands, Orange Groves, Turpentine Locations and Phosphate Lands.

NORTH CAROLINA SPECIALTIES

Orchard Farm and Timbered Lands, City Property, Rent Collections.

Moale & Chiles Real Estate and Insurance
27 Patton Ave., (2d fl)   Phone 661
General Agents United States Fidelity & Guaranty Co.

Club Cafe and Candy Kitchen
"A GOOD PLACE FOR REFRESHMENT"

Our Ice Cream manufacturing plant is absolutely clean and sanitary.
Prompt family delivery. Phones 110 and 111.
Catering for large parties and receptions. Special Creams.

HAYWOOD　　　462　　　HAYWOOD

Brown's Undertaking Parlors

S. H. BROWN

Lady Assistant When Desired

Phone 193-2 Rings

50 Patton Avenue
Asheville, N. C.

Established 1894

B. J. JACKSON

Carefully Selected Fruits and Vegetables

Stall No. 11, City Market

BUSINESS PHONES: 86 and 101

RESIDENCE PHONE 1596

　U S Post Office
　U S Courts
1　Postal Tel-Cable Co
　Blue Ridge B & L Assn
　Ray-Campbell Co, real est
3　Sunny Smoke Shop
　Robinson J G, kodaks
5　Hood H B, mlnr
7　St Charles Barber Shop
　　(College ends)
15　Walker C A, drugs
　New Sondley Bldg, offices
Rooms—
　1-3　Glenn E B Dr, phys
　4-6　Sondley F A L L D, atty
　9-10-11-12　Glenn C F, dentist
　15-16　Zimmerman C St V, phys
　17　Millard D R, atty
　☞Haywood continued
　Asheville Club
　Minor Chas L, phys
17　Stern Victor, jeweler
　Denoon M C Mrs, art gds
19-23　Meriwether Bldg
Rooms—
20　Winters M R
21　Chedester H C
22　Fisher R Z
23　Lange Chas
24　Radford S W
25　Ray S L
26　Smith L F
27　Wolf P W
29　Duckett T C
31　Robinson G S
34　Pagett B M
　Luther P A
　☞Haywood Continued
20　Marsteller & Co, real est
21　Club Cafe & Candy Kitchen
23　Yates & McGuire, gro's
25　Cruise J B Miss, hair gds
27　Y M C A
　Y M C A Bowling Alley
29-31　Halthenon Bldg (offices)
　Battle S W, phys
　Clemenger F J, phys
　Gruner Sanitarium
　Gruner E P Dr, baths
33　Allanstand Cottage Industries
33-35　Adelaide Bldg, offices
　Stevens & Orr, phys
　Brown A T Mrs
　Fanning F A
　Nelson J D

　Young Leona Miss
36　Woman's Exchange
　Woman's Exch Tea Room
　Adams Georgia Miss, nurse
　Sullivan M E Miss, nurse
—　Battery Park Cottage
　Millard Josephine Mrs
　　(Walnut Ends)
46　Hampton J E, phys
53　Elks Club
58　McKee A B, boarding
68　Corcoran P J
　Rock Ledge (The), board
72　Rohde H J
73-75　Briggs H H, phys
　Merrimon Louise A Miss, phys
74　Robinson J G
74½　Martorell G H Mrs
—　Christian Church
—　Asheville Auditorium
—　Asheville School of Musical Art
　　(Flint Begins)
88　Stroud C J Mrs
94　*Bryant & Clarke, pressing
95-97　St Lawrence's R C Church
96　Vacant
96-a　Davis G W
98　Palmer E I Mrs
98-a　Vacant
　tchr
101　Cauble P A
　Ninty Nine (The), board
102　Hays L E Mrs
102-a　Stradley Margaret Mrs
103　McCrary Frank
104　Vacant
104-a　Miller O O
106　McDowell B L Mrs, masseur
106-a　Weems Lacy
107-109　Avanmore (The), boarding
　Baker Josephine Mrs
108　Jellard R H
110　Vacant
112　Vacant
115　"Oak Cottage", board
　Brown J V
116　Vacant
119　Morrison Mary Mrs
　Elwood (The), board
124　Amiss J B Mrs
127　Campbell J M

Furniture and China Carefully Prepared for Shipment

Mahogany Furniture Hand Made & Carefully Reproduced

E. E. GALER
114 PATTON AVE.

Upholstering and Refinishing
PHONE - 1674

ROUGH AND DRESSED LUMBER
WHITE PINE AND YELLOW PINE
FLOORING A SPECIALTY
Hardwoods

Williams-Brownell Planing Mill Company
Mouldings and Interior Finish
Office: Southern Railway Tracks, Near Biltmore Station
Phone 729 *Planing Mill*

HAYWOOD 463 HAYWOOD

- Alabama (The), board
- 128 Bonnieview (The), boarding
- Amiss J B Mrs
- 135 Brown C N
- 139 Brown F F
- 147 Vance A C Mrs, furn rms
- (French Broad av Ends)
- 153 Robinson E J Mrs
- 161 Chunn J S
- 161½ Vacant
- (Montford av begins)
- 170 Hawthorne J E Dr
- 171 Hawkins V F
- 172 Harville C B Mrs, dressmkr
- 174 McIntyre P E
- 178 Brown E B
- 182 Carson Q M Miss
- Ward W A
- 186 Ingle J M
- 187 Boyce W A Mrs
- 194 Hamner C E
- 199 Fletcher M H Dr
- 200 Scott A L Mrs
- 207 Vacant
- 208 Ballard A M, phys
- Reeder J A Miss
- (Ann ends, Gudger begins)
- 216 McConnell Mollie Mrs
- 217 Haskell H S
- 217 (r) Haskell's Pepsi-Cola Bottling Works
- 223 Jones W M
- 231 Brown L V
- 232 Colwell A E
- 234 Hendrick J F
- 237 Vacant
- 238 Sanford —— Rev
- — Seventh Day Adventist Ch
- 239 Low W V
- 241 Mears P H Rev
- 249 Vacant
- 251 Robinson I R
- 255 Woodcock J A
- 258 Cowan J K
- 260 Maher W P
- 263 Vacant
- 264 Centerfit W H
- Pulliam Amelia Miss, nurse
- 271 Patton School for Boys
- Patton J C
- 275 Sullivan H H
- 278 Whitlock S K Mrs
- 279 Olive H J
- (Oakdale av begins)
- 291 Burton S P
- — Haywood St M E Church

HAYWOOD WEST—Continuation of Patton av and Haywood, s w from Buttrick
- 305 Crisp N L, gro
- 309 Tilson J H, shoemkr
- 311 Merrell W E, genl mdse
- 313 McMinn W J, drugs
- 315 Devine H P Furn Co
- 316 Smathers J L
- 317 *Vance Mark, gro
- 317½ Jordan J W, gro
- 319 Vacant
- 325 Johnston J V
- 327 Murdock Clara Mrs
- 328 McDonald E B Mrs
- 328 (r) Townsend W L
- 330 Baker H D
- Engle Henry
- 330 (r) Owen W E Mrs
- Freeman A E
- 333 Beachboard W M
- 334 Roberts & Crook, confrs
- 334 Rouse J A Rev
- Lipe Fred
- 334 (r) McCrumb Henry
- 334½ Dial Ada Mrs
- Tipton F T
- 336 Haywood Street Market, gros
- 337 Black J M, gro
- 339 Black J M
- 340 Williams W R
- Freeman R E L
- Scaffe J T
- 342 Crook R L, barber
- West End Pressing Club
- 343 Roberts P M, shoemkr
- 344 McAbee G W
- West End Grocery
- 346 Chandler T C Mrs, boarding
- (Spring ends)
- 347 Hoskovitz B H
- 349 Felmet Bros, gros
- 350 Vacant
- 350 (r) *McFee Mance
- *Manning Elijah
- 351 Black J H
- 352 Connor R H
- 353 Mills W F
- 356 Embler J M
- 357 Handley R G
- 359 Hough Matilda Mrs
- 361 DeVault W W
- 362 Eller T N
- 369 Green Bettie Mrs
- (Rector ends)

HUGHES
Transfer and Livery Co.

Automobiles for **HIRE**

TRUNKS 25c

Office:
401 Southside Avenue

PHONE 1405

Try our Hand Laundering. We strive to please in LAUNDERING and DRY CLEANING.

The Sanitary Home Laundry
No. 7 MONTFORD AVE.
PHONE - 1354

Mrs. Wilder's SANITARY HOME LAUNDRY turns out first class work in Laundering and Dry Cleaning. No. 7 Montford Ave., Phone 1354

HAYWOOD 464 HERREN AV

370 Hannah W W
371 Howie M G Mrs
373 Smathers Maggie Mrs
374 Beal C D
375 Lipe R P
376 Davis Harriet Mrs
    Allison Argus
379 Felmet F M
    Wilson W P
384 Vacant
385 Edwards W S
390 Harkins R W
391 Felmet A H
    (Jefferson Drive Begins)
405 Hall E S
408 Whitmore Sanitarium
    Whitmore S L Dr
409 Montgomery W S
415 Evans Jas
419 Sams J R
431 Rogers R B
441 Elkins Mark
    Barrett J J
445 Smart L P
    Revis Jas
    (Spring intersects)
458 Jay Mollie Mrs
462 Sams S J
470 (1) Potillo W L
    Webb R M
    Ramsey D T
470 (2) Wild J A, gro
    (Atkinson begins)
475 Ball H C
    Briggs M L
    Smith N H
477 Ingle A F
    Robinson Jas
478 Robertson Glenn
481 Sanders J M
    Cox F O
483 Sams L T
    Callahan C V
484 Farlow L A
    Lawrence T J
485 Dayton J H
488 Sircy J H
    Farlow Harley
— Vacant (new store)
    (Logan intersects)
492 O'Kelley Alvin
    Smith N H
493 King R P
    Metcalf J P
495 Solsbee G W
498 Radford Lula Miss

500 Vacant
501 Moser W M
502 Hammett Augustus, gro
504 Salvation Army Hall
    Sams Irving
506 King R P, shoemkr
508 Boyd H W
510 Sanders J M, gro
511 Mills W M, boarding
513 Crook J E, barber
514 Robinson W H
515 Boyd W H, eating hse
    (Roberts intersects)
523 Bradley N B, eating hse
525 Mears G A, genl mdse
527 Bradley J N, gro
    Rogers W F, fertilizers
529 Asheville Pkg Co
    (Sou Ry intersects)
— Asheville Cotton Mills
543 Westall J M & Co, lumber
545 Hill J F, gro
547-551 Olive H J, whse
549 Welch J L & Co, gros
551 Olive H J, gro
557 Jones W M, lumber
— Smith's Bridge

HAYWOOD ROAD—W Asheville

HAZZARD — Southeast from Eagle to Beaumont
  1 Ivy Levi, gro
    *Darden Texas
 16 *Wilson Laura
 23 *Anthony Jos, gro
 47 *Abbott Jas
 51 *Brown David
 59 *Coleman Chas
 65 *Sanders Sarah
 82 *Jones Rosa
 83 *Love Sarah
 87 *Love R P
 90 *Below Kate
 93 *Lyles J S
 98 *Williams Mary
 98 (r) *Dobey Amelia
100 *Dawkins Saml
102 *Smith Isaiah
104 *Latimer J S

HAZEL MILLS ROAD—W Asheville

HENRIETTA—N from 40 Josephine

HERREN AVENUE—W Asheville

BUICK — **ARBOGAST MOTOR COMPANY** — **OLDSMOBILE**
MAXWELLS — ACCESSORIES AND SUPPLIES — **DETROIT ELECTRIC**
52-60 N. Main Phones 302 and 1728

Asheville Dry Cleaning Co.
Telephones 835-836, All Dep't
MAIN, N. E. COR. COLLEGE

THE CLEANERS
Our Department for Oriental Rugs and Carpet Cleaning is prepared to serve you in all its branches.
E. S. Paine   O. E. Hansen

For Kindling "What am Kindling" Call
ENGLISH LUMBER COMPANY Phone 321

HIAWASSEE 465 HILL

HIAWASSEE—n w from Lexington av, 3 n of Patton av
- 7 *Burnett Chas
- 11 *Heard Mattie
  (Penland ends)
- 33 Starnes M J Mrs
  Cooper C S
- 36 Bradford M S Mrs
- 37 Glass Chas
- 38 Bradford J C
- 40 Paul C C
- 44 Blauvelt W H
- 49 Stevens F M, medicines
- 50 James W A Jr
- 51 Davis E W
- 56 Miller F B, painter

HIBERNIA—From 92 Black
- 1 Vacant
- 2 *Nesbitt Wm
- 3 *Davis Thos
- 4 *Wells Geo
- 5 *Burnon Wm
- 10 *Moon Wm L

HIBRITEN DRIVE—W from Pearson dr, 1 w of Santee

HIGHLAND—North from Chestnut, 3 e of Main
- 11 Stelling J H
- 16 Nance S S
- 17 Rogers W A
- 23 Barnett Jones
- 25 Pass R A
- 26 Vacant
- 27 Durrow W E
- 29 Vacant
- 33 Huffman A E
- 34 Atkins Jno
- 40 Tracey W D
- 42 Sherrill M C Mrs
- 43 Soncrant E R
- 45 Morgan G B
- 50 Haddon H B
  Clayton W B
- 54 Duvall LeRoy
- 60 Shook J B

HILDEBRAND—E from 10 Brick
- 15 *Erwin Virgil
- 20 *Ashe H L Rev
- 21 *Fletcher Henrietta
  *McDaniel Saml
- 22 *Green Theo
- 23 *Morris G W
- 26 *Steele Bruce
- 26½ *McIntire Thos
- 27 *Derumpley Prelow

- 28 *Long Nathan
- 29 *Flack Alex
- 29 (r) *Matthews Geo
- 31 *Vance Jas
- 32 *Johnson Lawrence
- 33 *Sanders Richard
- 34 Vacant
- 40 *St James A M E Church
- 41 *McDowell Elijah
- 42 *Barnum J R Rev

HILL—s w fr 30 Montford av
- 17 *McDavid Jos
  *Strachan Maude, nurse
- 20 *Evans A B
- 22 *Walker Thos
- 23 *Moore Anna
  *Smith Jane
- 28 *Moss Claude
- 29 *Jackson Sarah
- 30 *Davis Jos
- 31 *Vacant
- 34 *Frazier S D
- 35 *Taylor S F
- 36 *Whitmire Sarah
- 37 *Brown P B
- 38 *Simons Mary C, hairdresser
  (Gudger intersects)
- 47 Pearlman Barney, gro
- 48 *Clarke Nellie
- 52 *Hargraves Jonas
- 53 *Phinney Andrew
  (Bay intersects)
- 61 *Mulligan Wm
- 64 *Martin R J
  *Turner Perry
  *Avery Anna
- 67 *Coston Eugene, gro
- 70 *Swepson P J
- 70 (r) *Swepson Dorothy
- 71 *Bryan Julius
  (Maiden lane begins)
- 74 *Howell C T
- — *Hill St M E Church
- 81 *Hill Street School
- 84 *Livingston Hampton
  (Campbell intersects)
- 85 Sevier J D
- 95 *Torrence W G Dr
- 96 *Lipscombe C C
  (Oakdale av intersects)
- 118 *Steele Jesse
  *Greenleaf Jas
- 132 *Collins Chas
  (Buttrick ends)
- 140 *Wood Lee

BIGGEST BUSIEST BEST

ASHEVILLE STEAM LAUNDRY
Phones 1936 and 1937
43 to 47 W. COLLEGE

S. D. HALL
REAL ESTATE AGENT
—
Money Loaned
—
Notary Public
—
32 PATTON AVENUE
—
Phone 91

Founders, Machinists and Jobbers of Mill Supplies
PHONE 590
When in the market for pipe and fittings, let us make you Prices.
Carolina Machinery Co.
PHONE 590
If it's a Gas Engine let us figure with you, also on other kinds of machinery

LIFE INSURANCE COMPANY OF VA. OLDEST, LARGEST STRONGEST Southern Life Insurance Co.
ORGANIZED 1871
RICHMOND, VIRGINIA
Issues Industrial Policies from $8.00 to $900.00, with Premiums Payable WEEKLY on persons from two to seventy years of age
J. V. Moon, Superintendent, Rooms 3-4-5 Maxwelton Bldg., Asheville, N. C.

HILL 466 JEFFERSON DRIVE

D. TREXLER TIN SHOP

All Kinds of Roofing, Gutter and Conductor Work.

Phone 862

159 South Main St.

DR. C. H. MILLER

MECHANO-THERAPIST

14 N. Spruce St.
Phone 979
ASHEVILLE, N. C.

Hours by engagement

Drugless Healing of Disease

---

144 *Walker King
148 *Thomas Arthur
    *Brooks Tena
150 *Candler J G
152 *Poore J H
160 *Burton G W
163 *Robinson Wm
166 *Barton M H
167 *Aikens Frank
172 *Sheppard N E
176 *Wall J W
177 *Robertson Milton
180 *Jeffries Eugenia

HILLIARD LANE—West from 105 s Main
12 (15) Pittillo Kate Mrs, boarding
16 Brigmon E B Mrs, boarding
18 *Clemmons Otis, massage
    *Knight Bertha, hairdresser
18 (r) *Hull Garland

HILLSIDE—E from 415 n Main
16 Gibbs C B
29 *Davis Emma
    (West intersects)
34 Davis T E
44 Havener R A
48 Taylor A T
52 Henninger C G
56 Lyda E M
    (Center intersects)
64 McCall J F
65 Leeper H Y Rev
66 Lee Neil
73 Pugh C S
74 Batterham S R Mrs
83 Ray J E Capt
    (East intersects)
— Vacant
117 Ray A O
127 Ziegler E R P Mrs
134 Hunt F L Dr
135 Vacant
141 Ray S W
146 Constantine H B
149 Huntington E A Mrs
150 Smith F S
155 Davis W B
156 Barber G B
159 Alexander S D Mrs
165 Bennett Penelope Mrs
169 Vacant
    (Merrimon av intersects)
— "Bungalow" (The)
    Dunn W L Dr

    (Summit intersects)
243 Malone C W
    (Louisa intersects)
245 Jones Manning
    Jones W H
252 Voorhies M E Mrs
260 Wilson J B
266 Malone C N
270 Nixon W B
323 Owens Sarah Mrs
327 Buckner W N
335 Lingle P E
    Murdock D S
    (Clyde intersects)
341 Dickerson M J Mrs
349 Davenport O M
353 Buckner A L
    Sprinkle A P
— Foster G M

HOLLAND—N from 52 Chestnut
14 McDermott W R
18 Sinclair P D Dr
20 Hulme Y M
36 Herman G L
40 Rowe S N
44 Vacant
98 Tomlinson Peter
102 Eppes G W

HOLLYWOOD—N from 268 College
56 Bernard S G

HORSESHOE CURVE—S of Mud Cut, 1 w of s French Broad av

HUNT—West from Edgehill av
2 Briggs Chas
4 Bass Frank

INGLE—Depot section
3 *Bell Lillie
4 *Ryder C B
5 *Kemp Rebecca
7 *Moore Allison
8 *Wilson Bessie
10 *Penson Jno
14 *Hunter Dilcy
18 *Lanham Lit
19 Murray W W
20 Murray J W
22 *Thompson Myra
23 *Berry J A Rev

IRVING—(see Ervin)

JARRETT AVENUE—W Asheville

JEFFERSON DRIVE—Southwest from 319 Haywood

....**Asheville Cleaning and Pressing Club**....
Tailoring That Satisfies and Prices That Please
Steam and French Dry Cleaning of all delicate and fine wearing apparel for ladies and gentlemen. MESSENGER SERVICE IN THE CITY.
J. C. WILBAR, Prop. 4. N. Pack Square PHONE 389

CAROLINA COAL & ICE CO.
"M & W" INDIAN — Prompt Delivery — PHONE 130 — 50 PATTON AVE. — WEIGHTS ACCURATE

JEFFERSON DRIVE 467 LEXINGTON AV

12 Lambert H A Mrs, dressmkr
15 Betts R W
16 Crompton B L Mrs
20 Bryant G H
   Abbott T J
21 Adams O E
   Evans Hester Miss, nurse
22 Capps W C
26 Boone W H
   Byrd Oscar
29 Phillips S H
   Phillips D B Mrs, boarding
30 Viniarski B A
31-33 Vacant
38 Gooch T J
42 Davis H E Mrs
58 Pennel T L
62 Carter G D
90 Devine H P
92 Hampton B A
94 Crook H T
98 Hayes Edgar
99 Davis Louisa Mrs

JOHN—s e from 149 Bartlett
11 Early S T
15 McCall R A
16 Smith B M
17 Epley J N
34 Burgin A P
36 Vacant
42 Vacant
44 Burgin W B
57 Cashatt W H

JORDAN—s e from Latta
12 *Woodside J A
17 *Jordan Louisa
20 *Shade Isaac
26 *Randall Lawson
27 *Burgin Mary

JOSEPHINE—E from Merrimon av, 1 n of Hillside
16 Dickinson E C
18 Thompson E L Mrs
31 Britt W C
36 Whiteside J K
39 Selby Jos
40 Creek Martha Mrs
   (Henrietta intersects)
56 Enoch J L
   Glass E L
59 Patterson C W
60 Vacant
61 Young W W
62 Mitchell T L
67 Eller E E
78 Herron P G

80 Adams W M
81 Isom J D
83 Pool S R O
97 Lindsey J H
   Creasman L N
— Ball L R

KELLY—s w from Latta
KING—w from 402 Merrimon av
KNOB — s e from Circle to Ridge
6 *Steele Cora
7 *Jones H E
9 *Smith J H
15 *Clowney Lewis
17 *Moore Jackson
18 *Stinson G A, drayman

LATTA—S from 25 Clemmons
12 *Lyda Jackson
14 *Walker J M
14 *Walker Lucy
15 *Williams W M
16 *Love Addie
18 *Propes Laura
19 *Vance Wm
21 *Jackson Minnie

LEXINGTON AVE — North and south from Patton av, 1 w of Main
   ☞Going North
4 Sugarman Jacob, tailor
17 Berkeley Pool Room
18 Phipps J W, eating hse
21-23 Brown C L, blksmith
25-27 Bradford J M, painter
   Ashev Sign Co
30 Mountain City Laundry
32 Vacant
34 Barnes W E & Co, produce
36 Ownbey R L & Co, produce
38 Guy J L, produce
39-41 Chambers J K, livery
   (Walnut intersects)
59 Young S K, produce
   Rosen Max, coppersmith
69 *Campbell Robt
   *Creasman Kate, nurse
   *Witherspoon Preston
61 Robinson S D, stable
64 Vacant
77 Vacant
79 McCall J F, blksmith
81-93 Greer's Row
Rooms—
1 *Rumley Danl
2 *Maddox Newton

St. Rw'y — Electric Light and Power — Gas
ASHEVILLE POWER AND LIGHT COMPANY — PHONE 69

Poultry — Kiibler & Whitehead
CITY MARKET — PHONES, 195 and 694

Asheville Dray, Fuel and Construction Co.

Heavy Hauling of all kinds — 61-2 South Main — **WE FURNISH BUILDING STONE** — Moving Furniture a Specialty — PHONE - 223

LEXINGTON AV 468 LIVINGSTON

- 3 *Barber Jane
- 4 *Whiteside Lucy
- 5 *Young Jno
- 6 *Walker Lizzie
- 7 *Allison Nancy
- 8 *McComb Jno
- 9 *Johnson Hattie
- 10 *Alexander Mattie
- 11 *Snider Mattie
- 12 *Morgan Rose

(N Lexington av continued)
- 82 Wilson J H, stables
- Rosen Max, produce
- 82 (2d fl) Willis Nelson
- 84 Sternberg S & Co, skins

(Hiawassee begins)
- 93 Young & Robinson, gros
- 93½ *Avery Harper
- 97 Vacant
- 100 *Gibson Eva
- 101 *Gray Henry, furn repr
- Hoskins S B
- 104 *Littlejohn Hampton
- 109 *Phinney Elmore
- 110 *Keys M T
- 113 *Rodrick Mary
- 117 McGuire & Co, herbs
- 125 McConnell Wm C
- 127 Vacant

☞ Going South
- 7 Vacant
- 9 Webb W A, livery
- 11 Brown W B, live stock
- 10-12 Hackney & Moale Co, printers
- 14-16 Smith T C Dr, drugs (whol)
- 15-17 Asheville Auto Co
- 23 Higgins Carrie Miss
- 27-33 Slayden, Fakes & Co (Inc), whol gros
- 30 Vacant
- 34 Reisecker E A
- 39 Ray W S, livery
- 42 Citizens Transfer, stables

LIBERTY (North)—Fr Charlotte to H'side, 1 e of Merrimon av
- 18 Sullivan N B
- 19 Martin J C
- 21 Williams Leonore Miss
- 25 Moore J W
- 40 Robertson S L Mrs
- 43 Grove E W Dr
- 61 Vacant
- 70 Rawls R R
- 76 Vacant
- 85 Nichols J A
- Nichols J J
- 89 Lynch S A
- 90 Vacant
- 104 Freedlander S A

LIBERTY (South) — From Woodfin to Orange, 1 e of Merrimon av
- 3 Westerlund A M
- Randell D E
- 17 Maplewood (The)
- 21 Jewish Synagogue
- 25 Swartzberg M
- 27 Simpson Nicholas
- 29 Vacant
- 31 Levitt Morris
- 32 Keith J F
- 33 Diamond Morris
- 35 Swartzberg Isaac
- 37 Katz A H
- 39 Cohn C M
- 41 Finestein Saml
- 43 Seigle Harry
- 58 Sluder W R
- 60 Young M A Mrs
- 64 Londow Louis
- 68 Boon Chas
- 72 Burrows Harry
- 76 Clements J R
- Nash E W
- 78 Leidenger H H

LINCOLN AVENUE—Southeast from 94 Pine
- 7 *Harris Edwd
- 8 *Ponder Columbus
- 11 *McKesson Elsie
- 12 *Morris Walter
- 13 *Johnston J P
- 16 *Carter Dillard
- 17-20 *Vacant
- 18 *Richardson Jas
- 19 *Williams Marshall
- 22 (32) *Caldwell Augustus
- 22 *McCoy Alonzo
- 26 *Allman Waddey
- 28 *Derumpley Larkin
- 41 *Wilson Maggie
- 45 *Fleming Lee A
- 55 Underwood Jane Mrs
- 61 *Bruton Maggie
- 64 *Moore Clement

LIVINGSTON — N from 89 Victoria rd
- 22 Merchant L L, contr
- 29 Davis S N

DYNAMOS & MOTORS

Piedmont Electric Co.

64 Patton Av.
ASHEVILLE, N.C.

J. C. McPHERSON
SLATE AND TIN ROOFING
Galvanized Iron Work   Hot Air Furnaces
35-37 EAST COLLEGE STREET

PLUMBING STEAM AND HOT WATER HEATING
PHONE 133

MAPLE FLOORING — HARDWOOD LUMBER OF ALL KINDS

WOODWARD & SON
9th and Arch Sts., Richmond, Va.
See Adv. Opposite Page 188

LIVINGSTON   MADISON

- 33 Vacant
- 60 McDowell B L Mrs
- 64 Turner M L Mrs
- 71 Ward P W
- — Pease A E Mrs
- 72 *Livingston Presbyterian Ch
- 82 Goodlake Ella Mrs
- 93 Stewart A I Mrs, gro
- 94 Gates T L
- 95 Stewart A I Mrs
- 98 Jones W M
- 106 *Hall J A
- 108 *Winkler Rufus
- 116 *Gilliam Jno
- 118 *Eidson Douglas
- 128 *Bluford Fred
- 130 *Baird David
- 134 *Johnson Fannie, dressmkr
- 138 *Hicks Wm
- 142 *Leach Amanda
- 143 *Lenoir W H
- 146 *McKinney Whit
- 149 *Free Will Bapt Ch
- 150 *Washburn Louise
- 154 *Johnson Elbert
- 158 *Smith Edwd
- 160 *Kincaid Saml
- 164 *Hamrick Pink
- 174 *Harper Jos
- 178 *Stanback Jas, shoemkr
- 179 *Caldwell Jas
- 180 Ray Susan Miss, dressmkr
- 184 *Shuford Claude
- 188 *Glover David
- 190 *Chambers Geo
- 204 Whitted J O
- 212 McDarris Wm O, gro

LOCUST—N from 194 College
- 11 Thomas J W

LOGAN—s w fr 488 w Haywood
- 8 Smith Ross
- 10 McCallister D M
- 17 Vacant
- 23 Pruett C W
- 25 Brackett Gaither
- 26 Bradley J N
-    Rice Jas
- 28 Biggs S S Mrs

LOUIE—s w of Sou Ry Depot
- — *Moore Archibald
- — *Smith Jas
- — *Williams Elizabeth
- — Parris N F
- 9 Stricklin L E Mrs

- 25 Jones G N
- 33 Huff P J
- 34 Vacant
- 37 Waddell S C

LOUISA—N from 243 Hillside
- 12 Vacant
- 21 Cunningham J F
- 22 Vacant

LYMAN—West from Depot at junction of Roberts
- — Ashev Mica Co, warehouse
- — North Carolina Oil Co

McDOWELL—South from 16 Southside av
- 2 Nowell Sylvester, gro
- 12 *McDowell Lena
- 14 *Stewart Cora
- 16 *Miller Spencer
- 18 *Moss Crockett
- 20 *Pulliam Clarence
- 23 *Borden Mary
- 24 Lanning C G
- 25 *Moon Emma
- 26 Lyerly D K
- 27 *Sartor J R
- 29 *Watson L V Rev
- 31 *Powell Allen
- 32 Brown Maggie Mrs
-    Brown Alex, painter
- 34 Atkins Sarah Mrs
- 38 Blair Fannie Mrs
- 40 Johnson Kate Mrs
- 44 *Baird Cal
- 48 *Allison Belle
- 50 *Siler Dollie
- 58 *Smith M D Rev
- 64 Bocook F H
- 70 Justice W T
- — Patton J P

MADISON—South from Gray, w of Pearson Drive
- 2 *McCullough Squire
-    *Littlejohn Harriett
- 5 Duncan Elizabeth Mrs
- 8 *Wilson Chas
- 9 *McCullough Berry
- 12 *Piercey A
- 13 *Jeter Wm
- 14 *Johnson Harvey
- 23 Penland A M
- 23 Ward Sandy
- 36 *Reed Victoria
- 40 *Wilson Harrison
- 41 *Wilson Nea
- 42 *Matthews Mack
- 54 Grant Clara R Mrs

What Have You in Real Estate that You Don't Want?

What do You Want in Real Estate that You Haven't?

WESTERN CAROLINA REALTY CO.
J. W. Wolfe, Sec. & Treas.
On the Square
PHONE 974
10 N. PACK Sq.

H. A. BROWN & Co.
General Contractors
23 Temple Court Bldg.
Phone 341

—DEALERS IN—

Rough Building
and
all Kinds of
Crushed Stone

—OUR SPECIALTIES—

STONE FOUNDATIONS
CONCRETE WORK
and
EXCAVATING

Moale & Chiles — Real Estate and Insurance
City and Suburban Property   FARMS and TIMBER LANDS
27 Patton Ave., (2d fl) Phone 661

Candy Kitchen and Club Cafe "A GOOD PLACE FOR REFRESHMENT" Hot drinks on cold days. Cold drinks on hot days. The best drinks every day. Pure fruits and syrups blended "just right," served daintily. Our Ice Cream and Soda Water Department, Restaurant and Candy Departments are always kept up to the standard of nearest perfection. Phones 110 and 111. 19 and 21 Haywood St.

MADISON　　　470　　　MAIN

Brown's Undertaking Parlors

S. H. BROWN

50 Patton Avenue
ASHEVILLE, N. C.

Lady Assistant When Desired

Phone 193-2 Rings

THE MOORE Plumbing Company

16 N. Pack Square

PHONE 1025

Sanitary Plumbing, General Tin and Metal Work, Hot Air Furnaces

---

57 McNeely Jane E Mrs
58 Vacant
110 *Pearson Moore

MADISON AVENUE—North from 111 Broad
11 Cole J D
15 Henry L A
36 Lee E A Mrs
42 Winans F J
46 Horrich H H
48 *Daily Mary
49 Forestburg Mathias
50 Fields A J
59 Samuel Frank
60 Cain J A
61 *Cassel W M
64 Pinkins J J
69 Pursley E S
70 Hughes M M Mrs
71 Blackwell D D Mrs
78 Douglas G J
80 Hudson W D
83 Revis L A

MAGNOLIA AVENUE—West from 310 n Main
10 *Haynes Geo
14 *Arnold Jas
20 *Murphy Mary
26 *Jackson B J
30 *Williams Israel
34 *Greer Henry
35 *Robinson Alvin
37 *Thomas Margaret
39 *Robertson A M
40 Taylor W D
41 *Hooper Avery
42 Painter Z V
44 Edwards F O
　　(Flint intersects)
70 Vacant
71 Drummond C L Miss
71½ Cartmell Katharine Miss
73 Rhodes J J
75 Vacant
　　(——— intersects)
370 *Burnett Jackson
374 *Hunt Hattie
　　*Worford Jno

MAIDEN LANE—North from
71 Hill
9 *Cowans E O Rev
11 *Few Thos
15 Vacant
19 *Babb Jno
21 *Greer Louisa
27 *Shell Wm

*Posey Mary
30 *Conley Patsy
34 *Crawford Jno
35 Revis Geo
36 *Young Jno
　　*Scott Geo
　　*Gaither Adeline
40 *Brown Sallie
　　*Roseman Jas
　　*Whitson Wm
40 (r) Yarborough Mary Mrs
52 Parris Burnett

MAIN—North and south from Pack Square to city limits, one of the principal business streets of the city, and the dividing line for streets running east and west

☞ Going North
— Langren Hotel
　　Asheville Dry Cleaning Co
2 Langren Barber Shop
4-6 Asheville Paint & Glass Co
　　Langren Drug Store
7 Ashev & E Tenn R R Co
　　Weaverville Line
　　United States Cafe
　　Mosseller J S & Son, locksmiths
8 Vacant
9 Schochet J B Mrs, dry gds
11 Karres Bros, confrs
11½ Coffey Zora Mrs, furn rms
12 Finestein Saml, clothing
13 *Conley Lee, barber
13½ Sorrels G A, gro
15-17 Smathers J L & Sons, furn
　　Tillman J A, watchmkr
17½ Warren B W, furn rms
18 Vacant (store)
19 Featherston A A, gro
20 Vacant
21 Rich J R Co, plmbrs
22-24 Vacant
23 Ashev Barbers Supply Co
　　Tiller J T
　　Union Plumbing Co
25 Brown Hdw Co
26-28 Vacant
27 Moore W L, furn
29 Rockett O N, restaur
30 Shope & Patton, harness
31 Vacant
32 Jenkins J H, gro

The Battery Park Bank　　Capital - - $100,000.00
　　　　　　　　　　　　　　　Surplus and Profits, $110,000.00

ASHEVILLE, N. C.　　**City, County and State Depositary**

J. A. TILLMAN — work. Satisfaction guaranteed — **Jeweler** — I carry a nice line of Watches, Clocks and Jewelry, and make a specialty of repair — **17 N. Main St.**

MAIN 471 MAIN

- 33-35 Millard Livery Co
- 34 Excelsior P & P House
- 34½ Bryson Cora Mrs, board
  - Bryson U S, hackman
- 36 Harris-Barnett Dry Goods Co
- 36½ Panzerbeiter Georgia Mrs
  - Carson H B
  - Pegas J D
  - Psychoghio P D
  - Psychas D D
- 37 Barnett W L, gro
- 38 McConnell Bros, produce

(Walnut intersects)

- 39 Hotel Warren
  - Warren B W, real est
- 47 Monteeth Elisha
  - Monteeth E J Mrs, board
  - Ingle J B, gro
- 49 Whitt R Y, board
- 51 Cole Fulton, music tchr
- 52-60 Arbogast Motor Co
- 53 Fitzpatrick R L & Son, paints
- 53½ Creasman J H
- 55 Farmers Union, genl mdse
- 55½ Willis C P
- 57 Patterson W E & Co, furn
  - Havener R A, cabtmkr
- 57 (2d fl) Hall E S, mirrors re-silvered
- 58 Colonial (The), board
- 67-71 Enterprise Machine Co
- 70 Colonial (The), board
- 72 Ambler Bldg
  - Ambler C P, phys
  - Morris E C, phys
  - Woodbury W H, lumber
- 76 "Ozark" (The), board
  - Hammond L D Mrs
- — Masonic Temple & Scottish Rites Cathedral

(Woodfin intersects)

- 111 *Pritchett Albert
- 115 *Alexander Sherman

(Lexington av ends)
(Merrimon av begins)

- 130 Hyams Mord, gro
- 135 Allen M A Mrs, board
- 143 Starnes J R
- 144 Clark T S

(Cherry begins)

- 153 Eureka Boarding House
- 156 Chakales P E
- 159 Rembert C E Mrs, board
- 165 Loughran Frank
- 167 Finkelstein H L
- 179 Ford L B

(Starnes av begins)

- 210 Vacant
- 212 Voorhies H B
- 215 Sumner B H
- 234 Woodard Edwd
- 242 Buckner W W
  - Anders J H
  - Young Fredk
- 254 Patterson R O
- 258 Jones P M
- 264 Havener J M
- 266 Meek C A

(Chestnut intersects)

- 277 North Asheville Grocery
  - Hayes J F
- 292 Whyte Alex
- 298 Fry H A
- 306 Gentry J W
- 312 Dockery T L
- 318 Vacant

(Magnolia av begins)

- 319 Drake J R
- 320 Hensley S M
- 325 Hall R D

(Ocala begins)

- 331 Wilson W A, contr
- 332 Allison L C
- 336 Capehart M D Mrs
- 346 *Mills Richd

(Seney begins)

- 348-350 Vacant
- 357 Redmon T B
- 360 Hensley J H
- 361 Edwards L E
- 371 Taylor M L
- 372 Young J H
  - Bradford J M
- 382 White H Y
- 386 Holcombe Rosa Mrs
- 386 (r) Stevens G W
- 389 Reed J H
- 392-398 Vacant
- 394 Wheeler G W

(Hillside intersects)

- 415 Sherlin J L
- 417 Hart G G
- 418 Young J H, gro
- 421 Blackwell W S
- 424 McMahan Wm N
  - Banks Chas
- 425 Cauble D W, blksmith
- 434 Capehart Louis
- 436 Cauble D W
- 437 Banks R D

INSURANCE
- Insure your salary with us
- Never carry your own risk
- Safety is the best policy
- Unless you are a capitalist
- Rest easy if you have
- An accident we will
- Not keep you waiting to
- Collect your claim
- Every claim promptly paid

Imperial Mutual Life & Health Insurance Co.

Home Office: ASHEVILLE, N. C.

Phone 495

HOTEL OXFORD Redecorated and Refitted throughout. Recently enlarged to 60 rooms. Centrally located. Depot cars stop at entrance. Long distance telephone office upstairs. American and European plan. Rates 50c, 75c and $1 per day; special rates by week or month. C. H. Branson & Sons, Proprietors. Phone 1887. 50-54 South Main St. **Asheville, N. C.**

Williams-Brownell Planing Mill Company — *Hardwoods*

Lumber---Rough and Dressed Flooring a Specialty Moulding, Interior Finish, Etc.
Office, Plant and Yards on Southern Railway, Near Biltmore Station
WHITE PINE   Phone 729   YELLOW PINE

MAIN 472 MAIN

- 442 Murray Addie Mrs
- 443 Crank J C
- 448 Griffin J F
- 449 Davis J H
- 450 Wilson J R
- Rutledge Jas

(North begins)

- 467 Cannon & Haynes, gro
- 469 Haynes M E
- 481 Church G A
- 485 Berry P W

(Panola begins)

- 511 Buckner L M Mrs
- 521 Harden R W
- 557 Edwards Laura Mrs
- 559 Reed T J
- 560 Cannon C W

☞ Going South

- 1 Smith's Drug Store
- 1½ Johnston Bldg (offices)
  - Green & Goodman, real est
  - Patterson J R & Son, genl ins
  - Pisgah Lodge No 32 K of P Hall
  - U S Army Recruiting Station
- 2 Burton & Holt, furn
- 3 Levitt Morris, notions
- 4 Guarantee Shoe Store
- 5-7 Palais Royal, dry gds
- 6 Schas M S, cigars
- 6½ Asheville Dray, Fuel & Construction Co (Inc)
  - Asheville Concrete Pipe & Block Co
  - Sevier D E & J T, phys
- 8 Zageir R B, clothing
- 9 Fisher H L, confr
- 10 Grant's Pharmacy
  - Farmer E L Mrs, dressmkr
- 11 N Y Quick Lunch & Restaurant
- 11½ *Buckeye Sanitary Shaving Parlor
- 12-14 Southern Hotel (The)
- 13 Asheville Candy Kitchen
- 14 Donald & Donald, furn
- 14½ Woods F T H, real estate
- 15 Vacant
- 16 Racket Store (The), dry gds
- 17 Mumpower R E, dry gds
  - Nyberg Auto Sales Co
- 18 Jenkins G W, dry goods
  - Hinkle M L Mrs
  - Feezor H B Mrs, dressmkr
- 19 Vacant (store)
- 21 Falk's Music House
  - Gruner B F Mrs, corsets
- 21 (2d fl) Hare & Co, undertakers
  - Walton F A, real est
- 21 (3d fl) Y W C A Gymnasium
- 22 Gentry J C, dry gds
- 23-25 Finkelstein's Pawn Shop
- 24 Vacant
- 26-28 Hotel Paxton
- 27 Beaumont Furn Co
- 28 British Woolen Mills, tailors
- 29 Ashev Furn Co
- 29½ Batson Alice Mrs
- 31 Trakas N S & Co, fruits

(Eagle begins)

- 32 Globe Sample Co, shoes
- 33 Ashev Harness Co
- 33½ Eagles Hall
- 34 Vacant
- 35 Moore J C, furn
  - Noblitt M W
- 36 Psychas D D, eating hse
- 37 Davis J R, furn
  - Goldsmith W W Jr, watchmkr
- 37½ Goldsmith W W Jr
- 38 Vacant
- 38½ Salvation Army Hall
- 39 *Wilson J A, barber
  - *Weston Jos, shoemkr
  - *Sartor J A, cleaning
- 39½ *Faulkner Bennie P, hairdresser
- 40 *Greenlee & Loder, pool
- 41 Davis W A, gro
- 41½ Florida House (The)
  - Hudson H B Mrs
- 42 Champion Shoe Hospital
- 43 Jones W C, cigars
  - Gardner F K Dr, eye specialist
- 44 Woods S F, gro
- 45 Swannanoa Drug Co
- 46 Windsor Hotel Barber Shop

(Aston begins)

- 48-50 Windsor Hotel and Cafe
- 47-55 Swannanoa-Berkeley Hotel
- 54 Hotel Oxford
- 51 Gross W W
  - Gross Nola Mrs, board
- 52 Globe Furn Co

Asheville Electrical Co. — Electrical Contractors
HEADQUARTERS 74 CENTRAL AVENUE
W. Mansfield Booze, Manager
PHONE 377

Asheville Dry Cleaning Co. **THE CLEANERS**
Telephones 835-836, All Dep't
MAIN, N. E. COR. COLLEGE
Our Department for Oriental Rugs and Carpet Cleaning is prepared to serve you in all its branches.
E. S. Paine   O. E. Hansen

FOR BOX SHOOKS — **Call English Lumber Co.** **PHONE 321**

MAIN 473 MAIN

- 53 Swannanoa-Berkeley Hotel Barber Shop
- 55 Swannanoa-Berkeley Hotel Pool Room
- 56 Hollar Motor Co
- 57 Brux H B, paper
- 58-60 Wilson E F, stables
  - Tuttle A A, vet surg
- 59 Vacant (store)
- 60-68 Arbogast Motor Co
- 61-63 O K Auto Supply & Transit Co
- 62 Ashev F P Gas Machine Co
- 65-67 American Wagon Co
- 69-71 Johnson T P & Co, tinners
  - Wrenn & Garland, contrs
- 78 Henrietta (The)
  - Y W C A
  - Osborn G L Miss
  - Lance M W Mrs
- 90-92 Coca-Cola Bottling Co
- 91 Hull F A
- 97 *Westmoreland Maria
  - *Parks Tench
  - *Blakely Heywood
- 100 Sorrell F McD Mrs, boarding
- 101 Hilliard M E Mrs
  - Campbell J M
- 102 Austin E J Mrs
- 104 Vacant
  - (Hilliard lane begins)
- 111 Foster R P
- 123 Sawyer Clarence
- 128 Webster C N
- 129 Carmichael W C Dr
- 130 McClain R K
- 132 Burns D B
- 132½ Swearngan M A
- 134 Stikeleather Gilliland
- 134½ Reese Jas
  - Reese B H Miss, nurse
- 136 Salisbury J H
- 136½ Atkins M M Miss
  - Atkins E F Miss
- 137 Mears G A
- — Ashev T & S Co, whse
  - (Atkin begins)
- 145 Gudger W R
  - Gudger L M Mrs, dressmkr
- 149 Hermann J B
- 149 (r) Towe W P
- 153 Freck Carrie Mrs
  - Campbell N P Miss, dressmkr
- 153 (r) Freck C B
- 155 Leonardi J H, gro
- 155½ Freck Dollie Mrs
- 156 Leonardi J H
- 157 Swink Fred
- 158 Vacant
- 159 Trexler David, tinner
- 160 Stone P L
  - Peebles A L
- 161 Hayes C S, gro
- 161½ Clayton G H
- 162 Hunt H C
  - Capps M R
- 165 Swicegood D L
  - Ingram L F, paperhngr
  - Ingram C B Mrs, dressmkr
- 165½ Dillon J W
  - Conder F L
- 166 Trexler David
  - Swink Ella Mrs
- 166 (r) Smith Earl
- 167 Johnson W C
  - Dalton T S, contr
- 167½ Golay M M Mrs
- 173 Sneed C T
  - Sneed Mollie Mrs, boarding
- 174 Atkins Thos
- 174½ Featherston S M
- 175 Weaver M A Mrs
- 176 Swink Robt
- 178 Swink Robt, gro
  - (Southside av begins)
- 180 Swink J C
- 180 (r) Foster Zebulon
- 182 Taylor Jno G
- 184 Swink J J
- 190 *Lane Rachel
- 194 *Glascow Mary
- 195 *Bryant R H Dr
- 202 *Kemp E M
  - *Nipson J J
- 210 Vacant
  - (Valley ends)
- 215 *Garrett Mollie
- 217 Grant R M
- 219 *Cowan Wm
- 221 *Lytle Robt
- 223 *Davidson G H
- 237 Sugg J K
- 241 Cooke H E
- 245 Lasater W H
- 255 Alexander R D Mrs
- 255 (r) *Carter Henry
- 261 Youngblood T R
- 262 Buchanan S E
- 265 Nowell C E

BIGGEST BUSIEST BEST

Asheville Steam Laundry

Phones:
1936 and 1937

43 to 47
W. College Street

CHARLES H. HONESS

OPTOMETRIST AND OPTICIAN

Exclusive maker of
ATLAS SHUR-ON EYE GLASSES

THE
Home of Ce-Rite Toric Lenses

We make a specialty of correcting optical defects with properly fitted glasses.

54 Patton Avenue
Opposite Postoffice

Carolina Machinery Co. Founders, Machinists and Jobbers of Mill Supplies. We make all kinds of Castings in Iron, Brass or Aluminum.

WE ALSO FURNISH SKILLED MECHANICS FOR BOILER REPAIRS —— PHONE 590

LIFE INSURANCE COMPANY OF VA.

ORGANIZED 187

Richmond -:- Virginia

J. V MOON, Superintendent

Rooms 3-4-5- Maxweiton Bldg., Asheville, N. C.

All claims paid IMMEDIATELY upon receipt of satisfactory proofs of Death. Total payment to policyholders since organization, over $12,000,000.00. Is paying its Policyholders over $1,000,000.00 annually.

MAIN 474 MARKET

T. P. JOHNSON & CO.

SHEET METAL WORKERS

All Kinds of Roofing Guttering and Conductor Work Metal Ceilings, Skylights and Galvanized Iron Cornices

OFFICE and SHOP:
69-71 S. MAIN

Phone 325

DR. C. H. MILLER

Mechano-Therapist

14 N. Spruce Street
ASHEVILLE, N. C.

PHONE 979

Hours by Engagement

DRUGLESS HEALING OF DISEASE

- 269 Cobb J F
- 269 (r) Graham J B
-     Green Geo
-     Moody Chas
-     Mulwee Jno
-     Stepp G B
-     Dill J A
- 273 Norris O V
-     Parker Thos
- 277 Bird W H
-     (Bird Alley begins)
- 281 Smith R W
- 283 Clark H C
- 285 Miller T O
- 293 Brown C B, hackman
-     Wilson Theron
- 299 Sloan J B
- 303 Duckett E A Mrs
-     Moss Saml
-     Hollingsworth S O, shoemkr
- 315 Frady J B
- 317 Jones T W
- 321 Wilson Henry
- 323 Turner G B
- 323 (r) Tolley W D
- 323½ Lankford N T
- 324 Knight T B C
- 324 (r) O'Kelly B Z
- 326 Hawkins A N, gro
-     Israel F R
- 326 (r) Bass Jno
-     Townsend Wm
- 329 Dalton J T
- 330 Ingle J E
- 340 Langford Robt
- 345 Koon J N
- 447 Vacant (store)
- 357 Mason H E Mrs, dressmkr
- 358 Bishop J B
-     (McDowell intersects)
- 371 McPeeters & Mack, gros
- 371 (2d fl) Lanford S P
- 374 Branagan J J
- 375 Shuford E B
-     Baldwin C L
- 383 McDowell E E, contr
- 397 Welfley M L
- 401 Shehan G C
- 413 McDowell A E Miss
- 421 Waters W E
- 423 Kennedy Saml
- 425 Webb D H, gro
-     Bishop W H
-     Garren Virginia Mrs
-     Helton Marion

-     Parker Jas
- 428 St Joseph's Sanitarium
- 435 Garren Edwd
- 439 Robertson A H, shoemkr
- 441 Webb D H, blksmith
- 443 (433) McGuinn J A
- 453 Lanning A W, gro
- 458 Johnson A R & Co, gros
-     (Victoria Road begins)
- 460 Bourne J D
- 464 Jones J M
- 468 Moore C B
- — Forest Hill, boarding
-     Penniman W T Mrs
- — Normal & Collegiate Institute
- — Oakland Heights Presby Ch
- 515 Cosgrove T A Rev
- 556 Dawson Rufus
- 560 Moore J L
-     Murphy J J
- — Home Industrial School
- — Perry N R
- — *Tatum Benj
- — Newton Academy
- — Kenilworth Hall

MAPLE—East from 15 Reed
- 4 Champion H A Miss

MARCELLUS—West from 40 Merrimon av

MARGARET—Fr Courtland av
- 15 *Gibbs A L
- 23 *Houston Lee

MARJORIE—E from Market
- 12 McKinnish J W
-     Smith J R
- 16 Mitchell E M
- 20 Wilson H A Mrs
- — County Jail

MARKET—South from City Hall, 1 e of Main
- 8 Asheville Ice Co
- 16 Kelly M H, contr
- 18-22 Asheville Supply & Fdy Co
- 26 Asheville Mica Co
-     (Eagle intersects)
- — *Y M I Bldg
-     *Y M Institute
-     *Y M I Drug Store
-     *Torrence W G, phys
-     *Walker J W, phys
- — Murrough Noah, eating hse
-     *Y M I Pressing Club
- 44 *Masonic Temple
-     *Knights of Pythias Hall

ASHEVILLE CLEANING and PRESSING CLUB

TAILORING THAT SATISFIES and PRICES THAT PLEASE

Hats cleaned, banded and bound. Silk hats ironed. Buttons made to order in all sizes. Plain or with rims. PHONE 389

DYEING IN ALL SHADES Cleaned. Messenger Service.

Kid Gloves, Slippers and Plumes. Fancy Jabots and Ties. French Dry Cleaned. Ladies' and Gentlemen's suits Steam

J. C. Wilbar, Prop. 4 NORTH PACK SQ.

ASHEVILLE COAL CO. 6 North Pack Sq. Phone 40

M. & W. COAL

Electric Flat Irons — Asheville Power and Light Co. Phone 69

MARKET 475 MERRIMON PL

*Cannon & Oglesby, real estate
*N C Mutual Prov Assn
*Goodman E Z
*McGinness J H, tailor
72 *Allison Wm
74 *Asbury S A
76 *Peterson Matthew
78 *McClure Irvin
97 *Maxwell Mary
99 *Crosby Isaac
*Maxwell Ora
101 *Clifton Dora
103 *Rumley Wm
*Jeffries Wm
105-109 Vacant

MAX—South from 6 Knob
2 *Stinson W M
15 *Harrison Peggie
19 Vacant (new house)
— *Alexander W M, gro
23 *Wilson Jeremiah
27 *Mayfield Thos
31 *Sanford Geo
33 *Ritchie Jno
39 *Duckett Collier
*Simpson Casper
44 *Russell Louisa
48 *Wilson Jas
49 *Jordan McGee
52 *Earle Jos
55 *Garrett Vina
56 *Houston Wallace
59 *Macedonia Sanctified Ch
60 *Thompson Gabriel
63 *Davis Benj
*Cory Lula

MERRIMON AVENUE — Northeast from Main at junction of Lexington av
1 Swartzburg Moses
7 Snyder C H
17 Briggs Milton
18 Vacant
21 Vacant
21 (r) Henderson J H
23 Vacant
40 Diamond Annie Miss
52 Roselawn (The), boarding Collister E E
53 Rankin J E
64 Ringer P H Dr
(Orange intersects)
72 Morris Emma M Mrs
73 Northup W B
79 Ward Lizzie Mrs
82 Weaver F M
85 Porter A W Mrs
90 Shemwell Baxter
93 Patterson W E
99 Ashton C B
102 Mustin Eli
107 Schuessler C R Mrs
112 Merrimon M A Miss
(Chestnut intersects)
126 Lyman A J
135 Winn J A
Winn School for Boys (The)
Winn P P Rev
140 Pack Frances Mrs
156 Moore C A
157 McIntire F R
168 Hodges D M
175 Wright G H
176 Gibbs S H
179 Bledsoe J T
180 Williams B H
181 Penland R N
198 Vacant
(Seney ends)
201 Bryant M L
MacDonald J W
Wicker A C
203 Miller M S Mrs
205 Roth R H
206 Donnahoe P A
210 Nichols J W
211 Jenkins J H, gro
225 Allison G, D gro
(Hillside intersects)
— King H B
279 Vacant
285 Walden Winston
291 Johnson J E
297 Williams J S Rev
319 McCormick A H
333 Howe L W
348 Stockton M C Mrs
351 Vacant
365 Coston O M
393 Gillespie F E
(Coleman av begins)
403 Cheetham M L Mrs
407 Taylor T R
411 Tigar Wm
415 Fragge Lewis
— Ray J M Col

MERRIMON PLACE — East from 85 Merrimon av
1 Swayne A E
3 Ownbey A J Mrs

Meats — Kiibler & Whitehead
CITY MARKET PHONES, 195 and 694

WEAVERVILLE LINE NINE MILES BY TROLLEY FROM PACK SQUARE TO WEAVERVILLE

ASHEVILLE AND EAST TENNESSEE RAILROAD CO.

7 NORTH MAIN STREET   ASHEVILLE N. C.

| MILLER | 476 | MONTFORD |

MILLER—n e from 242 Beaumont
- 9 *Hobson Benj
- 13 *Grace Henry
- 17 *Mays Whitfield
- 24 *McElrath Edwd
- 24 (r) *Gash Jas
- 30 *Hunt Wooster

MINNESOTA AV—(Woolsey)

MONROE PL—E from n Main
- 34 Atkin S G Mrs
- 36 Vacant

MONTFORD AVENUE—North from 170 Haywood
- 7 Sanitary Home Ldy
- 9 Rhinehart M T, drugs
- 11 Wilder Eugene, phys
- 17 Mathis M D Mrs
- 22 Price Josephine Mrs
- Price B L, vet surgeon

(Cherry ends)
- 25 Ownbey & Son, gro
- 30 Sugarman Jacob
- Hetchel Elizabeth Mrs
- 33 McBrayer L B Dr

(Hill begins)
- 36 Coleman M J Mrs
- 41 Erwin R C
- 44 Hardee Mattie Mrs
- 45 Michalove S H
- 50 Hearn J M
- 51 Glenn J F
- 59 Ray H B
- 60 Alexander J R
- 65 Rorison E S Mrs
- 73 Fain N W
- 77 Vacant
- 80 Montford Av School

(Courtland av begins)
- 83 Schoepf J H
- 89 Gudger A L Mrs

(Bearden av ends)
- 102 Tennent J A
- 103 Bertolett M T Mrs, board "Montford Cottage"
- 108 Arbogast J C
- 111 Tennent Julia Miss, board
- 114 Wooldridge T J
- Myers C C
- 115 Witz Jos

(Blake intersects)
- 123 Johnson H C
- 124 Alexander J L
- 127 McCanless W J
- 133 Cobb A H
- 134 Gillis E W Mrs
- 139 Gudger Bessie C Mrs
- 140 Baird T G
- 143 Carr C T
- Kerr S E Miss
- 144 Swiggett W F
- 148 Vacant
- 152 Baird T G, gro

(West Chestnut intersects)
- 166 Tate J B
- 169 Craig Locke Hon
- 170 Donnell W H
- 171 Miller H A
- 174 Morrison T D
- 178 Mason W T
- 179 Rogers L B
- 182 Hodges C C
- 187 Abrahams A K Mrs
- 192 Sluder Erwin
- 193 Johnston M T Mrs
- Gibbon C M Mrs
- 194 Grant F R
- 199 Woodcock J E Mrs

(Cullowhee intersects)
- 200 Brown J A
- 208 Sherrill R J
- 211 Whiting W S
- 214 Sawyer J P Capt
- 228 Woodcock R J
- 230 Dwelle E C

(Soco intersects)
- 237 Allen H C
- 239 Stern Victor
- 242 Vacant
- 246 Duncan W F
- 247 McCandless J M
- 249 Hall A F
- 250 Vacant
- 257 Shoffner W H
- 260 Ross L S Mrs
- 263 Jones T A
- 264 Mason B C
- 276 Rudd C E
- 287 Vacant
- 288 Carter J H
- 296 Jordan C S Dr
- 397 Vacant

(Watauga intersects)
- 300 Stevens H B
- 311 Hewitt F R
- 312 Merrick Duff
- 320 Taylor W B
- 324 Harkins T J
- 327 Gould Edith Miss
- 332 Anderson J B

(Panola intersects)
- 333 Nichols Archibald

Electrical Supplies
PIEDMONT ELECTRIC COMPANY
ASHEVILLE, N. C.
64 PATTON AVE.

CONTRACTOR and BUILDER
J. C. McPHERSON
STEEL RANGES
35-37 E COLLEGE ST. PHONE 133
PLUMBING STEAM AND HOT WATER HEATING

400 South 9th St	**Montague Mfg. Co.**	Sash, Blinds, Doors
Richmond, Va.		Frames, Columns
See Bet. Pages 188-189	Rough and Dressed Lumber	Brackets, Mantels
		Porch Work, Etc.

MONTFORD 477 OAK

— Montford Park (city)
372 Hunter L E
377 Jones W W
381 Sumner F A
382 Robichaus E G
389 Mitchell F E
(Zillicoa intersects)
397 Fitzgerald W J
398 Murphy J D Judge
406 Evans P P
440 "Klondyke"
Coxe T C
450 Craddock J E
578 Glaser I W
585 Buckner R W
605 Allison C N

MORGAN AVENUE — West from 156 Asheland av
17 Mace E L
18 Vacant
26 Tomberlin Wm

MOUNTAIN—E from 22 Brick
1 *Colley Henry, gro
5 *Simonton W M
9 *England Edwd
15 *Shaw Lang
17 *Bearman Missouri
19 (1) *Alexander O G
19 (2) *Bly Hannah
19 (r) *Smith Lonnie
20 *Rees Martha
21 Vacant
25 *Porter A C
33 *Derumpley Lizzie
34 *Vacant
36 Fagan Max, gro
36½ *Robinson Essie
38 *Vance W M, gro
39 *Miller Lawson, gro
40 *Gray Porter, eating hse
*Liney Wm
(Pine intersects)
45 *Allen W A
48 *Hayes C H
49 Vacant (store)
52 *Bailey Nancy
55 *Holman Adam
56 *Martin Caleb
58½ *Bailey Geo
59 *Perrin Alice
62 *Crump Benj
65 *Orr Jane
68 *Grimes Maria
69 *Anderson Andrew
74 *Kesler Nellie A
*Martin Julia A, music tchr

77 *Beaumont Hotel
*Jones R P propr
78 *Hightower Mary
78½ *Martin F P
82 *Goodrum Sophia
90 *Smith Wm
91 *Mountain Street School
96 *Thompson Reuben
99 *Thompson Ida
105 *Webb E V
109 *Brown Ralph
114 *Goodrum Mary
119 *Rumley Jos
123 *Oglesby Thos
123 (r) *Baxter Worthy
131 *Lipscombe E H Jr

MURDOCK AVENUE—n w from Hillside, 1 w of Charlotte
— Brownhurst Greenhouses

NELLIE PARK—South from 200 Patton av

NELSON AVENUE—n e from Depot opp Freight Depot
22 Buckner H G
— Ensley R A
— Puckett W L

NEW—South from Beaumont
1 Davis Latimer
2 Davis Osborne
3-4 Knapp Mack
10 *James Edwd
15 *Williams Walter
30 *McDowell Smiley

NICHOLS HILL — Between View and Sou Ry

NORTH—E from 450 n Main
8 Evans J P
23 Banks V S
39 Jarvis A K
43 Haynes A L
49 Bates David
53 Jarvis J B
55 Lambert Moses
57 Vacant
— Johnson Omega Mrs

NORTH VIEW—n w from Center, 1 n of Hillside
15 Smith J W
23 Sorrels R Z
31 Jenkins G W

OAK—N from 173 College
18 Allport J H
Allport F D Mrs, furn rms
— High School
20 Restawyle (The), boarding

What Have You in Real Estate that You Don't Want?

What do You Want in Real Estate that You Haven't?

WESTERN CAROLINA REALTY CO.
J. W. Wolfe Sec. & Treas.

On the Square
PHONE 974
10 N. PACK SQ.

Brown-Carter Realty Co.
REAL ESTATE
23 TEMPLE COURT
PHONE 341
ASHEVILLE N. C.

FLORIDA SPECIALTIES
Grazing, Timbered, Farm Lands, Orange Groves, Turpentine Locations and Phosphate Lands.

NORTH CAROLINA SPECIALTIES
Orchard Farm and Timbered Lands, City Property, Rent Collections.

Moale & Chiles Real Estate and Insurance
27 Patton Ave., (2d fl) Phone 661
General Agents United States Fidelity & Guaranty Co.

Candy Kitchen and Club Cafe
"A GOOD PLACE FOR REFRESHMENT"

The very best ingredients with sanitary conditions in our Candy Manufacturing Department make possible the dainty, crisp confections sold here.

Bon Bons and Chocolates made every day, put up in neat, attractive boxes. Phones 110 and 111. 19 and 21 Haywood St.

| OAK | 478 | ORANGE |

Brown's Undertaking Parlors

S. H. BROWN

Lady Assistant When Desired

Phone 193-2 Rings

50 Patton Avenue
Asheville, N. C.

Established 1894

B. J. JACKSON

Carefully Selected Fruits and Vegetables

Stall No. 11, City Market

BUSINESS PHONES:
86 and 101

RESIDENCE PHONE
1596

    Ronci J L Mrs
24 Noland B M
26 Vacant
28 Bell J K
    Taylor D S
34 Brown E E
36 Great A & P Tea Co
    Handte J S
38 Wentworth (The), board
    Wells J B
41 Buckner H C
43 Smith S M
44 Cooper G W
    Nettles H L
54 Walton H S
56 Sevier D E Dr
60 Matthews Augustus Dr
— Cherokee Inn
    Misenheimer D W
OAK—(See also Biltmore)
OAKDALE AVENUE—North from 279 Haywood to Hill
8 *Greenlee Woodfin
14 *McCool C H
17 *Dale J F
20 *Bell C W
25 *Moore Geo
26 *Sloan Cora
29 *Bynum J B
30 *Hines Emerson
31 *Robinson Henry
34 *Kennedy Henrietta
35 *Vacant
37 *Tomlin Clinton
84 *Livingston Hampton
OAKLAND AV—(Victoria)
2 Garrett R U
655 Carpenter B C
— Doyle A B Mrs
    "Sunnybank"
OCALA—W from 325 n Main
16 Roberts J W
31 *Metz Jesse
35 *Arnold R L
36 *White Arthur
39 *Logan Jos
41 *Gilliam Richard
43 *Logan Augustus
OLIVE—South from McDowell, 1 e of Victoria av
18 Jarrett Otto
22 Jarrett E M
OLIVER—w from 82 Livingston
17 Vacant
19 *Burnham Floyd

21 *Davis Wm
23 *Manning Willis Rev
ORA—s w from 105 Bartlett, 1 w of s French Broad av
14 Mull R L
17 Estes P R
18 Misenheimer G W
25 Wilson A H
26 Blackwood J C
29 Michael W E
30 Gudger J H
34 Galvin J H
35 Wilson A E
37 Tennant W D
40 Vacant
51 Butler W S
55 Hunnicutt W J, phys
56-60 Vacant
59 McCallister W P
63 Goforth J A
67 Weddle W S
71 Seay J D
80 Eaton S C
83 MacLauchlin A M Rev
87 Cheek J H
    Cheek A E Mrs, boarding
88 Tate A A
92 McLean W H
95 Aldrich L P
96 Ora Street Presbyterian Ch
99 Lacy W G
117 *Jenkins S E
ORANGE—E fr 63 Merrimon
14 Lutz Michael
18 White C S
19 Wadsworth M C Mrs
21 Stokely R J
    Sproles W J
22 Ewell J L
23 Hyams Mord
25 Rankin A E
28 Fitzpatrick R L
33 Mims L A Mrs
35 Oliphant Edna Miss
36 Schartle J W
37 Blankenship — —
    (Liberty intersects)
47 Ware A B Dr
50 Shuford G A Judge
53 Chisolm Anna Mrs
53½ Sorrels Sallie Mrs
62 Tighe R J Prof
68 Keller W F
68½ Thompson L J Mrs
71 Orange Street School
73 Lettman Saml

Ye OLD BOOK SHOP

114 Patton Ave.   Phone 1674

BOOKS BOUGHT, SOLD OR EXCHANGED

Williams-Brownell Planing Mill Company

ROUGH AND DRESSED LUMBER
WHITE PINE AND YELLOW PINE
FLOORING A SPECIALTY
Hardwoods

Mouldings and Interior Finish
Office: Southern Railway Tracks, Near Biltmore Station
Phone 729   Planing Mill

ORCHARD 479 PACK SQ

ORCHARD—E fr 51 Central av
- 8 Vacant
- 10 Harmon T J
- 16 Sutherland W H
- 22 Reynolds N J Mrs
- 25 Proffitt H B
- 29 Scott E F
- 33 Bratman Regena Mrs
- 37 English J M
- 41 Hoffman David
- 51 Freeman R C
- 55 Hamrick M W
- 56 Wilson Wm
- 64 Bynum A E Mrs
- 37 Tennant W D

PACK SQUARE—The recognized center of the city, from which the principal business streets diverge

PACK SQ EAST—
- City Hall
- City Officials
- Fire Department
- Police Headquarters
- Police Court

City Market, Stalls—
- Asheville Fish Co
- City Fish Market
- Faulkner Bros, meats
- Globe Market, meats
- Goff W A, vegetables
- Guy J L, produce
- Hill's Market, meats
- *Jackson B J, vegetables
- Jarrett E C, vegetables
- Kiibler & Whitehead, meats
- Lutz Meat Co
- Lynch Mrs & Son, vegetables
- Marlow Bros, meats
- Mitchell T J, supt
- Star Market (The), meats

PACK SQ, NORTH—
- 2 Nichols Shoe Co
- 2 Whittington W P, phys
  - McBrayer L B, phys
  - Ray's Studio
- 4 Ashev Cleaning & pressing Club
  - Wilbar J C
  - Ashev Gazette News (The)
  - Evening News Pub Co
- 6 Ashev Steam Bakery
  - Young W W, barber
  - Ashev Coal Co
  - Whitson W R, atty
- 8 Crystal Cafeterian, restaur
  - Carpenter J E, jeweler
- 8 (2d fl) Petrie H P, tailor
- 8 (3d fl) Ashev Business College
- 10 Western Carolina Realty Co
  - Southern Coal Co
  - Goldsmith W W & Son, jewelers
- 10½ Brown Bldg (offices)

Rooms—
- 1-2 McCall R S, atty
  - Bennett O K, atty
- 3 James W A Jr, justice & notary
- 5-7 Way Eugene, atty
  - Carter H B, atty
  - Ball V J Mrs
  - Barnett W L
  - Whitaker Mary Mrs
  - **(N Pack Sq Continued)**
- 12 Jarrett E C, gro
- 12 (2d fl) Montague Loan Co
  - Rigsby J J, jeweler
- 12 (3d fl) Hall Julia Mrs
  - McQueen Hugh
  - Manley Geo
  - Ownbey P A
  - Patton Wm
- 14 Dunham's Music House
- 16 Golightly L O, furn
- 16½ Fountain Bldg (offices)
  - Union Art Studio
  - Ivey F T
  - Seawell C C
- 18 Singer Sewing Machine Co
- 18 (2d fl) Higgason Studio
- 20 Sproat A D Mrs, mlnr
- 20-22 Teague & Oates, drugs
  - Oates Bldg (offices)

Rooms—
- 200-202 Carolina Supply Co
  - Arbogast J C
  - Champion Lbr Co
  - North Carolina Merct Co
  - Pigeon River Ry Co
  - Tenn & N C R R Co
- 203-205 Jackson Lbr Co
  - Macon Lbr Co
  - Stevens & Anderson, attys
- 206 Baird-Wilford Realty Co
- 207 Malone C N, atty
- 208 Brown W P, atty
- 301 Ritter W M Lbr Co
- 302-303 Webb C A, atty

HUGHES Transfer and Livery Co.

Automobiles for HIRE

TRUNKS 25c

Office: 401 Southside Avenue
PHONE 1405

Try our Hand Laundering. We strive to please in LAUNDERING and DRY CLEANING.

The Sanitary Home Laundry No. 7 MONTFORD AVE.
PHONE - 1354

Mrs. Wilder's SANITARY HOME LAUNDRY turns out first class work in Laundering and Dry Cleaning. No. 7 Montford Ave., Phone 1354

PACK SQ　　　　480　　　　PACK SQ

305 Greenwood & Blackstock, hardwoods
306 Weaver Guy, atty
307 Gudger H A, atty
308-309 Bell L C, atty
400-402 Wells & Swain, attys
403-405 Craig Martin & Thompson, attys
406-408 Weaver Zebulon, atty
　　Murphy J D, atty
409-410 Styles J S, atty
Basement—
　　*Big 400 Pressing Club The
　　Creasman M A, notary
　　*Johnson G W
PACK SQ, NORTHEAST—
1 Bowles R E, paint
1½ McGarry Jos, photog
1-3 McIntyre Bldg
3 Stradley G F, gro
5 Vacant
PACK SQ, NORTHWEST—
1 Carmichael's Pharmacy
3 Pack Square Book Co
3½ Revell Bldg (offices)
Rooms—
9 Ingle F P, real est
15 Nitzer W A, real est
　　Revell O D, real est
16 Dixie Auto Service
　　Marwell Adv Service
　　Engraving School
　　(Pack Sq Continued)
5 *Bowman J W, barber
7 MacKay's Pharmacy
7½ *Swepson E W, cleaning
9 Princess Theatre
11 (2d fl) Carolina Amusement & Inv Co
　　Ware A B, dentist
13 Blomberg S I, dry gds
PACK SQ, SOUTH—
— Donahoe & Bledsoe, real est
— Franklin Hotel
— Bourne, Parker & Morrison, attys
　　Carolina Coupler Co
— Ravenel S P, atty
4 Pack Memorial Library Assn
　　Library Bldg, offices
Rooms—
1 Lusk V S, atty
2 Shuford G A, atty
　　Varnon T W, atty
3-4 Curtis Z F, atty

7-8-9 Jones & Jones, attys
　　Welch Gilmer, atty
10 Mountain School Dept Home
　　Mission Board Sou Baptist Convention
　　Brown A E Rev
11-12 Fortune & Roberts, attys
15 Posey J H
17 Davies Wm M, atty
19 Higgason L L
21 Sullivan M M
22 Adair E M
24 Plemmons — —
25 Mitchell T J
East Basement—
4 Waddell F N, magistrate
　　Watson D S & Co, real est
West Basement—
　　Batterham H, real est
　　(S Pack Sq continued)
6 Central Bank & Trust Co
Basement—
　　*McDonald Thos, barber
8 London Shop (The), art gds
Basement—
　　Gudger W R, magistrate
　　Jones F M, constable
10 Legal Bldg (offices)
Rooms—
201-202 Bernard S G, atty
　　Ashev Baseball Club
　　Blue Ridge Develop Co
206-208 Sinclair J A, dentist
　　Sinclair P D, dentist
209 Greco Frank, R R contr
210-211 Viavi Co
212 Cocke P C
214 Campbell J M, real est
215 Glenn J F, atty
　　Georgia Talc Co
217 Paquin Paul Dr
221 Terry P R, phys
223 Metropolitan Life Ins Co
225 Southern Land Auction Co
　　Praytor Laura Miss, stengr
301 Carolina Commercial Schl
　　Holman P L Miss, stengr
303-307 Russell E R, phys
303-314 Martin, Rollins & Wright, attys
310-312 Carolina Abstract & Title Co
315-319 Merrick & Barnard, attys
321 Burns D B, civ engnr

OLDSMOBILE — DETROIT ELECTRIC
ARBOGAST MOTOR COMPANY
ACCESSORIES AND SUPPLIES
52-60 N. Main　Phones 302 and 1728
BUICK — MAXWELLS

Asheville Dry Cleaning Co.
Telephones 835-836, All Dep't
MAIN, N. E. COR. COLLEGE

THE CLEANERS
Our Department for Oriental Rugs and Carpet Cleaning is prepared to serve you in all its branches.
E. S. Paine　　　O. E. Hansel

ALL KINDS
Hardwood Lumber

ENGLISH LUMBER CO.
Phone - - 321

PACK SQ   481   PARK SQ

325 Purefoy & Powell, phys
405-407 Weaver H B, phys
408-414 Dixie Mutual Life Ins Co
412-415 Carter Frank Judge
    Chedester H C, atty
417-421 Jones & Williams, attys
423-424 Fulgham J E, lbr
    Williams J M, lbr
425 Smith S M, lumber
501-507 Meacham & Rockwell, osteopaths
510 Hunt F L, dentist
512-515 U S Weather Bureau
527-528 Pelton H W, photog
    (S Pack Sq Continued)
12 Logan S T, tailor
14 Vacant
16-18 Reed Bldg (offices)
Rooms—
  2 Templeton S A Rev
  9 Brigmon Jodie Mrs
 13 Chambers J M
 14 Kroman Jenlnie Mrs
 19 Moore W M
 21-25 Bowman & Wright, dressmkrs
 22 Hall Martha Miss
    (S Pack Sq continued)
 20 Flower Mission and Associated Charities and Free Medical Dispensary
 22 Wolfe Bldg
    Wolfe W O, marble wkr
    Whiteside Ptg Co
    Whiteside E W
    Guischard G L, plmbr
    Goodlake A M, contr
    Jeanneret L W, watchmkr
PACK SQ. SOUTHWEST—
  1 Cash Grocery (The)
 1½ Amer Dairy Lunch Rest
  3 Evans Edwd, dentist
    Reisecker E A
  5 Central Cafe
 5½ Ideal Pressing Club
  9 Guffey J A, dry gds
  9 (2d fl) Reeves A F, phys
  9 (3d fl) Hermann J B, pool
 11 Green Ottis Hdw Co
 11½ Western Hotel
    Cowgill Anna Mrs
PALMER—(Victoria)
PANOLA—E from 327 Montford
  1 Bennett P R Dr

17 Scott C E
31 McFerren Pingree
32 Fanning Leslie
35 Tannahill Saml
36 Porter R F
44 Taylor W G
45 Glenn C F Dr
46 Whiteside J B, contr
47 Dills C M
50 Smith S S
PANOLA PL—From 32 Panola
  7 Sims J A Mrs
 41-44-83 Vacant
PARK AVENUE—South from 408 w Haywood
 — Park Avenue School
    (Park Pl begins)
 11 Warren L D
 17 Perkins A T
 23 Foister C F
 50 Long M D
 58 Davis S P
 65 Bruton D W
 68 McCoy T C
 69 Simmons W G
 75 Fitzgerald Mary Mrs
 76 (r) Pitts W W
    Redfern T E
 87 Jones C B
115 Coley B L
119 Williams W B
123 Tomlin H L
127 Perry L E
    (Jefferson Drive intersects)
130 Francis R L
131 Clement Ray
139 Rowe D G
140 Jones T B
    Fullam Clarence
144 Candler G W Mrs
145 Street J R
149 Reister W W
150 Monroe G A
157 Meacham W D
158 Davis J A
163 Dougherty J M
169 Campbell R W
174 Vacant
176 Poindexter F W
PARK PL—W from 23 Park av
  7 Brown G H, painter
  9 Rogers Nancy Mrs
PARK SQUARE—East from Roberts to Park Pl
 58 Tweed M N
 59 Callahan A R

BIGGEST BUSIEST BEST

Phones 1936 and 1937

ASHEVILLE STEAM LAUNDRY

43 to 47 W. COLLEGE

S. D. HALL
REAL ESTATE AGENT
—
Money Loaned
—
Notary Public
—
32 PATTON AVENUE
—
Phone 91

CAROLINA MACHINERY CO.
—US when you want machine work of any kind . . .

Founders Machinists and Jobbers of Mill Supplies
When in the market for heavy castings such as columns or building plates get our prices.   **Phone 590**

The Life Insurance Co. of Virginia
ORGANIZED 1871 RICHMOND, VA.

ISSUES ALL THE MOST APPROVED FORMS OF LIFE INSURANCE CONTRACTS from $500.00 to $25,000.00, with premiums payable quarterly, semi-annually and annually

J. V. Moon, Superintendent, Rooms 3-4-5 Maxwelton Bldg., Asheville, N. C.

PARK SQ 482 PATTON AV

D. TREXLER TIN SHOP

All Kinds of Roofing, Gutter and Conductor Work.

Phone 862

159 South Main St.

DR. C. H. MILLER

MECHANO-THERAPIST

14 N. Spruce St.
Phone 979
ASHEVILLE, N. C.

Hours by engagement

Drugless Healing of Disease

60-62 Vacant
61 Ellege J W
63 Ownbey Herman
64 Parris M A Mrs
65 Mills R C
66 Grice J B

PATTON AVENUE—West fr Pack Sq, the principal business street of the city
1 Barnard Bldg (offices)
Rooms—
  1 Edwards Bowley
    White Chas
  2 Peroulas Geo
    Peroulas Jno
  3 Anglin Z B
  4 Parker G B, contr
Basement—
  Antiseptic Barber Shop
☞ Patton av continued
4 Chackales & Pilalas, pool
  Ashev Shoe Shine Parlor
6 Gem Clothing Store (The)
7-9 Redwood H & Co, dept store
10-12 Ashev Dry Goods Co
11 Moore M V, clothing
13 Battery Park Bank
13½ Lee & Ford, attys
  Reynolds C G, atty
  U S Health & Accident Ins Co
  Ward C G
14 Ashev Barber Shop
  Barbee S A, cigars
15 Blomberg Louis, cigars
15½ Reynolds G S, atty
16 Crescent Jewelry Co
16 (2d fl) Waddell & Coxe
  Sluder J W
  Tennent J A, archt
  (Lexington av intersects)
18 Glaser I W, clothing
20 Patton Hotel
21-23 Bon Marche, dept store
22 I X L Dept Store
26-28 Kress S H & Co, notions
  Harkins Bldg
Rooms—
  3 Osteen T W, ins
    North State Mutual Life Ins Co
  4-6 Chambers E O, dentist
  8 Scott S A, ins
    Continental Casualty Co

9-11 Harkins & VanWinkle, attys
12 Lotspeich O P, broker
14 Comber Mrs
17-18 Fender J D
☞ Patton av continued
25 American Tailors (Inc)
27 Shoffner W H, jeweler
27 (2d fl) Moale & Chiles, real estate
30 Boston Shoe Store (The)
31 Raysor C A, drugs
31 (2d fl) Rutledge Fredk & Co, genl ins
32 Dew Drop Candy Parlor
32 Yuneeda Dairy Lunch
32 (2d fl) Hall S D, real est
  Chunn C H, archt
  Foller J J, tailor
32 (3d fl) McCanless J M, photog
33 Brown-Northup & Co, hdw
  Alexander Gustave, jeweler
  Brown-Gudger Bldg
  — Gudger V L, atty
34 Wachovia Bank & Trust Co
  Allen P R, ins
  Williamson W B, notary
  Hanes S M, notary
35 Law J H, chinaware
37 (2d fl) Mann I M, dentist
37 (3d fl) Florio Caryl
39 Rogers H T, stationery
39 (3d fl) C L U Hall
40-42 Peoples Dept Store (The)
  Maxwelton Bldg (offices)
Rooms—
  1-2 Weaver W T
    N C Electrical Power Co
  3-4-5 Life Ins Co of Va
  9 Spears E W, music tchr
  11 Allen P A
  19 Jones Otis
  23 Patterson Ernest
  24-25 Koyle W C
  26 Rhinehardt E T
  27 Beam Saml
  28 Sumner Frank
☞ Patton av continued
41 Whitlock Clothing Co
41½ The Little Smoke House
43 Allison's Drug Store
44 Amer Natl Bank Bldg
Rooms—
  21 Woodcock & Gillis, real est
  22-23 Aston Rawls, & Co

....**Asheville Cleaning and Pressing Club**....
Tailoring That Satisfies and Prices That Please
Steam and French Dry Cleaning of all delicate and fine wearing apparel for ladies and gentlemen. MESSENGER SERVICE IN THE CITY.

J. C. WILBAR, Prop.   4. N. Pack Square   PHONE 389

CAROLINA "M & W" INDIAN — Prompt Delivery

COAL

& ICE CO. PHONE 130 — 50 PATTON AVE. — WEIGHTS ACCURATE

PATTON AV 483 PATTON AV

24 Fork Ridge Coal Co
25 Virginia-Carolina Coal Co
26 Messler F M, real est and ins
27 Ashev Mercantile Agency
28 O'Rear Eva Miss, dressmkr
31-32 Imperial Mutual Life & Health Ins Co
33 Thomas F W, atty
34 Sykes C E, atty
35 Shemwell Baxter, capitalist
    Goode Frances Miss, stengr
37-38-39 Amer Furn Buyers Assn
    Kennett F S
    Amer Furn Mnfg Co
41-42 Ramsay J F, dentist
45 Varnon Realty Co
47-49 Hall B F, dentist
52 Villa Heights Co, real est
56 to 59 Whiting W S, lumber
61 Chiles Jake M
62 McCloskey J J Realty Co
63 (B) Hagan H J, dental supplies
66 Miller Ernest H
    Piedmont Directory Co
    Knoxville Directory Co
    Directory Library
    Asheville City Directory, office
69 Amer Natl Bank Store Rm
☞Patton av continued
45 Green Bros, furn
47 Brown-Miller Shoe Co
    Hyndman T L, shoe repr
47-53 Temple Court (offices)

Rooms—
  1-2 Toms C H, atty
  3 Daniel W H, atty
  4-5 Brown M W, atty
    Monteath A D, atty
  6-7-8 Board of Trade
    Retail Merchants Assn
  7 Rector J E, atty
  9 Underwood Typewriter Co
  10 Goldstein R C, atty
  11 Penland J D & Son, real est
  12 Carolina Hardwood Lbr Co
  14 Asheville Lbr Co
  15 Tonawanda White Pine Co
  16-17 English J M & Co, lbr
  18-19 Haynes & Gudger, attys
  20-21 Johnston Wm J, real estate
  23 Brown H A & Co, contrs

    Brown-Carter Realty Co
24 Shuford W E, atty
31 Hardwood Lbr Co
    McLean F L
32 Thomason G A
33 Henderson W P
34 Wynne E L
36 (front) Warren C M
36 (back) Haynes J W
38 Johnston A T
☞Patton av continued
— Field A M Co, jewelers
48 Citizens Transfer Co
    Grant H F Realty Co
    McDermott W R, notary
48-50 Drhumor Bldg (offices)

Rooms—
  2 Forbes & Campbell, real est
    Home B & L Assn
  3-4 Orr P B, phys
  6-8 Lynch J M, phys
  9-10-11 Pritchard A T, phys
    Millender M C, phys
  15 Socialist Reading Room
  16 Emanuel School of Shorthand
  17 Natl Special Sales Co
    (3d fl) Masonic Hall
☞Patton av continued
50 Brown's Undertaking Parlors
    Carolina Coal & Ice Co
51 Peerless-Fashion Stores Co
52 Henderson C E, jeweler
    Moore E J K Miss, art gds
53 Sawyer C R, gro
54 Honess C H, optometrist
55 Citizens Bank
    Paragon Bldg (offices)

Rooms—
  1-2 Burrows H S, tailor
  3 Lyman A J, real est
  4 Jefferson Standard Life Ins Co
    Smith A B, genl agt
  5-6 Aetna Life Ins Co
    Rickman T J, atty
    Lee G E, ins
  7-8 Mutual Life Ins Co
    Fitzpatrick R M, div supt
    Devenish A G Miss, stengr
  9 Mason B C, lumber
  10 Walker A E, publr
  11-12 Parker J M, dentist
  14-16 Smathers Wexler, dentist
  19-20 Pressley J M, shoe repr

LIGHT and POWER — **Asheville Power and Light Co.** PHONE 69

Poultry — **Kiibler & Whitehead** — CITY MARKET — PHONES, 195 and 694

Asheville Dray, Fuel & Construction Co.
6 1-2 South Main

COAL

Wood and Kindling
Stone and Sand
PHONE - 223

PATTON AV   484   PATTON AV

Sidebar: EVER READY FLASHLIGHTS — Piedmont Electric Company — 64 PATTON AVENUE — ASHEVILLE, N. C.

    (3d fl) Ashev Lodge 106 K of P
    ☞Patton av continued
    (Haywood begins)
56 Crystal Dairy Lunch
56½ Chakales & Pilalas, bootblacks
58 Mascari Chas, fruits
— U S Post Office
    U S Courts
    U S Revenue Office
    U S Marshal's Office
    Pritchard J C Hon
60 Sou Ry Ticket Office
    Sou Ry Dist Passngr Agt
    Ashev Transfer & Storage Co
60 Sou Ry Div Frt Agt
    Sou Ry Land & Industrial Dept
62 W U Tel Co
64 Piedmont Electric Co (The) Electrical Bldg

Rooms—
— Greater Western N C Assn
1 Pittsburg Life & Trust Co
2 Powell Geo S, real est
    Powell Murray Land Co
    Investors Land Co
    Carolina Electric Vehicle Co
7-8 Balfour Quarry Co
9 Garrett R U, real est
10-24 Tennent G S, oculist
    Tennent M L Mrs, wood carver
16-17 Faucette J W, dentist
21 Independent Scale Co
    ☞Patton av Continued
66 Brown Book Co
68 Vacant (store)
68 Elias & Hopson, tailors
    Prudential Ins Co
    Christian Science Reading Room
68 Moody H M Sales Co, mnfrs agt
    Murray Geo A, lumber
    Murray Lbr Co
70 Cosby B H, jeweler
    DeVault C W, extracts
76 Palace Theatre
78 Alexander L I, optician
78 Paris Millinery Shop
    Inland Press The, printers
    Alexander L I, optician
78 Smith Owen, phys

    Waddell C E, cons engnr
    Natl Cash Register Co
80-84 Morrison T S & Co, agri implts
81 Dreamland (The), moving pictures
86 Princess Air Dome
88 Lunsford W T, gro
90 Zindel's Model Bakery
    Zindel M K
91 Rhinehardt Bros, plmbrs
93 Battery Park Hotel, sample room
94 Bean S I & Co, marble Wks
95-97 McLean A L & Co, metal Wks
98 Smith W M, boarding
99-103 Sou Express Co
100 Henninger J C, shoemkr
    McLean & Anders, gros
102 Marquette Hotel
104 Asheville Power & Light Co
    (Asheland av begins)
110-112 Ashev Steam Bakery
    Morsell Bldg (The)

Rooms—
2 Baird J T, broker
4 Coleman Robinson & Co, lbr
14-15 Anderson J G Dr
17 Croker Wm
19 Elias L W, phys
20 Hunnicutt W J, phys
27 Arthur J P, atty
34 Hampton Wade
    3d fl Brock N, photog
    ☞Patton av continued
114 Galer E E, cabtmkr
116 Groves J A Grocery Co
118 Asheville Piano Co
    (Grove begins)
147 James J T
151-155 Patton & Stikeleather, livery
155½ *Justice J C, shoemkr
157 Burnette C B Miss
(French Broad av intersects)
167 Barton Jennie Mrs, dressmkr
167-a-169 Vacant
168 Sims J F, gro
169 Schaffe J T
169-a Henry E L
170 Asheville Marble Works
171 Sparks W G

J. C. McPHERSON
SLATE AND TIN ROOFING
Galvanized Iron Work   Hot Air Furnaces
35-37 EAST COLLEGE STREET

PLUMBING
STEAM AND HOT WATER
HEATING
PHONE 133

Yellow Pine White Pine Hardwoods See bet. pgs. 188-189	**LUMBER** SASH, BLINDS, DOORS	**WOODWARD & SON** Ninth and Arch Streets RICHMOND - VIRGINIA

PATTON AV   485   PENLAND

171-a Vaacnt
173 Duckett A L
173-a Neville Lucy Miss
   (Carter begins)
182 Sims J F
183 Reeves C H
195 Aspery Jos
   Honeycutt P L
   Tomberlin G G
   (Ann intersects)
208 Vacant
210 Newell W A Rev
211 Kilpatrick E M
214 Leverette P P
216 Wiley A L
218 Alexander Gustave
223 Vacant
   (Pearl begins)
224 Dunham H A
240 Kroger Wm, gro
242 Taylor M A Mrs
244 Baltimore Installment House
246 Green P F, confr
250 Farris M F, gro
   (Clingman av begins)
252-258 Carolina Creamery
264 Wild J A
266 Vacant
266½ Gardner G D Dr
268 Harkins R W, gro
270 West End Drug Store
270½ Medd Thos

PEARL—S from 223 Patton av
11 Hoyle C R
12 Revis H C
18 Treadway J R
21 Jones W J
25 Morris N E Mrs
26 Eaton J H
31 Elliott W A
36 Lutz W L
39 *Maxwell Hattie

PEARSON ALLEY—North fr W Haywood extd

PEARSON DRIVE—n w from Courtland av, 1 w of Montford
2 Vacant
6 Campbell R F Rev
9 Rhinehardt L F
14 Dukes E J Mrs
23 Cathey Geo
26 *Avery Tempie
   (W Chestnut intersects)
38 Rich A D Mrs, gro

39 Payne T T
42 Rich J J Mrs
55 Vacant
56 Lominac C M
58 (r) Payne A R
109 Shaw C D
110 Ledford Alice Miss
112 "Pines" (The)
   Allen Clara G Miss
128 *McCracken King
129 Vacant
143 Wagner J A Capt
144 *Summey Belle
   *Goodrum Henry
153 Lindsey F A
159-168 Vacant
167 Hortshorn F O
   (Watauga intersects)
183 Faulkner A W
207 Tennent G S Dr
208 Hawthorne Annie B Miss
216 Cocke C H
   Cocke R L Mrs
235 Vacant
240 Millender M C Dr
250 Burrell E C
265 Child M E Mrs
287 Morrison T S
301 Williamson W B
315 Jones B M
324 Brown D C
326 King P L
400 Haynes Jas
403 Hough Alice B Miss
408 Henderson C A
435 Settle Thos
436 Ledford Benj
454 Banks G B
458 Moore W J
   Roberson L W
— Newton R T
— "Riverside Park"

PENLAND—N fr 32 w College
4 *Carter Joe, horseshoer
— Armory Hall
24 Vacant
   (Walnut intersects)
51 Allen Jas, boarding
55 Dillingham H T
   Dillingham Grace Mrs, board
56 Seigler J B
59 Fuller Claud
62 Robinson S D
62½ McCoury C W
65 Duck D J

What Have You in Real Estate that You Don't Want?

What do You Want in Real Estate that You Haven't?

WESTERN CAROLINA REALTY CO.

J. W. Wolfe, Sec. & Treas.

On the Square
PHONE 974
10 N. PACK Sq.

H. A. BROWN & Co.

General Contractors
23 Temple Court Bldg.
Phone 341

—DEALERS IN—

Rough Building
and
all Kinds of Crushed Stone

—OUR SPECIALTIES—

STONE FOUNDATIONS CONCRETE WORK
and
EXCAVATING

Moale & Chiles Real Estate and Insurance
27 Patton Ave. (2d fl) Phone 661
City and Suburban Property FARMS and TIMBER LANDS

Club Cafe and Candy Kitchen
"A GOOD PLACE FOR REFRESHMENT"

The standards we work to in our Restaurant Department are: Cooking, perfect; Service, prompt and cheerful; Prices, moderate; Menu, everything in season. Parties and Banquets, Teas and Dinners. 19 and 21 Haywood St. Phones 110 and 111.

PENLAND 486 POPLAR

Brown's Undertaking Parlors

S. H. BROWN

50 Patton Avenue
ASHEVILLE, N. C.

Lady Assistant When Desired

Phone 193-2 Rings

THE MOORE Plumbing Company

16 N. Pack Square
PHONE 1025

Sanitary Plumbing, General Tin and Metal Work, Hot Air Furnaces

---

68 Morley W A
69 McKinney W C
   Wilson J H
75 McLean R L
76 Nele Philip, contr
80 Davis S R Mrs
81 Tiller B T
84 Dunn E C Mrs
   Bradford J B
85 Gregory Ella Mrs
88 West Virginia (The), board
   Hall G L

PENNSYLVANIA AVENUE
—W Asheville

PHIFER—W from 252 Asheland
6 Moore E D
14 Jarvis J A
15 Miller D Z
21 Kintz R E
23 Jacokes J W
24 White E L
25 Bradley L C
   (Grove intersects)
31 Middleton T F
32 Robbins H H Rev
33 Vacant
59 Green W H
60 Frady H F
61 Galyean E S
63 Sorrells J T
64 Hipp E L Mrs, dressmkr
75 Wallace J S
78 *Butler Wm

PHILIP—W from 79 Asheland av
10 Clampet B J
14 *Murrough Noah
22 Vacant
   (Grove intersects)
28 Wight A H Mrs
30 Drake W H
   Harrison H B
   Baldwin D P
32 Day C B Mrs
36 Prescott J F
44 Bernhard C H Rev
48 Greco Frank

PINE—S from 216 College
38 *Cogwell F V
   (Poplar intersects)
41 *Goodrum Sandy
41 (r) *Aiken Janie
42 *Henry Emanuel
45 *Evans S G
46 *Brooks Jno

48 *Eves Carrie
49 *Collett Thos
56 *Jackson Chas
74 *Harrison Moses
78 *Adair Siss
78 (r) *Bass Laura
80-82 *McDowell Mary, gro
81 *Miller Lawson
86 *Farr Josephine, eating hse
92 *Barnard Sallie
93 *Lattimore Jno
94 *Blackwell Alex
98 *Fowler Eliza J
103 *Alexander S E, eating hse
   *Reynolds Chas
104 *Doster Henry
   (Eagle intersects)
108 *Hunt Annie
112 *Caldwell Lonnie
116 *Teague Richard
118 *Jordan Ernest
120 *Hubbard Mattie
122 *Martin Thos
126 *Green Jas
130 *Nichols Lee
134 *Sartor Arthur
135 *Williams Henry
136 *Morris Thos
   *Thomas Blanche
139 *Wingate Marion
140 *Lord Moses
140 (r) *Burgin Ollie
— *First Baptist Church
— *Sims Thompson
143 *Salone Mary

PINE GROVE AVENUE—N from Livingston opp Olive
54 Lyda Alex
66 Beck J F
77 Parham W F

PLAZA—(See Biltmore)

POPLAR—East from junction of College and Valley
29 *Thomas David
40 *Johnson Emma
43 *Nance Della
45 Vacant
48 *Fowler J S
58 *Dickerson Amos
58 *Tucker Zela
58 (r) *Patton Robt
62 *Jackson Martha
63 *Moore J G
68 Head Lula Mrs
70 (66) No changed
   (Pine intersects)

The Battery Park Bank
Capital - - $100,000.00
Surplus and Profits, $110,000.00
ASHEVILLE, N. C.   City, County and State Depositary

J. A. TILLMAN   **Jeweler**   17 N. Main St.

I carry a nice line of Watches, Clocks and Jewelry, and make a specialty of repair work. Satisfaction guaranteed

POPLAR   487   RIDGE

- 80 Goodis Nathan, gro
- 89 *Haynes Lizzie
- 114 Campbell M E Mrs, dressmkr
- Stancill Alice Mrs, dressmkr
- 114 (r) *Baker Malinda
- 115 *Tomlin Alvin
- 117 *Revis Thos
- 119 Bates Andrew
- 120 Brackett Thos
- 122 *Vacant
- 123 *Fenderson E H
- 128 Brackett Hardy
- 129 *Martin Jas
- 130 Banks G V
- 134 Justice W S
- 134 (r) Jones J E
- 135 *Forney Jas
- 138 White A M Mrs, dressmkr
- 139 *Swann Irving
- 145 Miller P A
- 147 Vacant
- 151 (180) Vacant

PROXIMITY PARK — West end of Charlotte st

RALPH — Northeast from Southside av, w of Ora
- 12 *Counts Thos
- 16 *Francis Jas
- 18 *Lindsay Jas
- 20 *Knox Fannie
- 20 (r) Baldwin Pressley
- 22 *Foster Betsy
- 24 Guffrey Frank
- 28 Monk F H
- Buckner R B
- 48 *Clinton Daisy
- *Pickens Maria
- 58 *Austin Ella
- *Sims Jesse
- 62 *Simpson Lake
- 64 *Wilkins Edwd
- *Dukes Warren
- 72 Cabe M C Mrs
- 76 Monday B U
- 82 Riddle Thos
- 102 Baumberger J E
- Baumberger Margaret Mrs, boarding

RANDOLPH PL — (Grove Park)

REAR RALPH — From Southside av to Cavassa alley

RECTOR — n w from 94 Clingman
- 11 Killian J A
- 15 Crook W J
- 19 Vacant
- 20 Henninger J C
- Rector W G
- 21 Fox H J Mrs
- 25 Johnson G W
- 29 Burton S S
- 30-33 Vacant
- 39 Miller S F
- 43 Goldsmith R F

REDMON ALLEY — East from 84 East st
- 8 Hall Paralee Mrs
- 11 Taylor W L
- 12 Vest M A Mrs
- 15 Vacant

REED — North from 46 Baird
- 27 Vacant
- 32 Cline D W
- 46 Dr von Ruck's Library
- 45 Paquin Paul Dr
- 50 von Ruck Karl Dr

RESERVOIR — n e from College, 1 e of Cameron
- 1 Frady W B

RICHARD — West from Madison, 1 n of Gay
- 4 Patton M C
- Swinney Minnie Mrs
- 8 *McCoy Walter
- *Ray Elijah
- 10 *Ray Sidney
- 24 *Gaston A H

RIDGE — Southeast from junction of Hazzard and Pine
- 2 *Pearson J F
- 7 *Williams Elliott
- 12 *Bayson Wm
- 13 *Burgess Jennie L, nurse
- *Schaeffer C T Dr
- 17 *Jones Wm
- 20 *Pegram W T
- 21 *Conner D W
- 22 *Michael J H
- 25 *Jackson Hattie
- *Hughes J F Rev
- 30 *Nelson J R Rev
- 34 *Bogle Arthur
- 35 *Littlejohn Ellison
- 36 *Hunter M S
- 42 *Parks Jas
- 43 *Hamilton G F
- 44 *Harrison W E
- 48 *Dodd J P
- 55 *Ledbetter Martha

INSURANCE
- **I**NSURE YOUR SALARY WITH US
- **N**EVER CARRY YOUR OWN RISK
- **S**AFETY IS THE BEST POLICY
- **U**NLESS YOU ARE A CAPITALIST
- **R**EST EASY IF YOU HAVE
- **A**N ACCIDENT WE WILL
- **N**OT KEEP YOU WAITING TO
- **C**OLLECT YOUR CLAIM
- **E**VERY CLAIM PROMPTLY PAID

Imperial Mutual Life & Health Insurance Co.

Home Office: ASHEVILLE, N. C.

Phone 495

HOTEL OXFORD Redecorated and Refitted throughout. Recently enlarged to 60 rooms. Centrally located. Depot cars stop at entrance. Long distance telephone office upstairs. American and European plan. Rates 50c, 75c and $1 per day; special rates by week or month. C. H. Branson & Sons, Proprietors. Phone 1887. 50-54 South Main St. **Asheville, N. C.**

Williams-Brownell Planing Mill Company — *Hardwoods*

Lumber---Rough and Dressed Flooring a Specialty Moulding, Interior Finish, Etc.

Office, Plant and Yards on Southern Railway, Near Biltmore Station

WHITE PINE Phone 729 YELLOW PINE

Asheville Electrical Company
W. Mansfield Booze, Manager
74 CENTRAL AVE.
HEADQUARTERS
Phone 377

RIDGE — 488 — SENEY

- 56 *Jolly Lester
- 62 *Madison J A
- 63 *Staggs Jno
- 64 *Pearson Henry
- 70 *Gaines Thaddeus
- 71 *Ford Leo
- 72 *Brigman J C
- 73 *Bailey J D
- 75 *Long S G
- 76 *Sims Jas
- 79 *Faucett Giles
- *Ford Rosa
- 81 *Bennett Geo Rev

RIVERSIDE DRIVE — North from Haywood along east side of French Broad river

ROBERTS — s e from w Haywood, w of Park av
- 2 Vacant (store)
- 8 Ball E G, barber
- 9 Wyatt W H, genl mdse
- 10 Westmoreland B F, gro
- 12 Smith J E
- McCarson B
- 13 Wyatt W H
- 14 Buckner C B
- Fowler F B
- 19 Clark J W
- 25 Smathers P A
- Boyd C P
- (Buxton ends)
- 33 Calloway J M
- 34 Bryce S P, gro
- 36 Southern Mica Co
- 40 Cook Eli
- 41 Reynolds C Z
- Smith Douglas
- 42 Wells C M
- 45 Reynolds W A
- Dickson Matilda Mrs
- 55 Moore T F
- 56 Myers M L
- 60 Vacant
- 63 Roberts E G
- 64 Martindale W H
- 79 *Proctor Jno
- 81 *Berry Edwd
- 99 Williams Ernest
- *Clark Otis
- 101 *Freeman Jno
- Whiteside Jno
- 105 *Land B
- *Gaither Lucy
- 107 *Hellam Marjorie
- 120 *Banks W H
- 123 *Thompson S T

- 125 *Brooks Henry
- 127 *Brown Zelma
- 131 *Miller Cora
- *Morrisson Pinkney
- 133 *Crawford Lillian
- *Martin Carrie
- 156 Vacant
- — Ash Dray Fuel & Constr Co
- — Carolina Coal & Ice Co, yds
- — Asheville Grain & Hay Co

ST DUNSTAN'S ROAD — s w from Biltmore rd, Victoria
- 85 Arcouet M E Mrs
- 87 Fitzpatrick R M
- 89 Johnson W E

SAND HILL ROAD — (West Asheville)

SASSAFRAS — N from 90 Hazzard
- 5 *Porter Vina
- 6 Parker Jennie
- 14 De Vault Benj
- 15 *McDonald Thos
- 16 *Holmes Carrie
- 17 *Thompson Nannie
- 18 *Miller E G
- 21 *Hamilton Jas
- 26 *Sasportas Walter
- 28 *Steele Alice
- 36 *Copening Harvey
- 38 *McElrath Mamie

SANTEE — West from Montford av, 1 n of Watauga

SCOTT — E from 516 s French Broad av
- 27 *Morgan Ellison
- — *Beasley Wister
- 190 *Bradley Jno

SENEY — E from 336 n Main
- 5 Henderson W A
- 12 Boone M L Mrs
- 13 Brown W A
- 14 Mims W R
- 15 Anders B F
- Arrowood C C
- 16 Barrett J F
- (Center Begins)
- 23 Bean S I
- 24 Carter W R
- 25 *Walker Walter
- 29 Moseley J H
- 32 McMahon J R
- 36 Ingle F P
- 37 *Morgan Patrick
- 40 Crowell J A
- 44 Hart E P

Asheville Dry Cleaning Co.
Telephones 835-836, All Dep't
MAIN, N. E. COR. COLLEGE

THE CLEANERS
Our Department for Oriental Rugs and Carpet Cleaning is prepared to serve you in all its branches.

E. S. Paine   O. E. Hansen

Maple Flooring and Poplar Siding

English Lumber Co.
PHONE . . 321

SENEY 489 SILVER

45 Maxwell C N
　Powell J M
47 Frady G F
50 Sawyer J Y
　　(East intersects)
60-64 Redmon S M, gro
63 Vacant
64 Redmon S M
65 Ingle J V
69 *Alexander Rufus
70 Jarvis C F
75 Snyder A B Mrs
80 Pressley W H
81 Davis S F
　　(Fulton intersects)
91 Ashhton Jas
106 Mitchell J W
110 Gibson Eliza Mrs
111 Boyd J R
112 Vess R A
113 Ledbetter G W
　　(Holland intersects)
115 Ingle Clarence
118 Shytle C L
122 Terhune C G
126 Cleland Mary Mrs
SEVIER AV—n e from East at The "Winyah"
SHELLY PL—(Grove Park)
SHORT—N from 117 Cherry
　8 Gudger J M
　9 Young J G
　11 *McKee Arthur
　　 *Poole Green
　12 *Bolden Andrew
　15 *Hunt Sallie
　16 *Forney Henrietta
　19 *Hyatt R L
　23 *Fuller J E
　　 *Hardy Wm
　27 *Woodside Wm
　33 Howell F F
　36 *Thomas Susie
　45 *Cole Richard
　　 *Barton Lee
　　(Bearden av intersects)
　46 *Pearson E W
　47 *Saxton Hugh
　48 *Darden J B
　52 *Fall Lulu
　　 *Bason Henry
　54 *Greenlee Hattie
　　 *Littlejohn Geneva
　56 *Clark Eliza
　57 *Hairston R P Rev

SHORT BAILEY—(See Wallach)
SHORT McDOWELL — Near Victoria
　6 *Hemphill Ella
　8 *Watford Frank
　12 *Bolden Walter
　20 *Brooks Wm
　24 *Brown Belton
　28 *Phillips J H
　130 *Sumner Minnie
SHORT PINE—E fr 78 Pine
　4 *Ray Isaac
　5 *Gardner Taylor
　6 *Logan Eure
　8 Vacant
　151 *Flack Thos
SHORT ROBERTS — Southwest from 33 Roberts
　4 Rogers S J Mrs
　24 Sumner C E
　28 Ford Elizabeth Mrs
　30 King Monie Miss
　　 Crowell Alma Miss
　36 Presley M E Miss
　　 Hammett Augustus
　38 Miller Rena Mrs
　　 Sluder Minnie Miss
　118 Rice Eliza Mrs
　126 Chambers C E
SHORT STARNES — (See Starnes Place)
SHORT VALLEY—Southwest from 131 Velvet
　3 *White Marshall
　5 *Patterson Jno
　9 *Young Edwd
　　 *Moore Dennis
　13 *Postell Maude
　17 *Smith Carrie
　　 *Sanders Amanda
　19 *Clements Frank
　　 *Sanders Mattie
　25 *Foster Chas
　35 *Williams Lula
　113 *Hudson Lee
　　 *Roberts Mary
SHORT WOODFIN—North fr 52 Woodfin
SILVER—W fr 199 Asheland
　7 Steele W A
　8 Robinson L C
　10 Bean C L
　14 Kilpatrick R W
　15 Shipman J S
　18 Wagoner J D

BIGGEST
BUSIEST
BEST

Asheville Steam Laundry

Phones:
1936 and 1937

—

43 to 47
W. College Street

CHARLES H. HONESS
OPTOMETRIST
AND
OPTICIAN

Exclusive maker of
ATLAS SHUR-ON
EYE GLASSES

THE
Home of Ce-Rite
Toric Lenses

We make a specialty of correcting optical defects with properly fitted glasses.

54 Patton Avenue
Opposite Postoffice

IF in the market for a Gas Engine let us make you prices.
　its heavy castings, such as columns or building plates, see us.
　its a skilled mechanic for boiler work, see us.
　you want machine work of any kind phone 590.

CAROLINA MACHINERY CO.

FOUNDERS
MACHINISTS and
Jobbers of Mill
Supplies

Life Insurance Company of Virginia
ORGANIZED 1871
Home Office - Richmond, Va.

Has won the hearty approval and active support of the people by its promptness and fair dealing during the FORTY-TWO YEARS of its operation

J. V. Moon, Superintendent, Rooms 3-4-5 Maxwelton Bldg., Asheville, N. C.

SILVER 490 SOUTHSIDE AV

T. P. JOHNSON & CO.

SHEET METAL WORKERS

All Kinds of Roofing Guttering and Conductor Work Metal Ceilings, Skylights and Galvanized Iron Cornices

OFFICE and SHOP:
69-71 S. MAIN

Phone 325

DR. C. H. MILLER

Mechano-Therapist

14 N. Spruce Street
ASHEVILLE, N. C.

PHONE 979

Hours by Engagement

DRUGLESS HEALING OF DISEASE

---

19 Kilpatrick W P
24 *Wood Lee
25 Jones E J
28 Potillo W L
   Morgan E W
   (Blanton ends)
29 Goldsmith Z V
33 Vacant
SMITH—s w from 151 S'side av
12 Rickard J J
14 *Rice Theo
16 *Vernon Fannie
20 *Bruton Ora
22 *Penland Jno
26 *Ferguson Henry
28 *Gudger Chas
   (Bartlett intersects)
36 *Walker Emma
38 *Vernon Lizzie
46 *Angel Georgia
50 *Patton Vinie
SOCO—n e fr 201 Montford av
11 Buckner R G Dr
15 Cocke Ada Mrs
24 Mobley K M Mrs
27 Foreman J W Dr
28 Lawrence M P
32 Wells V L
38 Ladue Pomeroy
46 Hoyer Z M Mrs
SORRELL—s w from Beaumont to Atkin, 1 e of New
2 *Green Edith
4 *Foster Narcissa
4 (r) *Fuller J H
5 *Watts Mattie
7 *Gaither Jennie
8 *Williams Nellie
12 *Candler Richard
12 (r) *Tyson Presley
14 *Lynch Ida
14 (r) *Taylor Louise
15 *Proctor A K
   (Weaver intersects)
16 *Day Jno
17 *Lance J E, gro
23 Sorrell L F
26 *Proctor Elias
29 Brown Gustavus
SOUTHSIDE AVENUE—s w from 176 s Main to Depot
25 Young Annie Mrs
35 *Ashton Lena Mrs
53 Vacant
54 *Lundy Jane
90 *Thompson Elizabeth

94 *Abernathy Caroline
121 *Roberts Hattie
125 *Sanders Mamie, eating hse
128 *Galbraith Sallie
129 *McKee Thos
137 *Gudger Eddie
147 *Morgan Hattie
   (Phifer ends)
151 Harrison B A Mrs
160 Turner G B, shoemkr
162 Forster J S, gro
   (McDowell begins)
170 Jackson J F, gro
170½ Towe Jesse
172 Jackson J F
188 Hyatt W R
190 *Watson B S E, gro
195 Rickard J J, gunsmith
207 *Foster Oliver
221 *Young Blaine
225 *Murdock Chas
227 Gibson Wm
229 *Davis Reuben
231 *Nesbitt Jno
— *Southside School
238 Presley M H, gro
240 Allison E B
244 *Knox Fannie
248 *Logan Vernon
270 Sherlin Jno
272 Roberts Saml
   (Victoria av begins)
280 Isaac T L
283 Owens J L
286 Messer S M
   (Gaston begins)
292 Isaac T L, gro
296 Christopher C K
300 Bell C C
304 *Vacant
308 Plemmons J M
311 Vacant
   (Adams intersects)
327 Edwards J A
329 Moore W C
   Misenheimer M G
331 Call D H
333 Lunsford J C
   (French Broad av intersects)
343 Thrash P H
350 Heilig J H
369 Aiken C F
   (Ora ends)
370 Landreth A P, shoemkr
372 Southside Furniture Co
373 Hunter J C

ASHEVILLE CLEANING and PRESSING CLUB

TAILORING THAT SATISFIES and PRICES THAT PLEASE

Hats cleaned, banded and bound. Silk hats ironed. Buttons made to order in all sizes. Plain or with rims. PHONE 389

DYEING IN ALL SHADES Cleaned. Messenger Service.

Kid Gloves, Slippers and Plumes, Fancy Jabots and Ties, French Dry Cleaned. Ladies' and Gentlemen's suits Steam

J. C. Wilbar, Prop. 4 NORTH PACK SQ.

ASHEVILLE COAL CO.
6 North Pack Sq.   Phone 40

M. & W. COAL

SOUTHSIDE AV   491   STARNES AV

376 Glenn M F
382 Owens & Son, gros
    Owens J W
385 Whitener J W
390 Potts Jane Miss, boarding
394 West C C
394½ Blankenship J M
396 Capps Wakefield
3999 Landreth B P, fruits
401 Hughes Transfer & Livery Co
    Hughes R P
403 Lytle H F
407 Vacant
410 Suttle C N
410½ Swayngin S P
412-414 Hollar & Co, gros
418 Blair A B
    Blair M E Mrs, board
420 Union Store (The), clothing

SPEARS AVENUE—east from 319 Merrimon av
19 Burbage J H
25 Meyer Catherine Mrs
38 Smith D E Mrs

SPRING—West from junction of Haywood and Patton av
1-7 Vacant
8 Johnston J B
9 Langford J L
10 Gentry W M
11 Bradley Jos
    Morrow B R
16 Vacant
20 Madsen Christian
20 (2) Phillips C E Mrs
    Tilson Henry
24 Summey W C
    Hall M B
26 Quinton J R
28 Jackson W M
30 Simpson D M
32 Wallen E J
    Melton E B
34 Jackson J D
    Jordan Dyer
38 Evans C A
41 Gillis Robt
    Wyatt S W
47 Miller C
    Lumpkin Daniel
49 Huskey Jane Mrs
    Brown Jno
    Revis Joseph
65 Willis W A, gro
65 (r) Roberts P M

SPRUCE—North and south from 49 College
    Going North
12 Goff W A
14 Miller C H Dr
14 (r) *Dalrymple Larkin, painter
    *McDowell Elijah, shoemkr
15 "Dixie" (The), boarding
    Hatchell Bessie Mrs
17 Ramsey J L Mrs
    McDougle Artimecia Mrs, boarding
23 Fortune R G
24 Miller C H Dr
    Miller L R Mrs, board
    (Walnut ends)
35 Reeves R H Dr
38 Brown M W
45 "Elton" (The), boarding
    Watkins S N Mrs
48 "Old Kentucky Home"
    Wolfe Julia Mrs
57-65 "Belmont"
    Houser B A Dr
60 Bernecker Julius
    Bernecker Freda Miss, dressmkr
62 Miskelly C A Mrs
64 Nash E L
    Wolfe J W
66 Schochet J B
67 Jarvis W M
    Jackson Lonnie
— Beth Ha Teplutta Synagogue
73 Vacant
77 Killen F M
    Warren W W
    Going South
3 Blackwell B F
6 Lynch S S
10 Black T P
    Plemmons J R
12 Thompson W E
    McGhee Kittie Mrs
14 Cassada R E
    Cassada Maggie Mrs, board
16 Plemmons R L, board
20-22 Westall W H & Co
20½ Davis T E
36 Bishop D M
37 Vacant

STARNES AVENUE—West fr Main, 1 n of Cherry
4 Morrow C P Mrs

Gas Ranges   PHONE 69   **Asheville Power and Light Co.**

Meats   **Kiibler & Whitehead**
CITY MARKET   PHONES, 195 and 694

WEAVERVILLE LINE
NINE MILES BY TROLLEY FROM PACK SQUARE TO WEAVERVILLE

ASHEVILLE AND EAST TENNESSEE RAILROAD CO.
7 NORTH MAIN STREET — ASHEVILLE N. C.

STARNES AV — 492 — **VALLEY**

ELECTRIC FIXTURES
Piedmont Electric Co.
64 PATTON AVE.
ASHEVILLE, N.C.

---

5 "Lyons" (The)
   Trentham G W
18 Woody A I Mrs
   (Grady ends)
21 Bartlett C H
26 Moorman O P
30 Sanders T R
33 Smart C E Mrs, boarding
36 Glenn W E Dr
41 Glenn E B Dr
42 Steelman J A
47 Barker M C Mrs
48 Sams R B
51 Clark W H
54-55 Vacant
59 Rosenfeld N I
60 Hampton S A
   (Flint intersects)
65 Pickens C W Dr
   Aiken J P
71 Parham D W
75 Youge K M
   Sarasfield G L Mrs
76 Vacant
77 Petrie Hugh
78 Harrison F W Mrs
   (Starnes Place begins)
83 Pace B H
84 Orr J C
   Landreth M M
87 Young J T
90 Miller E H, publisher
91 Beerworth J A
93 Driver H L
94 Young L W
95 Clee F W
97 Vacant
99 Clark T G

STARNES PLACE—South fr 78 Starnes av
16 Piercy W H, carp
28½ Moore P R
80 Vacant
82 Wilson L C
84½ Lyerly W R

SUMMIT—West from 76 n Liberty
1 Bradley S O
3 Cobb P D
7 Hall H E
9 Hall E A

SUMMIT—(Biltmore)

SUNSET DRIVE—Northwest from Baird to city limits
— Doughty K E Miss
— Howland S H

SWAN—(See Biltmore)

SWANNANOA AVENUE—(W Asheville)

SYCAMORE—East from 48 s Main
— Caslar Sol, cider mnfr
37 *Forney Wm
37½ *Seventh Day Adventist Church
39 *Walker Emma
49 *Gaines Lillie
51 *Vacant
54 *Martin Lydia
60 Ledbetter L C, gro
  *Brown J B, shoemkr

TANNERY—Opp Hans Rees Sons Tannery

TIERNAN—W fr Bartlett
31 Hamilton W R B, contr
45 Muse J W
46 Murray School
53 to 63 Vacant
71 Hall Thaddeus
73 Vacant
75 Beacham W B
81 Sprouse Martin

TURNER—W from Buttrick
15 *Wofford Monroe
  *Bivins Henry
16 Revis Joseph
17 *Tucker Jno
  *Weaver James
20 Johnson E A
23 *Vance Mark
24 Johnson J V
27 *Wilson Florence
28 Spivey F A
29 *Moore Arthur
32 Ballard R B
35 Smith F L
  King M A
38 Plemmons J M

TUSKEE—N from 135 Pine to Eagle, 1 w of Hazzard
19 *Hill Saml
40 *Chisolm Thos
41 *Brown M A

VALLEY—s w fr 111 College
4 *Johnson Perry
16 *Johnson J W
— *Williams Ellen
— *Gudger Thos
— *Crawford C J
  (Poplar intersects)
35 *Lytle Louise
56-64 *Dobbins Jas, hackman

CONTRACTOR and BUILDER
STEEL RANGES
J. C. McPHERSON
35-37 E COLLEGE ST.
PHONE 133
PLUMBING STEAM AND HOT WATER HEATING

| VALLEY | 493 | VICTORIA RD |

MAPLE FLOORING
HARDWOOD LUMBER OF ALL KINDS

WOODWARD & SON
9th and Arch Sts., Richmond, Va.
See Adv. Opposite Page 188

60 *Bailey Julia
63 *Hunt Julia
64 *Dobbins Jas
   (Eagle intersects)
— Angel M Y, gro
78 *Redmon Maria
   *Hartman Alice, dressmkr
80 *Hadden T G Rev
81 *Young Jno
83 *Smith Louise
84 *Sample Alice
107 Smith Jno
109 *Sinclair Rachel
118 *Devinie Robt
119 *Durham Jane
123 *Morris Jas
127 *Slade Mayfield Rev
— *Catholic Hill School
133 *Dickson Isaac
136-137 Michalove I, gro
140 *Hampton Laura, eating house
141 *Green Pleasant
— *St Matthias Episcopal Ch
   (Catholic av begins)
147 *Jenkins Belle
153 *Ridley Jno
189 *McKesson Jeremiah
   (Beaumont intersects)
— City Stables
— Ledbetter L C

VANCE—N from 74 College
15 Kelly M H
16 Hill M A Mrs
18 Luther R H
   Kinsland Daisy Miss, nurse
   Lindsay Roberta Miss, nurse
   Owen Euphia Miss, nurse
19 Kerr J P
24 Buttrick W T
25 Whittington W P Dr
29 Fisher H L
27 Kennedy R V
29 Stanberry E E
30 McKay Edwin
32 Chambers J K
35 Kuchler E S Mrs
36 Miller M E Mrs
40 Justice C N
41 Hartzog P G
45 Marsh A H
46 Israel C W
47 Howatt J P
50 Enthoffer E J
51 Zageir R B

53 Schas Michael
54 McCall R S
   Cline T L
   Penland M A
55 Noland D G
58 Smith A B
59 Horton F L
61 Goode J C
64 Sluder C L

VELVET—Southeast from Eagle, 1 e of Spruce
7 *Harris Carl
   *Brooks Luther
9 (175) *Carson David
41 *Burns Wilson
43 *Knox Mattie
45 *Bailey Frank
46 Smith Josephine Mrs
47 *Flax Ida

VERNON HILL—(Victoria)
— Radeker E H Mrs
   "Sunnycrest"
— Littlefield A S
   "Ridgelawn"
— Montgomery S R
   "Spurwood"
— Adickes H F

VICTORIA AVENUE—S from S'side av, w of McDowell
6 Penland W H
   Creasman Henry
55 Brohun C B Mrs
69 Benson M M
77 McDowell W G
85 McDowell W W
93 Williams P U

VICTORIA ROAD—Southwest from 445 s Main
21 Harris J L
25 Campbell F M
33 Johnson T A
35 Vacant
41 "Chapel Cottages"
   Moore A E Miss, boarding
45 Moore A E Miss
53 McPeeters T C
75 Weaver Dick
77 Webb D H
86 Childs E P Prof
89 Goodrich F L Miss
101 Brux H B
146 Campbell J N
— Allen C J Genl
— Coachman J W
— St Genevieve College
— Hillside Convent

What Have You in Real Estate that You Don't Want?

What do You Want in Real Estate that You Haven't?

WESTERN CAROLINA REALTY CO.

J. W. Wolfe Sec. & Treas.

On the Square
PHONE 974
10 N. PACK SQ.

Brown-Carter Realty Co.
REAL ESTATE
23 TEMPLE COURT
PHONE 341
ASHEVILLE   N. C.

FLORIDA SPECIALTIES
Grazing, Timbered, Farm Lands, Orange Groves, Turpentine Locations and Phosphate Lands.

NORTH CAROLINA SPECIALTIES
Orchard, Farm and Timbered Lands, City Property, Rent Collections.

Moale & Chiles Real Estate and Insurance
27 Patton Ave., (2d fl)   Phone 661
General Agents United States Fidelity & Guaranty Co.

Club Cafe and Candy Kitchen
"A GOOD PLACE FOR REFRESHMENT"

Our Ice Cream manufacturing plant is absolutely clean and sanitary.
Prompt family delivery. Phones 110 and 111.
Catering for large parties and receptions. Special Creams.

| VICTORIA RD | 494 | WATAUGA |

Brown's Undertaking Parlors

S. H. BROWN

Lady Assistant When Desired

Phone 193-2 Rings

50 Patton Avenue
Asheville, N. C.

Established 1894

B. J. JACKSON

Carefully Selected Fruits and Vegetables

Stall No. 11, City Market

BUSINESS PHONES:
86 and 101

RESIDENCE PHONE
1596

— Cheesborough T P Dr
— McKee Henrietta Mrs
— Bull H K
— George Wm S
  "Knowllacre"
— Connally A T Mrs
  "Fernihurst"
— Jackson B M
  "Hillcote"
— Sternberg Siegfried
— Wright Frances Miss

VIEW—West from 25 Atkinson
8 Dayton T J
  Whittaker Solomon
12 Camp J B
16 Ramsey J L
  Brank C B
28 Vacant
32 Lunsford Anna Mrs
34 Bradley F E
38 Jones G W
44 Clontz Elizabeth Miss
48-52 Vacant

VIVIAN—N from Dortch av
22 Crowell P B
26 Roberts J C
28 Vacant
36 Martin Elizabeth Miss

WALLACH—Southeast from 138 Asheland av
1 Parker Alex
3 *McCorkle Wm
11 *Burgin Carrie
  *Hall Margaret
13 *Bailey Edwd
17 *Johnson Anna B
  *Allen Mary
17½ *Lyttle Francis
  *Copeland Della
19 *Johnson Beatrice
33 *Ponder Jas
38 *Anderson Henry
  *Brown Clarence
40 *Hart Minnie
42 *Peters Henry
  *Williams Fleming
43 *Wellman Mack
45 *Weaver Forrest
  *Saboid Jas
54 *Jones Susie
  *Gay Frank
56 *Berry Hester
75 *Gudger Susan
77 *Preston Mary
78 *Feimster Clarence

  *Taggart Mary
81 *Wilfong Jno
85 *Robinson Phylis
87 *Stroud Rhoda
91 Weaver Wm P
  Capps Jas
93 Carland Jno
115 *Anderson David
117 *Riggans Archie
121 *Beard Ernest
200 *Gudger Patton

WALNUT—W from 38 n Main
5 *Hellams M C, eating hse
7 *Hopkins J W & Son, blksmiths
9 Love F P & Son Drs, vet surgeons
  Creasman J H, livery
19 Westall J M & Co, lumber
  (Lexington av intersects)
— Western Carolina Auto Co
32 Asheville Tel & Tel Co
35 Ashev Tobacco Co
  (Penland intersects)
42 "Elm" (The), board
  Johnson P J
46 "Gray Gables," board
  Hughey R W
48 Penland J A
49 Miller J A
  Faulkner J H
50 Cooper H G Mrs
53 Clayton E S

WALNUT EAST—East from Main, 1 n of College
5 Warren B W, livery

WASHINGTON ROAD—North from 166 Chestnut
21 Lamb Mary R Mrs
27 Moore E J K Miss
28 Moale P R
39 Bragaw R M Mrs
70-78 Vacant
79 Moore J W
  Buckner J G
79 (r) Rodgers W R
79½ Douglas G J
80 Vacant
83 Steadman L A Miss, dressmkr
106 (200) Martin J V

WATAUGA—West from Montford av, 6 n of Haywood
14 Carr Omar
32 Vacant
36 Cain W S Rev

Furniture and China Carefully Prepared for Shipment

Mahogany Furniture Hand Made & Carefully Reproduced

E. E. GALER
114 PATTON AVE.

Upholstering and Refinishing
PHONE - 1674

ROUGH AND DRESSED LUMBER
WHITE PINE AND YELLOW PINE
FLOORING A SPECIALTY
Hardwoods

Williams-Brownell Planing Mill Company
Mouldings and Interior Finish
Office: Southern Railway Tracks, Near Biltmore Station
Phone 729 — *Planing Mill*

| WATAUGA | 495 | ZILLICOA |

- 37 Barnard A S
- 40 Green J B Dr
- 43 Williams J H Dr
- 44 McRae J P

WEAVER—E from 15 Sorrell
- 11 *Lee Henry
- 16 *Addington Jas
- 17 *Sheppard Chas
- 20 *Colley Georgia
- 21 *Boger Martin
- 22 *Howard Jesse
- 24 *Hill Clarence
- 26 *Vacant
- 33 *Gardner Q
- 138 *Palmer Cecil
- 139 *Johnson Thos

WEST—n w from Seney
- 10 Weir H M
- 31 Johnson H H
- 35 Sorrels C E
- 46 Krause Frank
- 47 *Porter Peter
- 49 *Clarke Ida
- 71 McKenzie H G
- 78 Starnes J H
- 80 Collins Benj
- 97 Ray Walter
- 107 Vacant

WILLIAM—n w from Atkinson
- 13 Revis S C
- 15 Duncan Lettie Miss
- 19 Hart W S
- 23 Ingle Mary Mrs
- 32 King Jesse
- 38 Spivey J T
- Beachboard J A
- 97 Taylor V T

WOODFIN—East from 79 n Lexington av
- 3 *Robinson Louisa
- 9 *Thompson Virginia
- 10 *Matthews Lewis
- 12 *Craig Caroline
  (Main intersects)
- 2 Asheville School for Girls
- 15 Piper Wesley
- 22 Spears J C Mrs
- 23 Featherston A A
- Featherston C M Mrs, bdg
  (Liberty ends)
- 24 Vacant
- 26 Sluder F S
- 31 Blomberg Louis
- 40 Waldrop Saml
- 41 Sluder L C
- 48 Britt W W

  (Spruce ends)
- 52 Williams J C
- 54 Seigle Harry, gro
- 55 Foster Jerome
- 58 Vacant
- 59 Kiibler R E
- Paulling A F
  (Central av begins)
- 64 Shook B F
- Carscaddon O C
- 65 Hale S P Mrs
- 68 Michalov Louis
- 71 Baker C P
- 72 Vacant
- 76 White E P
- Reese S P
  (Vance ends)
- 79 Johnson F L
- 82 Israel E M
- Reese S P
- 83 Vacant
- 87 Perkinson T J
- 91 Fitzgerald W E
- 92 Wolfe W O
- 95 Colvin & Davidson, contrs
- Colvin J G
- 104 Biggs Sanitarium
- Biggs A C Dr
  (Oak ends)
- 118 Case Gertrude Mrs
- 124 Logan S T
- 126 Ward P O
- 128 McLain J P
  (Charlotte begins)
- 137 Ford E K Miss
- 141 Ramsey S C
- 147 Davidson G H, contr
- 151 Henderson R H, carp
- 159 Brown R M
- Warner N J
  (Locust ends)
- 176 Suber Annie Mrs
- 176 (r) Simonton Amos
- 184 Goodrich J V
- 190 Bowles R E
- 194 Stradley G F
- 204 Brown E L

WOOLSEY AVENUE—A continuation of Merrimon av

ZILLICOA—Northeast from 389 Montford av
- 1 Mackay D McN
- 19 Cory W O Maj
- 49 Rumbough J E
- 75 Highland Hospital
- Carroll R S, phys

HUGHES
Transfer and Livery Co.

Automobiles for HIRE

TRUNKS 25c

Office:
401 Southside Avenue

PHONE 1405

Try our Hand Laundering. We strive to please in LAUNDERING and DRY CLEANING.

The Sanitary Home Laundry
No. 7 MONTFORD AVE.
PHONE - 1354

Association of American Directory Publishers

HEADQUARTERS,
202 EAST 12TH STREET, NEW YORK.

ORGANIZED NOVEMBER, 1898

J. L. HILL, President
R. H. DONNELLEY, 1st Vice-President
W. H. LEE, 2nd Vice-President
W. H. BATES, Secretary and Treas.

TRUSTEES

WM. E. MURDOCK, Boston
R. H. DONNELLEY, Chicago.
A. V. WILLIAMS, Cincinnati
J. L. HILL, Richmond, Va.
R. L. POLK, Detroit

W. H. BATES, New York
W. H. LEE, New Haven
E. M. GOULD, St. Louis
W. G. TORCHIANA, Phila.

THE OBJECTS OF THE ASSOCIATION ARE AS FOLLOWS:

FIRST:—To improve the directory business by the interchange of ideas, and by the exchange of competent employees.

SECOND:—To protect the public against fraudulent advertising schemes, operated under the name of directories, and to drive the promoters of such out of the business.

THIRD:—To provide permanent and continuous employment for honest and faithful directory canvassers.

FOURTH:—For the mutual advancement of the established and prospective interests of all who may become members of the Association.

$100 REWARD

The Association of American Directory Publishers will pay the above reward for the arrest and conviction of any one soliciting or collecting money on Fraudulent Directories, provided the conviction results in imprisonment of not less than 6 months. In case of arrest immediately telegraph W. H. Bates, Secretary, 202 East 12th Street, New York.

OR

PIEDMONT DIRECTORY COMPANY,
Asheville, N. C.

For Kindling "What am Kindling" Call
ENGLISH LUMBER COMPANY Phone 321

1913—Suburban Directory—1913
THE PIEDMONT SERIES

BILTMORE—Situated about 2 miles south of city.
BINGHAM HEIGHTS—Northwest of city bey French Broad river.
CHUNN'S COVE—East of city across the mountain (R D 2)
GRACE—North of city, beyond Woolsey (R D 1)
KENILWORTH—Southeast of city, beyond limits.
RICHMOND HILL—Northwest of city, beyond French Broad river.
SOUTH ASHEVILLE—Southeast of city, just beyond limits.
SOUTH BILTMORE—Located south of Biltmore.
VERNON HILL—Victoria.
WEST ASHEVILLE—West, across French Broad River (R D 3)
WOOLSEY—North of city, just bey limits (R D 1)

Biggest Busiest Best

Phones 1936 and 1937
ASHEVILLE STEAM LAUNDRY
43 to 47 W. COLLEGE

BILTMORE   497   BILTMORE

BILTMORE VILLAGE
ALL SOULS CRESCENT—S from Brook in Circle to Swan
1 Ericsson Eric (Christine)
2 McKain Annie Mrs
3 Vacant
4 Price A L (Mamie)
5 Elias L W Dr (Frances)
6 Nolan Fannie Miss
7 Kenney F W (Amelia)
9 Spann M E Miss, boarding
10 Griffin J T (Evangeline)
11 Bostick Elizabeth, wid B R
14 Rees H B (Elizabeth)
15 Cowdery L W (Florence V)
16 Swope R R Rev (Mary B)
ANGLE—East from Swan to All Souls' Crescent
— Biltmore Parish House
2 Spann M E Miss, boarding
3 Adams W S (Malinda)
5 Dodd T L (Mary)
  Dodd E W (Mary)
— All Souls' P E Church
BILTMORE PARK—
  Abernathy Chas (Martha)
  Bell Thos (Anna)
  Boynton Frank (Mary)
  Carter Fannie, wid Bruce
  Lipe J Frank (R)
  Presley Danl (Dora)
  Reed Jno
  Shuford Robt (Eliza)

BILTMORE ROAD—East of Sou Ry tracks
1 Lipe Jas C (Nancy)
  Clarke Sarah E, wid Robt
— Biltmore Shops, blksmiths
  Millholland L A
20 Waddell Chas (Ella)
BROOK—S from Plaza to Sou Ry
— Sou Ry Station
1 Biltmore Post Office
2 Sharpe F L (Jennie)
3 Keith N L, wid Dr H H
4 Hallyburton Lillie, wid J A
5 Baughan C R (Ida)
6 Dillard J P
7-8-9 Vacant
10 Warren S T (Bertha)
11 McGlone F H (Bertha)
— Trantham T L, gro
14 Luther B J & Co, livery
OAK—East from Swan to All Souls' Crescent
1-4 Vacant
2 Kitchin J P (Hesta)
3 Johnson H I (Addie)
5 Kerr — —
6 Waddell F N (Anna I)
PLAZA—West from Brook
1 Luther B J
2-5 Stoner A D, dry gds
3 Nurses Home
4 Dodd T L, meats
6-7 Vacant

S. D. HALL
REAL ESTATE AGENT
—
Money Loaned
—
Notary Public
—
32 PATTON AVENUE
—
Phone 91

Founders, Machinists and Jobbers of Mill Supplies

PHONE 590
When in the market for pipe and fittings, let us make you Prices.

Carolina Machinery Co.

PHONE 590
If it's a Gas Engine let us figure with you, also on other kinds of machinery

Asheville Dray, Fuel and Construction Co.

Heavy Hauling of all kinds
61-2 South Main
WE FURNISH BUILDING STONE
Moving Furniture a Specialty
PHONE - 223

BILTMORE 498 GRACE

DYNAMOS & MOTORS

Piedmont Electric Co.

64 Patton Av.
ASHEVILLE, N.C.

8 Biltmore Estate Industries
9 Vance Ella R, wid Jno P
10 Biltmore Drug Store
— Biltmore Estate Genl Office
RECTORY LANE—E from Biltmore rd, 1 s of All Souls' Crescent
SHORT—
2 Ravenel S P, atty
4 Vacant
SOUTHERN RY TRACKS—
Sou Ry Station
Sou Express Co
W U Tel Co
Biltmore Box Factory
— Gaston E L, lbr
U S Furn Mnfg Co
Vance C T
Williams-Brownell Planing Mill Co
Wright Horace
SWAN—South from Plaza to All Souls' Crescent
— Neeley Geo B (Ada M)
2 Reed F Julia, wid G W
3 Rankin M C, wid Alonzo
4 Praytor Edwd
5 Hoitt Chas A
VILLAGE LANE—E from All Souls' Crescent to limits
12 Cleveland E J, wid J S
— Biltmore Hospital
BINGHAM HEIGHTS —
Across French Broad River opp Riverside Park
Bingham Robt Col (Violet)
Bingham School (The)
Brookshire Frank
Dalton Jno (Olive)
Eve A Emerson
Eve Chas W (Kate E)
Greenwood E E Maj
Grinnan R T Maj (Sadie B)
Ingle Jas F (Nannie)
Ingle Robt (Kittie)
Lance Dill F (Hattie)
McKee S R Maj (Mary K)
Pike J Baxter (Daisy)
Turbyfill N H (Lizzie)

CHUNN'S COVE
(Cross mountain, R F D No 2)
*Anderson Lewis (Malinda)
Armstrong Flora, wid Eugene
Armstrong Wilbur W

*Bailey Elsie
Brown Paul
Broyles E E (Bessie)
Chunn's Cove Baptist Ch
Chunn's Cove Episcopal Ch
Chunn's Cove School
Crenshaw Jas W
Crook Edwd
Crook Jesse
*Davidson Lawrence
*Davis Wm (Mary)
DeVault Chas (Laura)
Evans Edwd Dr
Hildebrand D S (Oleatta)
*Holland Josephine
Jones D A (Nellie), genl mdse
Jones Edward (Esther)
Keenan J T (Bertha)
Laurel Springs Dairy
McIntyre Jas
Metz Joseph (Rhoda)
Metz Martha, wid T M
Oak Grove Dairy
Owen Wm T (Mary A)
Randall Alfred
Randall Burton C
Randall Chas R
Roberts Julius
Roberts Stella Miss
Roseland Dairy
*Reed Wm (Ella)
Shaft Albert (Laura)
Shaft Alvers (Josie)
Shaft Elizabeth Mrs
Smith Alfred (Emma)
Smith Mary Mrs
Smith Robt S
Stewart Augustus (Cora)
Stewart Edward D (Lottie)
Stewart Jno M
Stewart Wm (Rosa)
Whitson Geo M (Minnie)

GRACE
(R F D No 1)
Bassett H G (Bertha)
Billows Rest, board
Bowman C E Mrs
Burrell Jas (Maggie)
Carter Wm H (Emma)
Children's Home
*Coley Martha
Culvern G W (Elsie)
*Cuthbertson Baxter (Irene)

J. C. McPHERSON
SLATE AND TIN ROOFING
Galvanized Iron Work   Hot Air Furnaces
35-37 EAST COLLEGE STREET

MAPLE FLOORING
HARDWOOD LUMBER OF ALL KINDS

WOODWARD & SON
9th and Arch Sts., Richmond, Va.
See Adv. Opposite Page 188

GRACE 499 SOUTH ASHEVILLE

Davis Benj
Deal Jno (Lottie)
"Del Rosa Farm"
Dockery E J (Maggie)
Dockery J E (Mary)
Elkins Harvey
Felmet C L (Estelle)
Garland E F (Mary)
Garland G E, contr
Garland J N (Sarah)
Garland Jas (Mattie)
Grace Memorial Episco Ch
Grace School
Gragg F E (Agnes)
Green Jno F (Sue)
Greenwood J G (Pearl)
Greenwood Robt (Eliza)
Grindstaff T J (Mollie)
Haynes Washington Rev
Herron Jno R (Lizzie)
Johnson J E (Margaret)
Johnson S A (Carrie)
King H L (Mattie)
Kuykendall F H (Ella), blksmith
Kuykendall J W (Hettie)
Kuykendall Wm A (Bonnie)
Livingston Sue, wid L L
Lyman Chester Mrs
McBee U S (Vinie)
McConkey J N (Louise)
Melton G E (Lelia)
Miller Sylvester (Theodosia)
Mt Pleasant M E Church
Myers G T (America)
Myers Grover
Ottari Sanitarium
Randall J E (Sue), gro
Riddle Guy
Robertson S V (May)
Self J C (Gertha)
Smith Herbert (Kittie)
Stewart Danl W
Stewart N H (Mary)
Swain Cornelia Miss
Swain H E, wid J L
Swain J E, atty
Way Eugene
Way Martha J, wid C B
Willis Jas (Cynthia)

KENILWORTH
(Take Biltmore Car)
Baron A Zeta, wid Henry
Kenilworth Brick Works
Lance Henry (Allie)
McRary E H (Hettie)
Meyers Morris (Belle)
Nevercell Frank J (Ida H)
Redden Jno T (Etta)
Redden Robt (Blanche)
Rees Arthur F (Martha B)
Rees Arthur F Jr
Yarborough Martin (Sarah)

MONTFORD
(Across River opp Riverside)
Asheville Concrete Works
Montford Quarry

RICHMOND HILL
(Take Riverside Park Car)
Bame L Jackson (Annie)
Pearson J Thos
Pearson Marjorie H Miss
Pearson Richmond Hon (Gabrille T)
Rodgers Benj (Ethel)
Rodgers Clarence (Rosa)
Rymer Chas (Belle)
Smith Chas J (Alice)

SOUTH ASHEVILLE
(Take Biltmore Car)
*Avery Wm (Addie)
Bethel Rebecca
*Black Della
*Brackett Lou
*Brackett Raymond (Anna)
*Brown Julia
*Bryson Kate
*Burgin Delia
*Burgin Edwd
*Burgin Julia
*Burgin Wm (Margaret)
*Clark Andrew (Lula)
*Clayton Jesse (Angeline)
Collanter Peter (Lizzie)
*Cook Jno
*Cook Mary
*Davis Lettie
*Davis Saml (Daisy)
*Dalton Wm (Lucy)
*Fletcher David F (Ella)
*Gray Hattie
*Gray Squire (Rachel)
*Hemphill B Perry (Mary)
*Hill Logan (Emeline)
*Johnson Lee (Annie)

What Have You in Real Estate that You Don't Want?

What do You Want in Real Estate that You Haven't?

WESTERN CAROLINA REALTY CO.
J. W. Wolfe, Sec. & Treas.
On the Square
PHONE 974
10 N. PACK Sq.

H. A. BROWN & Co.
General Contractors
23 Temple Court Bldg.
Phone 341
—DEALERS IN—
Rough Building
and
all Kinds of
Crushed Stone
—OUR SPECIALTIES—
STONE
FOUNDATIONS
CONCRETE WORK
and
EXCAVATING

Moale & Chiles Real Estate and Insurance
27 Patton Ave., [2d fl] Phone 661
City and Suburban Property FARMS and TIMBER LANDS

Williams-Brownell Planing Mill Company — *Hardwoods*

Lumber---Rough and Dressed — Flooring a Specialty — Moulding, Interior Finish, Etc.
Office, Plant and Yards on Southern Railway, Near Biltmore Station
WHITE PINE — Phone 729 — YELLOW PINE

Asheville Electrical Co. Electrical Contractors
HEADQUARTERS 74 CENTRAL AVENUE
W. Manstield Booze, Manager
PHONE 377

SOUTH ASHEVILLE 500 SOUTH BILTMORE

- *Johnson Mattie
- *Keebler Edwd (Maggie)
- *Kemp Wade (Elizabeth)
- *Lance Jos (Mary)
- *Logan Lula
- *Lytle Jane
- *McLain Orange (Etta)
- *Mallory Aaron (Isabelle)
- *Miller Schofield (Corrie)
- *Mills Andrew
- *Patton Jas
- *Patton Saml
- *Payne Wm (Addie)
- *Powers Carl (Mollie)
- *Priestly Minnie
- *Ragsdale Benj
- *Ragsdale Nathaniel
- *Ramseur Jno (Minnie)
- *Richardson Rosa
- *Smathers Chas (Daisy)
- *Smathers Thos (Delia)
- South Asheville Cemetery
- South Asheville School
- *Southers Morris (Louise)
- *Tatum Clayton
- *Tatum Wm (Alice)
- *Thompson Blossom
- *Watson Howard
- *Watson Jno
- *Weaver Rufus (Sallie)
- *Weaver Vivian
- *White Virgil (Laura)
- *Wills Robt E (Sophia)

SOUTH BILTMORE
(Take Biltmore Car)

100 Ballard Robt (Dovie)
102 Whitaker S C, wid Dr A S
105 Cochrane Paul (Bonnie)
   Reeves A C
106 Cochrane Jas G (Jessie),
   Miller C L, wid Jacob
107 Vacant
108 Flanagan J M (Josie)
109 Lackman F C (Hattie E)
111 Tow J F (Nora)
112 Ingram M F (Dollie)
113 Green G A (Annie)
114 Yarborough Cleveland (Lou)
116 Maney M M (Ava)
— Brookshire J M
120 Wood Julia, wid Robt
122 Hull G D (Roxanna)
131 Lanning W H (Martha)

BOUNDARY—E from Summit
CHURCH—From Summit
1 Bostick W A (Crusia)
2 Maney J D (Rachel)
5 Roberts D S (Emma)
— S Biltmore M E Church
— Rowe Thos (Hattie)

HILL—East from Biltmore rd
IRVIN—From Summit
— Stephens V F (Nannie)

REED—From Irwin
1 Whitaker M S (Ada)
3 Lipe O H (Jennie)
5 Grove C E (Maggie L)
7 Waddell W D
11 Clapp Wm R (Annie)
   Clapp E B Rev
29 Sanders V A (Mary)
31 Bradford W C
   Rice N R, wid J C
— Reed C W (Annie W)

SUMMIT—
1 Hess Chas (Myrtle)
8 Dowtin R G (Agnes)
18 South Biltmore Baptist Ch
22 Hamilton J M (Rosa)
32 Creasman O F (Effie)
34 Oates W R (Emma)
36 Walton F A (Hattie)
37 Ray J H (Margaret)
   Lipe D B (Julia)
44 Marr W W Rev (Jeannette)
45 Gatlin M I, wid J W
46 Roberts E S, wid J W
54 Miller J H (Lennie)
57 Dunn —
58 Frady R E (Ethel)
60 Johnson M T (Laura)
61 Johnson M A (May)
62 Shroat J G (Bertha)
64 Barker J J Rev (Bettie)
65 Walton M M, wid A F
66 Shroat Arthur (Pollie)
*Anderson Henry (Minnie)
— Biltmore Supply Co
*Boozer Jas, gro
Butler Dock (Jane)
Creasman Z V (Mollie)
Creasman Eliza Mrs
Cochran M D (Ernestine)
Cochrane H J Mrs
Denton J F (Mollie)
Garren S M (Annie)
Hawes W E (Edith)
*Hall Chas (Hattie)

Asheville Dry Cleaning Co.
Telephones 835-836, All Dep't
MAIN, N. E. COR. COLLEGE

THE CLEANERS
Our Department for Oriental Rugs and Carpet Cleaning is prepared to serve you in all its branches.
E. S. Paine — O. E. Hansen

FOR BOX SHOOKS — **Call English Lumber Co.** PHONE 321

SOUTH BILTMORE   501   WEST ASHEVILLE

*Hamilton Walter (Beatrice)
Hawkins Nelson (Allhea)
Jackson B A
Jackson B M (Lola)
Justice Nancy, wid Jas W
*Kennedy Hattie A
Lipe Dudley (Katherine)
Lipe L A (Lee)
Myers C W (N L)
Nichols Chas (Cornelia)
Porter J A (Carrie)
Ponder E A (Addie)
Presley E F (Ethel)
Presley Melvin C
Reed W G (Ida)
Rhodes Lester (Dora)
Sharpe J Alex (Mollie)
Rogers J A (Mary)
Smathers Wexler Dr (Margaret)
South Biltmore Methodist Church
Stevens Wm H (Mamie)
Sumner Sallie E, wid T J
*Swepson Wm
Taylor W G
Torrence J W (Mamie)
Trantham T L (Lenora)
*Underwood Mary
Waddell C E (Eleanor)
*Williams Henry (Amanda)
Williams L J (Mollie)
Wolfe W F (Carrie)

VICTORIA

Brownson W C Dr (Elizabeth H)
ston st and Connallys Ridge)

WEST ASHEVILLE

Asheville's Largest Suburb
(R F D No 3)
Adams Anthony (Hattie A)
*A M E Zion Church
Alexander L E (Cecelia)
Alexander Nannie J Miss
Alexander R L (Sallie E)
Allison T C
Anders A B (Alice)
Anders J H (Eliza)
Anders Martha, wid Jno
Anders Philip (Julia)
Anderson C G (Fannie)
Anders J G Dr (Lottie L)
Anderson Jno
Anderson R L (Rosa)
Andrews T M (Cora J)
Asheville Electric Power Co, sub station
Asheville Packing Co
Atkinson E B (Annie J)
Atkinson H N, wid Natt
Avery Mary Mrs

Bailey G T (Belle M)
Bailey S S (Annie M)
Bailey Vennia Mrs
Baity J W (Georgia A)
Baker M B (Etta)
Ball D E (Annie)
Ball J E (Bricie)
Ball S J (Ida M)
Ballard C C (Ellen)
Ballard E R (Mary)
Ballard S C (F Eliza)
Ballew J M (Mary)
Ballinger J J (Miriam)
Balm Grove M E Church
Banks J A (Loretta)
Banks J G (T Elizabeth)
Banks J W (Lucy)
Banning Jas (Julia A)
Barnhardt Z E Rev (Kate)
*Barton G H (Harriet)
*Barton M H (Florence)
Beacham E W (Bessie M)
Beacham T C (Abbie), dairyman
Beacham T L (Sarah E)
Bell Edwd (Mylinda A)
Bell J B (Estella)
Bell Martha A, wid Jno
Bell Octavia, wid Jno M
Bishop A B (Sallie), meat mkt
Bishop J P (Mary A)
Bishop Larkin (Mary)
Bizzell A D (Effie G)
Bizzell R M (Edith B)
Black H C (Lizzie)
Blackwell Francis (Vestie)
Blue Mollie Mrs
*Boyd Benj (Carrie)
Boyles E J (Kate H)
Bradburn J H (Mary), gro
Bradley B V (Ada)
Bradley Callie, wid Fate
Bradley Clyde
Bradley G D (Emma T)
Bradley J W (Jeannette G)

BIGGEST BUSIEST BEST
Asheville Steam Laundry
Phones: 1936 and 1937
43 to 47 W. College Street

CHARLES H. HONESS
OPTOMETRIST AND OPTICIAN
Exclusive maker of ATLAS SHUR-ON EYE GLASSES
THE Home of Ce-Rite Toric Lenses
We make a specialty of correcting optical defects with properly fitted glasses.
54 Patton Avenue
Opposite Postoffice

Carolina Machinery Co. Founders, Machinists and Jobbers of Mill Supplies. We make all kinds of Castings in Iron, Brass or Aluminum.
WE ALSO FURNISH SKILLED MECHANICS FOR BOILER REPAIRS — PHONE 590

WEAVERVILLE LINE
NINE MILES BY TROLLEY FROM PACK SQUARE TO WEAVERVILLE

ASHEVILLE AND EAST TENNESSEE RAILROAD CO.
7 NORTH MAIN STREET — ASHEVILLE N. C.

Electrical Supplies
PIEDMONT ELECTRIC COMPANY
ASHEVILLE, N. C.
64 PATTON AVE.

| WEST ASHEVILLE | 502 | WEST ASHEVILLE |

*Bradley Jas (Alice)
*Bradley Jno (Rachel)
Bradley L E Mrs
*Bradley Louise
Bradley Mollie Miss
Bradley Rebecca Mrs
Bramlett P H (Nancy A)
Bramlett W R (Glenn)
Brewer Sarah Mrs
Briggs C C (Mattie)
Bright A L (Mary M), genl mdse
Britt G E (Nancy)
Britt W E (Mary I)
Brooks Julia Miss
Brooks Virginia Miss
Brown A E Rev (Lamanda)
Brown C E G (Myrtle)
Brown C V (Nannie)
Brown H A (Jennie G)
Brown Hester E Mrs, nurse
Brown J F (Lenora)
Brown J H (Nancy M)
Brown Mary J, wid M M
Brown W H (Clara)
Brown & Smith, stone quarry
Brownson W C Dr (Elizabeth H)
Bruce M A (Lillie B)
Bryson J A (Jane)
Buckeye Water Co
Buckner A S (Dora A)
Buckner H G (Annie)
Buckner H J (Mira)
Buckner J H (Anna)
Burgess Jno
Burnett Luther (Mary)
*Burton Lelia

Cain J B (Edith)
*Caldwell G H Rev
*Caldwell Gilbert Rev
Calloway Jno (Cynthia)
Calvary Baptist Church
Campbell J A (Bessie)
Canada H C (Minnie L)
Candler Lloyd (Nannie)
Candler Saml (Belle M)
Capps Wm R (Carrie R)
Carland J D (Nora)
Carland J T (Sarah A)
Carland W A (Estella)
*Carrington Fannie
Carson C G (Mary L)
Carter J E (Addie)
Carter W R (Sallie), gro

Carver G W (Mary)
Case Jno (Sarah)
Case W B (Zanie)
Cedar Hill Baptist Church
Chapman Chas (Berdie)
Chapman Millard (Effie)
Charles J M Mrs
Christopher Sallie L, wid Wm H
Chunn C H (Nannie)
Clark E G (Lula)
Clark Harley (Maude)
Clark J C B (Grace L)
Clark J M (May H)
Claudwoody F C (Jettie)
Clevenger J F (Lyda E)
Clodfelter J F (Beulah)
Cole E C (Della)
Cole Thos M Rev (Annie)
Cole W E R (Kate F)
Collins D C (Mary M)
*Collins Junius (Martha)
Coman Laura A, wid Jas R
Conley M S (Lethia)
Cook Julia N, wid Henry
Cooke Geo (Cora B)
Corn G W (Anna L)
Cornell Harriet A, wid Harrison T, gro
Courtney M P (Sarah A)
Cowan J W, contr
Cowan R E (Sophia R)
Cowan T H (Grace)
Cox Lila Mrs
Creasman E C (Lura)
Creasman E T
Creasman F O (Mary)
Creasman Hattie, wid Robt
Creasman L W (Eliza)
Creasman T F (Mantie)
Creasman R A (Lillian E)
Crook J E (Dove)
Crook J R (Julia A)
Crook Lyda (Lola E)
Crook Rebecca E, wid Jasper A
Crook Thos (Mollie)
Cross R D Rev (Virginia)

Dalton G R (Cora)
Dalton Rebecca, wid Patrick
Daves A D (Minnie)
Davis A P (Nancy L)
Davis D (Nancy L)
Davis L E Dr (Jennie E)
*Davis N C (Lizzie)

CONTRACTOR and BUILDER
J. C. McPHERSON
STEEL RANGES — 35-37 E COLLEGE ST. PHONE 133
PLUMBING STEAM AND HOT WATER HEATING

WEST ASHEVILLE

Dayton W W (Hattie L)
DeBrew Jno (Eskew L)
Dorland H P (Nettie)
Dougherty G W (Ruby D)
Drake Arlena T Mrs
Duckett F F (Florence)
Duckett H W (Mary)
Duckett J W (Maggie), contr
Duckett R L (M Elizabeth)
Earle J D (Bessie G)
Earwood W R (Susan)
Ebbs J A (Emma)
*Eddings C A (Emma)
Edwards Eva L, wid Jas N
Edwards Gwynn (Etta M)
Edwards J F (Lelia)
Edwards J H (Gertrude)
Edwards R B (Rosa)
Elkins Fannie B Mrs
Elkin H J (Burgin)
Elkins Jno (Augusta)
Elkins R N (M Elizabeth)
Elkins Susanna, wid Chas Y
Elkins U E (Stella)
Elkins W C (Finette)
Ellege A J (Cordie)
Ellege G C (Carrie)
Ellenburg J T (Maggie)
Eller Nannie, wid Jno C
Elmore Ernest (Kate)
Elmore G E (Fannie B)
Emery Thos (Annie)
Emery Noah
English Effie Mrs
Estes Ollie N A, wid Jno L J
Eubanks Susan, wid Jas M
Evans Dorcas, wid Chas A
Fairchild G W (C Eunice), gro
*Feimster Robt (Rebecca)
Felmet M V (Alice)
Floyd J W (Annie M)
Ford A L (Ethel)
Ford J T (May E)
Ford W G (Ida)
Ford W P (Sarah J)
Fordham M G (Irene)
Fore W J (Mary)
*Foreman Charlotte
Fort W H (Myra L)
Fowler J B M (Druscilla)
Fox J A (Nannie J)
Fox J H (Amanda)
Fox L N

Franklin O G (Effie)
Freeman A L (Ella)
Freeman Laura A, wid P Marion
Fullam J S (Dora J)
Galloway M W (Vaughtie)
Gardner G D Dr (Fannie L)
Garvin F B (Ollie)
Gasperson Chas (May)
Gasperson W O (Martha B)
Gentry J W (N Malissa)
Gheen Stella, wid Wm E
Gibson J A (Sallie), gro
Gilden C N (Mattie)
Glover Murray (Mollie E)
Goldsmith Franklin P
Gordon J W (Laura)
Gossett C T (Beatrice)
Gossett Ida C, wid Robt A
Graham G W (Nettie B)
Grahl W H (Julia)
Grant J T (Sallie)
Grant W T (Lura)
Grasty R M
*Graves Jno (Pattie)
*Greenlee G S (Sallie M)
Griffin Eliza C, wid Jno
Guthrie Oscar (Mamie)
Guthrie R W (Loretta)
Guthrie T K (Bertha)
Guthrie W A (Texie)
Hall A J (Lillie)
Hall S D (Lillie A)
Hall S C (Muncie)
Hames H E (Eliza J)
Hamlin J O (Nellie)
Hamlin Jacob (Elsie)
Hampton C M (Mary L)
Haney J E (Lena M)
Haney W B (Jane)
Hardin M M (Mollie D)
Hardin Sallie Miss, dressmkr
Harkins W W (Jessie B)
*Harris W H (Ella)
Harrison Caroline, wid Jesse
Harrison T J (Emma E)
Hawkins D H (Bertha)
Hawkins J L (Hester D)
Hawkins R C (Metta)
Hawkins Z B (Julia)
Hayes E L (Elizabeth)
Hayes R P (Lucy P)
Hebard E A Dr (Charlotte A)

Mrs. Wilder's SANITARY HOME LAUNDRY turns out first class work in Laundering and Dry Cleaning. No. 7 Montford Ave., Phone 1354

WEST ASHEVILLE 504 WEST ASHEVILLE

Henderson J L (Addie)
*Henderson J W Rev (Hattie R)
Henderson W P (Mary E)
Hendley R T (Sudie M)
Hendrix J W (Frankie)
Hendrix P L (Kate)
Hendrix W H (Cora)
Henry A L (Mantie)
*Henry G W (Addie)
Hensley G M (Mattie)
Hensley G W (Rebecca)
Hice C C (Della L)
Hill D F (Ruth E)
Hill J B (Delia), gro
Hill J F (Mary)
Hill W M (Lula)
Holcombe C L (Keturah T)
Holcombe W L (Beulah)
Hollifield Jefferson (Rena)
Hollingsworth Amelia Mrs
Hollingsworth J B
Hollingsworth R S (Kate)
Honeycutt Joshua (Mary E)
Howard V B (Carrie)
Howard W E (Ella)
Hughes Anna J Miss, nurse
Hughes G E (Love M)
Hughes Hannah M, wid Saml D
Hughes J R
Hughes Nancy, wid Robt Y
Hughes W H, gro
Hughey W C
Hugill H C (Kate)
*Hunt Butler (Love)
Hunter Belle Miss
Hyatt Nancy J, wid Jas M
Ingle E N (Mary C)
Ingle F B (Maggie)
Ingle J B (Sarah)
Ingle J E (Mary)
Ingle J V (Lottie)
Ingle J W (Wauneta)
Ingle M A (Claudia)
Ingle M M (Ollie J)
Ingle Mollie Miss
Ingle R E (Lillie C)
Ingram J M (Mamie E)
Israel R S (Lou)
Jackson A C, gro
James G C (Eva M)
Jarrett D T (Daisy)
Jarrett J N (Sadie)
Jarrett J W (Ida)

Jarrett Katherine B, wid Thos C
Jenkins M W (Grace)
Jenkins R L (Hattie)
Jenkins V J (Lola)
Johnson C M (Sarah S)
Johnson D W (Edith)
Johnson F J (Annie)
*Johnson Sarah A
Johnson School
Jones Anna, wid Patrick
Jones B B (Ida V)
Jones G H (Nannie)
Jones Herbert
Jones J H (Sarah A)
*Jones R J (Hattie)
Jones R L (Josephine)
Jones Stover (Kittie)
Jones T M (Hattie J)
Jones Theo E (Maggie)
Jones Z F (M Etta)
Joyner Chas (Nina), painter
Joyner J E (Rose)
Joyner J E Jr (Bessie)
Joyner J E & Son, contrs
*Justice J H
Kerr A W (Arah A)
Kesterson J W (Hattie)
King Arlington (Lucy)
King B C (Ollie)
King J W (Nora B)
*King Martha
Kiser Amanda, wid Louis I
Kiser C L (Lillian)
Knoblauch G H (Ruth)
Kraft W F (Dora)
Kuykendall E L (Vinna)
Kuykendall J A (Cora L)
Lail L P (Cora B)
Lamb J B (Elsie)
Lamb R S (Minnie A)
Lamb Thos A
Lance E B (Nannie)
Lance S B (Angeline)
Lane Jas (Lillie)
Lashley D A (Bessie G), florist
*Latimore J H (Mary)
Laughter Chas E (Mattie)
Laughter J F (Lector M)
Lawing C E (Olive)
Lawing T H (Susan B), gro
Lawrence J C (Lena)
Ledbetter Z T (Martha A)
Ledford E H
Ledford Eugene (Ella)

BUICK ARBOGAST MOTOR COMPANY OLDSMOBILE
ACCESSORIES AND SUPPLIES DETROIT ELECTRIC
52-60 N. Main Phones 302 and 1728
MAXWELLS -:-

Asheville Dry Cleaning Co.
Telephones 835-836, All Dep't
MAIN, N. E. COR. COLLEGE

THE CLEANERS
Our Department for Oriental Rugs and Carpet Cleaning is prepared to serve you in all its branches. :-:
E. S. Paine   O. E. Hansen

Hardwood Lumber — ALL KINDS

ENGLISH LUMBER CO. Phone - - 321

WEST ASHEVILLE

- Ledwell Kate, wid Jno
- *Lenoir Martha
- Lewis Susan, wid Jno
- Lewis Walker
- *Lincoln J P (Emma E)
- Lindsey M J Mrs
- Lineberry A J (Addie)
- Lineberry C M (Cora)
- Lineberry Elizabeth C, wid Jas
- Liner L N
- Logan Annie L Miss, music tchr
- Logan W E (Addie)
- London H R B (Martha A)
- London Jettie, wid Lee
- *Lowry J W (Ida)
- Lunsford J W (Ella M)
- Luther B F (Jennie E)
- *Lynch Jos (Etta)
- McAllister Wm (Ollie)
- McBee A C (Alice)
- McCarrell S P (Sarah)
- McCarson J E (Hannah)
- McCarson R B (Elsie)
- McCollum E D (Martha)
- McCurry J S (Nettie)
- McDaris L P (Hannah)
- McElroy J W (Anna)
- McElroy Lena Mrs
- McFarland G H (Pearle)
- McFarland Isabelle, wid Richd
- MsFarland J W (Create)
- McGlamery W A (Elvira)
- McIntyre J P (Angeline)
- McIntyre Lydia, wid Jas
- McKenzie C W (Callie F)
- McKinna G P (Lula)
- *McMickens O E (Nettie)
- *McMickens T M (Jane)
- McRary W S (Mary)
- Machin Jno (Sallie)
- Mack J A (Julia L)
- *Mackey Maria
- Maple Leaf Dairy
- Martin Wiley (Annie)
- Masters E H (Eva)
- Mayes M D (Roxie)
- Meadows M R (Delia V)
- Meadows U S (Bettie)
- Meece Geo W
- Merrimon J G (Blanche S)
- *Metcalf Peter
- Michaels Jas
- Miller Annie M Miss

- Miller C F (Bertha)
- Miller Clarissa E, wid Geo W
- Miller H D (Lola)
- Miller Hugh (Julia)
- Miller L G (Lucy)
- Miller Lawrence (Anna)
- Miller Lela E Miss
- Miller M (Harriet)
- Miller M L (Mollie)
- Miller Mary E, wid Wm R
- Miller R M (Nellie)
- Miller T H (Martha E)
- Miller W D (Mary E)
- *Miller Wm L (May)
- Mills J R (Theodosia)
- Mills Sarah A, wid Wm B
- Mills W A (Rebecca)
- Misenheimer J E (Kate)
- Mitchell A E (Geneva)
- Mitchell D F (Annie)
- Mitchell T J (Ada A)
- Moffit J W (Theodocia)
- Monday C U (Nellie)
- Moody B F (Mary J)
- Moody W C (Josephine)
- Moore A F (Carrie)
- Moore A H (Dora A)
- Moore A S (Sallie)
- Moore J L (Margaret)
- Moore L D (Lois)
- Moore R H (Julia)
- Moore Robt
- Morgan I M
- Morgan W R (Maude L)
- Morris H P (Martha)
- Morrison S E (Mary), gro
- Moses L J (Laura), contr
- Murphy L A
- Nicholson A S (Rachel)
- Nicholson D M (Agnes L)
- Nicholson E J (Maggie A)
- Nicholson E L (Allie M)
- Nicholson J H (Delia), gro
- Nicholson J R (Effie)
- Nix T F (Nettie)
- Noblitt T J (Fannie)
- Norris C O (Zola)
- Nuckles G C (Rosa B)
- O'Kelley T C (Martha E)
- Olive H J, genl mdse
- O'Rear W F (Minnie E)
- Orr P V Dr (Emma)
- Orr Sarah L, wid Jno P
- Owen J A (Ida)
- Owen J S (Addie R)

BIGGEST BUSIEST BEST

Phones 1936 and 1937

ASHEVILLE STEAM LAUNDRY

43 to 47 W. COLLEGE

S. D. HALL

REAL ESTATE AGENT

Money Loaned

Notary Public

32 PATTON AVENUE

Phone 91

CAROLINA MACHINERY CO.

—US when you want machine work of any kind . . .

Founders Machinists and Jobbers of Mill Supplies

When in the market for heavy castings such as columns or building plates get our prices. Phone 590

LIFE INSURANCE COMPANY OF VA. OLDEST, LARGEST STRONGEST Southern Life Insurance Co.

ORGANIZED 1871
RICHMOND, VIRGINIA

Issues Industrial Policies from $8.00 to $900.00, with Premiums Payable WEEKLY on persons from two to seventy years of age

J. V. Moon, Superintendent, Rooms 3-4-5 Maxwelton Bldg., Asheville, N. C.

WEST ASHEVILLE — WEST ASHEVILLE

D. TREXLER TIN SHOP

All Kinds of Roofing, Gutter and Conductor Work.

Phone 862

159 South Main St.

DR. C. H. MILLER

MECHANO-THERAPIST

14 N. Spruce St.
Phone 979
ASHEVILLE, N. C.

Hours by engagement

Drugless Healing of Disease

Owens Z W (Etta)
Ownsby Myra, wid Robt
Parker J P (Nora)
Parker R L (Nancy)
Parris A J (Levonia)
Patterson J M (Aviolena), contr
Patterson S Delano
Pelham C P
Pelham S D (Mamie D)
Penland Bros, blksmiths
Penland Jesse C (Bertha)
Penland J D (Susan)
Penland Jno (Mollie)
Penland L J (Hattie L)
Penland Luther J (Hattie, L)
Penland W C (Elizabeth M)
Perkins A F (Florence)
Peterson W A (Allie)
Phipps Thos R
*Pickens Jno (Lucinda)
Pinner G W (Alice S)
Pinner J D (Susan), contr
Pinner Jos (Texanna)
Pittillo R L (Ilah)
Plemmons A E (Maude E)
Plemmons C C (Lula F)
Plemmons J K (A Rosanna)
Plemmons Lee (Margaret)
Potts R P (Lillian L)
Presley T C (Bessie), gro
Putnam V S (Kate)
Radford Lula Miss
Ratcliff J J (Laura)
Ray Robt W (Vestie)
Rea Sarah O, wid Thos S
Rector J G (Ollie)
Rector Julius (Roxie)
Rector S L (Annie S)
Revis H G (Mollie)
Revis L M (Daisy E)
Reynolds B O (Lottie P)
Reynolds Cleveland (Lizzie)
Reynolds Dorcas M, wid Wm W
Reynolds J R (Maude J)
Reynolds W A (Lillie)
Rhodes G W (Sarah)
Rich C E (Stella)
Rich J O (Minnie)
Roberts E G (Mary A)
Roberts E W (Hester)
Roberts J A (Lottie C)
Roberts J C (Eliza J)

Roberts J M (Eliza)
Roberts J R (Pattie R)
Roberts M N
Roberts Mary E, wid Jacob R
Roberts R C (Mary E)
Robinson L B (Dora M)
Rogers J F (Betsy)
Rogers Thos (Allie)
Russell Arsenith S, wid Wm T
Russell C E
Russell J Z (Elsie)
Sams R B (Sue)
Sams T W (Omie)
Scott S A (Lula)
Searcy J B (May)
Searcy W G (Tina)
Sexton J H (Mattie A)
Shelton J F (Sarah A)
Shelton Theo D (Georgia)
Sheppard Frank (Zealie)
*Sheppard W A (Chaney)
Sherrill W H
Shipley B H (Debbie)
Shipley Jno (Essie)
Shirlin G C (Mary)
Shirlin H B (Maude)
Shook M P (Mabel G)
Shook O S (Minnie E)
Shultz G F (Carrie)
Sloop W R (Nannie E)
Sluder E H (M Etta)
Sluder J L (Mollie)
Sluder T J (Deliah)
Smith C Furman (Kathryn L)
Smith G W (Roxanna), gro
Smith Geo R (Lizzie)
Smith K D (Sarah)
*Smith O S (Anna)
Snider A M (Minnie)
Solesbee J W (Lulu)
Southwick C H (Debbie J)
Sparks H G (Lennie M)
Spivey Jerome (Josie)
Spivey R L (Ina)
Sprinkles M C (Bertie)
Staffon J B (Vera E)
Starnes G H (Theresa E)
Stevenson Albert
Styles J S (Eloise M)
Sudderth Geo (Rosa)
Sumner Conrad (Sallie)
Sumner E M (Lillie)
Sumner J H (Elizabeth)

....Asheville Cleaning and Pressing Club....
Tailoring That Satisfies and Prices That Please
Steam and French Dry Cleaning of all delicate and fine wearing apparel for ladies and gentlemen. MESSENGER SERVICE IN THE CITY.

J. C. WILBAR, Prop.   **4. N. Pack Square**   **PHONE 389**

CAROLINA COAL & ICE CO.
"M & W" INDIAN — Prompt Delivery — PHONE 130 — 50 PATTON AVE. — WEIGHTS ACCURATE

WEST ASHEVILLE — WOOLSEY

Sumner Lonnie (Eva)
Taylor J D (O E)
Taylor M B (Lillie J)
Taylor O C (Nicha)
Taylor R C (Jessie)
Teague I M (Ollie)
Teague J R (Hattie)
*Thomas Rachel
Thomason G M Mrs
Thompson C M (Mamie)
Tinsley S J (Cordelia)
Tilton Jennie, wid Harry D
Tow S M (Elizabeth J)
Tweed R H (Leona)
Tweed V T (Annie)
Van Valkenburg J F (Annie)
Vaughan H A (Cora)
Vaughan M L (Mary)
Vaughan Margaret, wid Wm
Wallace J C (Carrie)
Wallen R F (Lydia)
Walsh J P (Ovalina)
Wamboldt M M Rev
Warren C W (Johannah)
Warren F H (Ella)
Watkins J C (Ida L)
Watkins J E
Watts L C (Addie)
Weaver J H (Carrie L)
Webb A J (Bessie)
Webb C F (Clota)
Webb H T (Lessie)
Webb R Susan, wid M C
Weidler E P (Sadie)
Welch J L (Julia)
Wells H A (Lura), contr
Wells R M (Anna W)
West Asheville Cemetery
West Asheville Graded Schl
*West Ashev M E Zion Ch
Westall W B (Lula)
Whaley E S Miss
Wheeler M S (Lillie)
Whitaker J B (Kate)
White L H (Mallie B)
*Whiteside D M (Myra W)
Whitney A C (Irma)
Whitted R A (Lizzie)
Williams Jno (Mary)
Williams Nannie, wid Noah A
Williams R J (Mary)
Williams W J (Susie E)
*Wills Rufus (Kate)
*Wilson Alonzo (Lucy)
Wilson J L (M Catherine)
Wilson Margaret Mrs
*Wilson Saml (Carrie)
*Wilson Thos (Fannie)
Wilson W A (Hattie)
Winslow E L (Ida)
Wolfe J J (Josephine)
Woody C J (Laura E)
Woody P M (Althea)
Worley H B (Rena)
Worley Rachel M, wid Wiley J
Worley W M (Ella L)
Wright E B (Maggie)
Wright Lee
Wright W H (Altha A)
Wyatt S W (Mattie E)
Yarborough H T (Pink)
Yarborough L F (Florence)
Young A M (Florence), gro
*Young J W (Cora)
*Young W L (Carrie)
Young Wm (Sarah J)
Zimmerman Fredk (Bertha)

WOOLSEY
(R D 1—Take Merrimon av car)
Allman Jas T (May)
Bell Chas C (Edith)
Bishop T H (Mattie)
Bradley P P (Harriet)
Brock Ignatius W (Ora)
Buck Clara E, wid S C
Buckner E, wid M A
Bunn Roland (Annie)
Carter Garrett N (Flata)
Chambers Bathilda, wid R W
Chambers E O Dr
Cornell W S (Mary)
Davis Wm (Nellie)
Davis Wm A
Dennis Geo C
Dickerson G W (Annie)
Dillon C F (Fannie)
Duncan Anderson F (Virginia)
Eberman Edwin (Annie)
Evans Geo E (Eva)
Farr Susan, wid M F
Farr Wm (Eva)
Fritchey Emil (Julia)
Glenn Marshal R (Georgia), phys
Glenn Orr T, contr

St. Rw'y — Electric Light and Power — Gas
ASHEVILLE POWER AND LIGHT COMPANY — PHONE 69

Kiibler & Whitehead Poultry — CITY MARKET — PHONES, 195 and 694

Asheville Dray, Fuel & Construction Co.
6 1-2 South Main

COAL

Wood and Kindling
Stone and Sand
PHONE - 223

WOOLSEY 508 WOOLSEY

Glenn R B	Ray Alice Mrs
Glenn Robt B (Joanna)	Ray Alice C Mrs
Hale J H (Lenoir)	Ray Clarence F
Hall Mary Mrs	Ray Jas M (Alice)
Hamilton E G (Emma)	Ray Wayne S
*Hankins Lucy	Rayfield Eveline, wid W R
Harrison Andrew A (Kate)	Rayfield Thos C (Dora)
Jenkins Jas T (Jennie)	Reis Edwd P (Mary)
Kimberly Fannie Miss	Rice Mary A, wid C A
Kimberly Jno	Roath Warrington D
Kimberly Mary Miss	Roberson Frank D (Marietta)
Kimberly Thos M (Janie)	Roberson Jackson A (Mary)
Lingerfeldt Jno L (Alice)	Roberts Jno M (Margaret)
Long Robt A (Leonora)	Rogers C H (Josephine)
McConnell J H (Ella)	Sands Edwd L (Mary)
McFarland J P (Annie)	Sayre Martha E, wid W A
McGuire Edna, wid M L	Self G L (Minnie)
Maney Lorenzo D (Daisy)	Stowe Wm W (Bertha)
Maney Wm D (Hattie), gro	Swangum Emma, wid B S
Maney Wm E (Hattie)	Swann L W (May)
Masters Fredk P (Burr)	Taylor F D (Harriet)
Montgomery Geo W (Amanda)	Turnbull A L, wid R T
Moodie Jno E (Effie)	Walser Fred T Jr (Bruce)
Moore J C (Mattie)	Welborn Chas W (Lyda)
Moore Wm J (Maude)	Welborn Jno M (Cynthia)
Mumpower R E (Ida)	Welborn Jno Rev (Cynthia)
Newkirk Gus R (Laura)	Westall Jas M (Minnie)
Padgett Marion D	White Marintha E, wid J A
Padgett Robt R (Irene)	Woolsey Greenhouses
Poole Bros, dry cleaning	Williams Robt L (Sarah)
Poole Geo R (Lillian)	Wolf Saml M (Kate)
Ramoth Place, boarding	Woolsey Greenhouse, E C Dickinson propr
Poole Wm G (Wessie)	
Rawls Chas T (Sarah)	Woolsey Hall

EVER READY FLASHLIGHTS
Piedmont Electric Company
64 PATTON AVENUE
ASHEVILLE, N. C.

MR. MERCHANT:

Do you know that about the only establishment that makes money without advertising is the mint?

J. C. McPHERSON
SLATE AND TIN ROOFING
Galvanized Iron Work   Hot Air Furnaces
35-37 EAST COLLEGE STREET

PLUMBING
STEAM AND HOT WATER
HEATING
PHONE 138

1913—MISCELLANEOUS—1913

ASHEVILLE, N. C.

City, County, State, United States Government, Churches, Schools, Clubs, Secret Societies, and much other Useful Information.

NOTE—This is not a regular part of the Directory, but we desire to make it as complete as we can, therefore we will gladly insert any proper information furnished us in time.

CITY GOVERNMENT

(City Hall, e Pack Sq)

Asheville City Mayor—J E Rankin
Auditor—J M Clarke
Bacteriologist—L M McCormick
Building Inspr—C B Leonard
Chief of Police—D K Lyerly
Chief of Fire Dept—J H Wood
City Clerk — Lawrence W Young
City Engineer—B M Lee
Council Chambers—203 City Hall
Electrician—R B Hampton
Fire Chief—J H Wood
Health Officer—Dr L B McBrayer
Meat and Milk Inspr—L M McCormick
Plumbing Inspr—E M Israel
Police Matron—Miss Donnie Blackwell
Sanitary Inspector—W H Bird
Stable Foreman—J C Swink
Supt of Schools—Prof R J Tighe
Supt of Streets—J T Bostic
Supt Market—T J Mitchell
Supt Water Dept—Wm Francis
Tax Collector—C H Bartlett
Treasurer—J B Erwin

Board of Aldermen

First Ward—A B Sites
Second Ward—W R Patterson
Third Ward—W E Shuford
Fourth Ward—F Stikeleather
Montford—C W Brown
Victoria—W E Johnson
At Large—R L Fitzpatrick and R L Francis

Standing Committees

Water — Francis, Patterson, Sites
Fire—Stikeleather, Patterson, Fitzpatrick
Market House—Stikeleather, Brown, Francis
Parks—Johnson, Stikeleather, Brown
Lights—Johnson, Fitzpatrick, Stikeleather
Streets—Shuford, Sites, Stikeleather
Police—Fitzpatrick, Shuford, Patterson
Finance — Brown, Shuford, Stikeleather
Sanitation—Patterson, Stikeleather, Brown
Public Safety and Buildings—Patterson, Fitzpatrick, Sites
Sewers—Sites, Francis, Johnson
Special Tax—Shuford, Fitzpatrick, Sites
Franchise—Fitzpatrick, Brown
Auditorium—Brown, Francis, Johnson

Board of Health

J E Rankin, chairman
B M Lee, C W Brown

Police Department

Chief—D K Lyerly
Captains—C N Lominac, B H

Candy Kitchen and Club Cafe
"A GOOD PLACE FOR REFRESHMENT"

Hot drinks on cold days. Cold drinks on hot days. The best drinks every day. Pure fruits and syrups blended "just right," served daintily. Our Ice Cream and Soda Water Department, Restaurant and Candy Departments are always kept up to the standard of nearest perfection. Phones 110 and 111. 19 and 21 Haywood St.

CITY GOV 510 COUNTY GOV

Williams, M Sprouse
  1st Sergt—W G McDowell
  2d Sergt—F L Conder
  Patrolmen—J S Leverette, W W Britt, E A Hall, C J Ingle, C G Lanning, W H Centerfit, P L Stone, O M Davenport, M Y Angel, J M Bradley, W H Wyatt, Fred Jones, J E Murdoch, C H Snyder, C E Nowell, B M Collins
  Police Marton—Miss Donnie Blackwell

Police Court
(City Hall)

Convenes every morning (except Sunday) at 9 o'clock
  Police Justice — Junius G Adams

Fire Department
(e Pack Sq)

J H Wood, chf
L W Jeanneret, asst
Hose No 1—E M Israel, capt
L C Sluder—1st foreman
E W Davis—2d foreman
T H Brown—sec-treas
W D Ross—driver
L L Rhoads—driver
Hook and Ladder No 1—C L Payne capt
F H Hill—foreman
S A Rector—sec-treas

Fire Alarm Stations

In case of fire phone 1000
18 South Beaumont and Pine
21 Winyah Sanitarium
22 North Main and Hillside
25 Asheland av and Philip
29 Liberty and Hillside
31 Montford av and Zillicoa
33 Battery Park Hotel
34 Government cor Haywood
39 Pearson Drive and Watauga
41 Ora and John
44 Victoria rd and Livingston
47 Blanton and Phifer
48 Depot and Roberts
49 Jefferson Drive and Park av
55 "Ravenscroft"
66 Asheland av cor Patton av
77 Power Sta Avery st
127 Pine and Mountain
128 Central av and Orange
136 College and Pine
137 North Main and Starnes av
138 Montford av and Cullowhee
145 Chestnut and Charlotte
146 Jefferson Drive and West Haywood
153 Chestnut and Merrimon av
154 South French Broad av
163 Southside av and McDowell
164 Cumberland av and Blake
172 Valley and Atkins
173 The Manor, Charlotte
235 East and North Main
246 North Main and Woodfin
254 Cherry and Flint
262 Montford av and Haywood
324 Patton av and w Haywood
343 West Haywood and Roberts
352 French Broad and Patton av
364 Asheland av and Silver
425 Passenger Depot
432 South Main and McDowell
453 South Main and Southside
462 Pack Square and Patton av

Biltmore Fire Department
(Biltmore rd)

J C Lipe, chief

BUNCOMBE COUNTY GOVERNMETNT

(Court House, 57-71 College)
  Auditor—E M Lyda
  Register of Deeds — J J Mackey
  Sheriff—C F Williams
  Tax Collector—B A Patton
  Treasurer—T M Duckett
  Surveyor—O L Israel
  Coroner—Dr E R Morris
  County Atty—J E Swain
  Residing Judge—Frank Carter
  Solicitor—R R Reynolds
  Clerk of Court—Marcus Erwin
  Commissioners—E W Patton chairman
  Supt of Health—Dr D E Sevier
  Road Engineer—J C M Valentine
  Jailor—J V Jordan

Brown's Undertaking Parlors

S. H. BROWN

50 Patton Avenue
ASHEVILLE, N. C.

Lady Assistant When Desired

Phone 193-2 Rings

THE MOORE Plumbing Company

16 N. Pack Square
PHONE 1025

Sanitary Plumbing, General Tin and Metal Work, Hot Air Furnaces

---

The Battery Park Bank
ASHEVILLE, N.C.   City, County and State Depositary

Capital - - $100,000.00
Surplus and Profits, $110,000.00

J. A. TILLMAN — work. Satisfaction guaranteed — **Jeweler** — I carry a nice line of Watches, Clocks and Jewelry, and make a specialty of repair **17 N. Main St.**

STATE GOVETRNMENT
(Capitol at Raleigh)

Governor—W W Kitchin
Lieut Governor—W C Newland
Secy of State—J B Grimes
Auditor—B F Dixon
Treasurer—B R Lacy
Supt of Instruction—J Y Joyner
Atty General—T U Bickett
Com'r of Labor—M L Shipman
Senator (Buncombe)—J C Martin
Representatives (Buncombe)—R R Williams, E G Roberts
State Librarian—M O Sherrill
Com'r of Agriculture—(Elected by Board, Board appointed by General Assembly)
Governor's Council—Sec'y of State, Auditor, Treasurer and Supt of Public Instruction
State Board of Education—Composed of the Governor, Lieut Governor, Sec'y of State, Treasurer, Auditor, Supt of Public Instruction and Attorney General
Board of Public Buildings and Grounds—The Governor, Sec'y of State, Treasurer and Atty General
State Board of Pensions—The Governor, Auditor, Treasurer and Atty General

Supreme Court

The Supreme Court meets on the first Monday in February and last Monday in August

Chief Justice — Walter Clark, Raleigh, N C
Clerk—Thos S Kenan, Raleigh N C

The examination of applicants to practice law, to be conducted in writing, takes place on the first Monday of each term and at ro other time. The docket for the hearing of cases from the First Judicial District will be called on the Tuesday next succeeding the meeting of the court, and from other districts on Tuesday of each succeeding week, in numerical order, until all the districts have been called

Superior Courts

The State is divided into sixteen Judicial Districts, and for each a Judge and Solicitor are elected. Judges are elected by the State at large; the Solicitors by their respective Districts

Calendar Superior Courts Buncombe County

(Spring Term, 1911, to Fall Term, 1915, inclusive)

Criminal term, 2 weeks, 7th Monday after 1st Monday in March, April 24, 1911

Civil Term, 4 weeks, 12th Monday after 1st Monday in March, May 29, 1911

Spring Terms—Cvl, 2 weeks, 6th Monday before 1st Monday in March, Jan 22, 1912; Jan 20, 1913; Jan 19, 1914; Jan 18, 1915

Crm, 3 weeks, 4th Monday before 1st Monday in March, Feb 5, 1912; Feb 3, 1913; Feb 2, 1914; Feb 1, 1915

Cvl, 3 weeks, 1st Monday after 1st Monday in March, March 11, 1912; March 10, 1913; March 9, 1914; March 8, 1915

Cvl, 3 weeks, 6th Monday after 1st Monday in March, April 15, 1912; April 14, 1913; April 13, 1914; April 12, 1915

Crm, 2 weeks, 9th Monday after 1st Monday in March, May 6, 1912; May 5, 1913; May 4, 1914; May 3, 1915

Cvl, 2 weeks, 12th Monday after 1st Monday in March, May 27, 1912; May 26, 1913; May 25, 1914; May 24, 1915

Fall Terms—Cvl, 3 weeks, 6th Monday before 1st Monday in September, July, 24, 1911; July 22, 1912; July 21, 1913; July 27, 1914; July 26, 1915

Crm, 2 weeks, 3d Monday before 1st Monday in September, August 14, 1911; August 12,

---

INSURANCE

- **I**NSURE YOUR SALARY WITH US
- **N**EVER CARRY YOUR OWN RISK
- **S**AFETY IS THE BEST POLICY
- **U**NLESS YOU ARE A CAPITALIST
- **R**EST EASY IF YOU HAVE
- A**N** ACCIDENT WE WILL
- **N**OT KEEP YOU WAITING TO
- **C**OLLECT YOUR CLAIM
- **E**VERY CLAIM PROMPTLY PAID

Imperial Mutual Life & Health Insurance Co.

Home Office:
ASHEVILLE, N. C.

Phone 495

HOTEL OXFORD — Redecorated and Refitted throughout. Recently enlarged to 60 rooms. Centrally located. Depot cars stop at entrance. Long distance telephone office upstairs. American and European plan. Rates 50c, 75c and $1 per day; special rates by week or month. C. H. Branson & Sons, Proprietors. Phone 1887. 50-54 South Main St. **Asheville, N. C.**

Williams-Brownell Planing Mill Company — **Hardwoods**

Lumber---Rough and Dressed Flooring a Specialty Moulding, Interior Finish, Etc.
Office, Plant and Yards on Southern Railway, Near Biltmore Station
WHITE PINE   Phone 729   YELLOW PINE

STATE GOV 512 U S GOV

Asheville Electrical Company
W. Mansfield Booze, Manager
74 CENTRAL AVE.
HEADQUARTERS
Phone 377

1912; August 11, 1913; August 17, 1914; August 16, 1915

Cvl, 3 weeks, 3d Monday after 1st Monday in September, September 25, 1911; September 23, 1912; September 22, 1913; September 28, 1914; September 27, 1915

Crm, 2 weeks, 7th Monday after 1st Monday in September, October 23, 1911; October 21, 1912; October 20, 1913; October 19, 1914; October 18, 1915

Cvl, 4 weeks, 10th Monday after 1st Monday in September, November 13, 1911; November 11, 1912; November 10, 1913; November 9, 1914; November 8, 1915

Asylums and Hospitals

The Blind Asylum and Asylum for Colored Deaf and Dumb are located at Raleigh

The Deaf and Dumb Asylum for whites is located at Morganton

North Carolina Hospital—located at Raleigh

Eastern Hospital—located at Goldsboro

State Hospital — located at Morganton

The penitentiary is located at Raleigh

UNITED STATES GOVERNMENT

President—Wm H Taft, Ohio
Vice-Pres—Jas S Sherman
Speaker of the House—Champ Clark
Senators (N C) — Simmons and Overman
Congressman (10th Dist N C)—J M Gudger, Jr

UNITED STATES COURTS AND OFFICERS

United States Circuit Court of Appeals

Judges—Nathan Goff, Clarksburg W Va; Jeter C Pritchard, Asheville N C, and district as designated from time to time by the circuit judges

Clerk—H F Maloney, Richmond Va

UNITED STATES CIRCUIT COURT

(Western District of North Carolina)

Judges—Nathan Goff, Clarksburg, West Va, and Jeter C Pritchard, Asheville N C

Clerk at Asheville—W S Hyams

Deputy Clerk—Jas M Milligan (Greensboro)

Court convenes at Greensboro first Monday in April and October; at Statesville third Monday in April and October; at Asheville, 1st Monday in May and November; at Charlotte second Monday in June and December

UNITED STATES DISTRICT COURT

(Western District of North Carolina)

Judge—Jas E Boyd, Greensboro N C

Clerk—W S Hyams, Asheville

Deputy Clerk—Miss M L Rorison, Asheville N C

Court convenes at Greensboro first Monday in April and October; at Statesville third Monday in April and October; at Asheville first Monday in May and November; at Charlotte second Monday in June and December

District Attorney—A E Holton, Winston N C

Assistant District Attorney—A L Coble, Statesville, N C

Stamp Deputy—C B Moore, Asheville, N C

Internal Revenue Agent—R B Sams

United States Commissioner—R S McCall

UNITED STATES POSTOFFICE

Postmaster—W W Rollins
Assistant Postmaster — J C Bradford

Office hours—General delivery and stamp windows open from 8 a m until 8 p m. Money

Asheville Dry Cleaning Co.
Telephones 835-836, All Dep't
MAIN, N. E. COR. COLLEGE

THE CLEANERS
Our Department for Oriental Rugs and Carpet Cleaning is prepared to serve you in all its branches.

E. S. Paine   O. E. Hansen

Maple Flooring and Poplar Siding

English Lumber Co.
PHONE . . 321

U S GOV 513 BANKS

order windows open from 8 a m until 5 p m. Registry window open from 8 a m until 6 p m

City Delivery—Two deliveries excepting Sundays, in residence districts; leave office at 8:45 a m and at 4:15 p m

Three deliveries daily excepting Sundays in business district; leave office at 7:30 a m, 9:30 a m and 4:15 p m

Money Order and Registry Clerk—Jno N Bradley

Stamp Clerk—Miss Katharine C Rollins

General Delivery Clerk—Miss Florence Voorhies

Mailing Clerk—G M Foster

Superintendent Carriers—O L Fitzgerald

Distributors—E C Featherstone, R P Brown

Assistant Money Order Department—Miss Hattie D Rollins

Box Rent Clerk—Miss Louise L Branch

Stamper—Thos N Henry

Night Clerk—H B Henninger in charge

Assistant Night Clerk—S L Ray

City Letter Carriers—J F Cunningham, N W Fain, M M Hayes, Neil Lee, E L Mace, H B Ray, W F O'Rear, Fergus Stikeleather, Jr, J B Simpson, C W Parham, B F Good, J A Ware

Rural Letter Carriers

R F D 1—W E Fitzgerald
R F D 2—Fred P Masters
R F D 3—Chas N Monday
R F D 4—Robt E Cassada
R F D 5—Roy Schreyer
Special Delivery Messengers—J R Moore, J D Moore and C W Parham

Railway Postal Clerks—W P Abbey, W H Clark, T C Duckett, H G Cliff, E R Echerd, E H Fanning, J E Gudger, W W Gudger, J E Magwood, W F Michael, J F Phifer, C C Richardson, R C Roberts, E M Roland, R M Sanders, M A Whittemore, C F Wood, G P Younginer

Glen Rock Station of the Asheville Post Office—372 Depot st
J C Melton—Clerk in charge
W L Ray—Clerk

Asheville School Rural Station of the Asheville Post Office—Located at the Asheville School in West Asheville

Mail Messenger Service—Between the postoffice and the railway station
B L Eller—Contractor
J F Eller—Messenger
J P Eller—Messenger

U S Court House and Postoffice Building—
Custodian—J C Bradford
Janitors—E R Randall, Thos B Creasman and E M Kemp
Charwomen — Cornelia J Capehart and Louise Greer

United States Post Office—1 Brook, Biltmore
B J Luther—postmaster
R F D Carriers, Biltmore—
No 1—S M Garren
No 2—V F Stephens
No 3—A C Reeves

United States Weather Bureau
(512-514-515 Legal Bldg)
T R Taylor, observer in charge

United States Commissioner's Office
(10½ n Pack Sq)
R S McCall, commissioner

Internal Revenue
Agent's Office rms 210-212 Government Bldg
R B Sams—agt in charge
C M Justice—office dep collr

Banks
American National — Patton av cor Church; capital $300,000. L L Jenkins pres, C J Harris, J G Merrimon and Henry Redwood v-pres, A E Rankin and R E Currence cashrs

Battery Park — 13-15 Patton av; capital $100,000; Tench

BIGGEST BUSIEST BEST

Asheville Steam Laundry

Phones:
1936 and 1937

—

43 to 47 W. College Street

CHARLES H. HONESS

OPTOMETRIST AND OPTICIAN

Exclusive maker of
ATLAS SHUR-ON EYE GLASSES

THE
Home of Ce-Rite Toric Lenses

We make a specialty of correcting optical defects with properly fitted glasses.

54 Patton Avenue
Opposite Postoffice

IF in the market for a Gas Engine let us make you prices.
its heavy castings, such as columns or building plates, see us.
its a skilled mechanic for boiler work, see us.
you want machine work of any kind phone 590.

CAROLINA MACHINERY CO.

FOUNDERS MACHINISTS and Jobbers of Mill Supplies

LIFE INSURANCE COMPANY OF VA.
ORGANIZED 1871
Richmond -:- Virginia
J. V. MOON, Superintendent
Rooms 3-4-5- Maxwelton Bldg., Asheville, N. C.

All claims paid IMMEDIATELY upon receipt of satisfactory proofs of Death. Total payment to policyholders since organization, over $12,000,000.00. Is paying its Policyholders over $1,000,000.00 annually.

T. P. JOHNSON & CO.

SHEET METAL WORKERS

All Kinds of Roofing Guttering and Conductor Work Metal Ceilings, Skylights and Galvanized Iron Cornices

OFFICE and SHOP:
69-71 S. MAIN

Phone 325

DR. C. H. MILLER

Mechano-Therapist

14 N. Spruce Street
ASHEVILLE, N. C.

PHONE 979

Hours by Engagement

DRUGLESS HEALING OF DISEASE

BANKS 514 CHURCHES

Coxe pres, Erwin Sluder v-pres, J Eugene Rankin cashr, C Rankin asst cashr

Central Bank & Trust Co—s Pack Sq; capital $50,000; C W Brown pres, W B McEwen v-pres, Wallace B Davis cashr

Citizens Bank—Patton av cor Haywood; capital $50,000; Edwin L Ray pres, George A Murray v-pres, John A Campbell cashier

Wachovia Bank & Trust Co —34-36 Patton av; capital, $1,250,000; T S Morrison chairman, W B Williamson cashier, S M Hanes asst cashier, P R Allen mngr ins dept

Building and Loan Associations

Blue Ridge Building and Loan Assn; J E Rankin pres, Edwin L Ray sec-treas, A H Cobb auditor

Home Building & Loan Assn —Drhumor Bldg; F R Hewitt pres, H L Plummer v-pres, S L Forbes sect-reas

Business Organizations

Asheville Board of Trade—6-7-8 Temple Bldg

Frank Weaver, pres; Neptune Buckner, sec

Asheville Merchants Assn—6-7-8 Temple Court

Jas E Rector atty-sec, M F Hoffman treas

Cemeteries

Asheville Cemetery — Cemetery and Pearson Drive; W S Cornell supt, G H Cochrane asst

Hebrew Cemetery—Cemetery nr Pearson Drive

Newton Academy Cemetery—Biltmore rd; J J Murphy supt

South Asheville Cemetery—s Asheville nr Haw Creek rd; Geo Avery and Benj Ragsville trustees

West Asheville Cemetery—West Asheville; J B Searcy kpr

Christian Associations

Young Men's Christian Association—27 Haywood

Julius C Martin pres, Robt S Carroll v-pres, C E Reed rec sec, Thos J Rickman treas, Ed B Brown gen sec, C H Burt asst sec, R W Hammerslough office sec, Harry M Dill physical director

Young Women's Christian Association—60 s Main; Mrs M W Lance house sec

*Young Men's Institute—29 Eagle; W S Lee actg sec

CHURCHES—White

Baptist

Biltmore—S Biltmore; Rev W W Marr pastor; Sunday school 10 a m, preaching 1st and 3d Sundays 11 a m and 8 p m

Calvary—W Asheville; Sunday school 9:45 a m

Cedar Hill — W Asheville; Rev T M Cole pastor

Chunn's Cove—Chunn's Cove

First—College cor Spruce; Rev C B Waller pastor; Sunday school 9:30 a m; preaching 11 a m and 8:00 p m

North Asheville Mission—20 Centre; Sunday school 9:30 a m

West End—Buxton nr Roberts; Rev G P Hamrick pastor; Sunday school 9:30 a m, preaching 11 a m and 7:15 p m

Christian

Christian — Haywood opp Flint; Rev P H Mears pastor; Sunday school, 10 a m; preaching 11 a m

Christian Science

First Church of Christ, Scientist—66 n French Broad av; Sunday school 9:45 a m; services 11 a m

Episcopal

All Souls' (P E)—Biltmore; Rev R R Swope, rector; Sunday services 11 a m and 5 p m; Sunday school, 3:15 p m

Chunn's Cove—Chunn's Cove; Sunday school 10 a m

Grace Memorial—Grace; Rev W S Cain, rector; Sunday

ASHEVILLE CLEANING and PRESSING CLUB

TAILORING THAT SATISFIES and PRICES THAT PLEASE

Hats cleaned, banded and bound. Silk hats ironed. Buttons made to order in all sizes. Plain or with rims. PHONE 389

DYEING IN ALL SHADES Cleaned. Messenger Service.

Kid Gloves, Slippers and Plumes. Fancy Jabots and Ties, French Dry Cleaned. Ladies' and Gentlemen's suits Steam

J. C. Wilbar, Prop. 4 NORTH PACK SQ.

ASHEVILLE COAL CO. — 6 North Pack Sq. — Phone 40

M. & W. COAL

Asheville Power and Light Co. — Electric Flat Irons — Phone 69

CHURCHES

school 10 a m; services 11 a m and 4:30 p m on 2d and 4th Sundays

Trinity—Church cor Aston; holy com 8 a m; litany and holy com 11 a m; sermon 8 p m; Sunday school 10 a m

Hebrew

Beth Ha Tephilla Synagogue—Spruce nr Woodfin

Bickercholim Synagogue — s Liberty nr Woodfin; Ellis Fox rabbi

Lutheran

Emanuel Evangelical—French Broad av cor Philip; Rev C H Bernhard pastor; Sunday school 9:45 a m; preaching 11 a m

Methodist

Avery Street (M E)—85 Avery; Rev Jno Carver pastor; Sunday school 9:45 a m; preaching 11 a m

Balm Grove—W Asheville; Rev Zeb E Barnhardt pastor; Sunday school 9:45 a m; preaching 11 a m and 8 p m

Bethel M E (South)—Blanton cor Philip; Rev H H Robbins pastor; Sunday school 9:45 a m; preaching 11 a m and 7:45 p m

Biltmore—S Biltmore; Rev J J Barker pastor; Sunday school 9:45 a m; preaching 11 a m and 8 p m; 2d and 4th Sundays

Central (M E South)—Church nr Patton av; Rev Chas W Byrd pastor; Sunday school 9:45 a m; preaching 11 a m and 8 p m

Haywood (M E South)—w Haywood cor Patton av; Rev W A Newell pastor; Sunday school 9:45 a m; preaching 11 a m and 7:45 p m

Methodist Protestant—Haywood nr Montford av; Rev W D Fogleman pastor; Sunday school 9:45 a m; preaching 11 a m and 8:15 p m

Mt Pleasant—Grace; Rev J J Barker pastor; Sunday school 9:45 a m; preaching 11 a m and 8 p m, 1st and 3d Sundays

North Asheville (M E South)—51 Chestnut; Rev W E Poovey pastor; Sunday school 9:30 a m; preaching 11 a m and 7:30 p m

Presbyterian

First—Church nr Patton av; Rev R F Campbell pastor; Sunday school 9:30 a m; preaching 11 a m and 8 p m; prayer meeting Wed 4:30 p m

Oakland Heights—s Main nr Victoria rd; Rev T A Cosgrove pastor; Sunday school 9:45 a m; preaching 11 a m; prayer meeting Wednesday 8 p m

Ora Street—96 Ora; Rev A M MacLauchlin pastor; preaching 11 a m and 8 p m; Sunday school 3 p m

Roman Catholic

St Lawrence — 95-97 Haywood; Rev P G Marion pastor; masses daily 7:30 a m; Sunday low mass 8 a m and 11 a m

Seventh Day Adventist

Seventh Day Adventists—Haywood nr Ann; Rev — — Sanford pastor; preaching 11 a m; Sunday school 10 a m

Salvation Army—38½ s Main; Jno Bouters adj; services 8 p m every night (except Monday); Sunday school 2:30 p m

CHURCHES—Colored

Baptist

First—Pine cor Hazzard; Rev J F Hughes pastor

Free Will—149 Livingston; Rev Lee Harshaw pastor

Mt Zion—Eagle nr Velvet; Rev J R Nelson pastor

Provident—109 Black; Rev A J Berry pastor

Episcopal

St Matthias — Valley cor Beaumont; Rev J T Kennedy rector

Methodist

Berry Temple (M E)—246 College; Rev J P Morris pastor

Kiibler & Whitehead — Meats — CITY MARKET — PHONES, 195 and 694

WEAVERVILLE LINE NINE MILES BY TROLLEY FROM PACK SQUARE TO WEAVERVILLE

ASHEVILLE AND EAST TENNESSEE RAILROAD CO.

7 NORTH MAIN STREET   ASHEVILLE N. C.

CHURCHES 516 EDUCATIONAL

ELECTRIC FIXTURES
Piedmont Electric Co.
64 PATTON AVE.
ASHEVILLE, N.C.

Hopkins Chapel (M E Zion)—217 College; Rev J S Spurgeon pastor
St James (A M E)—40 Hildebrand; Rev J R Barnum pastor
St Paul (A M E Zion)—80 Hill; Rev L Watson pastor
Southside (A M E Zion)—Southside av nr Choctaw; Rev M D Smith pastor
West Asheville (M E)—W Asheville; Rev G H Caldwell pastor
West Asheville (A M E)—Haywood rd, W Asheville; Rev J W Henderson pastor

Presbyterian
Calvary Presbyterian Church—Eagle cor Velvet; Rev C B Dusenbury pastor
Livingston — 72 Livingston; Rev Chas Dusenbury pastor

Miscellaneous
Macedonia (Sanctified) — 59 Max; Rev —— Bennett pastor
Seventh Day Adventist—37½ Sycamore

CLUBS
Albemarle Club — Albemarle Park
Asheville Club—Haywood cor Battery Park pl
Asheville Country Club—Charlotte nr city limits
Elks Club — Haywood cor Walnut

EDUCATIONAL
(City Schools)
Supt's Office—207 City Hall; R J Tighe supt
Supervisors — Miss Mabelle Miller, penmanship; Miss Edith W Truitt, vocal music; Miss Margaret Atkins, drawing
School Committee—208 City Hall
Wm Jones, chmn; W B Northup, v-chmn; R J Tighe, sec; Dr T H Williams, Chas G Lee, H C Allen, Geo A Shuford

Asheland Avenue — 190-214 Asheland av: A H King, prin; Misses Helen Schartle, May Alexander, Nancy Carter, Edith Anderson and Willie Waters, teachers
High School — College cor Oak; R V Kennedy prin
F H Franks, E J Londow, Wm Meyer, Miss Fannie O'Brion, Kathleen Ware, Lillie Batterham, Gertrude Ennes, Rose Batterham, Mrs Delia B Weston, Mrs J C Wilson and Mrs Clara Akers, teachers
Montford Avenue—80 Montford av; C T Carr, prin
Misses Mamie Nixon, Cora Stockton, Mary Spann, Susan Dukes, Sue Reese, Eugenia Harrison and Mrs M L Bryant, teachers
Murray—46 Tiernan; Mrs M W Williamson, prin
Misses Minnie Lyda, Eugenia Rowe, Frances Suttle and Estelle Huston, teachers
Newton—Biltmore rd; Mrs Mary C Pickens tchr
Orange—Orange nr Central av; M K Weber, prin
Misses Mary A Pratt, Bessie E Moody, Emma Bernard, Susan Yeatman, Rena Nichols, Alice Halyburton, Lee Dennis, Mary Lanier Mamie Wright, Ruth Watts, Anna Carmichael and Margaret Ware, teachers
Park Avenue—Park av s e cor Haywood; Miss Queen Carson prin
Misses Olive M Irick, Hannah M Test, (Mrs) Irene Wortham, Eula Buttrick, Mattie Davis, Vienna Nichols and Mrs Elizabeth Haskell teachers
West Asheville—Haywood rd W Asheville; J W Bradley prin

(Colored)
Catholic Hill — Valley cor Catholic av; W S Lee prin
Hill Street—81 Hill; J H Michael prin
Mountain Street—91 Mountain; Emma H Fenderson prin

CONTRACTOR and BUILDER
STEEL RANGES
J. C. McPHERSON
35-37 E COLLEGE ST. PHONE 133
PLUMBING STEAM AND HOT WATER HEATING

South Side—Southside av nr McDowell; H A Lee prin

West Asheville — W Asheville; T M Elrod prin

Private Schools and Colleges

Asheville Mission Hospital Training School—Charlotte cor Woodfin, Dr W L Dunn, dean

Asheville Business College—n Pack Sq; H S Shockley prin

Asheville School (for boys)—Haywood rd; N M Anderson and C A Mitchell prins

Asheville School (for girls)—Main cor Woodfin; Miss E K Ford prin

Bingham School (The), (military)—Bingham Hts; Col Robert Bingham, A M LLD, supt; Maj R T Grinnan v-supt

Carolina Commercial School—Legal Bldg; Miss Pearl Holman prin

Emanuel School of Shorthand—Drhumor Bldg; Miss Sadie Emanuel prin

Home Industrial and Pease Memorial (Presby campus)—Victoria; Miss Florence Stephenson prin, Miss Josephine Bundy associate prin. Misses Grace M Maxwell, Elizabeth Rich, Helen D Fish, Elizabeth McKinstry, Bess M Martin, May Wilhelm, teachers

Pease Memorial House—Mrs Katherine S Byers, Mrs Evangeline G Benedict, Miss Edith M Thorpe, Miss Jeanie S Fuller, Mrs Mary Fortner, teachers

Johnson School — W Asheville; J M Ingram prin

Matney School—Cherry cor Flint; W W Matney prin

Normal and Collegiate Institute (Presby)—s Main cor Victoria rd

Prof Edward P Childs, pres; Miss Mary Hickok, prin; Miss May Hagenbach, supervisor of practice school; Miss Josephine Huston, director of music department; Miss Grace Hamilton, science; Miss Clara Belle Anderson, Latin; Miss Edith Morris, English; Miss Mary Sheak, domestic science, matron; Miss Laura Wiley, mathematics; Rev T A Cosgrove, Bible; Miss Edna White, physical culture; Miss Lois McKinney, history and German; Miss Ernestine Potter, domestic arts; Miss Susan Albright, assistant in music; Mrs Laura D Williams, matron; Miss Ella Bickerstaffe, cooking

North State Fitting School—157 Church; J M Roberts prin

Patton School for Boys—271 Haywood; J C Patton prin

St Genevieve College—Victoria; Mother DePlank in charge

Stevens Misses (The) — 15 Bearden av; Misses N B and E C Stevens prins

Winn School for Boys (The)—135 Merrimon av; Jas A Winn prin; Rev Paul P Winn asst prin

(Colored)

Allen Industrial Home and Asheville Academy—241 College; Miss A B Dole supt

HOSPITALS, HOMES AND CHARITABLE INSTITUTIONS

*Allen Industrial Home and School (for girls)—College nr Oak; Miss A B Dole supt

Asheville Mission and Associated Charities—20½ s Pack Sq

Asheville Mission Hospital, 5 Charlotte—Board of managers, Mrs Vance Brown pres, Dr M H Fletcher chief of staff

Clarence Barker Memorial Hospital and Dispensary, Biltmore. The rector and vestry of All Souls' church constitute the governing board. Miss M H Trist, supt

Buncombe County Home for Aged and Infirm, Leicester rd

Children's Home, Woolsey—Supported by the city of Asheville

City Hospital—3 miles west of city on French Broad river

Candy Kitchen and Club Cafe
"A GOOD PLACE FOR REFRESHMENT"

The very best ingredients with sanitary conditions in our Candy Manufacturing Department make possible the dainty, crisp confections sold here. Bon Bons and Chocolates made every day, put up in neat, attractive boxes. Phones 110 and 111. 19 and 21 Haywood St.

HOSPITALS   518   MILITARY

Brown's Undertaking Parlors

S. H. BROWN

Lady Assistant When Desired

Phone 193-2 Rings

50 Patton Avenue
Asheville, N. C.

Established 1894

B. J. JACKSON

Carefully Selected Fruits and Vegetables

Stall No. 11, City Market

BUSINESS PHONES:
86 and 101

RESIDENCE PHONE
1596

Faith Cottage (rescue home for unfortunate women)—43 Atkinson; L B Compton, supt

Highland Home (private)—75 Zillicoa; Dr R S Carroll, phys

Flower Mission and Associated Charities and Free Medical Dispensary—20 s Pack Sq, R J Tighe pres, J A Perry v-pres, W B Williamson treas, Mrs W G Smith sec, Mrs F P Wild genl sec

Meriwether Hospital (private)—24 Grove; Dr F T Meriwether prop; Miss N F Pitts supt

Mildred E Sherwood Home (private)—167 s French Broad av; Miss M E Sherwood, supt

Salvation Army Hall and Industrial Home—38½ s Main

Libraries

Directory Library—66 Amer Natl Bank Bldg

Pack Memorial Library—4 s Pack Sq; Miss Grace McH Jones librarian, Miss Ann T Erwin asst librarian

Socialist Reading Room—14-15 Drhumor Bldg

Medical Societies

Medical Society of Buncombe County—Meets 1st and 3d Monday night at City Hall. Dr H H Briggs pres, Dr G S Tennent sec

MISCELLANEOUS ORGANIZATIONS

Asheville Poultry and Pet Stock Assn, n Pack Square—J M Campbell pres

Mountain School Dept Home Mission Board Sou Baptist Convention—Library Bldg; Rev A E Brown supt

Pack Memorial Library Assn—4 s Pack Sq; Donald Gillis pres, S P Ravenel v-pres, Mrs A M Field sec, W B Williamson treas

Society Prevention Cruelty to Animals—Legal Bldg; J C Orr sec

Woman's Auxiliary Y M C A—Meets first Monday of each month in Y M C A Hall, Haywood nr Patton av

Woman's Exchange—36 Haywood nr Battery Park pl—Mrs C E Gibbs sec

PARKS

Albemarle (residential)—Charlotte extd

Aston Park—French Broad av opp Philip

City Park—Flint cor Magnolia av

Court House Park—rear Court House

Grove Park (residential)—Charlotte extd

Montford Park—Montford av s e cor Panola

Oak Park—Furman av opp Chestnut

Proximity Park (residential)—Charlotte extd

Riverside Park—on French Broad river northwest of city

SECRET SOCIETIES AND FRATERNAL ORGANIZATIONS

Masonic

Alpha Lodge of Perfection, A A S R—Meets every first Tuesday night at Drhumor Bldg

Ionic Council No 9, R and A M—meets third Thursday night at Drhumor Bldg

Asheville Chapter No 25, R A M—Meets every second Thursday night at Drhumor Bldg

Cyrene Commandery No 5, K T—Meets every fourth Thursday night at Drhumor Bldg

Mount Hermon Lodge No 118 A F and A M—Meets every first Thursday night at Drhumor Bldg

Military

First Brigade of N C N G—Staff Officers: S W Battle surg gen'l, Eugene B Glenn major surgeon, F J Clemenger adjt surg, Laurence W Young major First Infantry, commndg Asheville Post 1

Yᵉ OLD BOOK SHOP
114 Patton Ave.   Phone 1674
BOOKS BOUGHT, SOLD OR EXCHANGED

FLOORING A SPECIALTY — Mouldings and Interior Finish
Hardwoods Office: Southern Railway Tracks, Near Biltmore Station
Phone 729   **Planing Mill**

SECRET ORDERS   SECRET ORDERS

Company K, N C N G—Meets in Armory Hall every Thursday night; Chas I Bard, capt commndg; D E Penland 1st lieut, H E Johnston 2d lieut

Company F, First Infantry N C N G—Meets Armory Hall every Friday night; J H Koon, capt commndg; York Coleman, 1st lieut, Carl Felmet, 2d lieut

First Regiment Band, N C N G—Meets Armory every Thursday night; C N Webster director; Chas Glass, principal musician; J D Cole, drum major

Asheville Company No 6, U R K of P—Meets Castle Hall every Wednesday night; A L Duckett, capt commndg; G E Evans 1st lieut, F O'C Fletcher 2d lieut

B P O Elks
Asheville Lodge No 608—Meets every Wednesday night in hall at Elks Home, Haywood cor Walnut

C K of A
St Lawrence Branch No 826—Meets at 26 Patton av every 1st and 3d Sunday nights

Fraternal Order of Eagles
Aerie No 1377—Meets every Thursday night at Hall 33½ s Main

I O Heptasophs
Asheville Concalve No 405—Meets second and third Tuesday nights at C L U Hall

I O O F
Asheville Encampment No 2—Meets every Friday night at 18-20 Church

Blue Ridge Lodge No 205—Meets every Monday night at 18-20 Church

French Broad Lodge, No 172—Meets every Monday night at Biltmore Hall

Sulphur Springs Lodge No 186—Meets every Wednesday night in their hall, W Asheville

Pisgah Rebekah Lodge No 36—Meets every Friday night in Odd Fellows Hall, W Asheville

Swannanoa Lodge No 56—Meets every Tuesday night at 18-20 Church

Swannanoa Rebekah Lodge No 37—Meets every Thursday night at 18-20 Church

Jr O U A M
Asheville Council No 6—Meets every Monday night 3d fl Paragon Bldg

Emma Council No 253—Meets every Monday night in Odd Fellows' Hall, W Asheville

French Broad Council No 97—Meets every Thursday night at 1½ s Main

K and L of H
Blue Ridge Lodge No 1799—Meets second and fourth Tuesday nights at Pack Sq cor Main

K of H
Swannanoa Lodge No 646—Meets first and third Monday nights in Library Bldg

K of P
Asheville Company No 6 Uniformed Rank—Meets every Wednesday night at Castle Hall 1½ s Main

Asheville Lodge No 106—Meets every Friday night 3d fl Paragon Bldg; G P Younginer C C, W H Clark V C, Robt Lynn P, W H Krickhan M of W, W H Daniel M at A, S Nixon Rowe K of R & S, T M Duckett M of F, W H Zimmerman M of E, C E Case I G, M H Ramsey O G

Pisgah Lodge No 32—Meets every Tuesday night at Castle Hall, 1½ s Main; A G Barnett C C, R F Haskell V C, A T Morrison P, B M Jones K of R & S, E W Dodd M of F, D Harris M of E, E H Miller M of W, P P Brown M at A, Cloyd Pennell I G, Louis Lipinsky O G

West Asheville Lodge No 221—Odd Fellows Hall, W Asheville

HUGHES

Transfer and Livery Co.

Automobiles for **HIRE**

TRUNKS 25c

Office:
401 Southside Avenue

PHONE   1405

Try our Hand Laundering. We strive to please in LAUNDERING and DRY CLEANING.

The Sanitary Home Laundry
No. 7 MONTFORD AVE.
PHONE - 1354

Mrs. Wilder's SANITARY HOME LAUNDRY turns out first class work in Laundering and Dry Cleaning. No. 7 Montford Ave., Phone 1354

| SECRET ORDERS | 520 | UNIONS—LABOR |

Pythian Sisters—Meet at 1½ s Main

Modern Woodmen of America
Vance Camp No 13344—Meets at Ashev K of P Hall every 2d and 4th Wed nights of each month

National Union
Beaumont Council No 589—Meets every 2d Friday afternoon in the month at rms 1-2 Library Bldg

Red Men
Junaluska Tribe No 88 Improved Order Red Men—Meets every Wed evening at 8 o'clock in K of P Hall, 1½ s Main

Tahkeeostee Tribe No 51—Meets every Tuesday night in Odd Fellows' Hall, W Asheville

Royal Arcanum
French Broad Council No 701—Meets every second and fourth Monday at K of P Hall, 1½ s Main

Woodmen of the World
Balsam Camp No 1—Meets every Monday night in C L U Hall, 39 Patton av

Confederate Veterans
Zebulon Vance Camp No 681—Meets last Saturday in each month at Court House; F M Miller com

Sons of Confederate Veterans
Camp Johnston Pettigrew—Meets at Court House

G A R
Marion Roberts Post No 41—Meets fourth day of each month at homes of members

Daughters of the Confederacy
Asheville Chapter — Meets first Thursday of each month at 58 Haywood

Grand Order of the Confederate Veterans
R E Lee Camp—Meets once every month at the home of one of the members; Miss Julia Hatch sec

Grand Daughters of the Confederacy
Meet at Confederate Hall third Saturday in each month

UNIONS (LABOR)
(Hall over 39 Patton av)

Central Labor Union—Meets every Wednesday night in their hall at 39 Patton av

Amalgamated Assn of Street & Electric Ry Employees of Am—Meets every Monday night in C L U Hall

Plasterers—Meets every Wednesday night in C L U Hall

Retail Clerks International Protective Assn, Local No 141—Meets first and third Wednesday nights in C L U Hall, 39 Patton av

Stonemasons — Meets every Wednesday night in C L U Hall

Typographical No 263—Meets first Monday in each month at 5:15 p m in C L U Hall

Brotherhood of Locomotive Engineers—Swannanoa Division No 267—Meets every second and 4th Sunday at 9 a m—at Hall 18½ Church

Brotherhood of Locomotive Firemen, Blue Ridge Lodge No 455—Meets every 2d and 4th Sundays at Hall opp Sou Ry Passngr Station

United Commercial Travelers of America—Meets every 2d and 4th Saturday nights at K of P Hall 1½ s Main

United Brotherhood of Carpenters and Joiners Local Union No 384—Meets every Wednesday night in C L U Hall

When writing to advertisers please mention the City Directory

BUICK — MAXWELLS — OLDSMOBILE — DETROIT ELECTRIC
ARBOGAST MOTOR COMPANY
ACCESSORIES AND SUPPLIES
52-60 N. Main   Phones 302 and 1728

Asheville Dry Cleaning Co.
Telephones 835-836, All Dep't
MAIN, N. E. COR. COLLEGE

THE CLEANERS
Our Department for Oriental Rugs and Carpet Cleaning is prepared to serve you in all its branches.
E. S. Paine   O. E. Hansen

Lightning Source UK Ltd.
Milton Keynes UK
UKHW051116210820
368606UK00011B/844